Communications
in Computer and Information Science   1874

Rationale

The CCIS series is devoted to the publication of proceedings of computer science conferences. Its aim is to efficiently disseminate original research results in informatics in printed and electronic form. While the focus is on publication of peer-reviewed full papers presenting mature work, inclusion of reviewed short papers reporting on work in progress is welcome, too. Besides globally relevant meetings with internationally representative program committees guaranteeing a strict peer-reviewing and paper selection process, conferences run by societies or of high regional or national relevance are also considered for publication.

Topics

The topical scope of CCIS spans the entire spectrum of informatics ranging from foundational topics in the theory of computing to information and communications science and technology and a broad variety of interdisciplinary application fields.

Information for Volume Editors and Authors

Publication in CCIS is free of charge. No royalties are paid, however, we offer registered conference participants temporary free access to the online version of the conference proceedings on SpringerLink (http://link.springer.com) by means of an http referrer from the conference website and/or a number of complimentary printed copies, as specified in the official acceptance email of the event.

CCIS proceedings can be published in time for distribution at conferences or as post-proceedings, and delivered in the form of printed books and/or electronically as USBs and/or e-content licenses for accessing proceedings at SpringerLink. Furthermore, CCIS proceedings are included in the CCIS electronic book series hosted in the SpringerLink digital library at http://link.springer.com/bookseries/7899. Conferences publishing in CCIS are allowed to use Online Conference Service (OCS) for managing the whole proceedings lifecycle (from submission and reviewing to preparing for publication) free of charge.

Publication process

The language of publication is exclusively English. Authors publishing in CCIS have to sign the Springer CCIS copyright transfer form, however, they are free to use their material published in CCIS for substantially changed, more elaborate subsequent publications elsewhere. For the preparation of the camera-ready papers/files, authors have to strictly adhere to the Springer CCIS Authors' Instructions and are strongly encouraged to use the CCIS LaTeX style files or templates.

Abstracting/Indexing

CCIS is abstracted/indexed in DBLP, Google Scholar, EI-Compendex, Mathematical Reviews, SCImago, Scopus. CCIS volumes are also submitted for the inclusion in ISI Proceedings.

How to start

To start the evaluation of your proposal for inclusion in the CCIS series, please send an e-mail to ccis@springer.com.

Hector Florez · Marcelo Leon
Editors

Applied Informatics

6th International Conference, ICAI 2023
Guayaquil, Ecuador, October 26–28, 2023
Proceedings

 Springer

Editors
Hector Florez 🆔
Universidad Distrital Francisco Jose de
Caldas
Bogota, Colombia

Marcelo Leon 🆔
Universidad Ecotec
Guayaquil, Ecuador

ISSN 1865-0929 ISSN 1865-0937 (electronic)
Communications in Computer and Information Science
ISBN 978-3-031-46812-4 ISBN 978-3-031-46813-1 (eBook)
https://doi.org/10.1007/978-3-031-46813-1

This Springer imprint is published by the registered company Springer Nature Switzerland AG
The registered company address is: Gewerbestrasse 11, 6330 Cham, Switzerland

Paper in this product is recyclable.

Preface

The 6th International Conference on Applied Informatics (ICAI 2023) aimed to bring together researchers and practitioners working in different domains in the field of informatics in order to exchange their expertise and to discuss the perspectives of development and collaboration.

ICAI 2023 was held in blended mode at the Universidad Ecotec located in Guayaquil, Ecuador, during October 26–28, 2023. It was organized by the Information Technologies Innovation (ITI) research group that belongs to the Universidad Distrital Francisco Jose de Caldas. In addition, ICAI 2023 was proudly sponsored by Springer and Science Based Platforms.

ICAI 2023 received 132 submissions on informatics topics. Accepted papers covered Artificial Intelligence, Data Analysis, Decision Systems, Enterprise Information Systems Applications, Geoinformatics, Health Care Information Systems, Interdisciplinary Information Studies, Learning Management Systems, and Virtual and Augmented Reality. Authors of accepted submissions came from the following countries: Argentina, Colombia, Ecuador, Greece, India, Luxembourg, Morocco, Nigeria, Norway, Poland, Russia, Spain, United Arab Emirates, the UK, and the USA.

All submissions were reviewed through a double-blind peer-review process. Each paper was reviewed by at least three experts. To achieve this, ICAI 2022 was supported by 58 program committee members. PC members come from the following countries: Argentina, Canada, Chile, China, Colombia, Ecuador, India, Indonesia, Luxembourg, Morocco, Nigeria, Spain, and the USA. Based on the double-blind review process, 30 full papers were accepted to be included in this volume of Communications in Computer and Information Sciences (CCIS) proceedings published by Springer.

We would like to thank the staff of Springer for their helpful advice, guidance, and support in publishing the proceedings.

We trust that the ICAI 2023 proceedings open to you new vistas of discovery and knowledge.

October 2023   Hector Florez
                                                                             Marcelo Leon

Organization

General Chairs

Hector Florez	Universidad Distrital Francisco José de Caldas, Colombia
Marcelo León	Universidad Ecotec, Ecuador

Steering Committee

Jaime Chavarriaga	Universidad de los Andes, Colombia
Cesar Diaz	OCOX AI, Colombia
Hector Florez	Universidad Distrital Francisco José de Caldas, Colombia
Ixent Galpin	Universidad de Bogotá Jorge Tadeo Lozano, Colombia
Olmer García	Universidad de Bogotá Jorge Tadeo Lozano, Colombia
Christian Grévisse	Université du Luxembourg, Luxembourg
Sanjay Misra	Institute For Energy Technology, Norway
Ma Florencia Pollo-Cattaneo	Universidad Tecnológica Nacional Facultad Regional Buenos Aires, Argentina
Fernando Yepes-Calderon	Children's Hospital Los Angeles, USA

Organizing Committee

Marcelo León	Universidad Ecotec, Ecuador
Hegira Ramirez	Universidad Ecotec, Ecuador

Workshops Committee

Hector Florez	Universidad Distrital Francisco José de Caldas, Colombia
Ixent Galpin	Universidad de Bogotá Jorge Tadeo Lozano, Colombia
Christian Grévisse	Université du Luxembourg, Luxembourg

Program Committee Chairs

Hector Florez	Universidad Distrital Francisco José de Caldas, Colombia
Marcelo León	Universidad Ecotec, Ecuador

Program Committee

Fernanda Almeida	Universidade Federal do ABC, Brazil
Cecilia Avila	Fundación Universitaria Konrad Lorenz, Colombia
Joseph Bamidele Awotunde	University of Ilorin, Nigeria
Jorge Bacca-Acosta	Fundación Universitaria Konrad Lorenz, Colombia
Alejandra Baena	Universidad Antonio Nariño, Colombia
Carlos Balsa	Instituto Politécnico de Bragança, Portugal
Simone Belli	Universidad Complutense de Madrid, Spain
Hüseyin Bicen	Yakin Dogu Üniversitesi, Cyprus
Alexander Bock	Universität Duisburg Essen, Germany
Paola Britos	Universidad Nacional de Río Negro, Argentina
Robert Buchmann	Universitatea Babeş-Bolyai, Romania
Raymundo Buenrostro	Universidad de Colima, Mexico
Patricia Cano-Olivos	Universidad Popular Autónoma del Estado de Puebla, Mexico
Carlos Casanova	Universidad Tecnológica Nacional, Argentina
Jaime Chavarriaga	Universidad de los Andes, Colombia
Victor Darriba	Universidade de Vigo, Spain
Cesar Diaz	OCOX AI, Colombia
Silvia Fajardo-Flores	Universidad de Colima, Mexico
Mauri Ferrandin	Universidade Federal de Santa Catarina, Brazil
Hector Florez	Universidad Distrital Francisco José de Caldas, Colombia
Ixent Galpin	Universidad de Bogotá Jorge Tadeo Lozano, Colombia
Raphael Gomes	Instituto Federal de Goiás, Brazil
Daniel Görlich	SRH Hochschule Heidelberg, Germany
Jānis Grabis	Rīgas Tehniskā Universitāte, Latvia
Christian Grévisse	Université du Luxembourg, Luxembourg
Guillermo Guarnizo	Universidad Santo Tomas, Colombia
Alejandro Hossian	Universidad Tecnológica Nacional, Argentina

Gilles Hubert   Institut de Recherche en Informatique de
                             Toulouse, France
Manfred Jeusfeld   Högskolan i Skövde, Sweden
Rodrigo Kato   Universidade Federal de Minas Gerais, Brazil
Marcelo Leon   Universidad Ecotec, Ecuador
Keletso Letsholo   Higher Colleges of Technology, UAE
Isabel Lopes   Instituto Politécnico de Bragança, Portugal
Orlando Lopez-Cruz   Universidad El Bosque, Colombia
Hugo Peixoto   Universidade do Minho, Portugal
Diego Peluffo-Ordóñez   Mohammed VI Polytechnic University, Morocco
Tamara Piñero   Hospital Italiano de Buenos Aires, Argentina
Adam Piórkowski   AGH University of Science and Technology,
                             Poland
Florencia Pollo-Cattaneo   Universidad Tecnológica Nacional, Argentina
Filipe Portela   Universidade do Minho, Portugal
Pablo Pytel   Universidad Tecnológica Nacional, Argentina
Juan Camilo Ramírez   Universidad Antonio Nariño, Colombia
Vladimir Robles-Bykbaev   Universidad Politécnica Salesiana, Ecuador
José Rufino   Instituto Politécnico de Bragança, Portugal
Alber Sanchez   Instituto Nacional de Pesquisas Espaciais, Brazil
Sweta Singh   Savitribai Phule Pune University, India
German Vega   Centre National de la Recherche Scientifique,
                             France
Manuel Vilares   Universidade de Vigo, Spain
Fernando Yepes-Calderon   Children's Hospital Los Angeles, USA

Contents

Decision Systems

Enterprise Information Systems Applications

Geoinformatics

Health Care Information Systems

Interdisciplinary Information Studies

Learning Management Systems

Virtual and Augmented Reality

Artificial Intelligence

A Feature Selection Method Based on Rough Set Attribute Reduction and Classical Filter-Based Feature Selection for Categorical Data Classification

Oluwafemi Oriola[1,2]([envelope]) [iD], Eduan Kotzé[1] [iD], and Ojonoka Atawodi[3] [iD]

[1] University of the Free State, Bloemfontein, South Africa
[2] Adekunle Ajasin University, Akungba Akoko, Nigeria
oluwafemi.oriola@aaua.edu.ng
[3] University of Southern Mississippi, Hattiesburg, USA

Abstract. The main objective of feature selection in machine learning classification is to reduce the size of features by removing irrelevant and noisy features, with the goal of improving the accuracy and the efficiency of the classification model. Like continuous and mixed data classification, feature selection has been applied to better categorical data classification. On large datasets with tens of features, however, existing feature selection methods perform worse in terms of accuracy metrics than baseline categorical data classification models that involve full features. This paper presents a feature selection method that integrates Rough Set Attribute Reduction and Classical Filter-based feature selection method to improve the performance of categorical data classification. Two large categorical datasets from UCI repository are used to evaluate the method. Support Vector Machine, Random Forest and Multilayer Perceptron algorithms are used as machine learning classifiers. The results show that the proposed method outperforms existing feature selection models in terms of Accuracy, Precision, Recall, and F-measure for individual classes and their average weighted scores in both case studies. Benchmarking with baseline classification models, the best overall performance by the proposed method is obtained with Random Forest.

Keywords: Machine Learning · Feature Selection · Large Categorical Data · Classification · Joint Feature Selection Method

1 Introduction

The capabilities of machine learning algorithms in making use of complex inputs to solve problems have made many organizations to employ them in their applications. Machine learning algorithms rely on data in making decisions [1]. They are classified as unsupervised learning, supervised learning and semi-supervised

H. Florez and M. Leon (Eds.): ICAI 2023, CCIS 1874, pp. 3–15, 2024.
https://doi.org/10.1007/978-3-031-46813-1_1

learning technique [2]. Unsupervised learning technique relies on the relationship between features in the data to group the instances and are commonly used for clustering. In classification, supervised learning is mostly used when the labelled instances are large enough to classify unlabelled instances effectively; otherwise, semi-supervised learning technique is used.

Supervised learning techniques have been very effective in categorical data classification but require high execution time, especially when large datasets are involved [3,4]. In view of this, feature selection algorithms are applied to extract only relevant features [5].

Feature selection algorithms include filter-based [6], wrapper-based [4] and em-bedding feature selection algorithms [7,8]. The filter-based feature selection algorithms make use of simple and less computationally expensive steps to rank features based on different variable ranking criteria. They include Information Gain, Chi-Square Test and Pearson Correlation. The wrapper-based feature selection algorithms search for optimal prediction accuracy by selecting subsets of the dataset iteratively until the highest prediction accuracy is found. They tend to over-fit especially in cases of small datasets. Examples include Sequential Feature Selection and Cumulative Feature Selection. While both filter and wrapper-based feature selection algorithms work with training sets, embedding feature selection algorithms include variable selection in the training process without splitting the dataset into training and testing sets. Thus, it is unrealistic in real-life situation. Rough Set Attribute Reduction [9] on the other hand employs an approximate approach based on discernibility to reduce the number of attributes. In some applications, degree of dependency is used [10].

Although, filter-based feature selection appears appropriate for categorical data classification because of its simplicity and efficiency [11], however, they are less effective compared to other methods. Therefore, this paper exploits filter-based feature selection methods in supervised learning methods and improves the methods using Rough Set Attribute Reduction System. The paper contributes to knowledge by enhancing filter-based feature selection methods using Rough Set Theory for categorical data classification.

The rest of the paper is organized as follows: Sect. 2 presents the review of related works; Sect. 3 describes the proposed feature selection method; Sect. 4 discusses the steps used for the experimental analysis; Sect. 5 presents and discusses the results; and Sect. 6 concludes the paper by presenting the key achievements and areas for future works.

2   Related Work

Several works have explored hybrid feature selection methods for data classification, including categorical data classification.

Wang and Ke [12] work on outlier detection by exploring relevance, interaction, redundancy and complementarity of the features in categorical data. Their proposed model combines both dense subgraph-based feature selection and Relief methods. By using fourteen datasets with only mushroom dataset having more than 8,000 instances, their proposed method records 77% dimensionality reduction rate and least average AUC of 0.525 compared to other state-of-the-art feature selection methods. The algorithm does not perform well with mushroom dataset. Fuzzy Rough Computation performs better than the classical Fuzzy Rough Set and Rough Set in categorical data classification [13]. The model employs iterative computation strategy for implementing approximations and dependency functions. The limitation is that the performance of the algorithms however is not tested with machine learning classifiers.

Shu and Shen [14] develop incremental feature selection algorithms with varying feature values for single and multiple objects to handle dynamic incomplete data, which classic feature selection algorithms for single object (CFSV) with varying feature cannot handle very well. By evaluation with twelve UCI datasets, the proposed methods perform better compared to classic feature selection algorithms such as Mutual Information, Information Gain, Consist, ReliefF and CFSV. However, classic feature selection with J48 rather than incremental methods perform better for mushroom dataset [3] with highest accuracy of 98.92%.

In Abdoos et al. [15], sequential forward selection and sequential backward selection, both wrapper-based methods and Gram-Schmidt orthogonalization filter based method are combined. By using Support Vector Machine as classifier, the proposed method achieves improved speed and accuracy in classification of power quality events. Omuya et al. [16] develop a hybrid filter-based feature selection method based on principal component analysis and information gain. Application of the method to categorical data classification with Naïve Bayes, J48, Support Vector Machine and ZeroR shows that the model reduces data dimensionality and training time and improves accuracy, precision and recall.

Filter and wrapper-based methods are combined in the work of Peng et al. [11]. A preselection step with ROC curves are used to evaluate each feature. The proposed approach is applied to Sequential Forward Floating Search and the results show that the proposed approach improved the classification performance of the classical model and solves over-fitting problems. The limitation of the work is that the datasets used are small in size and contain numeric data. Eristi et al. [17] proposed K-means based Apriori algorithm for power quality event recognition, a categorical data classification problem. The algorithm optimizes the feature vectors and enhances efficiency, reliability and accuracy of the system. Although, the dataset is large with large feature size but it is not publicly available.

Chiew et al. [18] on the other hand propose an ensemble feature selection model for phishing detection. The framework has two phases: phase 1 selects the primary features using cumulative distribution function while phase 2 produces baseline features using function perturbation ensemble. The features from phase 1 are modified by perturbation to obtain secondary features. The results show that the Random Forest classifier model achieves 94.6% accuracy, which is best.

From the studies, the evaluated hybrid feature selection methods involving wrapper techniques perform better in terms of accuracy metrics than traditional feature selection techniques. However, wrapper techniques do incur higher computational costs compared to filter-based techniques. With large categorical data, classic filter-based feature selection methods perform better than incremental feature selection methods, with the highest accuracy of 98.92% in the case of Mushroom dataset [3]. In order to improve filter-based feature selection methods, the potentials of Rough Set Attribute Reduction techniques [9,13,14] are explored by integrating Rough Set Attribute Reduction Systems into classical filter-based approach. Both Mushroom [3] and Phishing Website Detection [21] datasets are also explored for their large sizes and high number of features.

3 Proposed Feature Selection Method

In this section, the proposed feature selection method is formulated. Firstly, the Information Gain, Chi-Square Test methods and Rough Set Attribute Reduction methods on which the proposed method is built are described.

3.1 Information Gain Feature Selection

Information Gain (IG) [1] is an entropy-based feature selection method that evalu-ates the worth of a feature by measuring the information gain with respect to the class. A high IG score indicates that the feature has a greater impact on the phish-ing website detection. The Weka's InfoGainAttributeEval [19] tool is used.

$$InfoGain(Class, Feature) = H(Class) - H(Class|Feature) \qquad (1)$$

where H is the entropy.

3.2 Chi-Square Test Feature Selection

Chi-Square Test (CH2), a filter-based feature selection method, is used to evaluate the relationship of a feature with the target variable. Chi-square value is small if the observed value is close to the expected value. A high value indicates high de-pendency between feature and target variable and eventually, high impact on the detection. Sci-kit Learn [20] is used for the computation of the value, which is given in Eq. 2.

$$X_c^2 = \sigma_{i=1}^n \frac{(O_i - E_i)^2}{E_i} \qquad (2)$$

where c is the degree of freedom, O is the observed value and E is the expected value. In the analysis, 23 features with highest values are also selected to avoid bias.

3.3 Rough Set Attribute Reduction

Rough Set Attribute Reduction (RS) [9] is the concept of indiscernibility (IND). Let I = (U, A) be an information system, where U is a non-empty set of finite objects and A is a non-empty finite set of attributes such that a: U → Va for every a ∈ A. Va is the set of values that attribute a may take. For any P ⊆ A, an associated equivalence relation IND(P) exists. The reduction of attributes is achieved by comparing equivalence relations generated by sets of attributes. Attributes are removed so that the reduced set provides the same predictive capability of the decision feature as the original. A Reduct, R, is defined as a subset of minimal cardinality of the conditional attribute set E such that $\gamma_R(F)$ = $\gamma_E(F)$. The algorithm is presented as follows:

Algorithm 1 : REDUCT (E, F)

E: the set of all conditional features;
F: the set of decision features.
$R \leftarrow \{\}$
do
      T ← R
      ∀ x ∈ (E-R)
      if $\gamma_{R \cup x}(F) = \gamma_E(F)$
          T ← R ∪ x
          R ← T
   until $\gamma_R(F) = \gamma_E(F)$
   return R

3.4 Proposed Feature Selection Method

The Reduct of the Rough Set Attribute Reduction Model is used to improve the existing feature selection models by applying certain guiding rules as presented in the flowchart in Fig. 1. This proposed model is applied to both IG and CH2 and they are referred to as RS-IG and RS-CH2, respectively.

4 Experimental Analysis

The analysis involves data collection, preprocessing, feature selection, classification and prediction. The framework for the process is presented in Fig. 2.

4.1 Data Collection

The datasets used in this study are collected from the University of California, Irvine repository (UCI). Phishing website detection [21]. It has 30 independent features cutting across different segments of URL and 1 binary class (phishing

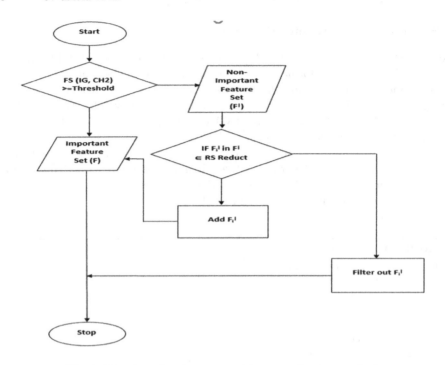

Fig. 1. Flowchart for the proposed feature selection method

and legitimate). The independent features are categorical and the categories include legitimate (value = 1), suspicious (value = 0) and phishy (value = −1), while the binary class categories include legitimate (value = 1) and phishing (value = 0). There are 11,055 instances in total, which are divided into 4,898 phishing and 6,157 legitimate instances. Table 1 presents the features and their categories.

Mushroom dataset [3]. It has 22 independent features and 1 binary class (poisonous = 0 and edible = 1). There are 8,124 instances in total, which are divided into 3,916 poisonous and 4,208 edible instances. Table 2 presents the features and their categories.

4.2 Data Preprocessing

The Waikato Environment for Knowledge Analysis (Weka) [19] Attribute-Relation File Format (ARFF) of the datasets is used. The datasets are cleaned by removing duplicate instances and null value. Each feature name is transformed to a single word. The Weka edit menu is used for the cleaning to maintain the integrity of the dataset.

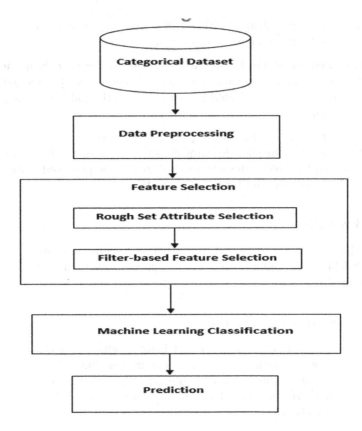

Fig. 2. Framework for the categorical data classification

4.3 Feature Selection

By applying the proposed feature selection to phishing website detection dataset, RS-IG produces 26 features and RS-CH2 produces 25 features. IG, CH2 and RS however produce 23 features each. For mushroom dataset, RS-IG produces 8 features and RS-CH2 produces 9 features. While 6 features from RS have the best matches, 5 most important features of IG and CH2 are used as it is in previous works [12,14].

4.4 Machine Learning Classification with Baseline Classifiers, Classical and Proposed Feature Selection Methods

In this subsection, the machine learning modelling steps with baseline model, classical feature selection methods and proposed feature selection methods are discussed.

Machine Learning Modelling with Baseline Model. These three popular machine learning classifiers, namely: SVM, RF and MLP are employed for the categorical data classification. Weka [19] is used for the analysis. This model is referred to as baseline model in this paper.

Machine Learning Modelling with Classical Feature Selection Methods. The three machine learning classifiers, that is, SVM, RF, and MLP are also employed to classify the selected features of IG, CH2 and RS. Weka [19] is used for the classification.

Machine Learning Modelling with Proposed Feature Selection Method. The three machine learning classifiers, that is, SVM, RF, and MLP are also employed to classify the selected features of the proposed feature selection method. Weka [19] is used for the classification.

4.5 Prediction

After the feature are extracted, the machine learning classifiers are evaluated using k-fold cross validation (k = 10) to prevent overfitting. Weka [19] is used for the analysis.

4.6 Performance Evaluation

All the feature selection methods and baseline classifier model are compared using accuracy, precision, recall and F-measure performance metrics. The equations for estimating the metrics are presented in Eqs. 3 to 6, where TP is true positive; TN is true negative; FP is false positive; FN is false negative; and l is the number of classes.

$$accuracy = \frac{TP + TN}{TP + FP + TN + FN} \tag{3}$$

$$Precision = \frac{\sum_{i=1}^{l} \frac{TP}{TP+FP}}{l} \tag{4}$$

$$Recall = \frac{\sum_{i=1}^{l} \frac{TP}{TP+FN}}{l} \tag{5}$$

$$F - measure = \frac{2 \times (Recall \times Precision)}{Recall + Precision} \tag{6}$$

5 Results

The results of the experimental analysis are presented and discussed in this section. Table 1 presents the accuracy performance of the feature selection methods (IG, CH2, RS, RS-IG, RS-CH2) and the baseline model (baseline), while Table 2 presents the respective precision, recall and F-measure for class (0) and class (1) as well as their weighted average performance.

Table 1. Accuracy performance of feature selection methods and classification algorithms

Classifiers	Model	Phishing Website Detection	Mushroom
SVM	IG	93.68	99.90
	CH2	93.73	89.86
	RS	93.79	99.80
	RS-IG	93.76	99.90
	RS-CH2	93.85	99.90
	Baseline	93.80	100.00
RF	IG	97.18	99.90
	CH2	97.02	96.55
	RS	97.20	99.90
	RS-IG	**97.32**	**100.00**
	RS-CH2	97.23	**100.00**
	Baseline	97.26	**100.00**
MLP	IG	96.42	99.90
	CH2	96.45	97.03
	RS	96.69	99.84
	RS-IG	96.80	99.86
	RS-CH2	96.81	**100.00**
	Baseline	96.79	**100.00**

Table 1 shows that among the feature selection methods, the proposed RS-IG feature selection method with RF classifier records the best accuracy of 97.32% for phishing website detection dataset compared to the highest accuracy of 97,26 by the baseline method. RS-IG and RS-CH2 methods with RF classifier and RS-CH2 method with MLP all record the best accuracy of 100% for mushroom dataset. This is comparable to the baseline accuracy of 100% for mushroom dataset. The classical filter-based feature selection and Rough Set Attribute Reduction methods however record worse performance compared to the baseline. The best scores are highlighted in bold.

For phishing website detection dataset in Table 2, RS-IG feature selection method with RF classifier records the best precision of 0.977 for phishing class, CH2 feature selection model with MLP classifier records the best precision of 0.976 for legitimate class, while RS-IG feature selection method with RF records the best precision of 0.973 for weighted average performance. Also, RS-IG and RS-CH2 feature selection models with RF classifier record the best recall of 0.962 for phishing class, RS-IG feature selection method with RF classifier records the best recall of 0.982 for legitimate class, while RS-IG feature selection method with RF records the best precision of 0.973 for weighted average performance. RS-IG feature selection method with RF classifier records the best F-measure of

Table 2. Precision, Recall and F-Measure performance of feature selection methods and classification algorithms

Classifiers	Model	Class	Phishing Website Detection			Mushroom		
			P	R	F1	P	R	F1
SVM	IG	0	0.940	0.916	0.928	1.000	0.998	0.999
		1	0.935	0.953	0.944	0.998	1.000	0.999
		W. Avg.	0.937	0.937	0.937	0.999	0.999	0.999
	CH2	0	0.940	0.916	0.928	0.935	0.849	0.890
		1	0.935	0.954	0.944	0.890	0.945	0.906
		W. Avg.	0.937	0.937	0.937	0.901	0.899	0.898
	RS	0	0.939	0.919	0.929	0.998	0.998	0.998
		1	0.937	0.953	0.945	0.998	0.998	0.998
		W. Avg.	0.938	0.938	0.938	0.998	0.998	0.998
	RS-IG	0	0.939	0.918	0.929	1.000	0.998	0.999
		1	0.936	0.953	0.944	0.998	1.000	0.999
		W. Avg.	0.938	0.938	0.938	0.999	0.999	0.999
	RS-CH2	0	0.941	0.919	0.930	1.000	0.998	0.999
		1	0.937	0.954	0.945	0.998	1.000	0.999
		W. Avg.	0.939	0.938	0.938	0.999	0.999	0.999
	Baseline	0	0.939	0.920	0.929	**1.000**	**1.000**	**1.000**
		1	0.937	0.953	0.945	**1.000**	**1.000**	**1.000**
		W. Avg.	0.938	0.938	0.938	**1.000**	**1.000**	**1.000**
RF	IG	0	0.976	0.960	0.968	1.000	0.998	0.999
		1	0.969	0.981	0.975	0.998	1.000	0.999
		W. Avg.	0.972	0.972	0.972	0.999	0.999	0.999
	CH2	0	0.974	0.958	0.966	0.993	0.935	0.963
		1	0.967	0.980	0.973	0.942	0.994	0.968
		W. Avg.	0.970	0.970	0.970	0.967	0.966	0.965
	RS	0	0.975	0.961	0.968	0.998	1.000	0.999
		1	0.969	0.981	0.975	1.000	0.998	0.999
		W. Avg.	0.972	0.972	0.972	0.999	0.999	0.999
	RS-IG	0	**0.977**	**0.962**	**0.970**	1.000	1.000	1.000
		1	0.970	**0.982**	**0.976**	1.000	1.000	1.000
		W. Avg.	**0.973**	**0.973**	**0.973**	1.000	1.000	1.000
	RS-CH2	0	0.975	0.962	0.969	1.000	1.000	1.000
		1	0.970	0.981	**0.976**	1.000	1.000	1.000
		W. Avg.	0.972	0.972	**0.973**	1.000	1.000	1.000
	Baseline	0	**0.977**	0.961	0.969	1.000	1.000	1.000
		1	**0.969**	**0.982**	**0.976**	1.000	1.000	1.000
		W. Avg.	**0.973**	**0.973**	**0.973**	1.000	1.000	1.000
MLP	IG	0	0.969	0.950	0.959	1.000	0.998	0.999
		1	0.961	0.976	0.968	0.998	1.000	0.999
		W. Avg.	0.964	0.964	0.964	0.998	0.999	0.999
	CH2	0	0.950	0.950	0.960	0.994	0.944	0.968
		1	**0.976**	0.976	0.968	0.950	0.995	0.972
		W. Avg.	0.965	0.965	0.965	0.971	0.970	0.970
	RS	0	0.970	0.955	0.962	1.000	0.997	0.998
		1	0.964	0.977	0.970	0.997	1.000	0.998
		W. Avg.	0.967	0.967	0.967	0.998	0.998	0.998
	RS-IG	0	0.970	0.958	0.964	1.000	0.997	0.999
		1	0.967	0.976	0.971	0.997	1.000	0.999
		W. Avg.	0.968	0.968	0.968	0.999	0.999	0.999
	RS-CH2	0	0.968	0.959	0.964	1.000	1.000	1.000
		1	0.968	0.975	0.971	1.000	1.000	1.000
		W. Avg.	0.968	0.968	0.968	1.000	1.000	1.000
	Baseline	0	0.964	0.942	0.953	1.000	1.000	1.000
		1	0.955	0.972	0.963	1.000	1.000	1.000
		W. Avg.	0.959	0.959	0.959	1.000	1.000	1.000

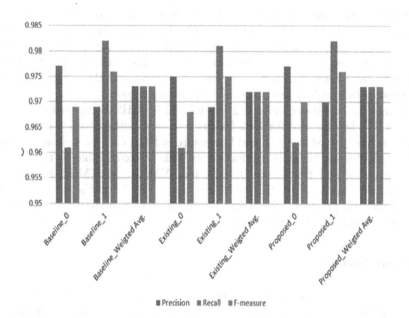

Fig. 3. Comparison of state-of-the-art Precision, Recall and F-measure of the Baseline, Existing and Proposed feature selection models for phishing website detection dataset

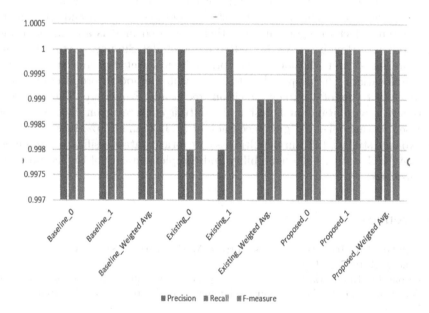

Fig. 4. Comparison of the state-of-the-art Precision, Recall and F-measure of the Baseline, Existing and Proposed feature selection models for mushroom dataset

0.970 for phishing class, RS-IG and RS-CH2 feature selection methods with RF classifier record the best F-measure of 0.976 for legitimate class, while RS-IG and RS-CH2 feature selection method with RF record the best F-measure of 0.973 for weighted average performance. The baseline with RF classifier record same recall and F-measure scores for legitimate class and the weighted average performance but slightly lesser scores for phishing class.

For mushroom dataset in Table 2, RS-IG and RS-CH2 feature selection methods with RF classifier and RS-CH2 feature selection method with MLP classifier record the best precision, recall and F-measure of 100% each for poisonous, legitimate class, average weighted performance. This is comparable to the baseline precision, recall and F-measure of 100% for SVM, RF and MLP. RS-IG however per-forms worse with MLP and SVM. Also, Fig. 3 and Fig. 4 illustrate the state-of-the arts precision, recall and F-measure for phishing website detection and mushroom datasets, respectively.

6   Conclusion

This paper has presented a novel feature selection method that employs Rough Set Attribute Reduction to enhance the important feature selection from categorical data by classical filter-based feature selection algorithms. The aim is to improve the accuracy performance of the feature selection-based machine learning classifiers over the inefficient machine learning classifiers that rely on full features. Rough Set Reduct is used to guide irrelevant feature filtering and improve important features prediction. In the study, Information Gain and Chi-Square Test feature selection algorithms and their improved models are explored and compared with Rough Set Attribute Reduction model. Support Vector Machine, Random Forest and Multilayer Perceptron Neural Network are employed for the classification. The proposed feature selection method records the best performance in terms of accuracy, precision, recall and F-measure. They perform impressively with Random Forest and Multi-layer Perceptron classifiers. The proposed feature selection gives accuracy of 97.32% and 100%, respectively in the two case studies. In future, multiclass categorical data classification and metrics like AUC, outlier detection ability and complementarity of the features will be considered.

References

1. Quinlan, J.R.: Induction of decision trees. Mach. Learn. **1**, 81–106 (1986). https:// doi.org/10.1007/BF00116251
2. Oriola, O., Kotzé, E.: Improved semi-supervised learning technique for automatic detection of South African abusive language on Twitter. S. Afr. Comput. J. **32**, 56–79 (2020)
3. Pinky, N.J., Islam, S.M., Alice, R.S.: Edibility detection of mushroom using ensemble methods. Int. J. Image Graph. Sig. Process. **11**, 55–62 (2019)

4. Babagoli, M., Pourmahmood, M., Vahid, A.: Heuristic nonlinear regression strategy for detecting phishing websites. Soft. Comput. **23**(12), 4315–4327 (2018). https://doi.org/10.1007/s00500-018-3084-2
5. Wah, Y.B., Ibrahim, N., Hamid, H.A., Abdul-Rahman, S., Fong, S.: Feature selection methods: case of filter and wrapper approaches for maximising classification accuracy. Pertanika J. Sci. Technol. **26**, 329–340 (2018)
6. Dharani, M., Badkul, S., Gharat, K., Vidhate, A., Bhosale, D.: Detection of phishing websites using ensemble machine learning approach. In: ITM Web of Conference (ICACC-2021), vol. 40, p. 03012, pp. 1–5 (2021)
7. Honest, N.: A survey on feature selection techniques. GIS Sci. J. **7**, 353–358 (2020)
8. Chandrashekar, G., Sahin, F.: A survey on feature selection methods. Comput. Electr. Eng. **40**, 16–28 (2014)
9. Chouchoulas, A., Shen, Q.: Rough set-aided keyword reduction for text categorization. Appl. Artif. Intell. **15**, 843–873 (2001)
10. Jensen, R., Shen, Q.: Rough set-based feature selection: a review. In: Rough Computing: Theories, Technologies and Applications (2007). https://doi.org/10.4018/978-1-59904-552-8.ch003
11. Peng, Y., Wu, Z., Jiang, J.: A novel feature selection approach for biomedical data classification. J. Biomed. Inform. **43**, 15–23 (2010)
12. Wang, L., Ke, Y.: Feature selection considering interaction, redundancy and complementarity for outlier detection in categorical data. Knowl.-Based Syst. **275**, 110678 (2023)
13. Wang, C., Wang, Y., Shao, M., Qian, Y., Chen, D.: Fuzzy rough attribute reduction for categorical data. IEEE Trans. Fuzzy Syst. **28**, 818–830 (2020)
14. Shu, W., Shen, H.: Incremental feature selection based on rough set in dynamic incomplete data. Pattern Recogn. **47**, 3890–3906 (2014)
15. Abdoos, A.A., Mianaei, P.K., Ghadikolaei, M.R.: Combined VMD-SVM based feature selection method for classification of power quality events. Appl. Soft Comput. J. **38**, 637–646 (2016)
16. Odhiambo Omuya, E., Onyango Okeyo, G., Waema Kimwele, M.: Feature selection for classification using principal component analysis and information gain. Expert Syst. Appl. **174**, 114765 (2021)
17. Erişti, H., Yildirim, Ö., Erişti, B., Demir, Y.: Optimal feature selection for classification of the power quality events using wavelet transform and least squares support vector machines. Int. J. Electr. Power Energy Syst. **49**, 95–103 (2013)
18. Chiew, K.L., Lin, C., Wong, K., Yong, K.S.C., King, W.: A new hybrid ensemble feature selection framework for machine learning-based phishing detection system. Inf. Sci. **484**, 153–166 (2019)
19. Garner, S.R.: WEKA: the waikato environment for knowledge analysis. In: Proceedings of the New Zealand Computer Science Research Students Conference 1995, pp. 57–64 (1995)
20. Pedregosa, F., Varoquaux, G., Gramfort, A., et al.: Scikit-learn: machine learning in Python. J. Mach. Learn. Res. **12**, 2825–2830 (2011)
21. Mohammad, R.M.A., MsCluskey, L., Thantah, F.: UCI Machine Learning Repository (2015)

Enhancing Face Anti-spoofing Systems Through Synthetic Image Generation

César Vega[✉][iD] and Ruben Manrique[iD]

Universidad de los Andes, Bogotá, Colombia
{c.vegaf,rf.manrique}@uniandes.edu.co

Abstract. This study introduces a strategy for synthetic image generation aimed at enhancing the detection capability of facial authentication systems (FAS). By employing various digital manipulation techniques, new synthetic fake images were generated using existing datasets. Through experiments and result analysis, the impact of using these new fake samples on improving the detection accuracy of FAS systems was evaluated. The findings demonstrated the effectiveness of synthetic image generation in augmenting the diversity and complexity of the training data. Fine-tuning using the enhanced datasets significantly improved the detection accuracy across the evaluated FAS systems. Nonetheless, the degree of improvement varied among systems, indicating varying susceptibility to specific types of attacks.

Keywords: Face Anti-Spoofing (FAS) · Presentation Attack Detection (PAD) · Digital Manipulation (MD) · Data Augmentation

1 Introduction

In the era of expanding intelligent workspace environments, the utilization of technologies like facial recognition has witnessed a notable surge across diverse domains, including but not limited to banking and security within restricted zones [10]. However, with the increasing popularity of these systems, there is a concurrent escalation in malicious activities aimed at compromising their integrity. Cyber attackers employ a range of tactics, encompassing presentation attacks utilizing printed photos or 3D facial masks [2,4], as well as digital manipulation attacks involving the creation of forgeries, such as DeepFakes [7,24].

Face Anti-Spoofing (FAS) systems have been developed to safeguard facial recognition systems. Early approaches in deep learning employed Convolutional Neural Networks (CNNs) to detect identity spoofing [7]. More recent advancements include anomaly detection methods [7] and liveness detection in images [23]. These approaches have been supplemented with widely adopted datasets. Notably, CASIA represents a comprehensive dataset for antispoofing model development, encompassing diverse ethnicities, modalities, and attack types [13,14,21]. However, the CASIA dataset lacks robust instances of digital manipulation, which is a prevalent type of attack in practice. According to [18] the

H. Florez and M. Leon (Eds.): ICAI 2023, CCIS 1874, pp. 16–30, 2024.
https://doi.org/10.1007/978-3-031-46813-1_2

generation of DeepFakes have grown by 16%, and the percentage of people who know how to create or use DeepFake applications has doubled since 2019, with 2% of the surveyed individuals in 2022 having this knowledge. Undoubtedly, these trends increase the risk of attempts at synthetic generation-based forgeries.

To overcome this limitation, data augmentation techniques have been proposed [5,22,25]. In this study, strategies for creating spoofing attack instances are presented, involving both simple face substitution and digital manipulation of images. Architectures based on probabilistic diffusion models for InPainting [15] were employed. These methods enable the generation of partially modified faces, which can be included as new examples of forgeries in existing datasets. This represents the primary contribution of this work.

To assess the effectiveness of FAS systems against artificially generated attack scenarios, three distinct FAS systems were chosen. Their performances were evaluated using metrics defined by the ISO/IEC 30107-3 standard. The selected FAS systems were evaluated both before and after undergoing Fine Tuning with the newly constructed datasets. The results of this evaluation, along with the corresponding discussion, constitute the second contribution of this study.

The structure of this paper is as follows: Sect. 2 provides an overview of the related work on FAS systems. Section 3 details the methodology employed for dataset construction and the selected FAS systems. Section 4 presents the experimental results. Subsequently, Sect. 5 and 6 offers a comprehensive discussion, future research directions, and concluding remarks, summarizing the key ideas and findings presented throughout the paper.

2   Related Work

Numerous investigations have been conducted to evaluate Facial Authentication Systems (FAS), with a particular emphasis on texture analysis to detect presentation attacks. Several approaches have focused on pixel-wise classification techniques, such as the automatic discovery of optimal pixel labels through pyramid supervision [24]. Additionally, there has been an exploration into effective methods grounded in the concept of Meta Patterns for enhancing the detection of deep forgeries [1]. Within the spectrum of deep texture-based features employed for robust forgery detection, notable techniques include Local Binary Patterns (LBP), Speeded-Up Robust Features (SURF), and Difference of Gaussians (DoG) [12].

The proliferation of digital manipulation attacks, predominantly facilitated by Generative Adversarial Network (GAN) architectures, encompasses the production of entirely or partially altered, photorealistic facial images through techniques such as expression swapping, attribute manipulation, and complete face synthesis. Confronting these attacks remains a formidable challenge for Facial Authentication Systems (FAS) [22], given that digitally manipulated content of this nature can be generated routinely via "no code" applications that effortlessly modify facial attributes through filter-based adjustments. The accessibility to digital manipulation technologies is widespread and does not necessitate specialized expertise or skills.

This presents both a potential hazard and an opportunity to bolster existing systems through the generation of additional training data. The generation of synthetic images via digital manipulation to enhance training datasets has received substantial attention across diverse domains. Synthetic imagery has proven pivotal in supporting endeavors such as facial alignment, facial recognition, 3D facial pose estimation, pedestrian detection, action recognition, among others [5]. Furthermore, these data can be continuously collected from diverse systems, making them potentially suitable for semi-supervised learning [25], and, in combination with adversarial learning could serve as a viable option to increase model defense to a wider range of attack types [25].

To summarize, research indicates that utilizing data augmentation during model training can yield advantages. It is suggested that the inclusion of synthetic images depicting counterfeit samples can aid in the precise classification of genuine samples [4,8,24]. This paper contributes to this line of research.

3   Methodology

This section outlines the methodology employed for generating synthetic images used for substitution-based presentation attacks and digital manipulation attacks. Furthermore, it elaborates on the training of models for facial authentication systems (FAS) and the evaluation of these models.

3.1   Generation of Image Sets

Considering the difficulty and time-consuming process involved in creating and subsequently classifying examples of presentation attacks [2,5,19,22], the following image sets were developed with the aim of generating a larger quantity of forgery images covering various attack scenarios such as presentation attacks and digital manipulation attacks.

Substitution-Based Image Set. This image set aims to provide many images for substitution-based presentation attacks while maintaining the image conditions by not covering the surrounding environment of the subject to be impersonated. The construction process of this dataset begins with the recognition of the face of the person whose face is to be substituted (see Fig. 1 - Person X (a)), and in the same frame (where the face is recognized), the face of the person to be impersonated is placed (see Fig. 1 - Person y (b)), which was previously recognized, resulting in images with direct substitution (see Fig. 1 - (c)).

To generate the dataset, different combinations of x/y were created using 20 individuals from the CASIA dataset [13,14,21]. For each of these 20 individuals, the first 8 videos were taken, resulting in the creation of approximately 6,900,000 images, which allows for the creation of around 25,000 videos. This approach enables the preservation of various impersonation contexts originally present in the CASIA image set, such as mask printing with and without simulated eye or facial movement (Fig. 2a), as well as recordings on a mobile device with different camera angles (Fig. 2b).

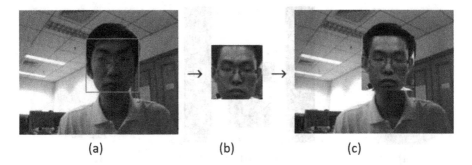

(a)   (b)   (c)

Fig. 1. Face substitution

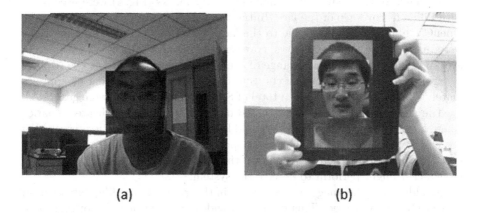

(a)   (b)

Fig. 2. Examples of face substitution

Regeneration-Based Image Set (InPainting). This image set is generated using probabilistic diffusion models for noise removal (RePaint) [15]. It requires an input image of a person X (see Fig. 3 - Person X (a)) and a binary black and white mask (see Fig. 3 - Binary Mask (b)), which is used to determine the segments that need to be regenerated in the image. Once the repainting model is applied, a new image is obtained (see Fig. 3 - Resulting Image (c)). By using appropriate masks with this method, we can preserve the original environment of the image and focus exclusively on facial elements. For generation, high-resolution images from CASIA were used, which had to be adjusted to allow the model to regenerate the image borders, resulting in a square resolution of 256×256.

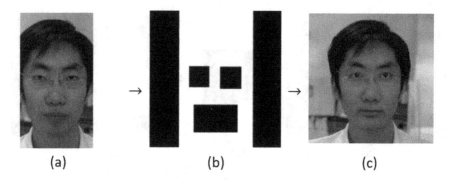

Fig. 3. Face InPainting

To generate the images, four different binary masks (Fig. 4) were used, each with different coverage of the face. Initially, masks were auto-detected using the OpenCV library[1]. However, due to the lack of accuracy, manual modifications were made to the mask as follows: coverage of eyes and mouth (a), coverage of eyes, nose, and mouth (b), coverage of eyes (c) and coverage of left eye (d).

From each mask, seven subsets were obtained, each consisting of approximately 400 images. As a result, a total of 8368 repainted images were generated.

The choice of these masks was based on the intention to replicate scenarios where facial authentication systems could be challenged by realistic presentation attacks. By creating masks that cover specific parts of the face, such as eyes, nose, and mouth, or even just one eye, the aim is to mimic the manipulations an attacker might perform to deceive the system.

In addition to the image sets generated in this research, the ffhq dataset from StyleGAN [11] was used. This dataset provides an additional set of images of digital manipulation attacks. In Table 1 a summary of the resulting datasets is shown. The total number of images in each set was randomly divided into three subsets: training, validation, and testing.

---

[1] https://github.com/opencv/opencv/tree/master.

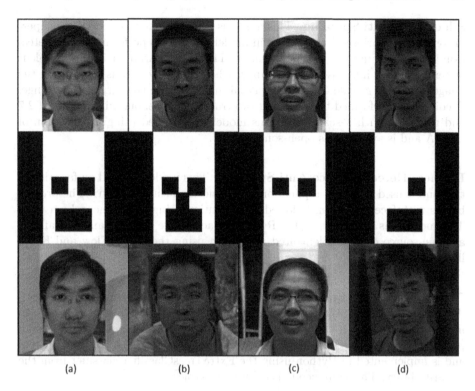

Fig. 4. Examples of images generated by the diffusion model

Table 1. Division of image sets

Image sets	Training	Validation	Testing	Total
CASIA	82536	16507	20635	119678
Substitution	4772300	954460	1193077	6919837
StyleGAN	160160	32032	40040	200200
Diffusion	5355	1339	1674	8368

3.2 Selected Models of FAS Systems

The selection of the FAS systems was based on the premise of addressing the issues present in the literature, particularly focusing on texture-based FAS approaches, which are widely used [5,19]. Within this category, the Silent FAS and Object FAS models were chosen. Additionally, FAS systems with face recognition capabilities, such as Liveness Detection FAS and Object FAS, were selected to determine the advantages and disadvantages of face detection in synthetically generated facial images, which are becoming increasingly sophisticated [3,22].

Silent Face Anti Spoofing. This model is primarily based on auxiliary supervision of the Fourier spectrum map in model training to perform liveness detection in an image in the frequency domain. The Silent FAS model adopts a silent or texture-based liveness detection approach. Firstly, the face is detected in the image, and then a scale of 2.7 and 4 is taken to increase the surrounding range. Prediction is performed by weighting two trained models, one with a scale of 2.7 and the other with a scale of 4. This model was trained using a derivation of CASIA and is available as open-source code[2].

Liveness Detection Face Anti Spoofing. This model is based on face detection and is used in a web application for biometric authentication[3]. The process begins with face detection, followed by validation using a deep neural network. This model was trained using the Replay-Attack image dataset[4] and is available as open-source code, implemented in Python using the TensorFlow and Keras libraries.

Objects Face Anti Spoofing. This model is based on the combination of two different color spaces: $CIE\ L^*u^*v^*$ and YC_bC_r, using histograms to classify an image as real or fake. It was trained using the Replay-Attack image dataset and a private database. This model utilizes an ensemble method with 10 decision trees and is implemented in Python using the ExtraTreesClassifier classifier from the sklearn library. The source code is openly available[5].

3.3   Datasets Preparation

The Sustitution, StyleGAN, and Diffusion datasets only contain examples of fake images (i.e., positive samples). To perform Fine Tuning of the FAS models, data balancing is necessary. A subset of real images from the CASIA* dataset was randomly selected for this purpose. Additionally, downsampling was applied to the generated fake images. The sizes of the resulting datasets after balancing are presented in Table 2.

Table 2. Size of datasets after balancing

Image Dataset	Fake	Real
Substitution	21000	20753*
StyleGAN	21000	20753*
Diffusion	6694	6694*

---

[2] https://github.com/minivision-ai/Silent-Face-Anti-Spoofing/.

[3] https://github.com/birdowl21/Face-Liveness-Detection-Anti-Spoofing-Web-App.

[4] https://www.idiap.ch/en/dataset/replayattack.

[5] https://github.com/ee09115/spoofing_detection.

Additionally, to perform the Fine Tuning process, the images need to be transformed according to the expected input of each FAS model, and in some cases, the output (i.e., labels). Table 3 provides a summary of the expected inputs/outputs for each model.

Table 3. Input and output formats for each FAS model

Silent FAS	Liveness Detection FAS	Object FAS
Input: 3D tensor (80, 80, 3)	Input: 3D tensor (32, 32, 3)	Input: Vector (1536)
Output: Binary	Output: One-hot encoding	Output: Binary

3.4 Model Evaluation

The evaluation of the models was performed using test datasets that included both substitution-based presentation attacks and digital manipulation attacks. The comparison will be made in terms of metrics outlined in ISO/IEC30107-3[6]. For this research, the standard labeling convention will be followed, where fake images are assigned the label 0 and real images are assigned the label 1. The metrics used for evaluation are detailed below:

– **Attack Presentation Classification Error Rate (APCER):** It is the proportion of presentation attacks incorrectly classified as genuine presentations (i.e., the error rate of fake images classified as real).

$$APCER = FP/(TN + FP) \qquad (1)$$

– **Average Classification Error Rate (ACER):** It is the average of the two error rates mentioned above.

$$ACER = (APCER + NPCER)/2 \qquad (2)$$

where, TP is the number of fake images classified as fake (true positives), TN is the number of real images classified as real (true negatives), FP is the number of real images classified as fake (false positives), and FN is the number of fake images classified as real (false negatives).

4   Experimental Setup

In this section, different experiments are conducted to evaluate the performance of the FAS models before and after Fine Tuning using the generated image sets. The experiments were conducted on three selected FAS models: Silent FAS, Liveness Detection FAS, and Object FAS.

---

[6] https://www.iso.org/standard/79520.html.

4.1 Experiment 1: Evaluation of the Performance of FAS Models Without Fine Tuning

In Experiment 1, the FAS models without Fine Tuning were evaluated. We aimed to observe the behavior of the models, without additional training rounds on our generated datasets. As shown in Table 4, the results demonstrate that all models achieved high error rates (APCER, ACER) in most of the evaluated image sets. Silent FAS achieved the best performance with an error of 0 in the CASIA dataset, but it clearly exhibited poor performance in the other datasets. This can be interpreted as a limitation in detecting digital manipulation attacks.

On average, Silent FAS exhibited an average APCER of 0.6795 and an average ACER of 0.3326. Liveness Detection FAS and Object FAS demonstrated average APCER values of 0.8141 and 0.6122, and average ACER values of 0.4820 and 0.3545, respectively. These results underscore the importance of considering the performance of FAS models across diverse image sets, as each model exhibits strengths and weaknesses in different scenarios. These findings highlight the importance of evaluating and comparing multiple FAS models on different datasets to gain a more comprehensive understanding of their performance and select the most suitable model for a specific presentation attack detection application.

Table 4. Experiment 1: Results of FAS models without Fine Tuning. The test subset was used for each dataset.

Image Dataset	Silent FAS		Liveness Detection FAS		Object FAS	
	APCER	ACER	APCER	ACER	APCER	ACER
CASIA	0	0	0.4496	0.5247	0.61	0.4986
Substitution	0.7517	0.3758	0.9099	0.455	0.8227	0.4114
StyleGAN	0.9729	0.4577	0.9153	0.4577	0.4681	0.2341
Diffusion	0.9934	0.4967	0.9815	0.4907	0.5478	0.2739
Averages	**0.6795**	**0.3326**	**0.8141**	**0.4820**	**0.6122**	**0.3545**

4.2 Experiment 2: Models Fine Tuning

In Experiment 2, the Fine Tuning process of the models was carried out using different image sets. Each image set's corresponding training set was used to fine-tune the model. The results are presented for both training and validation. The results on the test datasets are reserved for Experiment 3. For the models based on neural architectures, the number of epochs corresponding to the best checkpoint obtained in validation is reported, without exceeding 50 epochs.

Silent FAS. The results are presented in Table 5. Overall, it can be observed that the model achieved high accuracy (Acc) values and low loss values both in the training and validation sets for all evaluated image datasets.

Specifically, in the CASIA image dataset, the model with a scale of 4 achieved a training accuracy of 0.9968 and a loss of 0.0071, while in the validation set, it achieved an accuracy of 0.9938 and a loss of 0.0105. On the other hand, the model with a scale of 2.7 achieved a training accuracy of 0.996 and a loss of 0.0098, and a validation accuracy of 0.9948 and a loss of 0.0142.

For the Sustitution, StyleGAN, and Diffusion image datasets, the model also demonstrated solid performance in terms of accuracy and loss. These results indicate that the Fine Tuning process improved the performance of the Silent FAS model in detecting presentation attacks, demonstrating the effectiveness of this approach in fine-tuning the model for specific image datasets.

Table 5. Experiment 2: Accuracy/Loss obtained in the Fine Tuning process of Silent FAS using each image dataset

Image Dataset	Model with 4-scale					Model with 2.7-scale				
	Epochs	Acc	Loss	Acc_val	Loss_val	Epochs	Acc	Loss	Acc_val	Loss_val
CASIA	4	0.9968	0.0071	0.9938	0.0105	4	0.996	0.0098	0.9948	0.0142
Substitution	10	0.976	0.0335	0.9666	0.0462	9	0.9782	0.0295	0.9703	0.0395
StyleGAN	4	0.9999	0.0026	0.9991	0.0033	3	0.9975	0.0066	0.9961	0.0103
Diffusion	4	0.9998	0.0031	0.9981	0.0036	3	0.9986	0.0051	0.9992	0.005

Liveness Detection FAS. The results obtained are shown in Table 6. It can be observed that the model achieved high accuracy (Acc) values and low loss (Loss) values both in the training and validation sets for all evaluated image datasets.

Specifically, in the CASIA image dataset, the model achieved a training accuracy of 0.999 and a loss of 0.0008, while in the validation set, it achieved an accuracy of 0.9979 and a loss of 0.0007. In the Sustitution image dataset, the model exhibited a training accuracy of 0.9862 and a loss of 0.0362, and a validation accuracy of 0.9904 and a loss of 0.0215. As expected, similar to the Silent FAS model, the fine-tuning process proves to be effective with all datasets, indicating its effectiveness in handling different types of attacks.

Object FAS. The results obtained are shown in Table 7. The CASIA image dataset achieved the highest level of accuracy with a value of 0.9976, followed by the Sustitution image dataset with 0.9971, the Diffusion image dataset with 0.997, and finally the StyleGAN image dataset with 0.9976. These results indicate that the Fine Tuning process was effective in improving the performance of the Object FAS model in detecting fake images. Additionally, the accuracy values in the validation set (Acc_val) are also high, indicating that the model generalizes well to previously unseen data.

Table 6. Experiment 2: Accuracy/Loss obtained in the Fine Tuning process of Liveness Detection FAS using each image dataset

Image Dataset	Liveness model				
	Epochs	Acc	Loss	Acc_val	Loss_val
CASIA	40	0.999	0.0008	0.9979	0.0007
Substitution	40	0.9862	0.0362	0.9904	0.0215
StyleGAN	50	0.9993	0.0025	1	0.0009
Diffusion	40	0.867	0.2867	0.8734	0.2873

Table 7. Experiment 2: Accuracy obtained in the Fine Tuning process of Object FAS using each image dataset

Image Dataset	Decision Trees	
	Acc	Acc_val
CASIA	0.9976	0.9967
Substitution	0.9971	0.9944
StyleGAN	0.9976	0.9887
Diffusion	0.997	0.991

4.3   Experiment 3: Evaluation of FAS Model Performance After Fine Tuning

In Experiment 3, the Fine Tuning process was performed using all image datasets on the models. In contrast to Experiment 2, where Fine Tuning was conducted on individual datasets, in this experiment, Fine Tuning was performed collectively using all datasets, and evaluation was done on the test sets. The results obtained are summarized in Table 8. In terms of the APCER metric (Attack Presentation Classification Error Rate), both the Silent FAS and Diffusion models achieved an APCER of 0, indicating no false positives were detected in the classification of attacks. On the other hand, the StyleGAN model obtained an APCER of 0.2629, and the Sustitution model achieved an APCER of 0.4857.

Regarding the ACER (Average Classification Error Rate), the averages obtained were 0.1086 for Silent FAS, 0.0050 for Liveness Detection FAS, and 0.4814 for Object FAS. This indicates that the Liveness Detection FAS model had the best performance in terms of the average error rate, while the Silent FAS model had the lowest performance. Overall, it is evident that the Fine Tuning process improved the performance of the models when compared to the results of Experiment 1 (without Fine Tuning).

Table 8. Experiment 3: Results on the test sets after Fine Tuning with all image datasets

Image Dataset	Silent FAS		Liveness Detection FAS		Object FAS	
	APCER	ACER	APCER	ACER	APCER	ACER
CASIA	0	0.0602	0	0.0003	0.7817	0.5444
StyleGAN	0.2629	0.1314	0	0	0.9201	0.46
Diffusion	0	0	0	0	0.9502	0.4751
Substitution	0.4857	0.2428	0.0396	0.0198	0.892	0.446
Averages	**0.1872**	**0.1086**	**0.0099**	**0.0050**	**0.8860**	**0.4814**

5   Results Analysis

In this section, the analysis of the results obtained from the conducted experiments will be presented. The most relevant findings will be discussed, and corresponding conclusions will be drawn.

Firstly, it was observed that the strategy of generating synthetic images using presentation attacks and digital manipulation was effective in improving the performance of the evaluated FAS systems. The generated datasets allowed for increased diversity and complexity in the training data, resulting in an enhancement in attack detection capability.

Regarding the individual experiments, it was found that Fine-Tuning using presentation attack datasets had a positive impact on the Silent FAS and Liveness Detection FAS systems. These systems exhibited a significant improvement in detection accuracy metrics, with an average reduction in APCER of 25% and 83%, respectively. On the other hand, the Object FAS system did not show a significant improvement after Fine-Tuning with presentation attack datasets.

In the case of Fine-Tuning using digital manipulation datasets, it was observed that the Silent FAS and Object FAS systems demonstrated an improvement in detection metrics, with an average reduction in APCER of 61% and 13%, respectively. However, the Liveness Detection FAS system did not show a significant improvement after Fine-Tuning with digital manipulation datasets.

Regarding the analysis of the combined results from all datasets, it was found that the Liveness Detection FAS system showed the most significant improvement, with an average reduction in APCER of 83%. The Silent FAS system also exhibited a considerable improvement, with an average reduction in APCER of 25%. On the other hand, the Object FAS system showed a limited improvement, with an average reduction in APCER of 10%.

In conclusion, the results obtained demonstrate the effectiveness of the strategy of generating synthetic images in improving attack detection capability in the evaluated FAS systems. However, it was observed that the type of image dataset used in Fine-Tuning can have a significant impact on the results. Further research is needed to determine the most appropriate type of image dataset for each specific FAS system.

6   Conclusions and Future Work

This study employed strategies to artificially simulate presentation attacks and digital manipulation, resulting in the generation of new fake samples to complement existing anti-spoof datasets. The explored strategies have demonstrated improvements in the detection performance of three selected FAS systems, and the results are anticipated to provide a valuable resource for future research in the field.

FAS models trained without fine-tuning on the generated data exhibited a bad performance in terms of APCER metrics, with an average rate of 70% across the three FAS systems. However, after applying fine-tuning techniques, a noteworthy enhancement in APCER was achieved, with an average rate of 53% for the three FAS systems. The implementation of data augmentation techniques utilizing synthetic image generation exhibited positive outcomes, particularly for the Silent FAS and Liveness Detection FAS models. The Average Presentation Classification Error Rate (APCER) demonstrated improvements of 25% and 83% respectively.

In future research, further exploration will be conducted to investigate the correlation between the optimal type of image dataset for augmentation and the prevailing landscape of FAS architectures documented in the existing literature. Drawing from the knowledge obtained through the literature review, it is planned to assess FAS architectures that utilize feature extraction techniques, such as Local Binary Patterns (LBP) [17], Speeded-Up Robust Features (SURF) [20], and Difference of Gaussians (DoG) [9], for image representation. These approaches effectively capture the intrinsic textures inherent in the images. Lastly, to explore novel possibilities in synthetic image generation, we plan to implement and investigate state-of-the-art architectures such as CUT [16], Cycle-GAN [26], and DCLGAN [6]. Building upon recent successes reported in the literature, these approaches offer the potential for advancing the field of synthetic image generation for FAS systems.

References

1. Cai, R., Li, Z., Wan, R., Li, H., Hu, Y., Kot, A.C.: Learning meta pattern for face anti-spoofing. CoRR abs/2110.06753 (2021). https://arxiv.org/abs/2110.06753
2. Feng, H., et al.: Learning generalized spoof cues for face anti-spoofing. CoRR abs/2005.03922 (2020). https://arxiv.org/abs/2005.03922
3. George, A., Marcel, S.: Deep pixel-wise binary supervision for face presentation attack detection. CoRR abs/1907.04047 (2019). http://arxiv.org/abs/1907.04047
4. George, A., Mostaani, Z., Geissenbuhler, D., Nikisins, O., Anjos, A., Marcel, S.: Biometric face presentation attack detection with multi-channel convolutional neural network. CoRR abs/1909.08848 (2019). http://arxiv.org/abs/1909.08848
5. Guo, J., Zhu, X., Xiao, J., Lei, Z., Wan, G., Li, S.Z.: Improving face anti-spoofing by 3D virtual synthesis. CoRR abs/1901.00488 (2019). http://arxiv.org/abs/1901.00488

6. Han, J., Shoeiby, M., Petersson, L., Armin, M.A.: Dual contrastive learning for unsupervised image-to-image translation. CoRR abs/2104.07689 (2021). https://arxiv.org/abs/2104.07689

7. Hao, H., Pei, M.: Face liveness detection based on client identity using Siamese network. CoRR abs/1903.05369 (2019). http://arxiv.org/abs/1903.05369

8. Hernandez-Ortega, J., Fiérrez, J., Morales, A., Galbally, J.: Introduction to presentation attack detection in face biometrics and recent advances. CoRR abs/2111.11794 (2021). https://arxiv.org/abs/2111.11794

9. Huang, C., Huang, J.: A fast HOG descriptor using lookup table and integral image. CoRR abs/1703.06256 (2017). http://arxiv.org/abs/1703.06256

10. Innovatrics: Liveness Detection for Remote Identity Verification Solutions (2022). https://www.innovatrics.com/digital-onboarding-toolkit/liveness-detection/

11. Karras, T., Laine, S., Aila, T.: A style-based generator architecture for generative adversarial networks. CoRR abs/1812.04948 (2018). http://arxiv.org/abs/1812.04948

12. Kortli, Y., Maher, J., Alfalou, A., Atri, M.: A comparative study of CFs, LBP, HOG, SIFT, SURF, and BRIEF for security and face recognition (2018). https://doi.org/10.1088/978-0-7503-1457-2ch13

13. Liu, A., Tan, Z., Wan, J., Escalera, S., Guo, G., Li, S.Z.: CASIA-SURF CeFA: a benchmark for multi-modal cross-ethnicity face anti-spoofing. In: 2021 IEEE Winter Conference on Applications of Computer Vision (WACV), pp. 1178–1186. IEEE Computer Society, Los Alamitos (2021). https://doi.org/10.1109/WACV48630.2021.00122, https://doi.ieeecomputersociety.org/10.1109/WACV48630.2021.00122

14. Liu, A., et al.: Cross-ethnicity face anti-spoofing recognition challenge: a review. CoRR abs/2004.10998 (2020). https://arxiv.org/abs/2004.10998

15. Lugmayr, A., Danelljan, M., Romero, A., Yu, F., Timofte, R., Gool, L.V.: RePaint: inpainting using denoising diffusion probabilistic models. CoRR abs/2201.09865 (2022). https://arxiv.org/abs/2201.09865

16. Park, T., Efros, A.A., Zhang, R., Zhu, J.: Contrastive learning for unpaired image-to-image translation. CoRR abs/2007.15651 (2020). https://arxiv.org/abs/2007.15651

17. Rahim, M.A., Azam, M.S., Hossain, N., Islam, M.R.: Face recognition using local binary patterns (LBP). Glob. J. Comput. Sci. Technol. **13**, 1–8 (2013)

18. sarah.merker@iproov.com: Deepfake Statistics & Solutions – Protect Against Deepfakes (2022). https://www.iproov.com/blog/deepfakes-statistics-solutions-biometric-protection

19. Uricár, M., Krízek, P., Hurych, D., Sobh, I., Yogamani, S.K., Denny, P.: Yes, we GAN: applying adversarial techniques for autonomous driving. CoRR abs/1902.03442 (2019). http://arxiv.org/abs/1902.03442

20. Verma, R., Kaur, M.R.: Enhanced character recognition using surf feature and neural network technique (2014)

21. Wan, J., Guo, G., Escalera, S., Escalante, H.J., Li, S.Z.: Multi-modal Face Presentation Attack Detection. Synthesis Lectures on Computer Vision. Morgan & Claypool Publishers (2020)

22. Wang, M., Deng, W.: Deep face recognition: a survey. CoRR abs/1804.06655 (2018). http://arxiv.org/abs/1804.06655

23. Yu, Z., Li, X., Niu, X., Shi, J., Zhao, G.: Face anti-spoofing with human material perception. CoRR abs/2007.02157 (2020). https://arxiv.org/abs/2007.02157

24. Yu, Z., Li, X., Shi, J., Xia, Z., Zhao, G.: Revisiting pixel-wise supervision for face anti-spoofing. CoRR abs/2011.12032 (2020). https://arxiv.org/abs/2011.12032

Mapping Brand Territories Using ChatGPT

Luisa Fernanda Rodriguez-Sarmiento[1]([envelope]) [iD], Ixent Galpin[1] [iD],
and Vladimir Sanchez-Riaño[2] [iD]

[1] Facultad de Ciencias Naturales e Ingeniería, Universidad de Bogotá-Jorge Tadeo
Lozano, Bogotá, Colombia
[2] Facultad de Artes y Diseño, Universidad de Bogotá-Jorge Tadeo Lozano,
Bogotá, Colombia
{luisaf.rodriguezsa,ixent,vladimir.sanchez}@utadeo.edu.co

Abstract. Nowadays various tools, powered using artificial intelligence
technologies, enable us to automate mundane daily tasks. A well-known
recent example is ChatGPT, a large language model that generates seemingly coherent responses in conversations. This has paved the way for
wider interaction between users and artificial intelligence technologies.
On the other hand, in the field of advertising, defining brand territory
plays an important role in market research and the marketing or communication strategy that a brand implements with its customers. Brand
territory groups together a set of characteristics, attributes and values
that help a brand to establish a personality and differentiate it from its
competitors. Traditionally, mapping a brand territory is a largely manual, time-consuming process.

In this work, we propose an approach to automate this process, creating a more efficient way of mapping brand territory. Our approach
involves the webscraping of product reviews to obtain data set for subsequent analysis using ChatGPT. In this manner, we automatically determine customer perceptions with regards to certain dimensions. By analyzing customer reviews using this Large Language Model, we show that
it is possible to get a broader view of how consumers perceive specific
aspects of certain products or brands in an automated fashion.

Keywords: ChatGPT · brand territory · artificial intelligence ·
advertising · positioning · reviews

1 Introduction

A *brand territory* is a set of characteristics, attributes and values that define and
differentiate a brand in the marketplace. By having these criteria clearly defined,
it gives rise to what is known as the brand's personality, and the promise of value
that it gives to its customers and consumers [4]. A brand territory map may be

---

Supported by Jorge Tadeo Lozano University.

visualized using a two-dimensional Cartesian plane where the x- and y-axes represent different characteristics or dimensions of a brand, evaluated in relation to one another (see Fig. 12 for an example). Brand territories are fundamental elements in advertising and marketing, given the need for brands to be recognized and distinguished towards their consumers or a specific community, and in an increasingly competitive market [6]. Due to globalization, brand territory has received a boost in recent times, a boost associated with the increasingly evident need for differentiation [13].

Nowadays, action needs to be taken almost immediately, in the face of consumers who are becoming more demanding with the products they buy. Likewise, a standardization of consumer needs is occurring at the same time as the supply of products is increasing [8], making a group of people identify more with a brand. In addition to this, aspects such as company values, the tone of communication, among others, also have an influence. Brand territories are used for this type of analysis. However, techniques for defining a brand territory are largely manual, and the process of carrying out a mapping for brand can be cumbersome and time-consuming.

For this reason, it is useful to explore new techniques which allow brand territories to be developed more efficiently, using recent technologies that are beginning to become more widespread, in particular those in the area of artificial intelligence [24]. Furthermore, *Big Data* techniques are being used, which involve the analysis of massive data sets [11], and *web-scraping*, in which data is extracted from websites through the HTTP protocol used by web browsers [10]. The latter enables analysts to obtain and analyze relevant information from online shopping sites, making it easy to compare one brand against another, according to consumers opinions of their products.

In our work, we hypothesize that combining these previously described techniques with artificial intelligence approaches in possible solutions to the dilemma of how to collect and process relevant information on user behavior [14] in near real time, we can perform a deeper analysis of customer perception. This leads to quicker and more precise creation of brand territory maps, enabling advertising strategists to develop novel audience-targeting approaches. For this reason, in this work we combine web scraping and artificial intelligence approaches. We employ ChatGPT, a large language model to analyze information on online sales products and speed up the process of creating brand territory maps [21].

This paper is structured as follows: Sect. 2 presents related work. Section 3 presents methodology used. The remaining sections broadly follow the phases in the well-established CRISP-DM methodology used for data mining projects [23]: In Sects. 4 and Sect. 5 we present the *business understanding* and *data understanding* phases respectively. Subsequently, we discuss *data preparation* in Sect. 6. We carry out the *modeling* described in Sect. 7, the corresponding *evaluation* in Sect. 8. The final phase in CRISP-DM, *deployment*, is discussed in Sect. 9. Section 10 concludes.

2 Related Work

There are different techniques and methodologies for defining brand territories. One of them is based first on market segmentation, and thus finding in the same territory, a certain diversity of brands, to finally find the experience lived [8] by each customer. Other more complex techniques use market segmentation to find trends, unsatisfied needs and consumer motivations, while at the same time analyzing the image, strategies, weaknesses and positioning of competitors and the brand [9].

There are also techniques at the international level that implement artificial intelligence focused on advertising design, where there are systems that analyze the search keywords entered by users, quickly generate merchandising descriptions and, in turn, create advertising content [16].

On the other hand, there are a set of techniques that enable natural language analysis and manipulation [1] such as that provided by the NLTK library[1], or other Python libraries for text processing, such as tagging and sentiment analysis [7], such as TextBlob[2]. In its basic usage scenario, sentiment analysis is used to classify written customer reviews as negative, neutral or positive [12]. However, other fundamental aspects within a brand territory such as modernity or trustworthiness can not be measured [22] using these models.

As such, no research or documentation was found to support automated techniques for the creation of brand territory maps, applying artificial intelligence techniques. We therefore consider this work to present considerable novelty in this field.

3 Methodology

Figure 1 presents the concrete steps undertaken to carry out the process of generating a brand territory map from product reviews. As mentioned previously, the CRISP-DM methodology underpins these steps: the first three steps in the figure correspond to the *data preparation phase*, described in Sect. 6. Steps 4 and 5 correspond to *modelling* (see Sect. 7) and step 6 to *evaluation* (see Sect. 8).

Fig. 1. Steps to generate a brand territory map

---

[1] https://www.nltk.org/.

[2] https://textblob.readthedocs.io/en/dev/.

4   Business Understanding

Nowadays, it is possible to find a large number of options when buying products, making the market saturated and very competitive. As such, brands need to establish their own territory in order to stand out and have assertive communication with their audience. Thus, defining brand territory provides a basis for building an effective communication strategy and at the same time generating an emotional relationship with consumers [18]. The main objective of defining brand territory is to establish the brand's personality [4].

By defining a specific tone of communication, a brand can create a distinctive and recognizable identity, creating a long-term bond with its customers, and also connecting emotionally with them, because the brand is recognizable among its competitors and in the market in general. In addition to this, defining brand territory also helps to establish which values and attributes are to be associated with the brand image. Thus, these attributes can be tangible, such as product quality or customer service, or intangible, such as trust, modernity, or exclusivity. By communicating these attributes, the brand can influence the perception of its customers and differentiate itself from the competition.

Defining a personality and communicating specific attributes or values not only helps in brand communication, but also has the power to influence consumer decisions. By identifying with the brand and establishing a relationship with it, trust and preference for the brand is generated. This translates into competitive advantage and greater success in the marketplace. For advertising strategists, brand territory is an invaluable resource that allows them to understand brand identity, values, and communication, and to develop coherent messages that convey the desired message. Thus, they can have a guide to create advertising campaigns, choose communication channels and create relevant content. In addition to this, through brand territory, advertising strategists can capture the attention of the audience in comparison to their competitors, and in this way generate emotional connection, loyalty, brand preference, making the brand memorable, with a solid image and position in the market.

In short, brand territory is an extremely important resource, which must be understood to establish communication strategies, thus leading to the success and relevance of a brand in the competitive world of advertising, marketing and an increasingly demanding public saturated with advertising messages [17]. In this work, we use the following criteria which we deem to be representative for mapping brand territory for household goods: *esteem, reliability, modernity, quality* and *relevance*.

5   Data Understanding

The data set used in this study was collected from the website of Falabella Colombia[3], which markets a variety of household products. In 2018, Falabella was amongst the ten most valuable brands in Latin America [2]. The information

---

[3] https://www.falabella.com.co/falabella-co.

was obtained on 23 April 2023, and corresponds to the Home Electrics section, specifically in the categories of Washing Machines, Refrigeration and cooker, which were considered to be of interest due to the diversity of their reviews.

This site has a large number of products for sale, so initially there is a page that groups together all the products available, with basic product attributes: brand, name, discount, price, overall_rating and a link that redirects to another page, where users can view, in detail, all the characteristics of the product. This page contains more specific information about the product, which is extracted for subsequent analysis, as shown in Table 1.

Table 1. Extracted fields.

Type	Fields
Sales information	Brand, name, code, overall_rating, tags such as fast_shipping, discount, among others, full_price, discounted_price and CMR_discounted_price
Product specifications	Dimensions, warranty, and specifications specific to each product.
Customer Ratings	Rating between zero to five, comment_title, comment, comment_time, tags such as helpful_comment, recommend_the_product

In the data there are three types of prices: the full, non-discounted price of the product, the discounted price for the general public, and the discounted price for customers who have the Falabella CMR credit card. However, not all products have all three prices; it may be the case that only the full price is given. If there is no discount for the general public, the value No discount is given, and if there is no discount for customers with a CMR card, a value of No CMR discount is assigned.

The information was obtained by means of *web scraping* [19] techniques using the Python programming language and the Selenium[4] library, thus mapping the web page and collecting the data automatically. Based on the data collected, a total of 1240 products were obtained: 586 in cookers, 260 in refrigerators and 394 in washing machines as shown in Fig. 2. From this, a total of 844 customer reviews were collected, divided as shown in Fig. 3: 69 in cookers, 477 in washing machines and 298 in refrigerators. Although the cooker category has the most products, it has the lowest number of reviews.

It should be noted that some products do not have complete information: some are missing the brand name. Others, despite being the same brand, as can be seen in Fig. 4, which shows the number of reviews per brand, are not grouped correctly due to spelling or capitalization discrepancies. Finally, it was also found that there are products that do not have a comments section or, although they do have one, they do not have comments from customers.

---

[4] https://www.selenium.dev/.

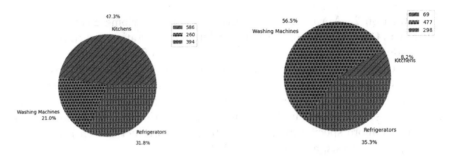

Fig. 2. Products by category   **Fig. 3.** Reviews by category

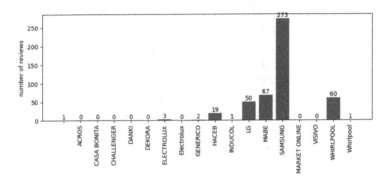

Fig. 4. Number of reviews per category (Washing machines)

6   Data Preparation

During the extraction of information through web scraping, transformations are made to the data types, such as the product code being converted from text format to number. The same applies to the overall product rating, the comment rating, and the number of ratings in the usefulness section of the comment. Also, we found that some reviews may have a title and no comments, or vice versa. To address this situation, we concatenated the title with the text of the comment, generating a single text field for the review. At the end of all data extraction, a JSON file is generated for each category [20].

In cases where a brand name is not specified for certain products, they are assigned the generic name Unspecified. For products that do have an identified brand, the first letter is capitalized, and lower-case letters are used for the rest of the letters, in order to standardize the brand names. This process is also applied to the product name.

Previously, it was determined that products could have three types of price: the total value of the product, the discounted value for the general public, and the discounted value for customers holding the CMR credit card. To clean up these fields, special characters such as dots, currency signs and spaces, as well as alphabetic characters, are removed, leaving only numeric characters. Once the numeric value is obtained, it is transformed from a text data type to a numeric data type. However, discounts that were labelled No discount or No CMR discount were left in the same form, without modification.

In the case of customer comments, the first letter is capitalized, and lower case is used for the rest of the characters. Then, special characters are removed, except for the full stop and the comma, so as not to remove the context of the comment. Furthermore, in relation to the time of publication of the reviews, since they are expressed in years, months and days, it was decided to standardize them in days. So first special characters are eliminated, and then each component is evaluated: if it corresponds to years, the number of years is multiplied by 365 days; if it corresponds to months, the number of months is multiplied by 30 days; and finally, the days are left as they are.

As can be seen, the transformations focus on sales information and product reviews. However, no data cleansing is performed on the product specifications, because each category has different specification fields, and even within the same product category not all products have the same characteristics, resulting in variability in the number of specification fields and the possibility that some products do not have them.

As a result, new JSON files are created with a different name, and the modifications made to the file containing the raw data, so that both files are retained in case they are needed later. Figures 5, 6 and 7 show the brands, categories, and number of reviews respectively. From these figures, we can see that the brands are not empty and are not repeated within the same category.

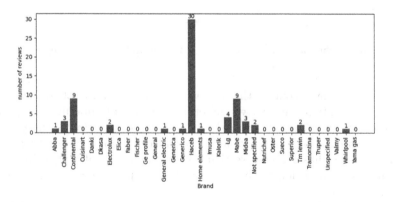

Fig. 5. Number of reviews by brand for the cooker category

The final phase of data preparation consists of grouping all the reviews of the different product files according to brand and category in a Python DataFrame [15]. For this, the file name is taken as the category, the value of the brand field and the product code is extracted. Subsequently, all product reviews are read, and the following validations are carried out:

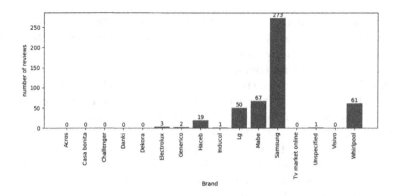

Fig. 6. Number of reviews by brand for the Washing Machines category

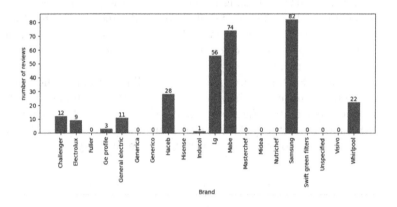

Fig. 7. Number of reviews by brand for the Refrigerators category

1. The product must contain the reviews section, if it does not, it means that it did not contain the reviews section at the time of obtaining the product information or an error occurred in its extraction. If this is the case, the product in question is ignored, and it is added to a table of event logs.
2. If the product has a review section, but no comments, it will still be added to the information log table, to show that the product was not taken into consideration.
3. If the product has a review section, and has comments, each comment will be evaluated:
   (a) If the comment is empty, it will not be taken into consideration, as it does not provide any information. It is therefore added to an informative log table.
   (b) If the review does have text, it will be added to an array along with the other reviews of the product.

Once this process has been carried out for each of the files, the comments are grouped by brand and category. This generates a single array of comments per brand and category.

7 Modeling

The next step is to make use of the ChatGPT language model, developed by OpenAI, a pre-trained model with a large amount of data and is based on a Transformer neural networks, known for its ability to handle relationships and large contexts in natural language processing. We use the ChatGPT API to interact with the GPT-3.5 model. By using the API, requests are sent to the platform to get responses generated by the model in an interactive fashion.

For this purpose, a JSON formatted object must be specified which must contain the model to be used and the message. This message is made up of two parts: first, the role, which in our case is the user, as we are sending requests; and second, the content, which provides the message that is sent so that the model responds. To this end, each of the reviews found in the previously constructed table is read and added to the text of the prompt that is sent to the ChatGPT model for the ChatGPT model to respond. The prompt is as follows:

```
Rate with a number from -5 to 5 the comment ''text of the review''
Where esteem, reliability, modernity, quality and relevance are
reflected. Example of your answer: esteem: 5, trustworthiness: 5,
modernity: 5, quality: 5, relevance: 5.
```

The prompt comprises four components:

1. **Instruction:** This contains the task for the model to perform, *i.e.*, "Rate the comment with a number from -5 to 5".
2. **Context:** This is where external information or additional context is added to give the model better answers, in this case it comprises the text of the review.
3. **Input data:** This is the entry or question we are interested in finding an answer to, *i.e.*, "Where esteem, reliability, modernity, quality and relevance are reflected".
4. **Output indicator:** This component indicates the type or format of output. In this case, an example of the expected output is given, i.e., "Example of your answer: esteem: 5, reliability: 5, modernity: 5, quality: 5, relevance: 5"

Once the prompt is sent, the API returns a JSON object with several metadata components, *i.e.*, id, model, number of tokens sent, the role, and the response provided by the model, among other data. An example of such a JSON object follows:

```
"{"id": "chatcmpl-7Oc4y8TqAPyzs14hYBbHJeEcMf7XZ","object": "chat.
completion", "created": 1686100604, "model": "gpt-3.5-turbo-0301",
```

"usage": {"prompt_tokens": 115, "completion_tokens": 31,
"total_tokens": 146}, "choices": [{"message": {"role": "assistant",
"content": "Esteem: 3, Reliability: 2, Modernity: 2, Quality: 3,
Relevance: 4"}, "finish_reason": "stop", "index": 0}]}"

Finally, the content of the response is obtained. In a few cases, for example if a review is too short, or does not contain enough information for the model to be able to rate it, it responds with the message "I cannot rate". Otherwise, we proceed to obtain each of the ratings by criteria (esteem, reliability, modernity, quality, relevance), so that finally a CSV file is saved, with the id of the review, id of the product, brand, category and ratings for the esteem, reliability, modernity, quality, relevance of the product respectively.

8 Results

After obtaining the result files, they are analysed by means of graphs in order to understand the distribution of the data. Box and whisker plots are used for each brand and criterion. An example of this is shown in Fig. 8, where the dispersion of the reliability data for each brand is observed.

The median is shown with a red line indicating the central position of the data, which indicates that 50% of the data is on the far right and the other 50% on the far left. However, we can observe cases such as Continental's, where the median value is 4 and the box of values is distributed between 3 and 4. This lack of whiskers allows us to identify that there is no significant variability in the data for the brand, meaning that there are no values outside the interquartile range and there are no outliers in this case.

In the case of Abba, Tm Lewin, and Unspecified we only have one review, meaning that they only have one rating for the brand and this does not provide us with sufficient information to determine the quartile ranks.

The above graph shows the ratings by brand in general, but it was decided to separate the information by category according to brand using box and whisker plots again to understand the distributions of the data. It should be noted that not all brands have products in each category, in the case of Fig. 9 a box and whisker plot is shown for the modernity criterion for each of the three categories.

Figure 9 shows that refrigerators and cookers have outliers, but that the distribution of these values is mainly towards positive ratings. While washing machines have more variety in their product ratings. However, in all three categories we can see that the median, represented by the green line, is about three, indicating that at least 50% of the ratings are above this value, suggesting that customers perceive the brand as modern.

Figure 10 presents a radar chart which plots the average ratings for each category according to the brand, in this case LG, which has a product presence across the three categories evaluated. According to these results, in general terms, LG stands out most in the Washing Machines category, where it scores best. However, it has a similar relevance in the refrigerator category. On the other hand, cookers show a lower estimation and reliability, although they are still

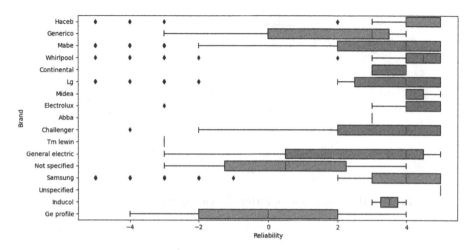

Fig. 8. Box-and-whisker plot showing reliability by brand

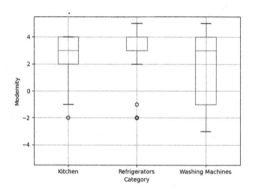

Fig. 9. Box and whisker diagram for **Mabe** brand grouped by category for the Modernity criterion

relevant to some extent. In summary, the criterion in which LG stands out the most is relevance, with positive ratings in all three categories. However, it is in the cooker category where it has the lowest scores, suggesting that the brand does not meet customer expectations.

Finally, the categories are evaluated by brand, to determine which one stands out the most for each criterion. However, as there are a large number of brands in each category, it was decided to select the five best scores in all criteria. As can be seen in Fig. 11, the cooker category is very similar in terms of rating, but the brands begin to differentiate in the other criteria evaluated. Whirlpool stands out in terms of reliability and modernity, but is on a par in quality and relevance with Electrolux.

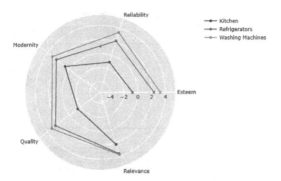

Fig. 10. Radar diagram of ratings by category for the LG brand

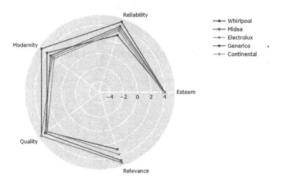

Fig. 11. Radar diagram by brand for the cooker category.

9   Deployment

In order to deploy a tool for use by publicists, we propose the creation of a dashboard containing brand territory maps from the data obtained. To do this, the average of the ratings by criteria and category is calculated. To make it more visually intuitive for advertising strategists to use in their analysis, the logos of the brands are placed. Figure 12 presents an example of a automatically generated brand territory map where reliability vs. modernity of the brands in the washing machines category is being compared. It can be seen that Inducol, despite being a reliable brand with a rating of 3, is perceived by customers as a not very modern brand, with a rating of −4, while the best perceived brand is Electrolux with a score of 4.6 for reliability and 4 for modernity.

These results, in the field of advertising strategists, can help to create strategies to improve the perception of a brand in the face of different criteria and that over time it is on a par with its competitors, by transmitting brand values with the hobbies and needs of the consumer, which delimits and integrates the contents and the rest of the company's communicative actions [5].

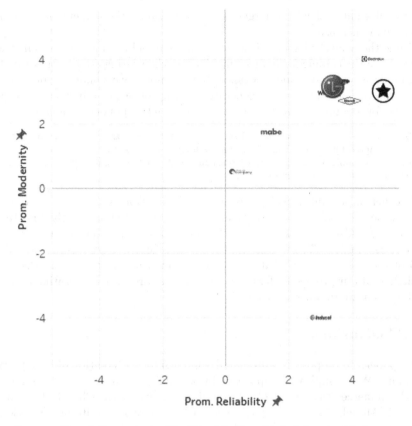

Fig. 12. Brand Territory for Washing Machines Reliability vs. Modernity.

9.1 Discussion

While in this work we demonstrate an approach for automatically generating a brandy territory map from an E-commerce site, we note that our approach has several, inherent, limitations. For example, our data set is obtained by means of web scraping. It should be noted that this technique cannot always be carried out on all websites due to blockages that occur on these pages resulting from company data protection policies. When many requests are made to a server, it can be detected as a denial of service attack and block the IP [3], among other reasons.

On the other hand, despite having a large amount of product information, it does not ensure that there is a significant number of reviews. Indeed, for the data set used in this study, only 17.5% of the products obtained had customer reviews. A similar case is that of the reviews: while 93.6% of the reviews had content to evaluate, the other 6.4% were empty, as customers gave their rating, but did not comment on the reason for their rating. It should be noted that in the case of a data set with a larger number of results, the percentage of empty reviews may increase.

While the ChatGPT model is a model that can help to identify certain characteristics of the comments as we could observe when rating esteem, trustworthiness, modernity, quality and relevance, there is not always enough information within the review comment to generate a rating on a per-criterion basis. For example, for a comment such as "Good", the model responded as follows:

```
I'm Sorry, as an AI language model, I cannot rate comments as I do not
have the capacity to evaluate or judge according to personal
criteria. My task is to provide coherent and useful responses
useful answers to users requests.
```

Another important aspect to consider is the cost of using the OpenAI API. At the time this study was undertaken, a credit of 5 USD during the first three months after subscribing was offered. Taking into account that the reviews can be short or long, for 777 requests that were made and were successful, only 0.19 USD of the free credit were utilized to carry out this study. We can therefore conclude that our proposal offers a cost-effective approach to generating a brand territory map in an automated fahsion.

10   Conclusions

In this paper, we propose an automated approach for the creation of brand territory maps. We exemplify the approach by scraping product reviews from a popular E-commerce website in Colombia. Subsequently, we use ChatGPT, a Large Language Model, to rate the reviews according to various criteria. Traditional text mining libraries are able to perform automated analysis of text but are limited to criteria such as negative/positive sentiment or subjectivity/objectivity. By using ChatGPT we are able to obtain ratings for diverse criteria deemed relevant to advertising strategists in brand territory mapping, in this case esteem, reliability, modernity, quality and relevance. Another advantage of using Chat-GPT is that minimal cleaning and preparation of the data is required, compared to traditional text mining techniques. The end result of our work is a dashboard which can be updated periodically in order to show how brand territory evolves over time, in a cost-effective manner, for use by advertising strategists.

We note that our approach has important limitations. In relation to the extraction of information, web scraping is impacted by changes to web pages and techniques to block web scraper bots, as well as being a legally gray area in many countries. However, many e-commerce sites provide APIs which could be used to obtain product review data instead of web scraping. Furthermore, if reviews are empty or too terse, they cannot be evaluated by ChatGPT. Although the costs in our study were moderate, as the amount of information increases, so will the cost of calls to the ChatGPT API.

We note that for advertising strategists, quickly obtaining a general vision of how the brand is behaving in relation to the proposed dimensions can be invaluable, even if it is of low precision. Further scrutiny of the quality and consistency of the ratings provided by ChatGPT is also needed. However, future work could usefully include a comparative evaluation between brand territory maps generated using our approach, and those created manually by experts. There is also further scope for future work exploring more advanced visualizations, for example, creating multidimensional or interactive brand territory maps.

References

1. Barrios Dominguez, L., Verdeja García, L.: Clasificación automática de los comentarios de los usuarios de aplicaciones de software. B.S. thesis, Universidad de las Ciencias Informáticas. Facultad 2 (2016)
2. BBC News Mundo: Cuáles son las 10 marcas más valiosas de américa latina. https://www.bbc.com/mundo/noticias-43874472
3. Condori Yujra, H.A.: Web scraping para la obtención de información actualizada de internet con push notifications para smartphone. Ph.D. thesis (2014)
4. Cruz Tarrillo, J.J., Haro Zea, K.L., Soria Quijaite, J.J.: Revisión sistemática: situación actual de la personalidad de marca para el posicionamiento estratégico. Tendencias **23**(1), 315–340 (2022)
5. Cuervas-Mons, F.T., San Emeterio, B.M.: Herramientas de marketing de contenido para la generación de tráfico cualificado online. Opción **31**(4), 978–996 (2015)
6. Díez, D., Castiblanco Laurada, C., Ríos Cardona, C.: Territorios de marca para el desarrollo sostenible: arquetipos en investigación y creación con grupos de interés de chec grupo epm (2022)
7. González, M., Organiche, E.C., Alfaro, A.J.J., Guillermo, I.C.A.: Analítica de textos en la detección de sentimientos aplicada a un call center automotriz. Tecno-Cultura, p. 54 (2021)
8. Gonzalez-Oñate, C., Martínez Bueno, S.: La marca territorio como elemento de la comunicación: factor estratégico del desarrollo turístico en cuenca/the brand territory as a communication: strategic factor in tourism development in cuenca (2013)
9. Kalieva, O.M.: Development of territory brand image: the marketing aspect. Rev. Eur. Stud. **7**, 23 (2015)
10. Khder, M.A.: Web scraping or web crawling: state of art, techniques, approaches and application. Int. J. Adv. Soft Comput. Appl. **13**(3), 144–168 (2021)
11. Kitchin, R., McArdle, G.: What makes big data, big data? Exploring the ontological characteristics of 26 datasets. Big Data Soc. **3**(1), 2053951716631130 (2016)
12. Lin, B., Zampetti, F., Bavota, G., Di Penta, M., Lanza, M., Oliveto, R.: Sentiment analysis for software engineering: how far can we go? In: Proceedings of the 40th International Conference on Software Engineering, pp. 94–104 (2018)
13. Lita, R.L., Osuna, M.T.B.: De la marca comercial a la marca territorio. Recerca: Rev. Pensament Anàl. 87–100 (2005)
14. Martínez, I.J.M., Terrón, J.M.A., Cobarro, P.d.H.S.: Smart advertising: innovación y disrupción tecnológica asociadas a la ia en el ecosistema publicitario. Rev. Latina Comun. Soc. (80), 21 (2022)
15. Pane, S.F., Prastya, R., Putrada, A.G., Alamsyah, N., Fauzan, M.N.: Reevaluating synthesizing sentiment analysis on COVID-19 fake news detection using spark dataframe. In: 2022 International Conference on Information Technology Systems and Innovation (ICITSI), pp. 269–274. IEEE (2022)

16. Qin, X., Jiang, Z.: The impact of AI on the advertising process: the Chinese experience. J. Advert. **48**(4), 338–346 (2019)
17. Ribeiro, M.B.R.S.P., et al.: A comunicação publicitária-a relação das estratégias de mensagem com os referentes culturais: o caso da publicidade televisiva portuguesa e os seus referentes culturais. Ph.D. thesis, Comunicación audiovisual e publicidade (2018)
18. Rodríguez, C., Chávez, R.M.A., Kuri, L.C.: Diagnóstico sobre la relación de la influencia emocional en el comportamiento del consumidor. Ciencias Adm. **1**, 23–32 (2019)
19. Sánchez-Riaño, V., Baez, L.C.S., Garcia-Bedoya, O., Sojo-Gomez, J.R.: Variables para la fase diagnóstica de un software piloto de planeación estratégica. VIS. REV. Int. Vis. Cult. Rev./Rev. Int. Cult. Vis. **9**(Monográfico), 1–15 (2022)
20. Toro Carrilero, J.D.: Creación de un sistema para autocompletar archivos readme (2022)
21. Vaswani, A., et al.: Attention is all you need. In: Advances in Neural Information Processing Systems, vol. 30 (2017)
22. Wang, Y., Lin, J., Yu, Z., Hu, W., Karlsson, B.F.: Open-world story generation with structured knowledge enhancement: a comprehensive survey. arXiv preprint arXiv:2212.04634 (2022)
23. Wirth, R., Hipp, J.: CRISP-DM: towards a standard process model for data mining. In: Proceedings of the 4th International Conference on the Practical Applications of Knowledge Discovery and Data Mining, vol. 1, pp. 29–39. Manchester (2000)
24. Zhou, C., et al.: A comprehensive survey on pretrained foundation models: a history from BERT to ChatGPT. arXiv preprint arXiv:2302.09419 (2023)

Predictive Modeling for Detection of Depression Using Machine Learning

Martín Di Felice[✉] ⓘ, Ariel Deroche ⓘ, Ilan Trupkin ⓘ, Parag Chatterjee ⓘ, and María F. Pollo-Cattaneo ⓘ

Grupo GEMIS, Facultad Regional Buenos Aires,
Universidad Tecnológica Nacional, Buenos Aires, Argentina
{mdifelice,parag}@frba.utn.edu.ar

Abstract. Predictive modeling techniques using artificial intelligence have shown promising potential in detecting and predicting depression in recent times, adding newer perspectives to mental health assessment and treatment. This paper presents a predictive modeling approach to detect the presence of depression using machine learning techniques. It presents predictive models to detect depression based on depression-related data of a student cohort containing demographic and academic data along with depression information collected through the Beck Depression Inventory questionnaire, in addition to scores such as the PHQ (Patient Health Questionnaire) score, GAD (Generalized Anxiety Disorder) score, and Epworth score, which provide insights into the severity and impact of depressive symptoms, anxiety symptoms, and daytime sleepiness, respectively. The methodology involves data collection and preparation, feature selection, model selection, and model training using machine learning techniques. The results show the performance metrics of different predictive models on various dataset versions generated through preprocessing steps such as normalization, feature encoding, and selection. The best metrics are compared and evaluated, where the Linear Discriminant Analysis model performed best in terms of AUC, F1 score, and other metrics in this specific cohort. Considering the recent advancements of machine learning, incorporating predictive modeling would be important to designing clinical decision support systems, for a comprehensive prediction and analysis of depression in different cohorts, to act as an assistive tool for mental health professionals.

Keywords: Artificial Intelligence · Depression · Mental Health · Predictive Model

1 Introduction

Mental health specifies the state of well-being of each individual in terms they can achieve their potential, cope with the normal stresses of life, live productively, and contribute to the community [1]. In the field of mental health, depression is a significant illness that disrupts an individual's mood, leading to feelings of sadness, disgust, and fear. This condition results in diminished interest and pleasure in everyday activities, lasting for extended periods of several weeks or more [2], greatly impacting one's mental

H. Florez and M. Leon (Eds.): ICAI 2023, CCIS 1874, pp. 47–57, 2024.
https://doi.org/10.1007/978-3-031-46813-1_4

well-being. Research indicates that a considerable portion of the global population is affected by depression. It can be categorized into various subtypes, with Major Depressive Disorder (MDD) being the most prevalent form, which is the focus of this study. It is estimated that approximately 5% of the world's population is affected by this particular type of condition [3–6].

In recent years, Artificial Intelligence has shown its application in different fields and healthcare is no exception. Especially in addressing problems that lack simple solutions and often rely on human intervention, AI techniques have often shown significant outcomes, benefiting from the computational prowess that enables faster processing and the handling of large datasets [7–10]. For the diagnosis of depression, there are specific clinical techniques, including standardized tests [11–13]. These tests can help to generate a score that can be used to determine depression levels, followed by the eventual analysis and diagnosis by a medical professional. With the application of AI techniques, advancements have been made in facilitating the diagnosis of MDD using text input from patients. Graham *et al.* [14] have reviewed several studies that address this area and concluded that although the application of these techniques still needs to be refined and improved, it potentially can help to diagnose better and faster, thus helping patients to have more personalized treatments. Tran *et al.* [15] also performed a systematic review and reached a similar conclusion, and they warned about privacy and confidentiality issues, which governments and organizations should safeguard. Morley *et al.* [16] addressed the ethical issues as well, not only regarding the usage of health mental data but also healthcare data in general, transforming this aspect into a key one at the time of working in this kind of research. The usage of these kinds of tools can improve the speed of diagnosis where the availability of professionals is not enough. However, as Higgins *et al.* [17] state, there is still a barrier that stops its incorporation in practice. This paper attempts to include a wide variety of dataset optimization techniques combined with the most popular AI binary classification algorithms in order to not only obtain the optimal result but also improve the perception of this kind of tool to contribute to its incorporation in real-life scenarios.

In this context of using artificial intelligence in facilitating the diagnosis of depression, this work aims to develop a predictive model to determine the presence of depression in a cohort based on its characteristics. Also, it provides the base for the development of a Clinical Decision Support System, to assist mental health professionals in reaching a faster and more precise diagnosis. The modeling pipeline consists of data preprocessing including transformations of the dataset, followed by the application of supervised machine learning models, and subsequent comparison in terms of their performance metrics. On the other hand, this predictive modeling is also proposed as a potential model for a clinical decision support system, applied to detect depression in cohorts with a specific set of characteristics.

This study continues in the following section by explaining the used methodology, then the results obtained by applying those methods, and finally, the last section presents the conclusions gathered from this study.

2 Methodology

The dataset selected for this study [18] is based on undergraduate students from the University of Lahore (n = 787), indicating if they suffer from depression or anxiety, and that related to those diseases. The dataset (Table 1) also presents demographic data and in addition to depression, includes data related to anxiety as well.

Table 1. Characteristics of the dataset

University year	First year: 35% Second year: 24% Third year: 23% Fourth year: 18%
Age (years)	20.26 ± 1.77
Sex (Female/Male)	Female: 52%, Male: 48%
BMI	23.41 ± 4.6
WHO BMI	Normal: 65% Overweight: 25% Underweight: 5% Class I Obesity: 4% Other: 1%
PHQ score	7.17 ± 4.42
Depression Severity	Mild: 44% None-minimal: 29% Moderate: 18% Moderately severe: 5% None: 2% Severe: 2%
Depressiveness	27%
Suicidal	8%
Depression diagnosis	8%
Depression treatment	7%
GAD score	6.88 ± 4.73
Anxiety severity	Mild: 38% None-minimal: 37% Moderately: 16% Severe: 9%
Anxiousness	25%
Anxiety diagnosis	8%
Anxiety treatment	8%
Epworth score	6.4 ± 4
Sleepiness	18%

This study focuses on the depression data gathered using the Beck Depression Inventory [13], a standardized method used to determine depression levels. It includes personal information about the patient such as Age, School Year, Sex, and BMI (the exact value and the category according to the WHO scale). Also, the dataset used in this study includes three key scores: the PHQ (Patient Health Questionnaire) score, the GAD (Generalized Anxiety Disorder) score, and the Epworth score. These scores provide valuable insights into the severity and impact of depressive symptoms, generalized anxiety symptoms, and daytime sleepiness, respectively. The PHQ score, ranging from 0 to 27, measures the frequency and severity of depressive symptoms experienced over the past two weeks, with higher scores indicating more severe symptoms. The GAD score, ranging from 0 to 21, assesses the severity of generalized anxiety disorder, with higher scores indicating higher levels of anxiety. Lastly, the Epworth score, ranging from 0 to 24, quantifies daytime sleepiness and the likelihood of falling asleep in different situations, with higher scores indicating a greater propensity for daytime sleepiness. These scores serve as standardized measures to evaluate the intensity and impact of symptoms, enabling a comprehensive assessment of mental health and sleep-related conditions. There are also binary data in responses to the patient's feelings regarding suicide, depression (whether the patient feels depressive or not, and if they received treatment or not), anxiety (the same as the previous feature, whether they feel anxious and if they were treated for that), and sleepiness. Finally, the Depression Severity and Anxiety Severity scores form from the PHQ and GAD scores respectively. Including these scores in the dataset allows for a more comprehensive analysis of the relationships between depressive symptoms, anxiety symptoms, and daytime sleepiness, contributing to a better understanding of these conditions and guiding potential interventions for improved mental well-being and sleep health.

The feature we use as the target variable is Depression Diagnosis, which is a binary feature, where only 8% of the records were marked as positive, indicating a highly imbalanced distribution.

The modeling pipeline (Fig. 1) consists of preprocessing, feature selection, model selection, and model training, followed by the interpretation of the results.

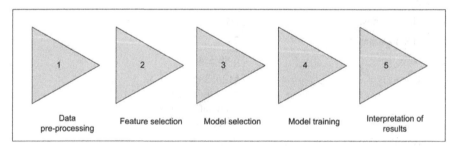

Fig. 1. Modeling pipeline.

As a part of the preprocessing module, several procedures have been applied to the data including the elimination of null values and redundant values that do not contribute any significant input to the dataset. These two procedures did not result in a significant decrease in the dataset size (<5%). Based on the characteristics of the dataset, Standard and MinMax data normalization techniques [19] have been applied. Also, 20% of the dataset is removed. That portion is kept separate to perform the validation of the chosen technique. The rows to be eliminated are chosen randomly.

As the first step of data analysis, to visualize the correlations among the features, a heatmap (Fig. 2) is designed based on the inter-feature correlations. A strong correlation has been observed between anxiety and depression features.

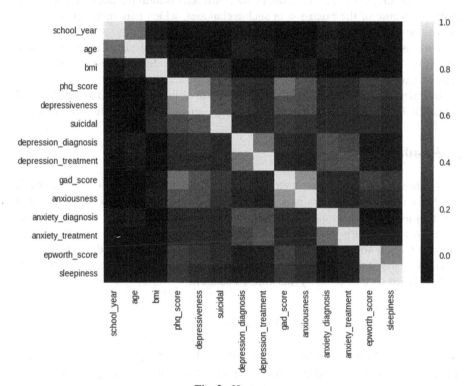

Fig. 2. Heatmap

Following the data preprocessing phase, based on the selected target variable (depression diagnosis), min-max scaling has been performed, followed by a preliminary feature selection using a correlation matrix generated based on all the dataset features. With the objective of selecting features, the process has been applied iteratively until it has no feature whose relationship surpasses the correlation ratio limit. On the other hand, features have been analyzed using the chi-square test to examine the differences between categorical variables.

For the preparation of the datasets for the predictive modeling, categorical features have been encoded using the one-hot method [20–22]. First, the 20% of the data is removed randomly, and that portion will be used for validation afterward. The remaining dataset has been optimally split, using 70% for training purposes, and the remaining 30% for testing. Concerning the predictive modeling, the following algorithms were used— Logistic Regression (*LR*), Ridge Classifier (*RIDGE*), Extra Trees (*ET*), Linear Discriminant Analysis (*LDA*), Light Gradient Boosting Machine (*LIGHTGBM*), Random Forest (*RF*), Extreme Gradient Boosting (*XGBOOST*), Gradient Boosting Classifier (*GBC*), ADABoost Classifier (*ADA*), Support Vector Machines (*SVM*), K-Nearest Neighbors (*KNN*), Decision Tree (*DT*), Naive Bayes (*NB*), and Quadratic Discriminant Analysis (*QDA*).

That list of algorithms covers the most known and popular classification AI techniques. The study purposely does not include Artificial Neural Networks as part of the analysis because of the extension of such techniques, which may merit another study that can be part of future work.

With its implementation in Python [23], subsequent analysis of the performance metrics of the predictive models has been performed to identify the most suitable model in this context.

In order to minimize errors and seek an optimal bias-variance tradeoff that will guarantee that the model won't underfit or overfit, cross-validation techniques are used.

3 Results

With respect to the performance metrics, among the different versions of the transformed data, the one-hot encoded min-max scaled version followed by the procedure of feature selection using the chi-square technique showed the optimal results. Through several procedures of comparison among the different transformed versions of the data, one-hot encoded version without scaling and feature selection also performed at par with the previous model. Table 2 shows the performance metrics of all the supervised models applied, based on the optimally transformed dataset.

Table 2. Results.

Model	Accuracy	AUC	Recall	Prec	F1	Kappa	MCC	Specificity
LDA	0.97	0.96	0.83	0.81	0.80	0.79	0.80	0.98
RF	0.97	0.95	0.83	0.81	0.80	0.79	0.80	0.98
LR	0.96	0.95	0.72	0.85	0.77	0.75	0.76	0.99
GBC	0.96	0.95	0.76	0.75	0.74	0.72	0.72	0.98
QDA	0.95	0.95	0.49	0.62	0.54	0.52	0.53	0.99
XGBOOST	0.97	0.94	0.83	0.81	0.80	0.79	0.80	0.98
LIGHTGBM	0.96	0.94	0.74	0.79	0.75	0.73	0.74	0.98
NB	0.95	0.94	0.43	0.70	0.51	0.49	0.52	0.99
ET	0.97	0.93	0.83	0.81	0.80	0.79	0.80	0.98
DT	0.97	0.91	0.83	0.81	0.80	0.79	0.80	0.98

(continued)

Table 2. (*continued*)

Model	Accuracy	AUC	Recall	Prec	F1	Kappa	MCC	Specificity
ADA	0.97	0.91	0.74	0.86	0.79	0.77	0.78	0.99
SVM	0.97	0.91	0.78	0.83	0.79	0.78	0.78	0.98
RIDGE	0.97	0.86	0.83	0.81	0.80	0.79	0.80	0.98
KNN	0.95	0.79	0.57	0.83	0.66	0.64	0.66	0.99

Analyzing the performance metrics of accuracy, the area under the curve (AUC), recall, precision, F1 score, Kappa, MCC, and Specificity, Linear Discriminant Analysis (LDA) showed the best performance. Also, Random Forest and Logistic Regression showed considerably fair performance in predicting. Finally, ADA Boost Analysis has the best Precision score.

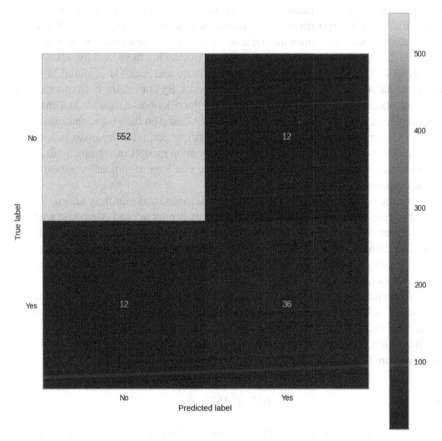

Fig. 3. Confusion matrix for LDA classifier.

With respect to the best-performing algorithm LDA Classifier, the confusion matrix (Fig. 3) highlights the performance of the algorithm in measuring the hit rate of the predicted class. In the context of this study, both reality and prediction in a classification model can be categorized as "yes" or "no". A "true positive" occurs when both the reality and prediction are "yes", indicating that the model is correct. Conversely, a "false positive" happens when the prediction is "yes" while the reality is "no", indicating an incorrect prediction. On the other hand, a "false negative" occurs when the model fails to detect a positive condition, in this case, depression, when the reality is indeed positive. This type of error (type II error) is considered more serious specifically in the context of detection of depression since it implies wrongly asserting a negative result when it should be positive. The problem with accuracy or hit rate arises when dealing with imbalanced classes. Accuracy represents the ratio of correctly classified cases to the total cases, encompassing both true positives and true negatives. Type II errors, or false negatives, refer to instances when the model incorrectly predicts a negative outcome for an originally positive observation.

Especially in the context of predicting depression, particular attention is necessary to false positives and false negatives, as their consequences can be substantial. To minimize the occurrence of false positives, it is important to prioritize high specificity. Conversely, a high recall is crucial to minimize false negatives, as it is less concerning to classify a patient as sick when they are not, compared to considering them healthy when they are actually sick. Striking a balance between specificity and recall is essential in order to achieve accurate and reliable classification outcomes. By optimizing both specificity and recall, the classification model aims to minimize the risk of misdiagnosis and ensure that patients receive appropriate care and interventions based on their true condition. Consequently, a comprehensive evaluation of false positives and false negatives is imperative for developing effective and trustworthy classification models in various fields, including healthcare, where accurate decision-making can have significant implications for patient outcomes and well-being.

Using the optimal dataset version, (one-hot encoded and min-max scaled, followed by feature selection), the ROC curve analysis was conducted and compared with other pre-processed dataset versions. Although all versions underwent preprocessing, the best version outperformed the others. The LDA algorithm was selected as the preferred model due to its ability to achieve the highest metrics among the evaluated algorithms. When dealing with imbalanced data the AUC metric is particularly important and LDA has the best performance but there are no other significant differences with the other algorithms, however, LDA also excels in other metrics, including the F1 score, which acquires more relevance [24] when the AUC value is high.

Finally, the reserved validation dataset is used to see how the chosen model (LDA) works with unknown data. These results are presented in Table 3.

Table 3. Validation.

Accuracy	AUC	Recall	Prec.	F1	Kappa	MCC	Specificity
0.93	0.84	0.44	0.89	0.59	0.56	0.6	0.99

The model predictions over the validation dataset show a similar accuracy and an even higher precision.

4   Conclusions

The proposed predictive models have successfully performed in predicting depression in the concerned dataset. Instead of performing as isolated models, it highlights the importance of developing comprehensive clinical decision support systems, to incorporate the computational power of the predictive models, as well as the multidimensional data related to the patients. A potential application of this study is its integration into a clinical decision support system for detecting depression. By incorporating this AI model as a foundation, the clinical decision support system can provide healthcare professionals with valuable insights, guidance, and evidence-based recommendations during the diagnostic process. The combination of the model's accuracy, additional clinical information, and the expertise of healthcare professionals can lead to more accurate and efficient depression detection, ultimately improving patient care and outcomes. However, it is essential to consider the ethical and legal implications associated with implementing AI in mental health diagnosis. Safeguarding privacy, ensuring informed consent, and maintaining a patient-centric approach is crucial to protecting individuals' rights and building trust in the use of AI technologies in healthcare.

The application of AI in mental health diagnosis holds tremendous potential. However, several challenges need to be addressed for its effective implementation in this field. One of the primary challenges lies in the availability of sufficient and diverse datasets for training and validating AI models. Mental health diagnosis is a complex process that involves considering various factors, such as symptoms, environmental and social influences, and comorbidities. Acquiring high-quality and comprehensive data that adequately captures these factors proves challenging, particularly due to the stigma associated with mental health conditions, which hampers data sharing and collection efforts. Another significant challenge is the need for transparency and interpretability of AI models. Some AI models operate as "black boxes," making it difficult to comprehend the underlying decision-making process. This lack of transparency can lead to concerns regarding the reliability and validity of AI-based diagnoses, which is particularly crucial in mental health, where decisions can profoundly impact individuals and their families. Therefore, efforts should be directed toward developing AI models that provide clear explanations for their predictions and enhance their interpretability. Additionally, the ethical development and validation of AI models are of paramount importance. Privacy and autonomy rights must be respected, and measures should be in place to prevent potential misuse of AI-based diagnoses for discriminatory purposes, such as denying individuals access to employment, insurance, or other opportunities. Ensuring responsible implementation of AI in mental health diagnosis requires adherence to ethical principles, guidelines, and legal frameworks.

In future lines of development, it is proposed to extend the implementation of this model to other datasets, broadening its predictive capabilities to encompass other mental health conditions, such as anxiety. Incorporating unsupervised models and natural language processing techniques can further enhance the system's ability to extract meaningful insights from diverse data sources and improve diagnostic accuracy. Furthermore, the application of Neural Networks can contribute to identifying behavioral rules specific to patients at risk of depression. By leveraging the power of Neural Networks, hybrid models that combine multiple classification approaches can be developed, further improving the accuracy and precision of mental health diagnosis. In this study, the usage of Neural Networks is not included due to a scope limitation.

In conclusion, despite existing challenges, the potential benefits of AI in mental health diagnosis are significant. By addressing the challenges of data availability, transparency, and ethical implementation, AI has the potential to revolutionize mental healthcare, leading to more accurate diagnoses, personalized treatment interventions, and improved patient outcomes.

Acknowledgments. This work has been supported and financed by the Cloudgenia group through its technical and operational initiatives.

References

1. Manwell, L.A., et al.: What is mental health? Evidence towards a new definition from a mixed methods multidisciplinary international survey. BMJ Open **5**(6), e007079 (2015). https://doi.org/10.1136/bmjopen-2014-007079
2. ICD-11 for Mortality and Morbidity Statistics. https://icd.who.int/browse11/l-m/en#/http%3a%2f%2fid.who.int%2ficd%2fentity%2f1563440232. Accessed 31 Mar 2023
3. Lim, G.Y., Tam, W.W., Lu, Y., Ho, C.S., Zhang, M.W., Ho, R.C.: Prevalence of depression in the community from 30 countries between 1994 and 2014. Sci. Rep. **8**(1), Article no. 1 (2018). https://doi.org/10.1038/s41598-018-21243-x
4. Diagnostic and Statistical Manual of Mental Disorders: DSM Library. https://dsm.psychiatryonline.org/doi/book/10.1176/appi.books.9780890425787. Accessed 23 Jun 2022
5. Bains, N., Abdijadid, S.: Major depressive disorder. In: StatPearls. StatPearls Publishing, Treasure Island (2023). http://www.ncbi.nlm.nih.gov/books/NBK559078/. Accessed 3 Apr 2023
6. Depressive disorder (depression). https://www.who.int/news-room/fact-sheets/detail/depression. Accessed 19 Apr 2023
7. Boden, M.A.: Artificial Intelligence. Elsevier (1996)
8. Tai, A.M.Y., et al.: Machine learning and big data: implications for disease modeling and therapeutic discovery in psychiatry. Artif. Intell. Med. **99**, 101704 (2019). https://doi.org/10.1016/j.artmed.2019.101704
9. 5 Trends Emerge in Gartner Hype Cycle For Emerging Technologies. Gartner (2018). https://www.gartner.com/smarterwithgartner/5-trends-emerge-in-gartner-hype-cycle-for-emerging-technologies-2018. Accessed 14 June 2022
10. Villars, R.L., Eastwood, M., Olofson, C.W.: Big Data: What It Is and Why You Should Care, p. 14 (2011)
11. Kroenke, K., Strine, T.W., Spitzer, R.L., Williams, J.B.W., Berry, J.T., Mokdad, A.H.: The PHQ-8 as a measure of current depression in the general population. J. Affect. Disord. **114**(1), 163–173 (2009). https://doi.org/10.1016/j.jad.2008.06.026
12. Kroenke, K., Spitzer, R.L.: The PHQ-9: a new depression diagnostic and severity measure. Psychiatr. Ann. **32**(9), 509–515 (2002). https://doi.org/10.3928/0048-5713-20020901-06
13. Beck Depression Inventory (BDI). https://www.apa.org. https://www.apa.org/pi/about/publications/caregivers/practice-settings/assessment/tools/beck-depression. Accessed 04 July 2022

14. Graham, S., et al.: Artificial intelligence for mental health and mental illnesses: an overview. Curr. Psychiatry Rep. **21**(11), 116 (2019). https://doi.org/10.1007/s11920-019-1094-0
15. Tran, B.X., et al.: The current research landscape on the artificial intelligence application in the management of depressive disorders: a bibliometric analysis. Int. J. Environ. Res. Public. Health **16**(12), Article no. 12 (2019). https://doi.org/10.3390/ijerph16122150
16. Morley, J., et al.: The ethics of AI in health care: a mapping review. Soc. Sci. Med. 1982 **260**, 113172 (2020). https://doi.org/10.1016/j.socscimed.2020.113172
17. Higgins, O., Short, B.L., Chalup, S.K., Wilson, R.L.: Artificial intelligence (AI) and machine learning (ML) based decision support systems in mental health: an integrative review. Int. J. Ment. Health Nurs. **32**(4), 966–978 (2023). https://doi.org/10.1111/inm.13114
18. Depression and anxiety data. https://www.kaggle.com/datasets/shahzadahmad0402/depression-and-anxiety-data . Accessed 19 Apr 2023
19. Patro, S.G.K., Sahu, K.K.: Normalization: a preprocessing stage. arXiv (2015). https://doi.org/10.48550/arXiv.1503.06462
20. Bruce, P.C., Bruce, A., Gedeck, P.: Practical Statistics for Data Scientists: 50+ Essential Concepts Using R and Python, 2nd edn. O'Reilly Media Inc, Sebastopol (2020)
21. Vance, W.: Data Science: Tips and Tricks to Learn Data Science Theories Effectively (2020)
22. García Herrero, J.: Ciencia de datos: técnicas analíticas y aprendizaje estadístico en un enfoque práctico. Alfaomega (2018)
23. Welcome to Python.org. Python.org. https://www.python.org/. Accessed 28 Oct 2022
24. Zou, Q., Xie, S., Lin, Z., Wu, M., Ju, Y.: Finding the best classification threshold in imbalanced classification. Big Data Res. **5**, 2–8 (2016). https://doi.org/10.1016/j.bdr.2015.12.001

Stock Price Prediction: Impact of Volatility on Model Accuracy

Juan Parada-Rodriguez$^{(\boxtimes)}$ ⓘ and Ixent Galpin ⓘ

Facultad de Ciencias Naturales e Ingeniería, Universidad de Bogotá-Jorge Tadeo
Lozano, Bogotá, Colombia
{juand.paradar,ixent}@utadeo.edu.co

Abstract. This research paper focuses on predicting stock prices using neural networks, and evaluating the impact of volatility on model accuracy. Two stocks, one non-volatile and one volatile, were selected to assess the effect of volatility on prediction precision using three types of neural networks: RNN, LSTM, and feedforward. The datasets used in this study include daily stock price information obtained from Yahoo Finance for the period from September 2020 to February 2023. Additionally, news articles were extracted to perform sentiment analysis. The NLTK sentiment library was utilized to classify sentiments as positive, negative, or neutral, and the results were averaged on a daily basis. The integration of these datasets aims to provide a comprehensive understanding of the factors influencing stock price behavior. The paper discusses the methodology used to train and evaluate neural network models based on the combined datasets. This research contributes to the field of stock price prediction and highlights the importance of considering volatility in achieving accurate predictions.

Keywords: Machine Learning · Neural Networks · Price Prediction · Stock Market · Sentiment Analysis · TensorFlow

1 Introduction

Accurate prediction of stock prices in the stock market is a significant challenge for investors. In recent years, the interest of retail investors has grown significantly, especially among individuals under the age of 35, driven by access to investment platforms and the search for lucrative financial opportunities [13]. In order to mitigate the risks associated with these investments, it is crucial to analyze and accurately predict stock prices.

In this paper, we evaluate the impact of volatility on the accuracy of a stock price prediction model based on neural networks. To conduct this study, we select two stocks, one considered non-volatile and the other volatile, in order to analyze how volatility affects the predictive capability of the model. The chosen stocks were carefully selected from the stock market, representing different levels of volatility.

H. Florez and M. Leon (Eds.): ICAI 2023, CCIS 1874, pp. 58–73, 2024.
https://doi.org/10.1007/978-3-031-46813-1_5

To achieve our objective, we implemented and compared three neural network models: RNN (Recurrent Neural Networks) [18], LSTM (Long Short-Term Memory) [19], and Feedforward Neural Networks [5]. These neural network architectures have proven to be effective in time series prediction and are therefore considered appropriate for addressing the stock price prediction problem.

The main objective of this study is to evaluate how volatility impacts the accuracy of neural network models in stock price prediction. The results obtained from the evaluation and comparison of the three neural network models will help identify which model is more effective at different levels of volatility. Additionally, this study contributes to advancing knowledge in the field of applying neural networks in stock price prediction and provides valuable insights for investors interested in the stock market, as well as the scientific and academic community involved in machine learning applied to finance [2].

The methodology employed in this article is based on the lifecycle architecture of data mining and analysis projects. Specifically, it follows the approach proposed by CRISP-DM (Cross Industry Standard Process for Data Mining), which provides a structured methodology for conducting data mining projects. This methodology starts with the analysis of the business problem and translates it into a technical data mining problem, thereby facilitating the execution of the project [20].

This document follows the following structure. Related works are presented in Sect. 2. The objective and approach of the article are described in Sect. 3. The understanding of the data used is explained in Sect. 4. Subsequently, data organization and preparation are carried out in Sect. 5. The modeling of neural networks is described in Sect. 6, while the obtained results are detailed in Sect. 7. Finally, conclusions are presented in Sect. 8.

2   Related Work

Table 1 presents previous work that uses various neural network architectures for the prediction of stock prices. Most of these networks focus on forecasting the future value of a specific stock within a given time period. As can be observed from the table, a wide range of different methods and neural networks have been used for prediction in the field of individual stocks and the stock market in general. The three most popular techniques are *feedforward networks* (e.g., , used by Hammad *et al.* [8] and Iguarán Cortés *et al.* [10]), *Long Short-Term Memory networks* (LSTM) (e.g., used by Cabezón *et al.* [3]), and *Recurrent Neural Networks (RNN)* (e.g., used by Dey *et al.* [4]). Other work, e.g., Pawar *et al.* [15] and Khoa *et al.* [11], concentrate on predicting the price of a widely recognized global index. In contrast, our paper, aims to predict prices for two stocks with different degrees of volatility, and compare the obtained results.

Table 1. Survey of related work

Paper	Topic	Techniques Used	Location
[8]	Predictive model of stock price variation based on neural networks and financial statement analysis	A feedforward neural network trained using one-step secant backpropagation	United States
[10]	Predicting the stock price of Ecopetrol in three time horizons: short-term (1 day), medium-term (5 days), and long-term (20 days)	Feedforward neural network with a hidden layer with nodes and a hyperbolic tangent activation function	Colombia
[12]	Implementation of a neural network for financial market prediction in the Mexican Stock Exchange	Multilayer feedforward network trained using the Backpropagation algorithm	Mexico
[15]	Stock price prediction	Two neural networks, LSTM and RNN, using historical data from S&P 500	India
[4]	Comparative analysis of recurrent neural networks in stock price prediction for different frequency domains (1 day, 3 days, and 5 days)	Using three neural network models (Simple RNN, LSTM, and GRU)	Bangladesh
[3]	Predicting electric demand in Spain using LSTM networks	Recurrent model consisting of an input layer, an LSTM hidden layer, a 0.2 Dropout layer, and an output layer	Spain
[11]	Stock price forecasting using backpropagation neural networks, presenting an approach with time-adjusted weighting factors and profits	Feedforward neural networks (FFN) and recurrent neural networks (RNN)	Korea
[17]	Cryptocurrency price projection based on tweets using LSTM	The LSTM recurrent neural network seeks to learn dependencies of future values	Perú
[9]	Stock market prediction with LSTM neural networks	RMSPROP, RNN, and SMA indicator	Colombia
[6]	Investment viability in an oil well	Key Performance Indicators	Colombia
[7]	Predictive model of stock price variation based on neural networks and financial statement analysis	Multilayer perceptron neural networks	Spain
[16]	Prediction of Telefónica stock price using data mining techniques	CART, Neural networks, Random Forest, Support Vector Machines, and Linear Regression	Spain
[14]	Prediction of stock prices in the banking sector	Log-normal and Montecarlo simulation	Colombia
[1]	Sentiment Identification on Tweets to Forecast Cryptocurrency's Volatility	Natural Language Processing (NLP)	Brazil

3   Business Understanding

The prediction of stock prices is a crucial task in the financial field, as it allows investors to make better informed decisions and improve their profit opportunities. In this context, the main objective of this article is to analyze and compare the effectiveness of different neural network models in predicting the prices of stocks belonging to two telecommunications companies: Verizon, which is listed on the New York Stock Exchange, and T-Mobile, listed on NASDAQ.

Understanding the results of this study has important implications for investors and financial market professionals. The findings and conclusions presented in this article can be used as a basis for the development of more informed investment strategies and the improvement of financial advisory systems. Additionally, the knowledge gained through this study can help investors better understand and manage the risks associated with market volatility.

The proposed study is relevant and significant due to the importance of accurate stock prediction in the financial market. Understanding how stock volatility can influence the performance of neural networks in price prediction is essential for making informed and strategic investment decisions. The results of this research can contribute to the field of finance and provide valuable information to investors and market professionals to enhance their prediction strategies and decision-making processes.

4   Data Understanding

In this section, a detailed analysis of the datasets used in the study is presented. The objective is to understand the nature of the collected data and how it was used to address the problem of stock price prediction based on neural networks, evaluating the impact of volatility on model accuracy.

4.1   Stock Price Dataset

To obtain the first dataset, the Yahoo Finance service[1] was used, which is a platform that provides financial information and market insights, with a particular focus on the United States. Two data files were downloaded, one for the Verizon stock, which is considered non-volatile due to its low standard deviation, and another for the T-Mobile stock, which is considered volatile. Both selected stocks are part of the telecommunications sector in the United States. The dataset used spans from September 2020 to February 2023, representing a total of 582 business days. These daily data contain relevant information including open prices, close prices, high and low prices, trading volume, and other relevant indicators.

4.2   News Dataset for Sentiment Analysis

The second dataset was generated by extracting news articles from different media sources using APIs. Services such as mediastacks[2] and gnews.io[3] were used

---

[1]   https://finance.yahoo.com.

[2]   https://www.medistacks.org.

[3]   https://gnews.io.

to collect news articles from the year 2020 to 2023. The choice of this dataset is based on the premise that the sentiments expressed in the news articles influence (or may reflect) the stock market behavior. To perform sentiment classification analysis, the NLTK.sentiment[4] library, was used for natural language processing in Python. This library enables each news article to be classified as positive, negative, or neutral.

4.3   Data Exploration

The initial analysis revealed primarily numerical data, such as daily open, high, low, and close prices, as shown in Fig. 1, as well as transaction volume. These data cover every business day from the period from 2020 to 2023 (Table 2).

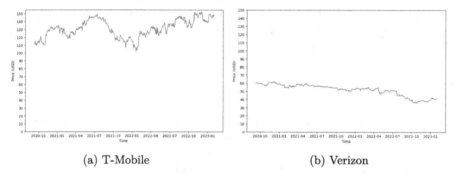

(a) T-Mobile   (b) Verizon

Fig. 1. Stock prices from 2020 to 2023

Table 2. Statistical measures of the stocks

Measure	T-Mobile		Measure	Verizon
Mean	105.39		Mean	53.60
Standard Deviation	30.155		Standard Deviation	6.10
Maximum	152.41		Maximum	62.07
Minimum	55.58		Minimum	35.34
Median	112.37		Median	55.28
(a) T-Mobile			(b) Verizon	

---

[4] https://www.nltk.org/index.html.

Average True Range (ATR). The Average True Range (ATR) is a technical indicator that provides a measure of the volatility of a financial asset [21]. The calculation of ATR involves determining the greatest difference among the following three values for each time period. Once these differences are calculated for each period, they are averaged to obtain the ATR. The higher the value of ATR, the greater the volatility of the stock.

$$PercentageRange = \frac{(Max - Min)}{Mean} \cdot 100 \tag{1}$$

In the case of T-Mobile:

$$PercentageRange = \frac{(152.41 - 55.58)}{105.39} \cdot 100 \tag{2}$$

$$PercentageRange = 91.83 \tag{3}$$

The percentage range of 91.83 indicates that T-Mobile stock has experienced a relative volatility of 91.83% in relation to its average prices. The higher the value of the percentage range, the higher the perceived volatility.

In the case of Verizon:

$$PercentageRange = \frac{(62.07 - 35.34)}{53.60} \cdot 100 \tag{4}$$

$$PercentageRange = 49.87 \tag{5}$$

The percentage range of 49.88 indicates that Verizon stock has experienced a relative volatility of 49.88% in relation to its average prices. Comparing the percentage ranges, we can see that T-Mobile has a higher percentage range (91.83%) compared to Verizon (49.87%). This indicates that T-Mobile is more volatile than Verizon, meaning it has experienced larger price fluctuations relative to its average. Therefore, in terms of volatility, T-Mobile is the more volatile stock compared to Verizon.

5   Data Cleaning and Preparation

Once the two datasets are obtained, they are integrated. Since the news data is extracted daily, it is necessary to combine it with the corresponding stock price data for each day. To do this, the sentiment analysis results of the news are averaged for each day. This approach allowed an overall view of the sentiment associated with each day and its potential influence on the stock price behavior. Thus, a combined dataset was obtained that includes both the financial information and the sentiments associated with each day.

In summary, the datasets used in this study consist of daily financial information for two stocks and sentiment classification analysis of news. This data is obtained from Yahoo Finance and various media sources using APIs. The integration of both datasets allows for a more comprehensive and balanced view of the factors that can influence stock price behavior (Table 3).

Table 3. Dataset attributes used for prediction

Attribute	Description
Date	Date on which the information is recorded
Open	Opening price of a stock over a period of time
High	Maximum price reached by a stock over a period of time
Low	Minimum price reached by a stock over a period of time
Close	Closing price of a stock over a period of time
Adj Close	Adjusted closing price of a stock considering corporate events
Volume	Volume of shares traded over a period of time
Content	Number of news articles related to the stock on that date
Positive sentiment	Positive sentiment score associated with the content of the news article about the stock (Range 0 to 1)
Negative sentiment	Negative sentiment score associated with the content of the news article about the stock (Range 0 to 1)
Neutral sentiment	Neutral sentiment score associated with the content of the news article about the stock (Range 0 to 1)

The data used in the construction of the prediction models was obtained following the previously established requirements, which consist of using only information from events between September 2022 and February 2023 using the Pandas Library. The training data contains only data corresponding to the months of September 2022 to January 2023. The test data set contains data for the month of February 2022. This data is reserved for evaluating the performance and accuracy of the models. By limiting the training data to the specific period mentioned, we ensure that the models are trained and evaluated using up-to-date information relevant to the target prediction period.

6   Modeling

Three different neural networks are created and trained with an architecture consisting of an input layer, a hidden layer and an output layer. The number of neurons in the hidden layer was varied in three different configurations: 5, 10 and 25 neurons. This resulted in a total of nine different networks for each stock. It is important to note that all networks were constructed using the same library and dataset, with the purpose of obtaining comparable results. The hyperbolic tangent (tanh) activation function was used along with the Adam optimizer. The hyperbolic tangent function is a commonly used activation function in neural networks due to its ability to generate values between -1 and 1. This allows the neural network to have a smoother output and less prone to errors. On the other hand, the Adam optimizer is an optimization algorithm commonly used in neural networks due to its ability to adapt the learning rate during training. For each network, 100 epochs were used during training. The number of epochs determines how many times the entire dataset is passed through the network during training.

7 Results

The performance of each model is evaluated using metrics including MSE, RMSE and MPE, to quantify the error in predicting stock prices. By evaluating these metrics over a period of 19 business days in the month of February 2022, we determine the effectiveness of each model in capturing patterns and trends, as well as its ability to generalize for future data.

Feedfoward Network. Figure 2 presents the results of the experiments conducted for the feedforward network. It is observed that as the number of neurons in the hidden layer increases, the prediction error decreases for both Verizon and T-Mobile. This pattern suggests that a higher number of neurons in the hidden layer improves the accuracy of the stock price prediction model.

Table 4. Summary of results for the feedfoward network

Neurons	T-Mobile			Verizon		
	MSE	MAE	RMSE	MSE	MAE	RMSE
5	0.053	0.191	0.23	**0.0176**	0.114	0.133
10	0.016	0.107	0.13	**0.014**	0.099	0.119
25	0.0073	0.071	0.087	**0.007**	0.066	0.085

Table 4 summarises the results obtained for the feedforward network for both stocks. It is observed that the model exhibits better performance and lower error as the number of neurons in the hidden layer increases. However, when comparing the results between the two analyzed stocks, no significant distinction in terms of error is observed. It is interesting to note that both stocks, with a hidden layer of 25 neurons, obtained very similar results, with an MSE of 0.0073 for T-Mobile and 0.0070 for Verizon.

Overall, the Verizon stock, considered a non-volatile stock, shows better performance in terms of all three errors metrics compared to the more volatile T-Mobile stock. This suggests that the volatility of a stock can influence the outcome of neural network prediction, making it more challenging to accurately predict the behavior of volatile stocks compared to non-volatile stocks.

Furthermore, it is important to mention that, despite the favorable results obtained in this study with the feedforward network, there are certain limitations in its ability to accurately predict stock prices. The static nature of this network architecture may hinder the capture of complex patterns and trends present in financial data. As such, the feedforward network lacks the ability to model long-term dependencies and temporal sequences that are inherent in stock prices.

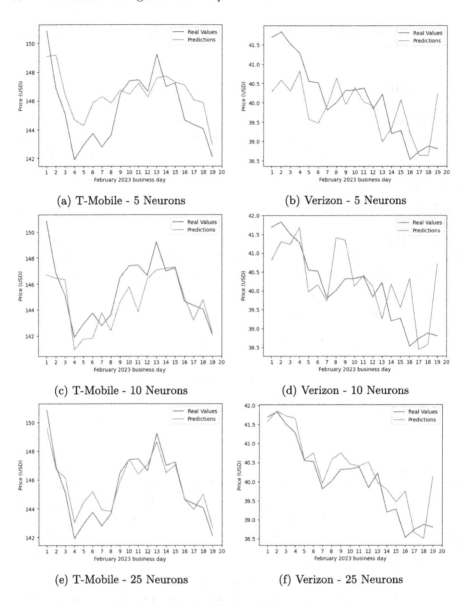

Fig. 2. Predictions for the feedfoward network

Therefore, in scenarios where greater consideration of temporal dynamics and the ability to capture complex relationships is required, it is worth exploring other neural network architectures such as LSTM or RNN, which are known for their ability to model and predict timeseries data.

LSTM Network. Figure 3 depicts the predictions for February 2022 obtained through experiments conducted with the LSTM network. It is observed that

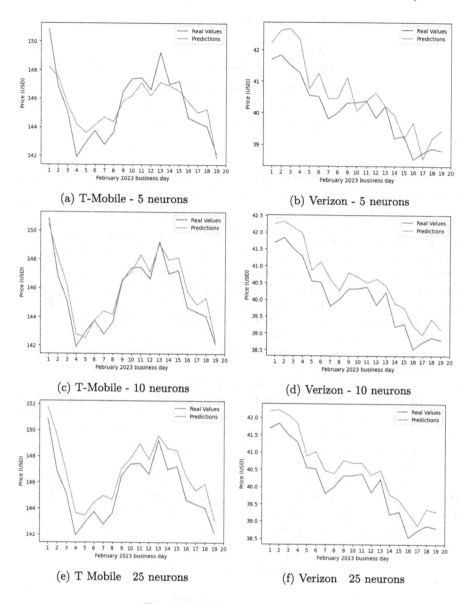

(a) T-Mobile - 5 neurons

(b) Verizon - 5 neurons

(c) T-Mobile - 10 neurons

(d) Verizon - 10 neurons

(e) T Mobile   25 neurons

(f) Verizon   25 neurons

Fig. 3. LSTM network predictions

this neural network architecture outperforms the feedforward architecture in predicting stock prices. This can be attributed to the inherent characteristics of the LSTM network, such as its ability to capture long-term dependencies, handle sequential data, and learn complex patterns. These capabilities enable the LSTM network to effectively adapt to the various time scales present in stock prices.

Table 5. Summary of LSTM network results

Neurons	T-Mobile			Verizon		
	MSE	MAE	RMSE	MSE	MAE	RMSE
5	**0.0037**	0.048	0.061	0.0054	0.0618	0.0735
10	0.0042	0.057	0.065	**0.0037**	0.054	0.0612
25	0.0058	0.063	0.076	**0.0026**	0.046	0.051

According to the results presented in Table 5, an interesting trait is observed in the case of the volatile T-Mobile stock. Despite increasing the number of neurons in the LSTM network, no improvement in prediction error was obtained. In fact, it can be observed that with 25 neurons, the error increases, with an MSE of 0.0058, compared to 10 neurons that achieved an MSE of 0.0042.

This result suggests that, for this particular stock, a higher number of neurons in the LSTM network does not necessarily result in an improvement in prediction accuracy, possibly due to overfitting. It is possible that T-Mobile stock exhibits patterns and characteristics that do not benefit from an increase in model complexity. Therefore, it is important to consider the specific characteristics of each stock when selecting the appropriate network architecture.

In general, the results support the choice of LSTM network as an effective tool for predicting stock prices due to its ability to capture long-term dependencies, handle sequential data, learn complex patterns, and adapt to different time scales. However, they also highlight the importance of considering the individual characteristics of each stock when tuning the hyperparameters of the neural network. As such, it is necessary to consider the specific features of each stock, such as volatility, when selecting the optimal number of neurons to achieve the best predictive performance.

Figure 4 shows that the recurrent neural network (RNN) achieves better results compared to the feedforward network. This indicates that the RNN's ability to process sequential data and capture contextual information over time is beneficial for stock price prediction.

Table 6. Summary of results for the RNN

Neurons	T-Mobile			Verizon		
	MSE	MAE	RMSE	MSE	MAE	RMSE
5	0.028	0.15	0.169	**0.011**	0.089	0.105
10	0.0084	0.077	0.092	**0.0092**	0.0783	0.098
25	0.0087	0.0767	0.0935	**0.003**	0.0457	0.0547

Based on the results provided in Table 6, we observe a similar scenario as previously seen in the LSTM model, where increasing the number of neurons in

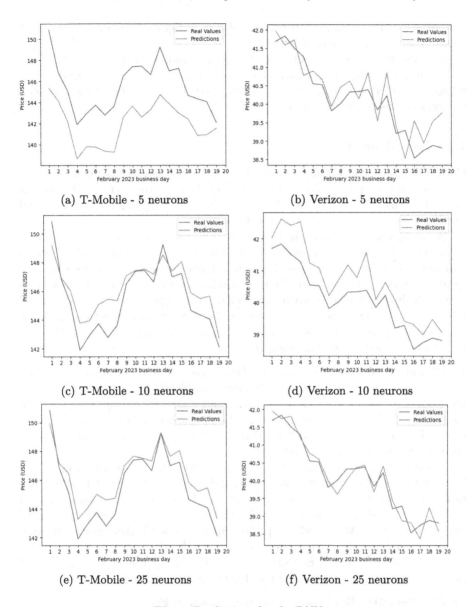

Fig. 4. Predictions for the RNN

the recurrent network does not lead to an improvement in the prediction accuracy for the T-Mobile stock. Despite efforts to increase the complexity of the model, it is found that the error either remains the same or even increases. This suggests the possibility of overfitting, where the model becomes too specialized to the training data and fails to generalize well to new data. It highlights the importance of finding the right balance between model complexity and generalization ability to avoid overfitting in neural networks.

This result may be attributed to the specific characteristics of the T-Mobile stock and its behavior in the market. It is possible that factors not captured by a higher number of neurons in the recurrent network influence the volatility and patterns of this particular stock.

7.1 Cross-Validation

Cross-validation is a technique that allows us to evaluate the performance of a model using multiple divisions of the dataset. In this study, cross-validation is applied to ensure that the models were evaluated in an unbiased manner and that the obtained results are statistically robust.

By using cross-validation in this study, more reliable measures of the performance of neural network models were obtained. This technique allows us to reduce the bias introduced by a single data partition. As a result, we can have greater confidence in model ability to generalize for future data and capacity to handle the inherent uncertainty in financial markets. The dataset was partitioned into 10 subsets, with each subset used as the test set once and the remaining 9 subsets used for model training in each iteration. Additionally, the folds were created by randomly selecting samples.

Feedforward Network. In cross-validation, the architecture previously found to exhibit best performance is used (i.e., with a hidden layer 25 neurons). According to the results presented in Fig. 5, some splits showed a relatively low mean squared error (MSE), indicating good prediction capability of the model in those cases. However, other splits exhibited higher MSE, suggesting lower prediction accuracy in those particular divisions.

These results indicate that model performance can vary depending on the input data used and their distribution at different time points. It is important to consider this variability when interpreting the results and assessing model ability to generalize to future data. Furthermore, the presence of splits with significantly higher MSE, such as split 9 and split 10 for Verizon stock, suggests that there are certain scenarios or patterns in the data that pose challenges for the feedforward neural network model. This may be due to the presence of nonlinear features or complex temporal dependencies in those specific datasets.

LSTM Network. Based on the findings shown in Fig. 5, the LSTM network demonstrates promising performance in predicting stock prices, as most of the splits exhibit low MSE values.

For Verizon stock, the LSTM network shows consistency in its performance, with relatively low MSE values in the majority of splits. This indicates that the LSTM network is capable of effectively capturing patterns and trends in Verizon's data. However, for T-Mobile stock, there is greater variability in the results. Some splits exhibit outstanding performance with very low MSE values, while others show poorer performance with higher MSE values.

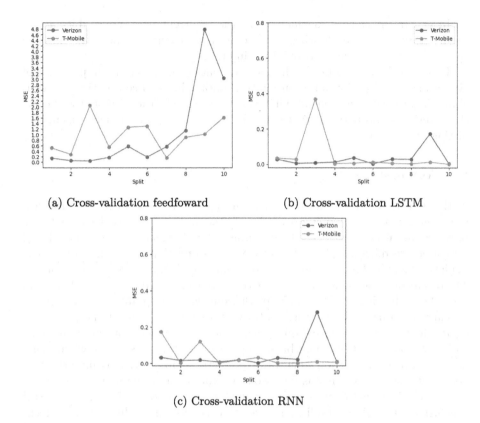

(a) Cross-validation feedfoward

(b) Cross-validation LSTM

(c) Cross-validation RNN

Fig. 5. Cross-validation

It is important to note that *Split 3* for T-Mobile stock displays a significantly higher MSE compared to other splits. This suggests that there are specific features or patterns in T-Mobile's data that are more challenging to capture for the LSTM network, resulting in lower prediction accuracy in that particular *split*.

Recurrent Neural Network. In Fig. 5 it can be observed that for Verizon stock, the MSE values range from 0.002673 (*split 6*) to 0.282497 (*split 9*). These results indicate some variability in the predictions of the network in each case, with significant variations in performance. It is noteworthy that the lowest MSE values were achieved in *split 4* and *split 10*, suggesting higher prediction accuracy for those specific scenarios.

On the other hand, in the case of T-Mobile stock, the MSE values obtained in each split range from 0.0015 to 0.1744. As with Verizon, there is considerable variation in the network's performance across different scenarios. However, it is worth noting that the lowest MSE was achieved in *split 2*, indicating higher prediction accuracy for that particular case.

In general, it can be concluded that the recurrent network exhibits mixed results in predicting both stocks. While accurate results are achieved in some splits, inferior performance is observed in others.

In summary, the results of the cross-validation highlight the importance of evaluating model performance on multiple data splits and considering the variability in performance. They also indicate the need to further explore the specific characteristics and patterns that can affect the accuracy of the networks in predicting stock prices.

8   Conclusions

In this study, the use of machine learning techniques, specifically neural networks, is explored to predict stock prices in the financial market. Using datasets provided by Yahoo Finance, three neural network models are developed and compared: Feedforward, LSTM, and RNN. We find that neural networks, particularly the LSTM model, demonstrate promising ability to predict stock prices. The results of these models were able to capture trends and patterns in historical price data, allowing them to make predictions with acceptable accuracy. Additionally, it is observed that the volatility of a stock can impact the prediction error. More volatile stocks exhibit a higher degree of uncertainty in predictions, indicating that volatility may be an important factor to consider when using neural network models for stock price prediction. However, it is important to note that this conclusion was based on one volatile and one non-volatile stock and experiments with more stocks would be needed to reach a more general conclusion. Overall, our findings suggest that the use of machine learning techniques, such as neural networks, can be a valuable tool for investors interested in the stock market. These techniques can provide additional information and analysis to support more informed investment decision-making. In conclusion, this study demonstrates the potential of neural networks for predicting stock prices and highlights the importance of considering volatility as an influential factor in prediction accuracy. These results may be of interest to both investors in the stock market and the scientific and academic community interested in the application of machine learning in finance.

References

1. de Araújo, R.C.F., Pinto, A.S.R., Ferrandin, M.: Sentiment identification on tweets to forecast cryptocurrency's volatility. J. Comput. Sci. **19**(5), 619–628 (2023). https://doi.org/10.3844/jcssp.2023.619.628
2. Ayala Jiménez, L., Letelier González, S., Zagal Morgado, P., et al.: Modelo de redes neuronales para la predicción de la variación del valor de la acción de first solar (2009)
3. Cabezón, M.: Predicción demanda eléctrica española. implementación de redes neuronales recurrentes en python (2018)
4. Dey, P., et al.: Comparative analysis of recurrent neural networks in stock price prediction for different frequency domains. Algorithms **14**(8), 251 (2021)

5. Eldan, R., Shamir, O.: The power of depth for feedforward neural networks. In: Conference on Learning Theory, pp. 907–940. PMLR (2016)
6. Falla Arango, J.D., et al.: Predicción de abandono de clientes en telecomunicaciones mediante el aprendizaje automático. Universidad de Bogotá Jorge Tadeo Lozano (2021)
7. Guevara, M.P., Moreno, E.: Propuesta de un modelo predictivo de la variación del precio de acciones basado en redes neuronales y análisis de estados financieros. In: Anales de la Universidad Metropolitana, vol. 12, pp. 103–123. Universidad Metropolitana (2012)
8. Hammad, A.A.A., Ali, S.M.A., Hall, E.L.: Forecasting the Jordanian stock price using artificial neural network. Intell. Eng. Syst. Through Artif. Neural Netw. **17**, 1–6 (2007)
9. Herrera Cofre, D.F., et al.: Predicción para el mercado de acciones con redes neuronales lstm (2020)
10. Iguarán Cortes, J.M., et al.: Aplicación de redes neuronales para predecir el precio de acciones en la bolsa colombiana (2019)
11. Khoa, N.L.D., Sakakibara, K., Nishikawa, I.: Stock price forecasting using back propagation neural networks with time and profit based adjusted weight factors. In: 2006 SICE-ICASE International Joint Conference, pp. 5484–5488. IEEE (2006)
12. Montañez, M.A.B., Hernández, A.O., Barrera, J.A.M., Castillo, S.L.: Redes neuronales en predicción de mercados financieros: una aplicación en la bolsa mexicana de valores (neural networks in financial market prediction: an application in the mexican stock exchange). Pistas educativas **40**(130) (2018)
13. Mundo, B.N.: Por qué muchos jóvenes están haciendo inversiones de riesgo (y por qué preocupa a las autoridades) (2022). https://www.bbc.com/mundo/noticias-59812479
14. Parody Camargo, E., Charris Fontanilla, A., García Luna, R.: Modelo log-normal para predicción del precio de las acciones del sector bancario. Dimensión empresarial **14**(1), 137–149 (2016)
15. Pawar, K., Jalem, R.S., Tiwari, V.: Stock market price prediction using LSTM RNN. In: Rathore, V.S., Worring, M., Mishra, D.K., Joshi, A., Maheshwari, S. (eds.) Emerging Trends in Expert Applications and Security. AISC, vol. 841, pp. 493–503. Springer, Singapore (2019). https://doi.org/10.1007/978-981-13-2285-3_58
16. Pham, P.A.: Predicción del precio de acciones de la empresa telefónica mediante técnicas de minería de datos (2022)
17. Regal, A., et al.: Proyección del precio de criptomonedas basado en tweets empleando lstm. Ingeniare. Revista chilena de ingeniería **27**(4), 696–706 (2019)
18. Sherstinsky, A.: Fundamentals of recurrent neural network (RNN) and long short-term memory (LSTM) network. Physica D **404**, 132306 (2020)
19. Staudemeyer, R.C., Morris, E.R.: Understanding LSTM–a tutorial into long short-term memory recurrent neural networks. arXiv preprint arXiv:1909.09586 (2019)
20. Wirth, R., Hipp, J.: CRISP-DM: towards a standard process model for data mining. In: Proceedings of the 4th International Conference on the Practical Applications of Knowledge Discovery and Data Mining, Manchester, vol. 1, pp. 29–40 (2000)
21. Yamanaka, S.: Average true range. Tech. Anal. Stocks Commodities-Magazine Ed. **20**(3), 76–79 (2002)

Data Analysis

Automated Diagnosis of Prostate Cancer Using Artificial Intelligence. A Systematic Literature Review

Salvador Soto[1]([envelope])(iD), María F. Pollo-Cattaneo[1]([envelope])(iD),
and Fernando Yepes-Calderon[2,3]([envelope])(iD)

[1] Universidad Tecnologica Nacional Regional Buenos Aires,
Grupo Gemis, Buenos Aires, Argentina
`salvasoman@gmail.com`, `flo.pollo@gmail.com`
[2] SBP LLC - RnD Department, 604, Fort Pierce, Fl 34950, USA
`fernando.yepes@strategicbp.net`
[3] GYM Group SA - Departamento I+R, Cra 78A No. 6-58, Cali, Colombia
`fernando@gym-group.org`

Abstract. Prostate cancer is one of the most preventable causes of death. Periodic testing, seconded by precursors such as living habits, heritage, and exposure to specific materials, help healthcare providers achieve early detection, a desirable scenario that positively correlates with survival. However, the currently available diagnosing mechanisms have a great opportunity of improvement in terms of invasiveness, sensitivity and timing before patients reach advanced stages with a significant probability of metastasis. Supervised artificial intelligence enables early diagnosis and excludes patients from unpleasant biopsies. In this work, we gathered information about methodologies, techniques, metrics, and benchmarks to accomplish early prostate cancer detection, including pipelines with associated patents and knowledge transfer mechanisms, intending to find the reasons precluding the solutions from being massively adopted in the standards of care.

Keywords: Prostate cancer · diagnosis · Artificial intelligence · Automatic pathology diagnosis

1 Introduction

The work presented contains an introduction to provide knowledge and context about prostate cancer, as well as the techniques currently applied to diagnose it. It is followed by the materials and methods section where the scientific methodology that supports the work and makes it replicable is explained in detail. In the results section, the results of the collection and processing of the systematic literature search are presented and analyzed. The findings are discussed and future lines of work are proposed, the conclusion of the work and the consulted bibliography are revealed.

H. Florez and M. Leon (Eds.): ICAI 2023, CCIS 1874, pp. 77–92, 2024.
https://doi.org/10.1007/978-3-031-46813-1_6

According to WHO [1], Cancer is a leading cause of death worldwide, accounting for nearly 10 million deceases in 2020, from which Prostate cancer (PCa) reported 1.41 million. PCa occurs when cells in the prostate gland begin to spread uncontrollably, and cell death (apoptosis) is delayed [2].

PCa is the second most common cancer in men worldwide [3]. Some regions are more affected than others, arguably due to cultural factors. In 2020, Guadeloupe presented the highest incidence rate normalized to 100,000 citizens, with 183.6 patients and 722 total casualties. The average world age-standardized rate was 30.7, with 1.4 million confirmed cases. According to the same report, Zimbabwe had the highest age-standardized rate of PCa mortality, with 41.7 casualties per 100,000 citizens and 868 total deaths. Recall that the age-standardized rate is a statistical method used to compare the incidence of events, such as disease or death, over time while considering differences in the age structure of a population.

Healthcare providers have correlated PCa primarily with habits and identified as risk factors the use of tobacco, alcohol consumption, unhealthy diet, sedentarism, and breathing highly polluted air. A secondary precursor of the affliction, with 13% of the cases in 2018, is attributed to infections, including Helicobacter pylori, human papillomavirus, hepatitis B and C viruses, and Epstein-Barr virus [4]. Contact with asbestos, contaminants such as aflatoxin, and drinking arsenic-loaded water are also possible triggers for the disease.

The Prostate Cancer Foundation (PCF) indicates that age is the biggest but not the only risk factor for PCa. Other essential precursors include heritage in that PCa patients' relatives are twice as likely to develop the disease. Race features are also crucial since African descent are about 75% more likely to suffer PCa than white men and 2.2 times more likely to die from the disease [5].

The World Cancer Research Fund International (WCRF),reported that being overweight or tall increases the risk of advanced PCa. Regarding dietary features, diets high in calcium in individuals presenting low vitamin E and low selenium concentration in blood plasma increase the risk of PCa [3].

PCa is considered a silent disease, not showing symptoms in the early stages. When present, symptoms often involve urination blockages due to an enlarged prostate or benign prostatic hyperplasia (BPH) [6].

The American Urological Association (AUA) recommends the screening test for PCa if the male falls into any of these groups: subjects between 55–69 years old, African American, family history of PCa, or symptoms like dull pain in the lower pelvic zone, a frequent need to pass urine, trouble passing urine, pain, burning or weak urine flow, blood in the urine, painful ejaculation, pain in the lower back, loss of hunger and weight, or bone pain [7].

The screening gold standard mechanisms include the prostate-specific antigen blood test (PSA) and the digital rectal exam (DRE). The PSA is the primary biomarker to detect early PCa exuberant expression in blood [8]. PSA derivates, their isoforms (free PSA, -2proPSA, prostate health index, hk2, PSA velocity or PSA doubling time), and novel urinary markers and biomarkers (PCA3) for screening to reduce PCa mortality provide limited evidence to conclude [7]. The DRE is a physical exam that characterizes the gland's shape, consistency, nodularity, or thickness by touching the anterior part of the rectum. DRE is safe and easy, and although the literature supports the efficacy of DRE, it cannot spot early Cancer by itself.

When both DRE and PSA tests are abnormal, healthcare professionals may suggest imaging the prostate gland with magnetic resonance imaging (MRI) or transrectal ultrasound (TRUS) [9]. Finally, prostate biopsy provides a cell-scale analysis through histology where cancer cells are visible under the microscope. However, state-of-the-art prostate biopsy requires an intra-rectal device and a needle passing through the anterior intestine wall to collect pieces of the gland. The histology allows the identification of prostatic carcinoma, at different degrees of colonization, including extraprostatic, perineural invasion, collagenous micronodules, and glomeruloid intraglandular projections [10].

Imaging with MRI creates volumetric representations of soft tissue that give doctors a clear picture of the prostate and nearby areas. Among the several MRI sequences, the multiparametric MRI (mp-MRI) is often used to image the prostate in patients with PCa symptoms. The volumetric images help physicians identify positive PCa areas and cancer spreading trends. The mp-MRI requires an anatomical MRI (T1 or T2) and diffusion-weighted imaging (DWI), dynamic contrast-enhanced (DCE), or MR spectroscopy, to look at other parameters of prostate tissue. The recurrent use of MRI is justified as it provides information to detect target areas for biopsy. Moreover, MRI combined with TRUS, as in MRI/ultrasound fusion biopsy with an endorectal coil, improves the detection accuracy [11].

Healthcare providers report MRI findings following the Prostate Imaging Reporting and Data System (PIRADS), which provides guidelines and standards to expedite the verdicts and assure traceability among laboratories. The PIRADS is also intended to avoid the use of biopsies and treatment for benign and subclinical disease [12].

Other complementary tests in PCa diagnosis include bone density scanning, also called dual-energy x-ray absorptiometry (DXA) that produces 2D images of bone using radiotracers such as Technetium-99m (Tc99m) complexed to a diphosphonate, either methylene diphosphonate (MDP) forming Tc99m-MDP or hydroxy-diphosphonate (HDP) forming Tc99m-HDP. DXA creates contrast in regions where irrigation is prolific, thus pointing to damaged bone. The DXA helps to determine if cancer has spread to the bones by injecting a small amount of low-level radioactive material and using a special camera to detect the levels of radioactivity, creating pictures of the skeleton with shadows depicting the affected regions.

The positron emission tomography scan (PET) uses radioactive isotopes (fluciclovine F18, sodium fluoride F18 or choline C11, Manganese-52, Copper-64, Rubidium-82) synthetically created in a laboratory with a limited radiating life. The isotope specific for the prostate reaches the gland through the bloodstream. Before the radioactive isotope returns to normal, it releases a positive charge that will hit a negative one inside the prostate. The collision between opposite charges creates gamma rays that travel in opposite directions. A gamma camera detects the rays and uses the delay between them to locate the emission point. When the radioactive molecules are created out of sugar, they rapidly travel to regions where the cells are avid of energy due to their accelerated metabolism, thus labeling the cancer cells [13].

The CT scan uses X-rays to make detailed, cross-sectional body images. In CT technology, electrons are created by thermogenesis and accelerated towards a plaque of tungsten or silver by an electrical field. When electrons strike the plaque, the reaction creates photons that are guided to the gate by the geometry of the plaque. The energy absorption of the internal structures of an object presented between the X-ray canyon and a matrix of detectors creates the contrast known as the X-ray image. The CT repeats this exercise in a circular trajectory to develop projections of the object under study and generate three-dimensional images of it through the Radon-transform [14].

Genetic tests are available for specific inherited gene changes, often used in men with a family history of cancer (BRCA or Lynch syndrome) and those with confirmed PCa and metastasis [15].

Gleason Score (GS) is a metric that evaluates the prognosis of men with PCa using samples from a prostate biopsy. Experts calculate the GS by adding the scores of the most significant areas in the sample tissue. The score ranges between 2 and 10; the lower the grade, the lower the size and cancer aggressiveness. GS helps physicians to plan treatment and determine prognosis [16].

According to Yu et al. [17], the relationship between PSA and PCa varies significantly between different studies, although positive biopsy results correlate with elevated serum levels of PSA. The use of the PSA level as a diagnostic decision-making tool for biopsies has a high rate of false-negative and false-positive results, leading to delayed diagnoses, unnecessary biopsies, and faulty treatment. Mp-MRI before TRUS-guided biopsy has a higher sensitivity for PCa but is less specific than a biopsy and PSA. The TRUS-guided biopsies for PCa diagnosis increase the risk of adverse events, including sepsis. Moreover, the result can yield a low risk with minimal risk of progression, resulting in overtreatment.

The biopsy samples undergo wax fixation, wax embedding, microscale sectioning, and staining before the tissues are ready for interpretation by a pathologist. The tissue preparation process has strict timing schemes that depend on the chemical used. Since sample preparation is not always automatic and a good verdict depends on the pathologist's expertise, histology may require more than one round of revision, which delays the emission of final reports [18].

In this work, we propose to explore the state of the art of the PCa, in terms of the type of methodologies, artifacts, benchmarks, key performance indicators, and problems or parts of the problem of PCa diagnosis and how researchers and physicians have approached these issues. The ulterior goal of this study is to provide insights and proposal to build a reliable pipeline for full diagnosis automation taking advantage of the benefits provided by AI-based methods.

2   Materials and Methods

This work employed the systematic literature review (SLR) methodology proposed by Barbara Kitchenham [19]. Regarding document classification, we adhere to Wieringa's strategy [20].

2.1 Research Questions

This study is based on the following research questions:

- RQ1. What developments have authors presented to diagnose and detect PCa using Artificial Intelligence (AI)?
- RQ2. What are the most accepted AI techniques currently diagnosing PCa?
- RQ3. Which metrics, measurements, or indexes derived from AI are applied to diagnose and detect PCa?
- RQ4. What is the form and nature of the data features used in Artificial Intelligence implementations to diagnose and detect PCa?

Documents Gathering Strategy: Kitchenham [19] suggests identifying key aspects towards bias reduction, predefined parameters, consistency, robustness, and replicability.

Search String Definition: The population comprises males at least 40 years old, and we are interested in prostate cancer diagnosis software, leading to keywords "prostate cancer" AND "software". The implementation implies technology and methodology applied to solve the problem. Then, we enforced the search string with: "segmentation" OR "classification" OR "regression" AND "automatic" OR "machine learning" OR "Artificial Intelligence". A set of methods for PCa diagnosis accompanied by measurements, metrics, and indexes are crucial for accomplishing our goal; therefore, the strings "diagnosis" AND "metric" OR "measurement" complements the search pattern.

Experimental Design: We fed the defined search string to specialized search engines – e.g., Google Scholar, IEEE Xplore, MDPI, Elsevier, Springer, and Wiley – and added "January 2020 to June 2022" as a dating constraint. We organized the results following an in-house mnemotechnic structure that, in addition to traditional bibliographic fields, records whether the techniques have been translated to commercial implementations or protected by patents. The gathered data are operationalized in lists of concepts and categories to build the response matrix where each row identifies an analyzed item. The operationalization transforms text or paragraphs into meaningful and representative tokens summarizing the article's content that answer the research question.

2.2 Study Selection Criteria

The Table 1, depicts the selection concepts used in this work.

2.3 Study Assesment

The search string yielded 719 articles. Then, after applying the inclusion and exclusion criteria, we labeled 132 articles indirectly related, 417 unrelated, 30 duplicates, and 47 discarded. The details can be observed in Fig. 1:

Table 1. Selection criteria

Inclusion criteria	Exclusion criteria
I1. Articles in English	E1. Systematic Literature Mappings (SMS) and Systematic Literature Reviews (SLR)
I2. For articles by the same author and focused on the same research, the most recent and complete one is taken	E2. Not accessible
I3. Articles published between January 2020 and June 2022	E3. Gray literature
I4. Articles that contain candidate strings in the title, keywords and/or in the abstract	E4. Articles whose content does not focus on the diagnosis or detection of prostate cancer

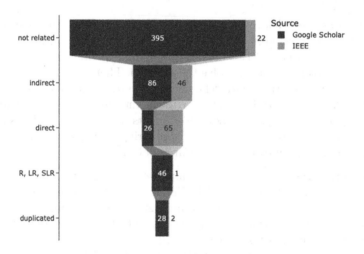

Fig. 1. Summary of article selection funnel

2.4 Data Extraction

In addition to standard bibliographic fields, we extracted the following data from each article: search engine and publisher, topic area, problem trying to solve, objectives, methods (used to provide a solution), and results. The extraction form is available in: [21].

2.5 Data Synthesis and Quality Verification

After thoroughly reviewing their content, we summarized the articles and answered the research questions. This content analysis yielded the material to categorize the documents, thus facilitating their further analysis and processing. Within the article classification, we also considered aspects such as pertinence,

used software, framework, methodology to propose a solution, level of completion, and reproducibility.

3   Results

The answers to the proposed research questions were operationalized and statistically processed. The summary form is available in: [21].

In Fig. 2 the reader can see a tree map of patents' distribution status, classification of the type of AI in terms of information transfer, and the kind of
technique used.

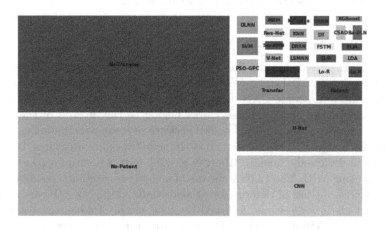

Fig. 2. Distribution of patent status, transfer learning, and techniques used in the
diagnosis and treatment of PCa

The 81.31% of the selected articles did not have or use any patented component or device to date. The 79.12% of the papers did not use any knowledge
transfer component or lacked reproducibility. Authors preferred the Convolutional neural network (CNN) in three of ten manuscripts. The second most used
technique was the U-shape neural network (U-Net), with a frequency of nearly
one over four works. The third most preferred group of techniques were the Logistic Regression (Lo-R), Random Forest (RF), Particle Swarm Optimized Gaussian Process Classifier (PSO-GPC), Deep Learning Neural Network (DLNN),
and Support Vector Machine (SVM). The fourth group with frequency one was
the group of Bayesian Deep Learning Networks (Ba-DLN), Cross-Modal Self-
Attention Distillation (CSAD), Deep Residual Neural Networks (DRNN), Deep
Residual Regression Networks (DRRN), Decision Tree (DT), Fuzzy Logic Model
(FLM), Feature Space Transfer Model (FSTM), K-Means, K Nearest Neighbors
(KNN), Lasso Regression (La-R), Linear Discriminant Analysis (LDA), Linear
Regression (Li-R), Long Shot Term Memory Neural Network (LSMNN), Multi-
Risk Model (MRM), Residual Neural Network (Res-Net), Swarm Artificial Neu-
ral Network (Sw-ANN), V-shape Neural Network (V-Net), and Xtreme Gradient
Boosting (XGBoost).

3.1   Contribution to Diagnosis and Detection of PCa

The 60.4% of the gathered articles proposed methods to improve the diagnosis and detection of PCa [22] with logistic regression to predict biochemical recurrence after surgery for high-risk PCa patients; 29.7% present tools that could be used to perform these tasks and its representative the work as in [23] with a deep learning regression for PCA detection using bi-MRI input. The 7.7% of articles occasionally propose a model or algorithm that improves at least one PCa diagnosis and detection workflow activity. Only 3.3% of the gathered documents presented an improvement directly linked to the metrics used to measure and estimate the presence or absence of PCa, as in [24].

3.2   AI Techniques

In [25], authors present a multi-site network that improves prostate segmentation with heterogeneous MRI data. With the same goal, [26] suggested a 3D adversarial pyramid anisotropic CNN of the prostate on MRI. Automatic histological image processing as in [27]. These works belong to the 36.26% of the articles that implemented a convolutional neural network as a solution to diagnosing and detecting PCa. The 24.17% mentioned U-shape network architectures, being the most cited and viewed Comelli, Albert et al. [28], with a device for prostate segmentation using MRI. The 12.08% the use of a based or combined residual neural network; 6.59% the use of random forest algorithm; 3.29% Naive Bayes, decision trees, and logistic regressions, followed by 2.2% usage of adversarial networks, Lasso regression, Xtreme Gradient Boosting, support vector machines, and deep learning neural networks. The rest mentioned using multivariate risk models, vgg19 architecture, ResNet50, gradient boosting machines, Ridge regression, K-medoids, K-means, IMSLIC algorithm, Adaboost, linear regression, and linear discriminant analysis.

Related image acquisition means, 13.2% mentioned the use of 3D images, 7.7% the use of MRI, 5.5% the use of T2W images, 6.6% MRI, 4.4% transrectal ultrasound, 3.3% multiparametric MRI, dynamic contrast-enhanced, diffusion-weighted images and whole slide histopathology images respectively; 2.2% biparametric MRI, TW1, apparent diffusion images, and voxel images each; and 1.0% 2D MRI images and PIRADS version 2 images. Regarding data treatment techniques, 4.4% mentioned transfer learning and 1.0% other strategies like pooling, bi-long short memory, conditional random fields, and one-hot encoding.

In Fig. 3 the reader can see the distribution of the benchmark KPI's values in boxplots detailed by the main architecture technique used and split by patent-base status as follows:

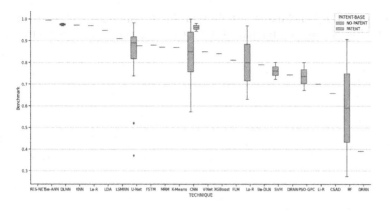

Fig. 3. Distribution of Benchmark KPI values by Technique and Patent-Base status.

The architecture with higher performance for the main KPI mentioned using the median was DLNN (0.9742). In the second place, the patent-related works that used CNN architectures showed a median performance of 0.962. The last group of the architectures with at least two occurrences in median performance descending order were U-Net (0.89), CNN without patent (0.85), Lo-R (0.79), SVM (0.76), PSO-GPC (0.73), and RF (0.59). The rest with one point of observation for median performance and relevant to mention: Res-Net (0.9984), Sw-ANN (0.9948), KNN (0.972), La-R (0.97), LDA (0.948), LSMNN (0.91), FSTM (0.88).

3.3 KPI's and Benchmarks

The most used accuracy testing metric in the analyzed papers was the Dice Score (DS) with the 37.4%, highlighting the work of Zhiqiang Tian et al. [29] with a graph CNN of MRI solution, and Accuracy (ACC.) with 35.2% of the papers, where D. Karimi et al. [30] proposed a deep learning Gleason grading of PCa from histopathology images. The Area Under the ROC Curve (AUC) was founded in (29.7%) of the articles, with artifacts such as 3D CNN with mp-MRI for segmentation [31]. The next step of KPI's, Sensitivity (SENS) and Specificity (SPEC) 14.3% and 13.2%, respectively. Athors did not specified any performance metric in a rate of 9.9%. The Jaccard Similarity Coefficient (JC) and Haussdorff Distance (HD) were cited in 7.7% each. Average Surface Distance (ASD) with 4.4%, Quadratic Kappa Coefficient, Cohen-Kappa Coefficient, Log Rank and F1-Score (3.3% respectively), Contrast group has Noise, Loupas, True Positive Rate, Positive and Negative Prediction Values, Correlation Coefficient Matthews, Root Mean Squared Error (2.2% each). In contrast, the remaining group included Completeness, R Squared, False Positive Rate, Clustering that-Medoids, Precision, and Recall, with 1.0% each. Regarding validation techniques, cross-validation was present in 3.3% of the articles, and 2.2% had to perform data augmentation to have enough information for training.

Regarding the benchmark distribution for the previous techniques architectures, the Fig. 4 presents boxplot distributions for the main architectures.

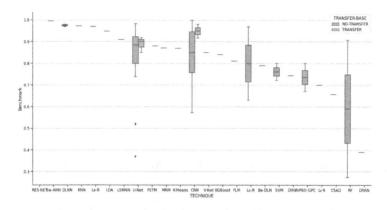

Fig. 4. Distribution of Benchmark KPI values by Technique and Transfer-Base status.

One of the most significant findings in this SLR is related to the KPI metrics in the classification task. The CNN architecture implementing transfer knowledge reported a median of 0.9483. The U-net, also using transfer knowledge, reported a median of 0.8839. Both CNN and U-Net medians were obtained with at least two observation points. The FSTM architecture with transfer knowledge claimed a KPI of 0.8800 and is the only method with a registered patent.

Table 2 indicates the metrics mentioned in at least three articles with the median value calculated. For DS 50% of the articles exceeded 0.8652, and the same proportion for ACC. with 0.92135; AUC 0.876, and SENS. 0.92; as follows:

Table 2. Distribution of frequencies and 50th percentile by metric.

Metric	frequency	50th percentile
DS	34	0.8652
ACC.	30	0.92135
AUC	27	0.876
SENS.	13	0.92
SPEC.	12	0.9091
HD	7	8.1
JC	7	0.77
ASD	4	1.335
LOG RANK	3	24.586

3.4 Data Source and Characteristics

The selected authors claimed to gather data from clinical facilities to which they have access at work.

Regarding public datasets, 15.4% used the Promise12 repository [32] such as He, Kelei et al. [33] within the title synergistic voxel level image processing for prostate segmentation. The 9.9% used the ProstateX dataset [34], and 8.8% of the articles did not precisely mention the data's origin nor provide details about the data's source. The 3.3% of the articles used the NCI-ISBI 2013 and ProstateX2 datasets [35], and 2.2% used PANDA, Prostate3T, CANCER IMAGING ARCHIVE, and The Cancer Genome Atlas, each one. Those that used other lesser-known datasets, with 1% in each case, included PROMIS, PROSTATEX17, UCI, PASCAL VOC 2012, DIAGSET, PRAD, GSE54460, HIPPA, U41RR019703, and Harvard Dataverse. In Summary, 7.7% of the articles combined at least 2 datasets, public or custom, to train and/or test their solutions.

5.5% of articles used whole-slide histopathological images (WSI) and diffusion weight images (DWI), 4.4% had Gleason label info, 3.3% made use of transrectal ultrasound images (TRUS), T1W images, and 2.2% of the articles used scan annotations and dynamic contrast-enhanced images (DCE). The devices used to scan were Phillips, Magnetom, Siemens (4.4%, each), Skyra, and Tesla (3.3% each). Regarding the origin of the custom data, the most frequent facility was Radboud Medical Center with 6.6%, Boston Medical Center, Universitas Indonesia Hospital (UI), and Kaggle, each with 2.2%.

In Table 3 25% of the samples exceeded 51 observations; 50% exceeded 120 observations or patients and the highest 25% of the samples exceeded 225 patients, as follows:

Table 3. Size sample percentile distribution

kth percentile	sample n
25	51
50	120
75	335

3.5 Research Type

According to the type of research, 76% of the articles propose a solution for one of the problems defined within the diagnosis and detection of PCa, such as Duran-Lopez, L. [36] with the contribution CNN based computer-aided diagnosis system for WSI PCa detection artifact. The remaining 24% propose to evaluate a technique, methodology, or approach to contribute to solving the research problem, as in the case of S. Iqbal et al. [37] that performed a comparison of deep learning techniques for PCa detection.

4   Discussion

Most of the reviewed proposals use frameworks or architectures based on deep learning convolutional neural networks to approach PCa Inherent challenges such as prostate segmentation, automatic localization of lesions, and pathologists' flow work. The mechanism for evaluating the general performance of these architectures are Dice Score, accuracy, sensitivity, and specificity since they are transversally related to classification. Most of the selected articles use clinical data from private institutions.

There is a significant drawback regarding the use of all possible available data. Since specialists have found correlations between heritage and other personal factors, such as race with PCa - and other cancer afflictions - one might hypothesize that personal data could be a set of useful features to improve the DS and confusion matrix scores. However, personal data is protected by strict regulations such as HIPAA [38]; therefore, scientists and developers can not include it in their developments. The work presented in [39] and patented [40] proposed a way to avoid this restriction within healthcare facilities. Consequently, personal data might be available, and AI developments can consider personal data while complying with the regulations. Preliminary quantifying attempts compatible with the mentioned fully automated platform for PCa and other cancer types have been reported to the scientific community in [41–44].

Clinical data, in contrast to recruited data, have high variability due to the purpose of the acquisition. Recall that healthcare providers order imaging to suit medical necessities and not research purposes; therefore, the data is acquired with many setups. Consequently, we could not find standard procedures or a baseline from which scientists start their developments. The filtered articles describe unique methods with few methodological coincidences. A good approach for a usable pipeline is to develop a pre-processing stage that allocates the images in a common space regardless of origin.

A second improvement opportunity exists in selecting or designing a common framework with standard tasks, metrics, and benchmark levels. We have identified a set of routine activities that should be standardized. 1. Dimensionality standardization of the image (2D, 3D, pixels, voxels), 2. Prostate segmentation, 3. Tissue classification, depending on the type of image source, 4. GS automatic estimation.

A third opportunity relies on how to merge or incorporate this technology or learning into the instruments (computer-aided, for instance) or procedures used today, aiming to provide a reliable, cheaper, faster, and standardized diagnosis. The database structure that supports the expected massive information should be shareable, available online, and capable of improving verdicts in time, feeding the framework with more observation data points.

A fourth opportunity is the combination of different types of information, tests, results, scenarios, risks, gradings, and stages in a standard way so that a patient with the first screening or another with some previous testing results can get into the pipeline straightforward to be classified and compared with patients having similar characteristics.

5   Future Work

Data standardization through robust pre-processing will be the first goal of the subsequent work. Then, we will focus on improving the quality of the histological information. As mentioned by [27,30,45–53], histological image processing currently depends on a series of manual tasks of a high level of difficulty and specialization by pathologists, which require preparation with a high level of meticulousness and attention so as not to lose the value of the information provided by the sample. As they are not obtained automatically or semi-automated, they are considered part of potential new lines of research that provide more accurate results in timely and precise detection.

On the other hand, there is an excellent opportunity for the use of learning transfer techniques and software-patented devices that make it possible to take advantage of the knowledge persisted in a standard data structure (understood as reuse) for its consultation and information retrieval, as well as its retraining capacity and adaptation to subfields or problems of classification or segmentation for all sort of cancer afflictions and several types of tissues other than those related to PCa.

Finally, our work will attain the integration of the standardized data with the most efficient AI-based classification methods, which will be improved with the use of enhanced histological results as supervised factors.

6   Conclusions

We designed a systematic literature review to discover the proposed developments in the context of PCa diagnosis using machine learning or artificial intelligence technologies. The SLR allows us to acknowledge the most accepted techniques of AI and know the metrics and benchmarks used in the PCa diagnosis framework.

The opportunities identified and listed in the discussion section suggest the development of a standard pipeline that could integrate the work reported as the most accurate. Still, we will need to standardize the data along the pipeline and improve the histological results' quality to be used as supervised factors. We will consider features such as data centralization and in-cloud service exploitation as priorities in the design from scratch.

References

1. Ferlay, J., Ervik, M., et al.: Global cancer observatory: cancer today. International Agency for Research on Cancer, Lyon (2020)
2. Elmore, S.: Apoptosis: a review of programmed cell death. Toxicol. Pathol. **35**(4), 495–516 (2007)
3. World Cancer Research Fund International: Prostate cancer statistics. Cancer Trends, Prostate cancer statistics (2023)
4. World Health Organization: Cancer. World Health Organization Fact Sheet, Detail, Cancer (2022)

5. Prostate Cancer Foundation. About prostate cancer. About Prostate Cancer (2023)
6. Urology Care Foundation. Prostate cancer-early-stage. Urology Health Organization (2023)
7. Carter, H.B., Albertsen, P.C., Barry, M.J., et al.: Early detection of prostate cancer: AUA guideline. J. Urol. **190**, 419 (2013)
8. Filella, X., et al.: Prostate cancer screening: guidelines review and laboratory issues. Clin. Chem. Lab. Med. (CCLM) **57**(10), 1474–1487 (2019)
9. The American Cancer Society medical and editorial content team. Prostate cancer early detection, diagnosis, and staging. Cancer A-Z, Prostate Cancer, p. 10 (2019)
10. Humphrey, P.A.: Histopathology of prostate cancer. Cold Spring Harbor Perspect. Med. **7**(10), a030411 (2017)
11. The American Cancer Society medical and editorial content team. Prostate cancer early detection, diagnosis, and staging. Cancer A-Z, Prostate Cancer, p. 24:25 (2019)
12. Weinreb, J.C., et al.: PI-RADS prostate imaging-reporting and data system: 2015, version 2. Eur. Urol. **69**(1), 16–40 (2016)
13. The American Cancer Society medical and editorial content team. Prostate cancer early detection, diagnosis, and staging. Cancer A-Z, Prostate Cancer, p. 26 (2019)
14. Herman, G.T.: Fundamentals of Computerized Tomography: Image Reconstruction from Projections. Springer, Heidelberg (2009). https://doi.org/10.1007/978-1-84628-723-7
15. The American Cancer Society medical and editorial content team. Prostate cancer early detection, diagnosis, and staging. Cancer A-Z, Prostate Cancer, p. 23 (2019)
16. National Cancer Institute. NCI dictionary of cancer terms. NCI Dictionary of Cancer Terms, p. G (2023)
17. Wei, Yu., Zhou, L.: Early diagnosis of prostate cancer from the perspective of Chinese physicians. J. Cancer **11**(11), 3264 (2020)
18. Gurina, T.S., Simms, L.: Histology, Staining. SataPearls Publishing-Europe PMC (2020)
19. Kitchenham, B.A., Dyba, T., Jorgensen, M.: Evidence-based software engineering. In: Proceedings of the 26th International Conference on Software Engineering, pp. 273–281. IEEE (2004)
20. Wieringa, R., Maiden, N., Mead, N., Rolland, C.: Requirements engineering paper classification and evaluation criteria: a proposal and a discussion. Requirements Eng. **11**(1), 102–107 (2006)
21. Salvador, S., Florencia, P.-C., Fernando, Y.C.: Automated diagnosis of prostate cancer using artificial intelligence. A systematic literature review. Extraction and Summary Forms (2023)
22. Bourbonne, V., et al.: External validation of an MRI-derived radiomics model to predict biochemical recurrence after surgery for high-risk prostate cancer. Cancers **12**(4), 814 (2020)
23. de Vente, C., Vos, P., Hosseinzadeh, M., Pluim, J., Veta, M.: Deep learning regression for prostate cancer detection and grading in bi-parametric MRI. IEEE Trans. Biomed. Eng. **68**(2), 374–383 (2021)
24. Javadi, G., et al.: Characterizing the uncertainty of label noise in systematic ultrasound-guided prostate biopsy. In: 2021 IEEE 18th International Symposium on Biomedical Imaging (ISBI), pp. 424–428. IEEE (2021)
25. Liu, Q., Dou, Q., Yu, L., Heng, P.A.: MS-net: multi-site network for improving prostate segmentation with heterogeneous MRI data. IEEE Trans. Med. Imaging **39**(9), 2713–2724 (2020)

26. Jia, H., et al.: 3D APA-net: 3D adversarial pyramid anisotropic convolutional network for prostate segmentation in MR images. IEEE Trans. Med. Imaging **39**(2), 447–457 (2019)

27. Schömig-Markiefka, B., et al.: Quality control stress test for deep learning-based diagnostic model in digital pathology. Mod. Pathol. **34**(12), 2098–2108 (2021)

28. Comelli, A., et al.: Deep learning-based methods for prostate segmentation in magnetic resonance imaging. Appl. Sci. **11**(2), 782 (2021)

29. Tian, Z., et al.: Graph-convolutional-network-based interactive prostate segmentation in MR images. Med. Phys. **47**(9), 4164–4176 (2020)

30. Karimi, D., Nir, G., Fazli, L., Black, P.C., Goldenberg, L., Salcudean, S.E.: Deep learning-based Gleason grading of prostate cancer from histopathology images-role of multiscale decision aggregation and data augmentation. IEEE J. Biomed. Health Inform. **24**(5), 1413–1426 (2019)

31. Arif, M., et al.: Clinically significant prostate cancer detection and segmentation in low-risk patients using a convolutional neural network on multi-parametric MRI. Eur. Radiol. **30**(12), 6582–6592 (2020)

32. Shirabad, J.S., Menzies, T.J.: The PROMISE repository of software engineering databases. School of Information Technology and Engineering, University of Ottawa, Canada (2005)

33. He, K., et al.: MetricUNet: synergistic image-and voxel-level learning for precise prostate segmentation via online sampling. Med. Image Anal. **71**, 102039 (2021)

34. Litjens, G., Debats, O., Barentsz, J., Karssemeijer, N., Huisman, H.: Cancer imaging archive wiki (2017). https://doi.org/10.7937/K9TCIA

35. Giger, M., Drukker, K.: SPIE-AAPM-NCI PROSTATE MR Gleason grade group challenge PROSTATEx-2: performance evaluation. American Association of Physicist in Medicine (2017)

36. Duran-Lopez, L., Dominguez-Morales, J.P., Conde-Martin, A.F., Vicente-Diaz, S., Linares-Barranco, A.: PROMETEO: a CNN-based computer-aided diagnosis system for WSI prostate cancer detection. IEEE Access **8**, 128613–128628 (2020)

37. Iqbal, S., et al.: Prostate cancer detection using deep learning and traditional techniques. IEEE Access **9**, 27085–27100 (2021)

38. Annas, G.J.: HIPAA regulations-a new era of medical-record privacy? (2003)

39. Yepes Calderon, F., Rea, N., McComb, J.G.: Enabling the medical applications engine. In: Florez, H., Diaz, C., Chavarriaga, J. (eds.) ICAI 2018. CCIS, vol. 942, pp. 131–143. Springer, Cham (2018). https://doi.org/10.1007/978-3-030-01535-0_10

40. Calderon, F.Y., McComb, J.G.: Enabling the centralization of medical derived data for artificial intelligence implementations. Technical report Patent No. US20200273551A1, Children Hospital Los Angeles (2020)

41. Espinosa, C., Garcia, M., Yepes-Calderon, F., McComb, J.G., Florez, H.: Prostate cancer diagnosis automation using supervised artificial intelligence. A systematic literature review. In: Florez, H., Misra, S. (eds.) ICAI 2020. CCIS, vol. 1277, pp. 104–115. Springer, Cham (2020). https://doi.org/10.1007/978-3-030-61702-8_8

42. Yepes-Calderon, F., et al.: EdgeRunner: a novel shape-based pipeline for tumours analysis and characterisation. Comput. Methods Biomech. Biomed. Eng.: Imaging Vis. **6**(1), 84–92 (2018)

43. Yepes-Calderón, F., Medina, F.M., Rea, N.D., Abella, J.: Tumor malignancy characterization in clinical environments: an approach using the FYC-index of spiculation and artificial intelligence. In: Tumor Progression and Metastasis. IntechOpen (2018)

44. Yepes-C, F., et al.: The 3D edgerunner pipeline: a novel shape-based analysis for neoplasms characterization. In: Medical Imaging 2016: Biomedical Applications in Molecular, Structural, and Functional Imaging, vol. 9788, pp. 681–685. SPIE (2016)
45. Matoso, A., Epstein, J.I.: Defining clinically significant prostate cancer on the basis of pathological findings. Histopathology **74**(1), 135–145 (2019)
46. Silva-Rodríguez, J., Colomer, A., Naranjo, V.: WeGleNet: a weakly-supervised convolutional neural network for the semantic segmentation of Gleason grades in prostate histology images. Comput. Med. Imaging Graph. **88**, 101846 (2021)
47. Chen, C.-M., Huang, Y.-S., Fang, P.-W., Liang, C.-W., Chang, R.-F.: A computer-aided diagnosis system for differentiation and delineation of malignant regions on whole-slide prostate histopathology image using spatial statistics and multidimensional densenet. Med. Phys. **47**(3), 1021–1033 (2020)
48. Koziarski, M., et al.: DiagSet: a dataset for prostate cancer histopathological image classification. arXiv preprint arXiv:2105.04014 (2021)
49. Bhattacharjee, S., et al.: Cluster analysis of cell nuclei in H&E-stained histological sections of prostate cancer and classification based on traditional and modern artificial intelligence techniques. Diagnostics **12**(1), 15 (2021)
50. Kalapahar, A., Silva-Rodríguez, J., Colomer, A., López-Mir, F., Naranjo, V.: Gleason grading of histology prostate images through semantic segmentation via residual U-net. In: 2020 IEEE International Conference on Image Processing (ICIP), pp. 2501–2505. IEEE (2020)
51. Pinckaers, H., Bulten, W., van der Laak, J., Litjens, G.: Detection of prostate cancer in whole-slide images through end-to-end training with image-level labels. IEEE Trans. Med. Imaging **40**(7), 1817–1826 (2021)
52. Wang, J., Chen, R.J., Lu, M.Y., Baras, A., Mahmood, F.: Weakly supervised prostate TMA classification via graph convolutional networks. In: 2020 IEEE 17th International Symposium on Biomedical Imaging (ISBI), pp. 239–243. IEEE (2020)
53. To, M.N.N., et al.: Deep learning framework for epithelium density estimation in prostate multi-parametric magnetic resonance imaging. In: 2020 IEEE 17th International Symposium on Biomedical Imaging (ISBI), pp. 438–441. IEEE (2020)

From Naive Interest to Shortage During COVID-19: A Google Trends and News Analysis

Alix E. Rojas[1]([⊠]) [ID], Lilia C. Rojas-Pérez[1] [ID], and Camilo Mejía-Moncayo[2] [ID]

[1] Universidad Ean, Bogota, Colombia
{aerojash,lcrojas}@universidadean.edu.co
[2] École de Technologie Supérieure, Montreal, Canada
camilo.mejia-moncayo.1@ens.etsmtl.ca

Abstract. Google Trends is a web-based tool for analyzing audience interests, tracking the popularity of events, and identifying emerging trends that could become a crowd purchase intention. The tool performs different combinations of trending queries and related topics at a given time and location until structured data, charts, and maps show a tendency, most relevant articles, and interest over time, among others. We consider data from January 2018 to December 2022, representing three typical times of the normal period before the pandemic, the outbreak period, and the widespread period. The analysis explored when people were more interested in certain products and when news about their scarcity appeared. The results showed that the pandemic gradually changed people's shopping concerns, which spread more throughout the week that the pandemic began. The study case used a validation process that compared real online data obtained from searches with offline data from official news portals of the same period. The comparative analysis established a relationship between trends and the scarcity of Ivermectin and face masks.

Keywords: Google Trends · Google News · COVID-19 · Search Interest · Scarcity

1 Introduction

The COVID-19 pandemic has left an indelible mark on people worldwide. It triggered widespread social and economic disruption, with business closures, job losses, and unrest across all industries. The implementation of quarantines as social distancing measures drastically altered daily routines and interpersonal interactions. As countries implemented various restrictions and lockdown measures to contain the spread of the virus, people turned to the internet for multiple purposes: remote work and learning, telemedicine, entertainment and media consumption, online shopping, information seeking, and virtual socializing, leading to a surge in online activities.

H. Florez and M. Leon (Eds.): ICAI 2023, CCIS 1874, pp. 93–106, 2024.
https://doi.org/10.1007/978-3-031-46813-1_7

The pandemic stimulated research in developing technological tools for health areas, education, and electronic commerce [14,23,24]. It also sparked increased interest in information related to COVID-19, including updates from health authorities, guidelines, and research results. People searched for news, medical information, prevention measures, and vaccination updates [20]. Hence, understanding the interests, doubts, and opinions people expressed and disseminated online during this period can be useful for planning responses to seemingly sudden events [4].

During crises like COVID-19, Google Trends data can inform us about people's concerns and interests in times of uncertainty [2]. We can explore concerns and topics that were top of mind for people during the pandemic by analyzing interest searches and pairing this data with online news in the same time frame to enhance the understanding holistically. Therefore, an exploratory study is proposed through two words that resonated during the pandemic: "ivermectin" and "face mask" using Google Trens and News API.

Having established the context, the following section describes related studies highlighting the importance of Google Trends analytics. The data collection details in the methodology section are defined, covering keyword selection, designated time frame, and geographic scope. Then, the results are characterized via trend charts and news headlines. Subsequently, the discussion section analyzes these findings, clarifying their implications between these two sources, and, finally, the conclusion section summarizes the fundamental conclusions of this exploratory study.

2   Background

Google first launched Google^{TM} Trends in May 2006, and since then, it has been available to the general public and has continuously updated and expanded its features to provide more robust and insightful data analysis tools [23]. Over the years, Google Trends has become widely used to track public interest and awareness of specific topics or events [18]. By examining search volumes and patterns, practitioners can understand the popularity and fluctuations in interest over time [23]. This information can be useful for studying public sentiment, identifying emerging trends, or monitoring the impact of public health campaigns or awareness initiatives [11,15].

Google Trends has been used in public health issues to find relationships between symptomatology and outbreaks during and after the COVID-19 pandemic [1,4]. Many studies have analyzed patterns related to Mpox in endemic and non-endemic countries. The authors observed search queries related to symptoms, self-diagnosis, and treatment options to understand public health concerns and monitor the spread of diseases [22]. This can aid in focusing resources and addressing crucial questions to advance scientific understanding of the virus [6,17]. This information helps gauge public engagement, identify areas where misconceptions or misinformation exist, and tailor public health communication campaigns accordingly [11]. By monitoring search queries related to COVID-19 symptoms or related terms, researchers have identified geographical hotspots or spikes of interest that may indicate potential outbreaks in specific regions [8].

Google Trends has also provided insights into information-seeking behavior through search trends to examine common queries, popular keywords, and related topics within the psychology [9] and e-commerce [18,26] domains. This kind of analysis can help in designing targeted interventions, creating educational resources, or tailoring communication strategies to meet the information needs of the public better. As forecasting data have been employed for predictive analytics by examining historical search trends, models to forecast future trends or predict outcomes in public opinion, consumer behavior, or market trends [15]. This can be valuable for businesses, social sciences, and public policy planning. Monitoring public sentiment and concerns by analyzing search trends for keywords related to mental health, anxiety, or social issues can provide insights into a crisis's emotional and psychological impacts [1]. This information can guide the development of support systems and mental health interventions.

To study the impact of policies, interventions, or significant events on public behavior or interest, it could be used to compare and assess search patterns before and after specific events, such as volatility markets [18], evaluate the effectiveness of interventions, measure changes in public attitudes or behaviors, and inform policy decisions [12]. Combined with news analysis, it could provide a comprehensive platform for monitoring news articles related to events from various sources. Researchers can analyze news articles' content, themes, and coverage to gain insights into media narratives, the dissemination of information, and the representation of different perspectives [25]. This can aid in understanding public discourse and media influence during the pandemic.

3   Materials and Methods

3.1   Google Trends

Google Trends, a Google Inc. portal, generates data available in real-time on geographical and temporal patterns according to specified keywords. Although it mirrors the search interest in particular topics, it increasingly allows people worldwide to explore global reactions to prominent events [19–21]. A spike for a specific topic does not reflect that a subject is somewhat "popular," only that, for some unspecified reason, there appear to be many users performing a search about a topic. It is important to note that while Google Trends provides valuable insights, researchers should consider its limitations. Google Trends represents the search behavior of Google users and may not fully capture the entire population's behavior.

Google Trends provides weekly information on the search frequency of keywords in the Google search engine. The search keyword is analyzed based on the searcher's category and location. In addition, this tool provides "Popular Searches" and "Top Charts," including top and rising searches that contain the search keyword [13]. This information is current and compares trends by providing past weekly charts. To measure and compare the popularity of search terms or topics over time, it uses the search volume index (SVI), which provides a relative value that indicates how much search interest there is for a specific term compared to the baseline period. The SVI captures the level of interest in a particular search term on a scale of 0–100. The baseline period, set to 100, serves as a reference point. Any value above 100 indicates higher search interest than the baseline period, and any value below 100 indicates lower search interest.

3.2 News API

News API (application programming interface) is a simple HTTP REST for searching for and retrieving articles, headlines, and other documents related to the news, both live and historical. This kind of API utilizes the HTTP protocol for communication; through this method, GET uses URLs to identify and access specific news. Being stateless, the server does not store client-specific information between requests, making each request independent and self-contained. It allows searching for articles with any combination of the request parameters: q, the keyword to search for in the article title and body; *searchIn*, the fields to restrict the q search; *from*, a date for the oldest article allowed; *to*, a date for the newest article allowed; *language*, the 2-letter ISO-639-1 code of the language to get headlines for; *sortBy*, the order to sort the articles in.

- q: "ivermectina"; "tapabocas"
- searchIn: 'title'
- from: 2018-01-01
- to: 2022-12-31
- country: 'co' (Colombia)
- sortBy: 'publishedAt'
- language: 'es' (Spanish)

3.3 Data Analysis

The present study aimed to explore the search terms "ivermectin" and "face mask," which garnered significant attention amid the COVID-19 pandemic. The term "ivermectin" was specifically chosen due to its medical relevance, public intrigue surrounding prospective treatments, and the starvation of this medication. On the other hand, the term "face mask" was chosen to represent consumer behavior and public health mandates, reflecting not only adherence to protective measures but also the tangible societal ramifications of supply shortages. These terms collectively unfold as portals to decipher people's health concerns, resource constraints, and their rippling repercussions across societal fabrics, rendering them apt focal points for this exploration. And since we were interested in a local analysis of Colombian territory, those search terms were used in Spanish. In addition, a third search term, "milk," was chosen as a control group in an experiment. This term suggests a "typical" trend since it is a consumer item belonging to the family basket that did not present a shortage in the pandemic, which could offer a contrasting viewpoint. Finally, a time window of 5 years is selected to explore a broader panorama before and during the pandemic, from January 1, 2018, to December 31, 2022.

Given the above, structured data from web searches was collected in a simple query with the following parameters:

- Search terms: "ivermectina", "tapabocas", "leche";
- location: Colombia
- time: From 2018 to 2022
- Others: "All Category" and "Web search"

4 Results

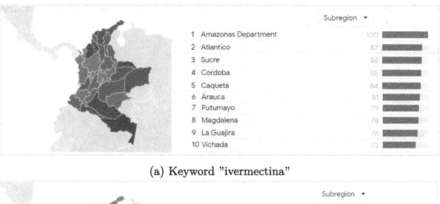

(a) Keyword "ivermectina"

(b) Keyword "Tapabocas"

Fig. 1. Interest by Colombian subregions. The darker blue area signifies a higher proportion of all queries. (Color figure online)

In Colombia, interest in the general search terms "ivermectin" and "mask face" for the last five years showed an increased trend for both search terms in the general category during the COVID period compared to the years before the pandemic. The results presented are normalized to represent relative popularity rather than absolute search volumes. Thus, corresponding the search interests of different terms or topics over time and across other regions is easier.

Figure 1 provides a visual summary of geographical distribution by regional administrative and economic divisions (departments). It depicts where the largest concentration of web searches are from people interested in the "ivermectin" and "face mask" terms during the 2018–2022 timeframe. Fig. 1a shows the departments with the highest SVIs for the term "ivermectin." Amazonas, Atlántico, and Sucre are the three departments that top the list. Fig. 1b shows the subregions with the highest SVIs for the term "face mask." The first is Bogota, Colombia's capital district and the most populous city, marked with a cross in the center of the map. It should be noted that values are calculated on a scale from 0 to 100, where 100 is the location with the most popularity as a fraction of the total searches in that location, and a value of 50 indicates a location that is half as popular. A value of 0 indicates a location with insufficient data for this term. A higher value means a higher proportion of all queries, not a higher absolute query count.

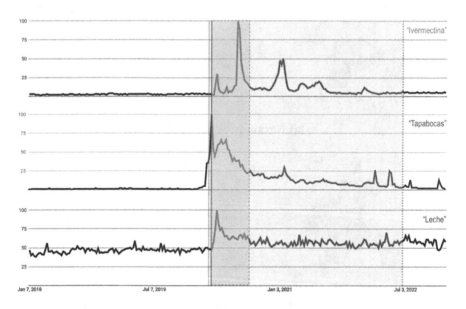

Fig. 2. From top to bottom, Google Trends results for the keywords "ivermectin", "face mask", and "milk" between 2018 and 2022.

Figure 2 illustrates the interest of three different terms on Google web searches: "ivermectin" at the top, "face mask" in the middle, and "milk" at the bottom. As the figure shows, a green line corresponds to the first week of March, in which the first case of COVID-19 in Colombia was officially confirmed. It matches the biggest spike in the chart for the term "face mask." Two weeks earlier, which witnessed an increase in the line, news was reported about the shortage of face masks in the country, as Table 2 shows. The purple line close to the dotted line is the week in which the vital simulacrum of the quarantine was established in the capital. The first dotted line marks the official start of the quarantine, and the second dotted line indicates the end of the quarantine.

The keyword "milk" was used as a control term since it is part of the family basket and for which we anticipated a monotonous trend, whereas, for the other two terms, we expected peaks with an upward trend in times of pandemic. However, the three terms presented a search peak just at the beginning of the pandemic in Colombia, the period in which the World Health Organization named coronavirus disease COVID-19. The face mask's bottom graph shows peaks from the third month of 2020 to the present, roughly coinciding with Ivermectin. This is simply because the face mask had a higher volume of internet searches, possibly because it became a must-wear product.

Figure 3 illustrates the interest of five related queries with "ivermectin" suggested by the tool due to their popularity. Fig. 3a shows the combination with the term "COVID-19," which only started to trend at the end of 2019. Fig. 3b represents the combination of the term "price." The tendency line comprises several little temporal spikes before the quarantine period but three big spikes during quarantine. Fig. 3c reflects "how to take the ivermectin." This tendency line is similar to the above, with more little spikes before quarantine and bigger spikes during quarantine. Fig. 3d shows a tendency line of stationary spikes related to "what is ivermectin for" that are more numerous during the outbreak. And finally, Fig. 3e shows spikes related to "ivermectin contraindications". Both Fig. 3d and 3e are highly related.

Table 1 shows that news about general communication discourages people from using Ivermectin and from talking about the scarcity of the pharmaceutical, while Table 2 lists news about face mask scarcity during the entire pandemic period. Both Table 1 and Table 2 show the news chronologically.

The highest SVI in the five years of observation for face masks and milk was at the beginning of the pandemic when the quarantine was made official, and the use of face masks for citizens became mandatory; clearly, this would indicate that people were concerned about health and food safety. Although the search interest for "ivermectin" is not at its highest in the observation window, comparing its SVI with those of the other terms, a few weeks later, it is already beginning to show signs of great public interest. Even it is noted that the keywords related to "ivermectin price" and "how to take ivermectin" were gaining popularity during the pandemic.

Now, when comparing two different sources of information, some indications can be observed to analyze. The first news about Ivermectin scarcity appeared in October 2020. Although the mask was sold out from the beginning of the pandemic, the Ivermectin was not, and maybe there was a chance that the search interest could give a sign of its future shortage. However, this trend is not easy to detect by the human eye due to the changing nature of this kind of data, which is affected by the complexity of online interactions and societal uncertainties.

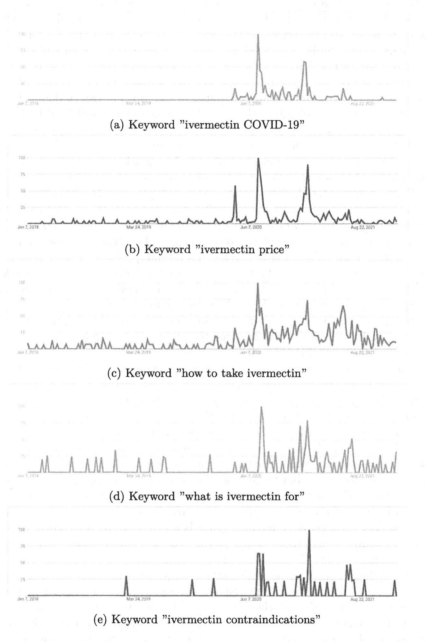

(a) Keyword "ivermectin COVID-19"

(b) Keyword "ivermectin price"

(c) Keyword "how to take ivermectin"

(d) Keyword "what is ivermectin for"

(e) Keyword "ivermectin contraindications"

Fig. 3. Google trend local web searches for terms related to "ivermectin" for the last five years. The y-axis is the SVI from 0 to 100, and the x-axis is the time scale.

Table 1. News headlines retrieved by News API regarding "ivermectin"

(1)	Ivermectin is not tested in Colombia to treat patients with COVID-19
	Source: La República
	Date: 10-02-2020
(2)	National Government Does Not Recommend Ivermectin As a Treatment for COVID-19
	Source: La FM
	Date: 13-07-2020
(3)	Invima gave free rein to the study to apply Ivermectin in the department of Valle
	Source: El Tiempo
	Date: 13-07-2020
(4)	Ivermectin and other drugs without proven efficacy against the Coronavirus that are promoted in Latin America
	Source: BBC
	Date: 14-07-2020
(5)	The laboratory that produces ivermectin denies that it works against COVID-19
	Source: El Espectador
	Date: 5-2-2021
(6)	What is Ivermectin, and why is there an increase in cases of poisoning in Colombia?
	Source: AS Colombia
	Date: 21-6-2021
(7)	Misinformation about COVID-19 leads to shortages of Ivermectin, a drug for animals
	Source: The New York Times
	Date: 30-9-2021
(8)	Ivermectin: How fake science invented a 'miracle' drug against COVID-19
	Source: El Tiempo
	Date: 8-10-2021

5   Discussion

Our analysis of Google Trends data on the key search terms chosen for this study from January 2018 to December 2022 revealed a national online interest in "facemask" went from irrelevant to a topic of national concern due to the shortage that it had already presented before the first case of COVID was confirmed in the country. The largest trend is concentrated in the departments of the Andean region of the country, where the largest number of inhabitants and the most economically important cities are located. "ivermectin" was of greatest

Table 2. News headlines retrieved by News API regarding "face mask"

(1)	The demand for face masks skyrocketed, and they are becoming scarce in Bogota
	Source: Portafolio
	Date: 27-02-2020
(2)	With used bra cups and corn cobs, children make face masks: Are they hygienic?
	Source: Pulzo
	Date: 9-3-2020
(3)	Because of Trump, Colombia could run out of N95 masks
	Source: Semana
	Date: 27-3-2020
(4)	Face mask: if you don't know how to use it, it's better not to touch it
	Source: AS colombia
	Date: 3-4-2020
(5)	What is the most effective mask against Coronavirus?
	Source: El País Cali
	Date: 14-10-2020
(6)	The Bogota Mayor's Office recommended that citizens use surgical masks and not cloth ones. What is the difference?
	Source: Semana
	Date: 27-1-2021
(7)	Manufacturer of N95 masks has 30 million units that, despite its effectiveness, cannot sell
	Source: Semana
	Date: 18-2-2021
(8)	Face mask waste increased by 9,000% between March and October 2020
	Source: El Espectador
	Date: 9-12-2021

interest to the departments of the coastal regions and the Amazon region, which was the most affected by fatal cases of COVID-19.

Ivermectin is an essential medicine for treating infections or parasitic diseases. It is primarily known for its effectiveness in treating onchocerciasis caused by the parasitic worm Onchocerca volvulus, transmitted through the bites of black flies. In combination with other drugs, it is used to treat lymphatic filariasis, a parasitic infection caused by filarial worms, including Wuchereria bancrofti and Brugia malayi. It has also demonstrated its effectiveness in treating strongyloidiasis, an intestinal infection caused by the roundworm Strongyloides stercoralis. In some cases, it is used to treat scabies, a highly contagious skin infestation caused by the mite Sarcoptes scabiei. Additionally, Ivermectin has been used to treat other parasitic infections, such as certain mites, lice infestations, and some helminthic infections [7]. However, it is ineffective against viral infections, such as COVID-19, and the World Health Organization and other health authorities have not recommended its use [5].

The dynamic surge in search interest for "ivermectin" observed during the pandemic underscores the profound influence of media coverage, online interactions, and societal uncertainties on public health-related information seeking. Analyzing this trend illuminates the intricate interplay of digital platforms and human behavior in disseminating and shaping medical narratives. The extensive news coverage spanning mainstream media and social platforms triggered an amplified curiosity about exploring Ivermectin as a potential COVID-19 treatment avenue. Furthermore, the rising tide of misinformation often propagated through online discussions and social media significantly increased search interest. The pandemic-induced anxiety and the dearth of definitive treatment options catalyzed this phenomenon as individuals sought to safeguard their well-being in an era of unprecedented health risks. This intricate web of factors demonstrates the need for computational models that can delineate the trajectories of information diffusion and unravel the fine-grained dynamics of public engagement with health-related content during crises.

This exploratory study exemplifies the critical role that intelligent algorithms and data analytics play in developing algorithms capable of discerning between reliable and dubious sources of information that can empower users to make informed decisions [3]. Moreover, as the pandemic has highlighted the speed and scale of information propagation, studying information cascades in a public health context could offer new insights into collective sensemaking and response patterns. Ultimately, the digital traces left behind during such critical junctures constitute a rich resource for computational researchers as they strive to comprehend the intricate relation between technological affordances and human behavioral responses in shaping the landscape of information dissemination.

5.1   Limitations

We understand that other search engines exist besides Google and that phrases and search volumes may change among regions. Additionally, digital infrastructure for internet coverage and accessibility varies within Colombian territory, as Fig. 4 shows. According to data from the World Bank, Fig. 4a is a heat map of internet use [10]. In Fig. 4b, it is easy to appreciate that there is no digital inclusion in all territories; the departments of the Andean and Atlantic regions are highlighted, whereas the Amazonic and Pacific regions are not [16]. Thus, the study may have some limitations. Given these restrictions, care must be taken to avoid assuming that the data displayed are absolute and precise. We suggest identifying research opportunities to delve into this area.

Given these restrictions, care must be taken to avoid assuming that the data displayed is absolute and precise; we suggest identifying research opportunities to delve into the area.

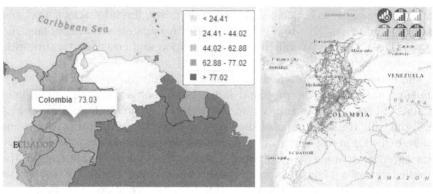

(a) Percentage of population using the Internet [10]

(b) Coverage of the most used mobile network [16]

Fig. 4. Cartography of Internet availability in Colombia

6 Conclusions

The convergence of data harnessed from disparate sources is a testament to the evolving landscape of information consumption. A more nuanced panorama unfolds by juxtaposing the trends mined from Google Trends with official news sources. The prominent spike in "ivermectin" searches during the COVID-19 pandemic is an outstanding example. This confluence of information streams elucidates the intricate interplay between media coverage, digital dialogues, societal anxieties, and the pursuit of reliable medical information. It accentuates the pivotal role computational models play in deciphering these complex interactions. It offers a glimpse into the potential of machine learning algorithms to discern credible sources amid the misinformation environment, ultimately advancing our capacity to make informed decisions.

Moreover, this hybrid approach to data analysis revealed another noteworthy peak in search interest related to "facial mask," occurring within a similar time window. It underscores the innate connection between information-seeking behavior and emerging circumstances as individuals navigate by searchers. The ability to extract such nuanced insights from the web underscores their potential in shaping informed responses across sectors as diverse as public health, commerce, and governance.

References

1. Alruily, M., Ezz, M., Mostafa, A.M., Yanes, N., Abbas, M., El-Manzalawy, Y.: Prediction of COVID-19 transmission in the united states using google search trends. Comput. Mater. Continua **71**(1), 1751–1768 (2022)
2. Chen, Y., Deng, X., Huang, Q., Luo, H.: Patterns and trends in online learning behaviors: Evidence from google analytics. In: 2021 IEEE International Conference

on Engineering, Technology & Education (TALE), pp. 961–964 (2021). https://doi.org/10.1109/TALE52509.2021.9678689

3. Dorado, R., Bramy, A., Mejía-Moncayo, C., Rojas, A.E.: Automatic acquisition of controlled vocabularies from Wikipedia using wikilinks, word ranking, and a dependency parser. In: Solano, A., Ordoñez, H. (eds.) CCC 2017. Communications in Computer and Information Science, vol. 735, pp. 32–43. Springer, Cham (2017). https://doi.org/10.1007/978-3-319-66562-7_3

4. Eka Prasetya, T.A., Kusuma Wardani, R.W.: Systematic review of social media addiction among health workers during the pandemic Covid-19. Heliyon **9**(6), e16784 (2023). https://doi.org/10.1016/j.heliyon.2023.e16784

5. FDA: Why You Should Not Use Ivermectin to Treat or Prevent COVID-19 (2021). https://www.fda.gov/consumers/consumer-updates/why-you-should-not-use-ivermectin-treat-or-prevent-covid-19

6. Florez, H., Singh, S.: Online dashboard and data analysis approach for assessing covid-19 case and death data. F1000Research **9** (2020)

7. Fox, L.M.: Ivermectin: uses and impact 20 years on. Curr. Opin. Infect. Dis. **19**(6), 588–593 (2006). https://doi.org/10.1097/QCO.0b013e328010774c

8. Gitin, A., Saikaly, S.K., Valdes-Rodriguez, R.: Public interest in sunscreens and sunscreen ingredients: a google trends study. Photodermatol. Photoimmunol. Photomed. **39**(2), 166–168 (2023)

9. Holland, M.R., Kahlor, L.A.: A google trends analysis of interest in nonbinary identities. Cyberpsychol. Behav. Soc. Netw. **26**(6), 401–407 (2023). https://doi.org/10.1089/cyber.2022.0304

10. ITU: Individuals using the internet (% of population). International Telecommunication Union World Telecommunication/ICT Indicators Database. The World Bank Group (2021). https://data.worldbank.org/indicator/it.net.user.zs?view=map

11. Jin, P., et al.: A google trends analysis revealed global public interest and awareness of nasal polyps. Eur. Arch. Otorhinolaryngol. **280**(6), 2831–2839 (2023)

12. Kim, Y., Kim, Y.: Global regionalization of heat environment quality perception based on k-means clustering and google trends data. Sustain. Cities Soc. **96** (2023)

13. Kornellia, E., Syakurah, R.A.: Use of google trends database during the Covid-19 pandemic: systematic review. Multidisc. Rev. **6**(2), 2023017 (2023). https://doi.org/10.31893/multirev.2023017

14. Mora-Beltrán, C.E., Rojas, A.E., Mejía-Moncayo, C.: An immersive experience in the virtual 3D VirBELA environment for leadership development in undergraduate students during the COVID-19 quarantine. In: Second International Workshop on Applied Informatics for Economy, Society, and Development (AIESD 2020), vol. 2714, pp. 42–52 (2020)

15. Mulero, R., Garcia-Hiernaux, A.: Forecasting unemployment with google trends: age, gender and digital divide. Empirical Econ. **65**, 587–605 (2022)

16. nPerf: 3G/4G/5G Coverage map, Colombia. https://www.nperf.com/es/map/CO/-/-/signal/. Accessed 20 Feb 2023

17. Pan, Z., Nguyen, H.L., Abu-Gellban, H., Zhang, Y.: Google trends analysis of covid-19 pandemic. In: 8th IEEE International Conference on Big Data, pp. 3438–3446 (2020)

18. Papadamou, S., Fassas, A.P., Kenourgios, D., Dimitriou, D.: Effects of the first wave of COVID-19 pandemic on implied stock market volatility: international evidence using a google trend measure. J. Econ. Asymmetries **28**, e00317 (2023)

19. Price, C., Morrison, S., Haley, M., Nester, C., Williams, A.: Searching for online information on the fit of children's footwear during the COVID-19 pandemic: an analysis of google trends data. J. Foot Ankle Res. **16**(1), 1–7 (2023)

20. Rizzato, V.L., Lotto, M., Lourenço Neto, N., Oliveira, T.M., Cruvinel, T.: Digital surveillance: the interests in toothache-related information after the outbreak of COVID-19. Oral Dis. **28**(S2), 2432–2441 (2022). https://doi.org/10.1111/odi.14012

21. Saegner, T., Austys, D.: Forecasting and surveillance of COVID-19 spread using google trends: literature review. Int. J. Environ. Res. Public Health **19**(19), 12394 (2022)

22. Shepherd, T., Robinson, M., Mallen, C.: Online health information seeking for Mpox in endemic and nonendemic countries: Google trends study. JMIR Formative Res. **7**, e42710 (2023). https://doi.org/10.2196/42710

23. Springer, S., Strzelecki, A., Zieger, M.: Maximum generable interest: a universal standard for google trends search queries. Healthcare Analytics **3**, 100158 (2023)

24. Tintín, V., Florez, H.: Artificial intelligence and data science in the detection, diagnosis, and control of COVID-19: a systematic mapping study. In: Gervasi, O., et al. (eds.) ICCSA 2021. LNCS, vol. 12957, pp. 354–368. Springer, Cham (2021). https://doi.org/10.1007/978-3-030-87013-3_27

25. Wong, A., Ho, S., Olusanya, O., Antonini, M.V., Lyness, D.: The use of social media and online communications in times of pandemic COVID-19. J. Intensive Care Soc. **22**(3), 255–260 (2021). https://doi.org/10.1177/1751143720966280

26. Wu, N., Mu, L.: Impact of COVID-19 on online grocery shopping discussion and behavior reflected from google trends and geotagged tweets. Comput. Urban Sci. **3**(1), 7 (2023). https://doi.org/10.1007/s43762-023-00083-0

Measuring the Impact of Digital Government Service: A Scientometric Analysis for 2023

Narendra Nafi Gumilang(✉) ⓘ, Achmad Nurmandi ⓘ, Muhammad Younus ⓘ,
and Aulia Nur Kasiwi ⓘ

Department of Government Affairs and Administration, Jusuf Kalla School of Government,
Universitas Muhammadiyah Yogyakarta, Bantul City 55183, Indonesia
aigilangnyagumilang@gmail.com

Abstract. This study explored the characteristics of digital government trends using research data from the Scopus database for 2012 to 2022. It used a qualitative descriptive method and software CiteSpace to analyze the data. Digitalization will help the community obtain appropriate services, produce collaborative practices, and allow digital innovation. The public sector is essential in public service issues and influences the economy, as it has the authority to issue and enforce regulations and policies. This study found that the number of publications on digital government has increased over the last ten years, with the UK being the region with the most journals. An analysis using CiteSpace Software revealed 11 related clusters, each with its discussion. Digital government transformation, efficient democratic responsiveness, transforming service delivery, and digitally-based enabler are discussed in detail. The research aims to identify best practices, media, and tools used to upgrade or start using digital services in governments. It is hoped that the results of this review can become capital for the government to make digital services even better, from administration to meeting the needs of the Indonesian.

Keywords: Digital Government · Public Service · E-Government · Scientometric Analysis

1 Introduction

Public services are obligatory things that the government of a country must provide. Public service is essential in conducting effective government and on the side of society. Public service can be used as a measure of the government's success in the execution of tasks and can also serve as a tool for performance [1]. Public services in this regard are all kinds of services the government provides to the general public. Public service can indicate whether the State has performed the administrative system only well or not. Despite the importance of a State doing fast and inexpensive public service, the opinion can make the service stuck because it does not want to change with the times.

The ratio of strategic value is not just the implementation of "faster and cheaper" than the current service plan. While "faster and cheaper" services would benefit traditional performance measurements and return on investment models, they could result

H. Florez and M. Leon (Eds.): ICAI 2023, CCIS 1874, pp. 107–121, 2024.
https://doi.org/10.1007/978-3-031-46813-1_8

in missed opportunities and lock inefficient structures by building complex and expensive IT systems around them [2]. It is imperative for public services to swiftly adjust to societal and technological advancements. Digital governance facilitates the expansion of services that effectively address the demands of contemporary society and the dynamic nature of the present era.

Digital government or bias is known as e-government, where the system of government or the way of government refers to the use of information technology. The digital government allows governments to change and improve the provision of public services, streamline administrative processes, and encourage citizens' involvement with the government of a country. Digital government can be a paradigm shift in the system of government that uses the power of information and technology (ICT) to make governance more efficient, accountable, transparent, and accessible to the general public. The development of digital technology can make governance more modern and reach many people from various layers, local, national, to global [3].

E-government has been implemented in Indonesia since 2003 through Presidential Decree No. 3 of 2003. Presidential Regulation Number 95 of 2018 defines e-government as an electronic-based government system (SPBE). E-Government improves public services by simplifying and combining data and information management processes. Services that involve the government, citizens, private companies, other government agencies, and their employees are carried out through E-Government. Since 2003, the Indonesian Ministry of Communication and Information has developed a Blueprint application for e-Government. The application blueprint is flexible because it does not depend on government policies and organizational structure changes. Local governments are given the freedom to translate and change it [4].

Digital government enables governments to innovate extensively because they can access many refractions and network with the outside world by entering the digital world. The public sector plays a vital role in public service issues and influences the economy. The public sector plays a vital role in an economy for several reasons. First, the Organization within it has the authority to issue and enforce rules and policies, including sanctions [5]. The realm of digital governance encompasses a wide-ranging influence on various domains, including economics, law, security, business, people, and international relations. The establishment of a digital government presence facilitates public access to government information and services. Additionally, the analysis of digital governance apps can be conducted using scientific tools, such as scientometric analysis, in order to gain insights about their advancements and effects.

Scientometric analysis tools have different strengths and weaknesses, so different types of analysts must work together to thoroughly analyze each aspect [6]. We can identify collaboration, effective writers, and research trends in digital governance with the aid of scientometric analysis. It helps us comprehend the effects of digital governance better. Different sorts of analysts must collaborate since different scientometric analysis techniques have varied strengths and drawbacks. Enhancing research and development in this area is crucial.

A government that ignores technology risks falling behind and becoming unstable. This study examines the impact of and reasons why digital governance has not been fully utilised. It contributes to knowledge expansion and the adoption of efficient and inclusive digital governance. Scientometric analysis aids in maximising the potential of digital government to solve issues and build a better future through enduring innovation, research, and collaboration.

2 Literature Review

The state apparatus or bureaucracy carries out public service regarding the fulfillment of civil affairs and the basic needs of society [7]. Public service can be used as a measure of government success in the execution of tasks and can also be used to measure performance [1]. In public service, a government can make an image for a bureaucratic performance because, in its journey, public service is not free of bureaucracy [8]. The bureaucracy still has some weaknesses in dealing with public services. According to Maryam [1], Public services provided by government bureaucracy have many problems, such as lengthy time, uncertainty, and costs, to make it difficult for communities to get a decent service. This leads to the lowest level of government service. Lips & Eppel [9] say that the development of complex public services helps us understand how the standards of digital public services are changing rapidly to meet new and growing needs.

Digital government, in short, is using technology to access and bring government services to society [10]. Von Haldenwang [11] argues that renewal thinkers should consider the often-limited capacity and willingness of public institutions to cooperate with one another. Digital government is very needed because of the accessibility that can reach many groups. However, not all groups are able to access digital-based services. According to Lee [12] that, information communication technology (ICT)-based practices cannot be successful for the community unless they are aware of and actively engage with government social media platformsple will be helpful if they can access the service properly. An in-depth conception and reflection of the main types of interactions between citizens and public officials, known as public meetings, assisted by digital public services created [13].

Digital government can be a solution for standardizing digital services that cover a range of resources, capacities, and needs of different local and city governments [14]. In practice, e-government is using the Internet to conduct government business and provide improved public services in a manner that prioritizes community service [15]. With many developments that will bring much change, according to Tangi [16], The applications, processes, cultures, structures, and responsibilities of old government officials will be transformed by digital technology. The use of technology in government is experiencing growth, and it takes time to become something good. Industry, government, and academia have assessed the e-government environment, two essential infrastructures that have emerged that help the research community understand this new phenomenon [17]. There are many things that cause studies or discussions about digital government to continue to grow. According to Opinion Moore [18] In areas such as democracy, decision-making, health care, education, integration, security, land surveys, and the provision of social services, digital governance through an e-government framework is essential. In order to do this, it is necessary to improve the system of work, as stated by Sensuse [19]. To improve the quality of public services, the use of digital governance requires a shift from "electronic" services to more "smart" services.

Digital government makes it possible to facilitate collaboration with outsiders. Collaboration can be done can be with anyone, as said Sari & Isnaeni [20] Interaction between government and society (G2C - Government to Citizen), government and companies (G2B - Government to Business), and relations between government (G2G) - Relationship) are all parts of e-government. Digital government or e-government cannot be carried out optimally in collaboration because, according to Rozikin [21] Overall, Indonesia's Government to Government (G2G) program is still in the early stages of implementing e-government, considering that many local governments have not implemented e-government, this stage is still limited to interaction with the community and has not fully reached the transaction stage.

Digital government can also create an open government that has many benefits. As stated by Meijer [22], open government is considered to have many benefits, such as being more efficient, reducing corruption, and increasing government legitimacy. This reason makes it very popular among politicians and policymakers. Interinstitutional collaboration, transparency of actions and operations, and citizen participation in Open Digital Government (ODG) increase confidence in using ODG services [23]. Not only is the government more open, but it will also increase a country's market potential, as said Ivanova [24]. Careful consideration of the impact of digital governance is crucial in order to comprehend its implications and facilitate its continued expansion. This will facilitate the optimisation of benefits and enable effective responses to the constant changes in the contemporary governance landscape.

3   Research Method

This research method uses a systematic review of the literature aimed at reviewing scientific articles on digital governance that have previously been published in the Scopus-indexed database. The selected articles are articles published over the last ten years, from 2012 to 2022. The data that appears on the scopus page is then re-filtered and obtained in 109 documents that are used as a database in this research. To obtain data that is systematically filtered and obtained using Scopus, it is searched using some keywords or queries like this:

((TITLE-ABS-KEY("digital government") AND TITLE-ABS-KEY("Public Service") OR TITLE-ABS-KEY(technology)) AND PUBYEAR > 2012 AND PUBYEAR < 2022 AND (LIMIT-TO (OA, "all")) AND (LIMIT-TO (DOCTYPE,"cp") OR LIMIT-TO (DOCTYPE,"ar")) AND (LIMIT-TO (LANGUAGE,"English"))).

After obtaining the data needed for this research using software in the form of CiteS-pac, which makes it possible to access the data needed in this scientometric research. Scientometric analysis tools have different strengths and weaknesses, so different types of analysts must work together to thoroughly analyze each aspect [6]. CiteSpace is a free program that is used to process data based on Java and is generally used to analyze the progress of science visually [25].

Figure 1 represents the stages of the research being carried out. The data collection process is carried out through the Scopus database with specific keywords to bring up the appropriate data. Scopus does not only document but also imports some data, such as graphics about publications, authors, the number of publications, and so on. This study

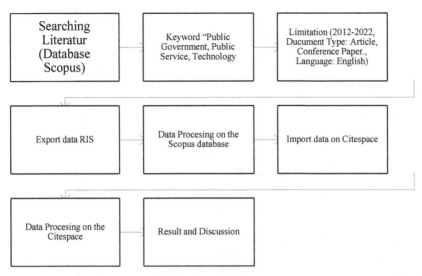

Fig. 1. Research Stages

also uses the Citespace application, which is helpful for mapping documents that have been obtained from Scopus. Citespace will bring up data visualizations from documents about digital government and public services that have been collected. After the required data has been collected, an analysis of the results can be carried out to fulfill this research.

4   Result and Discussion

4.1   Document by Year Digital Government

Publications growth of digital government and public service trends on the Scopus database from 2013 to 2022 is presented in Fig. 2.

Since 2013, there have been two publications about digital government on Scopus. Publications about digital government declined in 2014, with only one publication, and in 2015, there was no publication. Publications re-stick in 2016 with two publications; in 2017, there were seven publications increased; in 2018, there were 12; and in 2019, there were 18 publications. By 2020, the publication trend will fall back to just 14. Publications on the scope of digital government and public services rose again in 2021 with 19 publications and peaked in 2022 with the highest publication of 34 documents.

The graph above shows that from year to year, the government is more aware of the importance of digitizing their government. Even though there was a decrease in 2020 due to the presence of Covid-19, which required them to shift their focus to other things. In the following year, there was a surge in research on digital government because, at the time of Covid-19, all activities were shifted online, which required the government to innovate. Due to such demanding circumstances, e-government enables the amalgamation of public policies and services to promote inclusive economic growth, social development, and environmental protection [26].

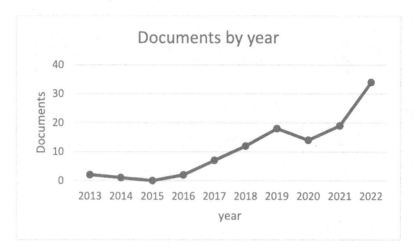

Fig. 2. Documents by year

4.2 Document by Source

There are five sources on the list that contributed to worldwide research of digital government and public service trends from 2016 to 2022. Figure 3 shows the sources with detailed information.

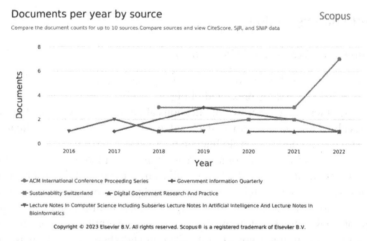

Fig. 3. Documents per year by source

The figure above shows that the ACM International Conference Proceeding Series published 13 documents, followed by the Government Information Quarterly, with seven documents. Sustainability Switzerland published six documents. It can be seen that starting in 2018, research on digital government and public services has been increasing in publication. In Fig. 3, it can be seen that starting in 2018, researchers have begun to be able to easily take references from this source because their publications are increasing.

4.3   Countries Contributions

There are ten countries that contributed to digital government and public service trends from 2012 to 2022. Statistical data of publications indexed by the Scopus database is provided below in Fig. 4.

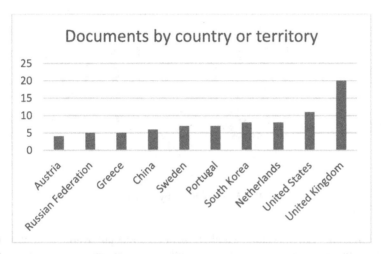

Fig. 4. Documents by country or territory

The survey looked at ten simple countries with the most publications on the scope of digital government and public services. The table below shows that the most published on the scope is the United Kingdom, with 20 documents. The dominant country in the study was the United States, with 11 publications, followed by the Netherlands and South Korea, with eight documents. Publications 7 documents have Portugal and Sweden. China, Greece, the Russian Federation, and Austria are the following four countries.

It can be seen that the United Kingdom has become a region that publishes research on digital government and public services. The United Kingdom is an advanced region and also conscious of technology, so it is not surprising that the advancement of digital services is at its forefront. The United States follows with the second-most publications. It is not surprising that the United States is a developed country and has made much progress in the field of government. It can be seen that their research on digital government is also massively carried out by researchers there. The top 10 countries and theories that issued documents on digital government and public services are famous for their initiative and willingness to grow. Covud-19 could be a leaping point or a basis for countries around the world to start digitalizing their governments because digitalization in the Covud-19 era can help in any sector, whether economy, health, or even education.

4.4   The Most Productive Authors

Referring to 109 analyzed documents, Fig. 5 top 10 most productive authors of digital government and public service trends from 2012 to 2022 indexed by the Scopus database in the specified period.

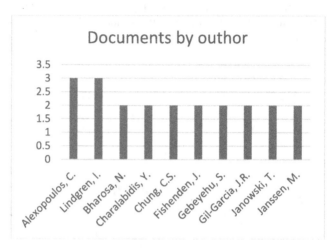

Fig. 5. Documents by author

The following section is the ten authors with the most publications on digital government and public services on Scopus. The authors in the table below are Alexopoulos and Lindgren, with three publications on Scopus. Eight other authors followed, with each publishing two documents in the Scopus, namely Bharosa, Charalabidis, Chung, Fishenden, J., Gebeyehu, S., Gil-Garcia, J.R., Janowski, T., and Janssen, M.

4.5   Mapping Visualization, Cluster Identification, and Analysis

Through citespace analysis, he produced 11 large clusters in which each cluster had its own point of discussion but was still related to each other, as shown in Fig. 6, which gave a cluster map taken using the citesapce application.

The results displayed from the citespace application can be displayed using some short descriptions that describe the cluster. Of the 11 clusters obtained, there are 0) digital government transformation, 1) efficiency democratic responsiveness, 2) transforming service delivery in this third cluster, 3) digitally-based enabler, 4) change agents, 5) bibliometric study, 6) best practice, 7) using the web, 8) electronic services, 9) collaborative platform, 10) artificial intelligence. The order of the clusters that appear is from the largest to the smallest cluster so that they can be identified quite easily. This analysis also provides data on what articles often appear when using the keywords digital government and public service.

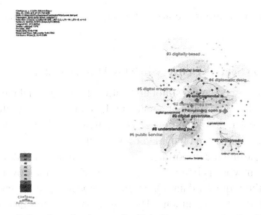

Fig. 6. Knowledge domain clusters in digital government and public services

4.5.1 Digital Government Transformation

This cluster has 34 members and a silhouette value of 0.898. It is labeled as digital government transformation by LLR, delivery processes by LSI, and artificial intelligence (0.84) by MI. The major citing article of the cluster is Bharosa, N "Inclusion through proactive public services: findings from the Netherlands: classifying and designing proactivity through understanding service eligibility and delivery processes."

This cluster has a discussion related to critical variables for creating service feasibility and service delivery so that they can be used to propose design principles to increase public service activity. The importance of increasingly proactive services is also included in this cluster discussion. Politicians are aware of the benefits of proactive governance, and the transition from reactive to proactive services is vast. The development of proactive services is a complex challenge that requires knowledge in many fields, including information technology, administration, data protection, and many areas of law (administrators, data defense, and human rights). In a general sense, proactivity refers to the transfer of citizen initiatives to governments and can be used in a variety of ways in the public sector. According to our research, we should discuss different levels of proactivity rather than considering them as dichotomy factors. Expanding the certification and delivery process is crucial to determine the possible level of proactivity [27].

4.5.2 Efficiency Democratic Responsiveness

This cluster has 31 members and a silhouette value of 0.97. It is labeled as efficient democratic responsiveness by LLR, the legal-rational process by LSI, and systematic review (0.69) by MI. The major citing article of the cluster is Ingram's "Assessing open government performance through Three public administration perspectives: Efficiency, democratic responsiveness, and legal-rational Process."

This laster discusses open government is necessary for a democratic society, coupled with the existence of digital government, making openness has been heralded by governments that use information and communication technology (ICT) without carrying out legal reforms whose institutions are needed to support accountability and transparency [28].

4.5.3 Transforming Service Delivery in This Third Cluster

This cluster has 29 members and a silhouette value of 0.99. It is labeled as transforming service delivery by LLR, government agency by LSI, and artificial intelligence (1.8) by MI. The major citing article of the cluster is Maruyama, M "Design teams as change agents: diplomatic design in the open data movement."

A discussion regarding the importance of digital designers and developers who must have data so that their work is better. Therefore, the role of the government is actually needed to provide the required data. Open data advocates see technology as a tool to rediscover citizenship and government. These groups indicate that space technologies are agents of change, diplomats, and supporters, in addition to experts in the design and development processes. These clusters are intended to investigate specialized CfA techniques that we call diplomatic designs, which combine participatory designs with agencies of change. Examples reveal that the primary goal of these individuals is to influence social change, with the technology they create only serving as a tool for that purpose [29].

4.5.4 Digitally-Based Enabler

This cluster has 18 members and a silhouette value of 0.96. It is labeled as a digitally-based enabler by LLR, public value by LSI, and Qatari experience (0.07) by MI. The major citing article of the cluster is Roy, JP "Service, openness and engagement as digitally- based enablers of public value? a critical examination of digital government in Canada".

This cluster discusses that public value creators can be the pivot for digital government transformation. A few arguments are presented in the discussion in an effort to clarify some of the major barriers to the creation of public value in the context of digital governance and to provide some fresh perspectives on how to do so while maximizing the use of digital innovation in government [30].

4.5.5 Change Agents

This cluster has 17 members and a silhouette value of 0.959. It is labeled as a change agent by both LLR and LSI and as artificial intelligence (0.03) by MI. The major citing article of the cluster is Maruyama, M "Design teams as change agents: diplomatic design in the open data movement."

This cluster discusses designer and developer experts who should have the same level as technical experts in obtaining government data. The responsibilities of government agencies include providing accessible and valuable data, enabling developers to use that data to create tools, and encouraging citizens to use new technologies. The objectives of one group may conflict with those of another group. This exposure investigates the usefulness of the diplomatic design approach, which emphasizes the craftsmanship and practice of negotiating using specific strategies, having this in mind [29].

4.5.6   Bibliometric Study

This cluster has 17 members and a silhouette value of 0.964. It is labeled as a bibliometric study by both LLR and LSI and as artificial intelligence (0.1) by MI. The major citing article of the cluster is Ravšelj, D "A review of digital era governance research in the first two decades: a bibliometric study."

This cluster has a discussion about the rise of digital technology, which has paved the way for the emergence of a new public governance model called the Digital Era Governance (DEG) model (often referred to as e-government, digital governance, e-governance, or governance digital governance) in which digital technology plays a central role. DEG research is a relatively new discipline marked by rapid development and evolution. Consequently, a comprehensive and in-depth strategy is required to comprehend the evolution of DEG research over time. In reviewing DEG research over the past two decades, this bibliometric study employs several established and innovative bibliometric approaches, including descriptive surveys, scientific production, network analysis, and thematic evolution. The results demonstrate the expansion of DEG research over the past two decades, particularly in recent years, as accelerated by some of the most pertinent articles published in prominent journals, with the majority of DEG studies conducted in developed nations [31].

4.5.7   Best Practice

This cluster has 13 members and a silhouette value of 0.953. It is labeled as bests practice by LLR, public service by LSI, and spatial planning (0.07) by MI. The major citing article of the cluster is Leão, HAT "Best practices and methodologies to promote the digitization of public services citizen-driven: a systematic literature review."

This cluster discusses public services that have become bigger and faster digital that the government uses. All levels of government are charged with providing services, protecting communities, and fostering economic growth. Although this is a long-term objective, citizens now expect the government to provide more excellent and quick delivery services. This paper presents a systematic review of the literature on the digitalization of government-provided services in several countries, motivated by the dearth of primary studies in the literature on the identification of the processes and methodologies used by governments and private companies to provide their services [32].

4.5.8   Using the Web

This cluster has 13 members and a silhouette value of 0.98. It is labeled as using the web by LLR, opportunities and challenges of using web 2.0 technologies in government by LSI, and using the web (0.01) by MI. The major citing article of the cluster is Sivarajah, U "Opportunities and challenges of using web 2.0 technologies in government".

In this cluster, the discussion that is published is related to public administration, which is assisted by the web making new opportunities for progress for the government. This technology has offered a series of new opportunities and difficulties for these governmental entities, and the discussion of Web 2.0 technology is more engaging than the old model of information provision or the construction of digital services. This study examines the potential presented to public authorities by Web 2.0 technologies and the obstacles that may need to be addressed by these authorities when incorporating these technologies into their work practices. The study does this by referring to previous research that has been conducted [33].

4.5.9 Electronic Services

This cluster has 13 members and a silhouette value of 0.982. It is labeled as an electronic service by both LLR and LSI and as a sensitivity review (0.03) by MI. The major citing article of the cluster is Luna-Reyes, LF, "Understanding public value creation in the delivery of electronic services."

This cluster discusses ways to analyze and define public value creation through electronic services. Using a process model to understand value creation through electronic services in Mexico is the subject of the current discussion. The ultimate goal of this unique initiative is to collect data through citizen surveys to understand the relationship between system quality, information quality, user satisfaction, system usage, and individual benefits [34].

4.5.10 Collaborative Platform

This cluster has 13 members and a silhouette value of 0.912. It is labeled as a collaborative platform by LLR, an environmental issue by LSI, and public health service (0.18) by MI. The major citing article of the cluster is Sapraz, M "Implicating human values for designing a digital government collaborative platform for environmental issues: a value-sensitive design approach."

This cluster aims to implicate essential human values for designing a Digital Government Collaborative Platform (DGCP). The conversations that take place in this cluster will play a role in the design of DGCP as an e-government solution, particularly for Environmental sustainability. The goal of this design is to construct successful collaboration for developing nations that have various socio-political and multicultural characteristics. In addition, the study made a contribution to the VSD literature by creating DGCP as an electronic service for the government [35].

4.5.11 Artificial Intelligence

This cluster has 12 members and a silhouette value of 0.98. It is labeled as artificial intelligence by LLR, artificial intelligence in the urban environment: smart cities as models for developing innovation and sustainability by LSI, and artificial intelligence (0.02) by MI. The major citing article of the cluster is Ortega-fernández, "Artificial intelligence in the urban environment: smart cities as models for developing innovation and sustainability."

This cluster discusses Smart City (Granada) in order to discuss which strategic technological actions to implement in different topical areas of action: the economy, sustainability, mobility, government, population, and quality of life. The advancement of better public administration, mobility, environment, economy, and quality of life in urban areas requires technological and digital innovation as well as AI. Consideration of the trend shift from functional systems to more sustainable and intelligent systems is crucial for the transformation of traditional cities into smart cities. For the financial structure to be optimized, the ICT infrastructure must be ready. It is necessary to combine a wide range of issues, including those relating to the environment, service quality, social behavior, etc. [36].

5   Conclusion

Government digital public services have advanced significantly in recent years. Fundamental changes in how governments connect with citizens and provide public services have been brought about by the digital revolution. We will highlight some of the key points that demonstrate the progress, advantages, and potential of digital public services. Digital government services have advanced significantly. Information and communication technology has been used by governments around the world to simplify and speed up administrative procedures. Online applications for documents, invoices, and registration are some examples of public services that are now easily accessible via digital platforms. This allows customers to buy the services they need with less time and effort.

According to the report, Various sectors, including the online economy and health care, embrace digital governance, which is very beneficial to society. For example, after the outbreak of COVID-19, more hospitals use online hospital registration, appointments, and access to electronic medical data. Through the penetration of online markets, digitization has allowed small and medium-sized business owners to thrive in the economy. All this shows how beneficial digital public services are for society.

Despite significant progress, government investment in the required technology infrastructure continues to rise as digital public services continue to expand. This requires better Internet connectivity, data security, and more dynamic and user-friendly software development. To ensure that everyone in the community, especially in rural areas and under-serving populations, has equal access to digital public services, the government also works with civil society. It is vital that the public actively participate in the decision-making process and monitor the growth of digital public services.

The public has benefited greatly from digital governance, which has reduced administrative barriers and improved the efficiency of public service provision, among others. Citizens no longer have to physically go to government offices to make requests, report problems, or ask for information. Greater comfort and accessibility is offered, especially for those with time or physical constraints. Moreover, because data and information are easily accessible by the public, digital governance also increases transparency and accountability of governments.

References

1. Maryam, N.S.: Mewujudkan good governance melalui pelayanan public. J. Ilmu Polit. dan Komun. 6(1) (2017). https://doi.org/10.56444/jma.v7i1.67
2. Fountain, J.E.: Beter public services for growth and jobs. NCDG Occas. (2007). http://www.megovconf-lisbon.gov.pt/

3. Osifo, O.C.: Examining digital government and public service provision: The case of Finland. In: Vrdoljak, E., et al. (eds.) 41st International Convention on Information and Communication Technology, Electronics and Microelectronics, MIPRO 2018. Institute of Electrical and Electronics Engineers Inc., pp. 1342–1347 (2018). https://doi.org/10.23919/MIPRO.2018. 8400242
4. Maria, E., Halim, A.: E-Government dan Korupsi: Studi di Pemerintah Daerah, Indonesia dari Perspektif Teori Keagenan. Ekuitas J. Ekon. dan Keuang. 5(1), 40–58 (2021). https://doi. org/10.24034/j25485024.y2021.v5.i1.4789
5. Nasrudin, A.: Sektor Publik: Definisi, Peran, Pro dan Kontra. cardasco.com. Accessed 23 Aug 2019
6. Hosseini, M.R., Martek, I., Zavadskas, E.K., Aibinu, A.A., Arashpour, M., Chileshe, N.: Critical evaluation of off-site construction research: A Scientometric analysis. Autom. Constr. 87(October 2017), 235–247 (2018). https://doi.org/10.1016/j.autcon.2017.12.002
7. Mukarom, Z., Muhibudin WIjaya, L.: Membangun Kinerja Pelayanan Publik: Menuju Clean Government and Good Governance. Pustaka Setia Bandung (2016)
8. Rinaldi, R.: ANALISIS KUALITAS PELAYANAN PUBLIK. J. Adm. Publik 1(Kolisch 1996), 22–34 (2012)
9. Lips, M., Eppel, E.: Understanding public service provision using digital technologies during COVID-19 lockdowns in New Zealand through a complexity theory lens. Glob. Public Policy Gov. 2(4), 498–517 (2022). https://doi.org/10.1007/s43508-022-00057-8
10. Silcock, R.: What is e-Government? Parliam. Aff. 54, 88–101 (2001)
11. von Haldenwang, C.: Electronic government (E-government) and development. Eur. J. Dev. Res. 16(2), 417–432 (2004). https://doi.org/10.1080/0957881042000220886
12. Lee, T.D., Park, H., Lee, J.: Collaborative accountability for sustainable public health: a Korean perspective on the effective use of ICT-based health risk communication. Gov. Inf. Q. 36(2), 226–236 (2019). https://doi.org/10.1016/j.giq.2018.12.008
13. Lindgren, I., Madsen, C.Ø., Hofmann, S., Melin, U.: Close encounters of the digital kind: a research agenda for the digitalization of public services. Gov. Inf. Q. 36(3), 427–436 (2019). https://doi.org/10.1016/j.giq.2019.03.002
14. Styrin, E., Mossberger, K., Zhulin, A.: Government as a platform: intergovernmental participation for public services in the Russian Federation. Gov. Inf. Q. 39(1) (2022). https://doi. org/10.1016/j.giq.2021.101627
15. Novliza Eka, P., Faizal, A., Astri, D.S.: Penerapan transformasi digital pada pelayanan publik di badan pengelola keuangan provinsi beNGKULU. J. Penelit. Sos. dan Polit. Juni 10(1) (2021)
16. Tangi, L., Janssen, M., Benedetti, M., Noci, G.: Digital government transformation: a structural equation modelling analysis of driving and impeding factors. Int. J. Inf. Manage. 60 (2021). https://doi.org/10.1016/j.ijinfomgt.2021.102356
17. Reece, B.: E-government literature review. J. E-Government, April 2015, pp. 37–41 (2008). https://doi.org/10.1300/J399v03n01
18. Moore, S.: Digital government, public participation and service transformation: the impact of virtual courts. Policy Polit. 47(3), 495–509 (2019). https://doi.org/10.1332/030557319X15 586039367509
19. Sensuse, D.I., Arief, A., Mursanto, P.: An empirical validation of foundation models for smart government in Indonesia. Int. J. Adv. Sci. Eng. Inf. Technol. 12(3), 1132–1141 (2022). https:// doi.org/10.18517/ijaseit.12.3.13442
20. Sari, T.P., Isnaeni, R.: E-Government : Teknologi Melawan Korupsi. J. Teknol. Inf. ESIT 83–88 (2019)
21. Rozikin, M., Hesty, W., Sulikah, S.: Kolaborasi dan E-Literacy: Kunci Keberhasilan Inovasi E-Government Pemerintah Daerah. J. Borneo Adm. 16(1), 61–80 (2020). https://doi.org/10. 24258/jba.v16i1.603

22. Meijer, A.J., Curtin, D., Hillebrandt, M.: Open government: connecting vision and voice. Int. Rev. Adm. Sci. **78**(1), 10–29 (2012). https://doi.org/10.1177/0020852311429533

23. Al Sulaimani, A.H.A., Ozuem, W.: Understanding the role of transparency, participation, and collaboration for achieving open digital government goals in Oman. Transform. Gov. People, Process Policy **16**(4), 595–612 (2022). https://doi.org/10.1108/TG-04-2022-0044

24. Ivanova, V., Poltarykhin, A., Szromnik, A., Anichkina, O.: Economic policy for country's digitalization: a case study. Entrep. Sustain. Issues **7**(1), 649–661 (2019). https://doi.org/10.9770/jesi.2019.7.1(46)

25. Setyowati, L.: Pengenalan Bibliometric Mapping sebagai Bentuk Pengembangan Layanan Research Support Services Perguruan Tinggi. JPUA J. Perpust. Univ. Airlangga Media Inf. dan Komun. Kepustakawanan **10**(1), 1 (2020). https://doi.org/10.20473/jpua.v10i1.2020.1-9

26. Castro, C., Lopes, C.: Digital government and sustainable development. J. Knowl. Econ. **13**(2), 880–903 (2022). https://doi.org/10.1007/s13132-021-00749-2

27. Bharosa, N., Oude Luttighuis, B., Spoelstra, F., Van Der Voort, H., Janssen, M.: Inclusion through proactive public services: Findings from the Netherlands: classifying and designing proactivity through understanding service eligibility and delivery processes. In: Lee, J., Pereira, G.V., Hwang, S. (eds.) 22nd Annual International Conference on Digital Government Research: Digital Innovations for Public Values: Inclusive Collaboration and Community, DGO 2021. Association for Computing Machinery, pp. 242–251 (2021). https://doi.org/10.1145/3463677.3463707

28. Ingrams, A.: Assessing open government performance through three public administration perspectives: efficiency, democratic responsiveness, and legal-rational process. Chin. Public Adm. Rev. **7**(1), 110–145 (2016). https://doi.org/10.22140/cpar.v7i1.120

29. Maruyama, M., Douglas, S., Robertson, S.: Design teams as change agents: Diplomatic design in the open data movement. University of Hawaii, Manoa, United States, pp. 1860–1869 (2013). https://doi.org/10.1109/HICSS.2013.170

30. Roy, J.P.: Service, openness and engagement as digitally-based enablers of public value? A critical examination of digital government in Canada. Int. J. Public Adm. Digit. Age **6**(3), 23–40 (2019). https://doi.org/10.4018/IJPADA.2019070102

31. Ravšelj, D., Umek, L., Todorovski, L., Aristovnik, A.: A review of digital era governance research in the first two decades: a bibliometric study. Future Internet **14**(5) (2022). https://doi.org/10.3390/fi14050126

32. Leão, H.A.T., Canedo, E.D.: Best practices and methodologies to promote the digitization of public services citizen-driven: a systematic literature review. Information **9**(8) (2018). https://doi.org/10.3390/info9080197

33. Sivarajah, U., Weerakkody, V., Irani, Z.: Opportunities and challenges of using web 2.0 technologies in government. In: Dwivedi, Y., et al. Social Media: The Good, the Bad, and the Ugly. I3E 2016. Lecture Notes in Computer Science. Springer, Cham, vol. 9844, pp. 594–606 (2016). https://doi.org/10.1007/978-3-319-45234-0_53

34. Luna-Reyes, L.F., Sandoval-Almazan, R., Puron-Cid, G., Picazo-Vela, S., Luna, D.E., Gil-Garcia, J.R.: Understanding public value creation in the delivery of electronic services. In: Janssen, M., et al. (eds.) Electronic Government. EGOV 2017. Lecture Notes in Computer Science, vol. 10428, pp. 378–385. Springer, Cham (2017). https://doi.org/10.1007/978-3-319-64677-0_31

35. Sapraz, M., Han, S.: Implicating human values for designing a digital government collaborative platform for environmental issues: a value sensitive design approach. Sustainability **13**(11) (2021) https://doi.org/10.3390/su13116240

36. Ortega-Fernández, A., Martín-Rojas, R., García-Morales, V.J.: Artificial intelligence in the urban environment: smart cities as models for developing innovation and sustainability. Sustainability **12**(19) (2020). https://doi.org/10.3390/SU12197860

Using Polarization and Alignment to Identify Quick-Approval Law Propositions: An Open Linked Data Application

Francisco Cifuentes-Silva[1,2]([✉])[ID], José Emilio Labra Gayo[2][ID],
Hernán Astudillo[3,4][ID], and Felipe Rivera-Polo[1]

[1] Biblioteca del Congreso Nacional, Valparaíso, Chile
francisco.cifuentes.silva@gmail.com
[2] Universidad de Oviedo, Oviedo, Principado de Asturias, Spain
[3] Universidad Técnica Federico Santa María, Santiago, Chile
[4] ITiSB - Universidad Andrés Bello, Viña del Mar, Chile

Abstract. Since the return of democracy in 1990 until the end of 2020, Chile's Congress has processed and approved 2404 laws, with an average processing time of 695 days from proposal to official publication. Recent political circumstances have given urgency to identifying those law propositions that might be shepherded to faster approval and those that will likely not be approved. This article proposes to classify law proposals, as well as parliamentarians and political parties, along two axes: *polarization* (lack of agreement on an issue) and *(political) alignment* (intra-party coincidence of a group's members regarding specific opinion), yielding four quadrants: (a) "ideological stance" (high polarization, high alignment), (b) "personal interests" (high polarization, low alignment), (c) "thematic interest" (low polarization, low alignment), and (d) "technical consensus" (low polarization, high alignment). We used this scheme to analyze an existing open-linked dataset that records parliamentarians' political parties and their voting on law proposals during 1990–2020. A simple visualization allows identifying a large set of propositions (1,643 = 68%) with technical consensus (i.e., low polarization and high alignment), which could have been quickly shepherded to approval, but instead took 687 days on average (i.e., essentially the same time as others). Wider adoption of this analysis may speed up legislative work and ultimately allow Congress to serve citizens more promptly.

Keywords: Data Analysis · Linked Open Data · Legal informatics · Polarization · Political alignment

1 Introduction

The creation of a new law in Chile is a complex process. Most legal norms start with the submission of an initiative or bill to Congress, which can be presented

Supported by Biblioteca del Congreso Nacional de Chile and ANID PIA/APOYO AFB220004.

H. Florez and M. Leon (Eds.): ICAI 2023, CCIS 1874, pp. 122–137, 2024.
https://doi.org/10.1007/978-3-031-46813-1_9

by the President or Congress members. It is then be revised by both the Senate and the Chamber of Deputies, and in most cases also by parliamentary committees, thus offering multiple opportunities for text modification, merge with other projects, revisions, and plenary debates, all of them allowing incorporation of the rainbow of ideological and thought perspectives represented in Congress. This complexity often generates a long processing time for each law, considering that each day many law proposals are submitted.

This phenomenon is so prevalent that the expression "laws sleeping in Congress" has become a metaphor to describe those bills already submitted but not yet addressed.

Chile's Library of Congress[1] has published several datasets (legal norms, parliamentary biographies, national budget, etc. [1,13,15]) as Linked Open Data (LOD) [2] that follow the FAIR principles [14] (Findable, Accessible, Interoperable, Reusable). The Chamber of Deputies and Senate also host an open data portal with legislative process data[2], which records voting on law proposals. These digitalization and availability of political and legislative data, using open data formats and semantic web technologies, bring new analysis possibilities.

With this Congress data, a novel analysis method of roll-call votes is presented to classify bills in one of four quadrants, where each quadrant defines the group behavior that Members of Congress have (ideological stance, personal interests, thematic/local interest, and technical consensus), and in turn, allows identifying latent issues associated with these types of behavior. These quadrants are established based on two main metrics, applied to each vote in the session room of a bill: political alignment (A) and polarization (P), which are both defined and calculated in a range from 0 to 100%, yielding a coordinate (A, P) which determines the quadrant to which the vote belongs.

Our proposal is to utilize the results of this analysis to identify projects that could undergo smoother processing because they have low polarization and high political alignment. Identifying these projects would allow to handle them with a simplified processing path and improve their processing time.

Although the above mention concepts of political alignment and polarization have been widely studied in political science[3], the use of semantic web technologies, and particularly its use in the field of open data, marks precedents in transparency that offer new analytical possibilities, enhancing reproducibility of results. Indeed, articles on data analysis of roll-call votes and similar topics [16–20], such as co-authorship of bills, have their focus only on sociological and political analysis, but not in the realm of process improvement.

The article continues as follows: Sect. 2 describes the data used and its acquisition method. Section 3 explains the concepts of polarization and alignment, along with the algorithms used for their calculation and the proposed quadrant logic. Section 4 details the developed data analysis. Section 5 provides a dis-

---

[1] Biblioteca del Congreso Nacional (BCN): https://www.bcn.cl.

[2] https://opendata.congreso.cl.

[3] Searching in Google Scholar by "political alignment" we found 22.100 results, and 203.000 by "political polarization".

cussion of the results, followed by Sect. 6 which presents the work conclusions. Finally, Sect. 7 discusses future work.

2   Datasets

The data of analysis (defined as a Political and Legislative Knowledge Graph), has been obtained from multiple sources, and consequently has been particularly processed and transformed for each case. The main sources of data are the Chilean Congress chambers, which have an open data portal[4] with XML Web Services and data about legislative process, as well as their own web pages. Another important source of data is the BCN Archive, specially the Political History portal and repository[5], which include parliamentarian biographies. Although these three data sources are common to both Congress chambers, they do not have a common standard or web service schema, hindering a clear and consistent integration of data published by each chamber separately. Indeed, in each chamber, Web services are published with different XML schema and details. For example, the roll-call of active senators and deputies have distinct and disjoint identifiers, and even name descriptors and dates are described under different standards and formats.

This problem also happens to other resource types, such as party membership and information about bills and voting, all of which are not integrated either (with the exception of bill number which is a functional code), and there are even restrictions on the limit of data allowed to harvest. This scenario has hampered data processing and curation.

However, thanks to an early strategic decision in 2011 [1] to adopt Semantic Web technologies in the BCN, the process of data integration has been undertaken incrementally and progressively over the years. As a result, to this day, there are several automated processes in place that facilitate data integration.

With regards to the mechanisms of data acquisition, it has been mixed, a part harvested from various XML Web services from the legislative congress open data page, as well as a web scrapping processing from the Congress chambers web pages. Once captured, the data has been curated, integrated and modeled in RDF using the Legislative Resources ontology (which includes bill voting), finally being published as Linked Open Data.

Thence, a variety of datasets and vocabularies have been published in RDF[6] at the LOD portal through its public SPARQL endpoint[7], among which are the bill voting and the biographies dataset, which are the data sources of this work.

2.1   Members of Congress and Political Parties Dataset

This dataset is composed of information from all Members of Congress and political parties that have been part of Congress since 1990. The data, published

---

[4] https://opendata.congreso.cl.

[5] https://www.bcn.cl/historiapolitica.

[6] Resource Description Framework: https://www.w3.org/RDF/.

[7] http://datos.bcn.cl/sparql.

as Linked Open Data in RDF, provides basic information about each person, their periods of membership to political parties and parliamentary positions.

Data were collected from a wiki (based on MediaWiki)[8] that includes biographical summaries of the main political actors in the nation history. This institutional wiki, developed in 2010, contains RDFa[9] marks that have been extracted and transformed into RDF triples, and subsequently the data used for analysis.

Although the database contains over 4,500 people related with the nation political history, the total number of Congress members who have participated in project voting during the period analyzed is 555.

This happens because many Congress members have been reelected in the same chamber or to the other chambers (usually from Chamber of Deputies to Senate), and because the voting record for the period is incomplete. Although this in part show the low turnover of Congress members in the last 30 years, in 2020 re-election limits where imposed [21] with retroactive effect, allowing a maximum of 2 terms of 8 years in Senate and a maximum of 3 terms of 4 years in the Chamber of Deputies.

2.2   Bills Dataset

A bill is a document presented in the National Congress, whose function is to propose a legal text to be discussed by the Congress and to create a new law. The presentation of a bill in Chile can be carried out at the initiative of the executive branch (a "Presidential Message"), or by a Congress member (a "Parliamentary Motion"). Generally speaking, each bill is recorded in legislative proceedings and enters a workflow that involves both chambers, where the proposed legal text is evaluated in full ("in general") and at its basic normative units ("in particular") by Congress members.

During this evaluation, votes are carried out to reach a consensus on the views of the lawmakers and define the final version of the law, which will be published. Processing a law involves great complexity according to its regulations, which will not be exposed in this article; the interested reader can browse the Ontology of Legislative Resources[10], which has an overview of the process in its main stages (Constitutional and Regulatory Procedures defined by *bcnres:TramiteConstitucional* and *bcnres: TramiteReglamentario* respectively), as well as various aspects that are currently processed, recorded and published as open data, including various types of entities, documents, and link properties.

Figure 1 shows the distribution, by type and year, of the bills published in RDF on the open data portal, differentiating Presidential and Congress members' initiatives. The data includes 21 bills prior to year 1990, which have been inserted in the database to digitize historical norms that are relevant or remain

---

[8] https://www.bcn.cl/historiapolitica/resenas_parlamentarias.
[9] Resource Description Framework in Attributes.
[10] https://datos.bcn.cl/ontologies/bcn-resources/doc/index.es.html.

in force, such as constitutions and other norms created during the 1973–1989 dictatorship period.

The graph shows data from 1978 onwards, although there is a bill that was created to build the history of the 1925 constitution. These data have been obtained mainly from three different sources: 1) the BCN project processing database, 2) a database created in 1990 that was replaced in 2010 by the Web services that provide the open data portal of the Congress (with which there is currently an automatic update service), and 3) by manual creation from the History of Law system [13].

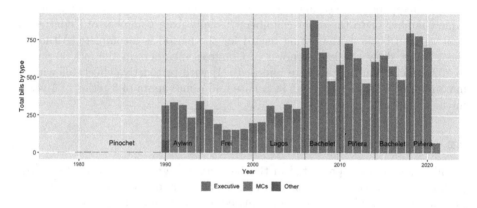

Fig. 1. Bills by type and year in the Chilean Congress

3   Polarization and Political Alignment Data Analysis

The main idea of the analysis is to characterize bills by two metrics: political alignment and polarization. For data analysis and charts we use the R language.

In this way, through SPARQL the voting events and votes of each bill are obtained, as well as the voting Members of Congress and their political party.

Based on these data, the coefficient of each vote is calculated using two algorithms:

1. Political alignment coefficient, which indicates the degree of cohesion in the vote that Members of Congress have with respect to their party (only in the context of voting).
2. Polarization coefficient, which indicates the degree to which the vote divides the group of voters into opposite poles.

Subsequently, the average values of each index are calculated for each bill, allowing the project to be characterized by a single value for each metric.

With these values at project level, a scatterplot is constructed with political alignment on the X axis and polarization on the Y axis.

Finally, on the diagram, quadrants associated with ranges are defined in the values of the indices (polarization $>= 50\%$ *high*, $<50\%$ *low*, alignment $>= 70\%$ *high*, $<70\%$ *low*), allowing four quadrants to be set.

A category has been assigned to these quadrants, which has been built inductively, taking as a reference the types of projects voted associated with each quadrant. Four categories arise:

1. **Ideological stance:** bills with high polarization and high alignment in voting; this category establishes a differentiation in the political axis between left and right, so projects voted are ideologically sorted.
2. **Personal interest:** bills with high polarization and low alignment in voting; this category establishes a differentiation between a parliamentarian and their political party, which indicates prevalence of personal interests over party principles.
3. **Thematic/local interest:** bills with low polarization and low alignment in voting; this category contains projects of thematic or local interest, so a parliamentarian is a representative of these interests, and the antagonism is against the disinterest of other Members of Congress.
4. **Technical consensus:** bills with low polarization and high alignment in voting; this category contains those projects where technical consensus was established, and with no political antagonisms in voting.

3.1   Metrics

This subsection describes the algorithms used to calculate the polarization and political alignment indexes.

Political Alignment. *Political alignment* will be defined as a characteristic that describes the degree of convergence or coincidence that occurs within a group of individuals with respect to a certain opinion.

Other variants of the political alignment (or just alignment) concept that are considered synonymous for the purposes of this article are party cohesion and party discipline [6].

This metric can be used both at the group level (political party or coalition), personal (Member of Congress depending on the group), by bill or by voting event.

In particular, in the case of Member of Congress votes on bills, the political alignment describes the degree of similarity in the votes of a group of parliamentarians from the same political party.

Stated in formal terms, we will describe the group alignment as follows:

$$A_g = \frac{\sum_{i=1}^{n} \frac{A_i * N_i}{N}}{N} = \frac{\sum_{i=1}^{n} N_i^2}{N^2} \tag{1}$$

where:

– A_g corresponds to group alignment.

- A_i corresponds to the alignment of the subgroup of individuals who voted for the option i
- N_i corresponds to the total number of individuals who voted for the option i
- N corresponds to the total number of individuals in the group.

where A_i is defined as follows:

$$A_i = \frac{N_i}{N} \tag{2}$$

where:

- A_i corresponds to the alignment within the group of those who voted for option i
- N_i corresponds to the total number of individuals who voted for option i
- N corresponds to the total number of individuals in the group.

In this way and simplifying with an example, if within the same group, in a specific vote the total number of individuals vote against, the alignment of the group is 100%, since they all vote the same.

In another hypothetical scenario, if half of the individuals from the same group (for example the same party) vote in favor, and the other half against, the group alignment is 50%, given that the group globally had an opinion divided, although internally there was alignment.

The published social science literature constantly refers to the Rice Index [7] (and variations [8]), to calculate the cohesion or degree of agreement within a voting event.

However, this indicator allows only having a single metric for a complete group under analysis (such as a political party for example), penalizing the entire group for the differences within it.

In our version of the political alignment coefficient, it is possible to associate an independent value for each person and vote, as well as for the entire project, obtaining more representative values from that perspective.

This, in turn, enables Members of Congress to be characterized through a metric associated with their alignment and the value of their vote. This offers a wider application range than the Rice-Index, without performing complex calculations.

For the cases described in the previous example but using the Rice-Index, the maximum alignment would correspond to 100%, but if the vote were divided exactly 50% within the group, the alignment value would be equal to 0%. The Fig. 2 describes the behaviour of Rice-Index, Cos-Rice-Index (variant) and Alignment metrics seen as functions.

Polarization. In the context of legislative votes, polarization will be defined as the lack of agreement on an issue, which leads to a universe of voters grouping into two politically opposed positions.

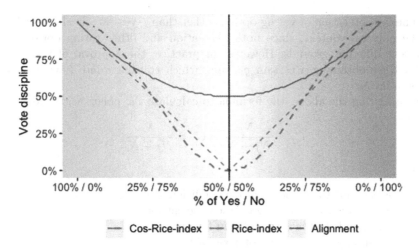

Fig. 2. Political alignment metrics behaviour

The level of polarization is maximum when there are two groups with an equivalent number of voters facing each other, while it is minimum when the voting universe votes for the same option.

The graph in Fig. 3 shows the behaviour of the polarization function when testing with different percentages of yes/no votes.

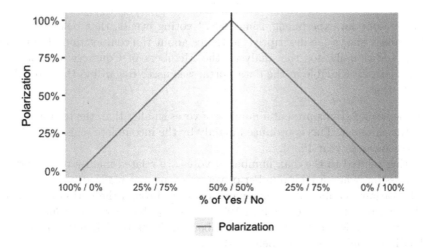

Fig. 3. Polarization metric behaviour

It is important to consider that for polarization only the extreme values (yes/no) are considered, therefore other types of votes are omitted for the calculation or normalized to one of the two options.

The interpretation of voting options other than – yes/no – is always relative to the political context, since both abstention and other voting options may represent different grounds. However, in practice, the approval of the vote is achieved by obtaining a certain *quorum*, which translates into having enough votes in favour.

Considering the above, the formula to calculate the polarization index is as follows:

$$C_f = \frac{N_f}{N_f + N_c} \wedge C_c = \frac{N_c}{N_f + N_c} \tag{3}$$

where:

- C_f corresponds to the polarization coefficient for votes in favor
- C_c corresponds to the polarization coefficient for the votes against
- N_f corresponds to the total votes in favour
- N_c corresponds to the total votes against

$$P_g = 1 - \sigma_p * \sqrt{2} \tag{4}$$

where:

- P_g corresponds to the degree of polarization within the group in voting
- σ_p corresponds to the standard deviation of the set C_f, C_c

4   Data Analysis

We have done an experiment using 15.874 voting events, that belong to 2.707 bills. Table 1 shows the descriptive statistics about the composition of data corpus[11]. Additionally, for the analysis, the Members of Congress and political parties dataset available in the data portal was used. Regarding the table data, we note that:

- Some voting events present a number of votes smaller than the total members of the chamber. This is produced mainly by the incomplete register of old bill votes (near to year 1990).
- Voting related to the max number of votes are related mainly to budget law discussion, when a high number of voting events are realized.
- The variant number of Members of Congress through the period also affects the register of votes. Indeed, in 1990 the lower chamber was formed by 120 deputies, while the Senate by 38 members. In 2020, the Chamber of deputies has 155 members and the Senate 43.

At this point, it is relevant to unveil some design decisions about the experiment:

---

[11] Data available in December 23th of 2020.

Table 1. Descriptive statistics of Roll call votes by bill in RDF

	Senate		Chamber of deputies	
	In general	*In particular*	*In general*	*In particular*
Min	4	13	39	45
1st Q	24	26	82	100
Med	29	32	99	205
Mean	35	77	153	707
3rd Q	34	53	141	507
Max	1.093	2.000	7.026	23.568
Total	57.189	52.960	439.698	726.655

- Only the types of votes Yes (+) and No (−) have been analyzed. Although there are other rarely used types, these are considered irrelevant in this experiment.
- It is possible to carry out this analysis considering general and particular votes separately, however, to simplify the experiment, both are used interchangeably.

The first thing that is possible to do is a characterization of the data under analysis.

In this sense, the graphs in Fig. 4 show in an aggregate way how the polarity and political alignment values are distributed for each camera according to the analyzed data.

When viewing the alignment and polarity distribution graphs in Fig. 4, in each of the chambers for the entire period, it is possible to affirm that in terms of political alignment, the senators have a behaviour much more aligned in their way of voting than the members of the Chamber of Deputies. Conversely, in the case of polarity, members of the Senate have a less polarizing behaviour than in the lower house.

Figure 5 shows a scatter diagram where each point represents a bill positioned in one of the four defined quadrants (similar to a Cartesian plane), according to its average polarization and alignment value.

It can be seen that the quadrant with the highest number of projects corresponds to the one with low polarization and high alignment, that is, the quadrant previously defined as *Technical Consensus*.

The way in which Members of Congress are grouped in these projects is better visualized in Fig. 6, which represents force graphs calculated with a distance function between Members of Congress given their voting form.

If the Members of Congress vote the same, their distance is 0, and if they vote differently, the distance is 1.

This calculation is performed for each voting event of the bill and for all Members of Congress, obtaining the average distance values in a bill for all pairs.

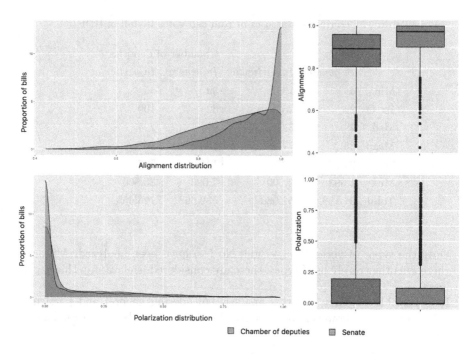

Fig. 4. Distribution of polarity in voting on bills for the Chilean Congress

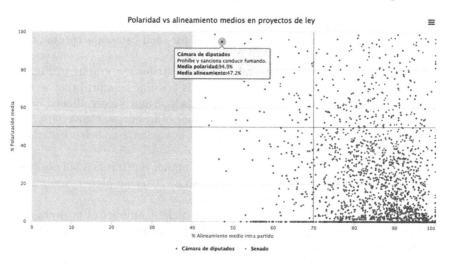

Fig. 5. Bills located in each defined quadrant

At the same time, the red and blue colours have been used to identify the Members of Congress associated with parties of the right or left.

In this way, it can be seen that in quadrant I, called *Ideological stance* (high polarization, high alignment), graphs are presented (one for each camera) where nodes of similar colour (same political tendency) are closely grouped and polarized with respect to the other group.

Discussions like the bill to decriminalize abortion[12] belong to this quadrant.

In quadrant II of *Personal interests* (high polarization, low alignment), nodes are not grouped by color, but proportionally polarized groups are displayed.

An example of bill in this quadrant is titled "Prohibit and penalize driving while smoking"[13].

In quadrant III of *Sectorial interests* (low polarization and alignment), voting has a diffuse ordering, and in fact some of them have missing votes due to absences, which may explain their lower number.

An example of this quadrant is the bill titled "Facilitate the call for municipal plebiscites"[14].

Finally, quadrant IV about *Technical consensus* (low polarization, high alignment), shows that the force graphs are gathered in only one group per chamber, and there is no equivalent distance difference in votes between Members of Congress.

An example of a bill in this quadrant is the one titled "Establish benefits for Health Sector personnel"[15].

It should be noted that for the analysis exercise, some data that did not fit with the designed tools were excluded. Examples of this are abstention-type voting, match (abstentions by pairs), non-voters due to absence, and others. However, it should be mentioned that these data do not represent a data volume greater than 2% of the total, therefore its weight is considered diluted for the experiment.

5 Discussion

Based on our method, the alignment graph in Fig. 4 shows that the Chamber of Deputies has a less disciplined behavior in voting compared to the Senate, since the trend in the distribution of the latter chamber shows a much larger bias towards 1 (fully aligned). This could be explained by various variables, such as the average age of the Members of Congress, political experience, etc.

Regarding polarization, the data distribution graph shows that although the behavior is similar in both houses, the Senate has a slightly less polarized behavior than the House of Representatives, since although in the analyzed group the Senate has less voting, shows a higher bias towards zero polarity than the Chamber of Deputies.

Regarding the analysis of bills in the context of the quadrants, the tool parsimoniously fulfills the function of characterizing each bill according to how it has been voted. Although a similar number of projects were randomly and manually analyzed (without the use of automatic text analysis) to identify a

---

[12] http://datos.bcn.cl/recurso/cl/proyecto-de-ley/9895-11.

[13] http://datos.bcn.cl/recurso/cl/proyecto-de-ley/3836-15.

[14] http://datos.bcn.cl/recurso/cl/proyecto-de-ley/4228-06.

[15] http://datos.bcn.cl/recurso/cl/proyecto-de-ley/4545-11.

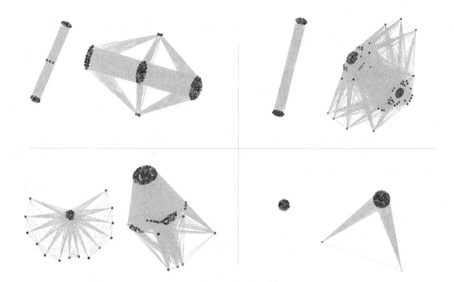

Fig. 6. Various graphs of forces of bills belonging to each quadrant

profile and conceptualize each of the four categories, it should be mentioned that in this aspect the analysis is qualitative based on inductive reasoning. However, it is considered valid to indicate that the tool can be useful for political actors, trying to predict the possible scenario that certain bills will face, with the idea of seeking strategies in advance to obtain the approval of quorums.

In the same vein, it can also be useful for the development of artificial intelligence systems associated with making political decisions, where it is necessary to incorporate weighting factors for decision-making based on historical data or associated with specific issues, or be applied to make optimizations to the legislative process, where those initiatives that will be approved more easily are identified to conduct their processing in a simplified way, and giving priority in discussion to those projects that generate greater polarization.

Notwithstanding this, by way of triangulation, the analysis agrees with other studies carried out, where the way in which legislators vote on bills has been analyzed:

- For example, in the US, when legislators vote on issues on which they do not have information [3], their decision is affected by the opinion of their voters. However, in other cases, the opinion may be influenced by interest groups, party leaders and their own preferences. This is similar to the categorization described above.
- Another study [4] suggests that congressmen can vote according to one of three motivational axes, within which are self-interest, exchange of favors and ideology. However, it is mentioned that a vote eventually indicates a direction or preference but not a vote intensity.

– An alternative perspective to this scenario is shown in another analysis [6], where the problem that arises when analyzing votes is presented when the data used is lacking in context. A scenario is presented where characteristics of the legislative work are erroneously inferred, as a result of the fact that only the roll call votes are rescued, but not those transmitted orally or that are partial, for which evidence associated with selection biases. Cases are presented about parliaments where all votes are registered, such as the US Congress, or in others where registration is on request, such as the European Parliament. A similar view is presented at [10] and at [11].

In any case, transparency in legislative votes affects the behaviour of the voters, allowing a greater citizen audit, and at the same time that the parties suffer fewer deviations compared to the case of not having public data [12].

Other analysis, such as identifying the specific parts of a norm that show greater differences based on their votes (in a project there may be few polarizing or aligned votes associated with specific articles), can be difficult in the current scenario, due to the absence of detailed descriptors in the data associated with each vote in open data format. While this information is available for download in PDF documents on the cameras' websites, obtaining, processing and publishing that part of the data is future work. However, it is considered valid to carry out the analysis at bill level, where there is both a descriptive title and the initiative text.

We consider that the potential for analysis provided by this tool and dataset is high, considering that it maintains a relatively constant growth. In addition the sets that coexist and interrelate are varied (and expanding) and they belong to a reliable and persistent source over time.

6   Conclusions

As seen through the analysis of voting data within Congress, it is possible to establish a categorization of bills based on ad-hoc defined indicators, in this case alignment and political polarization, which relate indicators to sociological categories.

From the perspective of algorithm explainability, this approach provides a clear idea for determining categories without introducing biases or hidden layers of data processing, which is of utmost importance in the political context to which it is applied.

In this way, the solution allows for an objective evaluation of the nature of a bill, taking into account implicit factors in politics (alignment and polarization) that on their own may seem like elements of analysis with limited utility for the improvement of the legislative process.

In this sense, undoubtedly the main motivation of this work is to make the legislative process more efficient, ideally allowing for the separation of the processing of projects based on their nature. This means that highly aligned and low-polarization projects can be processed more swiftly, resulting in a greater number of laws being passed. On the other hand, it enables focusing legislative efforts on projects that generate higher polarization, where there is a greater risk of legislative initiative rejection.

Considering that the legislative branch constantly bears a deteriorated image in the eyes of citizens [23][16], improvements to the process, such as those enabled by this type of analysis, contribute to enhancing the perception of trust in activities that are crucial to society but not highly regarded, such as politics.

From a data perspective, works like this, based on public information, highlight the importance of having high-quality, persistent, reliable, and readily available data. This, in turn, allows for the replication or repetition of experiments, which is particularly crucial today as it serves as one of the pillars of science and governmental accountability. It helps reduce corruption, enhances accountability, and strengthens democracy by enabling voters to make better-informed decisions [22].

7 Future Work

One of the areas we will focus on to continue and improve our work is modifying the way we establish quadrant boundaries. Currently, these boundaries are primarily defined geometrically, but we aim to shift towards a supervised training approach. This involves including the classification of bills by expert users and training a classifier that allows us to determine which quadrant a project falls into based on its characteristics, such as text, type of initiative, political tendencies of the authors, among others.

References

1. Cifuentes-Silva, F., Sifaqui, C., Labra-Gayo, J.: Towards an architecture and adoption process for linked data technologies in open government contexts. In: Proceedings of the 7th International Conference on Semantic Systems - I-Semantics 2011, pp. 79–86 (2011)
2. Berners-Lee, T.: Linked data-design issues (W3C). http://www.w3.org/DesignIssues/LinkedData.html
3. Butler, D., Nickerson, D., et al.: Can learning constituency opinion affect how legislators vote? Results from a field experiment. Q. J. Polit. Sci. **6**, 55–83 (2011)
4. Kau, J., Rubin, P.: Self-interest, ideology, and logrolling in congressional voting. J. Law Econ. **22**, 365–384 (1979)
5. Taylor, A.: Bill passage speed in the US house: a test of a vote buying model of the legislative process. J. Legis. Stud. **20**, 285–304 (2014)
6. Hug, S.: Selection effects in roll call votes. Br. J. Polit. Sci. **40**, 225–235 (2010). http://www.jstor.org/stable/40649430
7. Rice, S.: Quantitative methods in politics. J. Am. Stat. Assoc. **33**, 126–130 (1938)
8. Desposato, S.: Comparing group and subgroup cohesion scores: a nonparametric method with an application to Brazil. Polit. Anal. **11**, 275–288 (2003). http://www.jstor.org/stable/25791733

---

[16] https://ourworldindata.org/corruption#what-institutions-do-people-perceive-as-most-corrupt.

9. Lu, X., Gao, J., Szymanski, B.: The evolution of polarization in the legislative branch of government. J. Roy. Soc. Interface **16**, 20190010 (2019). https://royalsocietypublishing.org/doi/abs/10.1098/rsif.2019.0010

10. Roberts, J.: The statistical analysis of roll-call data: a cautionary tale. Legis. Stud. Q. **32**, 341–360 (2007), https://onlinelibrary.wiley.com/doi/abs/10.3162/036298007781699636

11. Poole, K., Rosenthal, H.: A spatial model for legislative roll call analysis. Am. J. Polit. Sci. **29**, 357–384 (1985). http://www.jstor.org/stable/2111172

12. Benesch, C., Bütler, M., Hofer, K.: Transparency in parliamentary voting. J. Public Econ. **163**, 60–76 (2018). http://www.sciencedirect.com/science/article/pii/S0047272718300604

13. Cifuentes-Silva, F., Labra Gayo, J.E.: Legislative document content extraction based on semantic web technologies. In: Hitzler, P., et al. (eds.) ESWC 2019. LNCS, vol. 11503, pp. 558–573. Springer, Cham (2019). https://doi.org/10.1007/978-3-030-21348-0_36

14. Wilkinson, M., et al.: The FAIR guiding principles for scientific data management and stewardship. Sci. Data **3**, 1–9 (2016)

15. Cifuentes-Silva, F., Fernández-Álvarez, D., Labra-Gayo, J.: National budget as linked open data: new tools for supporting the sustainability of public finances. Sustainability **12**, 4551 (2020). https://doi.org/10.3390/su12114551

16. Alemán, E.: Policy positions in the Chilean senate: an analysis of coauthorship and roll call data. Braz. Polit. Sci. Rev. (Online) **3** (2008)

17. Alemán, E., Calvo, E., Jones, M., Kaplan, N.: Comparing cosponsorship and roll-call ideal points. Legis. Stud. Q. **34**, 87–116 (2009)

18. Campos-Parra, H., Navia, P.: I won't scratch your back and you won't scratch mine. Cohesion in roll call votes in the chamber of deputies in Chile, 2006–2014. Colomb. Int. 171–197 (2020)

19. Toro-Maureira, S., Hurtado, N.: The executive on the battlefield: government amendments and cartel theory in the Chilean congress. J. Legis. Stud. **22**, 196–215 (2016)

20. Le Foulon Moran, C.: Cooperation and polarization in a presidential congress: policy networks in the Chilean lower house 2006–2017. Politics **40**, 227–244 (2020)

21. Presidencia, M.: Ley 21238 - reforma constitucional para limitar la reelección de las autoridades que indica (2020). https://www.leychile.cl/navegar?idNorma=1147301

22. Höffner, K., Martin, M., Lehmann, J.: LinkedSpending: openspending becomes linked open data. Semant. Web **7**, 95–104 (2016)

23. Ortiz-Ospina, E., Roser, M.: Corruption. Our World in Data (2016). https://ourworldindata.org/corruption

Utilizing Chatbots as Predictive Tools for Anxiety and Depression: A Bibliometric Review

María de Lourdes Díaz Carrillo$^{(\boxtimes)}$ ⓘ, Manuel Osmany Ramírez Pírez ⓘ, and Gustavo Adolfo Lemos Chang ⓘ

Universidad Ecotec, Samborondón, Ecuador
{mariadiaz,glemos}@est.ecotec.edu.ec, mramirez@ecotec.edu.ec

Abstract. This article addresses the impact of the implementation of medical chatbots as a tool to predict mental health disorders on society, focusing on the high prevalence of depression and anxiety worldwide. The promising potential of AI and psychological software agents, such as chatbots, to improve psychological well-being in the digital environment is highlighted. In order to analyze the scientific production related to the use of virtual assistants in the prediction of anxiety and depression, a comprehensive bibliometric review was conducted using the Scopus database. Subsequently, the study reveals the growing interest in medical chatbot development and research, notably from Australia, China, and the United States, which have made significant contributions. It identifies influential articles, authors, and journals that have significantly shaped this research domain. The analysis also underscores recurring keywords, with "depression" and "anxiety" emerging as central themes. This underscores their paramount importance in chatbot-based mental health prediction efforts and their potential to address these widespread mental health challenges. In conclusion, this article emphasizes chatbots' promising role in enhancing mental well-being through accessible, personalized support. While acknowledging inherent study limitations, it also points to prospective research directions. As technological advancements persist, chatbots are poised to play a pivotal role in promoting better global mental health outcomes.

Keywords: Mental health · Software · Anxiety · Depression · Well-being · Accessibility · Empathy · Interaction · Chatbots

1 Introduction

Mental health disorders can have a significant impact on society, affecting over 264 million people in the case of depression alone, while anxiety represents a concerning 3.76% of the global population [1]. Furthermore, depression is one of the leading causes of disability. In the working-age population, anxiety and depression are widely prevalent mental disorders worldwide, which can result in high rates of sick leave and impaired work performance [2].

© The Author(s), under exclusive license to Springer Nature Switzerland AG 2024
H. Florez and M. Leon (Eds.): ICAI 2023, CCIS 1874, pp. 138–153, 2024.
https://doi.org/10.1007/978-3-031-46813-1_10

In the current digital landscape, new solutions are being explored to address these issues and enhance psychological well-being. In this context, psychological software agents emerge as a promising tool that provides self-help interventions in digital environments [3].

These agents are designed to offer personalized support and guidance, giving individuals the opportunity to effectively manage and address their anxiety and depression. Leveraging technological advancements, psychological software agents can play a crucial role in promoting mental health and well-being [4]. Furthermore, their accessible and personalized nature makes them an appealing choice for those seeking to improve their emotional health.

By offering an innovative and tailored approach to individual needs, psychological software agents provide individuals with a practical and convenient tool to address their emotional challenges. As technology continues to evolve, these systems are expected to play an increasingly important role in mental healthcare and the promotion of greater emotional well-being [5]. These technological solutions offer an innovative opportunity to address emotional disorders in an accessible and convenient manner, providing support and resources to those in need in a digital format that caters to their needs and preferences [6].

In recent years, chatbot technology, mixed with AI techniques, has emerged as a promising tool for the early prediction of anxiety and depression disorders. Research in this field has underscored the importance of considering multiple factors when adopting digital mental healthcare technologies. Various studies have provided valuable insights into the design of human-machine communication-based interventions, emphasizing the need for personalization and adaptability to address individual user needs. [7]. These studies have also explored crucial aspects such as empathy and the quality of interaction in the user-technology relationship.

In this context, the study conducted by D. Y. Park and H. Kim [8] has provided valuable insights. Their findings offer practical guidelines for optimizing the effectiveness of zero-contact interventions and enhancing the user experience. With the continuous advancement of technology, virtual assistants are expected to play an increasingly relevant role in the early prediction and support of anxiety and depression disorders. The integration of these tools into digital mental health care environments opens new possibilities to reach a larger number of individuals and provide them with the necessary support for their emotional well-being [9]. For example, mental health chatbots were found to be an effective tool for managing depressive symptoms in young adults during the COVID-19 pandemic [10], offering an accessible and promising intervention option in times of need [11].

The results of a study conducted in India demonstrated that a conversational bot was able to effectively identify participants exhibiting symptoms of depression, suggesting that this technology could have a promising role in the early prediction of depression [12]. This non-clinical approach to early depression prediction using a conversational bot may have significant implications for early identification of depression and improving mental health outcomes in the population.

As time goes on, the development of technology is being considering the efficacy levels of virtual mental health assistants in identifying and supporting symptoms of anxiety and depression in various contexts, such as healthcare and psychotherapy[13]. Additionally, different motivating factors have been identified, such as comfort in interaction, reliability, and the absence of judgment during dialogue. These investigations have also revealed that the social role played by virtual assistants has a significant impact on the perception of the relationship between the user and the system, as well as on usage intentions [14]. For example, virtual assistants that adopt the role of a companion were perceived as more pleasant and trustworthy, resulting in a greater willingness to use them [15].

However, key interaction factors must be maintained, as studies have shown that low engagement can occur when applications are not user-centric or fail to address the user's most pressing concerns [16–18]. The lack of interactive or engaging features can also increase the risk of survey fatigue, where users become tired and fail to complete the assigned series of psychological questions [19].

This study draws inspiration from the search for an ideal chatbot system that offers appropriate emotional support to users and provides a comprehensive and sensitive virtual counseling environment, with a focus on empathy and sentiment analysis in chatbot development to enhance the quality of interaction and effectiveness of virtual counseling [20]. This innovative, technology-based approach demonstrates the potential of mental health chatbots as an effective tool for personalized behavioral activation and remote monitoring of mental health in the population [21].

This article will conduct a comprehensive bibliometric review of the scientific literature on the use of chatbots for the prediction of anxiety and depression. Through a structured and rigorous approach, relevant studies in this field will be identified, selected, and analyzed. Bibliometric techniques, such as co-citation analysis and keyword analysis, will be applied to obtain a detailed understanding of the knowledge network and current trends. The aim of this review is to provide a comprehensive and up-to-date overview of the state-of-the-art in the use of chatbots for the prediction of anxiety and depression, offering valuable insights for healthcare professionals, researchers, and technology developers. The findings will contribute to the advancement of knowledge in this rapidly growing field and serve as a foundation for future research in digital mental health.

2 Methodology

The research proposal has been conducted through a bibliometric review with the aim of analyzing the scientific production on chatbots for the prediction of anxiety and depression, identifying trends and gaps to provide relevant information for healthcare professionals and technology developers.

To achieve this objective, the following methodological steps are followed:

1. Database identification: Scopus is selected as the main database to retrieve relevant scientific literature in the field of chatbots used for anxiety and depression detection. Its strengths include its broad coverage, rigorous selection of high-quality data, capability for complex searches, provision of citation metrics, and integration with other tools. These features make Scopus a valuable tool for analyzing research trends, evaluating publication and author influence, and facilitating bibliometric analysis in the scientific community [22].
2. Definition of search criteria: The title category search function in Scopus was used with the key terms "Depression" or "anxiety" or "chatbot" or "interface". These terms were selected based on their relevance to the study topic.
3. Application of inclusion criteria: Inclusion criteria were applied to limit the search results. The following criteria were selected: "Open access" to access open-access articles, "last 10 years" to obtain the most up-to-date literature, "article" as the document type, and "English" as the publication language.
4. Data export: The available article data that met these criteria were selected and exported. This data included information such as the article title, authors, publication year, and journal.
5. Information processing: The exported data from Scopus was used as input in the Bibliometrix tool, which is a bibliometric analysis tool in the R programming environment [23]. This tool allowed for detailed analysis, including techniques such as co-citation analysis and keyword analysis.
6. Results Analysis with Python: In addition to the bibliometric analysis conducted with Bibliometrix, Python codes were developed using the Matplotlib library for generating visual graphs [24] and Pandas for data processing and generating statistical reports [25]. Collectively, these Python libraries enhance the capabilities of bibliometric analysis by providing flexible and powerful tools for visualizing, processing, and analyzing the obtained results.

In the realm of medical chatbots for anxiety and depression prediction, several critical questions drive our understanding. These dimensions span across geographical comparisons, publication frequencies worldwide, influential scientific contributions, prevalent research themes, notable researchers, trusted sources, and temporal trends. Together, they provide a comprehensive view of the current state and evolving dynamics in this critical field of study.

- What does the comparative analysis between Australia and China reveal about the trends in the production of articles on medical chatbots for predicting anxiety and depression?
- Which regions of the world have the highest publication frequencies in the field of medical chatbots for predicting anxiety and depression, according to the comparative analysis?
- What are the key findings from the analysis of citations and citation frequency in prominent scientific articles?
- What are the most prevalent keywords and recurring concepts in research related to the prediction of anxiety and depression through medical chatbots?

- Who are the prominent local authors in the field of research on anxiety and depression prediction through medical chatbots?
- Which scientific journals are prominent sources in the field of research on anxiety and depression prediction through medical chatbots?
- What are the trends in research topics regarding anxiety and depression through medical chatbots over time?

3   Analysis and Results

The analysis in this study is based on the provided CSV table reports from the Bibliometrix portal. The purpose is to conduct a thorough examination of these data, focusing on several key aspects such as the frequency of specific words used in the reports, the citation patterns of local authors, the relevant sources utilized, and the emerging topics that reflect production trends. Through this extensive analysis, we aim to obtain a deep understanding of the dynamics and patterns that characterize production across different countries. This valuable information can contribute significantly to decision-making processes and the identification of potential opportunities in this field.

3.1   Trends in the Production of Articles on Medical Chatbots for the Prediction of Anxiety and Depression: A Comparative Analysis Between Australia and China

Inspecting the provided Fig. 1, the production of articles related to medical chatbots measuring levels of anxiety and depression in two specific countries, Australia, and China, can be observed.

In the case of Australia, there is a progressive increase in article production over the years. In 2014, 179 articles were recorded, while in 2022, the highest number was reached with 1775 articles. This steady increase indicates a growing interest in the development and research of medical chatbots for the prediction of anxiety and depression in the country.

As for China, only one value is recorded for the year 2014, with 134 articles related to medical chatbots for the prediction of anxiety and depression. From this information, there is no subsequent data available to assess the evolution of production in this country.

These results suggest that Australia has been a more active country in the research and development of medical chatbots for the prediction of anxiety and depression compared to China, at least in the analyzed period. It is important to note that this analysis is based solely on the quantity of articles and not on their quality or impact.

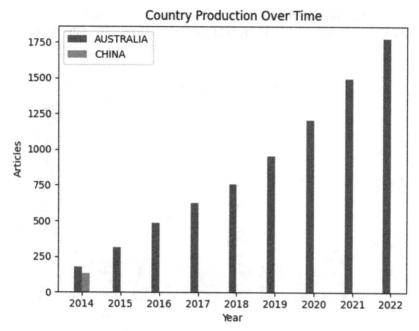

Fig. 1. Country production over time.

3.2   Comparative Analysis of the Production of Articles on Medical Chatbots for the Prediction of Anxiety and Depression in Different Regions of the World

Evaluating Fig. 2, we can observe the frequency of publications related to medical chatbots capable of measuring levels of anxiety and depression across different regions of the world. These data provide a broader perspective on the production and interest in this research area in various countries.

First and foremost, the United States (USA) stands out as the region with the highest publication frequency, boasting a total of 6,627 articles focusing on medical chatbots for predicting anxiety and depression. This figure highlights the leadership and prominence of the United States in driving research in this field.

Coming in second place, China exhibits significant frequency with 4,762 publications, indicating a high level of interest and activity in exploring medical chatbots for the prediction of anxiety and depression within the country.

The United Kingdom (UK) takes the third spot with 2,913 publications, followed closely by Australia with 1,775 publications. These two countries demonstrate substantial production levels compared to other regions.

Other notable countries such as the Netherlands, Turkey, Canada, Iran, Brazil, and Germany also exhibit considerable publication frequencies, albeit to a lesser extent when compared to the previously mentioned countries. These results underscore the global reach of research on medical chatbots for predicting anxiety and depression, with notable contributions from the United States and China. Furthermore, they reflect the widespread interest and activity in this field across diverse regions of the world.

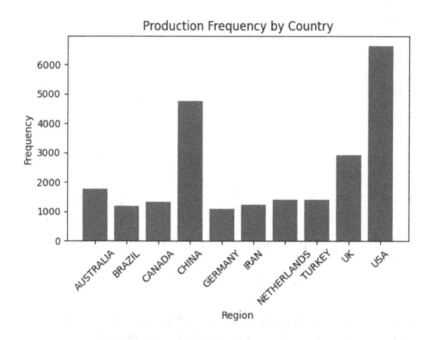

Fig. 2. Production frequency by country.

3.3   Analysis of Citations and Citation Frequency in Prominent Scientific Articles

Table 1 provides information on the total number of citations and the citation frequency per year for a series of scientific articles. Additionally, it includes the normalization of total citations, which represents the average citations per year for each article.

Firstly, the article "GRIFFITHS RR, 2016, J PSYCHOPHARMACOL" stands out with a total of 817 citations, indicating that it has been widely recognized and cited in scientific literature. This article also demonstrates a high citation frequency per year, with an average of 102.13 citations annually. Its total normalized citation score is 18.45, suggesting a significant influence in the field of study [26].

Another notable article is "STANTON R, 2020, INT J ENVIRON RES PUBLIC HEALTH" with a total of 728 citations and a citation frequency per year of 182. This article demonstrates a high citation rate per year, indicating ongoing relevance and impact in the research field. The total normalized citation score is 26.31, confirming its prominent influence in the field. Additionally, it can be observed that most articles in the table have a considerable number of citations and citation frequency per year, indicating that they have been widely recognized and cited in scientific literature [27].

Table 1. Citations and citation frequencies

Paper	Doi	Total Citations	Tc Per Year	Normalized Tc
Griffiths Rr, 2016, J Psychopharmacol (Griffiths et al., 2016)	https://doi.org/ 10.1177/026 9881116675513	817	102.13	18.45
Stanton R, 2020, Int J Environ Res Public Health (Stanton et al., 2020)	https://doi.org/ 10.3390/ijerph 17114065	728	182	26.31
Fitzpatrick Kk, 2017, Jmir Ment Heal (Fitzpatrick et al., 2017)	https://doi.org/ 10.2196/mental. 7785	725	103.57	20.21
Mazza Mg, 2020, Brain Behav Immun(Mazza et al., 2020)	https://doi.org/ 10.1016/j.bbi. 2020.07.037	708	177	25.58
Özdin S, 2020, Int J Soc Psychiatry[30]	https://doi.org/ 10.1177/002 0764020927051	688	172	24.86
Demirci K, 2015, J Behav Addict(Demirci et al., 2015)	https://doi.org/ 10.1556/2006. 4.2015.010	678	75.33	16.15
Ross S, 2016, J Psychopharmacol(Ross et al., 2016)	https://doi.org/ 10.1177/026 9881116675512	677	84.63	15.29
Chisholm D, 2016, Lancet Psychiatry(Chisholm et al., 2016)	https://doi.org/ 10.1016/S2215-0366(16)300 24-4	651	81.38	14.7
Santini Zi, 2020, Lancet Public Health(Santini et al., 2020)	https://doi.org/ 10.1016/S2468-2667(19)302 30-0	633	158.25	22.87
Liu Ch, 2020, Psychiatry Res (Liu et al., 2020)	https://doi.org/ 10.1016/j.psy chres.2020. 113172	612	153	22.12

3.4 Analysis of Keywords in Research on Anxiety and Depression Prediction Through Medical Chatbots

By examining Fig. 3, we can analyze the most prevalent words found in articles related to the prediction of anxiety and depression through medical chatbots. These data unveil the key terms and recurring concepts that are prominent in research within this field.

Topping the list is the word "depression" with 9217 occurrences, indicating its central focus and extensive investigation when it comes to medical chatbots and their predictive capabilities regarding anxiety and depression. The repeated use of the word "depression" underscores its significance in mental health discussions. It highlights the potential of chatbots and psychological software agents in addressing depression and other mental health challenges. This repetition also emphasizes the need for research and awareness surrounding depression. Overall, it emphasizes the central role of depression in the context of mental health and the potential of technology-based solutions like chatbots.

Following closely is the word "anxiety" with 7731 occurrences, signifying the significance and emphasis placed on analyzing anxiety within the context of medical chatbots.

The terms "female" and "male" appear with 6341 and 5671 occurrences, respectively, highlighting the interest in examining gender differences concerning anxiety and depression. The term "adult" surfaces with 5043 occurrences, suggesting that a substantial portion of the research revolves around predicting anxiety and depression in adults. The word "human" appears 4547 times, indicating the attention given to the interaction between chatbots and human users in the realm of anxiety and depression prediction.

Other noteworthy terms include "article" with 3702 occurrences, "humans" with 3323 occurrences, "middle aged" with 2848 occurrences, and "major clinical study" with 2552 occurrences. These terms shed light on aspects such as scientific publications,

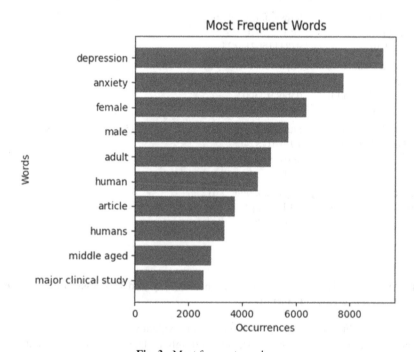

Fig. 3. Most frequent words.

the target population, and the significance of conducting major clinical studies in this specific area of research.

3.5 Prominent Local Authors in Research on Anxiety and Depression Prediction Through Medical Chatbots

Analyzing Fig. 4, the most cited local authors in articles related to anxiety and depression prediction through medical chatbots can be identified. These data provide insight into researchers whose work has had a significant influence in this field.

The author "WANG Y" stands out with 63 articles and a fraction of 8.86, indicating that their contributions have been significant and widely cited in relation to anxiety and depression prediction using medical chatbots. Another prominent author is "LI Y" with 51 articles and a fraction of 7.88, demonstrating their relevance and significant contribution in this research domain. "ZHANG Y" and "LIU X" are also notable authors, with 41 and 40 articles respectively, and fractions of 5.85 and 6.08. Their work has been recognized and cited in relation to anxiety and depression prediction through medical chatbots. Additionally, "ZHANG L," "LI J," and "WANG X" have made significant contributions with 40, 39, and 39 articles respectively, and fractions of 6.44, 5.37, and 5.12.

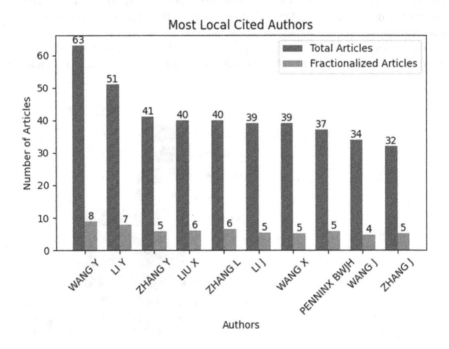

Fig. 4. Most local cited author.

Other authors such as "PENNINX BWJH," "WANG J," and "ZHANG J" have also been acknowledged in this field with 37, 34, and 32 articles respectively, and fractions of 5.69, 4.79, and 5.24.

3.6 Prominent Scientific Journals in Research on Anxiety and Depression Prediction Through Medical Chatbots

Reviewing Fig. 5, which showcases relevant sources in the context of articles on anxiety and depression prediction through medical chatbots, prominent scientific journals and publications in this research field can be identified.

The journal "PLOS ONE" leads the list with 192 articles, indicating its relevance and widespread dissemination in this area. It is closely followed by the "INTERNATIONAL JOURNAL OF ENVIRONMENTAL RESEARCH AND PUBLIC HEALTH" with 188 articles, highlighting its significance as a research source in the field.

Other scientific journals such as "FRONTIERS IN PSYCHIATRY" with 157 articles, "FRONTIERS IN PSYCHOLOGY" with 137 articles, and "JOURNAL OF AFFECTIVE DISORDERS" with 135 articles also stand out as relevant sources in this field.

Additionally, "BMC PSYCHIATRY" has 132 articles, "BMJ OPEN" has 59 articles, "DEPRESSION AND ANXIETY" has 57 articles, "SCIENTIFIC REPORTS" has 52 articles, and "NEUROPSYCHIATRIC DISEASE AND TREATMENT" has 45 articles, demonstrating their significant contribution to the scientific literature related to anxiety and depression prediction through medical chatbots.

These sources represent a wide range of renowned scientific journals in the field of mental health and psychology. Their high publication frequency on this topic indicates

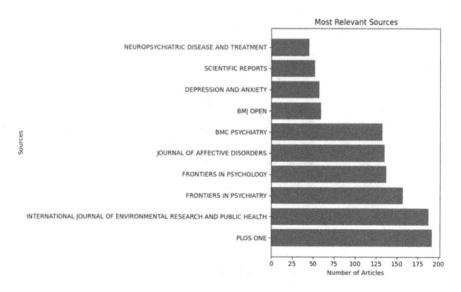

Fig. 5. Most relevant sources.

the interest and importance placed on research in anxiety and depression prediction using medical chatbots.

3.7   Trends in Research Topics on Anxiety and Depression Through Medical Chatbots Over Time

Analyzing the trends in research topics regarding anxiety and depression through medical chatbots over time reveals interesting patterns. The analysis of Fig. 6, depicting trending topics, reveals intriguing patterns in research themes on anxiety and depression throughout the studied years. In 2014, there was a notable interest in topics related to questionnaires, inventories, and assessment scales, as well as the concept of time. These subjects captured researchers' attention during that period.

Regarding specific topics, notable areas of focus include the study of motor activity, adaptive behavior, and postpartum depression in 2014 [36, 37]. These topics continued to be investigated in subsequent years, indicating sustained interest in understanding and addressing these areas. Starting from 2015, new relevant topics emerged, such as cognitive therapy, statistical analysis and numerical data, and exploratory behavior [38, 39]. These topics remained areas of interest until 2017 or 2018, indicating their importance in scientific research.

Lastly, it is noteworthy that depressive disorder was the most investigated and recurrent topic throughout the studied years, particularly in 2015, 2017, and 2018. This demonstrates the ongoing attention and dedication towards the study of this specific disorder.

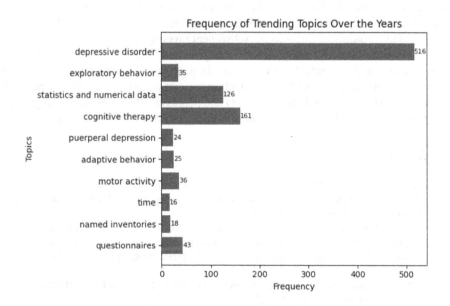

Fig. 6. Frequency of trending topics.

4 Conclusions

Following a comprehensive and rigorous analysis of the data obtained in this study, several notable conclusions can be drawn regarding the research question at hand. Primarily, the results unequivocally establish the validity of the hypothesis by confirming the causal link between the independent and dependent variables. The observed effects exhibit statistical significance and consistency, thereby providing robust support for the underlying theory and reinforcing the existing theoretical framework within the field of study.

The advancements in psychological software agents and chatbot technology have generated considerable interest due to their potential in addressing anxiety and depression, two prevalent mental health disorders affecting a substantial global population. These tools offer personalized support and guidance, empowering individuals to effectively manage their emotional well-being.

The utilization of psychological software agents and chatbots offers significant advantages, notably in terms of accessibility and convenience. These technologies enable individuals to access resources and support at any time and from any location, thereby obliterating geographical barriers and alleviating the economic burdens associated with mental health care. Moreover, engaging with a chatbot can create a less daunting and more comfortable environment for certain individuals, thereby facilitating help-seeking behaviors and fostering open communication regarding their emotions and concerns.

Conversely, the study has revealed limitations and identified potential avenues for future research. Despite concerted efforts to minimize biases and errors, it is imperative to acknowledge the inherent limitations of the employed methodology, such as sample size and the generalizability of findings to broader populations. Furthermore, specific thematic areas warranting further analysis and exploration have been elucidated, which may provide promising directions for subsequent investigations.

It is expected that psychological software agents and chatbots will assume an increasingly pivotal role in mental health care and the promotion of emotional well-being in the foreseeable future. As technological advancements persist, these tools are poised to be leveraged for early prediction of anxiety and depression disorders, facilitating timely interventions, and enhancing mental health outcomes across the population.

References

1. Ahmed, A., Ali, N., Aziz, S., et al.: A review of mobile chatbot apps for anxiety and depression and their self-care features. Comput. Methods Prog. Biomed. Update **1**, 100012 (2021). https://doi.org/10.1016/j.cmpbup.2021.100012
2. Hermosa-Bosano, C., Paz, C., Hidalgo-Andrade, P., et al.: Depression, anxiety and stress symptoms experienced by the ecuadorian general population during the pandemic for covid-19. Revista Ecuatoriana de Neurologia **30**, 40–47 (2021). https://doi.org/10.46997/revecuatneurol30200040
3. Wilson, L., Marasoiu, M.: The Development and Use of Chatbots in Public Health: Scoping Review. JMIR Hum. Factors **9** (2022)
4. Goonesekera, Y., Donkin, L.: A cognitive behavioral therapy chatbot (OTIS) for Health anxiety management: mixed methods pilot study. JMIR Form. Res. **6**, e37877 (2022). https://doi.org/10.2196/37877

5. Bendig, E., Erb, B., Meißner, D., et al.: Feasibility of a Software agent providing a brief Intervention for Self-help to Uplift psychological wellbeing ("SISU"). A single-group pretest-posttest trial investigating the potential of SISU to act as therapeutic agent. Internet Interv. **24** (2021). https://doi.org/10.1016/j.invent.2021.100377

6. Nicol, G., Wang, R., Graham, S., et al.: Chatbot-delivered cognitive behavioral therapy in adolescents with depression and anxiety during the COVID-19 pandemic: feasibility and acceptability study. JMIR Form. Res. **6**, e40242 (2022). https://doi.org/10.2196/40242

7. Yu, C.S., Hsu, M.H., Wang, Y.C., You, Y.J.: Designing a chatbot for helping parenting practice. Appl. Sci. (Switz.) **13**, 1793 (2023). https://doi.org/10.3390/app13031793

8. Park, D.Y., Kim, H.: Determinants of intentions to use digital mental healthcare content among university students, faculty, and staff: motivation, perceived usefulness, perceived ease of use, and parasocial interaction with AI chatbot. Sustain. (Switz.) **15**, 872 (2023). https://doi.org/10.3390/su15010872

9. Grové, C.: Co-developing a mental health and wellbeing chatbot with and for young people. Front Psychiatry **11**, 606041 (2021). https://doi.org/10.3389/fpsyt.2020.606041

10. Jiang, Q., Zhang, Y., Pian, W.: Chatbot as an emergency exist: mediated empathy for resilience via human-AI interaction during the COVID-19 pandemic. Inf. Process. Manage. **59**, 103074 (2022). https://doi.org/10.1016/j.ipm.2022.103074

11. He, Y., Yang, L., Zhu, X., et al.: Mental health chatbot for young adults with depressive symptoms during the COVID-19 pandemic: single-blind, three-arm randomized controlled trial. J. Med. Internet Res. **24**, e40719 (2022). https://doi.org/10.2196/40719

12. Kaywan, P., Ahmed, K., Ibaida, A., et al.: Early detection of depression using a conversational AI bot: a non-clinical trial. PLoS ONE **18**, e0279743 (2023). https://doi.org/10.1371/journal.pone.0279743

13. Jungmann, S.M., Klan, T., Kuhn, S., Jungmann, F.: Accuracy of a chatbot (ADA) in the diagnosis of mental disorders: comparative case study with lay and expert users. JMIR Form. Res. **3**, e13863 (2019). https://doi.org/10.2196/13863

14. Nißen, M., Rüegger, D., Stieger, M., et al.: The effects of health care chatbot personas with different social roles on the client-chatbot bond and usage intentions: development of a design codebook and web-based study. J. Med. Internet Res. **24**, e32630 (2022). https://doi.org/10.2196/32630

15. Lin, A.P.C., Trappey, C.V., Luan, C.C., et al.: A test platform for managing school stress using a virtual reality group chatbot counseling system. Appl. Sci. (Switz.) **11**, 9071 (2021). https://doi.org/10.3390/app11199071

16. Hungerbuehler, I., Daley, K., Cavanagh, K., et al.: Chatbot-based assessment of employees' mental health: design process and pilot implementation. JMIR Form. Res. **5**, e21678 (2021). https://doi.org/10.2196/21678

17. You, Y., Gui, X.: Self-diagnosis through AI-enabled chatbot-based symptom checkers: user experiences and design considerations. AMIA Annu. Symp. Proc. **2020**, 1354–1363 (2020)

18. Zhang, R., Li, F., Li, Y.: Design of a rehabilitation training system for older adults with mild cognitive impairment. In: Proceedings - 2018 11th International Symposium on Computational Intelligence and Design, ISCID 2018, vol. 2, pp. 107–110 (2018). https://doi.org/10.1109/ISCID.2018.10125

19. Ollier, J., Neff, S., Dworschak, C., et al.: Elena+ care for COVID-19, a pandemic lifestyle care intervention: intervention design and study protocol. Front. Public Health **9**, 625640 (2021). https://doi.org/10.3389/fpubh.2021.625640

20. Trappey, A.J.C., Lin, A.P.C., Hsu, K.Y.K., et al.: Development of an empathy-centric counseling chatbot system capable of sentimental dialogue analysis. Processes **10**, 930 (2022). https://doi.org/10.3390/pr10050930

21. Rathnayaka, P., Mills, N., Burnett, D., et al.: A mental health chatbot with cognitive skills for personalised behavioural activation and remote health monitoring. Sensors **22**, 3653 (2022). https://doi.org/10.3390/s22103653

22. Zyoud, S.H., Shakhshir, M., Abushanab, A.S., et al.: Bibliometric mapping of the landscape and structure of nutrition and depression research: visualization analysis. J. Health Popul. Nutr. **42**, 33 (2023). https://doi.org/10.1186/s41043-023-00378-2

23. Aria, M., Cuccurullo, C.: Bibliometrix: an R-tool for comprehensive science mapping analysis. J. Informetr. **11**, 959–975 (2017). https://doi.org/10.1016/j.joi.2017.08.007

24. Hunter, J.D.: Matplotlib: a 2D graphics environment. Comput. Sci. Eng. **9**, 90–95 (2007). https://doi.org/10.1109/MCSE.2007.55

25. McKinney, W., et al.: Data structures for statistical computing in python. In: Proceedings of the 9th Python in Science Conference, pp. 51–56 (2010)

26. Griffiths, R.R., Johnson, M.W., Carducci, M.A., et al.: Psilocybin produces substantial and sustained decreases in depression and anxiety in patients with life-threatening cancer: a randomized double-blind trial. J. Psychopharmacol. **30**, 1181–1197 (2016). https://doi.org/10.1177/0269881116675513

27. Stanton, R., To, Q.G., Khalesi, S., et al.: Depression, anxiety and stress during COVID-19: associations with changes in physical activity, sleep, tobacco and alcohol use in Australian adults. Int. J. Environ. Res. Public Health **17**, 1–13 (2020). https://doi.org/10.3390/ijerph171 14065

28. Fitzpatrick, K.K., Darcy, A., Vierhile, M.: Delivering cognitive behavior therapy to young adults with symptoms of depression and anxiety using a fully automated conversational agent (Woebot): a randomized controlled trial. JMIR Ment Health **4**, e778 (2017). https://doi.org/10.2196/mental.7785

29. Mazza, M.G., De Lorenzo, R., Conte, C., et al.: Anxiety and depression in COVID-19 survivors: role of inflammatory and clinical predictors. Brain Behav. Immun. **89**, 594–600 (2020). https://doi.org/10.1016/j.bbi.2020.07.037

30. Özdin, S., Bayrak Özdin, Ş: Levels and predictors of anxiety, depression and health anxiety during COVID-19 pandemic in Turkish society: the importance of gender. Int. J. Soc. Psychiatry **66**, 504–511 (2020). https://doi.org/10.1177/0020764020927051

31. Demirci, K., Akgönül, M., Akpinar, A.: Relationship of smartphone use severity with sleep quality, depression, and anxiety in university students. J. Behav. Addict. **4**, 85–92 (2015). https://doi.org/10.1556/2006.4.2015.010

32. Ross, S., Bossis, A., Guss, J., et al.: Rapid and sustained symptom reduction following psilocybin treatment for anxiety and depression in patients with life-threatening cancer: a randomized controlled trial. J. Psychopharmacol. **30**, 1165–1180 (2016). https://doi.org/10.1177/026988 1116675512

33. Chisholm, D., Sweeny, K., Sheehan, P., et al.: Scaling-up treatment of depression and anxiety: a global return on investment analysis. Lancet Psychiatry **3**, 415–424 (2016). https://doi.org/10.1016/S2215-0366(16)30024-4

34. Santini, Z.I., Jose, P.E., York Cornwell, E., et al.: Social disconnectedness, perceived isolation, and symptoms of depression and anxiety among older Americans (NSHAP): a longitudinal mediation analysis. Lancet Public Health **5**, e62–e70 (2020). https://doi.org/10.1016/S2468-2667(19)30230-0

35. Liu, C.H., Zhang, E., Wong, G.T.F., et al.: Factors associated with depression, anxiety, and PTSD symptomatology during the COVID-19 pandemic: Clinical implications for U.S. young adult mental health. Psychiatry Res. **290** (2020). https://doi.org/10.1016/j.psychres.2020.113172

36. Katon, W., Russo, J., Gavin, A.: Predictors of postpartum depression. J. Womens Health **23**, 753–759 (2014). https://doi.org/10.1089/jwh.2014.4824

37. Vliegen, N., Casalin, S., Luyten, P.: The course of postpartum depression: a review of longitudinal studies. Harv. Rev. Psychiatry **22**, 1–22 (2014)
38. Croxford, A., Notley, C.J., Maskrey, V., et al.: An exploratory qualitative study seeking participant views evaluating group Cognitive Behavioral Therapy preparation for alcohol detoxification. J. Subst. Use **20**, 61–68 (2015). https://doi.org/10.3109/14659891.2014.894590
39. Kalemenev, S.V., Zubareva, O.E., Frolova, E.V., et al.: Impairment of exploratory behavior and spatial memory in adolescent rats in lithium-pilocarpine model of temporal lobe epilepsy. Dokl. Biol. Sci. **463**, 175–177 (2015). https://doi.org/10.1134/S0012496615040055

Decision Systems

A Bio-Inspired-Based Salp Swarm Algorithm Enabled with Deep Learning for Alzheimer's Classification

Joseph Bamidele Awotunde[1], Sunday Adeola Ajagbe[2]([⊠]),
and Hector Florez[3]

[1] Department of Computer Science, Faculty of Information and Communication
Sciences, University of Ilorin, Ilorin 240003, Nigeria
awotunde.jb@unilorin.edu.ng
[2] First Technical University Ibadan, Ibadan, Nigeria
sunday.ajagbe@tech-u.edu.ng
[3] Universidad Distrital Francisco Jose de Caldas, Bogota, Colombia
haflorezf@udistrital.edu.co

Abstract. Alzheimer's disease is a progressive neurodegenerative disorder for which early identification is of paramount importance for a holistic treatment plan. Traditional methods of diagnosis require extensive manual interventions, making their scalability and reproducibility difficult. This paper presents a novel Bio-Inspired Salp Swarm Algorithm (BI-SSA) technique enabled by Deep Learning for the classification of Alzheimer's disease. The social behavior of birds and insects served as inspiration for the optimization technique known as BI-SSA which is able to identify useful solutions to complex problems with minimum manual interventions. This paper extends BI-SSA using Deep Learning which enables it to generate a more accurate and reliable diagnostic model. The model incorporates Alzheimer's disease-specific features such as age, gender, family history, and cognitive tests and employs an ensemble approach to improve the accuracy of the model. The proposed model is evaluated using a publicly available ADNI dataset. The results demonstrate that the model is able to correctly classify AD patients with an accuracy of 99.9%. Furthermore, our BI-SSA-based model outperforms traditional machine learning techniques and achieves better results with respect to sensitivity, precision, and accuracy of classification.

Keywords: Bio-inspired Model · Salp Swarm Algorithm · Deep Learning · Machine learning

1 Introduction

Alzheimer's disease (AD) is a neurological condition of the brain that permanently damages synapses involved in thinking and memory [3,8,11]. Dementia is ultimately caused by the cognitive decline brought on by this problem; the

H. Florez and M. Leon (Eds.): ICAI 2023, CCIS 1874, pp. 157–170, 2024.
https://doi.org/10.1007/978-3-031-46813-1_11

condition begins with mild protein breakdowns surrounding nerve cells and progresses to become a neurological type of dementia [32]. A clinical evaluation, a long history, a score on the Mini-mental State Examination (MMSE) that is lower than expected, as well as physical and neurobiological tests, are all necessary for the diagnosis of AD [15]. Resting-state functional magnetic resonance imaging (rs-fMRI) is a technique that provides undetectable ways to evaluate actual brain anatomy and changes in the brain [27, 28].

According to the 2015 Alzheimer Disease International Survey, 22.9 million individuals in Asia and 46.8 million people worldwide had dementia, with those numbers anticipated to double over the next 20 years. AD is primarily seen in adults. There are many potential computer-aided procedures for Alzheimer's categorization and early diagnosis. Deep learning (DL) models have been applied in the diagnosis of various diseases, where it is employed for voice, text, or image recognition, among other things. It consists of a lot of hidden layers that are used to model properties and update probabilities to get final results. The DL-based models may extract a lot of properties from a batch of input data, which aids in the accurate estimation of further data.

Compared to shallowly trained neural networks, the architecture of DL has a lot more hidden layers. It has been shown that DL is particularly good at identifying the patterns that exist in datasets. An effective artificial intelligence technique that supports computational models with several learning layers [29]. For instance, DL-based models can categorize AD and will help researchers and physicians more effectively diagnose brain disease. Convolutional Neural Networks (CNN) are frequently used for image recognition. The ADNI dataset was used in this study, which is a dataset of fMRI images of Alzheimer's patients' disease.

Salp Swarm Algorithm (SSA) is a new optimization algorithm with a limited history and extensive testing in diverse problem domains. Its performance is sensitive to parameter settings, making it difficult to predict its robustness. SSA's effectiveness decreases as problem dimensionality increases, making it less suitable for complex optimization problems. It also exhibits slower convergence rates, making it problematic for time-sensitive or real-time optimization problems. SSA is a bio-inspired optimization algorithm inspired by salps' swarming behavior, focusing on unique movement mechanisms and feeding behavior, varying effectiveness based on problem characteristics, parameters, and tuning.

In this study, the ADNI dataset is transformed into a comma-separated value (CSV) dataset, the dataset has the fMRI images of AD patients in a 3D image. It had information from two classes, the normal class and the Alzheimer's class, totaling 2652 rows and 4097 columns. The pre-processing was performed on the dataset in handling some traditional missing data to enter some reliable values into the data fields (utilized mean to fill in the empty spaces for the values). SSA was used for properties selection and reduction mechanism to avoid overfitting and get better performance results by the model in the classification of the dataset.

The combination of bio-inspired algorithms and DL techniques can be a powerful approach to solving complex problems like Alzheimer's disease classification. In this case, utilizing a SSA with a CNN-based model can offer potential benefits. SSA is a population-based optimization algorithm inspired by the collective behavior of Salps, which are gelatinous planktonic organisms. These organisms exhibit swarming behavior, where they collectively navigate their environment in search of resources. By modeling the behavior of Salps, SSA can be used to optimize solutions in various domains.

The paper is organized as follows. Section 2 presents some existing approaches to the classification and diagnosis of AD. Section 3 discusses the proposed framework using BI-SSA enabled with a CNN-based model. Section 4 discusses the experimental results and the comparison of the proposed model with cutting-edge models in the classification of AD, and finally, the paper is concluded in Sect. 5 with future direction.

2   Background

The proposed model is a cutting-edge method for categorizing Alzheimer's disease that blends the Bio-SSA with DL methods. While DL models might be employed for the actual classification task, the SSA might be utilized for feature selection, model parameter optimization, or data augmentation. The advantages of both approaches might be combined in this hybrid approach, which could increase the categorization of Alzheimer's disease's effectiveness and accuracy.

Many classification-based techniques for the diagnosis of mental deterioration or AZ illness have been proposed in recent years. There were different stages in this AZ, starting with a person who had no dementia symptoms and advancing to extremely trivial, minor, and moderate forms of dementia. Recent research shows promising markers for the early and precise diagnosis of AZ illness [2,7,24]. DL and ML techniques have been used in various studies to identify and diagnose AD [8,16,21]. Before the network can be utilized to detect AZ, it is necessary to train the model using large-labeled data samples. The accessible nature of large-labeled data is an intimidating issue. When a CNN is trained with a lot of datasets, it is expected to produce incredibly accurate and efficient results in the realm of medical images [12,31,34].

To use MRI to forecast the diagnosis of brain illnesses, a weakly supervised densely connected neural network (wiseDNN) was created by Lu et al., [20]. From the MRI, they first retrieved multiscale picture patches. The network was assessed using experimental results from the ADNI dataset. The accuracy of the four-stage recommended categorization approach was 96.5%. They were only evaluated on a small dataset, hence the wiseDNN was unable to offer a comprehensive answer. In a previous study of Liu et al., [18], the authors created a new strategy based on a deformation-based technique and tested it on the ADNI dataset to identify two groups of AD. Lu et al., [19] created a brand-new FCM-based Weighted Probabilistic NN (FWPNN) categorization technique. Then, 19 highly important traits connected to AD illness were selected using the multiple-criterion feature selection methodology. The experimental confirmation, which was thereafter employed, was done on the ADNI subset. The authors proposed a categorization accuracy of about 98.63% for the three types of AD diseases.

The numerous AZ-related illnesses were divided using deep CNNs. Several classifications and predictions of conversion risk utilizing transfer learning from previously trained ImageNet and five-fold cross-validation were examined and assessed for the GoogleNet and CaffeNet CNN architectures. Astonishing accuracy scores of 95.42% to 97.01% were reached by the CaffeNet. Duraisamy et al., [10] proposed a novel CAD approach for MR brain images to precisely identify both AD individuals and brain regions associated with AD. Awotunde et al., [7] used CNN to divide those with AD illness into two classes based on pictures of the hippocampal region obtained from MRI scans of the brain. The prediction model's accuracy for the three groups was 92.3%, 85.6%, and 78.1%.

The increasing AZ illness results in both physical and psychological dependence. A computer-aided diagnostic (CAD) system is required so that clinicians can make decisions right away. Agarwal et al., [2] proposed based on custom features, DL, and ML-based methods. These CAD systems usually have issues with class imbalance and overfitting since they need domain-expert knowledge and large datasets to extract deep features or train models. A novel method called CAD-ALZ is created to tackle these problems by identifying deep features using a ConvMixer layer and a blockwise fine-tuning technique on a relatively small initial dataset. Using six evaluation measures, including the F1-score of 99.61%, Kappa of 99.45%, accuracy of 99.61%, precision of 99.53%, sensitivity of 99.61%, and specificity of 99.09%, respectively. The suggested CAD-AZ model produced noteworthy results. The sensitivity and F1-score of the CAD-ALZ model were both 99.61%. A CNN-based DL model can be used to assess complex MRI scan information in clinical situations, according to Agarwal et al., [2], who presented the EfficietNet-b0 CNN is implemented using a novel approach called "fusion of end-to-end and transfer learning" to categorize different stages of AD.

An approach to improve recognition efficiency was suggested by [35]. It is also recognized that there is a second set of distinctive characteristics that guide the diagnosis of AD. Other morphological features are retrieved from the calculated AD Disease features and utilized to train the SVM classifier [35], which is used to predict the AD state. Their approach is assessed as they conduct tests by sequencing the detection of diseases. Many soft computing techniques have been used in the contemporary environment to quickly detect AD from MRI scans. There are numerous dimensionality elimination techniques used in many soft computing algorithms [17] because MRI images have a large number of features and a small number of subjects. Examples include Fisher's linear discriminate analysis (LDA) method [9], Principal component analysis (PCA) technique [30], and locally linear embedding (LLE) technique [33].

The current research had several serious shortcomings, such as disdain for binary classes and poor categorization preciseness for MCI higher levels. To aid in the early detection of AD, improved brain region segmentation still calls for more potent network architectures [22]. Investigating advanced sophisticated networks and other CNN pre-trained algorithms is necessary to produce successful classifiers for AD categorization [5,22]. Therefore, this study proposes a BI-SSA enabled with a CNN-based model for AD disease classification and diagnosis. The BI-SSA was used for feature selection and optimization of the CNN-based model for better classification performance. The proposed system was evaluated using the 1075 Alzheimer's Disease Neuroimaging Initiative (ADNI 1 1.5T) databases. The proposed framework aids in reducing the classification of the ADNI dataset's execution times.

3   Methodology

Pre-processing the dataset yields better performance outcomes by reducing the number of properties in the dataset and preventing overfitting in the model. The CNN architecture with the ideal hyper-parameter values, resulting in the highest performance and the fewest errors, was identified as having the following characteristics: ReLu is used as a normalized layer intermediate for the first and second convolution layers. There are then three convolution layers, three max-pooling layers, one flattened layer, three dense layers, and a final layer that is fully connected to the sigmoid activation function. The algorithm returns a value with the best possible hyper-parameter combinations. This produces the best performance metrics in comparison to approaches that are not optimized.

To develop a bio-inspired SSA enabled by deep learning for Alzheimer's disease classification, you could follow these general steps:

- **Data collection and preprocessing:** Gather a dataset consisting of brain imaging data (such as MRI or PET scans) from individuals with and without AD. Preprocess the data to extract relevant features and ensure it is in a suitable format for both the SSA and deep learning algorithms.
- **Salp Swarm Algorithm (SSA) implementation:** Design the SSA framework by defining the parameters, objective function, and update rules. The objective function should be tailored to the Alzheimer's disease classification task, such as maximizing classification accuracy or minimizing the classification error. Implement the swarm update rules inspired by the salp behavior, where each salp represents a potential solution.
- **Deep learning model integration:** Incorporate a DL technique, such as a CNN or a recurrent neural network (RNN), into the SSA framework. The DL technique will serve as the classifier for AD. You can train the DL technique using the labeled data from the dataset.
- **SSA optimization and deep learning training:** Initialize the salp swarm population and perform iterations of the SSA algorithm. At each iteration, update the positions of salps based on their current positions and the objective function. Simultaneously, update the deep learning model using a subset of the data, allowing it to learn from the salp swarm's collective behavior. This combination of SSA optimization and deep learning training helps enhance the classification performance.
- **Performance evaluation:** After the SSA optimization and deep learning training converge or reach a stopping criterion, evaluate the performance

of the integrated model. Use a separate validation dataset or cross-validation techniques to assess the classification accuracy, sensitivity, specificity, or other relevant metrics.

- **Fine-tuning and validation:** If necessary, fine-tune the model's hyperparameters or architecture based on the performance evaluation. Validate the model using an independent test dataset to ensure its generalization capability. Implementing and fine-tuning such a complex system requires expertise in both bio-inspired algorithms and deep learning. Additionally, obtaining high-quality and representative datasets is crucial for accurate classification. Collaborating with domain experts and conducting rigorous experiments can help ensure the reliability and effectiveness of the proposed approach for Alzheimer's disease classification.

3.1   The Bio-Inspired Salp Swarm Algorithm (BI-SSA)

The SSA is a nature-inspired optimization algorithm that is inspired by the collective behavior of salps, a type of marine organism. SSA was proposed by Mirjalili and Lewis in 2016 as a metaheuristic algorithm for solving optimization problems [23]. The algorithm imitates salps' swarming behavior in their natural environment, where they move in unison to find food and evade predators. In SSA, the search space is initialized at random with a population of solutions known as salps. Every salp stands for a possible resolution to the optimization issue. Exploration and exploitation are the two fundamental factors that control salp migration. Exploration enables the algorithm to look throughout a large portion of the solution space for promising locations, whereas exploitation concentrates on stepping up the search around the top solutions so far.

Numerous optimization issues, such as function optimization, feature selection, and engineering design, have been addressed by the Salp Swarm Algorithm. It is a comparatively straightforward and effective algorithm that gains from its parallelism and capacity to avoid local optima. The efficiency of SSA is nevertheless influenced by the nature of the problem and the parameter settings, much like any other metaheuristic algorithm. To acquire the best outcomes for a certain issue domain, settings might need to be carefully tuned. SSA is based on solutions where the population initialization is carried out randomly, just like other swarm-based approaches. The optimization issue might have a solution in each of these populations. A leader salp and a follower salp are the two groups into which the populations of SSA are divided. The chain is guided by the leader Salp, who is also obeyed by the other followers. Let x be the position of the salp, and F be the source of the food, the pack in the search space is aiming to achieve that. Equation 1 presents a matrix of a solution of n population.

$$X = \begin{bmatrix} x_1^1 & x_2^1 & \dots & x_d^1 \\ x_1^2 & x_2^2 & \dots & x_d^2 \\ \dots & & & \\ x_1^n & x_2^n & \dots & x_d^n \end{bmatrix} \tag{1}$$

The latest update to the leader salp position is presented in Eq. 2.

$$x_j^1 = \begin{cases} F_j + r_1((ub_j - lb_j)r_2 + lb_j), r_3 \geq 0.5 \\ F_j - r_1((ub_j - lb_j)r_2 + lb_j), r_3 \geq 0.5 \end{cases} \qquad (2)$$

where x_j^1 and F_j represent the positions of leader salp and source, respectively. r_1 is a random number in charge of balancing between the exploitation and exploration phases and the mathematical definition is presented in Eq. 3.

$$r_1 = 2_e - \left(\frac{4t}{T}\right)^2 \qquad (3)$$

where t is the number of the current iteration and T is the total number of iterations. Two uniformly produced random integers in the $[0, 1]$ range are the random numbers r_2 and r_3. r_3 The follower salps revise positions in accordance with Eq. 4.

$$x_i^j = \frac{1}{2}(x_j^i + x_j^{i-1}) \qquad (4)$$

where $i \geq 2$ and x_j^i represent the ith follower salp location vector at j^{th} dimension.

3.2   The Convolutional Neural Network Algorithm

A CNN architecture consists of a number of hidden layers.

- Convolution Layer: This layer calculates a cross-multiplication between the input and the weights, creating a complicated pixel matrix that is sent as an input to the following layer [6]. The convolution layer uses a variety of filters that replicate themselves throughout the whole input space and cycle through small, nearby portions of the input [7]. Its representation is presented in Eq. 5.

$$S(i, j) = (I * K)(i, j) = \sum_m \sum_n I(m, n)K(i - m, j - n) \qquad (5)$$

Where I is the image itself, K denotes the coefficient of the convolution filtering process, and (m, n) denotes the image's row and column, correspondingly.
- Normalization Layer: This layer carries out the element-wise activation procedure max $(0, x)$, also known as the ReLu extraction of features layer, which produces a corrected feature map [25].
- Pooling Layer: This layer undertakes down-sampling operations. Max-pooling can help by maintaining the most essential elements for identifying an image. The features get more efficient and minimal as you move up the levels by using max-pooling. The output of this layer is a pooled characteristic map, which is eventually smoothed and provided as an input to the following layer [1, 26].

- Fully Connected Layer: The automatic categorization of the image in the output layer, which happens after feature extraction, will be evaluated in this layer using the class scores [4,13,14].
- Sigmoid Activation Function: In neural networks, activation functions are important for understanding complex patterns. An artificial NN activation function transforms the input signals from the neurons into the output signals. According to their behavior and conduct, linear and non-linear activation mechanisms are the two main types of activation functions. The sigmoid activation function is the most widely utilized one because of NNs inherent non-linearity and computational simplicity. A non-linear activation function with an S-shaped curve, the sigmoid is also known as the logistic function.

The sigmoid function is used because it exists (0–1) when we create a model with the intention of predicting the probability as an output. The brilliance of these activation functions is that the value never approaches zero or exceeds one, which might cause an NN to stall out during learning. Large positive numbers will typically gravitate toward one, while large negative numbers will typically tend toward zero.

The convergence propensity identified through the function assessment is superior to competing methods because of the probabilistic replacement model used in this technique.

The critical and frequently repetitive process of choosing hyper-parameter values for a CNN design combines domain knowledge, experimentation, and computational resources. The performance, convergence, and effectiveness of the model can all be dramatically impacted by choosing the proper hyperparameter values. Hyper-parameter tuning in practice frequently entails experimenting with different values using methods like grid search, random search, or more sophisticated ones like Bayesian optimization. Iterative and based on a combination of theoretical knowledge, empirical findings, and available computational resources, the process is steered. It's crucial to remember that there is no one strategy that works for all problems, and the ideal hyperparameter can change depending on the particular dataset and issue you're trying to solve.

The present study makes use of the AD Neuroimaging Initiative (ADNI), a publicly available dataset on AD and associated dementia [9]. The characteristics of the participants in this study are listed in Table 1.

Table 1. The ADNI database demographic information on the participants.

Classification	Sex	Instances	Age (Mean ± SD)
Alzheimer	F = 132, M = 68	200	73.8 ± 7.5
Healthy Control	F = 73, M = 27	100	75.0 ± 7.2

3.3   The Measures for Measuring the Proposed Technique's Performance

The proposed model was evaluated using various performance metrics like accuracy, precision, F1-score, sensitivity, and specificity metrics. The equations for the metrics are presented in Eqs. 6 to 10.

$$Accuracy(ACC) = \frac{TP + TN}{TP + TN + FP + FN} \tag{6}$$

$$Precision(PR) = \frac{TP}{TN + FP} \tag{7}$$

$$Sensitivity(SE) = \frac{TP}{TP + FN} \tag{8}$$

$$Specificity(SP) = \frac{TN}{TN + FP} \tag{9}$$

$$F1 - Score = \frac{2 * PR * SE}{PR + SE} \tag{10}$$

The terms true positive (TP), true negative (TN), false positive (FP), and false negative (FN), respectively, were the few performance metrics used for the assessment of the proposed model to know how well the system performed when compared with other state-of-the-art models. The accuracy rate of the diagnosis is correlated with the SE, a critical diagnostic metric. The SP is crucial for evaluating the model's precision and for spotting medical problems. The PR explains how well the model can forecast the future. The ACC represents the anticipated accuracy of the framework. The harmonic is the PR, SE, and the F1-score.

4   Results

The experiment of the IB-SSA optimized CNN was performed on a Windows Operating System with 64-bit, Core(MT) i7-3520M Intel(R) at 2.90 GHz (4CPUs), with UHD Intel Graphics 670 model. The performance of the proposed model was tested to assess the model using various measures, the ability to be generalized, and adaptability. Two sets of experiments were conducted to evaluate the performance of the proposed model system. Using the bootstrapping process method, the scientific probabilities of the boxplots were generated. The training and interpretation processes were done utilizing the PyTorch architecture. By employing 80% for training and 20% for testing, the dataset is partitioned into different testing, validation, and training ratios.

Table 2 displays specific results for the proposed model on the ADNI dataset using the BI-SSA optimization enabled with the CNN-based model. Although the proposed model without the BI-SSA algorithm and the CNN-based model enabled with the BI-SSA technique performance was greatly good, the BI-SSA feature selection and optimized technique increased the accuracy of the AD

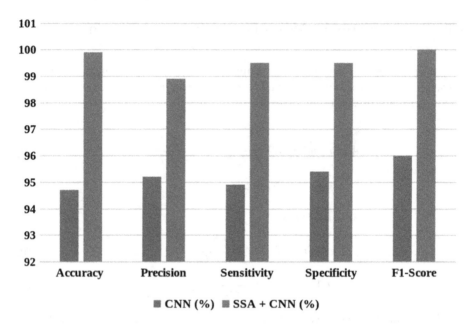

Fig. 1. Performance of the BI-SSA enabled with CNN-based model on ANDI dataset.

with an accuracy of 99.9%, with an increased accuracy of 3.9% against the model without the BI-SSA technique. The performance of the proposed model is shown in Fig. 1.

Table 2. Performance of the proposed model without and with BI-SSA technique an ADNI dataset.

Performance Metrics	CNN (%)	SSA + CNN (%)
Accuracy	94.7	99.9
Precision	95.2	98.9
Sensitivity	94.9	99.5
Specificity	95.4	99.5
F1-Score	96.0	1.0

All experiments were made of precisely the same dataset. To demonstrate the effectiveness of the recommended framework more clearly, an ablation study was also conducted. The proposed framework results performance is shown in Table 3.

Fully connected layers of CNN frameworks were initially trained using ImageNet datasets, and then they were retrained using the study dataset of ADNI images. Every training configuration was initially primed with a batch size of 32 and a learning rate of $1e-2$. After that, CNN designs were improved by BI-SSA

Table 3. Performance of the Proposed CCN-based model enabled with BI-SSA.

Techniques	Accuracy	Precision	Sensitivity	Specificity	F1-Score
Normal	97.00%	98.00%	98.00%	96.00%	99.00%
Mild Dementia	95.00%	97.00%	97.00%	96.00%	100.00%
Moderate Dementia	98.00%	96.00%	98.00%	98.00%	99.00%
Very Mild Dementia	97.00%	97.00%	98.00%	99.00%	99.00%
Proposed Model	100.00%	99.00%	100.00%	100.00%	100.00%

to meet the performance standards. This cosine annealing learning rate value was used. As a result, after every epoch, the results of the 50-epoch training process, the validation loss, and the validation accuracy were estimated, and the results are presented in Fig. 2. The validation loss values for the suggested

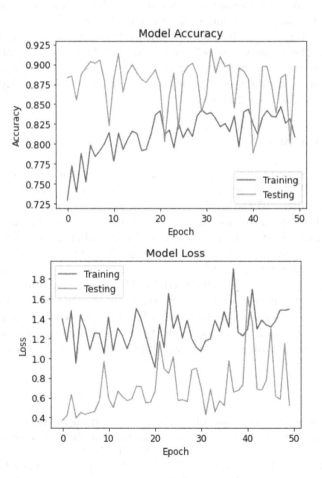

Fig. 2. Performance of the BI-SSA enabled with CNN-based model on ANDI dataset.

model had a constant structure after achieving saturation and showed an decline exponential.

The comparison of BI-SSA with a CNN-based model with some existing models further proved the need for the proposed model. The IB-SSA enabled with CNN-based framework was compared with other cutting-edge models that use the same ADNI dataset for objective evaluation of the framework.

The BI-SSA enabled with CNN-based model performed better when compared with some existing models using accuracy metrics. The existing models used the ANDI dataset to test the performance of their proposed models. The BI-SSA with a CNN-based model performed better than the existing DL-based algorithms and some hybrid ML methods. The outcomes showed that the BI-SSA enabled with a CNN-based model could successfully and precisely identify and predict AD from the ADNI dataset.

The performance of the proposed framework shows that the BI-SSA optimization employed for the optimization of the CNN-based model increases the accuracy of the proposed model by 99.9%, and the performance of other metrics used for the evaluation of the model performed better when compared with existing models. The proposed model hence, reduced the complexity of the model, memory consumption, removal of irrelevant features, and overfitting that can arise from the ANDI dataset. The proposed technique also shows highly impressive accuracy in AD prediction.

5   Conclusions

This study proposed BI-SSA enabled with CNN-based model to the classification of AD using ANDI for evaluation of the performance of the framework. The paper specifically used the BI-SSA algorithm for the optimization of the CNN-based for better performance, and the CNN was used for the classification of the AD dataset. To demonstrate the importance and efficiency of the proposed framework, extensive experiments using the ADNI dataset were performed. The BI-SSA with CNN-based model with an accuracy of 99/9% outperforms other start-of-the-art models using DL-based for AD classification. In the future, the proposed model will be tested on other related AD datasets to really show the effectiveness of the model. Besides, other Bio-Inspired optimization algorithms can be used with the CNN-based model to see their performance, and powerful feature selection can be used to improve the performance of the model.

References

1. Abdulraheem, M., Oladipo, I.D., Ajagbe, S.A., Balogun, G.B., Akanbi, M.B., Emma-Adamah, N.O.: Continuous eye disease severity evaluation system using siamese neural networks. ParadigmPlus 4(1), 1–17 (2023)
2. Agarwal, D., Berbís, M.Á., Luna, A., Lipari, V., Ballester, J.B., de la Torre-Díez, I.: Automated medical diagnosis of Alzheimer′s disease using an efficient net convolutional neural network. J. Med. Syst. 47(1), 57 (2023)

3. Ajagbe, S.A., Amuda, K.A., Oladipupo, M.A., Oluwaseyi, F.A., Okesola, K.I.: Multi-classification of Alzheimer disease on magnetic resonance images (MRI) using deep convolutional neural network (dcnn) approaches. Int. J. Adv. Comput. Res. **11**(53), 51 (2021)

4. Ali, M.D., et al.: Breast cancer classification through meta-learning ensemble technique using convolution neural networks. Diagnostics **13**(13), 2242 (2023)

5. Awotunde, J.B., Folorunso, S.O., Jimoh, R.G., Adeniyi, E.A., Abiodun, K.M., Ajamu, G.J.: Application of artificial intelligence for covid-19 epidemic: an exploratory study, opportunities, challenges, and future prospects. In: Artificial Intelligence for COVID-19, pp. 47–61 (2021)

6. Awotunde, J.B., Panigrahi, R., Khandelwal, B., Garg, A., Bhoi, A.K.: Breast cancer diagnosis based on hybrid rule-based feature selection with deep learning algorithm. Res. Biomed. Eng. **39**(1), 115–127 (2023)

7. Awotunde, J.B., Sur, N.S., Imoize, A.L., Misra, S., Gaber, T.: An enhanced residual networks based framework for early Alzheimer's disease classification and diagnosis. In: Dhar, S., Do, D.T., Sur, S.N., Liu, C.M. (eds.) ICCDN 2022. LNCS, vol. 1037, pp. 335–348. Springer, Heidelberg (2022)

8. Basaia, S., et al.: Automated classification of Alzheimer's disease and mild cognitive impairment using a single MRI and deep neural networks. NeuroImage: Clin. **21**, 101645 (2019)

9. Chu, C., Hsu, A.L., Chou, K.H., Bandettini, P., Lin, C., Initiative, A.D.N., et al.: Does feature selection improve classification accuracy? impact of sample size and feature selection on classification using anatomical magnetic resonance images. Neuroimage **60**(1), 59–70 (2012)

10. Duraisamy, B., Shanmugam, J.V., Annamalai, J.: Alzheimer disease detection from structural MR images using FCM based weighted probabilistic neural network. Brain Imaging Behav. **13**, 87–110 (2019)

11. Farooq, A., Anwar, S., Awais, M., Rehman, S.: A deep CNN based multi-class classification of Alzheimer's disease using MRI. In: 2017 IEEE International Conference on Imaging systems and techniques (IST), pp. 1–6. IEEE (2017)

12. Feng, C., et al.: Deep learning framework for Alzheimer's disease diagnosis via 3D-CNN and FSBI-LSTM. IEEE Access **7**, 63605–63618 (2019)

13. Hernandez, J., Daza, K., Florez, H.: Spiking neural network approach based on caenorhabditis elegans worm for classification. IAENG Int. J. Comput. Sci. **49**(4), 1–13 (2022)

14. Hernandez, J., Florez, H.: An experimental comparison of algorithms for nodes clustering in a neural network of caenorhabditis elegans. In: Gervasi, O., et al. (eds.) ICCSA 2021. LNCS, vol. 12957, pp. 327–339. Springer, Cham (2021). https://doi.org/10.1007/978-3-030-87013-3_25

15. Janghel, R.R.: Deep-learning-based classification and diagnosis of Alzheimer's disease. In: Deep Learning and Neural Networks: Concepts, Methodologies, Tools, and Applications, pp. 1358–1382. IGI Global (2020)

16. Janghel, R., Rathore, Y.: Deep convolution neural network based system for early diagnosis of Alzheimer's disease. IRBM **42**(4), 258–267 (2021)

17. Li, M., Yang, Z.: Deep twin support vector networks. In: Fang, L., Povey, D., Zhai, G., Mei, T., Wang, R. (eds.) CICAI 2022. LNCS, vol. 13606, pp. 94–106. Springer, Heidelberg (2022). https://doi.org/10.1007/978-3-031-20503-3_8

18. Liu, M., Zhang, J., Lian, C., Shen, D.: Weakly supervised deep learning for brain disease prognosis using MRI and incomplete clinical scores. IEEE Trans. Cybern. **50**(7), 3381–3392 (2019)

19. Long, X., Chen, L., Jiang, C., Zhang, L., Initiative, A.D.N.: Prediction and classification of Alzheimer disease based on quantification of MRI deformation. PLoS ONE **12**(3), e0173372 (2017)

20. Lu, D., Popuri, K., Ding, G.W., Balachandar, R., Beg, M.F., Initiative, A.D.N., et al.: Multiscale deep neural network based analysis of FDG-pet images for the early diagnosis of Alzheimer's disease. Med. Image Anal. **46**, 26–34 (2018)

21. Mehmood, A., Maqsood, M., Bashir, M., Shuyuan, Y.: A deep siamese convolution neural network for multi-class classification of Alzheimer disease. Brain Sci. **10**(2), 84 (2020)

22. Mehmood, A., et al.: A transfer learning approach for early diagnosis of Alzheimer's disease on MRI images. Neuroscience **460**, 43–52 (2021)

23. Mirjalili, S., Gandomi, A.H., Mirjalili, S.Z., Saremi, S., Faris, H., Mirjalili, S.M.: Salp swarm algorithm: a bio-inspired optimizer for engineering design problems. Adv. Eng. Softw. **114**, 163–191 (2017)

24. Murugan, S., et al.: Demnet: a deep learning model for early diagnosis of Alzheimer diseases and dementia from MR images. IEEE Access **9**, 90319–90329 (2021)

25. Odusami, M., Maskeliūnas, R., Damaševičius, R.: Pareto optimized adaptive learning with transposed convolution for image fusion Alzheimer's disease classification. Brain Sci. **13**(7), 1045 (2023)

26. Ojo, O.S., Oyediran, M.O., Bamgbade, B.J., Adeniyi, A.E., Ebong, G.N., Ajagbe, S.A.: Development of an improved convolutional neural network for an automated face based university attendance system. ParadigmPlus **4**(1), 18–28 (2023)

27. Saeed, F.: Towards quantifying psychiatric diagnosis using machine learning algorithms and big fMRI data. Big Data Anal. **3**(1), 1–3 (2018)

28. Sarraf, S., Tofighi, G.: Deep learning-based pipeline to recognize Alzheimer's disease using fMRI data. In: 2016 Future Technologies Conference (FTC), pp. 816–820. IEEE (2016)

29. Sawhney, R., Malik, A., Sharma, S., Narayan, V.: A comparative assessment of artificial intelligence models used for early prediction and evaluation of chronic kidney disease. Decis. Anal. J. **6**, 100169 (2023)

30. Suk, H.I., Lee, S.W., Shen, D., Initiative, A.D.N.: Deep sparse multi-task learning for feature selection in Alzheimer's disease diagnosis. Brain Struct. Funct. **221**, 2569–2587 (2016)

31. Wang, S.H., Phillips, P., Sui, Y., Liu, B., Yang, M., Cheng, H.: Classification of Alzheimer's disease based on eight-layer convolutional neural network with leaky rectified linear unit and max pooling. J. Med. Syst. **42**, 1–11 (2018)

32. Yagis, E., Citi, L., Diciotti, S., Marzi, C., Atnafu, S.W., De Herrera, A.G.S.: 3D convolutional neural networks for diagnosis of Alzheimer's disease via structural MRI. In: 2020 IEEE 33rd International Symposium on Computer-Based Medical Systems (CBMS), pp. 65–70. IEEE (2020)

33. Yu, S., et al.: Multi-scale enhanced graph convolutional network for early mild cognitive impairment detection. In: Martel, A.L., et al. (eds.) MICCAI 2020. LNCS, vol. 12267, pp. 228–237. Springer, Cham (2020). https://doi.org/10.1007/978-3-030-59728-3_23

34. Zhang, Y.D., Zhang, Y., Hou, X.X., Chen, H., Wang, S.H.: Seven-layer deep neural network based on sparse autoencoder for voxelwise detection of cerebral microbleed. Multimedia Tools Appl. **77**, 10521–10538 (2018)

35. Zhang, Y., et al.: Detection of subjects and brain regions related to Alzheimer's disease using 3d MRI scans based on eigenbrain and machine learning. Front. Comput. Neurosci. **9**, 66 (2015)

A Scientometric Analysis of Virtual Tourism Technology Use in the Tourism Industry

Sri Sulastri(✉), Achmad Nurmandi, and Aulia Nur Kasiwi

Universitas Muhammadiyah Yogyakarta, Kasihan, Indonesia
serinsry@gmail.com

Abstract. The study aims to analyze the characteristics of virtual tourism technology in the tourism industry over the past ten years. The development of digital technology and the increasing number of Internet users have had a significant impact on the productivity of the world of industry, especially the tourism industry sector. The concept of virtual tourism is one of the artificial intelligence technologies that uses simulation of travel sites in the form of images and videos containing sounds and text. The virtual tourism concept is an alternative effort to provide convenience in exploring tourist destinations armed with smartphones and internet networks. The study uses scientometric analysis to analyze data from 2013 to 2022 using the Scopus database and Citespace software. The number of publications on trends in virtual technology tourism and the tourism industry taken from the Scopuse search engine found 244 documents and has increased overall in the last ten years. Meanwhile, Scopus's data analysis shows that China (50) has the highest contribution to this research and the most dominant author in this research trend is Jung, TT (4). The research found that virtual tourism technology trends in the tourism industry consist of five (5) significant groups, namely technology acceptance, augmented reality, virtual reality experiences, tourism sector, and technology preparation. This research implies that it will help in the development of digital tourism in the world of the tourism industry.

Keywords: Digital Tourism · Virtual Tourism · Virtual Reality

1 Introduction

As the times change, the development of digital technology is increasingly rapid, this affects performance in the industAs the times change, the development of al world d[1]. The world of industry and digital technology cannot be separated because they are interconnected [2]. The industrial world needs digital technology to improve its production performance. Digital technology is understood to have the ability to analyze and solve problems in the industrial world [3]. Digital technology is a tool with a computerized system and automatic operation without the help of human labor [4]. Artificial Intelligence is one of the digital technologies underpinning the development of the industrial world. According to to H. A. Simon (1995) artificial intelligence is an area of research, application, and instruction related to computer programming to do something that in the human view is intelligent.

H. Florez and M. Leon (Eds.): ICAI 2023, CCIS 1874, pp. 171–185, 2024.
https://doi.org/10.1007/978-3-031-46813-1_12

Artificial intelligence has many benefits in everyday life such as assisting in the collection, processing, and analysis of data engaged in various fields to improve high-quality products, minimize errors, and time efficiency [6]. Along with the times, digital technology has played an important role in the tourism industry by using artificial intelligence in improving its service system [7]. This is driven by the activeness of the community which along with its development is increasingly dynamic in using the digital world [8]. In general, before the existence of digital technology, the tourism world used print media or newspapers to develop tourism [9]. The development of digital technology has changed the way of traveling with the concept of virtual tourism [10].

Virtual tourism is an alternative concept of tourism through artificial intelligence technology and internet networks that can replace tourism places virtually [11]. By using virtual tourism, tourists can see tourist attractions only using simulated tourist sites in the form of images and videos containing sound and text [12]. In addition, virtual tourism as an alternative effort in the tourism industry offers comfort in traveling, presents detailed tourism information, and offers assistance for those who have obstacles [13]. However, this new form of tourism was only acceptable to some tourists before the COVID-19 pandemic. The COVID-19 pandemic has caused various problems in the tourism industry because it substantially affects the development of tourism destinations, which has caused disruptions in the global tourism industry [14]. In fact, in the new normal period, tourism travel is also still limited, therefore stakeholders have begun to adopt the development of virtual technology as a strategy for developing tourism and reviving the global economy [15]. Not only that, there are studies that argue that the quality or features of virtual tourism still need to be studied again because they must cover all senses so that the physical tourism environment can be created entirely [16].

Various situations and conditions in the world of the tourism industry become challenges in developing tourism. However, the development of digital technology allows the creation of a sustainable tourism industry. Virtual tourism has been around for more than a decade, but most tourists are foreign to this type of technology and have begun to develop again after the post-COVID-19 pandemic [17]. Therefore, it is interesting for many researchers to know the use of virtual tourism in the current world of tourism globally. Therfore, this paper aims to analyze the trend of virtual tourism technology in the tourism industry over the past ten years using bibliometrics review and scientometric analysis based on the Scopus engine database.

2 Literature Review

Tourism is an activity associated with a relaxing or refreshing journey. According to Soekardijo (2003), tourism means a redirection of a person for a while to somewhere to enjoy peace. According to [18], tourism is a pleasure involving individuals with changing modern conditions with implications for the nation, citizenship, consumerism, cosmopolitanism, and globalization. Tourism is one of the drivers of the global economy because it has the potential to generate large incomes in a country [19]. Tourism helps in improving the construction infrastructure and boosts the scope of economic growth in a country [20].

As time goes by, the development of digital technology is increasing rapidly, impacting the tourism sector. Digital technology promises great potential for the future development of the tourism sector by focusing on the digitalization of tourism [21]. Digitalization of tourism has brought a lot of new products such as digital tourism, virtual tourism, and virtual reality. Digital tourism is a combination of physical and digital tourist attractions that are used to promote tourism potential and support the tourist experience [22]. Virtual tourism is a combination of virtual reality and the tourism industry that provides a travel experience without traveling and only using the internet [23]. Virtual tourism is the form of text, video, and audio tourist destinations where users can listen and view them using smartphones, laptops, or other technologies [12]. Virtual tourism becomes interesting because it allows one can visit tourist destinations in real time even all over the world without traveling [24].

Virtual reality is a digital technology that can create a real virtual environment and deliver innovations in the world of the tourism industry [25]. Virtual reality can visualize the real tourist environment in virtual affect the attitude of tourists in traveling and increase their intentions in visiting tourist destinations [26]. The use of virtual tourism shows that tourists who use virtual travel can follow hedonistic passions and experience travel experiences emotionally [27].

At the time of the COVID-19 pandemic, virtual tourism was on the rise, A Mura study (2017) explains that virtual travel could replace traveling around the world during the COVID-19 pandemic. Similar research [29] shows that virtual tourism can be another way to escape the isolation of COVID-19. However, there was an imbalance in the attitude of tourists toward virtual tourism during the Covid-19 pandemic [17]. Some studies show that the COVID-19 pandemic can affect the psychology and attitudes of tourists, such as stress, behavioral intentions, and sentiment. Therefore, every tourism product should be able to satisfy the tourist in its use [30].

3 Research Method

This study collected data trends related to virtual tourism technology and the tourism industry through the Scopus database from 2013 to 2022. Data collection is carried out using bibliometric studies with search strategies based on headings, abstracts, and keywords limited to open access, document types, and languages [31]. Therefore, the search queries are used as follows: (TITLE-ABS-KEY ("virtual") AND TITLE-ABS-KEY ("tourism") AND TITLE-ABS-KEY (technology)). Based on this search query, the study obtained 1267 documents related to virtual tourism technology and the tourism industry. Next, the document is filtered using the following search strategies: (TITLE-ABS-KEY ("virtual") AND TITLE-ABS-KEY ("tourism") AND TITLE-ABS-KEY (technology)) AND PUBYEAR > 2012 AND PUBYEAR < 2023 AND (LIMIT-TO (OA, "all")) AND (LIMIT-TO (DOCTYPE, "ar") OR LIMIT-TO (DOCTYPE, "cp")) AND (LIMIT-TO (SRCTYPE, "j") OR LIMIT-TO (SRCTYPE, "p")) AND (LIMIT-TO (LANGUAGE, "English")). Based on this strategy, it was found that there are 244 documents related to virtual tourism technology and the tourism industry. Then, the found data is displayed in documents by year, documents by country, authors' documents, types-based documents, sponsorship documents, documents with affiliates, sources-by-source documents, and topical documents consisting of journal articles and conference papers in English.

To analyze the data, this study uses the relevant data analysis techniques, namely Scientometric analysis. Scientometric analysis or knowledge mapping is a method of quantitative research using color theoretical graphs to find objective scientific understanding based on the data found [32]. The research also uses CiteSpace software that serves in conducting in-depth, chronological, and well-structured analyses of previous research in various fields, for example through data containing information of authors, institutions, and countries to analyze writers, agencies, and states that have made significant contributions in a particular field over decades [33].

4 Result and Discussion

The analysis of 244 scientific publications from the Scopus database resulted in a wide range of varied data. Scientific publications related to virtual tourism technology and the tourism industry from 2013 to 2022 have different perspectives. The research analyzed and classified data ranging from the year of the documents, research subjects, affiliates, authors, countries, and publication sources that most contributed to publications related to virtual tourism technology and the tourism industry. In addition, the study also provides mapping visualizations, cluster identification, and analysis which are an important part of the research findings.

4.1 Annual Publication Analysis of Virtual Tourism Technology and Tourism Industry

Research on virtual tourism technology and the tourism industry has been an outstanding research topic in the last ten years, this is due to the rapid development of digital technology. Therefore, the tourism industry is trying to adapt to digital technology developments to create sustainable tourism. Figure 1 below shows the growth trend of virtual tourism technology research publications and the tourism industry from 2013 to 2022. In 2013 and 2014, there were eight documents published each year. However, there was a decline in 2015 and 2016, there were 4 documents published. In 2017 there were 9 documents published. In 2018, there were 17 documents published. In 2019 there were 25 documents published, there was a significant increase in 2020, when there were 19 additional documents. Then, by 2020, there are 57 documents published. The year with the highest number of publications occurred in 2022, there were 2022 documents published.

The results showed that the growth trend of publications on virtual tourism technology and the tourism industry increased overall from 2013 to 2022 in the Scopus database. The findings are in line with research conducted by Gegung (2021) that the use of virtual tourism has been widely used to improve the sustainability of destinations and to explore the authenticity of the virtual tourist experience, as a substitute for the real-life experience after COVID-19. Based on the findings, 2020 is experiencing a significant increase in publication trends, this is in line with [17] the COVID-19 pandemic in early 2020,

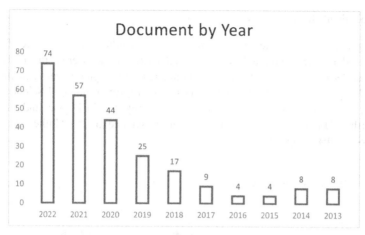

Fig. 1. Annual Publication Analysis of Virtual Tourism Technology and Tourism Industry based year document

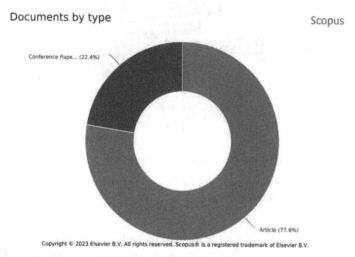

Fig. 2. Annual Publications Analysis of Virtual Tourism Technology and Tourism Industry based on document types.

urging the tourism industry to look for alternative solutions to understanding the effects of virtual tourism implementation, given the existence of activity restriction policies.

Figure 2 shows the analysis type of data based on the type of document, so in the publication, this study is dominated by type of article with a percentage of 77.6%, compared with conference paper type documents of 22.4% .

4.2 Analysis of Subject Area

Research on virtual tourism technology and the tourism industry has coverage of research topics. Based on the Scopus database, the most discussed trends were in the field of social sciences at 18.4% with 102 documents. Other research topics covered in this study include Computer Science (18%), Engineering (11%), Environmental Science (9.9%), Business, Management, and Accounting (9.2%), Energy (5.2%), Physics and Astronomy (5%), Earth and Planetary Sciences (4%), Materials Science (3.4%), Mathematics (3.4%) and others (12.4%) (Fig. 3).

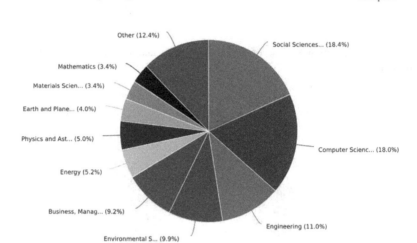

Fig. 3. Annual Publication Analysis of Virtual Tourism Technology and Tourism Industry based on the subject area of the document.

The results of the analysis showed that virtual tourism technology has a great influence on social science because the development of technology in tourism can influence social behavior such as the consumer behavior of tourists. In addition, virtual technology tourism is also discussed quite highly in the field of computer science and engineering, can be seen the comparison of social science and computer science only differed by 0.4% and engineering is in the third position (11%). Virtual tourism technology is discussed in science technology because in the tourism sector technology can be used load Mobile Augmented Reality Virtual Reality (VR), artificial intelligence (AI), and the Internet of Things. (IoT). This technology has the potential to boost positive changes in the tourism industry, as it can provide facilities that are easily accessible by consumers in the middle of the new normal era [35].

4.3 Analysis of Most Contributing Affiliates in Virtual Tourism and Tourism Industry Technology Publications

Figure 4 shows the affiliates that contributed the most to virtual tourism and tourism industry technology publication trends from 2013 to 2022. Manchester Metropolitan University ranks highest with the number of publications of 8 papers. Followed by the University of Surrey and the School of Business and Law with 5 papers. Then, Kyung Hee University, Universitat de Valencia, Hong Kong Polytechnic University, and Universitat Politecnica de Valencia with 4 documents. Next, the Ministry of Education of China, King Abdul Aziz University, and Hainan University with a total publication of 3 documents.

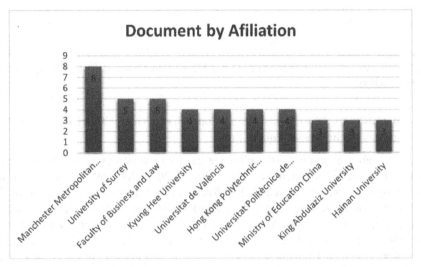

Fig. 4. Analysis of Most Contributing Affiliates in Virtual Tourism and Tourism Industry Technology Publications

4.4 Analysis of Most Contributing Author in Virtual Tourism and Tourism Industry Technology Publications

Based on the Scopus database of 244 analyzed documents, here is an analysis related to the authors who have had the highest contribution to the publication trends of virtual tourism technology and the tourism industry from 2013 to 2022. Based on the number of documents published, Jung, T. occupied the highest rank with the total number of publications of 4 documents. Followed by Deng had 3 documents, Fourkiotou had 3 papers, Jung T.H. had 3, Manglis had 3, Papadopoulou had 3, and Tom Dieck had 3. Then, Ammirato had two documents, Buhalis had two, and Chen had two (Fig. 5).

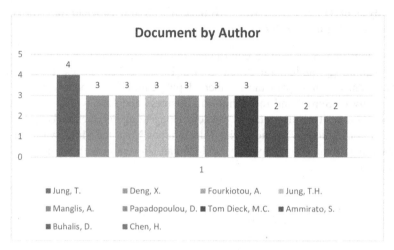

Fig. 5. Analysis of Most Contributing Author in Virtual Tourism and Tourism Industry Technology Publications

4.5   Analysis of the Most Contributing Countries in Virtual Tourism and Tourism Industry Technologies Publications

10 countries are contributing to this global research on virtual tourism technology publication trends and the tourism industry from 2013 to 2022. Publication statistics indexed by the Scopus Engine are provided in Fig. 6 below. Based on the analysis, China was the country that contributed the most to the publication trend of virtual tourism technology and the tourism industry from 2013 to 2022, contributing 50 documents. England ranks second with a total of 27 documents. Followed by Italy and Spain with 24 documents. South Korea donated 15 documents, Greece 11 documents, Indonesia 11 papers, the United States 11 documents, India 9 documents, and Portugal 9 documents.

The study finds the fact that China has become a pioneer in virtual tourism technology trends in the tourism industry as an effort to improve the tourist industry since the outbreak of COVID-19. China is taking quick steps and alternatives to limit the spread of the pandemic and policy to travel by leveraging the development of 5G digital technology, Virtual Tourism, and Artificial Intelligence [36]. One of the cities in China that has implemented Virtual Tourism is Tiongkok, for example, the Palace Museum, which is in the Forbidden City, has now launched the Virtual Reality Theatre Technology Palace Museum that can make it easier for visitors to see the conditions of the past using virtual tourism [37].

4.6   Analysis of Publication Sources

5 sources have the highest contribution to the publication trends of virtual tourism technology and the tourism industry from 2013 to 2022. Figure 7 below shows the publication source with detailed data information.

Figure 7 shows that Sustainability Switzerland ranks highest with a total of 25 papers published. The second place was occupied by the Journal of Physics Conference Series.

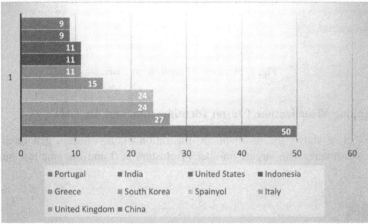

Fig. 6. Analysis of the Most Contributing Countries in Virtual Tourism and Tourism Industry Technologies Publications

Third place was held by the IOP Conference Series Earth and Environmental Science. Then, Applied Sciences Switzerland with 6 documents and Geojournal of Tourism and Geosites with 5 documents. Based on the Fig. 7 above publication each source experienced an increase in 2020. From this perspective, it can be concluded that in 2020 when the COVID-19 pandemic occurred it posed a variety of problems in the economic, educational, social, and cultural sectors, especially the tourism sector. Since the COVID-19 pandemic, travel activity has declined drastically. Therefore, virtual tourism technology has become one of the alternatives to improve the tourism industry since the spread of COVID-19.

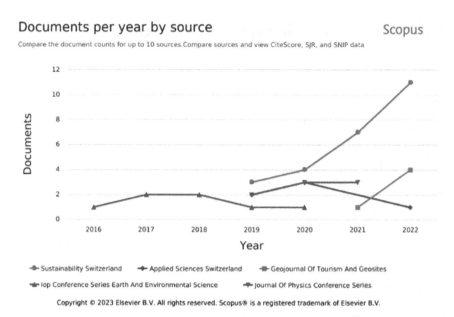

Fig. 7. Analysis of publication sources

4.7 Mapping Visualization, Cluster Identification, and Analysis

Figure 8 below shows the result of an illustration of the clusters generated by the CiteSpace software. The largest number of clusters is 0 and the smallest number is 5.

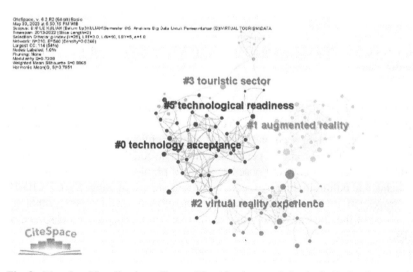

Fig. 8. Mapping Visualization, Cluster Identification, and Analysis Technology and Tourism Industry

CiteSpace software has a grouping function, in this function, the information analyzed is extracted using keywords designed as an alternative to knowing the constantly changing domains [38]. In addition, calculate the grouping findings using the log-likelihood ratio (LLR) [39]. In the publication trend of virtual tourism technology and tourism industry research from 2013 to 2022 with 244 documents used, CiteSpace provided the results of cluster analysis and found the 5 largest clusters. Five of the largest clusters were found, labeled #0, #1, #2, #3, and #5 (Table 1).

Table 1. Presents detailed information for each cluster.

Id Cluster	Size	Silhouette	Year	Label (LLR)
0	34	0,905	2019	Technology acceptance
1	31	0,881	2017	Augmented reality
2	26	0,828	2018	Virtual reality experience
3	13	0,928	2018	Touristic sector
5	10	0,936	2019	Technological readiness

The largest cluster consists of 34 members, **technology acceptance** with a silhouette value of 0.905. This cluster discusses the acceptance of technology in providing facilities to the tourism industry. Li et al. (2022). Revealed that there are new scales of assessment of the use of virtual tourism to tourists, such as scale of usability, convenience of use, risk of COVID-19 conditions, and attitudes toward technology acceptance. Furthermore, based on the scale of the assessment, it turns out that the use of virtual tourism technology has a significant impact on the acceptance of tourist technology, as they have considered the usage of virtualized tourism as a factor of convenience in traveling in the time of the COVID-19 pandemic [17]. However, on the other hand, there are still some things that disturb the convenience of tourists in using virtual tourism technology, the constraints of a complex operating system, unclear guidance, and expensive costs [40].

The second cluster consists of 31 members, that is, **argumented reality** with a silhouette value of 0.881. Based on the real arguments of tourists, they assume that virtual tourism technology is an effective technology and allows one to gain in-depth information about tourist destinations, such as museums [41]. This is because, virtual tourism can enhance the travel experience, encourage tourists to visit tourist destinations directly, and the desire to promote tourism destinations caused by pride [42]. However, unlike the Bharata study (2023) that found that the satisfaction experienced by tourists in using virtual tourism did not necessarily drive tourists' intentions to visit the sights.

In the third cluster, the **virtual reality experience** consists of 26 members with a silhouette value of 0.828. Based on the experience of using virtual travel, it turns out that virtual tourism technology can have a positive impact in improving the attitude and number of consumers when compared to previous travel experiences [44]. Same with research [45] that shows that the use of virtual tourism can affect consumer purchasing intentions and can boost tourism, especially in the culinary field. In addition, virtual tourism also presents features that are more interesting than other technologies [46].

Virtual tourism has different and higher levels of sensory information and some sites are very accurate with the world of tourism [44].

Next, on the fourth cluster is the **touristic sector**, consisting of 16 members with a silhouette value of 0.928. The tourism sector can help a country to boost economic growth [47]. One attempt to boost economic growth by enhaching 5G mobile networks designed to faciliate the use of technology as it can support the acceleration of social, economic, cultural, and tourism transformation digitally [48] [49]. The presence of this Internet network creates quality, innovative, and adaptive tourism concepts [50]. In the tourism sector, 5G networks are exploited to encourage long-distance tourism to enhance the real travel experience and bridge the gap between the physical and virtual worlds for tourism [48].

The last of the fifth clusters is **technological preparation**, consisting of 10 members with a silhouette value of 0.936. The COVID-19 pandemic has had a significant impact on life, its impact on flight cancellations, empty hotels and restaurants leading to bankruptcy, and tourist destinations starting to be crowded [51]. Virtual technology is expected to be able to revive the tourism industry from the impact of the COVID-19 pandemic [34]. Therefore, it is proposed the existence of a virtual tourism technology model that can enhance the virtual travel experience, the acceptance of technology in the community, encourage the intention of tourists to travel, and the use of virtual technology tourism [52]. Realizing this requires mature technology preparation so that it can simulate a virtual tourist spot [53].

5   Conclusion

The conclusions of the study show that the year 2022 has the highest number of publications in the publication trends of virtual tourism technology and the tourism industry indexed in the Scopus database from 2013 to 2022. China is the top contributing country of the ten countries with the highest rate of publication in this trend, with a total of 50 documents. Sustainability Switzerland is the most publishing source of virtual tourism technology and tourism industry trends, with a total of 25 publications. Later, Jung, T. was the most productive author in the publication trend of virtual tourism technology and the tourism industry, with a total of 4 papers. Furthermore, the affiliation with the most publications on this trend was achieved by Manchester Metropolitan University, with a total of 8 papers.

In addition, Scientometric analysis with CiteSpace software produced 5 major clusters in the publication trends of virtual tourism technology and the tourism industry from 2013 to 2022. These clusters include technology adoption, augmented reality, virtual reality experiences, the tourism sector, and technology readiness.Although the study outlines trends in the publication of virtual tourism technology and the tourism industry globally from 2013 to 2022, the study still has limitations in some ways as data is obtained only from the Scopus search engine with restrictions on all open access, types of article documents and conference papers, and English as the only language used. Therefore, recommendations for further research need to use data sources from the Web of Science as other global research database sources.

References

1. Barcena, A.: Digital Technologies for a New Future. Eclac Publication Digital Agenda for Latin America and the Caribbean, America (2021)
2. Asnidatul Adilah Ismail, R.H.: Technical competencies in digital technology towards industrial revolution 4.0. J. Tech. Educ. Train. **11**(3), 52–62 (2019). https://doi.org/10.30880/jtet.2019.11.03.008
3. Haleem, A., Javaid, M., Qadri, M.A., Suman, R.: Understanding the role of digital technologies in education: a review. Sustain. Oper. Comput. 3(February), 275–285 (2022). https://doi.org/10.1016/j.susoc.2022.05.004
4. Ng, W.: New Digital Technology in Education, 1st edn. Springer, Cham (2015). https://doi.org/10.1007/978-3-319-05822-1
5. Simon, H.A.: Artifical Intelligence: an empirical science. Artif. Intell. **77**(Artifical Intelligence), 95–127 (1995)
6. Nadimpalli, M.: Artifical intelligence risks and benefits. Int. J. Innov. Res. Sci. Eng. Technol. **6**(6), 1–4 (2017)
7. Filieri, R., D'Amico, E., Destefanis, A., Paolucci, E., Raguseo, E.: Artificial Intelligence (AI) for tourism: an European-based study successful AI tourism start-ups. Int. J. Contemp. Hosp. Manage **33**(11), 4099–4125 (2021)
8. Loader, B.D., Dutton, W.H.: A decade in Internet time the dynamics of the Internet and society. J. Info. Commun. Soc. **15**(5), 109–615 (2016). https://doi.org/10.1080/1369118X.2012.677053
9. Özturan, M., Roney, S.A.: Internet use among travel agencies in Turkey: an exploratory study. J. Int. Tour. Manage. **25**(2), 259–266 (2004). https://doi.org/10.1016/S-261-5177(03)00097-9
10. Pedrana, M.: Location-based services and tourism: possible implications for destination. Curr. Issues Tour. **17**(9), 753–762 (2014). https://doi.org/10.1080/13683500.2013.868411
11. Voronkova, L.P.: Virtual tourism: on the way to the digital economy. In: IOP Conference Series: Materials Science and Engineering, Lomonosov Moscow State University, Moscow, Russian Federation. Institute of Physics Publishing (2018). https://doi.org/10.1088/1757-899X/463/4/042096
12. Syahidi, A.A., Joniriadi, J., Waworuntu, N.H., Subandi, S., Kiyokawa, K.: Tour experience with interactive map simulation based on mobile augmented reality for tourist attractions in Banjarmasin City. IJICS Int. J. Inform. Comput. Sci. **6**(1), 22 (2022). https://doi.org/10.30865/ijics.v6i1.3900
13. Ionescu, C.A., et al.: The new era of business digitization through the implementation of 5g technology in Romania. Sustainability **13**(23) (2021). https://doi.org/10.3390/su132313401
14. Abbas, J., Mubeen, R., Iorember, P.T., Raza, S., Mamirkulova, G.: Exploring the impact of COVID-19 on tourism: transformational potential and implications for a sustainable recovery of the travel and leisure industry. Curr. Res. Behav. Sci. **2**(February), 100033 (2021). https://doi.org/10.1016/j.crbeha.2021.100033
15. El-Said, O., Aziz, H.: Virtual tours a means to an end: an analysis of virtual tours' role in tourism recovery post COVID-19. J. Travel Res. **61**(3), 528–548 (2022). https://doi.org/10.1177/0047287521997567
16. Kim, M.J., Lee, C.-K., Jung, T.: Exploring consumer behavior in virtual reality tourism using an extended stimulus-organism-response model. J. Travel Res. **59**(1), 69–89 (2020). https://doi.org/10.1177/0047287518818915
17. Li, Y., Liang, J., Huang, J., Yang, M., Li, R., Bai, H.: Would you accept virtual tourism? The impact of COVID-19 risk perception on technology acceptance from a comparative perspective. Sustainability **14**(19) (2022). https://doi.org/10.3390/su141912693

18. Franklin, A.: Tourism: An Intorduction. Sage Publications Ltd. (2003). https://doi.org/10.4135/9781446220108

19. Sánchez, E.C., Sánchez-Medina, A.J., Pellejero, M.: Identifying critical hotel cancellations using artificial intelligence. Tour. Manag. Perspect. **35**(November 2019), 100718 (2020). https://doi.org/10.1016/j.tmp.2020.100718

20. Momani, A.M.: Emerging technologies and their impact on the future of the tourism and hospitality industry. Int. J. Inf. Syst. Serv. Sect. **14**(1), 18 (2022). https://doi.org/10.4018/IJISSS.287579

21. He, Z., Wu, L., Li, X.R.: When art meets tech : the role of augmented reality in enhancing museum experiences and purchase intentions. Tour. Manage. **68**, 127–139 (2018). https://doi.org/10.1016/j.tourman.2018.03.003

22. Benyon, D., Quigley, A., O'keefe, B., Riva, G.: Prensence and digital tourism. AI & Soc. **29**(4), 521–529 (2013). https://doi.org/10.1007/s00146-013-0493-8

23. Neuburger, L., Beck, J., Egger, R.: The 'Phygital' tourist experience: the use of augmented and virtual reality in destination marketing. Tourism Planning and Destination Marketing, Chapter 9, pp. 183–202 (2018). https://doi.org/10.1108/978-1-78756-291-220181009

24. Verma, S., Warrier, L., Bolia, B., Mehta, S.: Past, present, and future of virtual tourism-a literature review. Int. J. Inf. Manage Data Insights **2** (2022). https://doi.org/10.1016/j.jjimei.2022.100085

25. Jayawardena, C.C.: What are the key innovative strategies needed for future tourism in the world? **11**(2), 235–247 (2019). https://doi.org/10.1108/WHATT-01-2019-0001

26. I Andersen, I.N.S.K., Kraus, A.A., Ritz, C., Bredie, W.L.: Desires for beverages and liking of skin care product odors in imaginative and immersive virtual reality beach contexts. Food Res. Int. (no. September 2017), 1 (2018). https://doi.org/10.1016/j.foodres.2018.01.027

27. Knobloch, U., Robertson, K., Aitken, R.: "Experience, emotion, and eudaimonia : a consideration of tourist experiences and well-being (2016). https://doi.org/10.1177/0047287516650937

28. Mura, P.: 'Authentic but not too much': exploring perceptions of authenticity of virtual tourism. Inf. Technol. Tour. 145–159 (2017)

29. Sparks, B.A., Browning, V.: The impact of online reviews on hotel booking intentions and perception of trust. Tour. Manage. **32**(6), 1310–1323 (2011). https://doi.org/10.1016/j.tourman.2010.12.011

30. Zhang: Would you enjoy virtual travel? The characteristics and causes of virtual tourists' sentiment under the influence of the COVID-19 pandemic. Tour. Manage. **88** (2022)

31. Lawelai, H., Iswanto, I., Raharja, N.M.: Use of artificial intelligence in public services : a bibliometric analysis and visualization. **12**(2), 798–807 (2023). https://doi.org/10.18421/TEM122

32. Zhong, B., Wu, H., Li, H., Sepasgozar, S., Luo, H., He, L.: A scientometric analysis and critical review of construction related ontology research. Autom. Constr. **101**(November 2018), 17–31 (2019). https://doi.org/10.1016/j.autcon.2018.12.013

33. Pan, X., Cui, M. Yu, X., Hua, W.: How is CiteSpace used and cited in the literature? An analysis of the articles published in English and Chinese core journals. ISSI 2017 - 16th International Conference on Science Information Conference Proceedings, vol. 2014, pp. 158–165 (2017)

34. Gegung, E.M.: International tourism and the COVID-19 pandemic: the use of virtual reality to increase tourism destination sustainability and how users perceive the authenticity of VR experiences. J. Kepariwisataan Indones. J. Penelit. dan Pengemb. Kepariwisataan Indones **15**(1), 9–15 (2021). https://doi.org/10.47608/jki.v15i12021.9-15

35. Wang, W., et al.: Realizing the potential of Internet of Things for smart tourism with 5G and AI. IEEE Netw. **34**(6), 295–301 (2020). https://doi.org/10.1109/MNET.011.2000250

36. Wu, J., Wang, J., Nicholas, S., Maitland, E., Fan, Q.: Application of big data technology for COVID-19 prevention and control in China : lessons and recommendations. **22** (2020). https://doi.org/10.2196/21980
37. Tech & Sci: China's Palace Museum takes visitors on VR Journey. news.cgtn.com (2020). news.cgtn.com/news/2020-10-21/China-s-Palace-Museum-takes-visitors-on-VR-jou rney-ULg0lSj7HO/share_amp.html. Accessed 8 June 2023
38. Chen, C.: CiteSpace A Pratical Guide For Mapping Scientific Literature. Nova Science Publishers Inc., New York (2016)
39. Dunning, T.: Accurate methods for the statistics of surprise and coincidence. Comput. Linguist. **19**(1), 61–74 (1993)
40. Cunneen, W.: 5 Problems with Virtual Reality Training They Don't Want You To Know (2022). https://roundtablelearning.com/, https://roundtablelearning.com/5-problems-with-virtual-rea lity-training-they-dont-want-you-to-know/. Accessed 9 June 2023
41. Lee, H., Jung, T.H., tom Dieck, M.C., Chung, N.: Experiencing immersive virtual reality in museums. Inf. Manage. **57**(5) (2020). https://doi.org/10.1016/j.im.2019.103229
42. Zeng, Y., Liu, L., Xu, R.: The effects of a virtual reality tourism experience on tourist's cultural dissemination behavior. Tour. Hosp. **3**(1), 314–329 (2022). https://doi.org/10.3390/tourhosp3 010021
43. Bharata, W.: Virtual reality experience in Indonesian tourism. Indones. J. Bus. Entrep. **9**(2), 334–345 (2023)
44. Alyahya, M., McLean, G.: Examining tourism consumers' attitudes and the role of sensory information in virtual reality experiences of a tourist destination. J. Travel Res. **61**(7), 1666–1681 (2022). https://doi.org/10.1177/00472875211037745
45. De Canio, F., Martinelli, E., Peruzzini, M., Marchi, G.: The use of virtual tours to stimulate consumers' buying and visit intentions: an application to the Parmigiano Reggiano cheese. Ital. J. Mark. **2021**(3), 209–226 (2021). https://doi.org/10.1007/s43039-021-00034-9
46. Wolf, S.: Virtual tourism, real experience: a motive-oriented approach to virtual tourism. In: 2023 CHI Conference on Human Factors Computing System, vol. 309, pp. 1–7 (2023). https:// doi.org/10.1145/3544549.3585594
47. Rasool, H., Maqbool, S., Tarique, M.: The relationship between tourism and economic growth among BRICS countries: a panel cointegration analysis. Future Bus. J. **7**(1), 1–11 (2021). https://doi.org/10.1186/s43093-020-00048-3
48. Vignaroli, L., et al.: The touristic sector in the 5G technology era: the 5G-TOURS project app-roach. In: 2020 IEEE Globecom Workshops, GC Wkshps 2020 - Proceedings, Rai Radiotele-visione Italiana, Italy: Institute of Electrical and Electronics Engineers Inc. (2020). https:// doi.org/10.1109/GCWkshps50303.2020.9367418
49. Xiaoling, P.: The transformation of artificial intelligence in the 5G era and the impact on educa-tion. In: 2022 IEEE 2nd International Conference on Electronic Technology, Communication and Information (ICETCI), pp. 903–907 (2022)
50. Batinic, I.: The role and importance of the internet in contemporary tourism in travel agencies business. IJCRSEE Int. J. Cogn. Res. Sci. Eng. Educ. 1(2), 1–4 (2013)
51. Kumar, S.: Impact of COVID-19 pandemic on tourism: recovery proposal for future tourism. Geo J. Tour. Geo Sites **33** (2020)
52. Yang, C., Yan, S. Wang, J., Xue, Y.: Flow experiences and virtual tourism: the role of techno-logical acceptance and technological readiness. Sustainability **14**(9) (2022). https://doi.org/ 10.3390/su14095361
53. Li-Xin, P.: The application of virtual reality technology to digital tourism systems. Int. J. Simul. Syst. Sci. Technol. **17**(18), 21–25 (2016)

A Tool to Predict Payment Default in Financial Institutions

D. Rivero(✉) ⓘ, L. Guerra ⓘ, W. Narváez ⓘ, and S. Arcinegas ⓘ

Pontifical Catholic University of Ecuador, Ibarra 100112, Ecuador
{dmrivero,lrguerra,smarginiegas}@pucesi.edu.ec

Abstract. Loans are financing services for clients of a bank and are one of the main activities in a financial institution since they are the means through which they make money. When a customer misses one or more payments cause grave problems at the bank at the point of crash. The bank loan manager to decide decides whether to approve or not the loan application using the client's financial and personal information. This decision always has associated risks. Currently, financial institutions, to reduce the risks associated with loan approval and take advantage of the large repositories of historical data from their clients, are using machine learning algorithms to identify if a client will comply with the loan payment. That information helps managers in their decision-making process. This paper presents the development of an application to support the process of authorizing or not a bank loan in the Acción Imbaburapak Savings and credit cooperative; to choose the model to use in the application, select after training three predictive methods. The analytical process followed the phases proposed by the KDD methodology. Three supervised classification methods were selected: logistic regression, decision trees, and neural networks. Since the neural network showed the best results during the evaluation, we chose this to build the application.

Keywords: Machine learning · bank loans · supervised learning · neural network

1 Introduction

Banking entities offer a variety of services to their customers, such as bank loans and credits, account management, among others. Of all these activities, bank loans and credits to legal or natural persons are one of its main activities, being its main source of income and therefore is where most of its capital is located. These activities, despite being lucrative, are the ones that generate the greatest risk for financial institutions, since there is a risk of approving loans that, due to non-payment of the loan and its interest, its capital is not recovered, causing significant losses. to the financial entity, being able to reach the extreme case of bankruptcy.

The default of payments in the credit portfolio is the main concern of risk managers in financial institutions, this scenario is known as credit risk. To reduce this risk, financial institutions need to validate and verify the documentation provided by loan applicants in order to find out if they have the necessary guarantees to grant the loan and, even so, it cannot be ensured that they are a client. Appropriate.

© The Author(s), under exclusive license to Springer Nature Switzerland AG 2024
H. Florez and M. Leon (Eds.): ICAI 2023, CCIS 1874, pp. 186–196, 2024.
https://doi.org/10.1007/978-3-031-46813-1_13

In recent years, due to the growing development of online banking applications and mobile applications, banks have large volumes of customer data, which facilitates the process of training models that can predict payment default [1]. Therefore, the challenge now is to find the learning model that best suits the characteristics of your customers.

Machine learning models have been used in various knowledge areas, such as financial business, human and medical resource management, and have shown to be successful in decision support systems [2]. In the case of bank loan support systems, different machine learning models have been used to predict whether the client has the characteristics to belong to the group of clients that pay their debts. These tools help the manager make the decision to approve or not the loan [3]. Among the algorithms that have been used to predict whether the client will comply with the loan payment in financial institutions, there are models developed using the Multiple Linear Regression (MLR) and Logistic Regression (LR) algorithms [4–6], algorithms of assembled methods have been used, such as Random Forests (RF) [7].

Support Vector Machines (SVM) have also been used in this domain, Pławiak, P. et al. [8] applied a Deep Genetic Cascade Classifier Set (DGCEC) which is a 16-layer system, in each layer one MSV was used, each classifier of the first layer is trained to improve the recognition of accepted or rejected borrowers, in layers 2 to 16, with the preprocessed data of the borrowers and the outputs of the classifiers of the first and the previous layers and applying a deep learning and the selection of genetic characteristics, the knowledge extraction process that leads to the final result by the method is carried out, generating the final output of the model, [9] proved that the K-Nearest Neighbors (KNN) algorithm coupled with parallelization produces good results for classification on large economic data. The models built Neural Networks have been used in [4].

Other approaches used are the search for models to customize the loans according to the requirements of the users to comfortably repay their loans at the best interest, thus reducing the risk of default [10] or strategic classification models in order to anticipate how users strategically modify the inputs under a given model to obtain the desired output [11, 12].

On the other hand, the need for intelligent applications that automatically replicate decision-making processes is greater every day, therefore, some banking applications allow customers to make loan applications online, thus expanding their model loan business. This expansion can cause inaccurate predictions, due to incomplete information from lenders. A solution to this problem has been to use the gradient boosting algorithm (LightGBM) based on decision trees [13, 14].

Despite the models developed to predict loan default, the particular characteristics of the clients of a bank in a region make it necessary to find a classification model that adapts to these characteristics. This paper describes the process that was carried out to find the classification model that most accurately predicted the possibility of default, as well as the development of a support application in the decision-making process for managers of the savings cooperative. And credit Acción Imbaburapak. To find the model, the data that characterizes the clients of this entity were selected and a set of models used in this domain were trained. Finally, the models were evaluated and the best of them was used in the development of the application.

The rest of the work is organized as follows, some general machine learning concepts and classification methods are presented in Sect. 2. Then, Sect. 3 describes the steps performed in this work to identify the set of features that describe the behavior of lenders and the training and selection of models. Section 4 shows the results obtained and the decision-making support system and finally the most relevant conclusions of this work are revealed.

1.1 Related Concepts

Classification: it is the process that partitions a data set X characterized by attributes in a set of disjoint groups, where the individuals of each group share common characteristics. Each group is called a category or class of the set. There are several methods to classify:

- Supervised classification: for each observation (x_i, $i = 1, ..., n$), for each observation there is a predictor measure and an associated response measure yi. It is desired to find a model that relates the response to the predictors, that is, the model that predicts the class given the attribute values, in order to accurately predict the response for future observations. These methods can be statistical (Logistic Regression, discriminant analysis) or from the field of Artificial Intelligence (Neural Networks, Rule Induction, Decision Trees, Bayesian Networks).
- Unsupervised classification: in this process each observation ($x_i = 1, ..., n$) has an associated response, that is, the class or category to which it belongs is not known, so the aim is to discover the groups of individuals whose similar characteristics allow them to be separated into different classes.

The supervised classification algorithms used in this work are described below.

- Logistic Regression (LR): This algorithm expresses the probability of a certain outcome ($Y = 1$ o $Y = 0$) as a function of the r-attributes of the observation ($x_{j,1}$, $x_{j,2}$, ... $x_{j,r}$). The attributes can be of any nature (continuous, discrete, dichotomous, ordinal or nominal). The result of the algorithm is to find the coefficients β_0, β_1 ... β_r, that best fit the sigmoid function. In this, the curve can take any value between ($-\infty$, + $-\infty$) and assign it to the output [0,1]. If the sigmoid goes towards positive infinity it becomes 1 and if it goes towards negative infinity, it becomes 0 [15]:

$$P(Y = 1) = \frac{1}{1 + ex(-\beta_0 - \beta_1 x_{1,r} - \cdots - \beta_r X_{n,r})} \tag{1}$$

- Decision trees (DT): it is a hierarchical tree structure formed by nodes of different types:
- The internal nodes represent each of the characteristics or properties to be considered to make a decision. The branch represents the decision based on a specific condition (i.e., probability of an event occurring).
- Decision nodes or end nodes represent the outcome of the decision.

Depending on the characteristics in the internal nodes, evaluations are carried out to form homogeneous subsets, which are indicated in decision nodes. The learning employs a divide-and-conquer strategy by performing a greedy search to identify optimal split points within a tree [16].

- Random Forests (RF): is a set of decision trees combined with bagging (assembled method), where different trees see different portions of the data. This is so that each tree is trained with different data samples for the same problem. In this way, when combining their results, some errors are compensated with others in order to obtain a prediction that generalizes better [17].
- Neural Network: It is a computational model. It consists of a set of units called artificial neurons, connected to transmit signals. The attribute values are the inputs that traverse the network, where it is subjected to various operations, producing output values. Each neuron is connected to others through links and each link is assigned a weight that serves to inhibit the activation state of adjacent neurons. A threshold function can be associated to the output of the neurons, which modifies the result value before propagating to another neuron. This function is known as the activation function [18].

2 Methods

This work is applied research. For the choice of the predictive model, the learning algorithms were trained with the set of selected attributes, this phase was called the data analytics phase. Once the predictive model was selected, the development phase was executed where the support application was built.

For data processing and model training, the scikit-learning library was used.

2.1 Data Analytics Phase

In this phase, the Knowledge Database Discovery (KDD) methodology was used [19]. The processes carried out were: selection, processing and transformation of the data used for training. Then the algorithms were selected and trained and finally the results obtained with the test data were evaluated and the model with the best results was selected.

2.2 Data Selection

To identify the data to be used in training the algorithms, the cooperative's credit manager, responsible for analyzing and approving the credits, was interviewed to identify some of the attributes used in the analysis of the requests. The database containing the information on the credits requested during the last 10 years was also reviewed. Once the characteristics were identified and their data was located in the financial institution's database, a table was created with all the customer data.

The characteristics were grouped by three aspects, the group of variables associated with personal data, geographic aspects and economic-credits that included delinquency variables such as the client's credit history, the applicable interest rate, the term of the loan. Variables of expenses and payments and balance. Table 1 shows the attributes selected as economic-credit data.

Table 1. Data obtained in the attribute selection phase.

Name	Description	Type
Create Date	Creation date	Date
Payment fee	Number of loan installments	Integer
Value	Requested credit amount	Float
interest rate	Applicable interest rate	Integer
Income	Total customer revenue	Float
Cats	Total customer expenses	Float
Months Economic Activity	Number of months that the applicant's work time or activity is justified	Integer
balance	Sum of assets plus liabilities	Float
Payment fee	Amount of the credit payment fee	Float
Number of fees	Number of installments	Integer
Number of credits	Number of credits that the client has had with the entity	Integer
Current debt	Value of the pending amount to be paid by the customer	Float
Guarantee	Does the client have guarantees or not?	Logic
Type of loan	Type of loan requested	Categoric
Account movements	Number of movements in the client's account before generating the loan	Integer

2.3 Data Preprocessing

In this phase, the quality of the data was analyzed and they were cleaned, eliminating atypical and lost data. As a strategy for the problem of missing data, based on the fact that there were not many rows with this problem with respect to the total volume of data (1%), the rows in which missing, null or duplicate data were found were eliminated.

First, the attributes that do not provide relevant information for model training were eliminated. Attributes referring to the geographic location of the client, such as parish and political division, were removed and replaced by the geographic area. The attributes loan number, loan assignment date, expense and equity values, and award date were also eliminated. Subsequently, it was validated if there were rows with null values or with negative values (integers or negative decimals). At the end of this process, 32,842 observations were obtained, with 5,998 approved credits, and 26,844 denied credits.

It was studied if any characteristic had atypical values, since these distort the results of the models. In this work, the extreme data, that is, those that deviated significantly from the mean, were eliminated. Figure 1 shows the box plot of the requested fee amount attribute, in this the presence of atypical values is observed, for which they were eliminated.

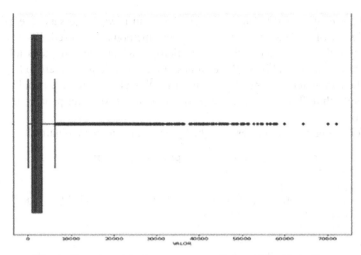

Fig. 1. Box plot of the loan amount attribute to identify outliers

2.4 Data Transformation

In this phase, the data is statistically manipulated in order to reduce the data set, extract important variables, detect outliers and anomalies, and determine the best configuration of the data under study. Data types were transformed from categorical to numeric as the models use numeric values for training. The modified attributes were gender, marital status, type of housing, level of education, type of guarantee.

We proceeded to identify the set of useful characteristics to adequately represent the bank's customers. To reduce the dimensionality of the data and therefore improve the behavior of the models, the number of features was decreased. A vertical reduction was performed by removing features that showed a dependency or correlation. To calculate the correlation, the Spearman method was used since when the distributions that followed the attributes were studied, it was observed that they did not follow a normal distribution.

The correlation study allowed us to see how strong the relationship that existed between the attributes of the data set was. Once the correlation values were obtained, it was identified that the attributes of the number of payment installments, amount requested, income, value of the installment are the important ones for training the models.

At the end, the numerical attributes were normalized. The final data set was made up of 10 attributes and 24092 observations, leaving as final attributes: Payment installment, number of installments, value, income, present debt, corporate credits, marital status, type of housing, guarantee, days of delay.

2.5 Data Mining

In this phase, two data sets were initially generated, the set to train the algorithms and the test set. 75% of the data was selected for training and 25% for testing. The selected algorithms were logistic regression, Decision Trees, Random Forests and Neural Networks (NN).

For the execution and training of each algorithm it was necessary to establish the values of a set of parameters, for this, different methods were used. For example, to train the algorithm associated with the LogisticRegression() method, the GridSearchCV function was used, it combines all the values of the possible parameters to find the best values. The parameters that needed to be set for this algorithm were penalty, log, and training algorithm. The values of the parameters obtained were: penalty l2, C: 0.01, solver: lbfgs.

The following code describes how the hyperparameters were obtained.

```
From sklearn.model_selection import GridSearchCV
X = numeric
Y= answer
X_train, X_test, y_train, Y_test = train_test_split(X,y,
test_size = 0,25, ramdom_state=42)
parameters = {
'penalty':['l1','l2'],
'C':no.logspace(-3,3,7),
'solver':['newton-cg','lbfgs','liblinear']
}
logist= LgisticRegression()
grid= GridSearchCV(logist,parameters,scoring="accu
racy",cv=10)
grid.fit(X_train,y_train)
```

The Fig. 2 shows the values obtained for the parameters.

To train the NN algorithm, the Keras library was used, which works together with Tesnsorflow. For the design of the network, 1 input layer with 10 neurons, two hidden layers with 50 and 10 neurons respectively, and an output layer were used, and 250 epochs were defined for training.

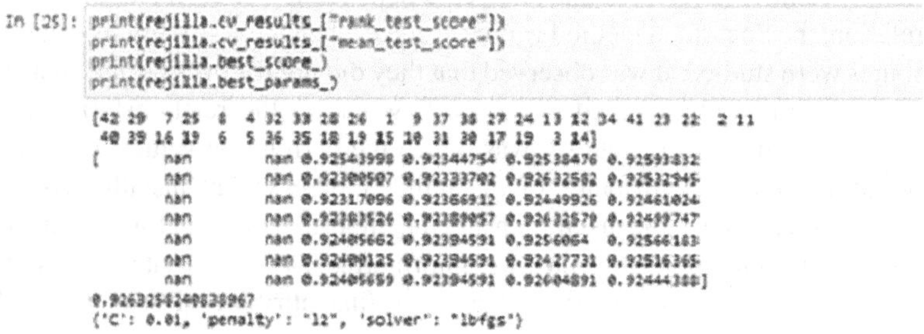

Fig. 2. Code and parameters to train the Logistic Regression model.

3 Results

After training the models, each one was validated. For this, the test data was used, obtaining as an output the set of labels (predictions) associated with the test case, with these data and the real labels of the tests, the confusion matrix was built and the precision, accuracy metrics were calculated and F1 score for each model. Table 2 shows the values of the confusion matrix and Table 3 presents the values obtained in each metric.

Table 2. Results of the confusion matrix of each model.

Method	True Positive	True Negative	False Positive	False Negative
Logistic regression	947	4602	260	214
Decision tree	760	4860	2	401
Random trees	834	4773	89	327
Neural networks	958	4609	290	166

Table 3. Metric values for each model

Method	Accuracy	Precision	Recall	F1- Score
Logistic regression	92%	78%	82%	80%
Decision tree	93%	100%	65%	79%
Random trees	93%	90%	72%	80%
Neural networks	92%	77%	85%	81%

In addition, the ROC curves of each model were generated to observe the relationship between Sensitivity vs. Specificity and the area under the curve (AUC) was also calculated. AUC values are shown in Table 4.

Table 4. AUC values for each model

Logistic regression	Decision tree	Random trees	Neural networks
0,881	0,827	0,854	0,971

4   Discussion

The metrics obtained showed that in terms of accuracy, the four methods had a very close value, varying only by 1%. The model generated by the decision trees and the random Forest had higher repetition but lower recall and F1 scores. Finally, the NN model, although its precision was not the best in terms of all the metrics, was the one that obtained the best values, which can be confirmed by observing the values thrown by the AUC, which indicates that the NN model has a higher AUC. It was concluded that the model with the best behavior was the one generated by the Neural Network. For this reason, it was used in the construction of the application.

5   Application Development

For the design, a micro-services-oriented style was chosen, which can be deployed in any entity's server and consumed by any application that requires it in the future. The service is only responsible for evaluating a loan application based on the model obtained in the training. To do this, the model generated during training was uploaded to the service.

The evaluteModel(parameterList) microservice was built, which receives as parameters a subset of the attributes required to make the prediction. The service, internally, calls the findCustomer() method to obtain the values of the missing attributes that are stored in the institution's DB. It then calls the model method (), this is responsible for creating the array with the attributes and calling the model evaluation function (predict()). Figure 3 presents the sequence diagram that describes the behavior of the evaluateModel() method. The GUI requests the evaluateModel() service and sends the values of the attributes that are requested in the interface, the service additionally needs other client attributes that are stored in the database, for this it calls the finAttributes() method to the entity CustomerDB, the service then loads the NN model and calls the predict() method to perform the prediction.

The interface of the loan management support application was also designed and built. This is used to request the values of the attributes that are not found in the database and to invoke the prediction method. The result of the prediction is displayed graphically, it indicates whether the model predicts that the client will pay the loan (green color) or if the client will not comply with the payments (red color), In addition, the value produced by the neural network is indicated (0 or 1 or a value very close to one of the extremes). Figure 4 presents the behavior of the application interface.

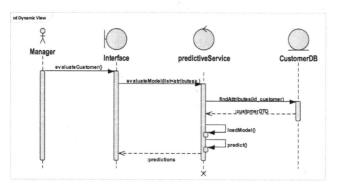

Fig. 3. Sequence diagram for the creation of the function

Fig. 4. Application interface that supports credit decision making

6 Conclusions

The use of statistical or computational models such as those used in this work are an excellent support tool to address the problem of credit risks. Models can reduce credit risk of default by classifying customers into paying and defaulting customers.

Different classification models have been used to predict defaults. For now, there is no general model to be used to predict defaults in a general way. The models are sensitive to the data you have and the selected attributes.

The results obtained in this study show the importance that the neural networks model represents as a prediction model and the application developed serves as a support tool to reduce the work that the manager must carry out in the analysis of the risk of non-compliance.

Developing the evaluation method as a service allows it to be used in mobile applications that make it easier for bank customers to make credit requests online in the future.

References

1. Lai, L.: Loan default prediction with machine learning techniques. In: 2020 International Conference on Computer Communication and Network Security (CCNS), pp. 5–9. IEEE (2020)
2. Tan, Z., Yan, Z., Zhu, G.: Stock selection with random forest: An exploitation of excess return in the Chinese stock market. Heliyon **5**(8), e02310 (2019)
3. Aslam, U., et al.: An empirical study on loan default prediction models. J. Comput. Theor.Nanosci. **16**(8), 3483–3488 (2019)
4. Alsaleem, M.Y., Hasqon, S.O.: Predicting bank loan risks using machine learning algorithms. AL-Rafidain J. Comput. Sci. Math. **14**(1), 149–158 (2020)
5. Nazemi, A., Heidenreich, K., Fabozzi, F.J.: Improving corporate bond recovery rate prediction using multi-factor support vector regressions. Eur. J. Oper. Res. **271**(2), 664–675 (2018)

6. Paredes, J.S.V.: Análisis de riesgo para préstamos bancarios. ILUMINATE, 47–60 (2020)
7. Gupta, R., et al.: The predictive value of inequality measures for stock returns: An analysis of long-span UK data using quantile random forests. Finan. Res. Lett. **29**, 315–322 (2019)
8. Pławiak, P., Abdar, M., Rajendra Acharya, U.: Application of new deep genetic cascade ensemble of SVM classifiers to predict the Australian credit scoring. Appl. Soft Comput. J. **84**, 105–740 (2019)
9. Soleymani, F., Masnavi, H., Shateyi, S.: Classifying a lending portfolio of loans with dynamic updates via a machine learning technique. Mathematics **9**(1), 17 (2021)
10. Barua, S., Gavandi, D., Sangle, P., Shinde, L., Ramteke, J.: Swindle: Predicting the probability of loan defaults using catboost algorithm. In: 2021 5th International Conference on Computing Methodologies and Communication (ICCMC), pp. 1710–115. IEEE (2021)
11. Levanon, S., Rosenfeld, N.: Strategic classification made practical. In: International Conference on Machine Learning, pp. 6243–6253. PMLR (2021)
12. Ghalme, G., Nair, V., Eilat, I., Talgam-Cohen, I., Rosenfeld, N.: Strategic classification in the dark. In: International Conference on Machine Learning, pp. 3672–3681. PMLR (2021)
13. Wang, D.N., Li, L., Zhao, D.: Corporate finance risk prediction based on LightGBM. Inf. Sci. **602**, 259–268 (2022)
14. Zhu, Q., Ding, W., Xiang, M., Hu, M., Zhang, N.: Loan default prediction based on convolutional neural network and LightGBM. Int. J. Data Warehouse Min. (IJDWM). **19**, 1–16 (2023)
15. Braga, L.P.V., Valencia, L.I.O., Carvajal, S.S.R.: Introducción a la Minería de Datos. Editora E-papers (2009)
16. IBM. https://www.ibm.com/es-es/topics/decision-trees#:~:text=Un%20%C3%A1rbol%20de%20decisi%C3%B3n%20es,nodos%20internos%20y%20nodos%20hoja. Accessed 05 Feb 2022
17. IA.net Homepage. https://www.iartificial.net/random-forest-bosque-aleatorio. Accessed 31 Jan 2022
18. Fernández, A.O.N.: Redes Neuronales (2021)
19. Fayyad, U., Piatetsky-Shapiro, G., Smyth, P.: From data mining to knowledge discovery in databases. AI Mag. **17**(3), 37 (1996)

Prediction Value of a Real Estate in the City of Quito Post Pandemic

Wladimir Vilca$^{(\boxtimes)}$, Joe Carrion-Jumbo, Diego Riofrío-Luzcando, and César Guevara

Universidad Internacional SEK, Digital School Faculty, Calle Italia N31 - 125 y Av. Mariana de Jesús, Quito, Ecuador
wladimir.vilca@uisek.edu.ec
https://www.uisek.edu.ec/

Abstract. Many real estate projects were paralyzed due to a lack of funding, and sales dropped significantly due to COVID-19. This article provides a method to predict the value of real estate in the city of Quito post-pandemic, using a methodology that compares different data mining techniques to achieve the best accuracy. In the end, it has been possible to classify the properties in different sectors of the population under study with a good level of value prediction. It can be concluded that the study based on a review of the appropriate literature, the comparison of different techniques, and the segmentation of the population is a basis for other studies that apply other techniques to further improve the level of prediction.

Keywords: machine learning · data · real estate · pandemic · appraisal

1 Introduction

The real estate area has been affected by the pandemic, and unemployment has become part of the deterioration of people's economies. "The pandemic has been a catalyst for changes in the perception of housing and in buyers' habits... single-family home sales skyrocketed during the first 7 months of 2021 compared to previous years", [6] said a professor at EAE Business School. The formation of real estate prices responds to the same logic as that of financial assets, where speculation is common [14].

According to the Association of Real Estate Housing Developers of Ecuador (APIVE), the net reserves of the sector between January and June 2021 grew by 44% compared to 2020, while visits to projects grew by 11% during the same period in 2021 versus the year before [3].

The experience of qualified professionals in an appraisal is important, and the particularity of the place where the property is located must be considered

---

Supported by Organization X.

since this can influence the moment of valuing a property and therefore cause its price to increase or decrease. Among other aspects of appraisal are mobility, measurement tools, etc. "Quito is located in the central region of the Ecuadorian highlands with a very irregular geographical context. (Metropolitan District of Quito, 2014).

This work proposes to apply machine learning techniques in order to forecast real estate values in the city of Quito. Applying algorithms is a simple way of facilitating the access and availability of information for the purpose of obtaining results in a more dynamic way.

The supervised learning process consists of training the neural network from a set of input data and their respective outputs. The learning algorithm adjusts the parameters of the network in such a way that the output generated by the ANN fits the data. Output is given some input [1].

In this type of learning, the figure "supervisor" is not conceived, and its main objective is to implement an output. It is based on the redundancy in the inputs, and the learning is extracted from the patterns that it obtains from the data input.

Below is a review of the literature related to the problem analyzed, the methodology applied, models, algorithms, and data used, then the results are presented for each model and geographical area under study, and the conclusions, limitations, and future work are presented.

1.1 Literature Review

There were three outstanding investigations that coincided with criteria and keywords such as "real estate + neural network" and applied variables such as: **area**, **price**, and others. The related works are the following:

1. Predictive analysis using Big Data for the real estate market during the COVID-19 pandemic. (Análisis predictivo utilizando Big Data para el mercado inmobiliario durante la pandemia del COVID-19) [16].
   It provides insight into the understanding of the applied machine learning models as well as which ones were the most accurate for real estate prediction. It collects data with web scraping, and the methodological steps were taken in building the machine learning models. Considering variables such as type of building, years old, size in square meters, room number, number of floors, garages, and other characteristics of the house, as well as proximity to universities, schools, shopping centers, and train stations as the characteristics most significant that affect the price.
2. Boost home price predictions by integrating geospatial networks [18]. The objective of this research was to predict the value of a house. The price is one of the most critical factors for buying a house, and highlighting the importance of the location and geospatial location, which is based on the installation of the neighborhood, also includes aspects such as room number, number of bathrooms, construction area, services, the proximity of the property to schools, train stations, and supermarkets, it is an area in a residential location whose environment is in harmony with the lifestyle of future buyers.

3. Real Estate Investing in Dubai: A Predictive and Time Series Analysis [19]. The objective of this research was to predict the house's value, considering that the price is a critical factor in the process of buying a house, as well as the geospatial location, which is based on the services of the neighborhood. Another aspect was considered, like the number of rooms and bathrooms, the construction area, etc. The study considers the proximity of the property to schools, train stations, and supermarkets as a residential location whose environment guarantees harmony for the future buyer's lifestyle.

2   Methodology

It is necessary to understand the process that an expert carries out and applies at the time of carrying out the appraisal. One of the methods they use is the so-called "comparison", which determines the value of the land in the value intervention area that does not have services and infrastructure "compared to another with homogeneous characteristics in the same area, for the same purpose and potentiality" [8].

The CRISP-DM (CRoss Industrial Standard Process for Data Mining) methodology will be used because it describes the key processes to carry out a data mining project

1. **Business understanding**: at the beginning, the objective is to obtain an overview of the real estate sector.
2. **Data preparation**: a phase that took a long time, since the selected data sets and their fields had to be cleaned before they could be used.
3. **Modelling**: in this phase, the analysis was carried out using the selected modeling techniques.
4. **Evaluation**: once the models were built and based on the metrics implemented, the evaluation was carried out.

2.1   Dataset

The web pages visited for the elaboration of this investigation were PROPERATI, PLUSVALIA, and REMAX, in which the web scraping tool was applied so that the information for the present project was collected.

2.2   Data Extraction

It was done by accessing the URL of the aforementioned real estate pages, where published information on houses is found and later saved in csv format. Among all of them, PROPERATI stands out because its portal allows downloading csv files, plus the data downloaded with the web scraping tool from the other web pages constitutes the data set for this project. It is necessary to highlight that the data obtained corresponds to the year 2020.

2.3 Data Transformation

In the transformation of the downloaded data set, the data of the collected properties was initially analyzed with the Excel tool; this was done with the purpose of visualizing the content of the information so that the starting point could be used to continue with the transformation process of the data.

2.4 Data Visualization

Once the data set was downloaded for the analysis of this work, it consisted of 288,984 observations and 24 columns or variables. The content of each column was analyzed, and its contribution to this research was verified. For a better understanding, all of this is described in detail in Table 1.

Table 1. Description of the variables.

Variable	Description
ad_type	Kind of property
Id	Automatically generated code numeric
start_date	Publication date
created_on	Post creation date
end_date	Finish date
Lat	Latitude
Lon	Length
l1	Country
l2	Province
l3	Canton
l4	Industry location name
l5	Industry name
l6	Neighborhood name
Rooms	Number of rooms
Bedrooms	Number of bathrooms
Area	Total area in of the property
Construction	Construction area
Price	Price in $
Surface	Area in
Currency	Currency USD
Description	Description of the user enters
Title	Post title
Price_period	Price periods

2.5   Column and Data Cleaning

For cleaning, we proceeded with the verification of the characteristics of the data. Columns were selected and eliminated due to their content, since many of these columns did not provide significant value for the present work. Table 2 shows the name of the variable and a brief description of its contents.

Table 2. Dropped Variables Table

Variable	Description
id	Generated Code Numeric and does not provide information.
created_on	Post creation date.
end_date	Finish date.
Surface	Area in m2
Currency	Currency USD
Description	Description that the user enters.
Title	post title
Price_period	Price periods

For the selection and cleaning of records within the data, the R-studio command was used, and the indications containing "9999-12-31" and empty were eliminated since they do not contribute to the data. According to the research "Model of Classification of Credit Risk Using Random Forest in a Finance Company of Ecuador", it should be checked if there are missing values that can generate errors when training the algorithm" [4].

2.6   Application of Automatic Methods

Some machine learning algorithms were applied, such as linear regression, decision trees, random forests, and neural networks, in order to respond to the proposed objective and later in the measurement of performance in models. In the implementation of the automatic methods, the open-source software R Studio was used, as well as Orange and Weka previously described in the theoretical framework section.

2.7   Algorithms and Key Parameters

A first aspect to consider is that there are several machine learning techniques that can classify, group, or predict data. The models used were:

- Linear Regression: The linear regression technique allows predicting the value of a variable from the values of another.

- Random Forest: The Random Forest algorithm works by aggregating the predictions made by multiple decision trees of variable depth. This method allows to correctly classify each variable based on a given objective.
- Decision Tree: Is a set of statistical algorithms that, through predictive methods, classifies data according to certain characteristics or properties, obtaining accurate and reliable models as a result. Initially.
- Neural network: Is a machine learning algorithm that can solve problems through machine learning, which trains neural networks with different structures for better results to be extracted with greater precision [11].

Also, the important parameters to verify for each method are:

- R2: A statistical measure that explains differences in one variable can be explained by the difference in a second variable.
- RMSE: Measure of the distance of the data points from the regression line
- CV: statistical measure of the dispersion of data points in a data series around the mean.

3 Results

The result of the transformation of the data through the visualization, analysis, and cleaning of the records allowed us to obtain a set of data ready to be used in the present project.

3.1 Data Analysis

Figure 1 shows the correlation of the variables that the data source has, with the largest circles being those with the best correlation and reaching the smallest circles with little correlation between the variables, obtaining the variables with the highest correlation of the area, construction, and price

Table 3 shows that for the large data set, we proceeded to segment some areas of the city of Quito into sectors; these sections are numbered from 1 to 7, since the downloaded data included said sectors. After that, their respective analyses were carried out.

Table 3. Sectors of Quito according to the downloaded data

Sector	Number
North of Quito	1
South of Quito	2
Valle de Tumbaco	3
Colonial Center	4
Valle de los Chillos	5
North Center	6
Others	7

3.2 Linear Regression

In this case, the price and area variables were used, and with both of them, it is possible to see the relationship between the **area** and the **price**.

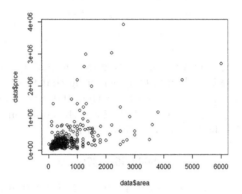

Fig. 1. Area and Price Scatter chart.

It shows, with small circles, the correlation dispersion of the data on the x axis. The area is in m2, and the y axis is the **price** in USD. We can observe the behavior of the data and its variations, which indicate that as the area of the property increases, so does the price.

Similarly, the correlation can be analyzed by means of Pearson's correlation, Table 4 shows the Pearson correlation by taking the **price** and **area** variables as parameters. When performing the correlation of the **price** and **area** variables, it is observed that there is a strong correlation between the two variables, and given that the p-value is less than 2.2e-16, it shows that there is a linear correlation as well.

Table 4. Pearson Coefficient Calculation

t	21.149
df	741
p Value	2.2e-16
Confidence Interval	95%
Cor	0.6135251

In this way, a linear regression model called "Modelo RL" can be proposed through the lm function of R, and later, the results can be displayed with summary (Modelo_RL), so that the results can be interpreted.

Table 5. Results of the estimation with the Linear Regression Model

Linear Regression Model	price vs Area
Estimated price	78644.45
Estimated Area	379.7
p Value	2e-16

Observing Table 5, once the Linear Regression model has been applied, the p-value is shown to be less than 0.05, considering that the model has a % confidence, as it has a significance value of less than 0.05. We can ensure that 0.05. We can ensure that the model is valid. To form the equation, we take the values of the coefficients. 78644.45 and 379.70 from Fig. 4.

$$x = 78644.45 + 379.70x \tag{1}$$

Equation 1 of the line allows us to predict the value of a piece of real estate with a certain area, according to the linear regression equation, just by moving x by the area in m2 of the real estate.

3.3   Random Forest

In the data set that is obtained when using the random forest, the possibilities of obtaining a more reasonable value for the properties by sectors are high since the decision is based on the results of multiple decision trees.

Table 6 shows the application of the Random Forest method. A partition of the data was created with 0.70 of the original data for building a model with Random Forest, where x represents the independent variables as well as the dependent variable. Ntree represents the number of trees that need to be generated. Later, we will make the prediction with the rest of the data. Resulting in the classification of real estate in each sector.

Table 6. Settings applied for Random Forest Model

Random Forest	Quito
Partition training data	0.7
X = Quito data	2:4
Y = Quito data	1
Number of trees	500

3.4   Decision Tree

We decided to use the area and construction variables of the real estate, but we had better influence using the **price**.

In the study of resolutions, it is possible to implement a decision tree to visually show the tree and thus, based on a set of variables, make the correct decision.

In Fig. 2, the algorithm shows the construction of the tree according to the data entered and its variables in the root node created by the tree. The **price** (real estate value)is taken as the main attribute, and at the first level we can observe 100% of the data, the first distinction made based on **price**. The properties with lower values than the one taken as a reference are 66% and the properties greater than said value correspond to 34%. The second distinction made corresponds to 34% and takes the **price** to be 25% lower than the referred **price** and 8% higher than this. For the third distinction, it takes construction, constructions smaller than 254 m$\hat{2}$ corresponds to 13%, and constructions greater than this value are 13%. The fourth distinction corresponds to 13% by taking real estate area, showing as a result that the area greater than 318 m$\hat{2}$ corresponds to 3% and less than this value is 9%.

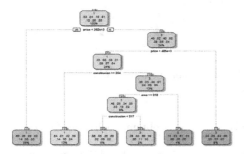

Fig. 2. Visualization tree using R

3.5   Neural Networks

Artificial networks are made up of nodes, or neurons," that receive, transmit, and send information; they are usually made up of layers. These networks are trained in a way that allows them to create, modify, or eliminate a connection between the nodes in order to provide a response.

The neural network method is applied. For the data presented in the present neural network, as input, there are all the independent variables that correlate with the **price** variable.

Figure 3 shows the input of the neural network and its output, which is the objective of the network. Its objective is the **price**, the presented neural network was carried out in 193 steps, which works with 9 neurons in the first layer and for the second layer 7 neurons.

4   Evaluation of Automatic Methods

This section shows the results of the performance measures after running the models on the seven data sets. The procedure for all models was the same in each case for both training and testing.

4.1   Results North Sector of Quito

Next, Table 7 shows the result of the performance measures generated by the models applied to the data in the northern sector of Quito.

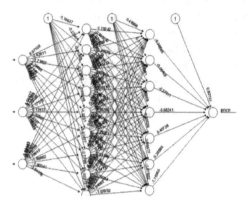

Fig. 3. Scheme neural network and its output

Table 7. Results obtained with the North Sector

	Linear Regression	Decision Tree	Random Forest	Neural network
R2	0.36	0.087	0.188	-0.57
RMSE	205148.504	245482.743	231397.99	322566.067
CV	1.0	1.25	1.18	1.65

Application result of the models concludes that the best determination co-efficient is the Linear Regression with a value of 0.36, likewise, it can be seen that the smallest **RMSE** error is the Linear Regression. This allows verifying that the prediction value of the property is close to the real one in the sector, and finally it is seen how the coefficient of variation is also lower in the Linear Regression.

4.2   Results of South Sector of Quito

In Table 8 It is shown that the best determination coefficient is linear regression with a value of 0.24, followed by random forest. This makes it possible to verify that the predicted value of the property is close to the actual value in the same sector. Also, it can be seen that the coefficient of variation is lower in random forests since the method coincides with the northern sector.

Table 8. Results obtained with the South Sector

	Linear Regression	Decision Tree	Random Forest	Neural network
R2	0.24	−0.40	0.125	−3.23
RMSE	44852.982	61047.422	48207.507	106028.419
CV	0.48	0.65	0.24	0.54

4.3   Results in the Valle de Tumbaco

Table 9 shows the performance of the Tumbaco Valley sector, in its results it indicates that the best coefficient of determination is Linear Regression with 0.62, followed by Random Forest with 0.54. For this sector, the neural network is the one with the lowest performance, it is shown that the value of the real estate with the southern sector of Quito is more economical than that of the Chillos Valley sector.

Table 9. Results in the Tumbaco Valley

	Linear Regression	Decision Tree	Random Forest	Neural network
R2	0.62	0.48	0.54	−0.78
RMSE	340741.160	396205.408	374709.079	490164.994
CV	0.69	0.80	0.21	0.99

4.4   Results Colonial Center Sector

As can be seen in Table 10, it is shown how the applied models do not contribute to the analysis; this is due to the fact that the data for this sector are small and consequently do not provide significant results, which is why they are excluded from this analysis.

Table 10. Results Colonial Center Sector

	Linear Regression	Decision Tree	Random Forest	Neural network
R2	−0.11	−0.19	−0.33	−12.97
RMSE	161446.168	49453.644	55661.92	163246.749
CV	0.98	0.30	0.34	0.33

4.5   Results of Valle de Los Chillos Sector

With the results of Table 11, it can be seen that the linear regression method has a higher coefficient of determination, followed by Random Forest; reviewing the previous results for the north sector 2.3, it can be deduced that the Linear Regression has a better impact on the sectors.

Table 11. Results of Valle de los Chillos Sector

	Linear Regression	Decision Tree	Random Forest	Neural network
R2	0.67	0.18	0.49	-1.2
RMSE	89926.373	143180.899	113115.389	240211.485
CV	0.49	0.79	0.62	1.3

4.6   Results Central North Sector

In Table 12 it is verified that the best determination coefficient is the linear regression method, and it can be seen that the low results are due to the scarce data sets of the north-central sector.

Table 12. Results Central North Sector

	Linear Regression	Decision Tree	Random Forest	Neural network
R2	0.07	−0.9	−0.4	−1.8
RMSE	147133.416	211231.11	183767.651	258027.961
CV	0,70	0.98	0.88	0.99

4.7   Other Sector Results

Table 13 As a result, for the other sector, the coefficient of determination with the greatest importance is Random Forest with 0.11 and its coefficient of variation is 0.86, which is lower compared to the other methods implemented.

Table 13. Other Sector Results.

	Linear Regression	Decision Tree	Random Forest	Neural network
R2	−0.13	−0.23	0.11	−1.17
RMSE	202503.134	211365.420	178830.719	280151.443
CV	0.98	0.99	0.86	1.36

4.8   Analysis of Results with ROC and AUC

From the analysis carried out and the results obtained with the applied methods, the so-called ROC analysis and AUC could be performed, which would allow verifying the classification performance of the applied methods.

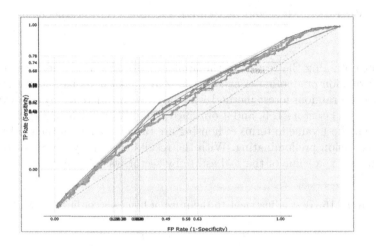

Fig. 4. Analysis of results with ROC and AUC

Figure 4 In the evaluation of the methods, it is observed that, for each method applied, the lower area of the **AUC** curve stands out with its respective value. In the ROC curve figure, the Y axis corresponds to the proportion of true positives over the total number of properties in the established sectors, and the X axis corresponds to the proportion of false positives over the total number of properties in the established sectors. Examining the ROC curve figure shows the "proportion of true positives" (Y axis) versus the "proportion of false positives" (X axis).

5   Discussion of Results

In this section, the techniques applied in the preparation of this work are detailed, as is their interpretation. In total, 1263 records were used, which, in the application of the chosen methods, had a partition of 70% for training and 30% for tests, since in this way it was possible to analyze the results obtained and their performance.

Table 14 was prepared as an explanation and summary of the techniques applied for each data set, showing the aforementioned percentages.

Table 14. Results obtained with the North Central sector.

Model	Regression, Decision Tree, Random Forest
Performance	Correlation of variables
Data	1263 individuals
Partition	Partition: 70%, Training 30%
Variables	14 sectors de Quito, Price, Area m2, Construction m2

After obtaining the results of the applied methods, it can be observed that linear regression predominates over sectors 2, 3, 5, and 6, unlike the other sectors in which the random forest method was the best. In reference to the RMSE, it is verified that sectors 1, 3, and 4 obtained a high value in housing; the sectors with the highest value in terms of housing are those areas, with the model called linear regression predominating. With the results thrown by RMSE distributed for each sector, a value of the real estate by sector was obtained.

Table 15. Best adjustment to the price of homes according to RMSE

Sector	RMSE
Norte	$ 251148,83
Sur de Quito	$ 65034,082
Valle de Tumbaco	$ 400455,160
Valle los Chillos	$ 146608,53
Centro Norte	$ 200040,03
Otros	$ 218212,679

Table 15 shows the average value of different neighborhoods using the automatic learning methods. It is evident that the sector with high capital gains, according to the cost of housing, is Valle de Tumbaco, and the sector with the lowest capital gains is the south of Quito.

The ROC curve shows the performance of classification models Table 16.

Table 16. ROC and AUC analysis

Model	AUC	Accuracy
Decision Tree	0.59	0.45
Random Forest	0.64	0.40
Neural Network	0.65	0.39
Linear Regression	0.66	0.65

Through the ROC and AUC analysis produced by the models applied to the Quito data, the Linear Regression presents the highest percentage of precision when predicting the value of the property in the data set.

6   Conclusions and Future Work

In this study, a process of obtaining data through the use of web scraping was proposed. This tool provided data from the different web portals available that are involved in the real estate branch. These datasets were widely used at the time of training the implemented models. In order to obtain satisfactory results, we used different machine learning techniques like linear regression, random forest, neural networks, and decision trees with different libraries to analyze this data. As a result, linear regression was the most effective way to determine the value of the property in comparison with the performance measures of: $R\hat{2}$, RMSE and CV implanted in the data set. The cleaning of the information and data processing contemplated the reduction of repeated records and empty data and the selection of relevant characteristics of the data in order to obtain an optimal data set and apply the methods described in this work. It is recommended for future work to take into account more variables than those considered in this work, such as years old, geographical location, remodeling, internal finishes, and number of bathrooms. As well as the use of other machine learning models.

This work is a first stage of the real estate analysis, and the percentage of the precision indicators can be improved since currently the AUC and accuracy do not exceed 75%, so it is advisable to explore other models and algorithms such as principal component analysis or multivariate linear correlation.

References

1. Chiarazzoa, V., Caggiania, L., Marinellia, M.: Modelo basado en redes neuronales para la estimación de precios de bienes raíces. ScienceDirect 811 (2014)
2. Concepto Jurídico. Bienes Inmuebles. Obtenido de conceptojuridico.com (2021)
3. Ekos   (2021).   https://ekosnegocios.com/articulo/el-sector-inmobiliario-se-dinamiza
4. Freire, J., Guevara, B.: Modelo de Clasificación de Riesgo Crediticio Utilizando Random Forest en financiera del Ecuador (2021). https://repositorio.uisek.edu.ec/handle/123456789/4256
5. García, C.: indrscompany (2022). https://www.indracompany.com/
6. Higueras, J.C.: El sector inmobiliario crece luego del rezago ocasionado por la pandemia. El telegrafo (2021)
7. Koller, S.: ¿Qué es el web scraping? (2022). https://seranking.com/es/blog/web-scraping/
8. Norma técnica de Valoración de los Bienes Inmuebles en el MDMQ. Normas Técnica para la valoración de bienes inmuebles urbanoss y rurales del Distrito Metropolitano de Quito (2019)
9. Realia. ¿Qué es el mercado inmobiliario? (2022). https://www.realia.es/que-es-mercado-inmobiliario

10. Rodríguez, T.: Discutiendo entre el Machine Learning y el Deep Learning ¿A qué nos referimos con cada uno? (2017). https://www.xataka.com/robotica-e-ia/machine-learning-y-deep-learning-como-entender-las-claves-del-presente-y-futuro-de-la-inteligencia-artificial
11. Shia, Y., Zhangb, Y.: The neural network methods for solving Traveling Salesman. Elsevier, 2 (2022)
12. Spiegato (2022). https://spiegato.com/es/que-es-un-conjunto-de-datos
13. Vozmediano, J.R.: Concepto de Valoración Inmobiliaria y Normativa Aplicable (2018). https://negocioinmo.com/concepto-de-valoracion-inmobiliaria
14. Zakaria, F., Fatine, F.A.: Towards the hedonic modelling and determinants of real estate's price. Elserver, 1 (2021)
15. García, C.: indrscompany (2022). https://www.indracompany.com
16. Grybauskas, A., Pilinkienė, V., Stundžienė, A.: J. Big Data (2021)
17. Plan de Uso y Gestión de Suelo del Distrito Metropolitano de Quito (2021). https://quito.gob.ec
18. Das, S.S.S., Ali, M.E., Li, Y.-F., Kang, Y.-B., Sellis, T.: Boosting House Price Predictions using Geo-Spatial Network Embedding (2020)
19. Krishna, N.: Dubai Real Estate Investment: A Predictive and Time Series Analysis (2021)

Simulation Model to Assess Household Water Saving Devices in Bogota City

Andrés Chavarro[1]([✉]) [iD], Mónica Castañeda[2] [iD], Sebastian Zapata[3] [iD],
and Isaac Dyner[4] [iD]

[1] Politécnico Grancolombiano, Bogotá, Colombia
achavarr@poligran.edu.co
[2] Tecnológico de Antioquia, Medellín, Colombia
mcastanr@unal.edu.co
[3] Universidad EIA, Medellín, Colombia
szapatar@unal.edu.co
[4] Universidad Jorge Tadeo Lozano, Bogotá, Colombia
idyner@unal.edu.co

Abstract. This paper examines the Bogotá River basin in the Andes of Colombia, which is in a vulnerable state. In the medium term, it would be difficult to meet the growing demand for water due to population growth and the risk of low rainfall. Therefore, this paper aims to determine the contribution to water system sustainability by measuring the impact of demand management measures to reduce water wastage through the adoption of household water-saving devices. This is an interesting topic, as few demand management measures have been applied in the Bogotá River Basin. In this sense, a system dynamics model has been developed to simulate the urban water system and the effect on water conservation of demand management measures that promote efficient use. The results show that water-saving taps are the most efficient micro-component, achieving up to 21% of water savings per year per household, while eco-efficient washing machines allow savings of up to 17% and toilets 7%. Consequently, after years of El Niño phenomenon, delays in works to expand supply or continued growth in demand, the water system could avoid a deficit situation with the policy of installing water-saving taps in households.

Keywords: Bogotá river basin · system dynamics modelling · urban water management · water conservation · water demand management · water-saving devices

1 Introduction

On a worldwide level, water consumption has increased by about 1% annually over the past 40 years [28]. It is projected that between 2016 and 2050, the global urban population facing water scarcity will increase from 933 million to 1700–2400 million [28]. Consequently, the development of alternative supply sources, such as wastewater utilization [29], becomes a crucial requirement for megacities.

There are different approaches to analyze the effectiveness of demand management measures based on the use of devices applied to urban water systems. From direct methods, that is, analyzing the implementation of installation programs for water-saving products [20], or through approaches not only of effectiveness but also of cost-effectiveness [13]. Although these methods are reliable for analyzing public policies ex post, they have limited ability to analyze the effectiveness of water demand management policies ex ante, because they do not observe the behavior of the modeled system and its response to interventions over the long term.

Another approach is to analyze alternatives for the future. In this sense, the Delphi method has been used to identify the most relevant measures to improve water supply according to a group of experts [11], as well as the development of simulation models to study the diffusion of technologies for water conservation [4].

In this context, system dynamics approaches are of particular interest. Unlike the Delphi method, System dynamics models allow to understand the (often complex) interactions between the subsystems that jointly determine the behavior of an urban water system [35].

System dynamics has been widely used in water demand management research [32]. [30] simulated the dynamic interactions between urban water demand, economy, climate and water conservation for the Macau region, China. They found that population is the main driver of urban water demand. By implementing water conservation measures (efficient use and reuse of wastewater), water demand was reduced by 17.5% [30]. In the case of Iran, the dominant approach is to use system dynamics to model the water-food-energy nexus and derive policies that contribute to water security. For example, [25] apply it to the Gavkhuni river basin in the centre of the country and find that the security of water supply and the stability of the energy sector are highly dependent on the food sector. [19] find similar results for Khuzestan province. Only [33] focus on urban water systems facing water scarcity. They analyse four demand and supply management measures, such as inter-basin transfers, wastewater treatment, price increases in times of scarcity, and the installation of household water-saving devices and leak detection. The main finding is that investment in the installation of devices and leak detection cannot stop the growth of the deficit, but it can reduce its growth rate.

For the Americas, [2] present a model and the results related to the demand for municipal water and its conservation potential for the water region of South Florida, United States, and find that the use of flow reducers has great potential to reduce demand.

For the Rio Grande border region between the United States and Mexico, [12] estimated changes in water quantity and quality due to climate change and measured their impact on community development. They showed that for the populations of Laredo and Reinosa, climate change affects water availability in conjunction with economic and population growth. The model suggests that policies such as: inducing more rational water consumption patterns, efficient water distribution systems in urban areas, increasing water recycling in industry and promoting conservation among residents will have a significant impact in tackling the problem.

Finally, there is an analysis of the dynamics of water management systems, and it is in Brazil. [21] assessed the sustainability of the Panaroá river basin in central Brazil between 2015 and 2018. Their assessment showed a medium level of sustainability.

They recommend effective demand management and the expansion of protected areas in the supply area. It is necessary to point out that no studies based on system dynamics modelling have been found that analyse feasible demand management alternatives that allow guaranteeing water supply in a South American city faced with increasing demand, climate change and supply management constraints.

Historically, the city of Bogotá has used supply management tools such as interbasin transfers and storage expansion to manage its water resources [14]. While these measures have helped overcome episodes of scarcity throughout the 20th century [18], it remains unclear if they can effectively handle threats to water resource availability, including droughts exacerbated by climate change, with only these inherently limited technical and operational tools. Green water scarcity has been caused by land-use changes favoring livestock, agriculture, and urbanization [3], as well as increasing demand resulting from economic and population growth.

In contrast to the valuable but insufficient supply management approach adopted by the city's policymakers to date, this work measures the effect of demand management measures to reduce water waste through the adoption of saving devices in households. In this regard, policies based on quantities, i.e., on saving water through devices will be analyzed. This will make it possible to reduce dependency on supply and give the population more tools to face possible scenarios of water scarcity caused by climate change and the probable permanent increase in consumption.

To achieve this objective, a System Dynamics (SD) model was developed that enables the simulation of an urban water system and the effect on water conservation derived from management measures that promote efficiency in use. SD represents the behavior of complex systems over time through differential equations, the model employs feedbacks cycles, delays, and non-linearity to do so [5, 26].

2   Overview of the Case Study

Bogotá watershed covers 5,894.65 km^2 and contributes 17% to Colombia's GDP, while also housing 20% of its population. The National Water Study spanning the past two decades exhibits the basin's substantial water vulnerability arising from inadequate supply. In concurrence with the growing population and changing climate, demand could surge by as much as 50% until 2050 [6].

In the center of the basin lies the city of Bogotá, which covers an area of 1,636.6 square kilometers. It is located at an elevation of 2,600 m above sea level, with an average annual temperature of 14 °C and approximately 1,050 mm of rainfall. The city's primary water supply comes from three swamp complexes: the Sistema Norte, Chingaza, and Sistema Sur. These sources provide 26%, 71%, and 3% of the available water, respectively [1]. It should be noted that since 1983, around 38.6% of the water supply comes from water transfers originating from the Orinoco basin of the Guatiquía and Blanco rivers [24].

For the city of Bogotá, the Supply and Sewerage Master Plan Update Report (2016) states that the three current systems have an installed capacity of 27.19 m^3/s based on the Continuous Reliable Flow (CRF). The unrestricted capacity, as per CRF, is 25.59 m^3/s. However, with technical, environmental, and concessionary restrictions, the water amount decreases to 20.04 m^3/s. With limitations imposed on account of the treatability capacity, given the current water quality conditions of the sources, the capacity falls further to 17.04 m^3/s [10].

Likewise, the average actual demand increases to 16.68 m^3/s. Based on the above information, the supply matches the demand, meeting the population's needs without any inconvenience. Due to this surplus, the local water company directly supplies Soacha, Gachancipá, and Tocancipá, and sells water blocks to eight municipalities, approximately amounting to 1 m^3/s.

The city's average household consumption is 122 L/person/day. According to the water company, this consumption varies based on the income level of the population. In Colombia, the population is divided into strata based on socio-economic levels for efficient targeting of public subsidies. Strata 1 and 2 encompass individuals with the lowest incomes, stratum 3 and 4 comprise the middle class, and stratum 5 and 6 include the wealthiest. Accordingly, Table 1 presents water consumption in the city (Table 2).

Table 1. Microcomponents % of total household use

Strata	Taps	Showers	Washing machines	Toilets	Average consumption per household (m^3/month)
1	41	15	24	20	10.28
2	40	15	19	25	10.37
3	39	17	20	24	10.25
4	32	18	18	32	11.24
5	31	19	18	32	13.23
6	33	18	15	32	15.3

Table 2. Microcomponent Water Conservation Potential

Device	Water saving	Water consumption by use (Average)	Cost (US Dollars)
Washing machine	76%	24%	416.1
Toilets	38%	20%	75.8
taps	55%	41%	106.6
Showers	26%	15%	135.8

Regarding the evaluation of public water management policies in Bogotá, an analysis of pricing policies was conducted. It was found that the combination of price increases and educational and awareness-raising campaigns following the breakdown of part of the supply network, which led to forced rationing in the 1990s, led to a notable reduction in per capita consumption [17]. Similarly, several researchers have found that price influences consumption habits among low-income populations, but it does not have the same effect on those with higher incomes [27].

For its part, the district's water policy has been developed since 2011 with the District Water Plan. This is further complemented by the Water Efficiency and Conservation Plan for the period 2017–2021. In terms of low-consumption technologies, the plan is founded on the diagnosis that two actions have been executed: 1) providing energy-saving devices in the company's restrooms, and 2) promoting the adoption of energy-saving devices by household users.

Various studies warn of a potential water scarcity crisis that could impact the city, the sub-basin, and the basin. Some argue that the city's water metabolism is unsustainable [23]. Others claim that the decrease in the natural plant cover, which reduces water supply and regulation, is caused by changes in land use for livestock pastures, urban expansion, mining, and agriculture [3, 15]. Finally, the basin could face water insecurity due to several reasons. These include delays in the planned expansion of storage capacity [8], the risk of earthquakes that could cause the failure of the supply line to the Sistema Norte treatment plant [10], reducing water transfer from the Guatiquía and Blanco Rivers is necessary. The slopes of these rivers have a high potential for hydric erosion, as documented in [3]. Furthermore, aerial rivers have faced deterioration due to deforestation in the Amazon [31].

Household Water Saving Devices
There are currently various household devices that can aid in water conservation, ultimately saving money and reducing water bills. It is important to note, however, that the amount of water saved may vary depending on the family's social class. This paper has previously addressed water-saving devices for households, including efficient washing machines, showers, faucets, and toilets.

3   Methods

The water system of the Bogotá River Basin is illustrated in Fig. 1. The system comprises of two main components: supply and demand. The former originates from rainfall and water transferred from the Orinoco basin.

The stored water is contained in reservoirs or dams, whose quantity and capacity are being expanded as more capacity under construction becomes operational. This occurs when the safety margin, which is defined as the minimum proportion required for supply to exceed demand and ensure supply, surpasses the set threshold (refer to negative loop L1). When the margin falls below the minimum, the policy of managing demand is activated, which decreases household consumption (see positive loop L2). On the other hand, increased consumption decreases the amount of available resources, which in turn reduces the margin and prompts the construction of supply capacity (refer to negative loop L3). The reduction of the margin results in the implementation of land-use policies to protect water resources, ultimately increasing water flow (refer to negative loop L4).

Figure 2 shows the main components of the built system dynamics model. This model is used to investigate the potential for water savings through the application of management measures to residential demand in the city of Bogotá.

Main Data and Equations
Table 3 shows the main data used in the computational model. These data are important for establishing the initial conditions.

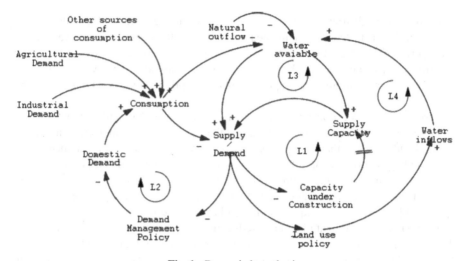

Fig. 1. Dynamic hypothesis

This paper presents a simulation model of the relationship between water supply and demand in the city of Bogotá. Special attention was given to the residential sector.

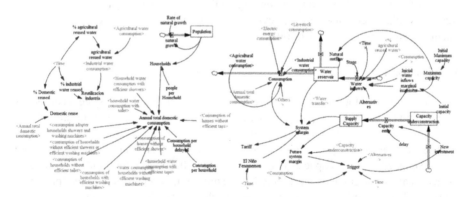

Fig. 2. Stock and flows diagram

Different scenarios were presented regarding the use of water-saving devices in households in the city of Bogotá. Table 4 shows these scenarios.

Bussines As Usual (BAU)

In the trend scenario, it is assumed that the water management policy is supply-oriented (expansion of storage capacity, which is carried out according to current official planning: optimisation of the supply system with 7 projects, representing a total increase in flow of 7.91 m^3/s available in 2026, and expansion of the Chingaza Phase I system, an additional 1.29 m^3/s available from 2032) [1]. In addition, it is assumed that there will be at least two El Niño episodes of one year duration within the simulated period (it is assumed that it

Table 3. Main Data

Variable	Data & Units	Source
Population	9.591.890 people served by the aqueduct of Bogotá in 2022	DANE Censo (2018)
Average annual growth rate of the population served by the Bogotá aqueduct in the period 2018–2035	0.86%	Own calculation based on DANE Censo (2018)
People per houshold	2.86	DANE Censo (2018)
Annual consumption per houshold	122 m^3/year/household	Own calculation based on Acueducto de Bogotá (2022) and DANE Censo (2018)
System margin	10.38%	Own calculation

Table 4. Simulation scenarios

BAU	Neither water saving device is adopted by households
Efficient washing machine	Households use only efficient washing machine, no additional water-saving device
Efficient toilets	Households with only efficient toilets and no additional water saving device
Efficient taps	Households with only efficient taps and no additional water saving device
Efficient showers	Households with efficient shower only and no additional water saving device

could occur in 2026 and the next one in 2031). It is assumed that there are no demand-side policies, i.e. there is no massive adoption of conservation devices by households.

Efficient Washing Machine
The supply conditions and the occurrence of El Niño are maintained, but a demand policy is introduced consisting of households gradually adopting an eco-efficient washing machine that achieves savings of 76% compared to a standard washing machine that uses 200 L per load.

Efficient Toilets
Supply conditions and the occurrence of El Niño are maintained, but a demand policy is introduced consisting of households gradually adopting a 3.7 L/flush toilet compared to the usual 6 L/flush, achieving a saving of 38.3%.

Efficient Taps
Supply conditions and the occurrence of El Niño are maintained, but a demand policy is introduced, consisting of the gradual adoption by households of 3 pressure reducers, which would save 55% of a daily consumption of 36.6 L/person/day, which includes brushing teeth, washing hands and cooking food.

Efficient Showers
The supply conditions and the occurrence of El Niño are maintained, but a demand policy is introduced, consisting in the gradual adoption by households of a shower that saves 26% compared to the one normally used in the city, which consumes 9.5 L per minute.

The main equations of the simulation model are then explained. There are two variables related to the water demand in the basin: consumption, which refers to the needs of the main economic agents in the area: agriculture, industry, electricity generation and residential (household) consumption. Water consumption and supply (i.e., storage and distribution systems) are used to calculate the system margin (SM). The functional form of the SM is given below (see Eq. 1). Under normal conditions, the system margin varies between 0 and 1 [8].

The system margin depends on the variation in the level of supply sources (e.g., level of reserves, inter-basin transfers) and storage capacity (quantity and capacity of reservoirs). Similarly, the margin can change depending on climatic conditions (variability of the rainfall regime) and the loss of supply capacity (from peatlands or the depletion of aquifers).

$$SM(t) = \frac{[\min(CS(t), WR(t)) - C(t)]}{C(t)} \tag{1}$$

where (SC) and (WR) represent supply capacity and water reserves, respectively (Chavarro et al., 2020).

For its part, consumption is defined as the sum of the water requirements that imply water flow that does not return to the basin [19], for which water consumption in the hydropower sector is assumed to be zero.

$$C(t) = Agr(t) + Pec(t) + Ind(t) + DC(t) \tag{2}$$

where Agr, Pec, Ind and DC represent agricultural, livestock, industrial and household consumption, respectively.

First, annual total residential consumption of water (rc) is calculated as the number of households (h) multiplied by the average consumption of water by household ($\bar{c}$).

$$rc(t) = H(t).\bar{c} \tag{3}$$

The average water consumption of a household ($\bar{c}$) varies according to the water saving device used.

In turn, household consumption is explained by consumption through taps (present in bathrooms and kitchens), use of toilets, showers and washing machines. Since the aim is to analyse the potential for water savings by implementing a policy of replacing inefficient devices with water-saving devices, Eq. 3 gives the total consumption of households that adopt device i.

$$WCA_i = H_i * (WC * (1 - \alpha) + WC * \alpha * (1 - \beta_i))   \tag{4}$$

where:

WCA_i is aggregate consumption of households that adopt the saving technology i.

i is washing machines, shower, faucets, toilets.

H_i is the number of households that adopt technology i.

WC is the consumption of each household.

α is the proportion of water consumption due to the use of toilets.

$\beta_i i$ s the proportion of water savings due to the use of saving toilets.

The number of households adopting conservation technology i follows a logistic curve whose shape depends on the impact of advertising or voice-to-voice communication on the adoption rate of device i. The number of households adopting appliance i is described by an integral equation (see Eq. 4), which indicates that the rate of change of adopting households per unit of time is equal to the rate of adopters.

$$H_i(t) = \int h_i(dt) + H_i(t_0)   \tag{5}$$

In turn, the number of households willing to adopt water saving devices Hwa_i is described in Eq. 5. It can be seen how it depends on the number of households that have already adopted the device and on the decision of each household to adopt, provided that the annualised value of what you must pay for water is less than the cost of the bill if you did not use the saving device.

$$Hwa_i = \left(H - Hp_i - H_i \right) * E_i   \tag{6}$$

where:

H is the total number of households in Bogotá.

Hp_i is the number of potential households adopting device i.

E_i is the effect of saving money on the bill if device i is used.

4   Results and Discussion

According to Fig. 3, the water supply has fulfilled the total demand during the analyzed period (2022–2050). Nevertheless, there might be a significant risk of a deficit in 2026 and 2031 in case of an El Niño-related phenomenon under current supply conditions. In such cases, the city usually launches a plan to enhance its supply capacity; on average, such works are completed 9 years later. This means that in 2031–2032, the supply will be expanded, resulting in two increases in level on the supply capacity line.

By 2026, the margin drops to about 1% before rebounding as new storage capacity starts to come on stream Thereafter, the system margin gradually declines, but no new capacity is built. The margin of the system exhibits a continual decline over time as long as consumption growth is consistent (refer to Fig. 4 for details).

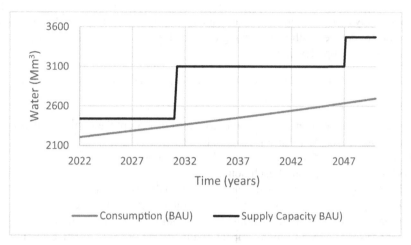

Fig. 3. Water consumption versus water supply capacity, BAU scenario

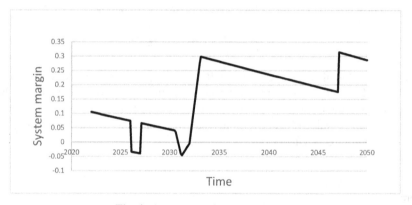

Fig. 4. System margin, BAU scenario

Figure 5 shows the varying effects of adopting different devices on the city's water consumption compared to the base scenario (BAU). It is important to note that this study assumes a sigmoid function for device adoption, whereby a small number of users are motivated to switch devices at the initial implementation of the policy. However, the number of adopters for each type of device increases rapidly through word-of-mouth and publicity, until adoption gradually slows down and reaches a ceiling. The results can be summarized as follows:

Efficient showers (ESHOWERS) have the lowest consumption savings among all scenarios. In the first year of the simulation, this policy allows for a saving of only 0.62 Mm3/year. By the end of the simulation, consumption is reduced by only 20.06 Mm3/year on average. Additionally, the effect of ESHOWERS on the system margin is minimal; in other words, the margin barely exceeds the demand.

Efficient toilets (EToilets) have a relatively low consumption-reduction rate compared to other scenarios. In the first year of the simulation, they only enable a saving of 1.21 Mm3/year and at the end of the simulation only 39.1 Mm3/year. The policy marginally increases funding to prepare for the possibility of the El Niño phenomenon occurring in 2026.

Efficient washing machines (EWM) can improve the reliability of the supply system. During the "El Niño" phenomenon, the margin system falls to around 2% with this policy, which is significantly better than the 0.095% that would occur in business as usual (BAU). While this measure alone cannot prevent the need to expand supply capacity, it can reduce the risk of shortages in the short term.

Efficient Taps (ETAPS) result in the highest consumption savings of all scenarios. In the first year of the simulation, it allows for a savings of 3.6 Mm3/year and only 114.95 Mm3/year at the end of the simulation. Average annual saving of 78.06 Mm3. The system margin is also strengthened, which would help avoid falling to eventual supply-demand parity in the business as usual (BAU) scenario when facing a possible El Niño phenomenon in 2026. If taps were massively installed, the supply would exceed demand by 2.28%. In the following years, the gap systematically widens, resulting in a water surplus of about 25% in the given year. This is a significant contribution to water security.

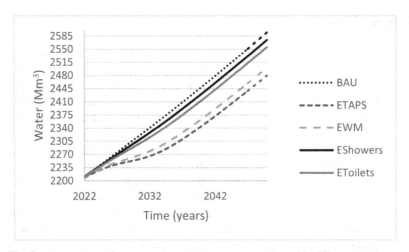

Fig. 5. Comparison of consumption: BAU vs. consumption with different appliances

Despite its efforts to reduce technical losses (leaks) or commercial losses (wrong connections, under-invoicing), the city's water company has not yet been able to reduce them to the levels required by law. For example, technical losses, as measured by the Non-Revenue Water Index (IANC), are 39% (Bogotá Aqueduct), whereas the limit tolerated by law is 25% (SSPD). In the same sense, according to Resolution 388 of 2014, commercial losses, measured as the Rate of Losses per Invoiced User (IPUF), allow a maximum of 6 m^3/month; however, the water company reports 6.89 m^3/month. In such a context, the cumulative savings that would be achieved by the combination of measures would compensate for the non-compliance with the loss target according to the IPUF index around the year 2024.

In addition to assessing the contribution of the implementation of domestic water saving devices to the management of water demand, the inclusion of a domestic wastewater reuse policy was simulated. This is not a new idea. Already in the World [29], the great untapped potential of this resource was highlighted. For the Colombian case, one of the strategies of the circular economy is that of reuse [7]. According to this study, four-year recovery targets of 20, 30 and 40% could be achieved in 2022, 2026 and 2030 respectively. Unfortunately, this has not yet happened, in part because regulatory changes to promote reuse were only made in November 2021 [22]. Based on this forecast and considering that 1) there are still no studies confirming that the water currently treated by the city meets the standards for reuse in agriculture or industry, and 2) there is still no storage and distribution infrastructure in place, more conservative targets were set for the simulation. It was therefore assumed that 10, 15 and 25% of domestic water reuse would be achieved in 2026, 2030 and 2040 respectively.

The reuse increases supply to such an extent that a new El Niño phenomenon around 2030–31 would have little or no impact on the reliability margin of the system, which would reduce the risk of shortages if the expansion of storage capacity planned for 2032 is delayed.

5 Conclusions

This paper succeeds in fulfilling its purpose, which was to present a computational model to measure water savings in households using efficient devices. In the same way, it provides estimates of the water saving potential of a policy for the implementation of efficient devices in households. The results suggest that the massive use of low-flow taps could save up to 78 million m^3 per year, or 2.47 m^3/s, which is a little more than half of the reliable continuous supply of the northern system (4.5 m^3/s) and almost five times the supply capacity of the southern system (0.5 m^3/s). Although this technological change represents a considerable economic effort for the average purchasing power of the city's inhabitants, there are alternatives that make it affordable for the entire population. Currently, there are around 3,353,800 households in the basin, of which 4.6% correspond to the richest [9], who can finance their own equipment. Likewise, it's possible to consider a contribution of these strata to co-finance the change of the poorest population, since the upper strata are the ones that consume the most water and the lower strata are the ones that consume the least, despite the fact that their consumption is subsidised in two ways: the vital minimum policy, which implies that only monthly consumption above 6 m^3/month is charged, and a tariff subsidy financed by the wealthiest. The remainder of the payment for the purchase of the appliance can be paid progressively with each bill, and part of it can be waived if there is evidence of a reduction in consumption, since for the water company less use of the distribution networks and less water consumption means lower long-term maintenance costs for infrastructure and raw water treatment.

Under the BAU scenario, the basin will be at risk of water scarcity if demand continues to grow while at least one El Niño event occurs before 2030 and the expansion of storage capacity takes at least 9 years to become operational. By massively increasing the use of water-saving taps, this risk can be mitigated, and the supply system can respond and adapt to more challenging conditions.

The capital alone discharges about 567 million m³/year, of which about 177 million m³/year (31% of the total) is treated with chemical primary treatment. If the treatment meets the standards for its multi-sectoral reuse (agricultural and industrial), it's possible to supply all the industrial and livestock needs and up to 38% of the agricultural water in the basin each year. This suggests that if the decision were taken to create the conditions to make use of its wastewater, the city could cease to be a destabilising factor in the ecology of the Bogotá River basin and become a determining factor in reducing the risk of shortages arising from climate change and reduce its dependence on water transfers. Steps are being taken in this direction with the construction of the Canoas wastewater treatment plant, which is expected to be operational in 2029 with a capacity of up to 16 m³/s. This will have a very positive impact on the entire lower river basin, whose economy is based on agriculture, and which is rapidly becoming a place of residence for the diaspora of Bogotá residents who decide to leave the city for calmer and warmer places. But it is not enough to treat wastewater. It is necessary to build the infrastructure to distribute treated water for non-human consumption. The key will be to capitalise on the fact that the Bogotá Water Company already sells water to 11 surrounding municipalities and plans to expand its coverage so that it becomes a regional supplier, taking advantage of the economies of scale that this brings.

Although the study examines a wide range of household water saving devices, it does not consider other water saving options such as the reuse of wastewater that reaches significant flows or the harvesting of rainwater. At present, and for the next 15 years, the conditions for their implementation are not in place, making it difficult to consider them as viable options. This is the case for wastewater treatment plants such as the Canoas plant, which has the potential to treat up to 18 m³/s of the 26 m³/s that the city discharges into the Bogotá River, but whose construction schedule has been delayed for several years. In addition, there is no independent channeling of storm water and wastewater, and no specific approved plans for such adaptation.

The model developed does not include a policy to encourage a change in habits. A next step in the research could be to estimate the long-term impact of reducing the time of use of micro-components, i.e., shortening the duration of showers, increasing the efficient use of washing machines, reducing the number of times they are used per week, or even facilitating the emergence of new business models based on rental or shared use (sharing economy).

Future research should explore the conservation potential of reviewing agricultural land use policies, limiting their extent and questioning the types of crops that are allowed. This would reduce the green water index [16]. This type of policy has been implemented in China, with results worth considering [34].

References

1. de Bogotá, A.: Almacenamiento y Embalses. (Storage and Reservoirs). https://www.acuedu cto.com.co/wps/portal/EAB2/Home/acueducto-y-alcantarillado/la-infraestructuraAcuedu cto/sistemas-abastecimiento/almacenamiento-y-embalses
2. Ahmad, S., Prashar, D.: Evaluating municipal water conservation policies using a dynamic simulation model. Water Resour. Manag. **24**, 3371–3395 (2010). https://doi.org/10.1007/s11 269-010-9611-2

3. ANLA. Reporte de análisis regional de la Subzona hidrográfica del río Bogotá (SZH-RioBog). (Regional analysis report of the Bogotá River hydrographic subzone) ANLA. Autoridad Nacional de Licencias Ambientales Bogotá, Colombia (2020)
4. Baki, S., Rozos, E., Makropoulos, C.: Designing water demand management schemes using a socio-technical modelling approach. Sci. Total Environ. **622–623**, 1590–1602 (2018). https://doi.org/10.1016/j.scitotenv.2017.10.041
5. Badham J.: A compendium of modelling techniques. Integration Insights No 12.The Australian National University. Canberra, Australia (2010)
6. Buytaert, W., De Bièvre, B.: Water for cities: The impact of climate change and demographic growth in the tropical Andes. Water Resour. Res. **48**, 1–13 (2012). https://doi.org/10.1029/2011WR011755
7. Centro de Ciencia y Tecnología de Antioquia – CTA. Propuestas de acciones y recomendaciones para mejorar la productividad del agua, la eficiencia en el tratamiento de aguas residuales y el reúso del agua en Colombia. (Proposals for action and recommendations for the improvement of water productivity, the efficiency of waste water treatment and the re-use of water in Colombia) Departamento Nacional de Planeación – DNP, Medellín, Colombia. https://www.dnp.gov.co/LaEntidad_/misiones/mision-crecimiento-verde/Documents/ejes-tematicos/Agua/INFORME_PROPUESTAS%20FINAL_18_05_18.pdf
8. Chavarro A., Castañeda M., Zapata S., Dyner I.: Future scenarios of water security: a case of Bogotá River basin, Colombia. CCIS 1277 ICAI 2020, pp. 251–265 (2020) https://doi.org/10.1007/978-3-030-61702-8_18
9. Cigüenza N.: Conozca cómo es el mapa de los estratos en las grandes ciudades de Colombia. (Learn about the map of the strata in the large cities of Colombia) (2019). https://www.larepublica.co/economia/este-es-el-mapa-de-los-estratos-en-las-grandes-ciudades-del-pais-2866032
10. de Bogotá, C.: Presente y futuro del agua para Bogotá D.C. (Present and future of water for Bogotá D.C.) Plan Anual de Estudios – PAE, Bogotá, Colombia (2020). https://www.ambientebogota.gov.co/documents/893475/1331774/4..+2020ER151328+-+2020IE150374+-+INFORME+PRESENTE+Y+FUTURO+AGUA.pdf/ed6d868d-e9cb-40a9-b7a0-60e3947f9d5b?version=1.0
11. de Andrade R., de Tarso-Marques S., Melo dos Santos S., Paiva-Coutinho A., Lopes-Coelho C., Silva-Pessoa, R.V.: Assessing alternatives for meeting water demand: A case study of water resource management in the Brazilian Semiarid region. Utilities Policy **61**, 100974 (2019). https://doi.org/10.1016/j.jup.2019.100974
12. Duran-Encalada, J.A., Paucar-Caceres, A., Bandala, E.R., Wright, G.H.: The impact of global climate change on water quantity and quality: A system dynamics approach to the US–Mexican transborder region. Eur. J. Oper. Res. **256**, 567–581 (2017). https://doi.org/10.1016/j.ejor.2016.06.016
13. Fidar, A.M., Memon, F.A., Butler, D.: Economic implications of water efficiency measures II: cost-effectiveness of composite strategies. Urban Water J. **14**(5), 531–553 (2017). https://doi.org/10.1080/1573062X.2016.1224361
14. Guhl-Nanneti, E.: La región hídrica de Bogotá. The hydric region of Bogotá Revista Academia Colombiana de Ciencias **37**(144), 327–341 (2013)
15. Huitaca consorcio - CAR.: Ajuste del plan de ordenación y manejo de la cuenca del río Bogotá. (Adjustment of the planning and management plan for the Bogotá River basin) Bogotá, Colombia (2019)
16. IDEAM.: Estudio Nacional del Agua 2022. (National Water Study 2022) IDEAM, Bogotá, Colombia (2023)
17. Ivanova, Y., Dominguez, E., Sarmiento, A.: Evaluación del efecto sobre el metabolismo hídrico de la ciudad Bogotá como respuesta al cambio en el modelo de gestión del agua en los

años 90. (Evaluation of the Effect on the Water Metabolism due to the Change in the Water Management Model in Bogotá during the 1990s) Ambiente y Desarrollo **22**, 1–10 (2018) https://doi.org/10.11144/Javeriana

18. Jiménez-Aldana, M., Santana-López, F.: Water distribution system of Bogotá city and its surrounding area, Empresa de Acueducto y Alcantarillado de Bogotá – EAB E.S.P. Procedia Eng. **186**, 643–653 (2017). https://doi.org/10.1016/j.proeng.2017.03.281

19. Keyhanpour, M.J., Musavi, S.H., Ebrahimi, H.: System dynamics model of sustainable water resources management using the Nexus Water-Food-Energy approach. Ain Shams Eng. J. **12**(2), 1267–1281 (2021). https://doi.org/10.1016/j.asej.2020.07.029

20. Koh, Y.R.: Attitude, behaviour and choice: the role of psychosocial drivers in water demand management in Singapore. Int. J. Water Resour. Dev. **36**(1), 69–87 (2020). https://doi.org/10.1080/07900627.2019.1617114

21. Marinho, H.L., dos Santos, T.M., Toná, B.H., Rocha, C., Passos, C.: Sustainability analysis of an urban basin in central Brazil. Journal of Environmental Engineering, **147**(11). American Society of Civil Engineers (2021). https://doi.org/10.1061/(ASCE)EE.1943-7870.0001912

22. Ministerio de ambiente y desarrollo sostenible. 23 november 2021 Resolución 1256. "Por la cual se reglamenta el uso de las aguas residuales y se adoptan otras disposiciones". (Decision 1256. "By which the use of wastewater is regulated, and other provisions are adopted") Bogotá, Colombia (2021)

23. Peña, A.: Simulación del ciclo urbano del agua en la ciudad de Bogotá. (Simulation of the urban water cycle in Bogotá city) Ph.D thesis, Universidad de Alicante, Alicante, España (2016)

24. Quinaxi - Esri Colombia: Bogotá y el agua. De los cerros orientales a la región hídrica. Una línea de tiempo. (2016). https://geoapps.esri.co/linea_del_tiempo_agua_bogota/#

25. Ravar, Z., Zahraie, B., Sharifinejad, A., Gozini, H., Jafari, S.: System dynamics modeling for assessment of water–food–energy resources security and nexus in Gavkhuni basin in Iran. Ecol. Ind. **108**, 105682 (2020). https://doi.org/10.1016/j.ecolind.2019.105682

26. Sterman, J.: Business dynamics: systems thinking and modeling for a complex world. Irwin/McGraw-Hill, Boston (2000)

27. Trout, C., Villegasa, D.: Estimación de la elasticidad precio de la demanda: un ejercicio para el consumo de agua residencial en Bogotá. (Estimation of the price elasticity of demand: an exercise for residential water consumption in Bogotá) Master thesis, Pontificia Universidad Javeriana, Bogotá, Colombia (2013)

28. UNESCO. The United Nations World Water Development Report 2023: partnerships and cooperation for water; executive summary. UNESCO. United Nations Educational, Scientific and Cultural Organization Paris, France (2023)

29. UNESCO World Water Assessment Programme. The United Nations world water development report, 2017: Wastewater: the untapped resource. UNESCO.United Nations Educational, Scientific and Cultural Organization Paris, France (2017)

30. Wei, T., Lou, I., Yang, Z., Li, Y.: A system dynamics urban water management model for Macau China. J. Environ. Sci. **50**, 117–126 (2016). https://doi.org/10.1016/j.jes.2016.06.034

31. Weng W.: Aerial river management for future water in the context of land use change in Amazonia. Ph.D thesis, Humboldt-Universität zu Berlin – Geographisches Institut, Berlin, Germany (2019). https://doi.org/10.18452/21097

32. Winz, I., Brierley, G., Trowsdale, S.: The use of system dynamics simulation in water resources management. Water Resour. Manag. **23**, 1301–1323 (2009). https://doi.org/10.1007/s11269-008-9328-7

33. Zarghami, M., Akbariyeh, S.: System dynamics modeling for complex urban water systems: Application to the city of Tabriz Iran. . Resour. Conserv. Recycl. **60**, 99–106 (2012). https://doi.org/10.1016/j.resconrec.2011.11.008

34. Zhang, D., Guo, P.: Integrated agriculture water management optimization model for water saving potential analysis. Agric. Water Manag. **170**, 5–19 (2016). https://doi.org/10.1016/j.agwat.2015.11.004

35. Zomorodian, M., Lai, S.H., Homayounfar, M., Ibrahim, S., Fatemi, S.E., El-Shafie, A.: The state-of-the-art system dynamics application in integrated water resources modeling. J. Environ. Manag. **227**, 294–304 (2018). https://doi.org/10.1016/j.jenvman.2018.08.097

Towards Reliable App Marketplaces: Machine Learning-Based Detection of Fraudulent Reviews

Angel Fiallos[1]($\boxtimes$) and Erika Anton[2]

[1] Universidad ECOTEC, Samborondón, Ecuador
afialloso@ecotec.edu.ec
[2] Fácil Emprendimiento Co, Guayaquil, Ecuador
eranton@facilemprendimiento.com

Abstract. Online reviews significantly influence consumer decisions, making the increasing prevalence of fake reviews in app marketplaces concerning. These deceptive reviews distort the competitive landscape, providing unfair advantages or disadvantages to certain apps. Despite ongoing efforts to detect fake reviews, the sophistication of fake review generation continues to evolve, necessitating continuous improvements in detection models. Current models often focus on precision, potentially overlooking many fake reviews. This research addresses these challenges by developing a machine learning model since experiments on app reviews were published on a popular App Marketplace. The developed model detects fake reviews based on the textual content and the reviewer's behavior, offering a relevant approach to enhancing the integrity of app marketplaces.

Keywords: Artificial · Intelligence · Fake · Reviews · Machine Learning · Marketplace · Random Forest · UMAP

1 Introduction

Currently, online reviews are an important indicator of the performance and popularity of a given product or service. Customers often take them into account when purchasing or making business decisions. Comments and ratings from other users give them an overview of the application's quality, functionality, and user experience [1]. Positive reviews can influence the decision to download, while negative reviews can deter potential users. Therefore, fake reviews could be a problem, as they are intended to influence readers' opinions artificially and are becoming increasingly prevalent in app stores [2]. Fake review generation is becoming a business, which increases the difficulty of detecting reviews.

Professionals consistently improve their efforts to make a review appear as natural as possible while tampering with the reputation of a given product, service, or business. Thus, a detection model needs to be constantly improved to address their changes in strategy/approach [3]. Also, most fake review detection models achieve high scores for only precision values, reflecting the proportion of samples classified by the model as fake when they are true positives. This could be misleading since the ratio of deceptive reviews is much smaller compared to truthful reviews. It is important to consider the recall score, as well, as it describes the proportion of fake samples that some models classify as fake. A model can report high precision but can also leave most of the fake reviews undetected.

Therefore, fake reviews can distort the competitive landscape. Apps with artificially inflated reviews may gain an unfair advantage, while those with falsely negative reviews may be unfairly disadvantaged. To contribute with a new approach that contributes to the detection and control of fake reviews, our team performed a series of technical analyses and experimentation with apps published between 2017 and 2020 on a popular App Marketplace to evaluate and develop a machine learning model that can detect these types of fake reviews, based on both the textual content and the behavior of the review's writer.

2   Related Work

Fake review detection is currently very relevant research, where the trend is to develop highly sophisticated statistical features from both the reviewers and the reviews to create an algorithm to make a determination. For instance, previous works characterized the behavior of fake reviewers from the metadata of their reviews [4] and used that information to develop a detection algorithm called SpEagle. It mainly leveraged patterns derived from the reviews' dates, polarity, statistics from ratings, and content similarity among reviews. Their model reported precision and AUC values of 90% and 70%, respectively, in their best setting. Other research [5, 6] also suggested that the most discriminant information is derived from behavior rather than just the review text itself and estimated groups of users that are likely to produce fake reviews.

This information was formulated in terms of the activity time windows of users, deviation of group ratings, and content similarity. These models achieved precision values of close to 100% and 71%, respectively. Martens et al. [7] utilized classical machine learning models along with features derived from ratings and dates of reviews. Those models were tested with decreasing values of dataset skew from 90% to 0.1%, achieving scores of AUC, precision, recall, and accuracy in the range of 90% to 100%, but significantly deteriorating as skew shifted to lower values.

Later, Li et al. [8] built upon previous work by incorporating semantic features extracted from the reviews using a novel Word2Vec-based technique, achieving a precision of 92% and an AUC of 78%, illustrating the importance of semantic understanding in fake review detection.

Shehnepoor et al. [9] took a different route, focusing on network-based features such as user-user and product-product networks in their study. Their model, named NetSpam, achieved an accuracy of 87% and an AUC of 84%, reinforcing the relevance of considering the network aspect of reviews in spam detection. Finally, Moosleitner et al. [10] proposes a method to detect fake text reviews by leveraging the consistent writing style exhibited by large language models like GPT-2. Specifically, the author uses features prominently used for authorship attribution to identify whether a text was automatically generated.

3 Methodology

In today's digital era, online reviews significantly shape consumer decisions. Yet, the surge of fake reviews threatens the trustworthiness of online platforms. Leveraging machine learning, we can combat this issue by automating the detection of deceptive reviews [11, 12]. This process starts with gathering a vast dataset of online reviews, which is then cleaned and preprocessed for analysis. Through this analysis, unique patterns distinguishing genuine from fake reviews emerge.

Using these insights, feature engineering extracts key attributes from the data, laying the foundation for the machine learning model. Once equipped with the appropriate algorithm, this model is trained to discern between genuine and deceptive reviews. After fine-tuning, it's deployed to actively identify and flag suspicious reviews in real time. Given the ever-changing nature of digital tactics, it's essential to periodically update the model to maintain its accuracy. Enhancing this approach, we present a detailed methodology for identifying fake reviews, as outlined in Fig. 1, providing a comprehensive roadmap for improved detection.

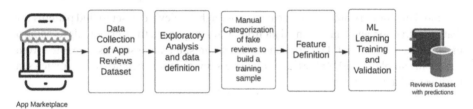

Fig. 1. Machine Learning Methodology for the identification of fake reviews.

3.1 Data Acquisition

The App reviews were collected through web scraping in the data acquisition phase. The process collected a total of 873,640 reviews in the English language, belonging to 1,812 different mobile apps published. Table 1 shows the primary columns from the review's dataset.

Table 1. Table captions should be placed above the tables.

Variable	Description
Review ID	The ID of the review
Reviewer ID	Review author's ID
Review content	Text of the review
Rating	Review's score
Thumbs up count	Thumbs up count for the review
Review created version	The version of the app when the review was published
Date/Time	The date the review was published
Reply content	The text of the reply by the app's publisher
Replied at	The ID of the review replied by the app's publisher

3.2 Exploratory Analysis

An initial exploratory analysis was carried out on the reviews dataset to find patterns for feature extraction and analyze the data from different perspectives prior to developing a machine learning model. Due to memory constraints, the analysis was computed from a random sample of 250,000 reviews. Figure 2 shows a visual capture of two reviews, a positive and a negative one.

Fig. 2. Visual capture of two App reviews.

First, the app reviews' distribution was analyzed in the Fig. 3. It indicated that most apps received less than 2K reviews, and that there was a considerable drop in the number of apps receiving 3K reviews or more.

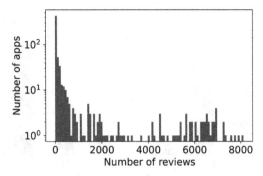

Fig. 3. Distribution of the number of reviews per application

The distribution of the length of the reviews (i.e., word count) was also analyzed in Fig. 4, and depicted a pattern typically found among reviews. Generally, the majority of the reviews are short, and few reviews have a lot of text, which follows a power law distribution [13]. There are some outliers, i.e., very long reviews. The number of words is an important factor in identifying fake reviews. For instance, short reviews like "Excellent" and "Great app!" are most likely to be fake if the user behavior associated with the reviews is also suspicious.

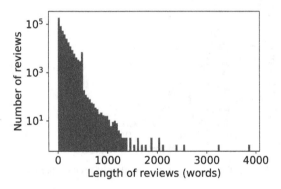

Fig. 4. Distribution of the length of the reviews

Ratings may also be leveraged to describe reviewer behavior and inform the identification of fake reviews. Figure 5 shows the rating distribution of all review's dataset, with most of the reviews having a rating of 1 or 5. An abundance of reviews with 1- or 5-ratings, especially when an app receives an unusual number of reviews of either rating in a short period of time, is a possible indicator of incentivized fake reviews.

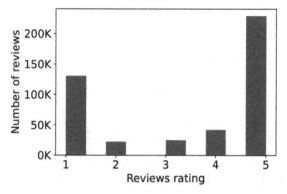

Fig. 5. Distribution of the reviews' ratings

Most of the reviewers tend to write only one review, as depicted in Fig. 6, which shows a histogram of the number of reviews per user. Fewer than 5K users have written more than 10 reviews. Additionally, there are outliers in this distribution, which may potentially be associated with fake reviewers.

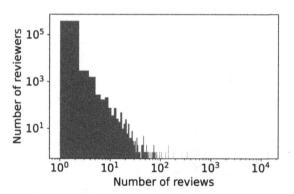

Fig. 6. Distribution of the number of reviews per user

In a more detailed analysis, the most common bigrams and trigrams in the reviews' text were extracted by calculating the term frequency–inverse document frequency or TFIDF representation, which statistically reflects the importance of words to a review in the dataset. Table 2 shows the summary of the most common bigrams and trigrams from the review's dataset.

The exploratory analysis informed the identification of features for fake reviews that were built into the machine learning model. We formulated the detection of fake reviews as a classification problem, i.e., each review will be assigned to one of two categories: truthful or fake.

Table 2. Most common bi-grams and tri-grams in reviews dataset

Bi-grams		Tri-grams	
Value	Count	Value	Count
(easy, use)	0.57%	(app, easy, use)	0.09%
(easy, use)	0.36%	(app, good, app)	0.03%
(great, app)	0.23%	(worst, app,ever)	0.03%
(can, not)	0.21%	(easy, use, app)	0.03%
(app, good)	0.20%	(easy, use, good)	0.03%
(nice, app)	0.17%	(mobile, banking, app)	0.03%
(use, app)	0.16%	(good, app, good)	0.03%
(customer, service)	0.16%	(good, easy, use)	0.02%

3.3 Manual Categorization

Before using a supervised machine learning approach, it was first necessary to categorize a training dataset manually by a human team. We designed a guide for data annotation to facilitate the categorization of reviews. It consists of a sequence of closed-ended questions whose answers determine whether a review is considered "Truthful" or "Fake." It includes a list of features based on qualitative variables, which support the final decision of the human who categorizes the review. Table 3 summarizes the features used in the guide design for data annotation.

Table 3. Data annotation Features for Manual Categorization

Feature	Description
Reviewer	The first part of the workflow is concentrated on the score given by the reviewer. This represents the average star rating (ranging from 1 to 5) that the reviewer has bestowed on any of the Applications. Average scores of 1 or 5 stars were deemed to have the highest probability of being fraudulent
Content	Subsequently, attention is shifted to the content of each review, which is evaluated using two methods: 1) Automated Classification, taking into account factors associated with the length of the text. 2) Hand-operated Classification, that considers language-related aspects such as grammar, spelling, writing style, and context
Rating	In the end, the emphasis shifts to the rating of the review, which is examined through an Automated Classification process. Reviews having ratings of 1, 4, or 5 stars were viewed as having the highest likelihood of being counterfeit

We manually labeled 1,320 reviews, which were applied to train and test the machine learning model. A review must meet at least one of the conditions listed under Truthful, and none of the conditions listed under Fake, to be considered Truthful. To the contrary, if it meets at least one Fake condition, it would be considered Deceptive. Table 4, shows some language-related aspects, used for manual categorization process.

Table 4. Language-related aspects for Manual Categorization

Truthful	Fake
The review employs descriptive words for the app and backs up this assertion with a corresponding declaration	The review is marred by grammatical, syntactical, or punctuation mistakes
While the review offers commendations, it also notes an aspect the user found unsatisfactory or wishes the app could enhance	The review touches upon unrelated topics, employing terms such as "Sir", "dude", and so on
The review shares critical commentary and substantiates the claim with proof or a detailed account of the problem	The review speaks to the app as though it were a person, or it's ambiguous who or what the review is referencing
The review conveys originality, wit, or sentiment in offering feedback about the app	The review confines itself to content that is apparent from the app's title or description
The review extends proposals or an appeal for action to the developers of the app	The review consists merely of a sequence of buzzwords (either positive or negative)
The review discusses advantages that the app offers	The objective or topic of the review is indistinct
The review acknowledges and critiques two or more functionalities of the app	The review includes random characters that do not express any particular significance

3.4 Feature Definition

The purpose of the feature definition is to establish the inputs to the machine learning model. The output will be the prediction whether the review is fake or not. For the input features, we have considered three types of features: behavioral, text-based features, and TFIDF-UMAP features [14]. Figure 7 is a summary of the features used in the machine learning experiments, based in previous approaches [15–17].

Behavioral features focus on explaining reviewer patterns in terms of review dates and ratings, from both the app and user perspectives. To this end, the metadata of each review in the dataset is analyzed and aggregated for apps and users. Also, raw text from reviews were analyzed to generate as much discriminant information as possible, complementing behavioral features.

We also included the statistical representation of words, specifically bigrams (2 consecutive words) and trigrams (3 consecutive words). The TF-IDF technique [18] calculates the frequency of bi-grams and trigrams in a review, and their representation over the entire dataset. Since TFIDF results in a high dimensional representation (20K

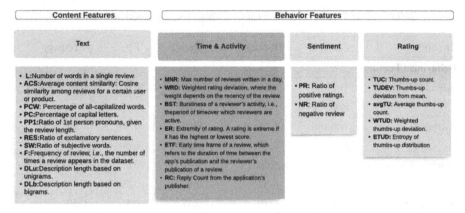

Fig. 7. Machine learning Features for fake reviews detection models

features), we conducted text preprocessing for the feature extraction pipeline, removing stop words, and used a dimensionality reduction technique (UMAP) to reduce the dimensionality to 15 features, thus reducing the training time and resources needed.

3.5 Machine Learning Training and Validation

In the endeavor to detect fake reviews, various machine-learning models were rigorously tested using distinct feature sets. The feature sets encompassed Behavioral Features, which focused on reviewer patterns like review dates and ratings; Text Features derived from the review content; and a combined set that integrated both with additional elements like bigrams processed via UMAP (Uniform Manifold Approximation and Projection).

The models employed in this study included Neural Networks, Adaboost, Random Forest, and Support Vector Machines. Each model's performance was evaluated across the different feature sets to determine its efficacy in distinguishing between genuine and deceptive reviews. The methodology underscores the significance of feature selection and the choice of an appropriate machine learning model in the quest to identify fake reviews effectively.

4 Results

After all machine models were selected for evaluation experiments, a training step was performed with 65% of the dataset and finally tested with the remaining samples. All Training, testing, and optimization sets had no overlap. The objective was to identify the model that consistently delivered superior performance across these feature sets. The model that stood out in terms of accuracy, precision, recall, and F1 score would be deemed the most suitable for deployment in a production environment to detect fake reviews. A detailed breakdown of the performance metrics for each model and feature set combination can be found in Table 5.

Table 5. Performance Metrics for the machine learning models experiments.

Truthful	Class	Precision	Recall	F1	Accuracy
Behavioral Features					
Neural Net	Truthful	0.69	0.58	0.63	0.62
	Fake	0.55	0.66	0.60	
Adaboost	Truthful	0.68	0.64	0.66	0.63
	Fake	0.58	0.62	0.60	
Random Forest	Truthful	0.68	0.63	0.66	0.63
	Fake	0.57	0.62	0.59	
Support Vector	Truthful	0.70	0.47	0.56	0.59
	Fake	0.52	0.75	0.61	
Behavioral Features + Text Features					
Neural Net	Truthful	0.79	0.72	0.76	0.74
	Fake	0.68	0.76	0.72	
Adaboost	Truthful	0.80	0.67	0.73	0.72
	Fake	0.65	0.78	0.71	
Random Forest	Truthful	0.82	0.80	0.81	0.79
	Fake	0.75	0.77	0.76	
Support Vector	Truthful	0.80	0.67	0.73	0.72
	Fake	0.65	0.78	0.71	
Neural Net Text Features + Behavioral Features + (bigrams/UMAP) dimensions					
Random Forest	Truthful	0.87	0.83	0.85	0.83
	Fake	0.80	0.84	0.81	
Adaboost	Truthful	0.84	0.80	0.82	0.80
	Fake	0.76	0.80	0.78	
Neural Network	Truthful	0.80	0.71	0.75	0.81
	Fake	0.68	0.77	0.72	

Then, we used the best model (Random Forest), determined by the accuracy score in the validation set, to generate predictions over the entire dataset. Table 6 shows the results of the prediction using only text features, and the results from combining text features and TFIDF-UMAP representation features.

The results show that when the models use all features, the models yield the best accuracy scores, with Random Forest being the best. To understand the predictions, we analyzed the features' relevance of the random forest model, since it consistently performed better than other models in most of the experimental settings. Figure 8 depicts the features' relevance:

Table 6. Results of the predictions on the dataset

Features employed	Percentage of Truthful Reviews	Percentage of Fake Reviews
Text	54.52%	45.48%
Text + TFIDF-UMAP	54.40%	45.60%
Text	54.52%	45.48%

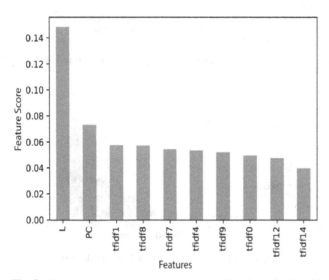

Fig. 8. Feature relevance in the selected Machine Learning Model

On the other hand, Fig. 8 shows that the reviews' length (L) has a considerable impact on model results, followed by percentage of capital letters in the review (PC) and the TFIDF-UMAP features calculated from the text representation of reviews. Behavioral features were not among the most important in detecting fake reviews, mainly due to the mixed distribution of these features among fake and truthful reviews. Thus, only text features and TFIDF-UMAP dimensions became inputs to the models for a validation procedure.

5 Discussion

We analyzed several aspects concerning the predictions over the entire dataset. First, we explored in Fig. 9 the distribution of reviews per category, and the tendency was similar for both categories: truthful and fake. Figure 10 shows the distribution of the predictions for a sample of 100 applications. It's possible to demonstrate that some apps receive a greater number of truthful reviews than fake ones, while other apps are overwhelmed by fake reviews, as depicted by the spikes. This finding suggests some apps struggle more with fake reviews than others; thus, these apps require more attention in the detection process.

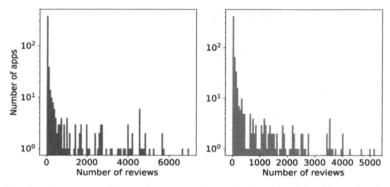

Fig. 9. Distribution of the reviews using the predictions of Random Forest Mode

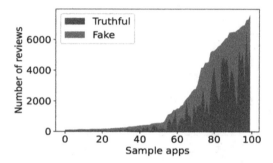

Fig. 10. Review prediction for 100 sample apps

Regarding the distribution of the reviews' content length (Fig. 11), there is a difference in the distribution of fake and truthful reviews. Both share similar distribution for long reviews, but very short reviews are more strongly associated with fake reviews.

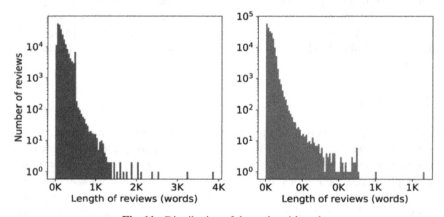

Fig. 11. Distribution of the reviews' length

Finally, we revisited the temporal distribution presented in the exploratory analysis, visualizing the predicted fake reviews with red dots for the top 3 apps.

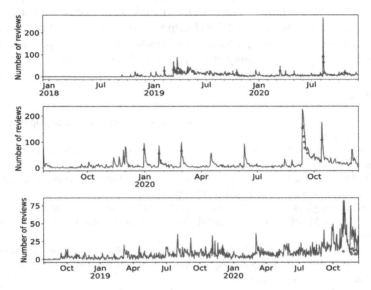

Fig. 12. Temporal distribution of fake reviews for the top 3 most reviewed apps

In Fig. 12, we show a sample of fake reviews (red dots) which are associated with spikes in the temporal distribution, or the number of reviews over time. This confirms our premise that abnormal or unusual activity may be related to fake reviews that should be identified and validated.

6 Conclusions

The exploratory analysis revealed patterns in the number of reviews received by apps, their content properties, ratings, and their reviewers' behavior. We noted a spike in the number of reviews in the temporal distribution. Further analysis revealed that fake reviews may have been behind that suspicious behavior. Overall, the averages of truthful and fake reviews across the apps were similar, each accounting for around 50% of the data; however, we found that some apps had a vast number of fake reviews (outliers) that may denote incentivized reviews.

The carefully designed features developed by our team, using not only the review's text but all related metadata (reviewer, app, creation date, etc.), provided discriminant information used in developing the machine learning model. Moreover, we calculated additional features related to behavior and TF-IDF that contributed to the performance improvement of the models.

For instance, the length of the reviews and the writing style (e.g., PC feature) significantly impacted the review's classification. Based on the results of our experiments with several machine learning models for detecting fake reviews, we found that simple models, such as Random Forest, outperformed more complex models based on neural networks. The Random Forest model obtains an F1 score of 83% on the validation set, using a small amount of labeled data through the proposed data annotation guide.

We conclude that our proposed methodology for fake review detection using machine learning approaches is feasible and could help several App Marketplaces to improve the quality of user-validated app reviews; it is feasible and could support several App Marketplaces to improve the quality of app reviews validated by users.

References

1. Luca, M., Zervas, G.: Fake it till you make it: reputation, competition, and yelp review fraud. SSRN Electron. J. (62) (2013)
2. Mayzlin, D., Dover, Y., Chevalier, J.: Promotional reviews: an empirical investigation of online review manipulation. Am. Econ. Rev. **104**(8), 2421–2455 (2014)
3. Wu, Y., Ngai, E., Wu, P.: Fake online reviews: Literature review, synthesis, and directions for future research. Decis. Supp. Syst. **132**, 113280 (2020)
4. Rayana, S., Akoglu, L.: Collective opinion spam detection: Bridging review. In: Proceedings of the 21th ACM SIGKDD International Conference on Knowledge Discovery and Data Mining (2015)
5. Kennedy, S., Walsh, N., Sloka, K., Foster, J., McCarren, A.: Fact or factitious? Contextualized opinion spam detection. In:Proceedings of the 57th Annual Meeting of the Association for Computational Linguistics (2019)
6. Mukherjee, A., Liu, B., Glance, N.: Spotting fake reviewer groups in consumer reviews. In: Proceedings of the 21st international conference on World Wide Web (2012)
7. Martens, D., Maalej, W.: Towards understanding and detecting fake reviews in app stores. Empirical Softw. Eng. (2019). https://doi.org/10.1007/s10664-019-09706-9
8. Li, S., Guojin, Z.: A deceptive reviews detection method based on multidimensional feature construction and ensemble feature selection. IEEE Trans. Comput. Soc. Syst. (2023)
9. Saeedreza, S., Mostafa, S., Reza, F., Noel, C.: NetSpam: a network-based spam detection framework for reviews in online social media. IEEE Trans. Inf. Forensics Secur. **12**(7), 1585–1595 (2017)
10. Moosleitner, M., Specht, G., Zangerle, E.: Detection of generated text reviews by leveraging methods from authorship. In: Datenbanksysteme für Business, Technologie und Web , Gesellschaft für Informatik e.V (2023)
11. Jindal, N., Liu, B.: Opinion spam and analysis. In: Proceedings of the 2008 International Conference on Web Search and Data Mining, pp. 219–230. ACM (2008)
12. Mukherjee, A., Liu, B., Glance, N.: Spotting fake reviewer groups in consumer reviews. In: Proceedings of the 21st International Conference on World Wide Web (2012)
13. Muchnik, L., Pei, S., Parra, L.C., Reis, S.D., Andrade, J.J.S., Makse, H.A.: Origins of power-law degree distribution in the heterogeneity of human activity in social networks. Sci. Rep. **3**(1), 1783 (2013)
14. McInnes, L., Healy, J.: UMAP: Uniform manifold approximation and projection for dimension reduction. ArXiv e-prints **03426**, 2018 (1802)
15. Elmurngi, E., Gherbi, A.: Detecting Fake Reviews through Sentiment Analysis Using Machine Learning Techniques (2018)
16. Mukherjee, A., Venkataraman, V.: Classification and Analysis of Real and Pseudo Reviews (2013)
17. Medhat, W., Hassan, A., Korashy, H.: Sentiment analysis algorithms and applications: a survey. Ain Shams Eng. J. **5**(4), 1093–1113 (2014)
18. Ramos, J.: Using TF-IDF to determine word relevance in document queries (2003)

Enterprise Information Systems Applications

Challenges to Use Role Playing in Software Engineering Education: A Rapid Review

Mauricio Hidalgo[1,3]([✉])[ID], Hernán Astudillo[2,3][ID], and Laura M. Castro[4][ID]

[1] Escuela de Informática y Telecomunicaciones - Universidad Diego Portales, Santiago, Chile
mauricio.hidalgo@mail.udp.cl, mauricio.hidalgob@usm.cl
[2] ITiSB - Universidad Andrés Bello, Viña del Mar, Chile
hernan@acm.org
[3] Universidad Técnica Federico Santa María, Santiago, Chile
[4] Universidade da Coruña, A Coruña, Spain
lcastro@udc.es

Abstract. Role playing is a teaching method widely used to enhance students learning and engagement, by allowing them to adopt specific roles and interact with others in simulating real-world scenarios, thus applying their theoretical knowledge in a practical context. In Software Engineering Education (SEE), role playing may help students to develop key skills (like teamwork, problem-solving, and critical thinking), to understand the complexities and challenges of software development, and to appreciate the importance of collaboration and effective communication. To use role playing effectively, SEE teachers need to understand the challenges that arising from using it. This paper presents the design, execution and results of a *rapid literature review* to identify these challenges. Several well known digital libraries (Web of Science, Scopus, and IEEE Xplore) yield 44 articles, which after inclusion/exclusion filters left a total of 23 articles. Key findings are that: (1) most role playing is used to teach skills linked to software development and teamwork/"soft skills", and secondarily to software design, quality assurance, and process management; rather than project management or quality assurance; (2) challenges and generic considerations for implementing role playing were identified; and (3) challenges for applying role playing in SEE were identified by virtue of the SE specialty classification. In summary, role playing is a mature teaching technique used to in other fields, and has made limited inroads in SEE, mainly in disciplines dear to agile development (like development and teamwork).

Keywords: Software engineering education · Role playing · Rapid review

1 Introduction

Software Engineering is a constantly evolving discipline that requires technical and soft skills. In the educational context, students prefer hands-on work to

© The Author(s), under exclusive license to Springer Nature Switzerland AG 2024
H. Florez and M. Leon (Eds.): ICAI 2023, CCIS 1874, pp. 245–260, 2024.
https://doi.org/10.1007/978-3-031-46813-1_17

theory [3]. In turn, SE teachers have used several approaches to address the socio-technical aspects, such as role-playing for improving the teaching-learning experience [4]. One popular method for improving the teaching-learning experience is role-playing [4]. For both pedagogical and ethical reasons, teachers must consider how formatting and preparation can impact learning outcomes [5]. This rapid review explores the use of role-playing in software engineering education to identify the challenges and considerations to take into account when implementing role-playing in the context of software engineering education.

The remainder of this paper is structured as follows: Sect. 2 introduces the theoretical background and the key concepts of SEE and Role Playing (RP); Sect. 3 relates some previous experiences of the use of RPin Engineering and SEE; Sect. 4 describes Rapid Review (RR) and the research protocol employed to guide our work; Sect. 5 presents the review's key findings of the study considering the generic and specific (for SEE) challenges and recommendations; Sect. 6 presents a results summary; Sect. 7 presents the possible threats to the study validity and the measures taken to mitigate them; and Sect. 8 summarises and concludes the paper.

2   Background Concepts

2.1   Software Engineering Education

Software Engineering Education (SEE) can be understood as the process of teaching students the principles, concepts and skills necessary to design, develop, test and maintain quality software. In this context, software developers education must adapt in the same way as the discipline itself, and not only with the recent addition of online training for computing skills [33]. While it is important to acknowledge and address the practical aspects of the technology, tools, and methodologies, students and teachers should also be equipped with skills that enable them to comprehend and master the ever-changing landscape of software development. Considering the above, [34] defines a (non-exhaustive) list of skills and knowledge that the software engineer must master like the theoretical foundations, design methods, technology and tools of the discipline. In addition, they have to be able to keep their knowledge up-to-date with respect to the new approaches and technologies, interact with other people, manage the development process, understand, model, formalize, analyse and recognize problems, reuse or adapt known solutions, and coordinate the work of different people. This list points to, in one hand, acquiring the theoretical foundations of a discipline (commonly accomplished through traditional schooling). However, managing a process includes the complexities of interpersonal interactions (with human stakeholders or teammates), and often demands hands-on experience and presents distinct challenges that vary based on the specific context. Hence, it is important that SEE incorporates techniques to allow students to develop relational skills through the practice of roles (like Role Playing), tasks, collaborative work and other areas that allow the development in a human scale environment.

2.2   Role Playing

Role playing educational activities have their origin in Role-Playing Games (RPGs) and, in view of that origin, they share a core base formed by rules for the game mechanics, stories (modules) that give meaning and context to the actions of characters, and means of social interaction through which a story is co-created [6]. The integration of character development with mastery design within a social context gives the potential to develop learning skills such as communication, problem-solving, and leadership, while presenting the learner with narrative agency within the curriculum [19]. Considering the above, role playing (sometimes referred to as role-play simulation in educational settings) is an experiential learning method in which learners are involved in a proposed scenario by representing an interacting part in it [20]. The two baseline concepts for role playing are:

- **Roleplayer or Interactor:** The person who develops or improvises a role as part of a scenario. Roles can be performed by individual students, in pairs, or in groups which can play out a more complex scenario [21].
- **Scenarios:** The scenarios are situations (not necessary a simulationin which two or more people act out in specific roles. The scenario is outlined by the teacher or professional, and while it must allow improvisation, it represents a safe and supportive environment where students will develop their own meaningful first-person experience [20].

In short, role playing exercises give students the opportunity to assume the role of a person or act out a given situation [22].

3   Related Work

The use of role playing as a pedagogical strategy in Higher Education has been the subject of interest and study in the academic community, and its applications are very diverse given the versatility of the roles and scenarios. In Engineering, a pilot study generating classroom STEM RP simulations to meet course learning objectives was conducted to gain deeper insight into the barriers to both adoption and sustained utilization of RP course content from several areas of engineering problem-solving [7]. In a closer environment to our speciality, [8] explores the potential of role engineering education and project development for engineering students using role playing in a case study for Human-Automation Systems, and [9] created and implemented a role-play case study in an undergraduate computing data mining course to improve ethical understanding of algorithms among computing students. In the SEE field two of the first role playing uses (not directly mentioned) were reported in 1987 [10,11], and expose an experience of teaching a senior-year course on software maintenance, centred around a maintenance project by the use of clients and groups roles and a maintenance project as scenario [10]; and a comprehensive description of one way of organizing and presenting a project course where components are well-trained advanced students, a minimal product, an elaborate engineering process, good tools, and task assignments for external participants, deliverables, and collateral duties [11]. Subsequently, new studies emerged in SEE to demonstrate that empirical study projects give students experience in research [12]; to allow acquiring competences by using Case Method and Role Play as instruments in several lectures of Software Engineering for teaching Finite State Machines [13]; by the proposing of an active learning approach that uses interactive role-play simulations in a virtual 3D environment for understanding Object-Oriented Software [14] and programming language concepts and skills by a Web-based Multiplayer Online Role Playing Game [15]; by the developing a two-and-a-half-day role-playing workshop for engineers that focuses on teaching the importance of RE, the background, rationale, and purpose of the requirements, as well as the actual requirements [16]; to present an assessment approach for teamwork performance in software engineering education for encourages and supports student active and collaborative learning by using an approach specially assessing teamwork performance of a team and each team member of the team [17]; and for giving the opportunity for students to appreciate the value of software design principles or even to learn how to apply principles in practice [18].

In summary, related work indicates that Role Playing is an intriguing approach in Software Engineering Education, fostering both relational and technical skills. This RR seeks to offer a more comprehensive insight into this aspect.

4   Research Method: Rapid Review

This section summarizes the Rapid Review (RR) research protocol employed as the research method to guide our work. Rapid Reviews (RR) are practice-oriented secondary studies, and their main goal is to provide evidence to support decision-making towards the solution, or at least attenuation, of issues practitioners face in practice [1]. Rapid Reviews were first mentioned in the literature in 1997, when [32] described the rapid health technology assessment program in the south and west regions of England, but did not provide a formal definition [31]. To characterise them, a rapid review is an accelerated way of conducting a systematic review of the scientific literature [31]. Unlike a traditional systematic review, which involves a long and detailed process, a rapid review seeks to perform a rapid evaluation of the existing evidence in a shorter period of time. The main objective of a rapid review is to provide a fast-delivered, summarized synthesis of the available evidence to inform decision-making in a specific context [30]. Considering the above, we will guide our research under this approach following the guidelines indicated in [2,30] for a RR process. Therefore, our RR protocol has the following assumptions:

- **Assumption 1.** The SEE teachers and researches have had time to adopt Role-Playing in the past 10 years.
- **Assumption 2.** The researches making empirical experiments with Role-Playing have documented their findings both positively and negatively.

- **Assumption 3.** There is no evidence on the challenges comprising the implementation of Role Playing in SEE beyond the "generic guidelines" (for any speciality) that can be found in the formal and grey literature.

4.1 Definition of Goal and Research Question

This Rapid Review (RR) is undertaken with the objective of providing a comprehensive perspective on the challenges associated with the utilization of Role-Playing in Software Engineering Education (SEE). To achieve this objective, we formulated the following research question:

- **Research Question (R.Q.).** "What's are the **challenges** to implementing role playing in software engineering education?" *Rationale:* Considering the diverse contexts within Software Engineering, compiling a list of challenges (and considerations) will empower educators and researchers to implement the Role Playing technique while tailoring it to the unique aspects of their courses or empirical experiments.

4.2 The Primary Studies Search and Selection Process

This section outlines the process employed to search and select primary studies for this paper. The process, depicted in Fig. 1, culminated in the identification of 23 selected papers for this RR. This selection was achieved through the following sequence of steps:

Search on Scopus, WoS and IEEE Xplore. A search was performed in the WoS and Scopus Databases and the IEEE Xplore digital library considering:

- The keywords: "Role Playing" and "Software Engineering Education"
- Date of searches: Papers published between January 2012 and March 2023.

Automated Duplicates Removal. The papers were filtered using a Python script that allowed us to eliminate documents with the same content.

Application of the Inclusion/exclusion Criteria. For this research we considered the inclusion (In) and exclusion (Ex) criteria. To be included in the RR, the paper must accomplish all of the next conditions:

- (In.) The paper must be in the context of SEE
- (In.) The paper should be explicit in the use of Role Playing
- (In.) The paper must report an empirical evidence-based
- (In.) The paper must be a primary study
- (In.) The paper must be written in English or Spanish

To be excluded in the RR, the paper must satisfy one (or more) of the next conditions:

- (Ex.) The paper publish date is lower than 2012
- (Ex.) The paper include the same author of other most recent paper with similar content
- (Ex.) The papers is not indexed in WoS or Scopus

Manual Papers Inclusion. The paper repository were complemented with suggested sources [30] considering the expertise in software engineering education of the research team. Notwithstanding, the suggested papers also went through the automated duplicate elimination process and the inclusion/exclusion criteria.

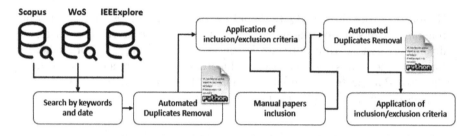

Fig. 1. Search and Selection Process

4.3   Data Extraction Process

Considering the [1,2] guidelines, a Rapid Review usually use a descriptive synthesis method rather than quantitative meta-analysis. For the extraction of data (necessary to answer the research question), a manual review process of the papers was carried out with the objective of generating a classification and a descriptive synthesis of each one of them. The following fields were considered to the data extraction for each paper:

- Description: Contains the description of the analyzed paper.
- Application domain (SE Category): Contains the main category to which the paper contributes in Software Engineering.

Category Classification. Among the 23 selected papers, the primary categorization within the field of Software Engineering yielded the following breakdown: 2 papers focused on Process Management, 2 on Quality Assurance, 2 on Software Architecture, 4 on Requirements Engineering, 5 on Teamwork and Soft Skills, and 8 on Software Development. This categorization information was integrated into the descriptive synthesis for each respective paper.

Descriptive Synthesis. For the descriptive synthesis, we chose to generate a summary that exposes the main ideas and/or proposals of each of the papers. Likewise, the classification of each paper towards a category of Software Engineering was included. The summary of descriptive synthesis is in Table 1.

Table 1. Rapid Review selected papers summary

N°	Paper Name	Short Description	SE Category
01	Role-playing software architecture styles	Propose an innovative use of role-playing as teaching strategy for architecture models of reference (i.e. layered, pipe filter, client-server, etc.)	Software Architecture
02	Applying Role-Playing game in Software Development	Application of Role-playing game where they elicit the software requirements through an interview with the teacher that plays the role of the end user	Software Development
03	Software Engineering Role-Playing Game: An interactive game for Software Engineering Education	Support the learning process through the simulation of a software company environment, challenging the students with the activities and problems from the development process management	Process Management
04	Towards a Role Playing Game for Exploring the Roles in Scrum to Improve Collaboration Problems	The goal of this study is to address such situations using an interactive role playing game-based approach among team members to improve collaboration	Teamwork / Soft Skills
05	Is role playing in Requirements Engineering Education increasing learning outcome?	Investigate whether a higher grade in a role playing project have an effect on students' score in an individual written exam in a Requirements Engineering course	Requirements Engineering
06	Swords and sorcery a structural gamification framework for higher education using role-playing game elements	This is achieved through implementing game elements to the entire second-year cohort (N = 34) of computer game development students, in the unit 'Engineering Software Systems'. The goal is to motivate and engage threat-risk students of the cohort with lower activity, attendance and involvement in the unit	Software Development
07	ATAM-RPG: A role-playing game to teach architecture trade-off analysis method (ATAM)	Describes ATAM-RPG, a role-playing game to support the teaching of ATAM by simulating stakeholder's interaction and trade-offs	Software Architecture
08	A Role-Playing Game for a Software Engineering Lab: Developing a Product Line	Report an experience of ours, showing how in the context of a software engineering course at University of Bologna our students tackled the task of developing a software product line consisting of four products which were variants of a basic shared asset	Software Development
09	A Capstone Course on Agile Software Development Using Scrum	Discusses the achievement of teaching goals and provides empirical evaluation of students' progress in estimation and planning skills	Process Management
10	Applying a maturity model during a software engineering course - How planning and task-solving processes influence the course performance	Report on a study and teaching approach where, in three successive semesters and at two different institutions, we started rating the process maturity of students solving tasks in our software engineering courses and transparently related the maturity levels to the task performances	Software Development

(*continued*)

Table 1. (*continued*)

N°	Paper Name	Short Description	SE Category
11	A pattern-based approach for improving model quality	Constructed a catalog of anti-patterns of correctness and quality problems in class diagrams, where an anti-pattern analyzes a typical constraint interaction that causes a correctness or a quality problem and suggests possible repairs to improve modelers' capabilities	Quality Assurance
12	Impact of Practical Skills on Academic Performance: A Data-Driven Analysis	Explores the correlation between practical (e.g., programming, logical implementations, etc.) skills and overall academic performance and analyzing the statistical features of students	Teamwork / Soft Skills
13	A Quest to Engage Computer Science Students: Using Dungeons Dragons for Developing Soft Skills	Explains a didactic approach for engaging students into active learning for developing soft skills and to make them aware of the importance of this topic in relation to their professional future	Teamwork / Soft Skills
14	Verification and Validation Model for Short Serious Game Production	Presents a model based upon requirements traceability and inspections to verify and validate the correct implementation of requirements and the successful production of quality short serious games	Quality Assurance
15	Cultural and linguistic problems in GSD: a simulator to train engineers in these issues	Work focuses on the development of a virtual training environment that can simulate global software development scenarios involving virtual agents (VAs) from different cultures	Software Development
16	Applying virtual reality to teach the software development process to novice software engineers	In this study, a virtual reality-based software development framework (VR-SODEF) is proposed, which provides an interactive virtual reality experience for learning software development tasks, from requirements analysis to software testing	Software Development
17	Role-Play as an Educational Tool in Auditing Skills	The primary objective of this research is to develop auditing skills: communication, problem solving, and teamwork by using three different role-play activities with 62 students in a bachelors of accounting degree at Walailak University	Teamwork / Soft Skills
18	Design of a course oriented to the comprehension of Agile Methods based on Teamwork, Role-play, and Class Project with a Real Client	Presents the methodological strategy developed in an undergraduate elective course, whose main objective was the comprehension of the philosophy of Agile methods in engineering students	Teamwork / Soft Skills
19	Evaluating Role Playing Efficiency to Teach Requirements Engineering	The objective of this study is to assess the use of role playing and role reversal in an intensive requirements engineering course and reports the experience teaching requirements engineering courses using role playing for four sessions of two hours each	Requirements Engineering

(*continued*)

Table 1. (*continued*)

N°	Paper Name	Short Description	SE Category
20	Leveraging Role Play to Explore Software and Game Development Process	This paper used role play techniques to engage the students more fully in the processes of development by creating a scenario in which the students have suddenly become the owners of an independent game studio	Software Development
21	Requirements Engineering Education using Expert System and Role-Play Training	This paper propose a method for use in requirements engineering education in a university, and based on 3 principles. (1) A type of expert system, (2) Group-work role-play training and (3) A software agent system	Requirements Engineering
22	Role Playing as a Method of Learning in Knowledge Engineering	This paper showns a Role Playing based procedure in wich Students are trained to interview experts to extract knowledge for intelligent systems and, at the same time, to argue their opinion	Requirements Engineering
23	Use of Role-play and Gamification in a Software Project Course	This paper discusses the use of team role-play activities to simulate the experience of working in a professional, game development studio as a means of enhancing an advanced undergraduate game design course	Software Development

5 Challenges to Role Playing Activity in SEE

In this section, we will examine the challenges outlined in the papers, acknowledging that they may fall into either a "generic" category or a "specific" category pertaining to one of the classifications within Software Engineering.

5.1 Generic Challenges

In several of the studied papers we noticed that Role Playing follows four generic steps to design an RP implementation [5]: (1) Preparation and explanation by the teacher, (2) Student preparation for the activity, (3) Develop of the Role Playing Activity and (4) Debrief and reflection of the experience. Notwithstanding this, there are challenges to be faced in each implementation and after a rigorous inspection of the 23 selected papers in light of the R.Q., several challenges were identified:

- **Time:** Designing, planning, executing, and assessing role playing activities requires a significant investment of time and dedication.
- **Adjustment period:** Students who are new to these types of activities will need an adjustment period to acquire the necessary skills for active participation. Otherwise, they may become distracted from the learning process.
- **Classroom setup:** Setting up the classroom for role-playing can be challenging, particularly when working within space constraints. Additionally, considering accessibility issues for both students and instructors can add to the complexity of the setup process.

- **SE subfield:** Given the breadth of Software Engineering, it is important to focus the Role Playing on a particular subfield. In this way, concrete results can be observed under defined scenarios.
- **Scenarios:** Considering the scenarios, one challenge is that improvisation can be allowed in a safe and supportive environment in which learners will develop their own expertise.

Notwithstanding the above, there are interesting points that remain unaddressed. These are:

- **Suitability for every student:** role play may not be suitable for every student, especially those who have special educational needs (e.g. ASD, Asperger Syndrome) and people who struggle with active participation or expressing themselves in class, because these activities can potentially generate anxiety and might hinder their overall performance.
- **Anti-bias:** depending on the context, certain role playing activities can be emotionally charged and confrontational; e.g. societal biases could cause problems for vulnerable students.
- **Professional profile:** in cases of higher courses, it was not possible to observe a profiling of students considering their technical skills or learning styles; hence, the results may not necessarily be the best for some particular students. For example, if a student whose *forte* is programming is assigned a management role, they may learn from the experience by virtue of not exploiting their core strength.

In any case, the aforementioned aspects correspond to the human aspect that is inherent to role playing (and to education in general).

5.2   SEE Category Challenges

In this section we will review, separately, the challenges extracted for each of the categories identified in the papers that make up the RR.

Requirements Engineering. The papers [24,35,37,38] researched on the application of role playing in Requirements Engineering Education and the following challenges and recommendations were identified:

- The assigned role must be clear (client, developer, etc.) to develop and understood the activities to teach the elicitation, analysis, specification and requirements validation.
- The scope of each role must be specified for the prioritization of requirements.
- If an actor in the developer team role needs clarification from the customer, such interaction must be allowed. Therefore, roles should change as little as possible during the ongoing Role Play.
- The use of standards for requirements and modeling tools can be included in the activities of each role of the development team.

No evidence of "requirements' change" situations was found in the papers reviewed.

Process Management. The use of role-playing simulations improved understanding of project management challenges and promoted hands-on learning [25,45]. Considering it, the following challenges and considerations were identified:

- The project (scenario) must be clear and include explicit limitations.
- Considering the limitations, the student must take choices rather than following instructions. E.g.: Choose between developers considering their programming language knowledge or select the life cycle.
- It's important to add some reality. Include "challenges" like team members may briefly leave the project because they are sick or on holiday [25].

Quality Assurance. Likewise, the quality assurance observed in [46,47] shows how role playing can focus on meeting quality standards. The following challenges and considerations were identified:

- Being a transversal process to the SW development stages, it must be clear which of these stages will be considered for the scenario.
- There must be roles to measure and examine if the work complies with the requirements and acceptance criteria and roles to ensure the execution of the processes.
- If the scenario contemplates the complete development cycle, students should be prevented from focusing directly on development and neglecting the analysis and design phases.

Software Architecture. In order to use role-playing games in this context, one must be clear about the "subcategory" that one intends to teach. In this case, the following challenges could be identified:

- Define a clear scenario to teach tradeoffs. The pros and cons of each component in the scenario should be included in each of the choices.
- To teach about architectural models, consider each architectural model to teach as an scenario [20]. Define a role to each component in the system including their functionalities, limitations and interactions with other components and parts of the system.

Teamwork/Soft Skills. In order to focus the Role playing on the development of Teamwork/Soft skills in SEE it is mandatory that the scenario and roles are linked to another category (e.g. development). Then, the challenges and recommendations found for this point in SEE are:

- Ensure to develop an scenario to learning the relationships between technology and society
- Must define clearly each role and their responsibility in the development team or the stakeholder.

Software Development. The use of role-playing is focus for the development process itself. Considering it, the following challenges and considerations were identified:

- Must specify any domain as a part of the scenario.
- Must define a clear and unique flow for each scenario.
- Must define clear requirements for the developers role and remove ambiguities.
- In domain implementation, ensure each team implements a different part of the common assets.

6   Results Summary

The review presented yields several interesting findings:

- Most studies found on *role playing in SEE focus on software development and teamwork/soft skills*; this tips the balance to the operational over the tactical and strategic aspects of the software development process.
- *Roles are usually attributed to humans*, but a role may also be associated (with the appropriate approach) to a software component.
- *Time and adjustment periods* are mentioned as part of the limitations of each study, and should be considered as a full part of the role playing.
- Scenarios should be defined according to the subfield to be developed and its constraints; likewise, the scenarios can be face-to-face, virtual, or mixed.
- The generic findings apply for any category in Software Engineering, but the specifically may apply to the main category in first instance.

Furthermore, it's noteworthy that specific critical aspects were conspicuously absent in all of the papers under review:

- There is no mention of cases where students have *special educational needs* (e.g.: A.S.D., Asperger Syndrome).
- No evidence was found of *how roles are assigned* to students; whether the study had a single general role for them or several, the assignment rationale was not made explicit.
- No evidence was found either of explicit addressing of **societal or other biases** that may occur.
- No cases could be found where the requirements were changing.

7   Threats to Validity

Several possible threats to the validity of our study were identified and mitigated:

- **Documents search:** the search was conducted across WoS, Scopus, and IEEE Xplore databases, primarily due to the accessibility constraints imposed by the nature of RR studies. This choice serves to reduce the potential risk of including papers whose source cannot be reliably verified.

- **Language:** all documents that were not in English or Spanish were excluded. This measure was taken to minimize the risk of misinterpreting documents written in languages not understood by the researchers.
- **Quality Appraisal:** although this step was omitted, it's important to note that our search and selection process focused exclusively on studies published in conferences and journals known for their stringent review processes.
- **Results:** the interpretation of the findings is constrained by the inherent limitations of the RR process.

8   Conclusions and Future Work

This paper presents a Rapid Literature Review (RR) focusing on the utilization of Role Playing in Software Engineering Education (SEE). The RR encompassed an examination of the WoS, Scopus, and IEEE Xplore databases, resulting in a selection of 23 papers. The majority of these papers revolve around software development and the enhancement of teamwork and soft skills, with a considerable emphasis on Requirements Engineering. This suggests that Role Playing, regardless of its potential in other areas, primarily contributes to skill development for product creation and team formation, targeting the operational aspects of the software development process. Moreover, while most papers delve into roles associated with "people," one paper, [20], stands out for its unique perspective, illustrating the assignment of roles to components. Conversely, the discussion concerning the design of scenarios is notably limited or entirely absent. This could potentially be attributed to the assumption that scenarios are inherently intertwined with the essence of Role Playing, and their formalization presents a challenge, given the various constraints such as space, modality, and time, among others, that may impinge upon them. Despite this observation, there is a discernible surge in interest surrounding the application of Role Playing in SEE. It becomes apparent that the challenges in implementing this approach center around operational planning considerations and the requisite focus on specific circumstances pertinent to the target group, i.e., the students who will engage with the technique. Moreover, our study, aligned with the research question, has unveiled a range of challenges and considerations relevant to the broad application of Role Playing, both in generic terms and within specific Software Engineering contexts. This compilation of insights serves as a valuable resource for educators aiming to integrate this technique into their SE courses and for researchers exploring the use of Role Playing in SEE. Finally, and as future work, an intriguing opportunity lies in the absence of student profiling based on their individual abilities or learning styles. This void presents the potential for the incorporation of tools like "Kolb's Learning Model," which can facilitate the development of Role Playing in a manner tailored to enhancing each student's strengths through the allocation of roles that align with their aptitudes.

Acknowledgments. This work has been partially supported by ANID under grant ANID PIA/APOYO AFB180002.

References

1. Cartaxo, B., Pinto, G., Soares, S.: Rapid reviews in software engineering. In: Contemporary Empirical Methods in Software Engineering, pp. 357–384. Springer, Cham (2020). https://doi.org/10.1007/978-3-030-32489-6_13
2. King, V.J., Stevens, A., Nussbaumer-Streit, B., et al.: Paper 2: performing rapid reviews. Syst. Rev. **11**, 151 (2022). https://doi.org/10.1186/s13643-022-02011-5
3. Erdogmus, H., Péraire, C.: Flipping a graduate-level software engineering foundations course. 2017 IEEE/ACM 39th International Conference on Software Engineering: Software Engineering Education and Training Track (ICSE-SEET), Buenos Aires, Argentina, pp. 23–32 (2017). https://doi.org/10.1109/ICSE-SEET.2017.20
4. Henry, T., LaFrance, J.: Integrating role-play into software engineering courses. J. Comput. Sci. Coll. **22**, 32–38 (2006)
5. Stevens, R.: Role-play and student engagement: reflections from the classroom. Teach. High. Educ. **20**, 1–12 (2015). https://doi.org/10.1080/13562517.2015.1020778
6. Cheville, R.A.: Linking capabilities to functionings: adapting narrative forms from role-playing games to education. High. Educ. **71**(6), 805–818 (2016)
7. White, A.R.: Pilot study and survey to increase adoption and sustained utilization of simulations using role-play course content. In: IEEE Frontiers in Education Conference (FIE), vol. 2022, pp. 1–15. Uppsala, Sweden (2022)
8. Ponsa, P., Vilanova, R., Amante, B.: The use of role playing in engineering curricula: a case study in human-automation systems. In: IEEE EDUCON 2010 Conference, pp. 1335–1341. Madrid, Spain (2010). https://doi.org/10.1109/EDUCON.2010.5492373
9. Hingle, A., Rangwala, H., Johri, A., Monea, A.: Using role-plays to improve ethical understanding of algorithms among computing students. In: 2021 IEEE Frontiers in Education Conference (FIE), pp. 1–7. Lincoln, NE, USA, (2021)
10. Andrews, J.H., Lutfiyya, H.L.: Experience report: a software maintenance project course. In: Thirteenth Conference on Software Engineering Education and Training, pp. 132–139. Austin, TX, USA (2000). https://doi.org/10.1109/CSEE.2000.827031
11. Mc Keeman, W.M.: Experience with a software engineering project course. IEEE Trans. Softw. Eng. **SE– 13**(11), 1182–1192 (1987)
12. Host, M.: Introducing empirical software engineering methods in education. In: Proceedings 15th Conference on Software Engineering Education and Training (CSEE&T 2002), pp. 170–179. Covington, KY, USA (2002). https://doi.org/10.1109/CSEE.2002.995209
13. Joseph, S., et al.: Teaching finite state machines with case method and role play. In: 2013 IEEE Global Engineering Education Conference (EDUCON), pp. 1305–1312. Berlin, Germany (2013). https://doi.org/10.1109/EduCon.2013.6530275
14. Jimenez-Diaz, G., Gomez-Albarran, M., Gomez-Martin, M.A., Gonzalez-Calero, P.A.: Understanding object-oriented software through virtual role-play. In: Fifth IEEE International Conference on Advanced Learning Technologies (ICALT 2005), pp. 875–877. Kaohsiung, Taiwan (2005). https://doi.org/10.1109/ICALT.2005.293
15. Chang, M., Kinshuk.: Web-based multiplayer online role playing game (MORPG) for assessing students' Java programming knowledge and skills. In: 2010 Third IEEE International Conference on Digital Game and Intelligent Toy Enhanced Learning, pp. 103–107. Kaohsiung, Taiwan (2010). https://doi.org/10.1109/DIGITEL.2010.20

16. Nakatani, T., Tsumaki, T., Tamai, T.: Requirements engineering education for senior engineers: Course design and its evaluation. In: 2010 5th International Workshop on Requirements Engineering Education and Training, pp. 26–35. Sydney, NSW, Australia (2010). https://doi.org/10.1109/REET.2010.5633111.

17. Chen, J., Qiu, G., Yuan, L., Zhang, L., Lu, G.: Assessing teamwork performance in software engineering education: a case in a software engineering undergraduate course. In: 18th Asia-Pacific Software Engineering Conference, pp. 17–24. Ho Chi Minh City, Vietnam (2011). https://doi.org/10.1109/APSEC.2011.50

18. Jarzabek, S., Eng, P.K.: Teaching an Advanced design, team-oriented software project course. In: 18th Conference on Software Engineering Education & Training (CSEET 2005), pp. 223–230. Ottawa, ON, Canada (2005)

19. Snow, C.: Dragons in the stacks: an introduction to role-playing games and their value to libraries. Collect. Build. **27**(2), 63–70 (2008)

20. Castro, L.M.: Role-playing software architecture styles. In: 20th IEEE International Conference on Software Architecture (ICSA 2023) (2023)

21. Bonwell, C.C., Eison, J.A.: Active Learning: Creating Excitement in the Classroom. The George Washington University, Washington, DC (1991)

22. Northern Illinois University Center for Innovative Teaching and Learning. Role playing. In: Instructional Guide for University Faculty and Teaching Assistants (2012). https://www.niu.edu/citl/resources/guides/instructional-guide

23. Svensson, R.B., Regnell, B.: Is role playing in requirements engineering education increasing learning outcome? Requirements Eng. **22**(4), 475–489 (2016). https://doi.org/10.1007/s00766-016-0248-4

24. Rueda, S., Panach, J.I., Cabotà, J.B., Valverde, F.: Applying role-playing game in software development subjects. In: ICERI2016 Proceedings, pp. 3532–3538 (2016)

25. Benitti, F.B.V.: Software engineering role-playing game: an interactive game for software engineering education. Int. J. Adv. Res. Comput. Sci. **2**(2), 6–9 (2011)

26. Akarsu, Z., Metin, Ö.O., Gungor, D., Yilmaz, M.: Towards a role playing game for exploring the roles in scrum to improve collaboration problems. In: Larrucea, X., Santamaria, I., O'Connor, R.V., Messnarz, R. (eds.) EuroSPI 2018. CCIS, vol. 896, pp. 254–264. Springer, Cham (2018). https://doi.org/10.1007/978-3-319-97925-0_21

27. McConville, J.R., Rauch, S., Helgegren, I., Kain, J.-H.: Using role-playing games to broaden engineering education. Int. J. Sustain. High. Educ. **18**(4), 594–607 (2017). https://doi.org/10.1108/IJSHE-08-2015-0146

28. Montenegro, C.H., Astudillo, H., Álvarez, M.C.G.: ATAM-RPG: a role-playing game to teach architecture trade-off analysis method (ATAM). In: 2017 XLIII Latin American Computer Conference (CLEI), pp. 1–9. Cordoba, Argentina (2017). https://doi.org/10.1109/CLEI.2017.8226416

29. Zuppiroli, S., Ciancarini, P., Gabbrielli, M.: A role-playing game for a software engineering lab: developing a product line. In: 2012 IEEE 25th Conference on Software Engineering Education and Training, pp. 13–22. Nanjing, China (2012)

30. Khangura, S., Konnyu, K., Cushman, R., Grimshaw, J., Moher, D.: Evidence summaries: the evolution of a rapid review approach. Syst. Control Found. Appl. **1**, 10 (2012). https://doi.org/10.1186/2046-4053-1-10

31. Hamel, C., et al.: Defining rapid reviews: a systematic scoping review and thematic analysis of definitions and defining characteristics of rapid reviews. J. Clin. Epidemiol. **129**, 74–85 (2021). ISSN 0895-4356

32. Best, L., Stevens, A., Colin-Jones, D.: Rapid and responsive health technology assessment: the development and evaluation process in the South and West region of England. J. Clin. Effectiv. **2**(2), 51–56 (1997)

33. Shaw, M.: Software engineering education: a roadmap. In: Proceedings of the Conference on the Future of Software Engineering, pp. 371–380 (2000)
34. Ouhbi, S., Pombo, N.: Software engineering education: challenges and perspectives. In: 2020 IEEE Global Engineering Education Conference (EDUCON), pp. 202–209. IEEE (2020)
35. Ouhbi, S.: Evaluating role playing efficiency to teach requirements engineering. In: IEEE Global Engineering Education Conference (EDUCON). Dubai, United Arab Emirates, pp. 1007–1010 (2019). https://doi.org/10.1109/EDUCON.2019.8725045
36. Decker, A., Simkins, D.: Leveraging role play to explore software and game development process. In: IEEE Frontiers in Education Conference (FIE), pp. 1–5. Erie, PA, USA (2016). https://doi.org/10.1109/FIE.2016.7757685
37. Nakamura, T., Kai, U., Tachikawa, Y.: Requirements engineering education using expert system and role-play training. In: 2014 IEEE International Conference on Teaching, Assessment and Learning for Engineering (TALE), pp. 375–382. Wellington, New Zealand (2014). https://doi.org/10.1109/TALE.2014.7062566
38. Kobrinskii, B.A.: Role playing as a method of learning in knowledge engineering. In: 2022 VI International Conference on Information Technologies in Engineering Education (Inforino), Moscow, Russian Federation, pp. 1–5 (2022)
39. Monasor, M.J., Vizcaíno, A., Piattini, M.: Cultural and linguistic problems in GSD: a simulator to train engineers in these issues. J. Softw. Evol. Proc. **24**, 707–717 (2012). https://doi.org/10.1002/smr.562
40. Gulec, U., et al.: Applying virtual reality to teach the software development process to novice software engineers. IET Soft. **15**(6), 464–483 (2021)
41. Maxim, B.R., Brunvand, S., Decker, A.: Use of role-play and gamification in a software project course. In: IEEE Frontiers in Education Conference (FIE), pp. 1–5. Indianapolis, IN, USA (2017). https://doi.org/10.1109/FIE.2017.8190501
42. Srisuwan, P.: Role-play as an educational tool in auditing skills, pp. 613–617 (2018). https://doi.org/10.1109/ICBIR.2018.8391271
43. Veldthuis, M., Koning, M., Stikkolorum, D.: A quest to engage computer science students: using dungeons & dragons for developing soft skills. In: Proceedings of the 10th Computer Science Education Research Conference (CSERC 2021), pp. 5–13. Association for Computing Machinery, New York, NY, USA (2022)
44. Rojas, A.E., Mejía-Moncayo, C.: Design of a course oriented to the comprehension of agile methods based on teamwork, role-play, and class project with a real client. In: 2019 International Conference on Virtual Reality and Visualization (ICVRV), pp. 212–216. Hong Kong, China (2019)
45. Mahnic, V.: A capstone course on agile software development using scrum. IEEE Trans. Educ. **55**(1), 99–106 (2012)
46. Barajas, A., Álvarez, F.J., Muñoz, J., Santaolaya, R., Collazos, C.A., Hurtado, J.A.: Verification and validation model for short serious game production. IEEE Lat. Am. Trans. **14**(4), 2007–2012 (2016)
47. Balaban, M., Maraee, A., Sturm, A., Jelnov, P.: A pattern-based approach for improving model quality. Softw. Syst. Model. **14**(4), 1527–1555 (2013). https://doi.org/10.1007/s10270-013-0390-0

Team Productivity Factors in Agile Software Development: An Exploratory Survey with Practitioners

Marcela Guerrero-Calvache[1]([⊠]) [iD] and Giovanni Hernández[2] [iD]

[1] Universidad de Nariño, San Juan de Pasto, Nariño, Colombia
marcela1396@udenar.edu.co
[2] Universidad Mariana, San Juan de Pasto, Nariño, Colombia
gihernandez@umariana.edu.co

Abstract. Agile software development (ASD) has favored the software industry thanks to the early delivery of value to customers and for providing certain advantages for their work teams, including increased productivity. Productivity in ASD is a relevant concept, it is still under study and is composed of a set of factors that allow to determine the performance of each of the members of a team. The purpose of this article is to compare professionals' perceptions of team productivity in ASD with productivity factors identified in a preliminary Systematic Literature Mapping (SMS). The study is oriented under the protocol for the construction of surveys in Software Engineering by Kitchenham and Pfleeger. As a result, the perceptions of 82 professionals working with agile methods were obtained, who associate productivity as an indicator of improvement within the team's processes and in the fulfillment of objectives to a client, this last aspect being also recurrent in the SMS. Finally, for the professionals only 22 factors are relevant for the evaluation of productivity highlighting Velocity, Communication, Work Capacity, Commitment, Team Leader, and Quality which are categorized into Meaning, Impact, Flexibility, and Socio-Human.

Keywords: Agile Software Development · Conceptions of Productivity · Perceptions of Software Industry Professionals · Productivity Measurement · Team Productivity Factors

1 Introduction

Organizations seek that with the use of agile methods they can permanently add value [1], thanks to the use of practices that strengthen the work towards the achievement of objectives, seek customer satisfaction, and with it, advance in the search for digital transformation [2]. In essence, the aim is to improve productivity.

The term productivity is generally approached from an economic perspective that comes from the late eighteenth century. In software engineering the concept only began to be understood in the seventies [3]. Since then, the purpose of defining productivity in this discipline has been influenced by various aspects, most of which are oriented under a traditional perception [4] based on lines of code (LOC) and as discussed [5–7] far from the values and principles that guide ASD.

Therefore, studying productivity in ASD has become a topic of great interest [8], because an agile development team generates data permanently in different places, through the use of various techniques and tools, but they do it without a unified vision of how to measure productivity [6]. In addition, the values and principles stated in the manifesto for agile software development are abstract when measuring team productivity [6]. Finally, it is evident that the information on this topic in this context is quite limited [6–8].

The motivation of this research is to carry out a comparative analysis between the perceptions of ASD team professionals on productivity and the factors identified in a Systematic Mapping Study (SMS) carried out in a previous phase. The article is organized as follows. Section 2 details related work. Section 3 shows the methodological design. Section 4 shows the results. Finally, Sect. 5 shows the conclusions.

2 Related Works

In [8] through an SMS, 616 studies were identified, eight of which were relevant for the extraction of information on the definition and measurement process of equipment productivity in ASD. The research allows an approach to the definition of team productivity in ASD. In addition, it establishes that it is composed of factors that generate an impact and contribute to the achievement of the objectives associated with the expectations coming from a client.

Regarding the conception of productivity, [8] found that, in the first place, it is composed of a set of factors [9–15] that become key elements to consolidate evaluation metrics that contribute to collecting valuable information that can be significant for decision making [6]. Thus, by knowing the behavior of the team, clear measures can be established to improve its productivity [5]. Secondly, productivity is associated with the fulfillment of objectives [8], which is related to the amount of work that a team has been able to generate with efficiency and quality, using resources optimally [9, 16] and satisfying the needs of a client [7, 10, 16–18]. Thirdly, productivity functions as an indicator of improvement [8] in software organizations [19, 20], allows to visualize the evolution of the project [16] towards its success [21] and contributes to evaluate the results achieved by a team [7]. Finally, productivity is also considered a relevant concept but remains abstract when translated into a measurement process [8].

In [8] it is also established that the measurement process is guided solely by productivity evaluation factors of which 63 were clearly identified. The factors were classified into four categories: Meaning, Impact, Flexibility, and High Performance [8].

The importance of the previous study lies in the fact that the previously defined factors are the starting point of this research because they are contrasted with the perceptions of software industry professionals through a comparative analysis as detailed in Sect. 3.

In [7] contrasts the conceptions of productivity at the team level from ASD perspective with the perceptions held by software industry professionals. This study describes productivity from both perspectives through three dimensions: input, process, and output. It highlights that productivity is related to customer satisfaction, activity management through knowledge transfer and time spent in meeting objectives. The study [7] is of great interest for this research since it proposes a way of approaching the understanding of productivity through productivity measurement dimensions.

In [22] a set of factors about the team productivity are defined, which contribute to continuous improvement processes. This study proposes a methodology for the classification of factors, specifically Socio-Human factors, which consists of phases: identification of factors that impact the productivity of a team, identification of predominant factors, selection of Socio-Human factors grouped according to their semantics, and evaluation and classification of the selected factors. The study allowed establishing 57 Socio-Human factors, which were classified into two groups: social and personal.

The previous study is relevant to this research because it shows the importance of a categorization of factors that affect team productivity and that these may be related to the social and human skills of the members.

In [23] the social and human factors that can influence the productivity of software development teams are considered to classify them. To achieve this, the study is oriented under a methodology based on a systematic review of the literature and evaluation processes with an expert in psychology. As a result, 13 social and human factors are presented, which were analyzed from a perspective of individual and group interaction and how they can favor the results of a software development team.

In [24], the productivity impact is analyzed, as of the team member perceptions about social and human factors. The results show that 13 factors are representative.

The two preliminary studies are important for this research because they show the importance of aspects related to social skills and relationships, and how they play a key role in the productivity of teams since the interaction between people is crucial in agile software development.

In [12] through the application of semi-structured interviews with software industry professionals from five organizations, the performance experience of teams using Lean and other ASD approaches is described. The study established that performance is associated with goal achievement and can be viewed from an individual, organizational, or market approach. It also identified thirty-three categories of performance factors, highlighting the importance of incorporating soft skills development into processes to improve performance.

The previous study is similar to this research in addressing performance perspectives through data collection techniques, which were categorized.

3 Methodology

3.1 Selection of Team Productivity Factors in ASD

The SMS conducted in [8] allowed establishing that the measurement process is oriented only by productivity evaluation factors of which 63 were clearly identified. The factors were classified into four categories: Meaning, Impact, Flexibility, and High Performance.

Subsequently, after analyzing in detail the definition of each factor in each of the selected studies in [8], it was identified that some of them had similarities. For example, the Team Capacity factor, being related to the amount of work the team can do in an iteration and being associated with a perception seen from a group approach, is merged with the Planning of Work factor and moved from the High-Performance Category to Meaning. The Need for Communication factor from the Meaning category is associated with the Communication factor from the Impact category and is retained in the latter classification. The Tools and Resource factor; and Cooperation and Collaboration from the Impact category are merged into the Resource and Collaboration factors respectively.

The transformations allowed to establish a reduction to 59 factors which were put into consideration by software industry professionals. Table 1 summarizes the factors selected for this study organized by each of the categories.

3.2 Gathering Perceptions of Software Industry Professionals

In this stage, the perceptions of software industry professionals on team productivity in ASD are obtained. For this purpose, the study was guided by the six (6) stages for the formulation and construction of a survey defined by authors Kitchenham and Pfleeger in [25].

Once the information on perceptions had been compiled, a contrast was made with the conceptions presented in the literature to identify similarities and differentiating aspects.

Setting Objectives. In this stage, the objectives of the collection instrument are defined. The objectives planned for this study are detailed below.

Obj. 1. Identifying the sociodemographic characteristics of professionals who use agile methods.
Obj. 2 Establishing the meaning and significance of team productivity for professionals who use agile methods.
Obj. 3. Determining how team productivity is measured by professionals who use agile methods.
Obj. 4. Establishing the level of relevance of the factors associated with team productivity in ASD.

Survey Design. The survey is designed as an instrument to collect data in a cross-sectional study [25] and is applied in the period between September and October 2022 to software industry professionals belonging to agile teams.

Developing a Survey Instrument. For the construction of the instrument, the results obtained in the SMS [8] are used, considering the conceptions of team productivity in ASD and the factors that involve its measurement.

For the design of questions, the questionnaire included closed questions in which multiple-choice answers were introduced; and open questions to deepen the perception of the respondent [25]. The questionnaire evaluated 73 items and the estimated time for its completion was 10 min. The instrument was organized into five sections. Table 2. describes each of them.

Survey Instrument Evaluation. For validation, a panel of two (2) experts was used to judge the content value of each question. Based on the recommendations made, adjustments were implemented. The questionnaire was implemented digitally through

Table 1. Classification of factors by category. Self-made based on [8]

Category	Definition	Factors
Meaning	Describes factors that define the productivity of a team, which is oriented under an individual or general perspective	Velocity, Work Capacity, Customer Satisfaction, Understanding job roles, Seeing the big picture, Ways to see success, Understanding Agile, Satisfaction with the programming experience, Satisfaction with the developed code, Team satisfaction, Team Capacity
Impact	Includes factors that positively, negatively, or neutrally influence the behavior of a team	Collaboration, Communication, Quality, Requirements handling by the Team, Iteration Length, Turnover rate (leavers), Turnover rate (newcomers), Team Stability index, Organizational support, Atmosphere, Decision power, Control of my own work, Re-organization, Distributed work, Goal setting, Testing, Duration to solve the calendaring task, Code performance, Team size, Resources, Unresolved conflicts
Flexibility	Determines the factors that affect the team when it is subjected to conditions involving changes	Improving the process, Organizational learning, Time investment, Adapting to change, Prioritization, Learning from failures, Getting buy-in, Work in progress, Lead Time, Meeting time per sprint, Percentage of missed tasks
High Performance	Establishes the factors that enable a team's performance to reach a higher level	Focus Factor, Team Leader, Inter-team relationship, Team Vision, Team spirit, Team setup, Reward, Personal development, Team identity, Pride, Social skills, Intrinsic motivation, Group Hedonic Balance, Confidence, Bonding, Commitment

the Google Forms tool (the form is available at the link https://forms.gle/4oV6s3nVjcyF xdJP7).

Finally, a pilot test was conducted with ten (10) professionals to identify difficulties in filling out the instrument. Based on the observations made, the pertinent changes were made.

Obtaining Valid Data. The selected population was the members of the software development teams that use agile methods. The sampling used was non-probabilistic of an

Table 2. Survey Sections.

Section	Description
General	Details the indications for filling out the instrument and the acceptance of the informed consent for the treatment of data
Sociodemographic information	Includes the questions related to the sociodemographic information of the professionals working in the Software Industry
Perceptions of Team Productivity in ASD	Inquires about the perception that the professionals of the software industry who use agile methods have about team productivity
Elements of measurement of Team Productivity in ASD	Contains questions related to how software industry professionals measure team productivity
Factors in measuring team productivity in ASD	The factors associated with the measurement of team productivity in agile software development in the categories: Meaning, Impact, Flexibility, and High Performance identified in [8] are presented for the respondent to determine the level of importance they have for the team

intentional type whose inclusion criteria were: to be a member of a software development team, making use of methods, techniques, and practices of agile software development.

3.3 Classification of Team Productivity Measurement Factors

Once the most relevant ASD team productivity factors for software industry professionals have been identified, they are categorized considering aspects in [8, 22–24].

4 Results

In this section, the results obtained in relation to the objectives proposed in the survey design and classification of the measurement factors are presented.

4.1 Perceptions of Software Industry Professionals

Socio-Demographic Characteristics of Professionals (Obj. 1). The results generated after applying the survey showed that 90.2% of the surveyed population is male (74) and the remaining 9.8% is female (8).

Regarding the country of residence, 93.9% of the professionals were from Colombia (77) and 6.1% from other countries (Mexico, Peru, Argentina, and the United States) (5). Regarding the city of residence, the most relevant cities are Pasto with 59.8% (49), Bogotá with 8.5% (7), and 3.7% (3) cities such as Cali and Ipiales, respectively.

Regarding the age of the respondents, 58.5% of the participants are between 24 and 36 years old, which indicates that currently professionals are linked to software companies from an early age. 15.9% between 20 and 24, 11% between 36 and 42, 14.6% between 42 and 50. Likewise, it was found that the maximum age identified was 50 years old.

Referring to the time that the professionals have been working in software construction projects, 73.2% have more than three years of experience in the area, 15.9% between 1 and 2 years, and only 11% have less than one year of experience.

Regarding the highest level of education obtained, 58.5% (48) of the respondents have attained undergraduate professional training, 24.4% (20) have a master's degree, 12.2% (10) have specialized training, 3.7% (3) are technologists, and only 1.2% (1) has basic and middle school training. The above data corroborate that the software industry is mostly made up of professionals.

According to the role played by professionals, it is found that most of the population (58) equivalent to 70.7% are Software Developers, followed by the position of project manager 6.1% (5), Scrum Master (4), Software Architect (4), Functional Analyst (4) with 4.9%, Technology Manager (2) and Agile Coach (2) with 2.4%; finally, Cybersecurity Engineer (1), Data Analyst (1), and Database Administrator (1) with 1.2% respectively.

Regarding the work modality within the organization, 63.4% (52) of the participants work remotely, 18.3% (15) work face-to-face, and 18.3% (15) work in a hybrid way.

According to the origin of the company where the participant works, 72% (59) are national and 28% (23) are foreign.

Determining the size of the company where the participant works, 36.6% (30) work in a large company, 28% (23) work in a small company, 24.4% (20) work in a medium-sized company, 6.1% (5) work in a micro-company, and 4.9% (4) do not know this information.

According to the agile method with which the professionals work in their teams, the first place goes to Scrum with 90.2% (74), the second with 31.7% (26) use Kanban, and 15.9% (13) use Extreme Programming. Other agile methods mentioned are ScrumBan, Lean, Agile UP, Spotify, and SAFe.

Sense and Meaning of Team Productivity for Professionals (Obj. 2). Once the concept of team productivity was consolidated in ASD considering the categories established in the Systematic Mapping Study described in a preliminary study presented in [8], it is continued by contrasting it with the perceptions of the 82 professionals of the software industry that were collected through the survey.

The results showed that 61% (50) of the professionals described productivity functions as an indicator of improvement within the team processes (see Fig. 1); 59.8% (49) stated that it is associated with the fulfillment of objectives according to customer needs; 53.7% (44) detailed that it is relevant for the organization to know the productivity of a team; 36.6% (30) stated that it is composed of a set of factors that generate an impact within the team, and only 6.1% (5) defined it as a purely abstract concept.

This has made it possible to establish the distance that exists between perceptions and the literature. In this sense, 87.5% of the theoretical references described in [8] state that productivity is composed of a set of factors that contribute to its measurement, while only 36.6% of professionals consider this idea. On the other hand, the professionals' orientation on productivity is focused as an indicator of improvement within the

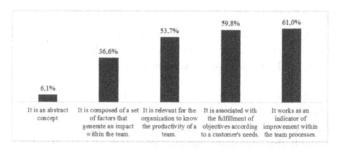

Fig. 1. Professionals' perceptions of team productivity in ASD. Source: Self-made.

team processes (61%), and in the literature this aspect is not so relevant. Nevertheless, both perspectives are recurrent in that productivity is associated with the fulfillment of objectives.

Measurement of Team Productivity by Professionals (Obj. 3). For the elements of team productivity measurement, the professionals were asked about three fundamental aspects: the indicators they use, how they measure it, and the tools they use.

It should be noted that the findings identified after the application of the survey showed a close relationship with the literature [8] because there was no evidence of a defined measurement process; on the contrary, all perceptions are oriented to establish factors that determine and influence team productivity in ASD in a subjective or intersubjective manner.

Regarding the indicators that professionals use to measure productivity in their team, it is determined that the ratio between the amount of work completed and planned (64.6%) is the most representative option by the respondents (See Fig. 2). This perception when related to the literature, is associated with the **Work Capacity** factor.

Software industry professionals consider that the work completed during an increment and iteration (58.5%) is another indicator of vital importance to measure productivity. This position when related to the literature is associated with the **Velocity** factor.

The evaluation of the fulfillment performed by the team is considered relevant in 54.9%, which is associated with the **Quality** factor according to the literature. The fulfillment of a customer's expectations is found to be 52.4%, which, according to the literature, is associated with the **Customer Satisfaction** factor.

Effective communication in the development of assigned tasks, with 47.6%, is associated with the **Communication** factor described in the literature.

Finally, interdependence in the development of assigned tasks (19.5%) and the use of work items in an iteration (9.8%) are the least highlighted options and are part of the **Collaboration** and **Resources** factors.

Secondly, the professionals were asked how they measure productivity in their team (see Fig. 3). It stands out that 32.9% of the respondents associate it with the relationship between the amount of work completed and the amount of work planned at the beginning of an iteration. This perception is associated with the **Work Capacity** factor described in [8].

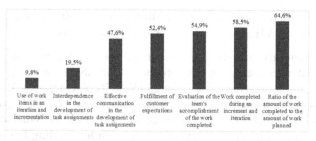

Fig. 2. Indicators to measure team productivity in ASD. Source: Self-made

The participants detail in 22% that team productivity can be measured by the amount of work that was completed in a given time (**Velocity Factor**). Another aspect to highlight is that professionals describe that task follow-up (19.5%), meeting objectives (14.6%), and holding meetings on an ongoing basis (8.5%) are key elements in measuring productivity.

Although these aspects do not have a direct relationship with a specific productivity factor, they nevertheless contribute to establishing that the review of tasks together with the holding of meetings on an ongoing basis makes the team's progress towards meeting objectives visible, determining the work completed and pending within an iteration.

Finally, the amount of work that a team can perform in an iteration (7.3%) (**Team Capacity Factor**) and customer satisfaction (4.9%) (**Customer Satisfaction**) Factor are other options mentioned by respondents.

Fig. 3. Measuring team productivity in ASD. Source: Self-made

Finally, in this section, when asked about the computational tools used by professionals to measure team productivity, Jira stands out with 34.9%, in second place is Easy Readmine with 13.3%, followed by Azure DevOps with 9.6%, then Trello with 8.4% and finally Excel with 7.2%. It is worth mentioning that in the findings identified in [8], no information was found in this regard.

Factors Associated with Relevant Team Productivity (Obj. 4). In this last section of the survey, participants are exposed to the factors for measuring team productivity in agile software development associated with the four categories identified in [8, 12]: Meaning, Impact, Flexibility, and High Performance, for them to evaluate the level of importance considering the following scale **Very High (VH), High (H), Medium (M), Low (L), and Very Low (VL)**.

It should be noted that those factors that exceeded 80% between the level of importance between VH and H are considered relevant for this research.

Meaning. Within this category, it was identified that, for the professionals, the relevant factors that allow measuring team productivity in ASD (See Fig. 4) are: the work completed during an increment and iteration (**Velocity Factor**) with 97.6%, the relationship between the amount of work completed and planned (**Work Capacity Factor**) with 89%, the fulfillment of customer expectations (**Customer Satisfaction Factor**) with 85.4%, the performance of each team member (**Understanding Job Roles Factor**) with 84.1%, the Satisfaction of the team members in the development of their activities (**Team Satisfaction Factor**) with 81.7%, and the amount of work the team can do in one iteration (**Team Capacity Factor**) with 80.5%.

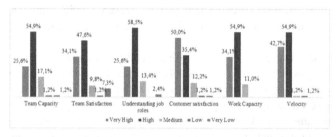

Fig. 4. Team Productivity Factors in ASD - Category Meaning. Source: Self-made.

Impact. Within the Impact category, it was identified that factors such as effective communication in the development of the assigned tasks (**Communication Factor**) with 92.7%, the evaluation of the fulfillment of the work performed by the team (**Quality Factor**) with 86.6%, the satisfaction of the team members in relation to the work environment (**Atmosphere Factor**), the precision and specification of the requirements (**Requirements handling by the team Factor**) with 85.4%, the goals set by the team (**Goal Setting Factor**) with 84.1% and the team's autonomy to make decisions (**Decision Power Factor**) with 80.5%, were perceived by software industry professionals at a VH and H level of importance (See Fig. 5).

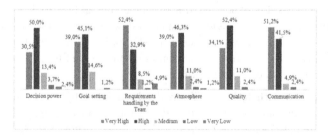

Fig. 5. Team Productivity Factors in ASD - Category Impact. Source: Self-made.

Flexibility. Within the Flexibility category, it was identified that factors such as: the organization's learning from the errors presented in a project (**Getting buy-in Factor**) with 86.6%, the team's learning from the errors presented in an iteration (**Learning from Failures Factor**) with 85.4%, the generation of new individual and team knowledge (**Organizational Learning Factor**) with 81.7%, and the maturity of the process used by the team (**Improving the Process**) with 80.5% were perceived by the professionals as relevant at the Very High and High levels (See Fig. 6).

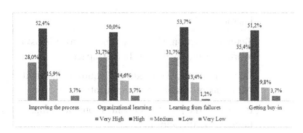

Fig. 6. Team Productivity Factors in ASD - Category Flexibility. Source: Self-made.

High Performance. Within the High-Performance category, the degree of willingness of a team member to collaborate with the other members (**Commitment Factor**) with 89%, the management, communication, and control of changes in the team (**Team Leader Factor**) with 86.6%, security in the achievement of the team's objective (**Confidence Factor**), the contribution of the members' complementary skills in the team's conformation (**Team Setup Factor**), the effect caused in the team as a result of developing quality work (**Pride Factor**), the degree of motivation of the team members (**Intrinsic Motivation Factor**), the ability of the members to work interdependently in the pursuit of an objective (**Social Skills Factor**) with 85.4% were perceived by software industry professionals with a Very High and High level of importance (See Fig. 7).

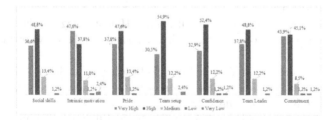

Fig. 7. Team Productivity Factors in ASD - Category High Performance. Source: Self-made.

4.2 Classification of Team Productivity Measurement Factors

The 59 ASD team productivity factors identified in [8] were classified into the following categories: Meaning, Impact, Flexibility, and High Performance. Subsequently, with the execution of the survey of 82 ASD team members, the importance of these factors was determined, establishing that only 23 of them were evaluated with a level of relevance between High and Very High.

According to the perception of the software industry professionals, the selected factors are grouped in the categories defined in Table 3.

Table 3. Relevant factors for professionals

Category	Factor
Meaning (6)	Team satisfaction, Understanding job roles, Customer satisfaction, Work Capacity, Velocity, Team Capacity
Impact (6)	Decision power, Goal setting, Requirements handling by the Team, Atmosphere, Quality, Communication
Flexibility (4)	Improving the process, Organizational learning, Learning from failures, Getting buy-in
High Performance (7)	Social skills, Intrinsic motivation, Pride, Team setup, Confidence, Team Leader, Commitment

Machuca and Gasca in [24] emphasize that; Socio-Human Factors are considered fundamental aspects within software organizations by providing benefits such as effectiveness in project management, efficiency of resources such as time and costs, and a positive impact on team productivity. The authors identified through a literature review 57 Socio-Human Factors [22] and after a debugging process they were reduced to thirteen [23].

When contrasting the factors described in Table 3 with those proposed in [22, 23] (see Table 4), it is established that, of the 23 factors identified in this research, 52.17% are related to Socio-Human factors. Therefore, the High-Performance category acquires a new meaning and is renamed Socio-Human because all the factors that constitute it (7) are related to them.

The above allows determining that the Socio-Human category plays an essential role to achieve high levels of performance in a team and that the software process being developed is successful.

On the other hand, it was identified five (5) factors (see Table 4) of the categories: Meaning, Impact, and Flexibility are also part of Socio-Human category; therefore, they are relocated in this new emerging category.

In a final debugging of factors, it was established that the Getting buy-in factor (initially belonging to the Flexibility category) is related to the Commitment factor in Socio-Human. For this reason, a merger of the two factors is made, finally obtaining 22 team productivity factors in ASD.

Figure 8 Summarizes the productivity factors categorized with the new classification: Meaning, Flexibility, Impact, and Socio-Human.

Table 4. Contrast of categories in [8] and Socio-Human Factors

Category defined in [8]	Factor	Socio-Human Factors to which it belongs according to [23]
High Performance	Social skills	Empathy and interpersonal relationship
High Performance	Intrinsic motivation	Motivation
High Performance	Pride	Work satisfaction
High Performance	Team setup	Team cohesion
High Performance	Confidence	Collaboration
High Performance	Team Leader	Leadership
High Performance	Commitment	Commitment
Impact	Decision power	Autonomy
Impact	Atmosphere	Work satisfaction
Impact	Communication	Communication
Meaning	Team satisfaction	Work satisfaction
Flexibility	Getting buy-in	Commitment

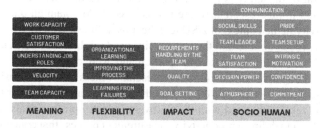

Fig. 8. Selected productivity factors. Source: Self-made

5 Conclusions

The research contributed to establishing that the process of measuring team productivity in ASD is oriented solely by factors. In a preliminary study, 63 factors were identified, which, after analyzing similarities between their definitions, were reduced to 59.

According to the information gathered through the design and validation of a survey and subsequent application to 82 software industry professionals, it is possible to determine the sociodemographic characteristics of the population, the sense and meaning of team productivity, the way it is measured, and the level of relevance of a set of associated factors compiled from the existing literature.

70.7% of the respondents are software developers, and 73.2% have been working on software construction projects for more than three years, which allows inferring that the collected perspectives are associated with a constant work product of the expertise built over a long period. Likewise, 90.2% of the professionals, work with the Scrum framework, one of the most used agile methods in organizations, especially in the IT sector.

The productivity perceptions of the professionals were very close to what is exposed in the literature, highlighting that, for them, productivity is an indicator of improvement within the team's processes and measures the degree or level of compliance with the objectives set by a client.

For professionals, productivity evaluation is determined by three fundamental aspects. First, there are the indicators used to measure productivity in a team. The relationship between the amount of work completed and planned, the work completed during an increment and iteration, the evaluation of the team's performance and the fulfillment of the client's expectations are the most representative ones. Secondly, the measurement process taken into account by the professionals is presented, focusing on Work Capacity and Velocity. Finally, it is identified that the most used computational tool to support the measurement of productivity is Jira.

The debugging of the categories associated with the measurement of team productivity in ASD allows proposing a reclassification of the factors in terms of: Meaning, Flexibility, Impact, and Socio-Human. In addition, of the 63 factors defined in the literature, only 22 are considered as the most relevant for software industry professionals, highlighting mainly the factors Velocity, Communication, Work Capacity, Commitment, Team Leader and Quality.

A limitation of the study is related to the perceptions of software industry professionals collected in this research, where it was possible to obtain an understanding of team productivity in the context of ASD and the most influential factors were identified. However, it is crucial to note that the sample size used might not be sufficient to generalize the results. In addition, most of the participants were of Colombian origin, which could limit the geographical and cultural representativeness of the conclusions.

As a future work, it is intended that, with the analysis carried out after the literature review and the results obtained with the Software Industry professionals, a conceptual model can be built to define a productivity measurement process that contributes to ASD teams.

References

1. Iqbal, J., Omar, M., Yasin, A.: Defining teamwork productivity factors in agile software development. Int. J. Adv. Sci. Eng. Inf. Technol. (2022). https://doi.org/10.18517/ijaseit.12.3.13648
2. Digital.ai, "State of Agile Report 2022," Annu. Rep. State Agil., vol. 13, pp. 1–22 (2022). https://stateofagile.com
3. Hernández-López, A., Colomo-Palacios, R., García-Crespo, Á.: Medidas de productividad en los proyectos de desarrollo de software: una aproximación por puestos de trabajo. Carlos III de Madrid (2014)
4. García-Crespo, Á., Hernández-López, A., Colomo-Palacios, R.: Productivity in software engineering: a study of its meanings for practitioners: understanding the concept under their standpoint. In: Proceedings of the 7th Iberian Conference on Information Systems and Technologies (CISTI 2012), pp. 1–6 (2012). https://ieeexplore.ieee.org/document/6263205

5. Hernández, G., Navarro, A., Jiménez, R., Jiménez, F.: Cómo los profesionales perciben la relevancia de las métricas de productividad para un equipo ágil de desarrollo de software. Revista Ibérica de Sistemas e Tecnologías de Información **E32**, 596–609 (2020)
6. Hernández, G., Martínez, Á., Jiménez, R., Jiménez, F.: Métricas de productividad para equipo de trabajo de desarrollo ágil de software: una revisión sistemática. TecnoLógicas **22**, 63–81 (2019). https://doi.org/10.22430/22565337.1510
7. Guerrero-Calvache, S.-M., Hernández, G.: Conceptions and perceptions of software industry professionals on team productivity in agile software development: a comparative study. Rev. Fac. Ing. 30 (2021). https://doi.org/10.19053/01211129.v30.n58.2021.13817. http://www.sci elo.org.co/scielo.php?script=sci_arttext&pid=S0121-11292021000400104&nrm=iso
8. Guerrero-Calvache, M., Hernández, G.: Team productivity in agile software development: a systematic mapping study, pp. 455–471 (2022). https://doi.org/10.1007/978-3-031-19647-8_32
9. Sj, D.I.K.: An Empirical Study of WIP in Kanban Teams (2018). https://doi.org/10.1145/323 9235.3239238
10. Mashmool, A., Khosravi, S., Joloudari, J.H., Inayat, I., Gandomani, T.J., Mosavi, A.: A statistical model to assess the team's productivity in agile software teams. In: Proceedings of the 2021 IEEE 4th International Conference and Workshop Óbuda on Electrical and Power Engineering (CANDO-EPE), pp. 11–18 (2021). https://doi.org/10.1109/CANDO-EPE54223.2021.9667902
11. Scott, E., Charkie, K.N., Pfahl, D.: Productivity, turnover, and team stability of agile teams in open-source software projects. In: Proceedings of the 2020 46th Euromicro Conference on Software Engineering and Advanced Applications (SEAA), pp. 124–131 (2020). https://doi.org/10.1109/SEAA51224.2020.00029
12. Fagerholm, F., Ikonen, M., Kettunen, P., Münch, J., Roto, V., Abrahamsson, P.: How Do Software Developers ExperienceTeam Performance in Lean andAgile Environments? (2014). https://doi.org/10.1145/2601248.2601285
13. Jung, M., Chong, J., Leifer, L.: Group hedonic balance and pair programming performance: affective interaction dynamics as indicators of performance. In: Proceedings of the SIGCHI Conference on Human Factors in Computing Systems, pp. 829–838 (2012). https://doi.org/10.1145/2207676.2208523
14. Dorairaj, S., Noble, J., Malik, P.: Understanding lack of trust in distributed agile teams: a grounded theory study. In: Proceedings of the 16th International Conference on Evaluation Assessment in Software Engineering (EASE 2012), pp. 81–90 (2012). https://doi.org/10.1049/ic.2012.0011
15. Melnyk, K., Hlushko, V., Borysova, N.: Decision support technology for sprint planning. Radio Electron. Comput. Sci. Control, 135–145 (2020). https://doi.org/10.15588/1607-3274-2020-1-14
16. Fatema, I., Sakib, K.: Factors influencing productivity of agile software development teamwork:a qualitative system dynamics approach. In: Proceedings of the 2017 24th Asia-Pacific Software Engineering Conference (APSEC), pp. 737–742 (2017). https://doi.org/10.1109/APSEC.2017.95
17. Ramírez-Mora, S.L., Oktaba, H.: Productivity in agile software development: a systematic mapping study. In: Proceedings of the 2017 5th International Conference in Software Engineering Research and Innovation (CONISOFT), pp. 44–53 (2017). https://doi.org/10.1109/CONISOFT.2017.00013
18. Sarpiri, M., Gandomani, T.J.: A case study of using the hybrid model of scrum and six sigma in software development. Int. J. Electr. Comput. Eng. **11**, 5342–5350 (2021). https://doi.org/10.11591/ijece.v11i6.pp5342-5350

19. Maldonado, M.A.: Factores que afectan la productividad en equipos Scrum analizados con pensamiento sistémico, Master Thesis, Universidad Nacional de Colombia, Medellín, Colombia 2017

20. Melo, C., de O,Cruzes, D.S., Kon, F., Conradi, R.: Interpretative case studies on agile team productivity and management. Inf. Softw. Technol. **55**(2), 412–427 (2013). https://doi.org/10.1016/j.infsof.2012.09.004

21. Iqbal, J., Omar, M., Yasin, A.: An empirical analysis of the effect of agile teams on software productivity. In: Proceedings of the 2019 2nd International Conference on Computing, Mathematics and Engineering Technologies (iCoMET), pp. 1–8 (2019). https://doi.org/10.1109/ICOMET.2019.8673413

22. Machuca-Villegas, L., Gasca-Hurtado, G.P.: Towards a social and human factor classification related to productivity in software development teams. In: Mejia, J., Muñoz, M., Rocha, Á., Calvo-Manzano, J. (eds.) CIMPS 2019. AISC, vol. 1071, pp. 36–50. Springer,Cham (2020). https://doi.org/10.1007/978-3-030-33547-2_4

23. Machuca-Villegas, L., Gasca-Hurtado, G.P., Restrepo Tamayo, L.M., Morillo Puente, S.: Social and human factor classification of influence in productivity in software development teams. In: Yilmaz, M., Niemann, J., Clarke, P., Messnarz, R. (eds.) EuroSPI 2020. CCIS, vol. 1251, pp. 717–729. Springer, Cham (2020). https://doi.org/10.1007/978-3-030-56441-4_54

24. Machuca-Villegas, L., Gasca-Hurtado, G.P., Puente, S.M., Tamayo, L.M.R.: Factores sociales y humanos que influyen en la productividad del desarrollo de software: Medición de la percepción. RISTI - Revista Iberica de Sistemas e Tecnologías de Informacao **E41**, 488–502 (2021)

25. Kitchenham, B.A., Pfleeger, S.L.: Personal opinion surveys. In: Shull, F., Singer, J., Sjøberg, D.I.K. (eds.) Guide to Advanced Empirical Software Engineering. pp. 63–92. Springer, London (2008). https://doi.org/10.1007/978-1-84800-044-5_3

Work-Life Interference on Employee Well-Being and Productivity. A Proof-of-Concept for Rapid and Continuous Population Analysis Using Evalu@

Fernando Yepes-Calderon[1,2]($\boxtimes$) and Paulo Andrés Vélez Ángel[1,2]

[1] Science Based Platforms, 405 Beact CT, Fort Pierce - Florida, USA
fernando.yepes@strategicbp.net
[2] GYM Group SA, Cra 78A No. 6-58, Cali, Colombia
http://www.strategicbp.net, http://www.gym-group.org

Abstract. The impact of work-life on employee well-being, family, and productivity is a prevalent concern in today's fast-paced and demanding work environments. This document presents the results of a pilot study that involves coherent data gathering, ease of massification of the tracking instrument used, and the possibility of continued observation to anticipate high-impact social disorders that affect the core of societies, the family. The research utilizes the SWING questionnaire, a widely used tool for measuring work-home interaction, to assess four types of synergies: positive work-to-home interaction, negative work-to-home interaction, positive home-to-work interaction, and negative home-to-work interaction.

The study employs the Evalu@ - data centralizer to gather information from populations that receive the tracking instruments in their smartphones. This approach enables fast and efficient data collection for posterior analysis providing researchers and practitioners with unexplored information and valuable insights into any field suitable for inspection.

The inference findings extracted from the presented exercise and other factors not included in this document will have a double-strike impact when spreading the methodology to a broader audience. The acquisition forms can continue pinpointing employees at risk of an unbalanced lifestyle to warn companies and individuals about low productivity with possible roots or consequences at home or home instability due to work factors. But more importantly, the exercise is a successful proof-of-concept to enable the participation of individuals in an organization with a hierarchical structure. We backed the findings with verifiable statistical procedures that will not take more than minutes to set up and a few more to yield results, a dynamic participation mechanism never envisaged before.

Keywords: Work-life interference · Swing questionnaire · Evalu@ · Employee well-being · Work performance · dynamic citizen sampling · citizen active participation · Swing questionnaire

H. Florez and M. Leon (Eds.): ICAI 2023, CCIS 1874, pp. 277–290, 2024.
https://doi.org/10.1007/978-3-031-46813-1_19

1   Introduction

Experts have recognized work-life balance as crucial for the employees' success and well-being [17]. Also, adverse consequences await organizations that ignore workers' quality of life by experiencing low engagement and declines in productivity [20]. Typically, workers spend more than half of their active hours at work or on work-related tasks. The time spent at the workplace, the nature of the functions performed, and the work environment collectively influence overall welfare [1] and families. The strategic importance of employee welfare for organizations and individuals is of utmost relevance, and researchers have displayed significant interest in this area due to the need for an adequate theoretical framework and comprehensive scientific instruments to assess quantifications of this nature at the workplace [16]. Authors have agreed that welfare is the compound of some separable interactions, and individuals can manifest it through a series of generalizable constructs [22]. Attempts to characterize the effect of work-life balance at Small and Medium-sized enterprises (SMEs) [21] is sufficient for diagnosis but needs systematization for continuous tracking and platform flexibility so the administrator can complement the survey with pertinent variables that are often local and specific to each studied population.

The Swing questionnaire has been widely used in the Nordic peninsula to diagnose workers' quality of life in all levels of commitment [2]. It was developed by Sabine Geurts and colleagues at the University of Nijmegen in the Netherlands [9]. The questionnaire measures four types of work-home interactions:

- Positive work-to-home interaction (PWH): This refers to how work experiences positively affect home life. For example, feeling energized and motivated at work may increase involvement and enjoyment in family activities.
- Negative work-to-home interaction (NWH). Refers to how work experiences negatively affect home life. For example, feeling stressed or exhausted at work may lead to decreased patience and increased irritability with family members.
- Positive home-to-work interaction (PHW). Refers to how home experiences positively affect work life. For example, feeling relaxed and refreshed after spending time with family may lead to increased focus and productivity at work.
- Negative home-to-work interaction (NHW). Refers to how home experiences negatively affect work life. For example, feeling worried or stressed about family matters may lead to decreased concentration and increased errors at work.

Various research studies have used the Swing questionnaire to examine work-home interaction and outcomes, such as job satisfaction, well-being, and work performance. The results of these studies suggest that work-home interaction can significantly impact work and home life. The validity of the instrument – the Swing –, has been tested before by several authors [8,10,11,18].

This article presents the pipeline for implementing the Swing tool to make it available for populations promptly. The system has reached a level of generalization that enables the implementation with no delays to any company, regardless of niche and localization. The platform captures the information through hand-held terminals and connects an API where extended analyses are available. The results section of this document is a non-exhaustive list of inference tests – as a proof of concept – where questions of management relevance are answered with statistical rigor.

2   Materials and Methods

To expeditiously reach a statistically significant quantity of samples and have the querying tool available for continuous data gathering even out of the scope of the current exploration, we employed the on-cloud data centralizer Evalu@ www.evalualos.com [23,24]. The online tool presents intuitive functions that facilitate the setup of online forms that a proprietary API synchronizes with native apps available for Android and Apple stores. Therefore, the questionnaires programmed in the platform are instantly available for unlimited users that can access the questionnaire everywhere, anywhere. Figure 1 depicts the configuration steps to run the data centralizer as a systematic tool for SWING endeavors. The reader is invited to observe the vertical timeline showing the setup process's efficiency.

2.1   Configuring Evalu@ for Swing Surveying and Complements

A user with sufficient permissions employs Excel files to define at least one container, one tracking instrument, and the desired indexes Evalu@ will use to report in the results link. The swing questionnaire is standard, with close-ended questions, but its application only yields significant results if confronted with lifestyle and status responses from the queried individuals. The surveying exercise ended with 44 questions, 22 specific to the Swing instrument (see Table 1) and 22 more grouped in a class that we named demographics (see Table 2).

In both, Tables 1 and 2, the Eval values column presents a $B - S - E$ (beginning number - step - ending number) format. Such as structure is a generalization to create a list starting in B that uses steps of size S until it arrives at number E., E.g., 0-1-5, creates the options' list $[0, 1, 2, 3, 4, 5]$. An exception happens when dealing with Boolean possibilities, in which case, the list is explicit, E.g., $[0, 1]$. Regardless of the method selected to create the options lists, there should be a one-to-one correspondence per row between the numeric values in the eval values columns and the elements listed in the Eval options column. The Evalu@ API provides functions to go back and forward from the numeric values to the concepts.

2.2   Swing Delivery to Handheld Devices

Since Evalu@ provides native interfaces for Android and Apple, the system synchronizes – with no delay – the configured tracking schemes. Access to the platform considers individual users that should sign up. Still, the administrators can

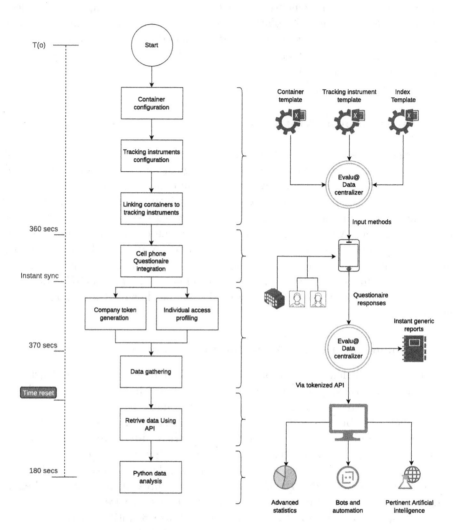

Fig. 1. Configuring Evalu@ for the specific proposes of the SWING Questionnaire. The timeline suggests that this device is made available in 370 s to a theoretically unlimited number of users. Services involving BOTs, advancing statistics, and Artificial intelligence implementations are available throughout the Evalu@ API

Table 1. Standard SWING survey with close-ended questions. The question with the underlined number were used in the inference analysis. Note that the negative and positive interactions are not labeled because we intend to go beyond the metrics extraction and explore the reasons for the psychological afflictions.

No	Category	Eval values	Eval options
1	Are you irritable at home because your work requires a high effort?	0—1—3	Never—Sometimes—Many times—Always
2	Is it difficult for you to meet your home obligations because you are constantly thinking about your job?	0—1—3	Never—Sometimes—Many times—Always
3	Do you have to cancel your plans with your partner/family/friends due to work commitments?	0—1—3	Never—Sometimes—Many times—Always
4	Your work schedule makes it difficult for you to meet your obligations at home?	0—1—3	Never—Sometimes—Many times—Always
5	Do you feel tired of participating in leisure activities with your partner/family/friends because of your work?	0—1—3	Never—Sometimes—Many times—Always
6	Do you have to work so hard that you don't have time for resting?	0—1—3	Never—Sometimes—Many times—Always
7	Do your work obligations make it difficult for you to stay relaxed at home?	0—1—3	Never—Sometimes—Many times—Always
8	Does your job require additional time that you would have liked to spend with your partner/family/friend?	0—1—3	Never—Sometimes—Many times—Always
9	Do problems at home make you so irritable that you take it out on your colleagues or coworkers?	0—1—3	Never—Sometimes—Many times—Always
10	Do you have difficulty concentrating on your work because of problems at home?	0—1—3	Never—Sometimes—Many times—Always
11	Problems with your partner / family / friends affect your job performance?	0—1—3	Never—Sometimes—Many times—Always
12	Do the problems you have with your partner /family/friends make you not feel like working?	0—1—3	Never—Sometimes—Many times—Always
13	After a nice day/week of work; Do you feel like participating in activities with your partner/family/friend?	0—1—3	Never—Sometimes—Many times—Always
14	Do you do better at home because of the things you've learned at work?	0—1—3	Never—Sometimes—Many times—Always
15	Do you fulfill your obligations better at home because you also do it at work?	0—1—3	Never—Sometimes—Many times—Always
16	Efficiently organizing your time at work made you learn to organize your time better at home?	0—1—3	Never—Sometimes—Many times—Always
17	Are you better prepared to interact with your partner/ family/friends as a result of the things you have learned at work?	0—1—3	Never—Sometimes—Many times—Always
18	After spending a fun weekend with your partner/family /friends; Is your job more enjoyable?	0—1—3	Never—Sometimes—Many times—Always
19	Do you take your responsibilities at work more seriously because you are forced to do the same at home?	0—1—3	Never—Sometimes—Many times—Always
20	Do you do better at work because you do the same at home?	0—1—3	Never—Sometimes—Many times—Always
21	Do you manage your time at work more efficiently because you have to do that at home too?	0—1—3	Never—Sometimes—Many times—Always
22	Do you have more self-confidence at work because your home life is well organized?	0—1—3	Never—Sometimes—Many times—Always

Table 2. List of complementary information requested to associate style-life, demographics, achievements, and work status with population-based findings extracted with the SWING questionnaire. The questions with underlined numbers were used in the inference exercises included in this document.

No	Criterio	Eval values	Eval options
1	Written consent. Do you agree to participate?	0 1	No—Yes
2	How old are you?	0—1—3	18-27—28-37—38-47—48 ó más (Years old)
3	Which is your gender?	0 1	Female—Male
4	What is your marital status?	0—1—5	Single—Married—cohabitation—Divorced—Widow(er)
5	Level of education?	0—1—7	Primary—Secondary—Technical—Bachelors—Specialty—Master—Doctorate—No study
6	Family structure?	0—1—5	Alone—Heterosexual couple with kids— Couple without kids—Monoparental with kids— LGBTI with kids—Extended family
7	How many dependents do you have?	0—1—8	None—1—2—3—4—5—6—7— more than 7
8	To which group do you belong?	0—1—9	Person with a disability—LGBTI—Indigenous—Afro-descendant—Victim of the armed conflict— Female head of household—Room—Raizal— None—Other
9	What is your stratification level?	0—1—5	E1— E2—E3—E4—E5—E6
10	What is your type of housing?	0—1—3	Owner—Family owned—Rented—Shared
11	Are you currently working?	0 1	No—Yes
12	What is your job about?	0—1—18	Agriculture—Fishing—Aquaculture—Livestock—Beekeeping—Industry—Construction— Mining and Energy—Health—Educational— Real Estate—Rental of machines and equipment—Financial—Communications—Transportation—Commerce—Tourism—Technological development —Others
13	What is the position you hold in the company?	0—1—5	Senior management—Director—Coordinator—Assistant—Operative—Other
14	How long have you worked at this company?	0—1—7	Less than 1 year—1 to 5 years—6 to 10 years— 1 to 15 years—16 to 20 years—20 to 25 years— 26 to 30 years—Over 31 years
15	What kind of contract do you have?	0—1—7	Indefinite Term—Fixed term one year— Fixed term less than one year—Service provision— Work or Labor—Apprentice and/or trainee— other—none
16	How many hours a day do you work?	0—1—20	0—1—2—3—4—5—6—7—8—9—10—11—12—13—14—15—16—17—18—19—20
17	In which area do you live?	0 1	Rural—Urban
18	How long does commuting (one way to work) take?	0—1—6	Less than 30 mins—Between 30 mins and 1 h— Between 1 and 1:30 h—Between 1:30 and 2 h— Between 2 and 2:30 h—Between 2:30 and 3 h— More than 3 h
19	How long does it take to commute (Only return home)?	0—1—6	Less than 30 mins—Between 30 mins and 1 h— Between 1 and 1:30 h—Between 1:30 and 2 h— Between 2 and 2:30 h—Between 2:30 and 3 h— More than 3 h
20	Are you registered in the social health system	0 1	No—Yes
21	Are you registered in the retirement system	0 1	No—Yes
22	Are you registered in labor-risks system	0 1	No—Yes

create a different code for companies and have several individuals working with the same credentials within a company domain. The latter option is highly convenient when dealing with sensible or data protected by confidentiality agreements since the system registers the user entry but does not know who is fulfilling the survey. Nevertheless, Evalu@ captures – in the background – the handheld MAC address to close the door to the possibility of multiple entries by users that could bias the querying exercise. The Figure 2 shows sections of the two forms (Swing and complementary information) as it looks in an Android handheld device.

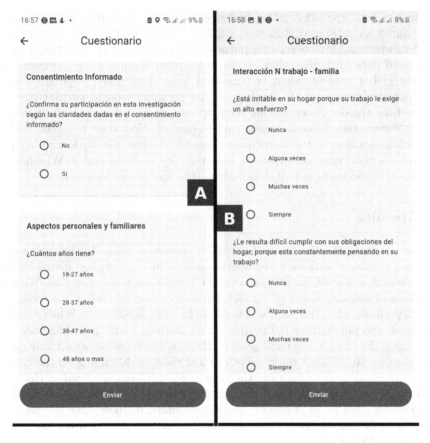

Fig. 2. Evalu@ displaying on its native app for smartphones. In panel A, the first section of the demographics form. In panel B, the SWING questions. Recall that Evalu@ displays the tracking instruments in the language defined by the administrator. Since we run this exercise in a Latin American country, the interface shows the instrument in Spanish.

2.3 Gathered Data and Sample Description

Evalu@ syncs the tracking schemes in real time; therefore, the survey administrators can reach a wide audience right after ending the configuration. In the particular case presented in this document, the administrator created credentials for two companies located in Bogotá - Colombia. The system registered 710 entries of 44 distinct records, each one. Evalu@ captured these values in 53.7 h.

2.4 Inference Exploration

Evalu@ collects the information holistically and in a coherent manner that is well suited for advanced statistics and feeds expert systems like Bots and AI implementations. Moreover, this purpose is the core of the API that enables organized data gathering after acquisition. Using Evalu@'s API, questions of current global interest might be answered from the studied population using mathematical inference [4]. Among all the possible hypotheses that one can derive from the data used in this work, we are interested in: 1. Define working habits differentiated between men and women, 2. How does a higher level of education manifest in the participant's wealth, 3. How the work stability provided by a good contract creates a better family ambient and 4. Whether the job-position redounds in irritability within the family environment.

3 Results

We have automated the tests of statistical inference using Python; therefore, answering other questions by comparing means in the samples' distribution if feasible at a mouse click. The exercises in Table 3 are not exhaustive. We have defined a significance $\alpha = 0.05$ for all the inference tests; therefore, we accept the null hypothesis when the p-value is smaller than the significance. When possible, we forced two populations in multiple class questions – such as Swing ones – by separating the ideal (never) and grouped the non-ideals (sometimes, many times, and always). Recall that the concept of ideal changes depending on the type of Swing interaction, in which case, the grouping is not always the same. However, in this document, we only analyzed negative interactions justifying the category never to be ideal in all studied cases. Additionally, in those exercises where it was impossible to set classes into two populations, we employed the analysis of variance (ANOVA) [7].

The five inference exercises proposed in Table 3, involve six questions of the socio-demographics group (Table 2 and two more from the Swing instrument. Table 4 presented the Gaussian statistics on the responses or status of the studied population and Fig. 3 recapitulates the percentual frequencies on each available option per question used in the inference analysis.

The first two hypotheses do not include Swing inputs but provide insight that could help to adjust public policies regarding genre equality and the impact of higher education. The Fig. 4 displays the population distributions for the

Table 3. Hypothesis questions with verdicts supported by inference tests and p-values.

Hypothesis	Inference test	p-value	Verdict
H_0: Women and men work the same hours	1.103	0.863	Reject H_0
H_0: Men work more than women	−1.103	0.274	Accept H_0
H_0: More education conducts to better lifestyle	2.650	0.003	Accept H_0
H_0: Task-executing at home is precluded by contract type	−5.934	1.43×10^{-7}	Accept H_0
H_0: Irritability at home is associated with job position	−6.760	5.6×10^{-9}	Accept H_0

Table 4. Numerical description of the distributions read on each question used in the presented analyses.

Question	From	Mean	Std	Min	25%	50%	75%	Max
Are you irritable at home because your work requires a high effort?	Swing Q:1	0.55	0.62	0.00	0.00	0.00	1.00	3.00
Is it difficult for you to meet your home obligations because you are constantly thinking about your job?	Swing Q:2	0.56	0.74	0.00	0.00	0.00	1.00	3.00
Which is your gender?	Dem Q:3	0.54	0.45	0.00	0.00	1.00	1.00	1.00
Level of education?	Dem Q:5	2.50	1.57	0.00	1.00	2.00	4.00	6.00
What is your stratification level?	Dem Q:9	1.38	1.00	0.00	1.00	1.00	2.00	5.00
What is the position you hold in the company?	Dem Q:13	3.75	1.17	0.00	3.00	4.00	4.00	5.00
What kind of contract do you have?	Dem Q:15	2.72	1.81	0.00	1.00	4.00	4.00	7.00
How many hours a day do you work?	Dem Q:16	8.21	1.76	0.00	8.00	8.00	8.00	20.0

gathered responses regarding working hours per genre (panel A) and lifestyle per education level (panel B).

Respecting the time men and women devote to work, the first hypothesis with a two-sided test rejected the null proposal of equals; then, we performed a one-sided test to settle the difference and concluded that men work more hours than women in the collected sample.

With reference to having a wealthier life due to a higher education level, the inference tests suggest accepting the null hypothesis; therefore, the higher the education, the more affluent the families. This exercise is possible due to the stratified society from where we extracted the samples.

The other two presented exercises involve Swing questions. The Fig. 5 displays the population distributions that relate the type of contract with difficulties executing tasks at home (Panel A), and irritability exacerbated possibly by job position is presented in Panel B.

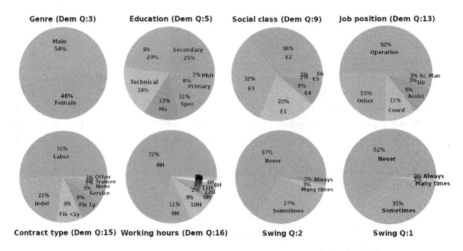

Fig. 3. Participants' status and preferences among the question used for the analysis in this document.

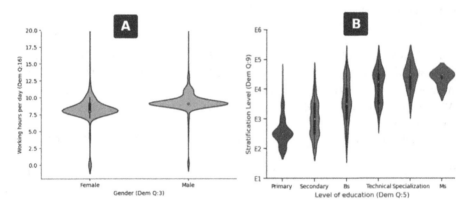

Fig. 4. Panel A. Although the distributions cover the same range of hours, the females work significantly fewer hours than males in the gathered sample. In Panel B, the higher the level of education, the wealthier the individuals and families.

The inference test regarding work position and irritability at home yielded acceptance of the null hypothesis. Consequently, we concluded that the studied population advertised a link between irritability at home and the individual position in the hierarchy imposed by the company. Such findings should turn on the alarms of the occupational health and safety management system since the issue affects the worker and all family members.

Finally, we tested the hypothesis that instability associated with contract types affects home obligations; accepting the null hypothesis is a crucial finding considering that labor informality in the explored region ascends to 57.5% [3,14].

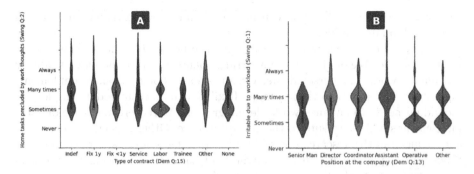

Fig. 5. Attempting to find the reasons for psychological afflictions by analyzing Swing responses to the light of socio-demographics. In panel A, the response distributions per type of contract related to incapacity to disconnect from job assignments. In Panel B, we explore possible relations between irritability at home and the position held inside a company or unemployment.

4   Discussion

This manuscript presents a reduced set of feasible statistical analyses with data collected through a system we set up and launched in minutes. Although its usability and robustness, the system can theoretically reach millions quickly since the Evalu@ platform syncs handheld devices in real time. In this opportunity, we implemented the Swing instrument and delivered it to a relatively narrow audience collecting 31.240 records in 3.222 min. The gathered data was a resource for inference tests, and correlations ran offline throughout the Evalu@ API. The Swing questionnaire was accompanied by 22 questions of local pertinence thanks to the flexibility provided by the data centralizer.

The study intends to examine the impact of work-life interference on employee well-being and productivity. The results shed light on several important findings and implications extracted from the demographics alone and combined with the Swing instrument. These analyses are presented as evidence of rapid and continued tracking feasibility. The reader is invited to size the dimensions of the exercise and consider how many social and labor-related questions it may respond to by observing the number of variables in Tables 1 and 2 that remained unexplored together with their possible combinations.

The system pinpointed a gender disparity in working hours, with men working more than women. Such a finding is relevant since it seems to argue against actual international policies enforced by the United Nations agenda to 2030 (goal 5 - gender equality) and highlights the need for organizations to address and rectify any gender imbalances in workload distribution, as it can have consequences such as generating the phenomena that the law supposes to eliminate [5,6].

Higher levels of education were associated with higher socioeconomic status, indicating the role of education in shaping individuals' social and economic circumstances. This finding suggests that promoting access to education and supporting continuous learning can improve employees' work-home interaction and overall quality of life.

The type of contract was found to influence home obligations. This finding implies that flexible or rigid working arrangements can affect employees' ability to balance work and personal life. Organizations should consider implementing policies and practices that promote flexibility and accommodate employees' individual needs to enhance work-life integration. Moreover, making more stable contracts will contribute to the general welfare. Other aspects to consider – and included in this research – would lead to possible solutions, e.g., commuting times and displacement expenses might hold part of the missing resources to better contracts to the light of remote working.

Other Authors have explored Swing [9] and other similar instruments, such as the Maslach Burnout Inventory (BMI) [12] and the Copenhagen Burnout Inventory (CBI) [13], in different environments and societies [15,19]. Those authors have proposed modifications to bring pertinence to their studies. We consider that pertinence can be accomplished by going beyond the pure metrics yielded by the instruments and complementing the survey with socio-demographics that can be cross-correlated with the responses found in the psychological test. Moreover, the socio-demographics push us to abandon the diagnosis domain and look at the possible causes of stress by tracking population tendencies.

The Swing questionnaire, accompanied by demographics with local pertinence, empowers the tracking instrument to be a valuable and reliable tool for measuring work-home interaction experiences. Moreover, the presented setup remains available for tracking the effect of mitigation strategies, providing researchers and practitioners with a robust device for further investigations in this field and others not event alike.

5   Conclusion

We presented a research exercise that automated a standard tool and complemented it with demographics to derive region-pertinent results. This proof-of-concept also derived conclusions with statistical support and intuitive reports promptly. The presented pipeline is a missed instrument within human resource departments, which often run programs without the certainty of the numbers and mathematically valid procedures. Recall that a simple change in the scope of this tool might provide us with an active participation instrument that precludes representation, a desired scheme in hierarchical organizations at all scales.

References

1. Adams, J.M.: The value of worker well-being. Public Health Rep. **134**(6), 583–586 (2019)
2. Alhumoudi, R.S., Singh, S.K., Ahmad, S.Z.: Perceived corporate social responsibility and innovative work behaviour: the role of passion at work. Int. J. Organ. Anal. (2022)

3. Arango, L.E., Flórez, L.A.: Regional labour informality in Colombia and a proposal for a differential minimum wage. J. Dev. Stud. **57**(6), 1016–1037 (2021)
4. Avigad, J.: Reliability of mathematical inference. Synthese **198**(8), 7377–7399 (2021)
5. Bennedsen, M., Simintzi, E., Tsoutsoura, M., Wolfenzon, D.: Do firms respond to gender pay gap transparency? J. Financ. **77**(4), 2051–2091 (2022)
6. Cook, C., Diamond, R., Hall, J.V., List, J.A., Oyer, P.: The gender earnings gap in the gig economy: evidence from over a million rideshare drivers. Rev. Econ. Stud. **88**(5), 2210–2238 (2021)
7. Emerson, R.W.: ANOVA and T-tests. J. Vis. Impairment Blindness **111**(2), 193–196 (2017)
8. Geurts, S., Bakker, A.B., Demerouti, E.: Recovery experiences as buffers against work-home interference. J. Appl. Psychol. **94**(6), 1355 (2009)
9. Geurts, S., Taris, T.W., Bakker, A.B.: Development and validation of the swing questionnaire: a multidimensional measure of work-home interference. J. Occup. Organ. Psychol. **79**(4), 465–483 (2006)
10. Ingunza Lastra, N., Carrasco Muñoz, M.: Validez y confiabilidad del cuestionario de interacción trabajo-familia (swing) en trabajadores de una empresa minera de la libertad, perú. bol.redipe **8**(8), 144–152 (2019). https://revista.redipe.org/index.php/1/article/view/807, [Internet]
11. Kinnunen, U., Geurts, S., Taris, T.W.: Work-home interference and well-being: a meta-analysis. Work Stress **21**(3), 219–237 (2007)
12. Koeske, G.F., Koeske, R.D.: Construct validity of the maslach burnout inventory: a critical review and reconceptualization. J. Appl. Behav. Sci. **25**(2), 131–144 (1989)
13. Kristensen, T.S., Borritz, M., Villadsen, E., Christensen, K.B.: The Copenhagen burnout inventory: a new tool for the assessment of burnout. Work stress **19**(3), 192–207 (2005)
14. Mondragón-Vélez, C., Peña, X., Wills, D., Kugler, A.: Labor market rigidities and informality in Colombia [with comment]. Economía **11**(1), 65–101 (2010)
15. Mościcka-Teske, A., Merecz, D.: Polish adaptation of swing questionnaire (survey work-home interaction-Nijmegen). Med. Pr. **63**(3), 355–369 (2012)
16. Pradhan, R., Hati, L.: The measurement of employee well-being: development and validation of a scale. Global Bus. Rev. **23**, 385–407 (2019). https://doi.org/10.1177/0972150919859101
17. Roopavathi, S., Kulothungan, K.: The impact of work life balance on employee performance. J. Interdisc. Cycle Res. **12**, 31 (2021)
18. Shimada, K., Shimazu, A., Geurts, S.A., Kawakami, N.: Reliability and validity of the Japanese version of the survey work-home interaction-Nijmegen, the swing (swing-j). Community Work Fam. **22**(3), 267–283 (2019)
19. Shimada, K., Shimazu, A., Geurts, S.A., Kawakami, N.: Reliability and validity of the Japanese version of the survey work-home interaction-Nijmegen, the swing (swing-j). Commun. Work Family **22**(3), 267–283 (2019)
20. Shuck, B., Reio, T.: Employee engagement and well-being. J. Leadersh. Organ. Stud. **21**, 43–58 (2013). https://doi.org/10.1177/1548051813494240
21. Susanto, P., Hoque, M.E., Jannat, T., Emely, B., Zona, M.A., Islam, M.A.: Work-life balance, job satisfaction, and job performance of SMEs employees: the moderating role of family-supportive supervisor behaviors. Front. Psychol. **13**, 906876 (2022). https://doi.org/10.3389/fpsyg.2022.906876
22. Wijngaards, I., King, O.C., Burger, M.J., van Exel, J.: Worker well-being: what it is, and how it should be measured. Appl. Res. Qual. Life **17**(2), 795–832 (2021). https://doi.org/10.1007/s11482-021-09930-w

23. Yepes-Calderon, F., Yepes Zuluaga, J.F., Yepes Calderon, G.E.: Evalu@: an agnostic web-based tool for consistent and constant evaluation used as a data gatherer for artificial intelligence implementations. In: Florez, H., Leon, M., Diaz-Nafria, J.M., Belli, S. (eds.) ICAI 2019. CCIS, vol. 1051, pp. 73–84. Springer, Cham (2019). https://doi.org/10.1007/978-3-030-32475-9_6
24. Yepes Zuluaga, J.F., Gregory Tatis, A.D., Forero Arévalo, D.S., Yepes-Calderon, F.: Evalu@ + sports. creatine phosphokinase and urea in high-performance athletes during competition. a framework for predicting injuries caused by fatigue. In: Florez, H., Pollo-Cattaneo, M.F. (eds.) ICAI 2021. CCIS, vol. 1455, pp. 290–302. Springer, Cham (2021). https://doi.org/10.1007/978-3-030-89654-6_21

Geoinformatics

Comparative Analysis of Spatial and Environmental Data in Informal Settlements, from Point Clouds and RPAS Images

Carlos Alberto Diaz Riveros[1]([✉]) [iD], Andrés Cuesta Beleño[1] [iD],
Julieta Frediani[1] [iD], Rocio Rodriguez Tarducci[2] [iD], and Daniela Cortizo[2] [iD]

[1] Universidad La Gran Colombia, Bogotá, Colombia
{carlos.diaz3,Andres.cuesta}@ugc.edu.co
[2] Universidad Nacional De La Plata, La Plata, Argentina

Abstract. Although there is access to QGIS, ArcGIS, MappingGIS platforms, with extensive historical and current information, environmental and spatial data, paradoxically, there is little analysis of the data from these platforms on urban structures that contribute to decision making, and even less on informal settlements; Paradoxically, there is little analysis of the data from these platforms on urban structures that contribute to decision making, and even less on informal settlements, we start from this problem question: the lack of knowledge coupled with little use or implementation of geoinformatics in municipal planning offices, have allowed the uncontrolled and uncontrolled growth of informal settlements, therefore, their problems are becoming more complex every day? In addition to this hypothesis, could we infer from geoinformatics possible solutions to informal settlements, guiding the steps of government authorities, seeking to support decision making, promoting welfare and protection of vulnerable communities there? In this exercise, which will be presented with the support of geoinformatics, we intend to present the results of a comparative analysis on issues related to critical environmental aspects in informal settlements -such as water courses and flood plains-. Seven informal settlements are analyzed: three in La Plata (Argentina), two in Mocoa and two in Villavicencio (Colombia). The method seeks the interrelation of geometric information from point clouds, and radiometric information from orthomosaic images of Piloted Aerial Systems (RPAS), to then classify the variables, with the objective of generating new information derived from the analysis, which. The images resulting from the crossing of information generating new spatialities will be made available to communities, public and private entities.

Keywords: Geoinformatics · environmental spatialization · informal settlements · point clouds · RPAS images

The original version of the chapter has been revised. An error in the author's name has been corrected. A correction to this chapter can be found at https://doi.org/10.1007/978-3-031-46813-1_31

1   Introducción

Geoinformatics today is presented as an unavoidable tool for the analysis of the territories from different areas, although it is costly for municipal administrations, because of this, it seeks to consolidate through some of the platforms that allow access to information of maps of Colombia, such as GEOPORTAL in https://www.igac.gov.co, Colombia in maps in https://www.Colombiaenmapas.gov.co maps - Datos Abiertos Colombia in https://www.datos.gov.co Portal Servicio Geol'ogico Colombiano in https://www.sgc.gov.co among others, with Qgis software, due to its versatility, will allow to compare in a direct, clear and concrete way. The parallel or comparison will be made of seven informal settlements: the cases of El Rincón, Abasto Nuevo and La Aceitera, in La Plata, Argentina, in El Brillante, Playa Rica in Villavicencio, and the Yanacona indigenous cabildo, and Nueva Betania in Mocoa - Colombia, informal settlements in Argentina, in the city of La Plata, The study was carried out from three environmental and spatial data scopes, critical environmental aspects in informal settlements such as watercourses and flood plains, recognizing and classifying the variables: vulnerability, threats, risks and mitigation, in order to provide new information that offers new possibilities for solutions in decision making. These platforms are still little used, given the need to understand the problems that go beyond physical deficiencies, such as social, cultural and psychological ones, which affect the quality of life of the inhabitants of the area. This study has as objectives, to publicize the possible solutions of this geoinformatics tool, the speed in time, and versatility in reaching possible solutions and therefore results in informal settlements.

2   Methodology

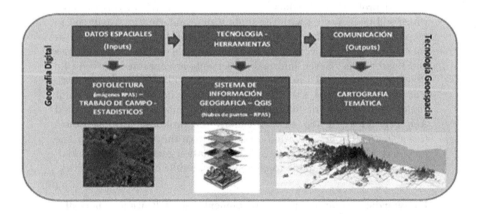

Fig. 1. methodological design. Own elaboration 2023

As Del Rco, J. y Beltrán [1] point out, "to know and analyze space requires data, the raw material; to interpret and manage it requires technological tools and, to make it known and transform it, communication (...); three interrelated and indissoluble aspects that make up an open system: the tool of networked geography is technology, which consumes data (inputs) and produces communication (outputs)". In this framework, Geographic Information Systems are the tool par excellence for analyzing territories that are blurred in the digital world as mentioned by [1]. For his part, [6] points out that "the development experienced by GIS is related to that which has given rise to the constitution of a new scientific and technical discipline, called geomatics (or geospatial technology) that integrates all the sciences and technologies used for the knowledge of the territory and the management of spatial databases, including geographic information systems, remote sensing or remotely and global satellite navigation systems". All of which enable the acquisition, storage, retrieval, management and interpretation of spatially referenced in- formation. Data today come from multiple sources, from traditional sources (statistics, maps, archival documents) to new ones (artificial satellites, remote sensing, photo-interpretation), comment [6] all of which are processed by modern computer techniques.

From images obtained from a remotely piloted aerial system (RPAS) it is possible to generate detailed topography. The advantage of this methodology is the speed in obtaining high precision digital surface models (DSM) and terrain models (DTM) and their corresponding orthophotography, at a very low cost, as well as the possibility of obtaining information at large scales or "in detail", due to the capacity of RPAS to fly at "low altitudes" and obtain high resolution images. The use of RPAS images contributes not only to the generation of orthophotos, he mentions it from his experience [4] but also of reliable topographic products for medium-sized projects that require detailed information at affordable costs. The main advantages of RPAS are: obtaining and processing spatial data in short periods of time. Converting a LIDAR point cloud to a Digital Elevation Model (DEM) with the LAStools add-on in QGIS 3 Digital Elevation Models (DEM) are a digital representation of the visible surface of the earth that allow numerical determination of heights or elevations with respect to a reference surface. Unlike digital terrain models (DTM), DEMs describe the features and elements present on the earth's surface, both anthropogenic and natural. DEMs are used in various applications and disciplines such as cartography, photogrammetry, civil engineering, geodesy and geophysics, and are therefore a product in demand by a wide range of users. The applications of DEMs or DTMs are varied, for example: Generation of con- tour lines, Generation of slope maps, Creation of relief maps, Flight planning in three dimensions, Geometric rectification of aerial photographs or satellite images, Reduction of gravity measurements, also called terrain or topographic correction, Projects of large engineering works, Tracing of topographic profiles, Volume calculations, Environmental risk analysis (IGN).

2.1 Study Areas

The three study areas are characterised as follows: La Plata (Buenos Aires, Argentina), Mocoa (Colombia) and Villavicencio (Colombia).

2.1.1   La Plata, Buenos Aires, Argentina. La Plata (capital of the Province of Buenos Aires, Argentina) is the fourth most populated city in the country with 772,618 inhabitants [5]. It is located 56 km from the Autonomous City of Buenos Aires and southwest of the Río de La Plata. [2] Its main characteristic is that it was designed under hygienist standards and planned from its foundation based on a scheme in which the urban area was demarcated, as opposed to the areas destined for intensive and/or extensive agricultural activities from a ring road. Over the years, the city grew beyond these limits and formed the urban peripheries.

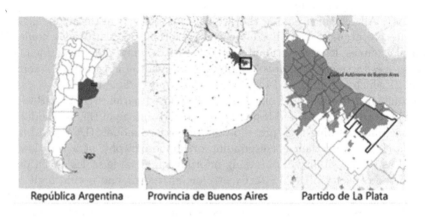

República Argentina   Provincia de Buenos Aires   Partido de La Plata

Fig. 2. Location of the La Plata district. Source: Own elaboration 2023

With regard to environmental aspects see Fig. 2, the La Plata district is located on an alluvial plain, where two different topographical zones can be distinguished, called the coastal plain and the high plain. The first occupies small sectors on the border with the districts of Ensenada, Berisso and Magdalena, where the lowest elevations are found. The second zone comprises almost the entirety of the District, with a main interfluve of flat relief, which acts as a watershed between the two main watersheds, the Río de la Plata to the north, and the Samboromb'on River to the south [3]. The district of La Plata is partially located on the basins of the Pereyra and San Juan streams and entirely on the basins of the Carnaval, Mart'ın, Rodr'ıguez, Don Carlos, del Gato, P'erez, Regimiento, Jard'ın Zool'ogico, Circunvalaci'on, Maldonado, Garibaldi and El Pescado streams. Two main basins can be highlighted according to the amount of population that settles on them: the basin of the arroyo del Gato, and the basin of the arroyo Maldonado. Flooding is the result of heavy or continuous rainfall that exceeds the absorption capacity of the soil and the carrying capacity of rivers, streams and coastal areas. This causes a given watercourse to overflow its channel and flood adjacent lands. Flood plains are the orographic part of a watercourse (river, stream, lake) that can be inundated by rising water. They are therefore "flood prone" and a danger to development activities if their vulnerability exceeds an acceptable level, is clarified by [14]. In 2013, the Partido de La Plata experienced the worst flooding in its history, and it is therefore important to pay special attention to this problem.

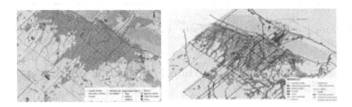

Fig. 3. Left. Environmental aspects, Partido de La Plata, Buenos Aires, Argentina. Source: Own elaboration 2023. **Right**. Informal settlements, La Plata, Buenos Aires, Argentina. Source: Own elaboration 2023.

In relation to the informal habitat, there are 163 informal settlements in the interior of the Party where 20,491 families live in extremely precarious and vulnerable situations see Fig. 3. 60 % of the informal urbanisations are crossed by streams, or are located on flood plains. In relation to the distribution of informal urbanisations, the basins of the district with the highest concentration are: Pereyra, Carnaval, Martin Rodr'ıguez, El Gato, Maldonado, Garibaldi, Pescado y Abascay, Circunvalaci'on and Diagonal 74. Of these, Pereyra, Garibaldi and Abascay are the ones that cover the largest areas in the territory, however, they have very little population in comparison with the others. The basins of the Gato and Maldonado streams are the ones with the highest number of informal urbanisations, with 60 in the Gato stream basin (40 %) and 20 in the Maldonado stream [3] basin (20 %).

2.1.1.1 El Rincón The informal settlement is located on the northern axis of the Partido, and is divided into three neighbourhoods: Rincón I, II and III, where 190 families live. Are located on the Carnaval-Martin basin, on the banks of the Carnaval stream. See Figs. 5 y 6, (Fig. 4).

Fig. 4. Left. Case 1, El Rincón. Source: Own elaboration based on Google Earth, 2023. Center. Case 2, Abasto Nuevo and Right. Case 3, La Aceitera.

NEIGHBOUR HOOD 1	AMOUNT OF FAMILIES	SURFACE HECTARES	YEAR OF ORIGIN	ACCESS TO ELECTRICITY	ACCESS TO SEWERS	ACCESS TO SAFE WATER
EL RINCON I	58	3	Decade of 2000	Formal connection with domestic meter	Drainage of septic chamber and cesspool	Domestic Well Water Pump
EL RINCON II	122	4.82	Decade of 2000	Formal connection with domestic metering system	Drainage only to cesspit or hole	Domestic well water pump
EL RINCON III	10	10.42	Decade of 2000	Irregular Grid Connection	Drainage only to cesspit or hole	Irregular connection to the water network

Fig. 5. Comparative graph of the population characteristics of the informal settlements, El Rincón I, II, y III.

2.1.1.2 Abasto Nuevo Neighbourhood is located in Abasto, on the southern axis of the city. see Figs. 7 y 8.

NEIGHBOUR HOOD	AMOUNT OF FAMILIES	SURFACE HECTARES	YEAR OF ORIGIN	ACCESS TO ELECTRICITY	ACCESS TO SEWERS	ACCESS TO SAFE WATER
ABASTO NUEVO	160	42	2015	Irregular grid connection	Drainage only to cesspit or hole	Irregular connection to the water network

Fig. 6. Comparative graph of the population characteristics of the informal settlement Abasto nuevo.

2.1.1.3 La Aceitera Neighbourhood is located in the catchment area of the Pescado stream. see Figs. 9 y 10.

NEIGHBOUR HOOD	AMOUNT OF FAMILIES	SURFACE HECTARES	YEAR OF ORIGIN	ACCESS TO ELECTRICITY	ACCESS TO SEWERS	ACCESS TO SAFE WATER
LA ACEITERA	180	10.21	Decade of 1990	Irregular grid connection	Drainage only to cesspit or hole	Domestic well water pump

Fig. 7. Comparative graph of the population characteristics of the informal settlement La Aceitera.

2.1.2   Mocoa, Putumayo, Colombia was founded on September 29, 1563. This municipality is located on the Amazonian foothills, to the north of the department of Putumayo see Fig. 1. Physiographically, it comprises a varied range of geoformas that range from high mountain slopes to slightly undulating plains. It includes mountainous areas, corresponding to Laderas Altas de Cordillera, whose geomorphological characteristics are slopes greater than 75 %. The territory contains great water wealth, and many of its water currents cross the urban area of the municipality, generating in some areas a potential to be susceptible to torrential floods that influence the growth and development of the municipality.

Fig. 8. NLevels of territorial location in Colombia, the department of Putumayo and the municipality of Mocoa. Source: Elaboration with information from the DANE Geoportal, Consulted on July 6, 2023.

2.1.3   Villavicencio, Meta, Colombia. Villavicencio (capital of Meta, Colombia) is the 22nd most populated city in the country with 558,299 inhabitants, that's how he mentions it [13]. It is located 86 km from the capital of Colombia and south of the Guatiquia River. Its main characteristic was of spontaneous conformation and built since its foundation with cadastral lot was delimited the urban area. After 119 years, the city grew beyond these limits and formed the 4 radial road rings, see Fig. 12.

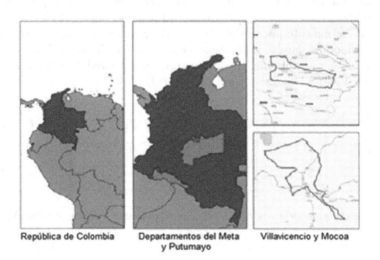

República de Colombia   Departamentos del Meta   Villavicencio y Mocoa
y Putumayo

Fig. 9. Location of Villavicencio. SOURCE: Own elaboration based on maps of the world 2023.

Villavicencio is located in the alluvial fan between the Guatiquia and Guayuriba river basins, where the canals originate, and belongs to the Pleistocene-Upper Holocene Price period. These wetland fluvial-lacustrine deposits overlie a basement that locally is represented by Cretaceous-Tertiary sedimentary rocks, [10] makes known, the whole depositional model is controlled by thrust fault systems that belong tothe system. These types of soils are less bearing, besides being in a high Seismicity level, level 1; it makes the construction system used in the study territory take greater relevance, since they have not suffered from collapse of buildings during earthquakes. This shows the great ability, skill, technique and performance of the builders of the XIX and XX centuries, makes known [11]. Threat and risk areas that cannot be mitigated by natural or technological phenomena, so the location of human settlements restricts the possibility of urbanization. The rivers that border the city, to the north the Guatiquia, to the south the Ocoa, and is covered by more than 9 secondary surface tributaries, and more than 45 streams called "can˜os". Floods are recurrent due to lack of planning and spontaneous generation, according to studies of [15] although today mitigation of hazards and risks is being carried out. In Villavicencio the natural landscape is piedmont, which allows a wide visualization of each of the components: mountain, highlands and plains, generating several incomparable visual foci of landscape, providing them with a unique landscape value in the region; it has visuals on mountain, highlands and plains. These environmental, natural or scenic values must be preserved. The number of informal settlements in Villavicencio amounts to 588. The consolidated number of legal and illegal neighborhoods in Villavicencio (year 2019), Legal are 325, Illegal are 263 and the total is 588, which would correspond in percentages to legal neighborhoods 55.27 %, [12] and illegal neighborhoods 44.73 %.

As will be indicated in the planimetry the greatest are three, the risks and threats of flooding, landslide by mass removal, and technological threat; aggravating or further aggravating the problem to these 30 and 33 settlements are in communes 4 and 8 respectively see Fig. 13, (Fig. 11).

Commune	1	2	3	4	5	6	7	8	0	Total
Neighborhoods	56	51	24	89	114	29	75	71	79	588
Illegal	25	21	15	30	44	11	31	33	53	263

Fig. 10. Illegal neighborhoods 2019 V/cio. Source: urban development office. Municipal archives.

2.1.3.1 Playa Rica He Playa Rica informal settlement is located in the northwest axis of Villavicencio, and is home to 33 families, with 163 inhabitants, located approximately 100 m from the large river. See Figs. 12 y 13.

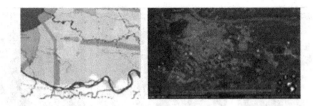

Fig. 11. Left. Left Map 11C + 12 Urban Land Activity Area Plan - Playa Rica and El Brillante. Right: Location of settlements: Playa Rica and El Brillante.

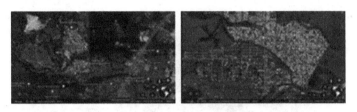

Fig. 12. Left. Left Case 1, Playa Rica. Source: Own elaboration based on Google Earth, 2023. Right. Case 2, El Brillante. Source: Own elaboration based on Google Earth, 2023.

Settleme nt	Age	# Dwellings	Locati on	Risk	Area m2	Access to electrici ty	Access to sewerage	Access to aquedu ct
Playa Rica	1980	185	Comu na 8	flood	153761,2 6	Formal Connecti on With Househo ld meter	Drainage	Aqueduc t

Fig. 13. Comparative graph of the population characteristics of the informal settlement Playa Rica. **2.1.3.2. El Brillante** The El Brillante informal settlement is located in the northeast axis of Villavicencio, and is home to 30 families, with 128 inhabitants, located approximately 300 meters from the Maizaro river to the north and the Ocoa river to the south. See Fig. 14.

Settleme nt	Age	# Dwellings	Locati on	Risk	Area m2	Access to electrici ty	Access to sewerage	Access to aqueduct
El brillante	2020	965	Comu na 4	flood	802791,0 1	Formal Connecti on With Househo ld meter	Drainage	Aqueduct

Fig. 14. Comparative graph of the population characteristics of the informal settlement El Brillante.

2.1.3.2. El Brillante The El Brillante informal settlement is located in the northeast axis of Villavicencio, and is home to 30 families, with 128 inhabitants, located approximately 300 m from the Maizaro river to the north and the Ocoa river to the south. See Fig. 14.

Fig. 15. Informal settlement El Rincón, Nuevo Abasto, La Aceitera in La Plata.

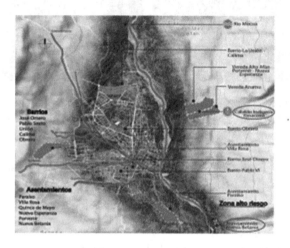

Fig. 16. Urban area of Mocoa and some informal settlements

2.2   Point Cloud Method and UAV Portraits

In geoinformatics it seeks to make spatial information available, in order to guide rural and urban planning; through a process it starts with the capture of information, classifies it, then stores it, processes it, generates the output in an image and then disseminates it. Some of its branches, Cartography, Geodesy, Global Navigation Satellite Systems, Remote Sensing, Spatial Analysis, and Web Mapping; will be the support to combine the point cloud of an unmanned aerial vehicle UAV, or RPAS, with orthomosaic, in order to recognize characteristics in informal settlements, which allow to classify them, and thus collaborate with municipal administrations in the improvement of informal settlements projecting plausible solutions for the quality of life.

2.3   Data Acquisition

In Colombia, the information found on informal settlements; what was expected was a series of analytical cartographies that would provide a synthesis of the

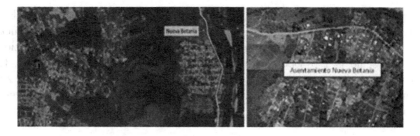

Fig. 17. The Nueva Betania settlement and its transition area with the urban area of Mocoa Note: This photograph was taken by the Self-Sufficient Territorial Planning with Integral Training research group called GOTAFI, 2015. The parceling process is shown with determined environmental limitations and distant from the urban area of Mocoa. Source: Self-sufficient Land Management Group with Comprehensive Training GOTAFI and Adaptation. Own elaboration.

dynamics present in the study territories, and infer possible solutions, be they programs or projects. On the contrary, the information found was a dis- jointed cartography of national and municipal levels that differ in scales, which does not allow a quick, clear and concrete access to information, analysis, or conclusive deductions. As well as governmental documents, National Unit for Disaster Risk Management (UNGRD), technical reports of INGEOMI- NAS, municipal planning secretary, P.O.T., PMGRA, Villavicencio, as primary sources; doctoral and master thesis, as secondary sources. The data of water courses, flood plains and natural reserves, were taken from P.O.T., PMGRA, of Villavicencio, documents of 2015, it became necessary to update such information to 2023, with the support of the planning secretary, with the group of neighborhood legalization; as for the regulations of 2017, 2021 and 2023, it will be presented at the end of the results.

2.4 Data Processing

In Argentina, information on informal settlements comes from both secondary sources (National Organisms - National Registry of Popular Neighbour- hoods - and Provincial Organisms - Provincial Registry of Slums and Settle- ments) and primary sources resulting from research projects carried out at the Institute for Research and Policy on the Built Environment -IIPAC- and from academic works - Doctoral and Master's Theses. These sources have guaranteed access to up-to-date information but, as in the Colombian case, the information is disjointed at the national and provincial levels, and there are no records at the municipal level. The aforementioned disarticulation is fundamentally based on the disparity of theoretical and methodological criteria regarding the conception of informal habitat. On the other hand, information on relief, hydrography and flood plains was taken from the National Geographic Institute (IGN). In the case of Argentina, georeferenced information on the physical environment at the national level was taken from the IGN. This information was cross-referenced with provincial and local data on informal settlements, also geo-referenced. From the analysis of this cross-referenced data, thematic cartography was constructed using GIS. In the case of Colombia, planimetries were taken from the national level, the scale is 1:100000, from the municipal level the scale is 1:5000, this information found was classified and mapped digitally, updating data to 2023 for analytical, diagnostic, conclusive and prospective purposes, in this process it was possible to reach the results.

3   Results

The topics addressed in the characterisation of the informal settlements studied in Argentina and Colombia are: watercourses, flood plains and nature reserves. Coincidentally in both cases, after analysing them, they have provided a clear picture of the situation that characterises them: populations with high environmental vulnerability due to their proximity to streams and occupation of flood plains resulting, among other things, from the lack of risk management, weaknesses in the protection of management zones and environmental protection of water bodies by governments at the local-provincial-national level, and insecurity due to environmental and technological threats. In short, these are populations that are "distant" from the interest of governments. Because they are territories that began their development spontaneously, and that in the case of Colombia have been regularised in the last year, but not in the case of Argentina, they form "neighbourhoods" with a future that could be consolidated after two or three more phases, oriented towards quality of life, in the ideal of SDG 1: End poverty, SDG 8: Decent work and sustainable development, SDG 10: Reducing inequalities, SDG 11: Sustainable cities and communities, SDG 13: Climate action.

3.1   Characterization of the Experimental Area

In the case of the city of La Plata, the cases of El Rincón, Abasto Nuevo and La Aceitera present similar problems with regard to the three variables analysed - watercourses, flood plains and nature reserves - which are described below. In relation to the informal residential occupation of the flood plains, it is possible to recognise in the three cases analysed a regular grid pattern organised without respecting the irregularity generated by the towpath, informally invading the natural course of the stream. This situation leads to the following conflicts: i. Overflowing of stream beds flooding the surrounding areas due to heavy and persistent rainfall, insufficient carrying capacity of the beds, overflowing of water from the rainwater network at the point where it meets the beds. In the same way, the deficiency of the piping where it meets the urban layout. ii. The lack of reservoirs - large basins of absorbent land - prepared to receive water when the containment capacity of the conduits and/or streams is exceeded by heavy rainfall. iii. Insufficient pedestrian linkage of both banks; poor maintenance in the watercourses. Likewise, linked to this type of informal residential occupation is the proliferation of rubbish dumped by neighbours, whether from housing and/or productive activities, which affects the quality of the water in nearby streams and threatens the native flora and fauna, affecting the quality of life of the population.

3.1.1 Results Related to the la Plata, Argentina. In the case of Nuevo Abasto, located in the upper basin of the El Gato stream, the growing greenhouse technology is having negative consequences on the territory, see Fig. 15. The waterproofing of the soil as a result of the plastic cover of intensive fruit and vegetable production and insufficient ditching means that rain cannot infiltrate the soil, and every time it rains, large bodies of water are formed which run off into the natural watercourses and improvise paths for this purpose.

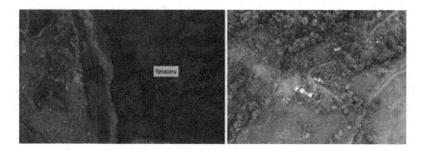

Fig. 18. Yanacona settlement in the process of being formed Note: The Yanacona indigenous community is located in a territory assigned by the Mocoa Municipal Mayor's Office. Its internal organization of the territory is dispersed and in keeping with the existing vegetation. Source: Adaptation. Own elaboration.

In relation to the nature reserves of the district of La Plata, they are not directly affected by the three settlements studied. In this sense, in the case of the La Aceitera settlement, although its location is close to the protected area of the El Pescado stream, it does not affect it. Nuevo Abasto is located in the horticultural belt of La Plata, an area considered protected until the Land Use Ordinance of 2000, but not in the last Ordinance of 2010. Although the informal settlements studied show some weaknesses, little preparation in terms of hazards, risks and disasters or disaster reduction; the informal settlements El Rincón, Abasto Nuevo, La Aceitera, located in La Plata Argentina, El Brillante and Playa Rica in Villavicencio and the Yanacona indigenous cabildo, and Nueva Betania in Mocoa, both in Colombia.

3.1.2 Results Related to the Mocoa and Villavicencio, Colombia have similar problems in the first two of the three study variables water courses, flood plains and nature reserves, the third are different; they will be presented below:

3.1.2.1 Results related to the Nueva Betania and Yanacona Yachay Wasi settlements

Regarding the identification of forms of occupation of the territory, in these two informal settlements rural and/or country-type houses with low densities are identified, without access to all public services, with ecological effects, and situations of threats, flood risks and danger of continuing with processes of appropriation of conservation areas, see Fig. 16. The process of urban consolidation and articulation is remote, although inside the town hall there is a better process of construction of the habitat, [7] unlike the case of Nueva Betania, where internal social relations are more difficult to bear. The affectations in terms of flooding and environmental deterioration presented and exposed in the territory of these settlements, increasingly deteriorate the study population, who were affected in their forced displacement from the beginning of their location in said place, see Fig. 16.

Note: The water structure of the urban area of the city of Moco is appreciated with its morphological manifestations and identification of two informal settlements, case studies, Yanacona and Nueva Betania, disjointed from the urban area. Source: Adapted from Google Maps and Google Earth, 2023. Own elaboration.

Today the trends identified in the transformation of urban land, in the dynamics of territorial growth and the uncertainty of water wealth, constitute great challenges associated mainly with losses of natural coverage, biodiversity, conservation of human life and ecological connectivity, presenting in the city a progressive deterioration in the main ecological structure, related to the water course, the floods presented and the existing natural reserves. Notoriously affecting the study sites in this municipality called Nueva Betania and Yanacona Yachay Wasi. Characteristics of the zones, With specific relation to the settlements Nueva Betania and the Yanacona indigenous council, they present the following characteristics: They present deficient communication for the normal functioning of land mobility, [9] reaffirming a delay and lack of support for adequate territorial development, see Fig. 17. The settlements located in Mocoa: Yanacona indigenous cabildo, and Nueva Betania are located in the following areas, the three maps for each settlement water courses, flood plains and natural reserves.

The Yanacona Cabildo is located to the east of the urban area of Mocoa (Fig. 18) and presents an organic territorial organization in accordance with the existing biomes in the place. However, the vision of said community is pessimistic in terms of its territorial and housing development; [9] because the basic needs of health, employment, housing, public services, are deficient and the solution to these problems is not clearly seen in the near future. Additionally, a large part of these problems has had to be solved by the community itself and on other occasions, with the collaboration of the government and non-governmental institutions. They are victims of the Colombian armed conflict and have been brutally dispossessed of their ethnic territories, generating a rupture of the social fabric, deterioration of customs and loss of ancestral spirituality.

3.1.3 Results Related to the Villavicencio, Colombia.

As it has been possible to analyze the informal housing occupation of flood plains it is possible to recognize in the two cases analyzed. El Brillante and Playa Rica in Villavicencio a regular plot organized in an orthogonal rectangular shape of half a block respecting the irregularity generated by the layout of the can˜o campo alegre, next to the Ocoa river and can˜o grande, with can˜o Tela, respectively; although if invading in an informal way, draining in some sectors approximately 400 ml of the natural course of can˜o campo alegre, and thus building them. Although the situation is unmanageable, it brings about conflicts: I. Overflowing of the riverbeds, flooding neighboring areas during the rainy season for nine months of the year, influenced by the climatic phenomena of El Nin˜o and La Nin˜a, since their banks are not very high and the surrounding morphology presents a slightly sloping relief, added to the low carrying capacity of the riverbeds. Also, the sewage system is inadequate. II. The absence of reservoirs -large absorbent soil sin charge of collecting the water when the rivers overflow is overcome due to heavy rains. III. The need for pedestrian linkage on both shores; the scarcity of maintenance in the watercourses; IV. Playa Rica extended to the edge of the large canals and Tela, increasing the risk of flooding, which is difficult to mitigate or reduce due to the high cost of intervention works. On the other hand, in this type of informal settlements, there is a proliferation of garbage that is thrown by the neighbors, affecting the quality of the water quality of the watercourses, threatening the ecosystems and consequently the flora and fauna, affecting the quality of life of the inhabitants. The nature reserves near El Charco wetland are not directly affected by Playa Rica.

4   Conclusions

One of the good practices supported by government entities and NGOs is highlighted, it is related to the accompaniment of these informal settlements to generate trust at the beginning of defining actions in the intervened territory; such as planting shrubs and trees to protect the environment on the banks of water currents; In addition, initiate and accompany the communities in organization processes, especially the Yanacona community to develop collective productive processes, who collaboratively develop activities to improve their living conditions. However, poor public services hinder their good intentions.

References

1. Del Río, J., Beltr'an, G.: Geografía en red y datos: la materia prima. Serie: Geografía en red de la reflexión la acción, libro II. (1ạ ed). España (2021)
2. CISAGUA, An'alisis ambiental del Partido de La Plata. Aportes al Ordenamiento Territorial (2006)
3. Tarducci, R.R.: Informalidad urbana en el partido de La Plata. Análisis del proceso de ocupaci'on y apropiación territorial, 1989- actualidad. Tesis doctoral. UNLP (2020)

Prospects of UAVs in Agricultural Mapping

Paulo Escandón-Panchana[1,2,4(✉)] (iD), Gricelda Herrera-Franco[3] (iD),
Sandra Martínez Cuevas[1] (iD), and Fernando Morante-Carballo[2,4,5] (iD)

[1] Universidad Politécnica de Madrid, ETSI Topografía, Geodesia y Cartografía, c/Mercator 2,
28040 Madrid, Spain
pc.escandon@alumnos.upm.es, sandra.mcuevas@upm.es
[2] Centro de Investigaciones y Proyectos Aplicados a Las Ciencias de La Tierra (CIPAT),
ESPOL Polytechnic University, P.O. Box 09, 01-5863 Guayaquil, Ecuador
fmorante@espol.edu.ec
[3] Facultad de Ciencias de La Ingeniería, Universidad Estatal Península de Santa Elena, P.O.
Box 240204, La Libertad, Ecuador
grisherrera@upse.edu.ec
[4] Geo-Recursos y Aplicaciones GIGA, ESPOL Polytechnic University, P.O. Box 09, 01-5863
Guayaquil, Ecuador
[5] Facultad de Ciencias Naturales y Matemáticas, ESPOL Polytechnic University, P.O. Box 09,
01-5863 Guayaquil, Ecuador

Abstract. The food security of most rural sectors depends on traditional agricultural practices. Geomatics tools contribute to traditional agricultural practices through Unmanned Aerial Vehicles (UAVs) in smart agriculture, agricultural mapping and improving sustainable agricultural production. The study's objective is to explore the application of UAVs in agricultural mapping through a literature review of the use of this tool in agriculture. The methodology of this review performs a literary search on the application of UAVs to explore the structure, dynamics and domain of this area of knowledge. Subsequently, the analysis includes scientific contributions, the most relevant authors, evolution of themes and trends in sustainable agriculture. The results show that the countries with the greatest scientific contribution in this area of knowledge are the United States (USA) and China. The predominant themes are monitoring plant phenology/crop detection, status/evaluation of agricultural soils, irrigation applications/water resources and agricultural yield. UAV use, and their fusion with other technologies is a technological trend contributing to agricultural mapping through thematic maps and object-based image analysis in digitising sustainable farming activities and practices.

Keywords: UAV · Agriculture · Agricultural mapping · Sustainability ·
Geomatics

1 Introduction

Agriculture is an important activity that responds to the food needs of a dynamically growing global population [1]. To meet this need, soil-related agricultural practices, methods, and crop monitoring must be improved through geomatics, artificial intelligence (AI), and the Internet of Things (IoT) technologies. These technologies hold significant potential for agricultural production and result in smart agriculture [2]. Smart agriculture produces useful results on the suitability of soils for crops through geomatic tools such as Unmanned Aerial Vehicles (UAVs), which collect and process information for crop management and monitoring easily and efficiently [3, 4]. Geospatial information is organised and projected through thematic maps that depend on agricultural activity.

Agricultural mapping provides relevant information on soil state, crops, agricultural production, and pest identification and allows decisions to be made in the agricultural field to improve crop yields [5]. However, agricultural mapping requires periodic information for the preparation of agricultural land, cadastral delimitation, vegetation identification, and crop inventory [6]. In addition, it uses different geospatial tools and techniques, such as the spatial resolution of sensory data using satellites, aircraft and UAVs in agricultural management [7].

A UAV, also known as a drone, is an uncrewed aircraft controlled remotely by an operator. Incorporates various types of multispectral and hyperspectral cameras to acquire aerial images [8]. These images are processed in high spatial-temporal resolution in close ranges and various applications associated with crop management [9]. In addition, vegetation indices are extracted from these images that contribute to the farmer's decision-making. For example, the normalised difference vegetation index (NDVI) provides data on crops' biomass, diseases, and nutritional status [10]. Also, the red edge normalised difference index (NDRE) analyses the chlorophyll of the forest canopy [11].

Different studies associated with agricultural activities use UAVs in agrarian mapping. For example, in Córdoba, in southern Spain, they used a UAV with a visible spectrum camera to acquire high-resolution images of wheat agricultural land. This study considered visible spectral indices for vegetation mapping, which allowed the detection and management of weeds. In addition, it achieved precision and spatial-temporal consistency in the planting season [12]. Also, in Traibuenas, Navarra, Spain, they evaluated the seasonal variability of the water state in a vineyard through thermal images that allowed the mapping of the water state. In this study, UAV provided very high-resolution images (pixel < 9 cm) to obtain crop water stress indices (CWSI) that estimated the patterns of variation in water status [13].

In Rothamsted Research, United Kingdom, the study by [14] analysed a method to determine crop height and growth rate, using high spatial resolution (1 cm/pixel) 3D digital models, photogrammetry, UAV with a red camera, green and blue (RGB). This study obtained a novel spatial mapping of crop height variation at field and plot scales. On the other hand, south of Kauai, Hawaii, the study by [15] demonstrated the safe operation of long-duration, slow-flying UAVs for remote sensing plant crowns in an agricultural region. These authors used a local area network (LAN) to control the camera and a wide area network (WAN) to send control commands. The acquired images provided a mapping of weed outbreaks and identification of irrigation and fertilisation problems. Also, in southern China, the study of [16] generated an accurate weed cover map using

UAV imaging and a convolutional neural network. This study found an accuracy of 88.3% in the recognition of weeds to guarantee the yield of rice crops.

Additionally, in the Center Val de Loire region, France, the study by [17] mapped diseased areas in vineyards to provide fast and accurate treatments. This study used deep learning segmentation on UAV visible and infrared images for pest detection, achieving 92% detection on the vine and 87% on the leaf.

UAV use in agriculture is a recent issue; studies are required to expand the scientific and technological challenge to increase agricultural productivity and production quality. Under this approach, the research question arises: How are UAVs used in agricultural mapping to obtain sustainable agriculture?

The study's objective is to explore the application of UAVs in agricultural mapping through a literature review of the use of this tool in agriculture.

2   Methodological Approach

This review used bibliometric analysis to explore the structure, dynamics, and domain-specific knowledge of UAV use in agricultural mapping. The bibliometric analysis uses statistical tools such as mapping techniques to represent available bibliographic information in indexed databases and identify trends [18, 19].

This study used a scientific database, Scopus, which provides high-quality indexed documents. Scopus is one of the largest databases of peer-reviewed scientific literature with international publishers [20]. Figure 1 presents the research process, highlighting the search equation and the types of documents this study includes (i.e., articles and conference papers). The search equation used title, abstract and keywords with Boolean operators: (TITLE-ABS-KEY (uav) OR TITLE-ABS-KEY (unmanned AND aerial AND vehicle) AND TITLE-ABS-KEY (agricultural AND mapping) OR TITLE-ABS-KEY (agricultural AND cartography)) AND (LIMIT-TO (DOCTYPE, "ar") OR LIMIT-TO (DOCTYPE, "cp")). The search was carried out in June 2023 and provided 440 documents. Eight documents were excluded for record availability and 23 for languages other than English. Therefore, the analysis had a total of 409 documents. The analysis of results used the statistical program RStudio version R-4.1.2, in addition to the Biblioshiny web, to study bibliometric indicators [21].

Finally, the study identified the scientific contribution by year, country, and author, the co-occurrence of keywords and the evolution of themes involved in using UAVs in agricultural mapping.

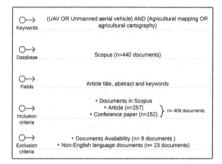

Fig. 1. Research process.

3 Bibliometric Review

3.1 Annual Publications and Citations

This research topic is recent, and its editorial peak occurred in 2020. Figure 2 shows the number of publications and annual citations that establish an upward trend in the study period, highlighting the publication of 403 documents and 7036 citations between 2012−2023. These results show that the use of UAVs in agricultural mapping is a relatively new research topic that captures the attention of the agricultural sector.

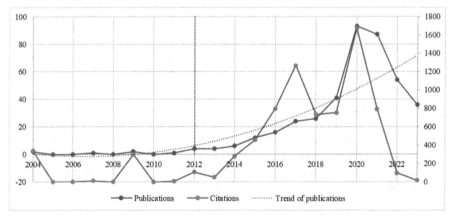

Fig. 2. Annual scientific contributions and citations.

3.2 Analysis of Contribution and Collaboration by Country

The scientific collaboration represents the interrelation or a network between countries, where the nodes are the authors and the links are the global co-authorships [22]. In applying UAVs in agricultural mapping, at least 48 countries have collaborated in this area of knowledge. The five main countries that present the greatest contribution by the authors are China, the USA, Germany, Spain and Italy; these represent 52% of the total contribution. Figure 3 shows the greatest collaboration (thick red line) between the USA and countries such as China, Denmark, Australia, Italy and Korea. In addition, the USA and China are prominent as the main contributing and collaborating countries. These countries highlight their studies on yield mapping, crop production and disease prediction through multi-scale image processing—also the applications of precision agriculture, irrigation, groundwater management and agricultural soil analysis.

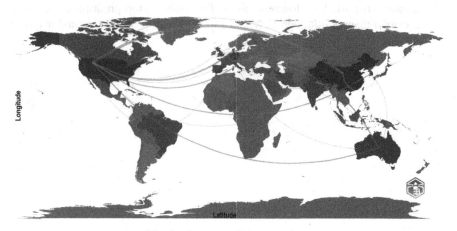

Fig. 3. Country collaboration map.

In addition, Fig. 4 presents the scientific collaboration according to the number of citations. The cooperation of researchers with different institutions in the world highlights the most cited countries, such as the USA with 1078, China with 1042 and Spain with 845 citations.

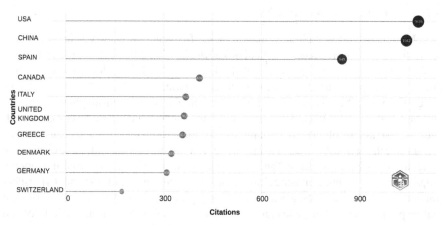

Fig. 4. The top ten countries, according to the number of citations.

3.3 Most Relevant Authors

Figure 5 shows the authors with the greatest scientific contribution to the subject of study, such as Habibb A, affiliated with Purdue University, which has eight relevant documents and 1.68 articles in collaboration with other authors. His studies focus on automated orthorectification of images over agricultural fields, using UAVs for rover mapping, high-throughput phenotyping, and farm management. Similarly, Zhang Y, affiliated with the University of Chinese Academy of Sciences, has eight papers and 1.49 collaborative articles. However, his studies analyse crop production estimation and vegetation mapping through UAV and LíDAR for crop monitoring and irrigation management.

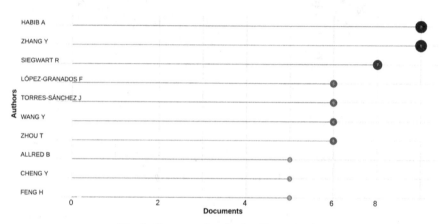

Fig. 5. Top ten authors' scientific production.

3.4 Document Analysis - Tree Map

Tree Map represents graphic information on the frequency of keywords in abstracts of scientific documents related to the field of knowledge [23, 24]. In Fig. 6, the rectangle's dimensions represent the frequency of the keywords, and the colours represent their interrelationship. In this study, the most frequent terms are "UAV", "antennas", "agricultural robots", "remote sensing (RS)", "mapping", "vegetation mapping", "crops", and "agriculture". "UAV" and "spatial resolution" suggest that the studies propose evaluations of spatial resolution in vegetation, detection of crop diseases and changes in the soil surface through UAV images to improve decisions and economic development of the agricultural sector. In addition, "antennas" and "data acquisition" are used in mapping crops and water channels in agricultural fields by processing multi-spectral, hyperspectral and thermal infrared images to monitor crop growth. Also, "RS" and "soil" suggest that mapping studies of organic matter, erosion and soil moisture through RS, UAV and GPS are essential for data processing in precision agriculture applications.

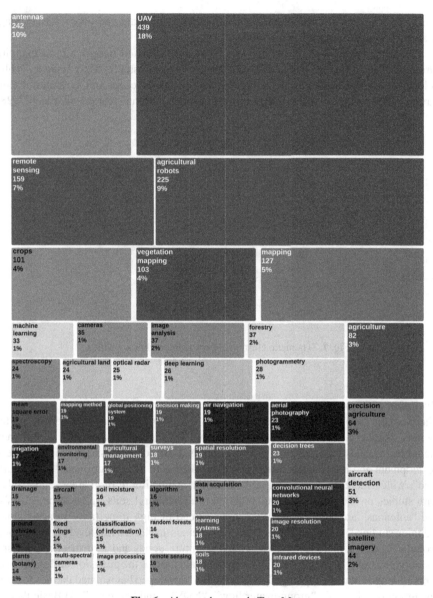

Fig. 6. Abstract keywords Tree Map.

3.5 Conceptual Structure

Co- occurrence Network

The conceptual structure presents the interrelation of the relevant topics in three clusters (Fig. 7). Cluster 1, "UAV, RS and precision agriculture" (green colour), considers the issues associated with crop phenology, agricultural soil state and object-based image analysis for early agricultural monitoring [25].

Cluster 2 "Mapping" (red colour) includes topics related to agricultural mapping through robotics, surveys and aerial navigation [5, 26]. Cluster 3, "UAV imagery" (blue colour), has topics related to detecting vegetation, weeds, crops and agricultural yield through AI techniques such as deep learning and convolutional neural networks [27, 28].

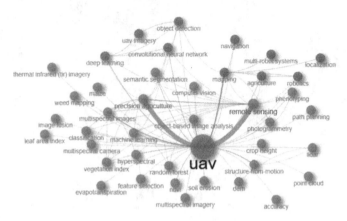

Fig. 7. Thematic cluster network using author keywords.

Evolution of Themes

The thematic map divides the research topics into four categories that depend on the themes' degree of importance and development [29]. Figure 8 presents the evolution of the subject of study through the authors' keywords. 1) Motor themes have a high degree of development and importance. The topics associated with this category are "agricultural land", which includes the agricultural expansion estimation in rural areas, and "soils", with studies on the state and contamination of agricultural soils. In addition, "UAVs" and "antennas" are technologies that show a trend of high importance in agricultural mapping studies. 2) Emerging themes are new themes that have a low level of importance, "robotics", which includes studies related to future aerial and terrestrial agricultural phenotyping, and "air navigation" used in the evaluation of the precision and stability of drones for agricultural mapping. 3) Niche themes, developed but isolated themes focused on "infrared radiation", "groundwater flow", "NDVI", and "biomass". 4) Basic themes are fundamental and transversal research themes based on "agriculture" and "agricultural mapping" for pest control, vegetation, soil cover, drainage systems and improvements in agricultural production.

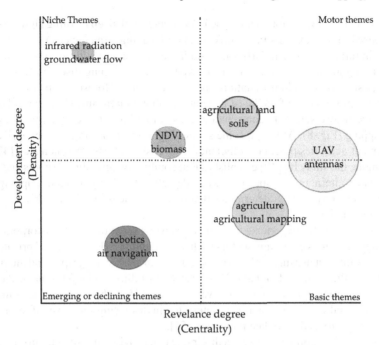

Fig. 8. Evolution of themes.

4 Discussion

This study provides a scientific documentary reference associated with using UAVs in agricultural mapping, which promotes research on rural challenges such as spatial-temporal monitoring, crop census, and agricultural territory management. In addition, it contributes to the digitisation of agricultural management practices for decision-making by the farmer, companies, government entities and educational entities, achieving sustainable food security.

UAV in agriculture is an innovative technology that transforms traditional agricultural activities into smart practices. Some studies highlight UAVs use in agricultural mapping, managing to improve water quality metrics and optimal irrigation scheduling in urban-rural agricultural areas [30, 31], crop and environment monitoring in various environments for timely control of food security [32, 33], collection of tree height/crown volume information for crop disease detection [17, 34] and watershed boundary mapping for soil erosion reduction [35]. Similarly, other studies consider UAVs important in mapping weeds through NDVI for crop protection and reducing the use of pesticides [36–38]. Also, UAVs are crucial for the phenotyping of plants, specifically to know their traits [39].

Fusing UAVs with other technologies has become an effective alternative for data acquisition in smart agriculture. For example, the study by [40] highlights applying photogrammetric techniques to UAV images to measure the canopy in woody crops. Another study combines UAVs with a conventional neural network, providing an effective way to extract and add spatiotemporal features for vegetation mapping [41]. Also, the studies of [42, 43] complemented the UAV images with deep learning algorithms and object-based image analysis in identifying and managing strategic crop cover for food security in rural sectors. Similarly, other studies combine agricultural robotics with AI, deep learning algorithms, and multi-robot systems for mapping disease identification, plant exposure to ground-air radiation, and detection of the forest canopy [44–46].

UAVs represent one of the latest generation robotic platforms. However, robotics is a new topic whose scientific contribution reflects low importance in applying agricultural mapping (Fig. 8). Although some studies highlight its use in different agricultural management activities/practices, efficiency, low costs and easy maintenance [47, 48]. For example, the study by [49] establishes that combining agricultural robots and UAVs represents an alternative to speed up weed detection time in grassland mapping. Furthermore, the study by [50] determines that many advances in robotics drive real-time sensing and mapping.

The UAV industry experiences significant development due to the incorporation of technology in various economic sectors such as agriculture [51]. Public and private companies show interest in using UAVs in mapping, topography, videography and monitoring [52]. Despite the estimated global UAV market (89.1 billion dollars) for the next decade and its exponential application trend in various topics [53], there are private companies with commercial purposes that are not interested in disclosing sensitive information on the use of UAV tools due to data protection [54].

Agricultural mapping represents a discipline that provides geospatial information on crops and soil properties. In addition, it allows evaluation of the suitability of agricultural land to ensure sustainable production, food security and environmental protection.

5   Conclusions

This study identified the use of UAVs in agricultural mapping, with relevant research in monitoring plant phenotyping and crop detection (32%), soil evaluation (14.3%), irrigation/water resources applications (13%), agricultural yield (13%), and a low percentage of studies related to efficient fertilization, use of pesticides, proper weed management, and efficient disease management. In addition, the fusion of technologies such as AI, robotics, and deep learning algorithms is crucial because they transform traditional agricultural practices into modern and novel approaches. Agricultural mapping is essential for managers to develop accurate and sustainable agricultural policies that improve local farmers' well-being and the population's food security.

UAV is a technology that, in the last decade, has increasingly contributed to agricultural mapping, providing multispectral, infrared and hyperspectral images of different farm activities. They contribute to elaborating thematic maps (e.g., NDVI maps) that, combined with other indices, constitute agricultural mapping tools with valuable crop and soil management information. Studies focused on the automatic detection of agricultural plots through evolutionary computation are recommended, which allows for specifying suitable soils for crops and sustainable agrarian yield.

References

1. Navia, J., Mondragon, I., Patino, D., Colorado, J.: Multispectral mapping in agriculture: terrain mosaic using an autonomous quadcopter UAV. In: 2016 International Conference on Unmanned Aircraft Systems (ICUAS), pp. 1351–1358. IEEE (2016). https://doi.org/10.1109/ICUAS.2016.7502606

2. Tsouros, D.C., Bibi, S., Sarigiannidis, P.G.: A review on UAV-based applications for precision agriculture. Information **10**, 349 (2019). https://doi.org/10.3390/info10110349

3. Aslan, M.F., Durdu, A., Sabanci, K., Ropelewska, E., Gültekin, S.S.: A comprehensive survey of the recent studies with UAV for precision agriculture in open fields and greenhouses. Appl. Sci. **12**, 1047 (2022). https://doi.org/10.3390/app12031047

4. Jakob, S., Zimmermann, R., Gloaguen, R.: The need for accurate geometric and radiometric corrections of drone-borne hyperspectral data for mineral exploration: MEPHySTo—A toolbox for pre-processing drone-borne hyperspectral data. Remote Sens. (Basel) **9**, 88 (2017). https://doi.org/10.3390/rs9010088

5. Christiansen, M., Laursen, M., Jørgensen, R., Skovsen, S., Gislum, R.: Designing and testing a UAV mapping system for agricultural field surveying. Sensors **17**, 2703 (2017). https://doi.org/10.3390/s17122703

6. Rokhmana, C.A.: The potential of UAV-based remote sensing for supporting precision agriculture in Indonesia. Procedia Environ. Sci. **24**, 245–253 (2015). https://doi.org/10.1016/j.proenv.2015.03.032

7. Yue, J., et al.: Estimation of winter wheat above-ground biomass using unmanned aerial vehicle-based snapshot hyperspectral sensor and crop height improved models. Remote Sens. (Basel) **9**, 708 (2017). https://doi.org/10.3390/rs9070708

8. Radoglou-Grammatikis, P., Sarigiannidis, P., Lagkas, T., Moscholios, I.: A compilation of UAV applications for precision agriculture. Comput. Netw. **172**, 107148 (2020). https://doi.org/10.1016/j.comnet.2020.107148

9. Gašparović, M., Zrinjski, M., Barković, Đ., Radočaj, D.: An automatic method for weed mapping in oat fields based on UAV imagery. Comput. Electron. Agric. **173**, 105385 (2020). https://doi.org/10.1016/j.compag.2020.105385

10. Allred, B., et al.: Overall results and key findings on the use of UAV visible-color, multispectral, and thermal infrared imagery to map agricultural drainage pipes. Agric. Water Manag. **232**, 106036 (2020). https://doi.org/10.1016/j.agwat.2020.106036

11. Simic Milas, A., Romanko, M., Reil, P., Abeysinghe, T., Marambe, A.: The importance of leaf area index in mapping chlorophyll content of corn under different agricultural treatments using UAV images. Int. J. Remote Sens. **39**, 5415–5431 (2018). https://doi.org/10.1080/01431161.2018.1455244

12. Torres-Sánchez, J., Peña, J.M., de Castro, A.I., López-Granados, F.: Multi-temporal mapping of the vegetation fraction in early-season wheat fields using images from UAV. Comput. Electron. Agric. **103**, 104–113 (2014). https://doi.org/10.1016/j.compag.2014.02.009

13. Santesteban, L.G., Di Gennaro, S.F., Herrero-Langreo, A., Miranda, C., Royo, J.B., Matese, A.: High-resolution UAV-based thermal imaging to estimate the instantaneous and seasonal variability of plant water status within a vineyard. Agric. Water Manag. **183**, 49–59 (2017). https://doi.org/10.1016/j.agwat.2016.08.026

14. Holman, F., Riche, A., Michalski, A., Castle, M., Wooster, M., Hawkesford, M.: High throughput field phenotyping of wheat plant height and growth rate in field plot trials using UAV based remote sensing. Remote Sens. (Basel) **8**, 1031 (2016). https://doi.org/10.3390/rs8121031

15. Herwitz, S.R., et al.: Imaging from an unmanned aerial vehicle: agricultural surveillance and decision support. Comput. Electron. Agric. **44**, 49–61 (2004). https://doi.org/10.1016/j.compag.2004.02.006

16. Huang, H., Deng, J., Lan, Y., Yang, A., Deng, X., Zhang, L.: A fully convolutional network for weed mapping of unmanned aerial vehicle (UAV) imagery. PLoS ONE **13**, e0196302 (2018). https://doi.org/10.1371/journal.pone.0196302

17. Kerkech, M., Hafiane, A., Canals, R.: Vine disease detection in UAV multispectral images using optimized image registration and deep learning segmentation approach. Comput. Electron. Agric. **174**, 105446 (2020). https://doi.org/10.1016/j.compag.2020.105446

18. Niknejad, N., Ismail, W., Bahari, M., Hendradi, R., Salleh, A.Z.: Mapping the research trends on blockchain technology in food and agriculture industry: a bibliometric analysis. Environ. Technol. Innov. **21**, 101272 (2021). https://doi.org/10.1016/j.eti.2020.101272

19. Velasco-Muñoz, J., Aznar-Sánchez, J., Belmonte-Ureña, L., López-Serrano, M.: Advances in water use efficiency in agriculture: a bibliometric analysis. Water (Basel) **10**, 377 (2018). https://doi.org/10.3390/w10040377

20. Luo, J., Han, H., Jia, F., Dong, H.: Agricultural Co-operatives in the western world: a bibliometric analysis. J. Clean. Prod. **273**, 122945 (2020). https://doi.org/10.1016/j.jclepro.2020.122945

21. Ragazou, K., Garefalakis, A., Zafeiriou, E., Passas, I.: Agriculture 5.0: a new strategic management mode for a cut cost and an energy efficient agriculture sector. Energies (Basel) **15**, 3113 (2022). https://doi.org/10.3390/en15093113

22. Bouchenine, A., Abdel-Aal, M.A.M.: Towards supply chain resilience with additive manufacturing: a bibliometric survey. Supply Chain Anal. **2**, 100014 (2023). https://doi.org/10.1016/j.sca.2023.100014

23. Khuram, S., Rehman, C., Nasir, N., Elahi, N.S.: A bibliometric analysis of quality assurance in higher education institutions: implications for assessing university's societal impact. Eval. Program Plann. **99**, 102319 (2023). https://doi.org/10.1016/j.evalprogplan.2023.102319

24. Abdollahi, A., Ghaderi, Z., Béal, L., Cooper, C.: The intersection between knowledge management and organizational learning in tourism and hospitality: a bibliometric analysis. J. Hosp. Tour. Manag. **55**, 11–28 (2023). https://doi.org/10.1016/j.jhtm.2023.02.014

25. Ma, L., et al.: Evaluation of feature selection methods for object-based land cover mapping of unmanned aerial vehicle imagery using random forest and support vector machine classifiers. ISPRS Int. J. Geoinf. **6**, 51 (2017). https://doi.org/10.3390/ijgi6020051

26. Chakraborty, M., Khot, L.R., Sankaran, S., Jacoby, P.W.: Evaluation of mobile 3D light detection and ranging based canopy mapping system for tree fruit crops. Comput. Electron. Agric. **158**, 284–293 (2019). https://doi.org/10.1016/j.compag.2019.02.012

27. Nevavuori, P., Narra, N., Linna, P., Lipping, T.: Crop yield prediction using multitemporal UAV data and spatio-temporal deep learning models. Remote Sens. (Basel) **12**, 4000 (2020). https://doi.org/10.3390/rs12234000

28. Chhikara, P., Tekchandani, R., Kumar, N., Chamola, V., Guizani, M.: DCNN-GA: a deep neural net architecture for navigation of UAV in indoor environment. IEEE Internet Things J. **8**, 4448–4460 (2021). https://doi.org/10.1109/JIOT.2020.3027095

29. Bose, S., Mazumdar, A., Basu, S.: Evolution of groundwater quality assessment on urban area- a bibliometric analysis. Groundw. Sustain. Dev. **20**, 100894 (2023). https://doi.org/10.1016/j.gsd.2022.100894

30. Miswan, M.S., Hamdan, R., Roffe, N.I., Wurochekke, A.A.: Land used mapping using unmanned aerial vehicle (UAV) along parit rasipan drainage system. Int. J. Sustain. Constr. Eng. Technol. **13** (2022). https://doi.org/10.30880/ijscet.2022.13.04.025

31. Park, S., Ryu, D., Fuentes, S., Chung, H., O'Connell, M., Kim, J.: Mapping very-high-resolution evapotranspiration from unmanned aerial vehicle (UAV) imagery. ISPRS Int J Geoinf. **10**, 211 (2021). https://doi.org/10.3390/ijgi10040211

32. Tocci, F., et al.: Advantages in using colour calibration for orthophoto reconstruction. Sensors **22**, 6490 (2022). https://doi.org/10.3390/s22176490

33. El Hoummaidi, L., Larabi, A., Alam, K.: Using unmanned aerial systems and deep learning for agriculture mapping in Dubai. Heliyon. **7**, e08154 (2021). https://doi.org/10.1016/j.hel iyon.2021.e08154

34. Tagarakis, A.C., Filippou, E., Kalaitzidis, D., Benos, L., Busato, P., Bochtis, D.: Proposing UGV and UAV systems for 3D mapping of orchard environments. Sensors **22**, 1571 (2022). https://doi.org/10.3390/s22041571

35. Grau, J., et al.: Improved accuracy of riparian zone mapping using near ground unmanned aerial vehicle and photogrammetry method. Remote Sens (Basel). **13**, 1997 (2021). https://doi.org/10.3390/rs13101997

36. de Camargo, T., Schirrmann, M., Landwehr, N., Dammer, K.-H., Pflanz, M.: Optimized deep learning model as a basis for fast UAV mapping of weed species in winter wheat crops. Remote Sens. (Basel) **13**, 1704 (2021). https://doi.org/10.3390/rs13091704

37. Deng, J., Zhong, Z., Huang, H., Lan, Y., Han, Y., Zhang, Y.: Lightweight semantic segmentation network for real-time weed mapping using unmanned aerial vehicles. Appl. Sci. **10**, 7132 (2020). https://doi.org/10.3390/app10207132

38. Jiang, R., et al.: UAV-based partially sampling system for rapid NDVI mapping in the evaluation of rice nitrogen use efficiency. J. Clean. Prod. **289**, 125705 (2021). https://doi.org/10.1016/j.jclepro.2020.125705

39. Manish, R., Lin, Y.-C., Ravi, R., Hasheminasab, S.M., Zhou, T., Habib, A.: Development of a miniaturized mobile mapping system for in-row, under-canopy phenotyping. Remote Sens. (Basel) **13**, 276 (2021). https://doi.org/10.3390/rs13020276

40. López-Granados, F., et al.: Monitoring vineyard canopy management operations using UAV-acquired photogrammetric point clouds. Remote Sens. (Basel) **12**, 2331 (2020). https://doi.org/10.3390/rs12142331

41. Feng, Q., et al.: Multi-temporal unmanned aerial vehicle remote sensing for vegetable mapping using an attention-based recurrent convolutional neural network. Remote Sens. (Basel). **12**, 1668 (2020). https://doi.org/10.3390/rs12101668

42. Chew, R., et al.: Deep neural networks and transfer learning for food crop identification in UAV images. Drones. **4**, 7 (2020). https://doi.org/10.3390/drones4010007

43. de Castro, A.I., et al.: Mapping cynodon dactylon infesting cover crops with an automatic decision tree-OBIA procedure and UAV imagery for precision viticulture. Remote Sens. (Basel) **12**, 56 (2019). https://doi.org/10.3390/rs12010056

44. Gabrlik, P., Lazna, T., Jilek, T., Sladek, P., Zalud, L.: An automated heterogeneous robotic system for radiation surveys: design and field testing. J. Field Robot. **38**, 657–683 (2021). https://doi.org/10.1002/rob.22010

45. Rangarajan, A.K., Balu, E.J., Boligala, M.S., Jagannath, A., Ranganathan, B.N.: A low-cost UAV for detection of Cercospora leaf spot in okra using deep convolutional neural network. Multimed Tools Appl. **81**, 21565–21589 (2022). https://doi.org/10.1007/s11042-022-12464-4

46. Tian, Y., et al.: Search and rescue under the forest canopy using multiple UAVs. Int. J. Rob. Res. **39**, 1201–1221 (2020). https://doi.org/10.1177/0278364920929398

47. Wang, T., Chen, B., Zhang, Z., Li, H., Zhang, M.: Applications of machine vision in agricultural robot navigation: a review. Comput. Electron. Agric. **198**, 107085 (2022). https://doi.org/10.1016/j.compag.2022.107085

48. Yang, Z., et al.: UAV remote sensing applications in marine monitoring: knowledge visualization and review. Sci. Total Environ. **838**, 155939 (2022). https://doi.org/10.1016/j.scitot env.2022.155939

49. Valente, J., Hiremath, S., Ariza-Sentís, M., Doldersum, M., Kooistra, L.: Mapping of Rumex obtusifolius in nature conservation areas using very high resolution UAV imagery and deep learning. International J. Appl. Earth Observ. Geoinform. **112**, 102864 (2022). https://doi.org/10.1016/j.jag.2022.102864

50. Nex, F., et al.: UAV in the advent of the twenties: where we stand and what is next. ISPRS J. Photogramm. Remote. Sens. **184**, 215–242 (2022). https://doi.org/10.1016/j.isprsjprs.2021.12.006
51. Edulakanti, S.R., Ganguly, S.: Review article: the emerging drone technology and the advancement of the Indian drone business industry. J. High Technol. Manag. Res. **34**, 100464 (2023). https://doi.org/10.1016/j.hitech.2023.100464
52. Stöcker, C., Bennett, R., Koeva, M., Nex, F., Zevenbergen, J.: Scaling up UAVs for land administration: towards the plateau of productivity. Land Use Policy **114**, 105930 (2022). https://doi.org/10.1016/j.landusepol.2021.105930
53. Volovelsky, U.: Civilian uses of unmanned aerial vehicles and the threat to the right to privacy – An Israeli case study. Comput. Law Secur. Rev. **30**, 306–320 (2014). https://doi.org/10.1016/j.clsr.2014.03.008
54. Kayad, A., et al.: How many gigabytes per hectare are available in the digital agriculture era? A digitization footprint estimation. Comput. Electron. Agric. **198**, 107080 (2022). https://doi.org/10.1016/j.compag.2022.107080

Health Care Information Systems

Gross Motor Skills Development in Children with and Without Disabilities: A Therapist's Support System Based on Deep Learning and Adaboost Classifiers

Adolfo Jara-Gavilanes and Vladimir Robles-Bykbaev(✉)

GI-IATa, Cátedra UNESCO Tecnologías de apoyo para la Inclusión Educativa,
Universidad Politécnica Salesiana, Cuenca, Ecuador
{ajarag,vrobles}@ups.edu.ec

Abstract. Fundamental or Gross Motor Skills (GMS) are a set of essential skills both for basic movement activities and physical activities. Properly developing them is vital for children to develop a healthy lifestyle and prevent serious illnesses at an older stage of life, like obesity and cardiorespiratory problems. This is a problem for therapists because they must attend to many children lacking this skill set, and it's even more time-consuming with children with disabilities. Therefore, this work presents a system that can assist therapists in giving therapy to more children with and without disabilities. To reach this goal, the system is divided into 3 phases: first, the data preprocessing phase, where images from 3 postures are collected: sitting, static crawling, and bound angle. Then all the images are resized. Model construction is the second phase. It consists of implementing the MoveNet algorithm that helps detect human posture through 17 key points of the body. Then, this algorithm is applied to the dataset created to obtain the coordinates from the postures collected. After that, an Adaboost model is created and trained, and tested. Next, the MoveNet algorithm is assembled with the Adaboost model to predict the three postures in live action. Then comes the third phase: model evaluation. This step includes evaluating the model assembled at Instituto de Parálisis Cerebral del Azuay (IPCA). Finally, the results of this evaluation are presented.

Keywords: education · gross motor skills · artificial intelligence · machine learning

1 Introduction

Fundamental or Gross Motor Skills (GMS) are considered a pillar for physical activities because they oversee moving large muscles [18]. For example, crawling, sitting, walking, or running [7]. Therefore, the right development of these skills is crucial as a child as they are linked to a healthy level of body mass index, better cardiorespiratory shape, greater social development, stronger language

H. Florez and M. Leon (Eds.): ICAI 2023, CCIS 1874, pp. 325–337, 2024.
https://doi.org/10.1007/978-3-031-46813-1_22

skills, and finer cognitive development [5,19]. Instead, the lack of these skills has four huge impacts on the development of children. First, children who haven't developed GMS early may have trouble developing it throughout their entire life [14]. Second, children are more likely to experience lower self-esteem. Third, children are more prone to higher anxiety levels [18]. Fourth, the lack of GMS is related to academic failure [19].

Research has shown that many children today are not developing adequate gross motor skills, and this is a cause for concern. According to a study conducted by the Centers for Disease Control and Prevention (CDC) in 2018, only 24% of children between the ages of 6 and 17 met the guidelines for physical activity, which include engaging in moderate to vigorous physical activity for at least 60 min per day [2]. This lack of physical activity can have negative consequences on a child's health, including increased risk of obesity, cardiovascular disease, and type 2 diabetes.

There are several related works and fields of study that are relevant to the importance of gross motor skills in childhood development. One such area is physical therapy. Physical therapists work with children to develop customized treatment plans that are tailored to their individual needs and goals. These treatment plans often include a variety of interventions, such as exercises, stretches, and manual therapies, that are designed to improve strength, balance, coordination, and mobility [6]. Physical therapists may also work with children to address any underlying conditions or injuries that may be impacting their gross motor development, such as cerebral palsy, spina bifida, or sports-related injuries. By working with physical therapists, children can improve their gross motor skills and overall physical function, which can have a significant impact on their quality of life and ability to participate in activities that are important to them.

Even though GMS is important for the reasons described above, only 50% of children demonstrate competency through these skills [4]. Therefore, to create an intervention plan, it is necessary to know how GMS are divided into different categories of movements, which are the following 3:

- Locomotion: it is related to any movement that a child performs to move from one location to another. For instance: crawling, rolling, walking, climbing [15]. These actions are vital for assessing the child's ability to move within their environment.
- Stationary: it involves movement in a fixed or stationary place. For example, balance, rising, bending, and turning [21]. These movements are crucial for evaluating the child's posture stability and control while stationary.
- Manipulation: it refers to controlling objects in different manners. For example: catch, throw, move, hang on an object [19]. This category's significance lies in evaluating the child's fine motor skills and their ability to interact with objects in different therapeutic contexts.

The classification into these categories provides a structured framework for assessing a wide range of movements exhibited by children with disabilities during therapy sessions. By understanding the specific movements within each category and their connection to posture assessment, therapists can better tailor their interventions to address different aspects of a child's physical capabilities.

A therapist must commit and divide his time with a child to practice the categories described above to ensure that the child develops the GMS. Finishing a session with a specific child lacking these skills can take a lot of time. This can be even more complex if a child has a disability. For that reason, new technological tools with the help of artificial intelligence and machine learning should be implemented to assist therapists in addressing more patients effectively.

For these reasons, in this work, we present a machine learning classifier and an artificial intelligence algorithm to predict 17 key points of a body to reach the following goal: to develop a system that can accurately identify and monitor the correct posture of children with and without disabilities in real time. By achieving this, therapists can efficiently redirect their focus to other children, confident in the knowledge that the posture of the child under consideration is being appropriately monitored. This will optimize the therapist's ability to manage multiple children simultaneously and enhance the overall effectiveness of therapy sessions. This work focuses on stationary movements only. The decision to exclusively focus on stationary movements within this study is primarily rooted in the need to establish a solid foundational understanding of posture control and alignment. By concentrating on stationary movements, we are able to meticulously analyze the fundamental aspects of posture without the added complexity of dynamic motion. The system is divided into 3 phases: first, the data preprocessing phase, where images from 3 stationary postures are collected: sitting, static crawling, and bound angle. Then all the images are resized to the camera dimensions. Model construction is the second phase. It consists of implementing the MoveNet algorithm in an Nvidia Jetson Xavier NX. It helps detect human posture through 17 key points of the body. Then, this algorithm is applied to the dataset created to obtain the coordinates from the postures collected to produce numerical data. After that, an Adaboost model is created, trained, and tested with the coordinates extracted. Next, the MoveNet algorithm is blended with the Adaboost model to predict the three stationary postures in live action. Then comes the third phase: model evaluation. This step includes evaluating the model assembled at Instituto de Parálisis Cerebral del Azuay (IPCA). Finally, the results of this evaluation are presented and discussed.

This paper is organized as follows. Section 2 presents the related works. Section 3 describes the methodology, the movement lightning algorithm, and the Adaboost classifier, it also illustrates the experimental setup and the dataset. Section 4 shows the results obtained. Section 5 expresses the limitations of this work. Section 6 narrates the conclusions of this work.

2   Related Work

In [11], the researchers proposed a hybrid model to detect and recognize human postures. They made use of the human body using the galvanic skin response dataset. The model created included a Convolutional Neural Network (CNN) and a Long-Short Term Memory (LSTM). The combination of those formed the final model. They extracted different features including skew, percentile, SR, SD, mean, and kurtosis to feed the model. The hybrid model reached 98.14% accuracy, 98% precision, 98% recall, and 98% f-score.

In [13], the authors made use of 2 transfer learning models: AlexNet, and VGG16 with hyperparameter optimization, a Convolutional Neural Network (CNN), and a Multilayer Perceptron (MLP) to be able to identify different human poses. They worked with the MPII human posture dataset. After all the models were trained and tested, they yielded the following percentage of accuracy: AlexNet 91.2%, CNN 87.5%, VGG16 90.2%, and the MLP 89.9%.

In [14], the researchers conducted a study to research the impact of a structured movement activity program related to the development of GMS in children aged 3 to 5 years. 136 children were part of this study over 24 weeks. They were divided into 2 groups: 28 children for the intervention group and 108 for the comparison group. The last group only performed free-play activities. The McCarthy Children's Psychomotricity and Aptitude Scales (MSCA) battery of psychomotor tests evaluated the GMS development. At the end of the study, the intervention group yielded better results at movement coordination for their right arm ($F_{1,134}$ = 14,389, p = 0.000, $\eta2$ = 0.097). Same for leg coordination ($F_{1,134}$ = 19,281, p = 0.000, $\eta2$ = 0.126) as the comparison group.

In [3], the authors created a system for posture detection. The system consists of 1 control center and two sensors placed in the leg and another in the spine. The system contains the following devices: two Arduino Nano development boards, two MPU 6050 modules that have both an accelerometer and gyroscope, a Bluetooth module, and an external dual-port battery for powering the device. Also, an application was created to receive the data. This system detected and alert when a posture was mistakenly performed.

In [9], the authors proposed a six-month controlled trial to help develop physical activity and GMS. It counted 150 children aged between 3 and 5 years and six educators. The trial consisted of structured physical activity lessons and unstructured physical activity sessions. Gross motor skills were assessed using the Test of Gross Motor Development (2nd edition) and physical activity was measured objectively using GT3X+ Actigraph accelerometers. As a result of this trial, four out of 5 children improved their GMS, and the same for physical activities.

3   Methodology

Following the models selected are going to be described. These models were selected because is critical to ensure accurate and efficient pose estimation. For our study, we selected the MoveNet algorithm due to its ability to provide real-time and high-quality human pose estimation. MoveNet utilizes a lightweight deep learning architecture, optimized for mobile and edge devices, making it suitable for real-time applications. It has demonstrated robustness and accuracy in estimating human body poses across different scenarios and viewpoints.

Additionally, we incorporated the Adaboost classifier into our pose estimation. Adaboost is an ensemble learning algorithm that combines multiple weak classifiers to create a strong classifier. It has been widely utilized in various machine learning tasks and has shown excellent performance in classification problems. By integrating Adaboost into our system, we aimed to enhance the accuracy and robustness of the pose estimation results obtained from the MoveNet algorithm

The approach presented in this article distinguishes itself from previous methods in terms of the detection methodology employed. While previous approaches have utilized CNNs connected to an ANN or MLP, our method leverages the MoveNet model to extract 17 key points representing the body. Subsequently, these key points are fed into the Adaboost classifier to accurately classify the pose performed by the child. This novel combination of the MoveNet model and Adaboost classifier enhances the accuracy and robustness of pose estimation in our methodology.

3.1   Models

- Adaboost: it's a boosting technique that generates a series of stumps to create a robust classifier. The difference between a stump and a decision tree is that a stump is not as deep as a decision tree. In the training phase of this technique, the first stump is going to generate an error, and this error is used for the next stump to improve its prediction, and so on with the rest of the stumps generated [16]. Also, this error is employed for the weight value that each stump has for the final decision. Thus, a stump with a lower error has a higher value for the final decision. Next, Table 1 the parameters with which the different models were configured to select the best model.

Table 1. Parameters tested for the Adaboost model.

Classifier	Parameters
Adaboost	tree_depth=2, 3, 4, 5
	learning_rate=0.00001, 0.0001, 0.001, 0.01, 1
	n_estimators=50,100,150,200,250,300,350,400,450,500
	algorithm= samme, samme.r
	cross_validation=5, 7, 10

- MoveNet: It's a model that detects 17 key points from the body [1]. Figure 1 shows an example of the key points that are detected. Hence, it can be used for pose estimation. It was developed by Google and IncludeHealth [8]. It's a bottom-up model that makes use of Tensorflow object detection API. It also implements MobileNet V2 as the feature extractor [12]. There are 2 versions of it: MoveNet Lightning which is mainly used for high performance in latency-critical applications. The other one is MoveNet Thunder, its target is high-performance applications [10].

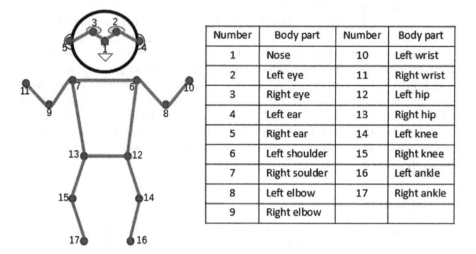

Number	Body part	Number	Body part
1	Nose	10	Left wrist
2	Left eye	11	Right wrist
3	Right eye	12	Left hip
4	Left ear	13	Right hip
5	Right ear	14	Left knee
6	Left shoulder	15	Right knee
7	Right soulder	16	Left ankle
8	Left elbow	17	Right ankle
9	Right elbow		

Fig. 1. The 17 key points that MoveNet detects for pose estimation.

3.2 Proposed Method

The method created to reach the proposed goal is divided into 3 phases:

Data Preprocessing:

1. Data gathering: in this step, images from 3 poses are gathered: crawling, static crawling, and bound angle.
2. Image resize: after the data was gathered, all the images were resized to 640 × 480.

Model Construction:

3. MoveNet implementation: in this stage, the MoveNet algorithm is implemented in the embedded system: Nvidia Jetson Xavier NX.
4. Keypoints extraction: after MoveNet was implemented, it was applied to the data gathered to extract the coordinates from the 17 key points that MoveNet yields. Thus, a .csv file is created with this numerical data.
5. Model training and testing: once we obtain the numerical data, a machine learning algorithm is trained and tested. The dataset was divided into 70% for training and 30% for testing. In this case, Adaboost was the classifier selected for this step.

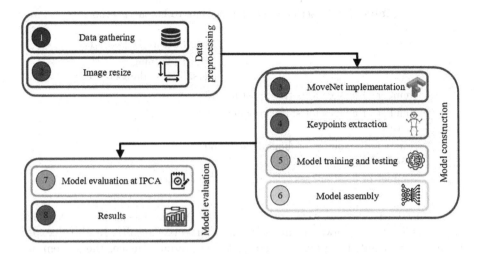

Fig. 2. Method implemented for this work, which is divided into 3 phases: data preprocessing, model construction, and model evaluation.

6. Model assembly: once we have the trained model, it must be assembled with the MoveNet algorithm to be able to predict the pose in live action.

Model Evaluation:

7. Model evaluation at IPCA: in this step, the model assembled in the previous step is tested in live action at IPCA with children with disabilities.
8. Results: Finally, the results obtained at IPCA are presented (Fig. 2).

3.3 Dataset Description

The images recollected come from 2 datasets from Kaggle: Yoga Posture Dataset [17], and Yoga Pose Image classification dataset [20]. These datasets are for yoga pose classification. Yoga contains many poses, where three poses have an exact match to the ones that are needed for this work. For example, the chair pose (Utkatasana) is identical to the sitting posture, the only difference being that in exercises for GMS, a chair is needed. Then, the cat pose (Marjaryasana) is the same as the static crawling posture in GMS. Finally, the easy pose (Sukhasana) matches the bound angle posture for GMS. Therefore, only images with the yoga pose described were selected to create our dataset. Following, Table 2 shows a summary of the final dataset:

3.4 Experimental Setup

The experiments were conducted at Instituto de Parálisis Cerebral del Azuay (IPCA). A screen was placed in the room. A camera was laid down at a height

Table 2. Dataset description according to human posture.

Datasets	Yoga Posture Dataset [17]
	Yoga Pose Image classification dataset [20]
Number of images for sitting posture	73
Number of images for static crawling posture	102
Number of images for bound angle posture	50
Number of total images	225

of 0.75 m. These devices were connected to an Nvidia Jetson Xavier NX. The child was located 2 m away from the camera for better results. In all the experiments carried out, the physical therapist was present. Hence, the system and the therapist could verify the children's postures.

Two experimental scenarios were outlined for the study, and their specifics are elaborated upon below. Both scenarios involved the participation of the same group of 8 children, with ages spanning between 8 and 16 years. The group consisted of one 3-year-old child, one 8-year-old, three 9-year-olds, one 10-year-old, one 13-year-old, and one 16-year-old.

1. **Scenario one: system accuracy without therapist's aid for child's correct posture.** This scenario was developed to explore how accurate the system would be without the therapist's direct intervention. It means the therapist would only give instructions about the posture the child should perform. Therefore, the therapist wouldn't help the child to make the correct posture. Once the child was correctly located, the therapist announced the position to be performed. The order was seating, crawling, and bound angle posture. The child had to stay in each position for 5 s, then he would switch to the next posture announced by the therapist. Every second the system would take the accuracy metric to later obtain a mean to get the results.

2. **Scenario two: system accuracy with therapist's intervention for child's correct posture.** This scenario examined how accurate the system would be with the therapist's intervention. Hence, first, the therapist would announce the posture to be performed and then would help the child to execute the correct posture. After the child was perfectly located, the therapist the postures in the same order as Scenario One. As soon as the therapist stopped helping the child, he had to stay in that posture for 5 s.

4   Experiments and Preliminary Results

First, the best Adaboost model is going to be explained. This model reached 94% accuracy and 93% precision. To reach these results, the dataset was divided into

70% for training and 30% for testing. The model had the following configurations: tree_depth was set to 5, the learning_rate was 1, the n_estimators were 300, the best algorithm was same and the number of folds for cross_validation was 5.

4.1 Results Scenario One

In this segment, after 8 children were tested without the therapist's help to do the right posture, the mean of each child for each posture is calculated. Following the results obtained:

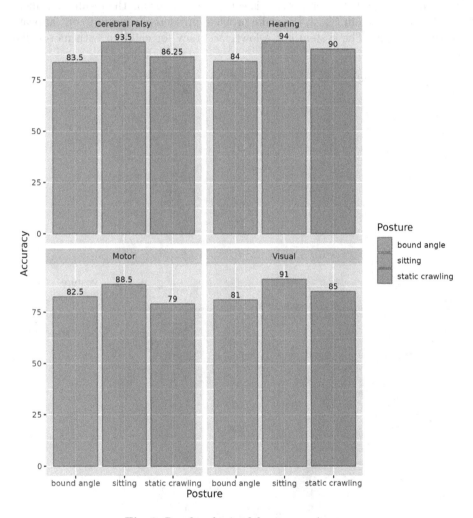

Fig. 3. Results obtained from scenario one.

As can be seen in Fig. 3, the system had a little bit of difficulty with children with motor disabilities, especially for static crawling. This is due to their difficulty moving certain parts of their body. Another important outcome that can be seen is that the system has a lower accuracy prediction for the bound angle posture, but still, it's a good accuracy because it stays higher than 80% in each case. The same with the other postures.

4.2 Results Scenario Two

In this segment, after the same 8 children were tested in scenario one, they were tested with the therapist's help for the children to do the right posture. Then the mean of each child for each posture is calculated. Following the results obtained:

As can be seen in Fig. 4, the same problem presented in scenario one appears in this scenario. The system got a lower accuracy for children with motor dis-

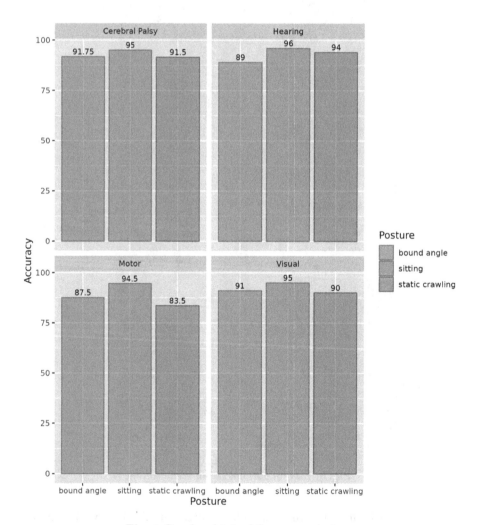

Fig. 4. Results obtained from scenario two.

abilities, but in this scenario, with the help of a therapist, the results were better than scenario one.

5   Limitations

The main limitation of this study is the amount of data recollected. The dataset created contains 225 images that aren't equally distributed. With more data, the Adaboost model could achieve higher results and therefore better results when testing the system in live action. To restrain this problem, more datasets containing the same poses as described in this paper should be discovered on public platforms.

Another limitation is the number of postures the system can predict. This problem is due to the lack of data to solve GMS problems. There aren't GMS datasets to predict the posture of a person or a child. To solve this problem, data should be gathered in schools with the consent of parents and the schools. This would take some time, but it would help create systems to aid therapists with patients with GMS problems.

6   Conclusions

In conclusion, this study successfully achieves its intended objective of accurately detecting the posture of children with disabilities, both with and without the assistance of a therapist, in order to ensure correct posture alignment. Thus, a therapist doesn't necessarily need to be present at the moment of the session. Therefore, therapists could attend to more patients. First, during the image preprocessing phase, the dataset created ended up with 225 images of 3 postures: sitting, static crawling, and bound angle. Then, all the images were resized to 640 × 480. Second, in the model construction phase, the MoveNet algorithm was implemented and applied to the dataset to be able to gather the coordinates of 17 key points of a human body. After that, an Adaboost model was trained and tested. The best model reached 94% of accuracy and 93% precision. The best parameters of this model were: tree_depth was set to 5, the learning_rate was 1, the n_estimators were 300, the best algorithm was samme, and the number of folds for cross_validation was 5. At last, for this phase, the Adaboost model and the MoveNet algorithm were assembled to be able to be used in live action. Third, in the model evaluation phase, the system was tested at IPCA with 8 children for 2 scenarios that were explained in the experimental setup. Finally, the results for each child were shown and the system proved that it's capable of having great accuracy at prediction for each scenario. For that reason, the system created can be used to help children perform therapy sessions without the help of a therapist. In this manner, therapists could attend to more patients. It is worth mentioning that this study has made significant strides in the development of a posture recognition system for children with disabilities, the limitations arising from the lack of comprehensive data for predicting a broader spectrum of postures, integral to Gross Motor Skills (GMS) development, warrant careful consideration. Consequently, as we contemplate the practical implications of the proposed system, we must recognize the importance of contextualizing its outcomes within the parameters of this data limitation. Looking ahead, efforts to expand the dataset and enhance the system's capacity to predict a wider array of postures could undoubtedly contribute to further advancements in assisting children with disabilities in achieving their motor skill development goals.

For future work, we propose the following lines:

- To implement a different pose detection algorithm like PoseNet.
- To train and test other machine learning algorithms like XGboost, Random Forest, and Catboost, among others.
- To gather more data from different postures that are commonly performed during therapy sessions to develop GMS.

Acknowledgements. This research has been supported by the "Sistemas Inteligentes de Soporte a la Educación Especial (SINSAE v5)" research project of the UNESCO Chair on Support Technologies for Educational Inclusion.

References

1. Movenet: Ultra fast and accurate pose detection model, December 2022. https://www.tensorflow.org/hub/tutorials/movenet
2. Physical activity facts, July 2022. https://www.cdc.gov/healthyschools/physicalactivity/facts.htm
3. Adochiei, F.C., Adochiei, I.R., Ciucu, R., Pietroiu-Andruseac, G., Argatu, F.C., Jula, N.: Design and implementation of a body posture detection system. In: 2019 E-Health and Bioengineering Conference (EHB), pp. 1–4 (2019)
4. Barnett, L.M., et al.: Correlates of gross motor competence in children and adolescents: a systematic review and meta-analysis. Sports Med. **46**(11), 1663–1688 (2016)
5. Burns, R.D., Brusseau, T.A., Fu, Y., Hannon, J.C.: Gross motor skills and cardiometabolic risk in children: a mediation analysis. Med. Sci. Sports Exerc. **49**(4), 746–751 (2017)
6. Furtado, M.A.S., et al.: Physical therapy in children with cerebral palsy in brazil: a scoping review. Dev. Med. Child Neurol. **64**(5), 550–560 (2022). https://onlinelibrary.wiley.com/doi/abs/10.1111/dmcn.15067
7. Gonzalez, S.L., Alvarez, V., Nelson, E.L.: Do gross and fine motor skills differentially contribute to language outcomes? A systematic review. Front. Psychol. **10**, 2670 (2019). https://www.frontiersin.org/articles/10.3389/fpsyg.2019.02670
8. Jo, B., Kim, S.: Comparative analysis of openpose, posenet, and movenet models for pose estimation in mobile devices. Traitement du Signal **39**(1), 119–124 (2022)
9. Jones, R.A., Okely, A.D., Hinkley, T., Batterham, M., Burke, C.: Promoting gross motor skills and physical activity in childcare: a translational randomized controlled trial. J. Sci. Med. Sport **19**(9), 744–749 (2016). https://www.sciencedirect.com/science/article/pii/S1440244015002066
10. LeViet, K., Chen, Y.: Pose estimation and classification on edge devices with movenet and tensorflow lite, August 2021. https://blog.tensorflow.org/2021/08/pose-estimation-and-classification-on-edge-devices-with-MoveNet-and-TensorFlow-Lite.html

11. Liaqat, S., Dashtipour, K., Arshad, K., Assaleh, K., Ramzan, N.: A hybrid posture detection framework: integrating machine learning and deep neural networks. IEEE Sens. J. **21**(7), 9515–9522 (2021)
12. Osigbesan, A., et al.: Vision-based fall detection in aircraft maintenance environment with pose estimation. In: 2022 IEEE International Conference on Multisensor Fusion and Integration for Intelligent Systems (MFI), pp. 1–6 (2022)
13. Ren, Z., Wu, J.: The effect of virtual reality games on the gross motor skills of children with cerebral palsy: a meta-analysis of randomized controlled trials. Int. J. Environ. Res. Public Health **16**(20) (2019). https://www.mdpi.com/1660-4601/16/20/3885
14. Ruiz-Esteban, C., Terry Andrés, J., Méndez, I., Morales, Á.: Analysis of motor intervention program on the development of gross motor skills in preschoolers. Int. J. Environ. Res. Public Health **17**(13) (2020). https://www.mdpi.com/1660-4601/17/13/4891
15. Schott, N., El-Rajab, I., Klotzbier, T.: Cognitive-motor interference during fine and gross motor tasks in children with developmental coordination disorder (DCD). Res. Dev. Disabil. **57**, 136–148 (2016). https://www.sciencedirect.com/science/article/pii/S0891422216301470
16. Tang, D., Tang, L., Dai, R., Chen, J., Li, X., Rodrigues, J.J.: MF-Adaboost: ldos attack detection based on multi-features and improved Adaboost. Futur. Gener. Comput. Syst. **106**, 347–359 (2020). https://www.sciencedirect.com/science/article/pii/S0167739X19310544
17. Tyagi, M.: Yoga posture dataset, September 2022. https://www.kaggle.com/datasets/tr1gg3rtrash/yoga-posture-dataset?select=Utkatasana
18. Veldman, S.L.C., Jones, R.A., Okely, A.D.: Efficacy of gross motor skill interventions in young children: an updated systematic review. BMJ Open Sport Exerc. Med. **2**(1) (2016). https://bmjopensem.bmj.com/content/2/1/e000067
19. Veldman, S.L., Santos, R., Jones, R.A., Sousa-Sá, E., Okely, A.D.: Associations between gross motor skills and cognitive development in toddlers. Early Hum. Dev. **132**, 39–44 (2019). https://www.sciencedirect.com/science/article/pii/S0378378218307461
20. Verma, M., Kumawat, S., Nakashima, Y., Raman, S.: Yoga-82: a new dataset for fine-grained classification of human poses. In: IEEE/CVF Conference on Computer Vision and Pattern Recognition Workshops (CVPRW), pp. 4472–4479 (2020)
21. Webster, E.K., Ulrich, D.A.: Evaluation of the psychometric properties of the test of gross motor development-third edition. J. Motor Learn. Dev. **5**(1), 45–58 (2017). https://journals.humankinetics.com/view/journals/jmld/5/1/article-p45.xml

TP53 Genetic Testing and Personalized Nutrition Service

Jitao Yang$^{(\boxtimes)}$

School of Information Science, Beijing Language and Culture University,
Beijing 100083, China
yangjitao@blcu.edu.cn

Abstract. TP53 is one of the tumor suppressor genes found to be highly correlated with human tumor development, this gene can sense stress or damage to cells and prevent cell division or trigger cell death, thereby preventing the proliferation of damaged cells. The P53 protein encoded by TP53 has an anti-tumor effect and is known as the "guardian of the genome". The mutation of TP53 gene eliminates a key cell safety mechanism, making it the trigger of cancer. In this paper, we first described the relationship between TP53 gene and tumors, and discussed the application of TP53 gene in tumor prediction and treatment, then we developed a TP53 genetic testing service to evaluate the cancer suppression ability of tumors, so that to help individuals to establish a scientific and reasonable lifestyle in a timely manner, and better grasp the initiative of health. Further, we describe the interaction between TP53 gene and nutrition and its impact on the occurrence and development of cancer. Finally, based on the analysis of the genetic testing results and food frequency questionnaires, we developed a personalized nutrition service to reduce the risk of developing the diseases with high genetic risk score.

Keywords: TP53 tumor suppressor gene · genetic testing · personalized nutrition · personalized lifestyle

1 Introduction

The TP53 gene is one of the important tumor suppressor genes, which has the effect of inhibiting cancer. Over 50% of cancers are accompanied by mutations in the TP53 gene. The mutation of TP53 gene not only leads to the loss of its cancer inhibitory function, but also promotes the occurrence and development of cancer.

The TP53 gene is located on the short arm of human chromosome 17 and is a regulatory factor in the cell growth cycle. It is associated with important biological functions such as cell cycle regulation, DNA repair, cell differentiation, and apoptosis [1].

The p53 protein was first discovered in 1979 that the tumorigenic virus SV40 can form complexes with it, and the transfer of cloned p53 into cells can cause

H. Florez and M. Leon (Eds.): ICAI 2023, CCIS 1874, pp. 338–350, 2024.
https://doi.org/10.1007/978-3-031-46813-1_23

cell carcinogenesis [2], therefore for the first 10 years, it was generally believed that TP53 was a proto-oncogene. Later, it was found that the TP53 gene was divided into two types: wild type and mutant type, and its products also had wild type and mutant type. Wild-type P53 protein inhibits the division of cells with DNA damage and chromosomal aberrations, thereby preventing the transmission of aberrations to daughter cells, with a broad spectrum of tumor suppressive effects. In contrast, mutations/deletions of the TP53 gene are closely related to the occurrence and development of tumors [3]. Studies have shown that forced expression of wild-type P53 protein can block oncogene mediated transformation in cultured primary rat embryonic fibroblasts [4,5], therefore, TP53 is considered an important tumor suppressor gene. This gene has homozygous mutations in approximately 50–60% of human cancers, resulting in reduced protein binding ability to specific DNA sequences that regulate the TP53 transcription pathway [5].

In this paper, we developed a TP53 genetic testing service and a personalized nutrition service, so that to reduce the risk of developing the diseases caused by TP53 mutations. This paper is organized as follows. Section 2 describes the relationship between TP53 gene and tumors; Sect. 3 introduces the application of TP53 gene in tumor prediction and treatment; Sect. 4 demonstrates the TP53 genetic testing service; Sect. 5 explains the interaction between TP53 gene and nutrition and its impact on the occurrence and development of cancer; Sect. 6 gives the personalized nutrition service; Sect. 7 concludes the paper and proposes future research directions.

2   TP53 Gene and Tumors

In the field of cancer research, TP53 is one of the tumor suppressor genes found to be highly correlated with human tumor development to date. This gene can sense stress or damage to cells and prevent cell division or trigger cell death, thereby preventing the proliferation of damaged cells. The P53 protein encoded by TP53 has an anti-tumor effect and is known as the "guardian of the genome" [6]. The mutation of TP53 gene eliminates a key cell safety mechanism, making it the trigger of cancer.

After studying 10225 patient samples from 32 different types of cancer from the cancer genome map, the study found that TP53 mutations were more common in patients with lower survival rates among all studied cancer types [7]. The research has also shown that TP53 mutations are closely related to genomic instability, suggesting the role of normal proteins in monitoring chromosome integrity. In most TP53 mutant tumors, there is an increase in oncogene amplification and deep deletion of tumor suppressor genes. The TP53 mutation has a profound impact on the genomic structure, expression, and clinical prospects of tumor cells.

Somatic mutation in TP53 gene is one of the most common changes in human cancer, and germline mutation is the root cause of Li-Fraumeni syndrome [8], which is prone to multiple early-onset cancers. Most mutations are single base substitutions distributed throughout the entire coding sequence. Their different types and locations may reveal the nature of mutagenic mechanisms related to the etiology of cancer. Therefore, TP53 mutation is also a potential prognostic and predictive marker, and a target for drug intervention [9].

2.1   TP53 Somatic Mutations and Tumors

Almost all types of cancer will have somatic cell TP53 mutations. The probability of somatic cell TP53 mutations in ovarian cancer, esophageal cancer, colorectal cancer, head and neck cancer, laryngeal cancer and lung cancer is about 38%–50%, and that in primary leukemia, sarcoma, testicular cancer, malignant melanoma and cervical cancer is 5%. Mutations are more common in advanced or aggressive cancer subtypes [10–12]. Over the past 20 years, TP53 germline mutations have been detected in approximately 500 households or individuals with complete or partial LFS characteristics.

2.2   TP53 Germline Mutations and Tumors

The T53 germline mutation is the root cause of Li-Fraumeni syndrome (LFS). LFS is a family aggregation disease with early onset tumors, including sarcoma, breast cancer, brain tumor and adrenal cortical cancer [13]. Over the past 20 years, TP53 germline mutations have been detected in approximately 500 households or individuals with complete or partial LFS characteristics [14]. LFS is usually considered a rare syndrome, however, when TP53 germline mutation screening was carried out for patients with early-onset cancer and patients without family history selection, 2%–3% TP53 mutations were found [15]; when 525 patients with family history of cancer were screened, 91 (17.3%) TP53 mutations were found [16]. Based on these results, TP53 mutations may lead to approximately 17% of familial cancer cases, and TP53 germline mutations may be more common than previously recognized, with TP53 germline mutations occurring in approximately 1 out of 5000 to 20000 newborns [15,16].

2.3   TP53 Polymorphism

The TP53 P72R (rs1042522) polymorphism has been extensively studied in experiments and population studies. Significant racial differences have been observed, with the frequency of the P72 allele being approximately 17% in the Swedish Sami population and 63% in Africans (Yoruba people). A study showed the correlation between the SNP and the living latitude of Asian people, and suggested that the difference in allele frequency might be due to adaptation to winter temperature differences [17].

To investigate the correlation between TP53 P72R polymorphism and the risk of chronic B-lymphoblastic leukemia (B-CLL), a case-control study was conducted in Khartoum Oblast, Sudan from April 2017 to April 2018. In this study, 110 patients with B-CLL and 80 healthy volunteers (control group) were included. All patients were examined by physical examination, whole blood count and immunophenotype to confirm the diagnosis. This study indicates that the Pro/Pro genotype is 10 times more susceptible to increased risk of chronic B lymphocyte leukemia compared to the Arg/Arg genotype population [18].

Many studies have explored the relationship between TP53 P72R polymorphism and bladder cancer risk. A meta-analysis included 22 applicable studies, 3791 cases of bladder cancer and 4917 controls; the results showed that TP53 P72R polymorphism was significantly associated with Asian susceptibility to bladder cancer; in addition, in bladder cancer cases, this polymorphism also shows a positive association with tumor stage/smoking status [19]. A meta-analysis consisting of 17 case-control studies involving 2371 prostate cancer cases and 2854 controls showed that the Pro/Pro genotype of the p53 P72R polymorphism was associated with an increased risk of prostate cancer, especially in Caucasians [20]. Another meta-analysis involving 32 genome-wide case-control population studies involving 15336 subjects (6924 cases and 8412 controls) showed that p53 P72R polymorphism is associated with susceptibility to osteosarcoma. However, the occurrence and development of osteosarcoma is a complex, multi-step, and multifactorial process, and potential mechanisms still need to be studied in the future [21].

A study in the Czech Republic involving 240 patients with pancreatic cancer and a control group (1827 people in total) showed that carriers of the TP53 P72R polymorphism variant Pro allele had an increased risk of pancreatic cancer (OR: 1.73; 95% CI: 1.26–2.39; P = 0.001). The genetic variation of TP53 may help, alone or in combination with other risk factors, to change the genetic susceptibility to pancreatic cancer and other gastrointestinal cancers [22].

Upper gastrointestinal cancer is the main cause of cancer-related deaths in northwest China, with many similarities in histological types, risk factors, and genetic variations. Researchers conducted a case-control study on trial subjects from high incidence areas of upper gastrointestinal cancer in China, using multiple logistic regression analysis to evaluate the correlation between TP53 P72R polymorphism and the risk of gastric and esophageal cancer. The results showed that compared to the Pro allele, the Arg allele was associated with an increased risk of gastric cancer (1.810×) and an increased risk of EC (2.285×). The risk of developing gastric cancer (OR smoking = 2.422, OR drinking = 5.152) or esophageal cancer (OR smoking = 5.310, OR drinking = 8.359) is further increased among carriers of the Arg allele who smoke or drink simultaneously. The TP53 P72R polymorphism is not associated with survival rates in gastric and esophageal cancer (p > 0.05) [23].

A case-control study conducted in Taiyuan, China examined the correlation between single nucleotide polymorphisms (SNPs) at two TP53 loci rs2078486 and rs1042522, as well as their potential interactions with environmental factors and cancer risk. Research has confirmed that the polymorphism of TP53 rs2078486 and rs1042522 loci may affect cancer risk. In addition, research has shown a potential synergistic effect of TP53 rs2078486 SNP with smoking and indoor air pollution exposure on lung cancer risk [24].

In addition, many studies have found the association between TP53 gene and different cancers. A recent study confirmed the association of a rare variant in TP53 with the risk of glioma, the most common primary brain tumor. The study genotyped the SNP rs7878222 in 566 glioma patients and 603 controls. The mutant "C" allele (the allele frequency in the control group was 1.1%) was associated with a 3.5-fold increase in glioma risk (OR = 3.54; P = 0.0001). The rs78378222 SNP is the first confirmed rare susceptibility mutation in glioma [25]. Another study genotyped the TP53 rs78378222 SNP in 1329 melanoma patients, 1096 head and neck squamous cell carcinoma patients, 1013 lung cancer patients and 3000 cancer free controls, and found that the mutation at this locus had a protective effect on the risk of SCCHN (OR = 0.41; 95% CL = 0.21–0.79) [26]. A study including 364 invasive serous ovarian cancer cases and 761 non Hispanic white controls showed that rs2078486 and rs12951053 SNPs of TP53 gene were associated with ovarian cancer risk [27]. A study in 2021 analyzed seven SNPs of four breast cancer susceptibility genes in 734 Chinese breast cancer patients and 672 age-matched healthy controls, and the results showed that rs12951053 in TP53 was positively correlated with lymph node negative breast cancer [28].

3   The Application of TP53 Gene in Tumor Prediction and Treatment

3.1   TP53 Genetic Testing and Ultra Early Warning Detection of Tumors

The TP53 gene is a tumor suppressor gene and is the most common mutated gene in human malignant tumors. Compared with the wild-type, the anti-tumor function of P53 protein in TP53 mutated individuals is reversed. In vivo experiments have confirmed that Trp53 gene knockout mice have a higher risk of developing cancer, so this gene is also considered a guardian of the human body. The detection of mutant TP53 can serve as a marker for early cancer detection, prediction, and prognosis.

3.2   The Impact of TP53 Gene on Cancer Treatment and Prognosis

The TP53 gene can be applied to the study of various tumor mechanisms, evaluate the diagnosis and treatment outcomes of tumors. A study published in January 2022 showed that mutations in the TP53 gene can be detected in non-small cell lung cancer tissue samples, with approximately 60% of patients experiencing mutations. Patients with TP53 gene mutations have poor response to radiotherapy and chemotherapy, are prone to metastasis, and can be used as a prognostic indicator for treatment effectiveness and prognosis [29].

As an important tumor suppressor gene, TP53 gene plays an important role in the occurrence and development of tumor cells, and has good application prospects. Preclinical trial studies have yielded positive results, such as the ability to inhibit the malignant phenotype of various solid tumors in humans by introducing the wild-type TP53 gene. Pharmacological methods that stimulate the function of wild-type P53 proteins or induce P53 mutant proteins to restore wild-type function are also being developed [30]. However, they are still in the exploratory stage and require further research on their mechanisms of action, so that to make TP53 gene therapy another promising method for tumor treatment.

4 TP53 Genetic Testing Service

The purpose of TP53 genetic testing is to provide a more comprehensive assessment of the cancer risk for individuals. Through TP53 genetic testing, the genetic carrying capacity and cancer suppression ability of tumors can be evaluated, helping individuals establish a scientific and reasonable lifestyle in a timely manner, and better grasp the initiative of health. TP53 genetic testing can help individuals actively avoid environmental risk factors that trigger tumors, making cancer prevention and treatment more targeted and organized.

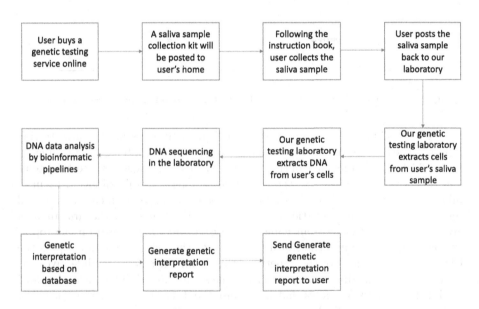

Fig. 1. The process of the TP53 Tumor Suppression Genetic Testing service.

We developed a "TP53 Tumor Suppression Genetic Testing" product to assess the cancer risk for individuals, and a personalized nutrition service to reduce the risk of cancer based on genetic testing result and lifestyle assessment questionnaire. The process of the genetic testing service is described in Firuge 1. The genetic testing service includes the genetic testing items of: Squamous Cell Carcinoma of the Head and Neck, Chronic Lymphocytic Leukemia, Bladder Cancer (male), Prostate Cancer (male), Ovarian Cancer (female), Breast Cancer (female), Pancreatic Cancer, Osteosarcoma, Esophageal Cancer, Lung Cancer,

Colorectal Cancer, Gastric Cancer, and Glioma. Each disease's risk score is calculated using genetic risk score (GRS) [31] algorithms or polygenic risk scores (PRS) [32] algorithms.

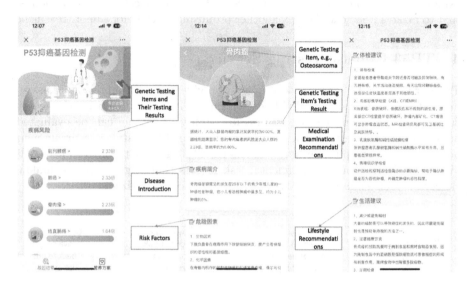

Fig. 2. The screen shots of the TP53 Tumor Suppression Genetic Testing report.

Figure 2 is the screen shots of the TP53 Tumor Suppression Genetic Testing report (since our customers are chinese, therefore the user interface is in chinese). Figure 2 left is the homepage of the report which lists all the genetic testing items and their testing results (*i.e.*, the risk of developing a certain disease). Figure 2 middle and right are the screen shots of the second level page which gives a detail testing result for each genetic testing item. In Fig. 2 middle, the first module gives the genetic testing item name (*e.g.*, Osteosarcoma disease) on the top of the page, and then gives the testing result (*e.g.*, the risk score of developing the Osteosarcoma disease) of the genetic testing item, the second module gives the introduction of the disease that describes the symptoms of the disease, the third module gives the risk factors that may cause the disease. In Fig. 2 right, the first module gives the medical examination recommendations that list the medical examination techniques and instruments to check the disease risk, the second module gives the lifestyle recommendations to reduce the risk of developing the corresponding disease.

5   The Interaction Between TP53 Gene and Nutrition and Its Impact on the Occurrence and Development of Cancer

There is a complex interaction between TP53 and nutritional metabolism. TP53 has been found to regulate energy metabolism and antioxidant defense, and metabolic changes are hallmarks of cancer cells. The rapid growth and division of cancer cells require precursors of energy and macromolecular metabolism [33, 34]. Nutritional status also affects the stability, expression level, and signaling pathway of TP53, thereby affecting the occurrence and development of cancer.

5.1   The Effect of TP53 Mutation on Nutritional Metabolism

TP53 and carbohydrate metabolism. The p53 has been found to regulate glycolysis, pentose phosphate pathway (PPP), mitochondrial oxidative phosphorylation, lipid and nucleotide metabolism, and importantly, to regulate cellular responses to oxidative stress [33].

TP53 and fat synthesis. Tumor cells strongly require the synthesis of fatty acids (FA) for rapid cell membrane production and intracellular signal transduction [33]. Wild type p53 can stimulate the expression of FAs in mitochondria β-Oxidize and block the biosynthesis of FAs acting on FASN (fatty acid synthase) and ACLY (ATP citrate lyase), thereby blocking the formation of new phospholipid membranes to support rapid growth and division of tumor cells.

5.2   The Effect of Nutritional Status on TP53 Gene

Vitamin C, as a powerful antioxidant, exhibits cytotoxic effects on cancer cells and is considered a dynamic chemotherapy agent for cancer patients [35]. Vitamin C promotes cancer cell apoptosis by regulating p53 [35]. Vitamin C activates SIRT1, leading to deacetylation of p53, dissociation of CBL-p53 complex, and ultimately leading to cell apoptosis. The presence of p53 can also affect the cytotoxicity of vitamin C [36]. The cytotoxicity of vitamin C is positively correlated with p53 expression, and the reactivation of p53 can make cancer cells more susceptible to oxidative stress, making them more sensitive to vitamin C and enhancing their cytotoxicity.

Vitamin D is involved in various biological processes, such as calcium homeostasis, cell proliferation, and differentiation, and has anti-tumor effects in various cancers, but its deficiency is associated with cancer risk [37]. Vitamin D and p53 signaling can protect cells from spontaneous or carcinogen induced malignant transformation [38]. The crosstalk between vitamin D and p53 signaling has been shown to occur at different levels, with a genome-wide impact, and is highly important for many malignant tumors, including non mucinous skin cancers. These interactions include p53 passing the POMC derivatives of α-MSH and ACTH upregulate the ability of skin pigmentation, protect the skin from UV induced DNA damage and skin photocarcinogenesis, but also inhibit the skin synthesis of vitamin D. In addition, the p53 status can determine the biological effects of vitamin D on cancer cells [38,39]. P53 and its family members are involved in the direct regulation of vitamin receptor (VDR) genes. The VDR responsive element (VDRE) is overexpressed in the promoter sequence that binds to mutant p53, increasing the accumulation of VDR in the nucleus. High levels of VDR in human cancer tissues and cancer cell lines indicate that vitamin D has more effective pharmacological effects on cancer cells [37]. In addition, mutant p53 can convert vitamin D3 from a pro apoptotic agent to an anti apoptotic agent, affecting the normal cell cycle and thus affecting the occurrence and development of cancer [39].

Vitamin B3 is associated with skin and mucosal protection, and vitamin B3 deficiency can lead to leprosy. In skin cancer patients, vitamin B3 deficiency and hypoxia-inducible factor-1α (HIF-1α) are positively correlated with the expression level of p53. After taking vitamin B3 orally for one week, the expression levels of HIF-1α and p53 in skin cancer patients' tissues were significantly reduced compared to before taking B3, while there was no significant change in the placebo group [40].

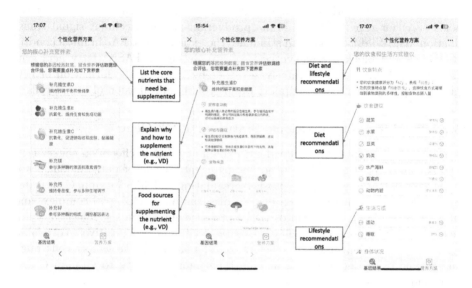

Fig. 3. The screen shots of the personalized nutrition report.

6   Personalized Nutrition Service

TP53 is an important tumor suppressor gene, and mutated TP53 genes with acquired functions not only lose their inhibitory effect on cancer, but may also be modified as promoting factors for cancer occurrence. There is a complex interaction between p53 and nutritional metabolism, which can regulate energy metabolism and antioxidant defense, providing energy and precursors of macromolecular metabolism for the rapid growth and division of cancer cells. The lack or excess of some nutrients can affect the stability, expression level, and TP53 signaling pathway of TP53 genes, thereby affecting the occurrence and development of cancer. The interaction between TP53 gene and nutrition should be considered in cancer prevention and treatment.

To reduce the risk of developing the diseases with high risk score, we further provide a personalized nutrition service based on the analysis of the genetic testing results and food frequency questionnaires FFQs [41]. Food frequency questionnaires is used to acquire individuals' diet situation and disease history, so that we can understand an individual's daily intake of nutrients. Combining the genetic data and diet data together, we calculate personalized nutrition supplementation solution for each individual.

Figure 3 demonstrates the screen shots of the personalized nutrition report. Figure 3 left lists the core nutrients that need be supplemented. Click the nutrient's name in Fig. 3 left, a drop down box will be opened as shown in Fig. 3 middle which explains why and how to supplement the nutrient (e.g., supplementing vitamin D can maintain calcium and phosphorus balance and bone health), and provides the food sources for supplementing the nutrient (e.g., the foods rich in vitamin D include trout, cheese, egg yolk, sardine, mushroom and etc.). In Fig. 3 right, the report gives the diet and lifestyle recommendations, the diet recommendations module suggests the personalized foods including vegetables, fruit, beans, dairy, seafood, meat, offal and etc., the lifestyle recommendation module gives suggestions for sports and sleep.

Based on our personalized nutrition supplementation solution, we can further produce nutrition box for each customer, that the customer can place the nutrition box order online, then our system will order the nutrition factory to produce customized nutrition box for each customer. Each customer will have his/her unique nutrition box, and each customer's name will printed on the box.

7 Conclusions

TP53 gene is closely related to the occurrence and development of tumors. In this paper we first introduced the TP53 gene and p53 protein, and we surveyed the relationship between TP53 gene and tumors. We developed a "TP53 Tumor Suppression Genetic Testing" product to assess the cancer risk for individuals to help individuals actively avoid environmental risk factors that trigger tumors, making cancer prevention and treatment more targeted and organized. Additionally, lifestyle is also closely related to disease, therefore apart from genetic testing data, we use food frequency questionnaire to understand individuals' diet situation and disease history, so that to provide a personalized nutrition service to reduce the risk of cancer based on genetic testing result and lifestyle data. The TP53 genetic testing service has been delivered online and has used by many customers.

In the near future, we will add physical examination data and sports watch data to our data model to provide more comprehensive personalized nutrition service for customers, so that to provide better service to reduce the risk of developing the diseases related to TP53 gene.

Acknowledgment. This research project is supported by Science Foundation of Beijing Language and Culture University (supported by "the Fundamental Research Funds for the Central Universities") (Approval number: 23YJ080003).

References

1. Kaur, R.P., Vasudeva, K., Kumar, R., Munshi, A.: Role of p53 gene in breast cancer: focus on mutation spectrum and therapeutic strategies. Curr. Pharm. Des. **24**(30), 3566–3575 (2018)
2. DeLeo, A.B., Jay, G., Appella, E., et al.: Detection of a transformation-related antigen in chemically induced sarcomas and other transformed cells of the mouse. Proc. Natl. Acad. Sci. U.S.A. **76**(5), 2420–4 (1979)
3. Levine, A.J., Oren, M.: The first 30 years of p53: growing ever more complex. Nat. Rev. Cancer **9**(10), 749–58 (2009)
4. Finlay, C.A., Hinds, P.W., Levine, A.J.: The p53 proto-oncogene can act as a suppressor of transformation. Cell **57**, 1083–1093 (1989)
5. Baugh, E.H., Ke, H., Levine, A.J., et al.: Why are there hotspot mutations in the TP53 gene in human cancers? Cell Death Differ. **25**(1), 154–160 (2018)
6. Lane, D.P.: p53, guardian of the genome. Nature **358**(6381), 15–6 (1992)
7. Donehower, L.A., Soussi, T., Korkut, A., et al.: Integrated analysis of TP53 gene and pathway alterations in the cancer genome atlas. Cell Rep. **28**(5), 1370-1384.e5 (2019)
8. Schneider, K., Zelley, K., Nichols, K.E., Garber, J.: Li-Fraumeni syndrome. In: Adam, M.P., et al. (eds.) GeneReviews [Internet]. University of Washington, Seattle, Seattle (WA) (1999). Accessed 21 Nov 2019
9. Olivier, M., Hollstein, M., Hainaut, P.: TP53 mutations in human cancers: origins, consequences, and clinical use. Cold Spring Harb. Perspect. Biol. **2**(1), a001008 (2010)
10. Petitjean, A., Mathe, E., Kato, S., et al.: Impact of mutant p53 functional properties on TP53 mutation patterns and tumor phenotype: lessons from recent developments in the IARC TP53 database. Hum. Mutat. **28**(6), 622–9 (2007)
11. Wang, Y., Helland, A., Holm, R., et al.: TP53 mutations in early-stage ovarian carcinoma, relation to long-term survival. Br. J. Cancer **90**, 678–685 (2004)
12. Langerod, A., Zhao, H., Borgan, O., et al.: TP53 mutation status and gene expression profiles are powerful prognostic markers of breast cancer. Breast Cancer Res. **9**, R30 (2007)
13. Li, F.P., Fraumeni, J.F.J., et al.: A cancer family syndrome in twenty-four kindreds. Cancer Res. **48**, 5358–5362 (1988)
14. Olivier, M., Goldgar, D.E., Sodha, N., et al.: Li-Fraumeni and related syndromes: correlation between tumor type, family structure, and TP53 genotype. Cancer Res. **63**, 6643–6650 (2003)
15. Lalloo, F., Varley, J., Moran, A., et al.: BRCA1, BRCA2 and TP53 mutations in very early-onset breast cancer with associated risks to relatives. Eur. J. Cancer **42**, 1143–1150 (2006)
16. Gonzalez, K.D., Noltner, K.A., Buzin, C.H., et al.: Beyond Li Fraumeni syndrome: clinical characteristics of families with p53 germline mutations. J. Clin. Oncol. **27**, 1250–1256 (2009)
17. Shi, H., Tan, S.J., Zhong, H., et al.: Winter temperature and UV are tightly linked to genetic changes in the p53 tumor suppressor pathway in Eastern Asia. Am. J. Hum. Genet. **84**, 534–541 (2009)
18. Mohammed Basabaeen, A.A., Abdelgader, E.A., Babekir, E.A., et al.: TP53 Gene 72 Arg/Pro (rs1042522) single nucleotide polymorphism contribute to increase the risk of B-Chronic lymphocytic leukemia in the Sudanese population. Asian Pac. J. Cancer Prev. **20**(5), 1579–1585 (2019)

19. Zhang, L., Wang, Y., Qin, Z., et al.: TP53 codon 72 Polymorphism and bladder cancer risk: a meta-analysis and emphasis on the role of tumor or smoking status. J. Cancer **9**(19), 3522–3531 (2018)
20. Lu, Y., et al.: Association of p53 codon 72 polymorphism with prostate cancer: an update meta-analysis. Tumor Biol. **35**(5), 3997–4005 (2014). https://doi.org/10.1007/s13277-014-1657-y
21. Wang, X., Liu, Z.: Systematic meta-analysis of genetic variants associated with osteosarcoma susceptibility. Medicine (Baltimore) **97**(38), e12525 (2018)
22. Naccarati, A., Pardini, B., Polakova, V., et al.: Genotype and haplotype analysis of TP53 gene and the risk of pancreatic cancer: an association study in the Czech Republic. Carcinogenesis **31**(4), 666–70 (2010)
23. Cao, J., Chen, Z., Tian, C., et al.: A shared susceptibility locus in the p53 gene for both gastric and esophageal cancers in a northwestern Chinese population. Genet. Test. Mol. Biomarkers **24**(12), 804–811 (2020)
24. Li, Y., Chang, S.C., Niu, R., et al.: TP53 genetic polymorphisms, interactions with lifestyle factors and lung cancer risk: a case control study in a Chinese population. BMC Cancer **13**, 607 (2013)
25. Egan, K.M., Nabors, L.B., Olson, J.J., et al.: Rare TP53 genetic variant associated with glioma risk and outcome. J. Med. Genet. **49**(7), 420–1 (2012)
26. Guan, X., Wang, L.E., Liu, Z., et al.: Association between a rare novel TP53 variant (rs78378222) and melanoma, squamous cell carcinoma of head and neck and lung cancer susceptibility in non-Hispanic Whites. J. Cell Mol. Med. **17**(7), 873–8 (2013)
27. Schildkraut, J.M., Iversen, E.S., Wilson, M.A., et al.: Association between DNA damage response and repair genes and risk of invasive serous ovarian cancer. PLoS ONE **5**(4), e10061 (2010)
28. Wang, S., Zhang, K., Tang, L., et al.: Association between single-nucleotide polymorphisms in breast cancer susceptibility genes and clinicopathological characteristics. Clin. Epidemiol. **13**, 103–112 (2021)
29. Zhao, Z., Wan, J., Guo, M., et al.: Expression and prognostic significance of m6A-related genes in TP53-mutant non-small-cell lung cancer. J. Clin. Lab. Anal. **36**(1), e24118 (2022)
30. Seemann, S., Maurici, D., Olivier, M., et al.: The tumor suppressor gene TP53: implications for cancer management and therapy. Crit. Rev. Clin. Lab. Sci. **41**(5–6), 551–83 (2004)
31. Igo, R.P., Jr., Kinzy, T.G., Cooke Bailey, J.N.: Genetic risk scores. Curr. Protoc. Hum. Genet. **104**(1), e95 (2019)
32. Ruan, Y., Lin, Y., Feng, Y., et al.: Improving polygenic prediction in ancestrally diverse populations. Nat. Genet. **54**, 57–3580 (2022)
33. Perri, F., Pisconti, S., Scarpati, G.D.V.: p53 mutations and cancer: a tight linkage. Ann. Transl. Med. **4**(24), 522 (2016)
34. Levine, A.J.: p53: 800 million years of evolution and 40 years of discovery. Nat. Rev. Cancer **20**, 471–480 (2020)
35. Xiong, Y., Xu, S., Fu, B., et al.: Vitamin C-induced competitive binding of HIF-1α and p53 to ubiquitin E3 ligase CBL contributes to anti-breast cancer progression through p53 deacetylation. Food Chem. Toxicol. **168**, 113321 (2022)
36. Kim, J., Lee, S.D., Chang, B., et al.: Enhanced antitumor activity of vitamin C via p53 in cancer cells. Free Radic. Biol. Med. **53**(8), 1607–15 (2012)
37. Li, M., Li, L., Zhang, L., et al.: 1,25-Dihydroxyvitamin D3 suppresses gastric cancer cell growth through VDR- and mutant p53-mediated induction of p21. Life Sci. **15**(179), 88–97 (2017)

38. Reichrath, J., Reichrath, S., Vogt, T., Romer, K.: Crosstalk between Vitamin D and p53 signaling in cancer: an update. Adv. Exp. Med. Biol. **1268**, 307–318 (2020)
39. Stambolsky, P., Tabach, Y., Fontemaggi, G.: Modulation of the vitamin D3 response by cancer-associated mutant p53. Cancer Cell **17**(3), 273–85 (2010)
40. Liu, T., Yang, H., Mou, Y., Zhang, H.: Correlation of changes in HIF-1α and p53 expressions with vitamin B3 deficiency in skin cancer patients. G. Ital. Dermatol. Venereol. **154**(5), 513–518 (2019)
41. Affret, A., El Fatouhi, D., Dow, C., et al.: Relative validity and reproducibility of a new 44-item diet and food frequency questionnaire among adults: online assessment. J. Med. Internet Res. **20**(7), e227 (2018)

Interdisciplinary Information Studies

Changes in the Adaptive Capacity of Livelihood Vulnerability to Climate Change in Ecuador's Tropical Commodity Crops: Banana and Cocoa

Elena Piedra-Bonilla$^{(\boxtimes)}$ ⓘ and Yosuny Echeverría ⓘ

Universidad Ecotec, Km 13 1/2 Vía Samborondón, Samborondón, Guayas, Ecuador
epiedrab@ecotec.edu.ec

Abstract. Climate change can cause negative impacts on agriculture. This paper aims to analyze the changes in the adaptive capacity of livelihood vulnerability to climate change in Ecuador's Tropical Commodity Crops: Banana and Cocoa. We used the adaptive capacity factor from the livelihood vulnerability index approach, using secondary data from the Survey of Agricultural and Livestock Surface and Production of Ecuador from 2020 to 2022. The results showed that for the banana crops, the livelihood strategy has remained stable, the sociodemographic profile was improving, and the social network got worse in 2021 during the pandemic. Regarding cocoa, the sociodemographic profile has the lowest values of the major components. Lastly, the adaptive capacity was much better in 2022 for both crops, so farmers were becoming more prepared for climate hazards, but they could have better improvement. The policy implications are that agricultural assistance and insurance access should be improved to reduce climate vulnerability.

Keywords: adaptive capacity · vulnerability · banana · cocoa · climate change

1 Introduction

Due to its potential socioeconomic impacts [1], climate change is one of society's most critical threats. Records of the average global temperature from 1860 to 2015 indicate that 1986–2005 was 0.63 °C warmer than 1850–1900, and 2006–2015 was 0.87 °C warmer than 1850–1900 [2]. Climate change could have more negative than positive effects on the agricultural sector because crops are susceptible to climate conditions [3]. According to Dell et al. [4], higher temperatures reduce agricultural output. So, it is crucial to develop adaptive mechanisms to reduce climatic risks.

In that sense, Ecuador also shows climatic evidence of these changes. For example, from 1960 to 2010, the Ecuadorian Coast presented, on average, a 33% increase in precipitation and a 0.6 °C increase in average temperature. In contrast, the Ecuadorian Amazon gave, on average, a 1% reduction in rainfall and a 0.9 °C increase in average temperature [5]. Both regions are producers of bananas and cocoa. Thus, climate change may impact the agricultural sector, as there are forecasts of temperature increases of up to 4 °C and increased precipitation throughout the country by 2050 [6]. For example,

H. Florez and M. Leon (Eds.): ICAI 2023, CCIS 1874, pp. 353–368, 2024.
https://doi.org/10.1007/978-3-031-46813-1_24

pessimistic scenarios indicate increased average annual rainfall in the equatorial Pacific [3].

The objective is to analyze the evolution of changes in the adaptive capacity of livelihood vulnerability to climate change in Ecuador's Tropical Commodity Crops: Banana and Cocoa.

2 Literature Review

Farmers' perceptions of climate variability are a complex process that includes a variety of psychological constructs, such as knowledge, beliefs, attitudes, and practices related to how the local climate has varied [7]. Farmers' perceptions, mitigation efforts, and tactics for adapting to climate change are influenced by socioeconomic, institutional, and environmental factors [8].

A study conducted in the Kenyan highlands identified socioeconomic, institutional, and environmental explanatory variables. The research shows six main determinants in three sets of predictors that influence farmers' perceptions of climate variability, including TLU, agricultural training, soil fertility status, soil erosion, and changes in farm production and planted forest cover as significant factors influencing perceptions of climate variability. Total TLU positively predicted farmers' perceptions of climate variability. This implied that smallholders with high TLU were likelier to perceive climate variability. Another significant variable was access to agricultural training; agricultural training impacts farmers with early warning systems and indicators of climate variability and agrarian information dissemination.

On the other hand, the findings show that education and group membership negatively influenced farmers' adoption of crop rotation, while arable land, agricultural training, soil fertility status, and soil erosion positively influenced adoption. However, the age of the household head and access to credit negatively influenced intercropping adoption, while household size, remittances, and changes in agricultural production positively influenced intercropping adoption. Unexpectedly, group membership and access to credit significantly and negatively affected farmers' adoption of crop rotation and intercropping, respectively. Smallholder farmers are faced with adopting strategies based on perceived benefits. Group membership might have influenced farmers to perceive crop rotation as having lower benefits. The gender of male household heads and access to credit were inversely related to barriers to adopting adaptation measures in smallholder agriculture for all agroecosystems. Education, crop diversification, extension services, land tenure, farmer group affiliation, dependence on external inputs, distance from the market, and risk experience showed the most robust relationships with barriers over the different agroecosystems in the study area [9].

Furthermore, in a study of 327 smallholder farmers in the Far Western Province, Nepal, most farmers reported higher barriers in most economic and techno-informational dimensions. Explanations for higher variance in adaptation barriers included gender of household head, access to credit, farming practice, and experience of climate risk, and these were inversely related to adaptation barriers. Variables with a positive relationship with borders included dependence on external inputs, dependence on monsoon rains, off-farm income, and distance to market. Variables such as household size, farm size, land tenure, and distance to market did not show a significant relationship with barriers. Correlation analysis showed mainly an important inverse relationship between farm management and economic and environmental obstacles for all agroecosystems [10].

Another study of 200 farmers in Hainan, China, revealed that the farmer's age is essential in determining adaptive behavior. The coefficient of age is negative, which shows that as the farmer's age increases, his adaptive attitude decreases. The coefficient of gender was significant and positive, indicating that the adaptive behavior of farmers is different for male and female farmers; therefore, gender differences affect the adoption of adaptations differently: the probability of adopting adaptations is higher for male farmers than for female farmers. In addition, the coefficient of non-farm income positively affects farmers' adaptation behaviors, indicating that wealthier farmers present a more remarkable ability to purchase and plant new varieties and better planning horizons. On the other hand, farmers' training coefficients and their access to credit are positive. The study also inferred that perceived changes in temperature, precipitation, rainfall, and flooding significantly affect farmers' adaptation behavior positively, suggesting that if farmers are aware of the threats of climate change, it would be an essential determinant for taking agricultural adaptation measures [11].

Another study carried out in Brazil indicates that most farmers (38.6%) have less than five agricultural hectares; therefore, with such a small area, it is more difficult to obtain a financial return, which causes a limited propensity adaptive due to its reduced financial capacity. It also mentions that about 28% of farmers had access to agricultural credit in the last year; this access allows the producer to achieve adaptation mechanisms to climate change and allows the use of new technologies, such as crop diversification [12].

Research involving 200 households in Mozambique in the districts of Moma and Mabote identified regarding access to credit that more than 92% of households said that they had not approached their local government for help in the last month. Mabote households reported borrowing money more frequently and receiving more in-kind assistance from family and friends relative to the number of times they lent or provided assistance in the past month than Moma households. In addition, with an agriculture dependency index of 0.312, there is a high percentage of households in Moma where their income depends solely on agriculture on average. In Mozambique, household heads farmed for 21.7 ± 14.4 years, raising animals for 6.8 ± 7.0 years, and natural resource harvesting for 6.8 ± 11.1 years as ways of coping with variable rainfall [13].

An additional study carried out in the municipalities of Brazil [14] studies the influence of climate variability on categories of crop diversification; the research shows that the membership does not significantly relate these categories to groups, irrigation, and population density, Non-farm income, access to credit, and women farmers. In addition, the likelihood of municipalities falling into the Very Diversified group was negatively impacted by technical support, average size, asset index, and youthful producers between 25 and 45 years old. Therefore, due to their expertise and established practices, older farmers may be more likely to enhance crop diversification.

Ecuador is highly vulnerable to climate change because of its geographical and climatic diversity, sensitivity to periodic El Niño and La Niña events, reliance on rapidly diminishing glaciers, and sensitive highland wetlands [15]. Given these challenges, the peasant Social Security SSC protects the Ecuadorian rural population, which is a special regime of Mandatory Universal Insurance for independent agricultural workers and artisanal fishermen.

3 Methodology

3.1 Study Area

Since before being considered a Republic, Ecuador was already an agro-exporting country, the experience of the cocoa and banana boom led to an exploitation of the comparative advantages that have allowed it to be considered one of the economies with more resources in the fifties until the seventies, placing it among the main competitors of banana fruit, followed by cocoa. One of the most representative activities within the economy of Ecuador is the cultivation of bananas, which is of great importance for the country's economic development. The banana sector figures as the second item of non-oil exports, reaching 104,731,409 banana boxes exported during the first quarter of 2020, according to the report of the Association of Banana Exporters of Ecuador [16], which implies an increase of 9.92% compared to 2019 in the same period, where the first three months of the year presented a higher export volume than in 2019, exceeding in each of them the 30 million banana boxes. On the other hand, Ecuador is the world's leading producer of fine and flavor cocoa, accounting for 70% of the world's total, followed by Indonesia with only 10% [17]. This type of cocoa is used to prepare select and gourmet chocolates internationally to be qualified as the best in the world [18]. Because of this recognition, the bean is highly coveted and is in great demand in international markets.

To illustrate the economic importance of bananas and cocoa in Ecuadorian exports, it can be seen in Fig. 1 that the agricultural shares of these two products add up to more than 60% from 2018 to 2021. Additionally, traditional agricultural exports (36.8% of total exports), such as bananas, cocoa, coffee, shrimp, and tuna, will match oil exports (36.8% of total exports from January-July in 2021 in Ecuador [19]. However, for the first quarter of 2020 and 2021, traditional exports exceeded oil exports in FOB value by 22.12% and 2.75%, respectively. Therefore, these agricultural products are paramount for foreign trade and the country's foreign exchange generation.

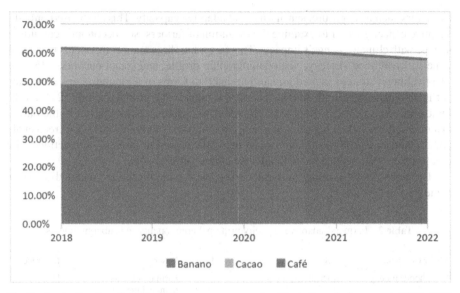

Fig. 1. Agricultural participation of bananas, cocoa, and coffee in Ecuadorian exports 2018–2022. Source: SIPA, 2022

3.2 Source of Data

The data source is the Survey of Agricultural and Livestock Surface and Production (ESPAC) of the National Institute of Statistics and Census (INEC). The ESPAC is a survey that provides information on Ecuadorian agricultural production for an annual period with provincial and national statistical representativeness. It used the Multiple Sampling Framework with a sample of 3,469 Agricultural Production Units (UPA) [20]. The crops used in this survey are bananas for export (*Musa × paradisiaca*) and cocoa bean (*Theobroma cacao L.*) CCN51 variety. The data available for the variables for analysis were from 2020 to 2022. However, the number of banana and cocoa farms varies in the different study periods (Table 1).

Table 1. Representative samples of farms from the ESPAC survey (2020–2022)

Year	Banana farms	Cocoa farms
2020	481	2490
2021	506	3302
2022	506	3315

3.3 Data Analysis

The livelihood vulnerability index (LVI) approach, developed by a study in Africa [13], was used to study adaptive capacity. According to IPCC [2], vulnerability is influenced by factors such as exposure, sensitivity, and adaptive capacity. This study used only the adaptive capacity factor to examine the evolution of farmers' socioeconomic conditions to cope with climate change's impacts. This factor has three main components that determine it: Livelihood strategy, Sociodemographic profile, and social networks [13, 21]. The livelihood strategy is predominantly related to forms of agricultural diversification but is also associated with sources of income outside the productive unit [21]. At the same time, the sociodemographic profile refers to different characteristics of the farmer that may influence their capacity to manage the impacts of climate change (Aroca et al., 2022; Hahn et al., 2009). Finally, social networks represent farmers' interactions with groups or institutions to cope with adverse climate effects [21].

The variables describing the farmer's socioeconomic profile are detailed below in Table 2:

Table 2. Farmers' adaptive capacity principal components and subcomponents

Major Component	Subcomponent	Unity	Description	References
Livelihood strategy	Diversification	%	Farm production is a monoculture	[13]
	Family labor	%	Farms that have only family labor	
	No Legal status of the property	%	Farms that do not own the land	[12]
Sociodemographic profile	Dependency ratio	%	Percentage of dependent people ($<$ 15 years and $>$ 65 years old)	[21]
	Schooling	%	Farmers have not attended secondary school	[21]
	Gender	%	Women head of household	
	Culture	%	Farmers who define themselves as indigenous or *montubios*[1]	
Social Network	No access to government agricultural kit[2]	%	Farms that have not received an agricultural extension	
	No access to the internet	%	Farms with no access to the internet	
	No Social Security	%	Farms with no social security	
	No access to agricultural insurance	%	Farms with no access to credit	

Various subcomponents embrace each major component for the analysis [21]. Nevertheless, since each subcomponent is assessed using a distinct scale, it becomes essential

---

[1] The *Montubios* have cultural characteristics and customs typical of the Ecuadorian coastal peasantry. It is a minority group of the Ecuadorian population.

[2] The government agricultural kits include subsidized products such as seeds, fertilizers, and agro-inputs.

to normalize each into an index. The index standardization ($index_{S_d}$) is the ratio of the difference between the observed value and the minimum value of the subcomponent and the range of maximum and minimum values of this [13]:

$$index_{S_{djt}} = \frac{S_{djt} - S_{mint}}{S_{maxt} - S_{mint}} \tag{1}$$

where S_d is the observed value of the subcomponent in d province, of j crop, in t year; S_{min} and S_{max} are the minimum and maximum values for each subcomponent determined using data from the total provinces in t year. For subcomponents with relative values such as 'Percentage of farmers with no access to the internet,' the minimum and maximum values were set at 0 and 100, respectively.

After calculating the index standardization, the value of each major component ($M_{d_{it}}$) for d province, of j crop, in t year is calculated through the subcomponents averaged:

$$M_{d_{ijt}} = \frac{\sum_{i=1}^{n} index_{S_{dijt}}}{n} \tag{2}$$

where the $index_{S_{dijt}}$ represents the index standardization of the i subcomponent by d province, of j crop, in t year, that make up each major component and n is the number of subcomponents in each major component.

Finally, the livelihood vulnerability of adaptive capacity ($LV - AC_{d_{jt}}$) is calculated by the weighted average of the three seven major components, for d province, of j crop, in t year:

$$LV - AC_{d_{jt}} = \frac{\sum_{i}^{m} W_{mi} M_{d_{ijt}}}{\sum_{i}^{m} W_{mi}} \tag{3}$$

where W_{mi} is the weight of each major component, determined by the number of subcomponents that make up each major component, to confirm the equal contribution of all subcomponents to calculating the livelihood vulnerability of adaptive capacity. For this research, adaptive capacity was scaled from 0 (high adaptive capacity) to 1 (least adaptive capacity).

It should be noted that vulnerability studies are usually conducted on primary and cross-sectional data [13, 21]. This study conducted a vulnerability analysis with secondary and panel data to show changes over the period. This was a complex process since dealing with databases from different years meant having different database formats and not having standardized variable names. For this, the data was accurate in the software Stata 18, and the process of the maps in the software Qgis 3.22.7.

For time series analysis, secondary data need to be of high quality, maintaining the same sampling methodologies and questionnaires, as missing variables make it impossible to study changes in vulnerability.

4 Results and Discussion

4.1 Evolution of Harvested Area and Yield

Cocoa has the largest planted area, with an average of 228 thousand hectares. Cultivated bananas had an area of approximately 158 thousand hectares (Table 3). Then, it is observed that the average banana yield was 31.16 mt/ha, which would rank lower than Guatemala (47.85 mt/ha), Costa Rica (46.85 mt/ha), and the Philippines (31.75 mt/ha) [22]. Likewise, the Ecuadorian cocoa yield (0.46 mt/ha) would be after Peru (0.94 mt/ha) and Ghana (0.55 mt/ha) [22].

Table 3. Descriptive statistics on means of harvested area, production, and yield 2018–2021

Variable	Unit	Banana	Cocoa
Harvested area	ha	158,045.28	227,741.91
Production	mt	6,478,255.25	121,077.53
Yield	mt/ha	31.16	0.46

Note: ha = hectare. mt = metric tons
Source: Research results

According to Fig. 2, about the evolution of the harvested area, it is observed that banana crops did not maintain a trend but had a growth peak in 2019. In the case of cocoa, it had moderate growth in the harvested area; however, it was an atypical year in 2018.

On the other hand, export banana yields have mostly stayed the same throughout the study period. In the case of cocoa, it is observed that the yield has a slight decrease.

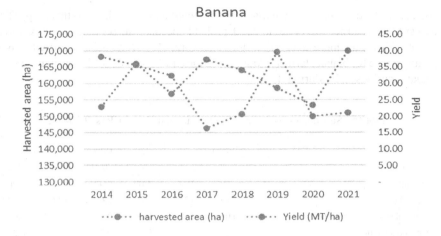

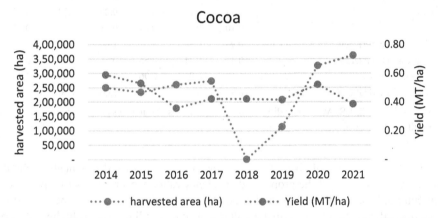

Fig. 2. Evolution of harvested area, production, and yield of banana and cocoa (2018–2021)

4.2 Evolution of Livelihood Vulnerability in the Adaptive Capacity of Banana and Cocoa

The values of the subcomponents for bananas and cocoa for 2020 to 2022 are presented in Table 4. The results of banana farmers showed that many subcomponents, such as diversification, the legal status of the property, government agricultural kit, and agricultural insurance, have not changed. However, the banana crop is more of a monoculture, making it more vulnerable to climate risks. The legal status showed that most of the farmers owned the property. Then, access to the governmental agricultural kit is low, like farm insurance. These public policies were part of the *Gran Minga Agropecuaria* Program that lasted until 2021 because it was a policy of the government in power [23]. The rest of the subcomponents have varied during the period. Family labor was reduced in the final period. The percentage of dependent people has increased a little bit. The schooling levels have increased for banana farmers. Few women farmers are dedicated to banana production, and scarce indigenous and *montubios* are related to this crop. Then, access to the Internet was better in 2020, probably because the pandemic context forced people to look for more integration in the network. However, social security has been getting worse for banana farmers. Many Ecuadorian workers stopped contributing to the social security system during the pandemic.

Table 4. Subcomponents values for Bananas and Cocoa UPAs 2020–2022

Subcomponent	Banana			Cocoa		
	2020	2021	2022	2020	2021	2022
Diversification	1.00	0.97	1.00	0.90	0.91	0.90
Family labor	0.16	0.21	0.08	0.68	0.78	0.70
No Legal status of the property	0.05	0.06	0.06	0.03	0.05	0.04
Dependency ratio	0.20	0.27	0.26	0.28	0.27	0.26
Schooling	0.43	0.36	0.28	0.69	0.74	0.70
Gender	0.17	0.14	0.14	0.23	0.24	0.24
Culture	0.10	0.04	0.04	0.41	0.37	0.34
No access to government agricultural kit a	0.90	0.89	–	1.00	0.99	–
No access to the internet	0.41	0.71	0.56	0.75	0.83	0.79
No Social Security	0.82	0.92	0.96	0.68	0.69	0.70
No access to agricultural insurance, a	0.85	0.82	–	1.00	1.00	–

Note: a – The 2022 ESPAC survey did not include questions about access to governmental kit and agricultural insurance

Instead, the results of cocoa farmers showed that values for diversification, family labor, the legal status of the property, dependency ratio, gender, access to government agricultural kits, social security, and agricultural insurance stayed the same. Nevertheless, diversification and access to agricultural insurance still need to be higher. Most of the farmers owned the properties. There are more indigenous and *montubios* farmers in the cocoa crops. Access to the internet was better in 2021, too. However, any cocoa farmer can access agricultural kits and insurance, so they could not benefit from the *Gran Minga Agropecuaria* Program.

The results of the major components and adaptive capacity from both crops are presented in Table 5. For the banana crops, the livelihood strategy has remained stable. The sociodemographic profile of banana farmers was improving, probably because the schooling level was improved. The social network got worse in 2021 during the pandemic. Lastly, the adaptive capacity was much better in 2022, so banana farmers are becoming more prepared for climate hazards.

Regarding cocoa farmers, the livelihood strategy got worse in 2021 but could perform better in 2022. The sociodemographic profile has the lowest values of the major components and was reduced in 2022. Social network values were decreasing, so this major component was improving. Again, the adaptive capacity was better in 2022.

Table 5. Major Components values for Bananas and Cocos UPAs 2020–2022

Major component	Banana			Cocoa		
	2020	2021	2022	2020	2021	2022
Livelihood strategy	0.40	0.41	0.38	0.54	0.58	0.55
Sociodemographic profile	0.23	0.20	0.18	0.40	0.40	0.38
Social Network	0.74	0.84	0.76	0.86	0.88	0.74
Adaptive Capacity	0.46	0.49	0.31	0.60	0.62	0.42

In Fig. 3, it is shown that social network has the worst performance in both crops, livelihood strategy, and socio-demographic profile. It also shows that the major components have remained the same for a long time. Nevertheless, these results are from the country level. There are differences when the results are shown by province (Fig. 4). For example, Carchi and Manabí provinces had the least capacity for banana crops in 2020 and 2021, respectively. In 2022, Chimborazo province has the least adaptive capacity for banana crops.

Regarding cocoa, almost all provinces had this crop production. The Napo province had the worst performance in adaptive capacity in 2020 and 2021. In 2021, Cañar also did poorly in adaptive capacity. Nevertheless, both crops had better performance in adaptive capacity in 2022. Nevertheless, both crops had better performance in adaptive capacity in 2022.

Vulnerability studies help to support policies to reduce the adverse effects of climate shocks. This study contributes to the planning of climate change adaptation programs, showing the need to improve aspects such as schooling level, access to information, agricultural insurance, and social security. Thus, these programs require the transversal participation of several public and private institutions linked to education, agriculture, connectivity, and financing, especially for the provinces with less adaptive capacity. Likewise, agricultural programs that provide kits are insufficient to generate adaptive capacities if producers have low social and financial conditions to withstand climate shocks.

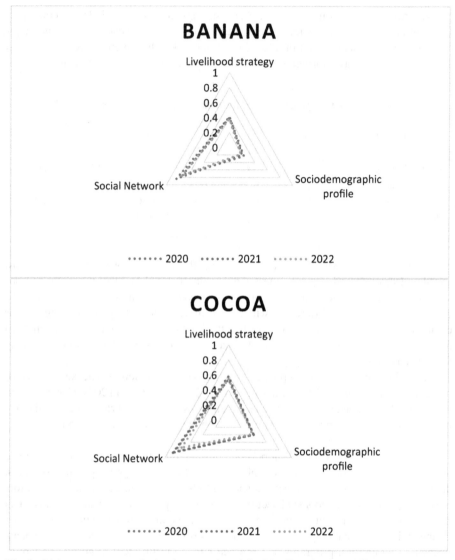

Fig. 3. Major components of adaptive capacity of the Livelihood vulnerability for banana and cocoa, 2020 – 2022.

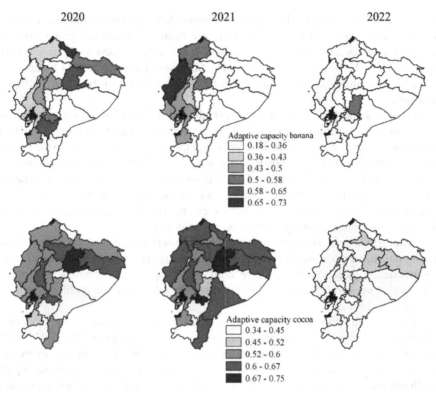

Fig. 4. Adaptive capacity of the Livelihood vulnerability for banana and cocoa, 2020 – 2022.

5 Conclusion

This study proposed to analyze the changes in the adaptive capacity of the vulnerability of livelihoods to climate change of Ecuadorian banana and cocoa producers from 2020 to 2022. These two products were considered because they are the essential staples in Ecuador's traditional non-oil exports and have a share of more than 60% of exports. Climate change may have more negative than positive effects on crops because they are susceptible to weather conditions. Therefore, understanding the evolution of the socioeconomic conditions of Ecuadorian farmers allows us to understand the limitations and strengths they have as producers to face the impacts of climate change. The adaptive capacity factor was identified with three main components that determine it: Livelihood strategy, Sociodemographic profile, and social networks available within the study area.

This research showed that Cocoa has the largest planted area, with an average of 228 thousand hectares. Cultivated bananas had an area of approximately 158 thousand hectares. On the other hand, export banana yields have varied little throughout the study period, but in the case of cocoa, it is observed that the yield has a slight decrease. The results show that the farmers of these two agro-export products are going through a phenomenon of masculinization and aging in the rural area, which could compromise the continuity of production. The banana crop is more of a monoculture, making it more vulnerable to climate risks. The results of banana farmers showed that the schooling levels have increased, few women farmers are dedicated to banana production, and scarce indigenous and *montubios* are related to this crop. Access to the Internet was better in 2020. However, social security has been worsening for banana farmers, and many Ecuadorian workers stopped contributing to the social security system during the pandemic.

Instead, the results of cocoa farmers showed that diversification and access to agricultural insurance still need to be higher. Most of the farmers owned the properties, and there were more indigenous and *montubios* farmers in the cocoa crops. Access to the internet was better in 2021, but any cocoa farmer can access agricultural kits and insurance, so they could not benefit from the *Gran Minga Agropecuaria* Program. Lastly, the adaptive capacity was much better in 2022, so banana and cocoa farmers are becoming more prepared for climate hazards; however, the social network has the worst performance in both crops, livelihood strategy, and sociodemographic profile.

About policies, the first step is to have public institutions that generate accessible and quality data to carry out studies related to vulnerability. This information will allow the construction of indices, which must be validated. Thus, the results will help formulate policies that need to be transversal to improve socio-demographic profiles, livelihood strategies, and social networks.

In conclusion, this research can serve as a basis for studies related to the production of bananas and cocoa and the competitiveness of national production. The results imply that knowledge is critical to involve farmers in superior forms of production where they can improve the cultivation of their products. As communities face the genuine impacts of climate change, adaptation measures have a high stake, and intervention is essential.

Acknowledgments. The authors gratefully acknowledge comments and suggestions by the anonymous reviewers. The authors thank Nancy Johnson for the thoughtful suggestions on the manuscript versions. Author EPB gratefully acknowledges the Mentoring Program for Women Agricultural Economists in the Global South, which is a collaboration of African Women in Agricultural Research and Development (AWARD) and the International Association of Agricultural Economics (IAAE) through its International Committee of Women in Agricultural Economics (ICWAE).

This study was part of the research project "Estimation of the impact of extreme weather on the performance of Ecuador's agro-export sector," funded by Ecotec University.

References

1. Dell, M., Jones, B.F., Olken, B.A.: What do we learn from the weather? The new climate-economy literature, J. Econ. Lit. **52**(3), 740–798 (2014). https://doi.org/10.1257/jel.52.3.740
2. Allen, M.R., et al.: Framing and context. In: Global Warming of 1.5°C. An IPCC Special Report on the impacts of global warming of 1.5°C above pre-industrial levels and related global greenhouse gas emission pathways, in the context of strengthening the global response to the threat of climate change, sustainable development, and efforts to eradicate poverty [Masson-Delmotte, V., et al. (eds.)]. Cambridge University Press, Cambridge, UK and New York, NY, USA, pp. 49–92 (2018). https://doi.org/10.1017/9781009157940.003

3. IPCC.: Climate Change 2014: Synthesis Report. Contribution of Working Groups I, II, and III to the Fifth Assessment Report of the Intergovernmental Panel on Climate Change [Core Writing Team, R.K. Pachauri and L.A. Meyer (eds.)]. IPCC, Geneva, Switzerland, p. 151 (2014)
4. Dell, M., Jones, B., Olken, B.: Temperature shocks and economic growth: evidence from the last half century. Am. Econ. J.: Macroecon. **4**(3), 66–95 (2012)
5. Ministerio del Ambiente, Agua y Transición Ecológica, "Tercera Comunicación Nacional del Ecuador a la Convención Marco de las Naciones Unidas sobre el Cambio Climático" (2017). https://www.ambiente.gob.ec/tercera-comunicacion-nacional-del-ecuador/ (accedido 16 de julio de 2023)
6. BID, "Vulnerability to Climate Change and Economic Impacts in the Agriculture Sector in Latin America and the Caribbean I Publications" (2020). https://publications.iadb.org/public ations/english/viewer/Vulnerability-to-Climate-Change-and-Economic-Impacts-in-the-Agr iculture-Sector-in-Latin-America-and-the-Caribbean.pdf (accedido 16 de julio de 2023)
7. Whitmarsh, L., Capstick, S.: Perceptions of climate change, in Psychology and climate change: human perceptions, impacts, and responses, San Diego, CA, US: Elsevier Academic Press, pp. 13–33 (2018)
8. Mango, N., et al.: Awareness and adoption of land, soil and water conservation practices in the Chinyanja Triangle. South. Afr. Int. Soil Water Conserv. Res. **5**(2), 122–129 (2017)
9. Mairura, F., et al.: Determinants of farmers' perceptions of climate variability, mitigation, and adaptation strategies in the central highlands of Kenya. Weather, Clim. Extremes **34**, 100374 (2021)
10. Lamichhane, P., et al.: What motivates smallholder farmers to adapt to climate change? Insights from smallholder cropping in far-western Nepal. Anthropocene **40**, 100355 (2022)
11. Gao, J., et al.: Climate change resilience and sustainable tropical agriculture: farmers perceptions, reactive adaptations and determinants of reactive adaptations in Hainan. Atmosphere **13**(6), Art. n° 6, China (2022). https://doi.org/10.3390/atmos13060955
12. Piedra-Bonilla, E., Cunha, D., Braga, M.: Diversificação agrícola na bacia hidrográfica do Rio das Contas. Bahia Geosul **34**, 280–306 (2019)
13. Hahn, M., Riederer, A., Foster, S.: The Livelihood Vulnerability Index: a pragmatic approach to assessing risks from climate variability and change—A case study in Mozambique. Glob. Environ. Change **19**(1), 74–88 (2009)
14. Piedra-Bonilla, E.B., da Cunha, D.A., Braga, M.J.: Climate variability and crop diversification in Brazil: An ordered probit analysis. J. Cleaner Prod. **256**, 120252 (2020)
15. Mills-Novoa, M., et al.: Governmentalities, hydrosocial territories & recognition politics: the making of objects and subjects for climate change adaptation in Ecuador. Geoforum **115**, 90–101 (2020)
16. Asociación de Exportadores de Banano del Ecuador: Informe I Trimestre 2020, AEBE, vol. 141 (2020)
17. Instituto de Promoción de Exportaciones e Inversiones, Dirección de Inteligencia Comercial e Inversiones – PRO ECUADOR. https://www.proecuador.gob.ec/estudios-de-inteligencia-comercial/. Accessed 03 Sep 2023
18. Ministerio de Agricultura y Ganadería. MAGAP impulsa proyecto de reactivación del Cacao Fino y de Aroma (2017). https://www.agricultura.gob.ec/magap-impulsa-proyecto-de-reacti vacion-del-cacao-fino-y-de-aroma/. Accessed 03 Sep 2023
19. Central Bank of Ecuador, Evolution of the Trade Balance by Products January -June 2022
20. INEC: Encuesta de Superficie y Producción Agropecuaria Continua (ESPAC): Metodología (2022)
21. Arifah, D., Salman, Yassi, A., Demmallino. E.: Livelihood vulnerability of smallholder farmers to climate change: a comparative analysis based on irrigation access in South Sulawesi, Indonesia. Reg. Sustain. **3**(3), 244–253 (2022)

Context and Characteristics of Software Related to Ecuadorian Scientific Production: A Bibliometric and Content Analysis Study

Marcos Espinoza-Mina(✉) ⓘ, Alejandra Colina Vargas ⓘ, and Javier Berrezueta Varas

Ecotec University, Samborondón, Ecuador
mespinoza@ecotec.edu.ec

Abstract. In view of the predominance of Information Technologies in different contexts, it is known that the use of software and data in the field of scientific research has increased; however, it is not possible to clearly determine the environment and the use given to them. The present study proposes a bibliometric and content analysis of publications with Ecuadorian affiliation, which allows us to recognize the characteristics and context of the use of software as a work tool. The study was developed in four stages: selection of documents, bibliometric analysis, network analysis and content analysis. A total of 4028 documents were extracted from the WoS and Scopus databases, analyzing 117 at the content level. Among the main tools used were R Studio, VOSviewer and QualCoder. Among the institutions generating this production are the Universidad Politécnica ESPOL, the Universidad Politécnica Salesiana and the Universidad de las Fuerzas Armadas ESPE. There is a high rate of collaboration with Spanish authors. Finally, the studies are strongly oriented towards "Professional, scientific and technical activities", are of the "Experimental" type, and have mainly referred specifically to proprietary software.

Keywords: Ecuadorian research · software · authorship · affiliation

1 Introduction

Today's environment is dominated by Information Technology (IT). Specialists have the central task of strategically and accurately identifying those areas that can potentially improve their efficiency, with the support offered by hardware, software or new IT-related value-added services [1].

In the field of scientific research, the use of software and digital data has increased significantly in recent years. There are many domain-specific peculiarities in the use of software by researchers; both the amount and the purpose of its application vary significantly [2]. Unfortunately, although citation standards exist, there is no rigor in software citation practices in scientific production [3]. This makes automatic detection and unambiguous removal of software mentions a problem for your study [2].

Bibliometrics provides information on a topic, the trend of future research, critical points of research, scientific collaborations, among other things [4]. However, it is

© The Author(s), under exclusive license to Springer Nature Switzerland AG 2024
H. Florez and M. Leon (Eds.): ICAI 2023, CCIS 1874, pp. 369–389, 2024.
https://doi.org/10.1007/978-3-031-46813-1_25

not enough to know only the bibliometric attributes of a subject when conducting a tecnological assessment, or the assessment of other disciplines [5].

Content analysis is a research technique that provides answers to open-ended questions. The words and phrases mentioned in a document reflect important contents; however, they may also involve multiple meanings. Therefore, in order to achieve the reliability of this technique, it is necessary to ensure the correct organization of the significant contents in codes and categories, together with an adequate structuring of the results of this process [6]. The objective of this research was to carry out a bibliometric study strengthened with the content analysis of publications with Ecuadorian affiliation, which allows the recognition of the characteristics and the context of the use of software as a technological and scientific tool.

2 Methodology

According to the topic of interest to be worked on, a method for the development of the research is established. Based on the definitions and adoptions of [7] and [8], the scheme and steps required for the development of a bibliometric study with content analysis are shown in Fig. 1. Several computer tools were used in the different stages. For document selection and bibliometric analysis, mainly the R Studio software and the Bibliometrix package were used. VOSviewer software was used for network analysis and QualCoder for content analysis.

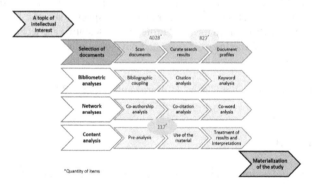

Fig. 1. Method for bibliometric study with content analysis

3 Results

The results of the study are organized below according to the four stages defined in the method, which are: document selection, bibliometric analysis, network analysis, and content analysis.

3.1 Selection of Documents

3.1.1 Scan Documents

In February 2023, the records of the scientific production of Ecuador related to software were consulted from the Web of Science (WoS) and Scopus databases. The word "software" was searched for in the title, abstract and keywords, of the scientific production of the last ten years, that is, from 2013 to 2022, with the filter by country of Ecuador. This search generated 1691 results in WoS and 2337 in Scopus.

3.1.2 Curate Search Results

Two filters were added to the extracted documents, the first by "type of document", restricting it exclusively to articles, and the second by "type of access", so that only open access documents would be shown in the list. Finally, a total of 377 WoS articles and 450 Scopus articles remained, whose references were exported to files with ".bib", ".csv" and ".txt" extensions for further processing.

3.1.3 Documents Profiles

Within the study period from 2013 to 2022, it can be observed that the annual production recorded is variable, and there is a positive trend (see Fig. 2). The growth rates were: for WoS 45.74%, and for Scopus 44.81%. The latter database regularly surpasses WoS in the number of annual papers.

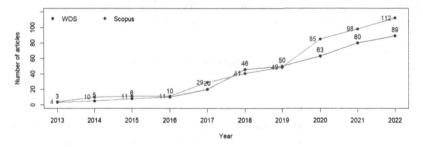

Fig. 2. Total articles per year for WoS and Scopus

Although the scientific production analyzed was selected with a filter by country of Ecuador, affiliations from 39 other countries were identified. Due to the filter, Ecuador heads the list of the country with the highest number of articles. Likewise, the rest of the countries have a solid international collaboration (inter-country index above 0.50), i.e. with Ecuador. Spain, USA, Chile and Mexico stand out in terms of number of articles. See details in Table 1.

Table 1. Top ten countries by number of articles

WoS						Scopus					
A	B	C	D	E	F	A	B	C	D	E	F
Ecuador	217	0.57713	94	123	0.567	Ecuador	208	0.5826	71	137	0.659
Spain	61	0.16223	0	61	1.000	Spain	50	0.1401	0	50	1.000
Usa	14	0.03723	0	14	1.000	Chile	15	0.0420	0	15	1.000
Chile	11	0.02926	0	11	1.000	Usa	11	0.0308	0	11	1.000
Mexico	7	0.01862	0	7	1.000	Mexico	7	0.0196	0	7	1.000
Argentina	5	0.01330	0	5	1.000	Italy	6	0.0168	0	6	1.000
Peru	5	0.01330	0	5	1.000	Argentina	5	0.0140	0	5	1.000
Colombia	4	0.01064	0	4	1.000	Brazil	5	0.0140	0	5	1.000
United Kingdom	4	0.01064	0	4	1.000	Colombia	5	0.0140	0	5	1.000
Brazil	3	0.00798	0	3	1.000	Cuba	4	0.0112	0	4	1.000

(A) Country (B) Articles (C) Frequency (D) Intra-country collaboration index (E) Inter-country collaboration index (F) Inter-country relationship.

A total of 1296 different affiliations are reported for WoS and 1262 in Scopus. Table 2 shows the 10 institutions with the highest number of registered articles. The count depends on the affiliation of each of the authors involved in a scientific production; due to this, the list also includes foreign institutions, in addition to the Ecuadorian ones. Among the Ecuadorian institutions are ESPOL Polytechnic University, Universidad Politécnica Salesiana, Universidad de las Fuerzas Armadas ESPE, Universidad de las Américas, Universidad San Francisco de Quito, and Universidad de Cuenca.

Table 2. Top ten institutions by number of articles

WoS			Scopus		
A	B	C	A	B	C
Espol Polytech Univ	83	0.02786	Espol Polytechnic University	57	0.02205
Univ Politecn Salesiana	45	0.01510	Univ Politécnica De Madrid	31	0.01199
Univ Fuerzas Armadas Espe	40	0.01342	Univ De Las Américas	30	0.01160
Univ Politecn Madrid	40	0.01342	Univ Fuerzas Armadas Espe	29	0.01121
Univ Cuenca	38	0.01275	Univ San Francisco De Quito	27	0.01044
Univ San Francisco Quito	35	0.01174	Universidad De Cuenca	26	0.01005
Univ Las Américas	26	0.00872	Univ Técnica Particular De Loja	24	0.00928
Univ Politecn Valencia	26	0.00872	Univ Politécnica Salesiana	23	0.00889
Univ Tecn Particular Loja	25	0.00839	Univ Técnica De Manabí	18	0.00696
Univ Tecn Manabi	21	0.00704	University Of California	17	0.00657

(A) Affiliations (B) Number of articles (C) Proportion.

3.2 Bibliometric Analysis

3.2.1 Bibliographic Coupling

The "Bibliographic Coupling Network Analysis" function of VOSviewer returns the number of citations received by an author, when using "author" as the unit of analysis [9]. For the required calculation the default author thesaurus of VOSviewer was used. Within the selection criteria, the minimum number of documents of an author is defined as five, and the minimum number of citations of the author's documents that have received citations is defined as one.

A total of 1577 authors were obtained in WoS and 1915 in Scopus, of which eleven and ten meet the specifications in the extracted data, respectively. Figure 3 shows "Montalvan-Burbano, Nestor" and "Marrero Ponce, Y." as the authors who most agree with others, citing one or more articles together, in WoS and Scopus, respectively.

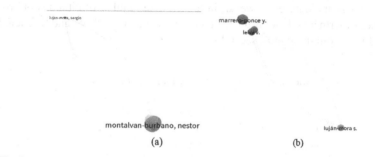

(a)   (b)

Fig. 3. Visualization of bibliographic coupling analysis by authors (a) WoS, (b) Scopus

Additionally, the "Bibliographic Coupling Network Analysis" utility is used in VOSviewer, selecting "Sources" as the unit of analysis; identifying in it the number of citations received from a source. The items to be obtained were limited to five as the minimum number of documents from a source, and one for the minimum number of citations received from a source. The result was 201 and 260 sources, of which fourteen and thirteen of them meet the guidelines already defined.

Of the sample obtained, thirteen and twelve sources from the two scientific databases used are strongly connected, being the most representative sources or journals "IEEE Access", followed by "Sustainability", as they show greater size in the circle and its label, both for WoS and Scopus, see Fig. 4.

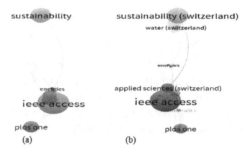

Fig. 4. Analysis of bibliographic coupling by source (journals): (a) WoS, (b) Scopus

3.2.2 Citation Analysis

Due to the filter applied, Ecuador has the highest number of citations by volume of related articles in the dataset; however, in the average number of citations of articles, the countries of Armenia, Estonia and Netherlands stand out in WoS, and Sweden, Italy and United Kingdom in Scopus, see Table 3.

Table 3. Top ten countries by number of citations

WoS			Scopus		
A	B	C	A	B	C
Ecuador	988	4.55	Ecuador	1280	6.154
Spain	330	5.41	Spain	286	5.720
Armenia	192	96.00	Italy	175	29.167
Usa	144	10.29	Chile	122	8.133
Netherlands	119	59.50	Sweden	101	33.667
Estonia	74	74.00	Usa	90	8.182
Chile	71	6.45	Argentina	85	17.000
United Kingdom	63	15.75	United Kingdom	64	21.333
Switzerland	51	25.50	Switzerland	59	19.667
Finland	47	15.67	Finland	58	19.333

(A) Country (B) Total Citations (C) Average Article Citations.

3.2.3 Keyword Analysis

The WoS publications have a total of 1764 keywords suggested by the author (Author's Keywords) and in the case of Scopus there are 1888. The keywords associated by the databases themselves (Keywords Plus) for WoS were 1185 and Scopus 3743. Discarding the keywords "Ecuador" and "software", the following terms should be highlighted: "COVID-19", "bibliometric analysis", "human", "performance", "article", "software engineering", "system", "education" and "female", see Table 4.

Table 4. Top ten relevant keywords

WoS				Scopus			
Author Keywords		Keywords-Plus		Author Keywords		Keywords-Plus	
A	B	A	B	A	B	A	B
Ecuador	15	Software	33	Ecuador	21	Software	91
Software	11	Design	17	Bibliometric Analysis	11	Human	83
Covid-19	9	Performance	17	Covid-19	9	Article	71
Software Engineering	9	System	17	Education	8	Female	64
Bibliometric Analysis	8	Model	15	Software Engineering	7	Ecuador	62
Monitoring	8	Management	14	Telemedicine	6	Humans	56
Cloud Computing	7	Diversity	11	Co-Occurrence	5	Male	51
Simulation	6	Quality	10	Latin America	5	Adult	42
Analysis	5	Conservation	9	Machine Learning	5	Controlled Study	35
Co-Occurrence	5	Identification	9	Simulation	5	Aged	24

(A) Keywords (B) Articles.

3.3 Network Analysis

3.3.1 Co-authorship Analysis

Co-authorship analysis comprises the identification and study of the generation of a link when two researchers appear in the same publication. As for the co-authorship maps, whose unit of analysis was the author, the minimum values of choice were defined as having five documents per author and one author citation, in order to identify the most visible author (WoS with 1177, and Scopus with 1815). Of which eleven and ten meet the criteria defined in WoS and Scopus.

From the sample obtained, five authors are strongly connected in WoS and four in Scopus, from which it is deduced that the node with the largest diameter of the network refers to the productivity per author; as well as collaboration with the number of links between the nodes of the network [10]. Being productive "Montalvan-Burbano, Nestor", followed by "Carrion-Mero, Paul" in both WoS and Scopus, see Fig. 5.

As for the co-authorship map, whose unit of analysis was countries, the minimum values of choice for an organization were defined as having five documents and one citation to the institution's documents in WoS and Scopus, in order to identify the most visible organization. The result was WoS with 64, and Scopus with 68, with research on the topic under study. There are 22 items linked in the resulting networks in WoS and 24 in Scopus; see Fig. 6.

In WoS and Scopus, it was found that, in the case of Ecuador, the country that stands out most for its productivity, relationship and assertive and frequent communication with authors from other countries [10], ivs Spain.

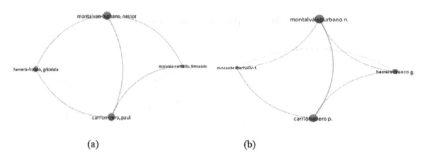

Fig. 5. Visualization of co-authorship analysis by author. (a) WoS, (b) Scopus

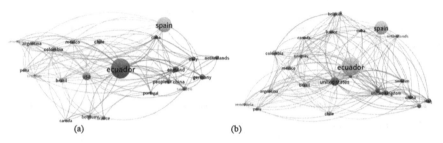

Fig. 6. Visualization of co-authorship analysis by countries (a) WoS, (b) Scopus

3.3.2 Co-citation Analysis

Co-citation analysis is also performed in VosViewer, to identify when two items are cited by the same document [9]. The author is established as the unit of analysis, the thesaurus of default authors is included and the minimum value of citations of an author is limited to ten, resulting in 14813 and 45566 authors, where 25 and 282 meet these criteria, both in WoS and Scopus, respectively. From the data reported in WoS, the most cited author was "Herrera-Franco, G.", while in Scopus the most cited author was "Montalvan-Burbano, N.", see Fig. 7.

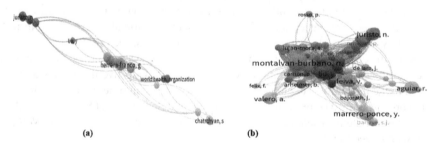

Fig. 7. Visualization of co-citation analysis by cited authors. (a) WoS, (b) Scopus

3.3.3 Co-word Analysis

From the execution of the algorithm of analysis and identification of trends in topic, creating maps based on Vosviewer data texts, criteria were established to simplify the visualization [11], where the unit of analysis was title and abstract, frequency greater than 30, counting method "Full counting", and the default thesaurus of topics. A total of 11559 and 13821 terms, respectively, were obtained from the total number of selected articles in the WoS and Scopus databases. The number of words appearing together are 54 for WoS and 64 in Scopus. The resulting word networks in Fig. 8, identifies the pairs of terms, showing a larger size those tags with a higher frequency of occurrences, for WoS "software", "analysis", "study" and "system". In the case of Scopus, "software", "study", "system" and "model" are located in the center of the map because they are highly interrelated.

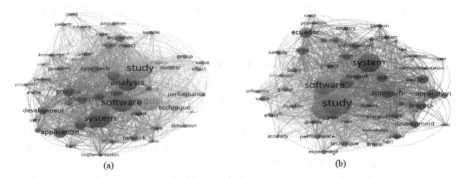

(a)   (b)

Fig. 8. Visualization of co-word analysis of keyword occurrences (a) WoS, (b) Scopus

3.4 Content Analyses

3.4.1 Pre-Analysis

The number of articles extracted in the bibliometric analysis was 377 from WoS and 450 from Scopus. By establishing a maximum acceptable error of 10%, the estimated sample percentage of 50%, and the desired confidence level of 90%, it is calculated that a content analysis should be performed on 58 and 59 documents, respectively.

The samples were taken from the total extracted from each database, following for WoS, the rule of representativeness, provided by the same database through the relevance of the articles, and for the Scopus sample, the rule of homogeneity considering articles from the last year of the study period.

After a first review, a repeated article was found in the databases, and through the reading of the abstracts, those that are not relevant to the study, which in the case of WoS were two and Scopus was only one. The respective documents are removed and other articles are taken from the extracted universe to complete the calculated sample numbers. Two objectives were defined for the study, their categories and codes, see Table 5. Finally, the files are downloaded in "pdf" format for the respective analysis of the summaries and conclusions.

Table 5. Code Table

Objectives	Categories	Associated codes
Identify the context of scientific research that makes use of software	Economic activities	According to page 19 in [12]
	Type research	According to page 110 in [13]
	Geographical region benefited	According to [14]
Recognize the characteristics of software referenced in scientific publications	Distribution software	Open Source Software, Free Software, Proprietary Software, Freeware
	Device Support	Server, Desktop, Mobile

3.4.2 Use of the Material

QualCoder open source software was used for the qualitative processing of the selected articles. The documents were reviewed one by one and the codes and their respective categories were created.

3.4.3 Treatment of Results and Interpretations

Within the categories covering the objective "Identify the context of scientific research that makes use of software", see Table 6, it was found that, of the 117 documents evaluated, the economic activities toward which the studies are mostly oriented are "Professional, scientific and technical activities" covering 38% of the total; somewhat distanced are "Human health care and social assistance activities" and "Agriculture, Forestry and Fishing", both with 11%.

The classification "Professional, scientific and technical activities" covers a wide range of research and development areas; these include forensic genetics focused on haplogroups, the development of new antibiotics through DNA regulation, the implementation of a robot based on the electronic communication interface for emerging countries, the use of CEINCI LAB in seismic engineering, data compression algorithms and electrical systems, lava flow monitoring in remote volcanoes, characterization of pathogen exposure through environmental pathways, interoperability of software systems, promising medicine for anticancer vaccines, code analysis in software repositories, quality control in software development, among other relevant topics.

The research was of the Experimental type, under this coding 32 studies were identified; in Case study and Descriptive 27 and 26 documents emerged, respectively. In the Experimental area, a number of studies have been carried out in various research areas. These include the analysis of bibliometrics, with the application of state-of-the-art technology, experiments with wind turbines, the search for new molecules, simulation of quadruped robots, development of robots for locomotion in small intestines, study of composite materials, quasi experiments with young people aged 11 to 13 years, biomass surveys, temperature analysis in asphalt replacement, electricity and statistical code studies, database identification, design of charging stations, use of neural networks, study of concrete structure when replacing sand, oil extraction, and controlled experiments for quality assessment in an IDE (Integrated Development Environment).

As expected, when delimiting the research to studies in Ecuador, the main beneficiary region of the production is South America, with 31 studies; then, it is necessary to highlight the second region, which is Europe with 11 works. In Europe, several studies and research have been carried out in countries such as Italy, the Netherlands, France, Denmark, Germany and Spain. These studies cover a wide variety of areas, ranging from science and technology to medicine, engineering and social sciences.

Table 6. Coding result to identify the context of scientific investigations

A	B	C	D
Economic activities	Administrative and support services activities	2 (2)	[15, 16]
	Agriculture, Forestry and Fishing	13 (11)	[17–29]
	Arts, Entertainment and Recreation	2 (2)	[30, 31]
	Construction	2 (2)	[32, 33]
	Exploitation of mines and quarries	5 (4)	[34–38]
	Financial and insurance activities	2 (2)	[39, 40]
	Human health care and social assistance activities	13 (11)	[41–53]
	Information and Communication	12 (10)	[54–65]
	Manufacturing industries	10 (9)	[66–75]
	Professional, scientific and technical activities	45 (38)	[77–120]
	Supply of electricity, gas, steam and air conditioning	5 (4)	[121–125]
	Teaching	3 (3)	[126–128]
	Water distribution, Sewerage, Waste management and sanitation activities	3 (3)	[129–131]
Type research	Case study	27 (22)	[28, 31, 33, 37, 39, 43, 55, 62, 69, 70, 73, 75, 83, 86, 92, 94, 98, 103–105, 108, 109, 112, 114, 115, 117, 120]
	Correlational	17 (14)	[19, 23, 43, 47, 51, 53, 57, 66, 80, 82, 91, 111, 116, 119, 123, 128, 129]
	Descriptive	26 (21)	[15–18, 29, 30, 38, 41, 42, 44, 46, 54, 56, 64, 66, 76, 78, 79, 82, 84, 85, 87, 88, 99, 122, 130]
	Documental	13 (10)	[20, 22, 26, 50, 58, 59, 74, 87, 89, 93, 97, 126, 131]
	Experimental	32 (26)	[21, 24, 27, 32, 35, 36, 39, 40, 45, 48, 49, 52, 60, 61, 65, 67, 68, 71, 72, 75–77, 81, 88, 96, 101, 102, 106, 118, 121, 124, 125, 127]
	Explanatory or casual	2 (2)	[15, 78]
	Historical	8 (6)	[25, 63, 90, 95, 100, 107, 110, 113]
Geographical region benefited	Africa	1 (2)	[125]
	Asia	2 (4)	[84, 131]
	Europe	11 (22)	[18, 26, 31, 39, 44, 50, 68, 70, 73, 81, 99]
	North America	4 (8)	[39, 44, 81, 131]
	Oceania	1 (2)	[70]
	South America	31 (62)	[15, 17, 19–21, 23, 25, 26, 30, 32–34, 36, 38, 42, 43, 46, 47, 50, 73, 78, 81, 82, 85, 91, 97, 106, 113, 119, 127, 128]

(A) Categories (B) Associated codes (C) No. of studies (%) (D) Studies.

In the first category "Distribution software", which covers the objective "Recognize the characteristics of software referenced in scientific publications", see Table 7, it is evident that most of them have referenced "Proprietary Software" with 69% of the total.

In the study, several proprietary software tools and programs were used to carry out the analysis and research. These included databases such as Scopus, modeling and simulation programs such as MATLAB/Simulink, SureDesign, LeDock and Adsorption V10. In addition, data visualization and analysis tools such as ArcGIS and Rockworks were used. In the case of the second category, the studies give almost no direct reference to the type of equipment on which the software operates, among the few that could be recognized there is a greater presence of "Mobile" devices, comprising 47% of the total.

Table 7. Coding result to recognize the characteristics of the referenced software

A	B	C	D
Distribution software	Freeware	1 (3)	[48]
	Open Source Software	8 (28)	[17, 20–22, 74, 77, 79, 81]
	Proprietary Software	20 (69)	[18, 23, 27, 34, 39, 48, 49, 51, 66, 69, 76, 77, 79, 80, 97, 121, 123, 124, 129, 131]
Device Support	Desktop	5 (29)	[16, 54, 58, 63, 105]
	Mobile	8 (47)	[42, 54, 56–59, 62, 108]
	Server	4 (24)	[41, 77, 85, 88]

(A) Categories (B) Associated codes (C) No. of studies (%) (D) Studies.

4   Conclusions

For the recognition of the characteristics of the software and the context in which it is applied, within the scope of Ecuadorian scientific production, two significant scientific content databases were used, WoS and Scopus.

When applying the search and filters in the defined databases, 377 references of articles were obtained in WoS and 450 in Scopus. With these references the bibliometric analysis is performed, within the period 2013 to 2022, which has the following results:

From 2013 to 2022 there is a positive growth in the number of research papers referring to software, in WoS (45.74%), and Scopus (44.81%). The countries of Spain, USA, Chile and Mexico stand out for the number of articles and international collaboration in the development of studies with Ecuadorian affiliation. Among the Ecuadorian institutions with the greatest production in the subject matter addressed are: ESPOL Polytechnic University, Universidad Politécnica Salesiana and Universidad de las Fuerzas Armadas ESPE.

The analysis of bibliographic coupling networks presented "Montalvan-Burbano, Nestor" and "Marrero Ponce, Y.", as those authors who most coincide with others, citing one or more articles together for WoS and Scopus, respectively. Another result raises the most representative sources; by coupling with other journals, are "IEEE ACCESS", followed by "Sustainability". For the average number of citations of articles, the countries of Armenia, Estonia and Netherlands stand out in WoS and Sweden, Italy and United Kingdom in Scopus.

In the word analysis, terms such as "COVID-19", "bibliometric analysis", "human", "performance", "article", and "software engineering" stand out. Montalvan-Burbano, Nestor" followed by "Carrion-Mero, Paul", are the authors with the highest productivity due to their strong connection in the co-authorship analysis. Under this same analysis, it was obtained that, among the authors from Ecuador and Spain, they stand out for the relationship they have. The co-citation analysis shows "Herrera-Franco, G." for WoS and "Montalvan-Burbano, N." for Scopus. The trend of terms obtained through co-word analysis were "software", "analysis", "study" and "system" for WoS, and "software", "analysis", "study" and "model" for Scopus.

The content analysis of a sample of 117 documents was carried out, following rules of representativeness and homogeneity. Two objectives were set: "Identify the context of scientific research that makes use of software" and "Recognize the characteristics of software referenced in scientific publications". The most significant results are presented below: The economic activities towards which the studies are oriented are "Professional, scientific and technical activities", "Human health care and social assistance activities" and "Agriculture, Forestry and Fishing".

The research was mainly of the "Experimental", "Case study" and "Descriptive" type. The beneficiary regions of the productions are "South America", since Ecuador is part of it, and "Europe". The studies have mostly referred to "Proprietary Software". Although very little is stated about the type of equipment used in the studios, it was found that they make use of "Mobile" devices. Due to the rapid evolution and use of information technologies, added to the increase in scientific production of the characteristics defined in this work, there is interest in carrying out a new study in the short term, which will allow the evaluation of new areas of application.

References

1. Alt, R., Leimeister, J.M., Priemuth, T., Sachse, S., Urbach, N., Wunderlich, N.: Software-defined business: implications for IT management. Bus. Inf. Syst. Eng. **62**(6), 609–621 (2020). https://doi.org/10.1007/s12599-020-00669-6
2. Schindler, D., Bensmann, F., Dietze, S., Krüger, F.: The role of software in science: a knowledge graph-based analysis of software mentions in PubMed Central. PeerJ Comput. Sci. **8**, e835 (2022). https://doi.org/10.7717/peerj-cs.835
3. Kruger, F., Schindler, D.: A literature review on methods for the extraction of usage statements of software and data. Comput. Sci. Eng. **22**(1), 26–38 (2020). https://doi.org/10.1109/MCSE.2019.2943847
4. Li, J., Hou, Y., Wang, P., Yang, B.: A review of carbon capture and storage project investment and operational decision-making based on bibliometrics. Energies **12**(1), 23 (2018). https://doi.org/10.3390/en12010023
5. Soehartono, A.M., Khor, K.A.: Critical assessment of technological development: what can bibliometrics reveal? Sch. Assess. Rep. **2**(1), 4 (2020). https://doi.org/10.29024/sar.11
6. Takahashi, Y., Uchida, C., Miyaki, K., Sakai, M., Shimbo, T., Nakayama, T.: Potential benefits and harms of a peer support social network service on the internet for people with depressive tendencies: qualitative content analysis and social network analysis. J. Med. Internet Res. **11**(3), e29 (2009). https://doi.org/10.2196/jmir.1142
7. Khanra, S., Dhir, A., Mäntymäki, M.: Big data analytics and enterprises: a bibliometric synthesis of the literature. Enterp. Inf. Syst. **14**(6), 737–768 (2020). https://doi.org/10.1080/17517575.2020.1734241
8. Bardin, L.: El análisis de contenido, 2a edn. Akal Ediciones, Madrid (1996)
9. van Eck N.J., Waltman, L.: VOSviewer Manual, p. 54 (2022)
10. Rodríguez Gutiérrez, J.K., Gómez Velasco, N.Y.: Redes de coautoría como herramienta de evaluación de la producción científica de los grupos de investigación. Rev. Gen. Inf. Doc. **27**(2), 279–297 (2017). https://doi.org/10.5209/RGID.58204

11. Galvez, C.: Análisis de co-palabras aplicado a los artículos muy citados en Biblioteconomía y Ciencias de la Información (2007–2017). Transinformação **30**(3), 277–286 (2018). https://doi.org/10.1590/2318-08892018000300001
12. INEC - Ecuador, "Clasificación Nacional de Actividades Económicas," (2012)
13. Bernal, C.A.: Metodología de la investigación. Colombia: Pearson Educación (2010)
14. Homeland Security, "Geographic Regions," Homeland Security (2023). https://www.dhs.gov/geographic-regions
15. Romero-Subia, J.F., Jimber-del Rio, J.A., Ochoa-Rico, M.S., Vergara-Romero, A.: Analysis of citizen satisfaction in municipal services. Economies **10**(9), 225 (2022). https://doi.org/10.3390/economies10090225
16. Kostakis, V., Niaros, V., Dafermos, G., Bauwens, M.: Design global, manufacture local: exploring the contours of an emerging productive model. Futures **73**, 126–135 (2015). https://doi.org/10.1016/j.futures.2015.09.001
17. Veliz, K., Chico-Santamarta, L., Ramirez, A.D.: The Environmental profile of ecuadorian export banana: a life cycle assessment. Foods **11**(20), 3288 (2022). https://doi.org/10.3390/foods11203288
18. Del-Aguila-Arcentales, S., Alvarez-Risco, A., Carvache-Franco, M., Rosen, M.A., Yáñez, J.A.: Bibliometric analysis of current status of circular economy during 2012–2021: case of foods. Processes **10**(9), 1810 (2022). https://doi.org/10.3390/pr10091810
19. Grupo de Investigación en Energía, Universidad Politecnica Salesiana. Ecuador et al., "TRNSYS Modeling of flat plate and vacuum tube solar collector systems for residential use under equatorial middle altitude climate condition. Renew. Energy Power Qual. J. **20**, 121–125 (2022). https://doi.org/10.24084/repqj20.240
20. Arcentales-Bastidas, D., Silva, C., Ramirez, A.: The environmental profile of ethanol derived from sugarcane in Ecuador: a life cycle assessment including the effect of cogeneration of electricity in a sugar industrial complex. Energies **15**(15), 5421 (2022). https://doi.org/10.3390/en15155421
21. Iñamagua-Uyaguari, J.P., Green, D.R., Fitton, N., Sangoluisa, P., Torres, J., Smith, P.: Use of unoccupied aerial systems to characterize woody vegetation across silvopastoral systems in Ecuador. Remote Sens. **14**(14), 3386 (2022). https://doi.org/10.3390/rs14143386
22. Mejía, V.C., et al.: Automatic control system for cane honey factories in developing country conditions. Processes **10**(5), 915 (2022). https://doi.org/10.3390/pr10050915
23. Martínez-Balderramo, L.Á., Cheme-Rodríguez, S.D., Baquerizo-Crespo, R.J., Riera, M.A.: Simulation of an anaerobic digestion system for agricultural residuals generated in the province of Manabí. Afinidad J. Chem. Eng. Theor. Appl. Chem. **79**(596) (2022). https://doi.org/10.55815/400722
24. Quezada Moreno, W.F., Quezada-Torres, W.D., Mera-Aguas, M.C., Medina-Litardo, and R.C., Proaño Molina, M.Y.: The essential oil of Mentha viridis L, chemical characterization and the relationship with its biological activities. Afinidad J. Chem. Eng. Theor. Appl. Chem. **79**(596) (2022). https://doi.org/10.55815/401284
25. Fouet, O., et al.: Collection of native *THEOBROMA CACAO* L. accessions from the Ecuadorian Amazon highlights a hotspot of cocoa diversity. Plants People Planet **4**(6), 605–617 (2022). https://doi.org/10.1002/ppp3.10282
26. Revelo, H.A., López-Alvarez, D., Landi, V., Rizzo, L., Alvarez, L.A.: Mitochondrial DNA variations in colombian creole sheep confirm an iberian origin and shed light on the dynamics of introduction events of african genotypes. Animals **10**(9), 1594 (2020). https://doi.org/10.3390/ani10091594
27. Espinoza, J., Pacheco, H.: Use of an unmanned aerial vehicle as an alternative to assess the nutritional status of thecotton crop. Rev. Fac. Agron. Univ. Zulia **39**(1), e223919 (2022). https://doi.org/10.47280/RevFacAgron(LUZ).v39.n1.19

28. Garcia, B.F., Bonaguro, Á., Araya, C., Carvalheiro, R., Yáñez, J.M.: Application of a novel 50K SNP genotyping array to assess the genetic diversity and linkage disequilibrium in a farmed Pacific white shrimp (Litopenaeus vannamei) population. Aquac. Rep. **20**, 100691 (2021). https://doi.org/10.1016/j.aqrep.2021.100691

29. Ortiz-Olivas, M., Hernández-Díaz, J., Fladung, M., Cañadas-López, Á., Prieto-Ruíz, J., Wehenkel, C.: Spatial Genetic Structure within and among Seed Stands of Pinus engelmannii Carr. and Pinus leiophylla Schiede ex Schltdl. & Cham, in Durango, Mexico. Forests **8**(1), 22 (2017). https://doi.org/10.3390/f8010022

30. Carpio-Arias, T.V., et al.: Relationship between perceived stress and emotional eating. A cross sectional study. Clin. Nutr. ESPEN **49**, 314–318 (2022). https://doi.org/10.1016/j.cln esp.2022.03.030

31. Ashrafzadeh, M.R., et al.: Assessing the origin, genetic structure and demographic history of the common pheasant (Phasianus colchicus) in the introduced European range. Sci. Rep. **11**(1), 21721 (2021). https://doi.org/10.1038/s41598-021-00567-1

32. Vásquez-Álvarez, P.E., Flores-Vázquez, C., Cobos-Torres, J.-C., Cobos-Mora, S.L.: Urban heat island mitigation through planned simulation. Sustainability **14**(14), 8612 (2022). https://doi.org/10.3390/su14148612

33. Merchán-Sanmartín, B., Aucapeña-Parrales, J., Alcívar-Redrován, R., Carrión-Mero, P., Jaya-Montalvo, M., Arias-Hidalgo, M.: Earth dam design for drinking water management and flood control: a case study. Water **14**(13), 2029 (2022). https://doi.org/10.3390/w14 132029

34. Villalta Echeverria, M.D.P., Viña Ortega, A.G., Larreta, E., Romero Crespo, P., Mulas, M.: Lineament extraction from digital terrain derivate model: a case study in the Girón–Santa Isabel Basin, South Ecuador. Remote Sens. **14**(21), 5400 (2022). https://doi.org/10.3390/rs14215400

35. Pérez Bayas, M. Á., Cely, J., Sintov, A., García Cena, C.E., Saltaren, R.: Method to develop legs for underwater robots: from multibody dynamics with experimental data to mechatronic implementation. Sensors **22**(21), 8462 (2022). https://doi.org/10.3390/s22218462

36. Garcia-Troncoso, N., Baykara, H., Cornejo, M.H., Riofrio, A., Tinoco-Hidalgo, M., Flores-Rada, J.: Comparative mechanical properties of conventional concrete mixture and concrete incorporating mining tailings sands. Case Stud. Constr. Mater. **16**, e01031 (2022). https://doi.org/10.1016/j.cscm.2022.e01031

37. Viana Da Fonseca, A., Cordeiro, D., Molina-Gómez, F., Besenzon, D., Fonseca, A., Ferreira, C.: The mechanics of iron tailings from laboratory tests on reconstituted samples collected in post-mortem Dam I in Brumadinho. Soils Rocks **45**(2), 1–20 (2022). https://doi.org/10.28927/SR.2022.001122

38. Oleas, N.H., Meerow, A.W., Francisco-Ortega, J.: Genetic structure of the threatened Phaedranassa schizantha (Amaryllidaceae). Bot. J. Linn. Soc. **182**(1), 169–179 (2016). https://doi.org/10.1111/boj.12444

39. Rodriguez-Marin, M., Saiz-Alvarez, J.M., Huezo-Ponce, L.: A Bibliometric analysis on pay-per-click as an instrument for digital entrepreneurship management using VOSviewer and SCOPUS data analysis tools. Sustainability **14**(24), 16956 (2022). https://doi.org/10.3390/su142416956

40. Rodríguez-Insuasti, H., Montalván-Burbano, N., Suárez-Rodríguez, O., Yonfá-Medranda, M., Parrales-Guerrero, K.: Creative economy: a worldwide research in business, management and accounting. Sustainability **14**(23), 16010 (2022). https://doi.org/10.3390/su1423 16010

41. Ayala-Ruano, S., et al.: Network science and group fusion similarity-based searching to explore the chemical space of antiparasitic peptides. ACS Omega **7**(50), 46012–46036 (2022). https://doi.org/10.1021/acsomega.2c03398

42. Beltrán-Iza, E.A., Noroña-Meza, C.O., Robayo-Nieto, A.A., Padilla, O., Toulkeridis, T.: Creation of a mobile application for navigation for a potential use of people with visual impairment exercising the NTRIP protocol. Sustainability **14**(24), 17027 (2022). https://doi.org/10.3390/su142417027

43. Bautista-Valarezo, E., Espinosa, M.E., Michels, N.R.M., Hendrickx, K., Verhoeven, V.: Culturally adapted flowcharts in obstetric emergencies: a participatory action research study. BMC Pregnancy Childbirth **22**(1), 772 (2022). https://doi.org/10.1186/s12884-022-05105-z

44. Rodríguez, S., Motta, F.D., Balbinotto Neto, G., Brandão, A.: Waiting list for liver transplantation: clinical and economic burden. Arq. Gastroenterol. (2022). https://doi.org/10.1590/s0004-2803.202204000-87

45. Yan, Y., Zhang, B., Páez Chávez, J., Liu, Y.: Optimising the locomotion of a vibro-impact capsule robot self-propelling in the small intestine. Commun. Nonlinear Sci. Numer. Simul. **114**, 106696 (2022). https://doi.org/10.1016/j.cnsns.2022.106696

46. Camacho-Leon, G., et al.: Attitudes towards depression of Argentinian, Chilean, and Venezuelan healthcare professionals using the Spanish validated version of the revised depression attitude questionnaire (SR-DAQ). SSM - Popul. Health **19**, 101180 (2022). https://doi.org/10.1016/j.ssmph.2022.101180

47. Rodríguez-Fernández, A., et al.: Maternal factors associated with non-exclusive breastfeeding in haitian immigrant women in Southern Chile. Nutrients **14**(15), 3173 (2022). https://doi.org/10.3390/nu14153173

48. Haider, M., Yousaf, S., Zaib, A., Sarfraz, A., Sarfraz, Z., Cherrez-Ojeda, I.: Diagnostic accuracy of various immunochromatographic tests for NS1 antigen and IgM antibodies detection in acute dengue virus infection. Int. J. Environ. Res. Public Health **19**(14), 8756 (2022). https://doi.org/10.3390/ijerph19148756

49. Aguiar-Salazar, E., Villalba-Meneses, F., Tirado-Espín, A., Amaguaña-Marmol, D., Almeida-Galárraga, D.: Rapid detection of cardiac pathologies by neural networks using ECG signals (1D) and sECG images (3D). Computation **10**(7), 112 (2022). https://doi.org/10.3390/computation10070112

50. Carrazco-Montalvo, A., et al.: Omicron sub-lineages (BA.1.1.529 + BA.*) current status in Ecuador. Viruses **14** (6), 1177 (2022). https://doi.org/10.3390/v14061177

51. Yousaf, M., Aslam, T., Saeed, S., Sarfraz, A., Sarfraz, Z., Cherrez-Ojeda, I.: Individual, family, and socioeconomic contributors to dental caries in children from low- and middle-income countries. Int. J. Environ. Res. Public Health **19**(12), 7114 (2022). https://doi.org/10.3390/ijerph19127114

52. Oubahmane, M., Hdoufane, I., Bjij, I., Jerves, C., Villemin, D., Cherqaoui, D.: COVID-19: In silico identification of potent α-ketoamide inhibitors targeting the main protease of the SARS-CoV-2. J. Mol. Struct. **1244**, 130897 (2021). https://doi.org/10.1016/j.molstruc.2021.130897

53. Alam, M.Z., et al.: Population genetics of Leishmania (Leishmania) major DNA isolated from cutaneous leishmaniasis patients in Pakistan based on multilocus microsatellite typing. Parasit. Vectors **7**(1), 332 (2014). https://doi.org/10.1186/1756-3305-7-332

54. Alpala, L.O., Quiroga-Parra, D.J., Torres, J.C., Peluffo-Ordóñez, D.H.: Smart factory using virtual reality and online multi-user: towards a metaverse for experimental frameworks. Appl. Sci. **12**(12), 6258 (2022). https://doi.org/10.3390/app12126258

55. Sharma, P., Singh, A.K., Leiva, V., Martin-Barreiro, C., Cabezas, X.: Modern multivariate statistical methods for evaluating the impact of whatsapp on academic performance: methodology and case study in India. Appl. Sci. **12**(12), 6141 (2022). https://doi.org/10.3390/app12126141

56. Molina Ríos, J.R., Honores Tapia, J.A., Pedreira-Souto, N., Pardo León, H.P.: Estado del arte: metodologías de desarrollo de aplicaciones móviles," 3C Tecnol. Innov. Apl. Pyme **10**(2), 17–45 (2021). https://doi.org/10.17993/3ctecno/2021.v10n2e38.17-45

57. Molina Ríos, J.R., Honores Tapia, J.A., Pedreira-Souto, N., Pardo León, H.P.: Comparativa de metodologías de desarrollo de aplicaciones móviles," 3C Tecnol. Innov. Apl. Pyme **10**(2), 73–93 (2021). https://doi.org/10.17993/3ctecno/2021.v10n2e38.73-93

58. Armijos Carrión, J.L., Morocho Román, R.F., Redrován Castillo, F.F., Torres Apolinario, D.A.: Estado del arte: métricas del desarrollo de software móvil. 3C Tecnol. Innov. Apl. Pyme **10**(3), 17–37 (2021). https://doi.org/10.17993/3ctecno/2021.v10n3e39.17-37

59. Cárdenas Villavicencio, O.E., Zea Ordóñez, M.P., Valarezo Pardo, M.R., Ramón Ramón, R.A.: Comparativa de tendencias de desarrollo de software móvil. 3C TIC Cuad. Desarro. Apl. Las TIC **10**(1), 123–147 (2021). https://doi.org/10.17993/3ctic.2021.101.123-147

60. Tello-Oquendo, L., Lin, S.-C., Akyildiz, I.F., Pla, V.: Software-Defined architecture for QoS-Aware IoT deployments in 5G systems. Ad Hoc Netw. **93**, 101911 (2019). https://doi.org/10.1016/j.adhoc.2019.101911

61. J. A. Herrera Silva, L. I. Barona López, Á. L. Valdivieso Caraguay, and M. Hernández-Álvarez, "A Survey on Situational Awareness of Ransomware Attacks—Detection and Prevention Parameters," *Remote Sens.*, vol. 11, no. 10, p. 1168, May 2019, doi: https://doi.org/10.3390/rs11101168

62. Martinez, D., Ferre, X., Guerrero, G., Juristo, N.: An agile-based integrated framework for mobile application development considering ilities. IEEE Access **8**, 72461–72470 (2020). https://doi.org/10.1109/ACCESS.2020.2987882

63. J. R. Molina Ríos, M. P. Zea Ordóñez, M. J. Contento Segarra, and F. G. García Zerda, "Comparación de metodologías en aplicaciones web," *3C Tecnol. Innov. Apl. Pyme*, vol. 7, no. 1, pp. 1–19, Mar. 2018, doi: https://doi.org/10.17993/3ctecno.2018.v7n1e25.1-19

64. R. Flores Moyano, D. Fernandez, N. Merayo, C. M. Lentisco, and A. Cardenas, "NFV and SDN-Based Differentiated Traffic Treatment for Residential Networks," *IEEE Access*, vol. 8, pp. 34038–34055, 2020, doi: https://doi.org/10.1109/ACCESS.2020.2974504

65. Chamba, J., Sánchez, M., Moya, M.J., Noroña, J., Franco, R.: Simulación de movimiento de un robot hexápodo en entornos de realidad virtual. Enfoque UTE **10**(1), 173–184 (2019). https://doi.org/10.29019/enfoqueute.v10n1.456

66. Mayacela, M., Rentería, L., Contreras, L., Medina, S.: Comparative analysis of reconfigurable platforms for memristor emulation. Materials **15**(13), 4487 (2022). https://doi.org/10.3390/ma15134487

67. Carrión-Coronel, E., Ortiz, P., Nanía, L.: Physical experimentation and 2D-CFD parametric study of flow through transverse bottom racks. Water **14**(6), 955 (2022). https://doi.org/10.3390/w14060955

68. Abad-Coronel, C., Palomeque, A., Mena Córdova, N., Aliaga, P.: Digital volumetric analysis of CAD/CAM polymeric materials after tooth brushing. Polymers **14**(17), 3499 (2022). https://doi.org/10.3390/polym14173499

69. Olivera-Montenegro, L., Bugarin, A., Marzano, A., Best, I., Zabot, G.L., Romero, H.: Production of protein hydrolysate from quinoa (chenopodium quinoa willd.): economic and experimental evaluation of two pretreatments using supercritical fluids' extraction and conventional solvent extraction. Foods **11**(7), 1015 (2022). https://doi.org/10.3390/foods11071015

70. Ortiz Lizcano, J.C., et al.: Colored optic filters on c-Si IBC solar cells for building integrated photovoltaic applications. Prog. Photovolt. Res. Appl. **30**(4), 401–435 (2022). https://doi.org/10.1002/pip.3504

71. Guaman, D., Delgado, S., Perez, J.: Classifying model-view-controller software applications using self-organizing maps. IEEE Access **9**, 45201–45229 (2021). https://doi.org/10.1109/ACCESS.2021.3066348

72. Minchala, L.I., Peralta, J., Mata-Quevedo, P., Rojas, J.: An approach to industrial automation based on low-cost embedded platforms and open software. Appl. Sci. **10**(14), 4696 (2020). https://doi.org/10.3390/app10144696

73. Vergara, A.M.C., et al.: A matrilineal study on the origin and genetic relations of the Ecuadorian Pillareño creole pig population through d-loop mitochondrial DNA analysis. Animals **11**(11), 3322 (2021). https://doi.org/10.3390/ani11113322
74. Minchala, L.I., Ochoa, S., Velecela, E., Astudillo, D.F., Gonzalez, J.: An open source SCADA system to implement advanced computer integrated manufacturing. IEEE Lat. Am. Trans. **14**(12), 4657–4662 (2016). https://doi.org/10.1109/TLA.2016.7816994
75. García, C., Castellanos, E., García, M.: UML-based cyber-physical production systems on low-cost devices under IEC-61499. Machines **6**(2), 22 (2018). https://doi.org/10.3390/machines6020022
76. Köksal, Z., et al.: Targeted Y chromosome capture enrichment in admixed South American samples with haplogroup Q. Forensic Sci. Int. Genet. Suppl. Ser. **8**, 97–98 (2022). https://doi.org/10.1016/j.fsigss.2022.09.034
77. Arévalo, J.M.C., Amorim, J.C.: Virtual screening, optimization and molecular dynamics analyses highlighting a pyrrolo[1,2-a]quinazoline derivative as a potential inhibitor of DNA gyrase B of Mycobacterium tuberculosis. Sci. Rep. **12**(1), 4742 (2022). https://doi.org/10.1038/s41598-022-08359-x
78. Flores-Vázquez, C., Angulo, C., Vallejo-Ramírez, D., Icaza, D., Pulla Galindo, S.: Technical development of the CeCi social robot. Sensors **22**(19), 7619 (2022). https://doi.org/10.3390/s22197619
79. Aguiar-Falconí, R.R., Cagua-Gómez, B.J.: Sistema Computacional 'CEINCI LAB' como una herramienta para la enseñanza de Ingeniería Sísmica-Estructural. DYNA **89**(222), 74–82 (2022). https://doi.org/10.15446/dyna.v89n222.101814
80. Amaya, L., Inga, E.: Compressed sensing technique for the localization of harmonic distortions in electrical power systems. Sensors **22**(17), 6434 (2022). https://doi.org/10.3390/s22176434
81. Vasconez, F.J., Anzieta, J.C.,. Vásconez Müller, A., Bernard, B., Ramón, P.: A near real-time and free tool for the preliminary mapping of active lava flows during volcanic crises: the case of hotspot subaerial eruptions. Remote Sens. **14**(14), 3483 (2022). https://doi.org/10.3390/rs14143483
82. Köksal, Z., et al.: Testing the Ion AmpliSeq^{TM} HID Y-SNP Research Panel v1 for performance and resolution in admixed South Americans of haplogroup Q. Forensic Sci. Int. Genet. **59**, 102708 (2022). https://doi.org/10.1016/j.fsigen.2022.102708
83. Ortíz, J.F., et al.: Pulvinar sign, stroke and their relationship with fabry disease: a systematic review and metanalysis. Neurol. Int. **14**(2), 497–505 (2022). https://doi.org/10.3390/neurolint14020041
84. Viera, R.T.: Lexical richness of abstracts in scientific papers in anglophone and non-anglophone journals, 3L Southeast Asian. J. Engl. Lang. Stud. **28**(2), 224–239 (2022). https://doi.org/10.17576/3L-2022-2802-15
85. Sosa-Moreno, A., et al.: Characterizing behaviors associated with enteric pathogen exposure among infants in rural Ecuador through structured observations. Am. J. Trop. Med. Hyg. **106**(6), 1747–1756 (2022). https://doi.org/10.4269/ajtmh.21-1099
86. Reyes, J., Fuertes, W., Arévalo, P., Macas, M.: An environment-specific prioritization model for information-security vulnerabilities based on risk factor analysis. Electronics **11**(9), 1334 (2022). https://doi.org/10.3390/electronics11091334
87. Computer and Decision Science Department, Universidad Nacional de Colombia, Medellín, Colombia, D. M. T. Ricaurte, M. K. V. Cabezas, Faculty of Electrical and Computer Engineering, Escuela Superior Politécnica del Litoral, ESPOL, Guayaquil, Ecuador, C. M. Z. Jaramillo, and Computer and Decision Science Department, Universidad Nacional de Colombia, Medellín, Colombia, "Representing Interoperability Between Software Systems by Using Pre-Conceptual Schemas," Int. J. Electr. Eng. Inform. **14**(1), 101–127 (2022). https://doi.org/10.15676/ijeei.2022.14.1.7

88. Romero, M., et al.: A novel network science and similarity-searching-based approach for discovering potential tumor-homing peptides from antimicrobials. Antibiotics **11**(3), 401 (2022). https://doi.org/10.3390/antibiotics11030401
89. Nina, H., Pow-Sang, J.A., Villavicencio, M.: Systematic mapping of the literature on secure software development. IEEE Access **9**, 36852–36867 (2021). https://doi.org/10.1109/ACCESS.2021.3062388
90. Corral, A., Sánchez, L.E., Antonelli, L.: Building an integrated requirements engineering process based on Intelligent Systems and Semantic Reasoning on the basis of a systematic analysis of existing proposals. JUCS - J. Univers. Comput. Sci. **28**(11), 1136–1168 (2022). https://doi.org/10.3897/jucs.78776
91. Arcos-Medina, G., Mauricio, D.: Identifying factors influencing on agile practices for software development. J. Inf. Organ. Sci. **44**(1), 1–31 (2020). https://doi.org/10.31341/jios.44.1.1
92. Santos, A., Vegas, S., Uyaguari, F., Dieste, O., Turhan, B., Juristo, N.: Increasing validity through replication: an illustrative TDD case. Softw. Qual. J. **28**(2), 371–395 (2020). https://doi.org/10.1007/s11219-020-09512-3
93. Sayago-Heredia, J., Pérez-Castillo, R., Piattini, M.: A systematic mapping study on analysis of code repositories. Informatica, 619–660 (2021). https://doi.org/10.15388/21-INFOR454
94. Rosero, R.H., Gomez, O.S., Rodriguez, G.: Regression testing of database applications under an incremental software development setting. IEEE Access **5**, 18419–18428 (2017). https://doi.org/10.1109/ACCESS.2017.2749502
95. Flores, P., Alvarez, M., Torres, J.: Identifying difficulties of software modeling through class diagrams: a long-term comparative analysis. IEEE Access **10**, 28895–28910 (2022). https://doi.org/10.1109/ACCESS.2022.3157290
96. Gomez, O.S., Aguileta, A.A., Aguilar, R.A., Ucan, J.P., Rosero, R.H., Cortes-Verdin, K.: An empirical study on the impact of an IDE tool support in the pair and solo programming. IEEE Access **5**, 9175–9187 (2017). https://doi.org/10.1109/ACCESS.2017.2701339
97. Palacios, K., Guerra, J.: Software aplicado en investigaciones científicas de las universidades del Ecuador: estudio de mapeo sistemático. Cienc. UNEMI **15**(39), 14–26 (2022). https://doi.org/10.29076/issn.2528-7737vol15iss39.2022pp14-26p
98. Longmore, S.N., et al.: Adapting astronomical source detection software to help detect animals in thermal images obtained by unmanned aerial systems. Int. J. Remote Sens. **38**(8–10), 2623–2638 (2017). https://doi.org/10.1080/01431161.2017.1280639
99. Guaman, D.S., Alamo, J.M.D., Caiza, J.C.: A systematic mapping study on software quality control techniques for assessing privacy in information systems. IEEE Access **8**, 74808–74833 (2020). https://doi.org/10.1109/ACCESS.2020.2988408
100. Ríos, J.M., Pedreira-Souto, N.: Approach of agile methodologies in the development of web-based software. Information **10**(10), 314 (2019). https://doi.org/10.3390/info10100314
101. Sandobalin, J., Insfran, E., Abrahao, S.: On the effectiveness of tools to support infrastructure as code: model-driven versus code-centric. IEEE Access **8**, 17734–17761 (2020). https://doi.org/10.1109/ACCESS.2020.2966597
102. Cruz, M., Bernárdez, B., Durán, A., Guevara-Vega, C., Ruiz-Cortés, A.: A model-based approach for specifying changes in replications of empirical studies in computer Science. Computing **105**(6), 1189–1213 (2023). https://doi.org/10.1007/s00607-022-01133-x
103. Bardier, C., Székely, D., Augusto-Alves, G., Matínez-Latorraca, N., Schmidt, B.R., Cruickshank, S.S.: Performance of visual vs. software-assisted photo-identification in mark-recapture studies: a case study examining different life stages of the Pacific Horned Frog (Ceratophrys stolzmanni). Amphib.-Reptil. **42**(1), 17–28 (2020). https://doi.org/10.1163/15685381-bja10025

104. C. E. Anchundia, C.E., Fonseca, C.E.R.: Resources for reproducibility of experiments in empirical software engineering: topics derived from a secondary study. IEEE Access **8**, 8992–9004 (2020). https://doi.org/10.1109/ACCESS.2020.2964587

105. J. R. Valdés-Martiní *et al.*, "QuBiLS-MAS, open source multi-platform software for atom- and bond-based topological (2D) and chiral (2.5D) algebraic molecular descriptors computations," *J. Cheminformatics*, vol. 9, no. 1, p. 35, Dec. 2017, doi: https://doi.org/10.1186/s13 321-017-0211-5

106. Gaviria, A., et al.: Genetic polymorphisms of 12 X-STRs in the Ecuadorian population. Forensic Sci. Int. Genet. Suppl. Ser. **7**(1), 677–679 (2019). https://doi.org/10.1016/j.fsigss. 2019.10.135

107. Mejia, P., Martini, L.C., Grijalva, F., Larco, J.C., Rodriguez, J.C.: A survey on mathematical software tools for visually impaired persons: a practical perspective. IEEE Access **9**, 66929–66947 (2021). https://doi.org/10.1109/ACCESS.2021.3076306

108. Rodas-Silva, J., Galindo, J.A., Garcia-Gutierrez, J., Benavides, D.: Selection of software product line implementation components using recommender systems: an application to wordpress. IEEE Access **7**, 69226–69245 (2019). https://doi.org/10.1109/ACCESS.2019. 2918469

109. García-Jacas, C.R., et al.: Choquet integral-based fuzzy molecular characterizations: when global definitions are computed from the dependency among atom/bond contributions (LOVIs/LOEIs). J. Cheminformatics **10**(1), 51 (2018). https://doi.org/10.1186/s13321-018-0306-7

110. Santos, A., Gomez, O., Juristo, N.: Analyzing Families of Experiments in SE: A Systematic Mapping Study. arXiv, Aug. 02, 2018. Accessed 03 June 2023. http://arxiv.org/abs/1805. 09009

111. Martínez-Santiago, O., et al.: Exploring the QSAR's predictive truthfulness of the novel N-tuple discrete derivative indices on benchmark datasets. SAR QSAR Environ. Res. **28**(5), 367–389 (2017). https://doi.org/10.1080/1062936X.2017.1326403

112. Cuesta, S.A., Mora, J.R., Márquez, E.A.: In silico screening of the drugbank database to search for possible drugs against SARS-CoV-2. Molecules **26**(4), 1100 (2021). https://doi. org/10.3390/molecules26041100

113. Urquía, D., Gutierrez, B., Pozo, G., Pozo, M.J., Espín, A., Torres, M.D.L.: Psidium guajava in the Galapagos Islands: population genetics and history of an invasive species. PLoS ONE **14**(3), e0203737 (2019). https://doi.org/10.1371/journal.pone.0203737

114. Larco, A., Peñafiel, P., Yanez, C., Luján-Mora, S.: Thinking about inclusion: designing a digital app catalog for people with motor disability. Sustainability **13**(19), 10989 (2021). https://doi.org/10.3390/su131910989

115. Cuadros, J., Dugarte, N., Wong, S., Vanegas, P., Morocho, V., Medina, R.: ECG multilead QT interval estimation using support vector machines. J. Healthc. Eng. **2019**, 1–14 (2019). https://doi.org/10.1155/2019/6371871

116. Crespo-Martinez, E.: Análisis de vulnerabilidades con SQLMAP aplicada a entornos APEX 5. Ingenius **25**, 104–113 (2020). https://doi.org/10.17163/ings.n25.2021.10

117. Abad-Coronel, C., et al.: Analysis of the mesh resolution of an. STL exported from an intraoral scanner file. J. Esthet. Restor. Dent. **34**(5), 816–825 (2022). https://doi.org/10. 1111/jerd.12889

118. García-Jacas, C.R., Contreras-Torres, E., Marrero-Ponce, Y., Pupo-Meriño, M., Barigye, S.J., Cabrera-Leyva, L.: Examining the predictive accuracy of the novel 3D N-linear algebraic molecular codifications on benchmark datasets. J. Cheminformatics **8**(1), 10 (2016). https://doi.org/10.1186/s13321-016-0122-x

119. Poulakakis, N., et al.: Description of a New galapagos giant tortoise species (chelonoidis; testudines: testudinidae) from cerro fatal on santa cruz Island. PLoS ONE **10**(10), e0138779 (2015). https://doi.org/10.1371/journal.pone.0138779

120. Congacha Aushay, E.P., Santillán Castillo, J.R., Guerra Salazar, J.E., Barba Vera, R.G.: Empleo de una aplicación informática como estrategia didáctica para el desarrollo de aptitudes académicas," Rev. Educ. 398–413 (2018). https://doi.org/10.15517/revedu.v42i2.27472

121. Ochoa, D., Martinez, S., Arévalo, P.: Extended simplified electro-mechanical model of a variable-speed wind turbine for grid integration studies: emulation and validation on a microgrid lab. Electronics **11**(23), 3945 (2022). https://doi.org/10.3390/electronics11233945

122. Universidad Politécnica Salesiana, Sede Guayaquil. Ecuador Grupo de Investigación en Energías, Universidad Politécnica Salesiana, Cuenca. Ecuador, D. Segovia-Muñoz, X. Serrano-Guerrero, and A. Barragán-Escandon, "Predictive maintenance in LED street lighting controlled with telemanagement system to improve current fault detection procedures using software tool). https://doi.org/10.24084/repqj20.318

123. Lema, M., Pavon, W., Ortiz, L., Asiedu-Asante, A.B., Simani, S.: Controller coordination strategy for DC microgrid using distributed predictive control improving voltage stability. Energies **15**(15), 5442 (2022). https://doi.org/10.3390/en15155442

124. Tamay, P., Inga, E.: Charging infrastructure for electric vehicles considering their integration into the smart grid. Sustainability **14**(14), 8248 (2022). https://doi.org/10.3390/su14148248

125. Pillay, E., Kumarasamy, M., Adu, J., Thirumuruganandham, S.P., Paruk, A., Naidoo, M.: Feasibility analysis of energy recovery using PATs in water distribution networks. Water **14**(7), 1150 (2022). https://doi.org/10.3390/w14071150

126. Vairinhos, V.M., Pereira, L.A., Matos, F., Nunes, H., Patino, C., Galindo-Villardón, P.: Framework for classroom student grading with open-ended questions: a text-mining approach. Mathematics **10**(21), 4152 (2022). https://doi.org/10.3390/math10214152

127. Universidad Técnica Estatal de Quevedo, Ecuador and J. Coutinho Dos Santos, "Improving Speaking Fluency Through 4/3/2 Technique and Self-Assessment. Teach. Engl. Second Foreign Lang.-TESL-EJ, vol. 26, no. 4 (2022). https://doi.org/10.55593/ej.26102a1

128. Cruz Pérez, M.A.: Propuesta metodológica para el empleo del software educativo como recurso didáctico en la formación investigative. Rev. Cienc. PEDAGÓGICAS E Innov. **7**(2), 21–30 (2019). https://doi.org/10.26423/rcpi.v7i2.288

129. Escuela de Ingeniería Química, Facultad de Ciencias Químicas, Universidad de Cuenca, Cuenca, Ecuador, M. Vera, S. Astudillo, Centro de Estudios Ambientales, Departamento de Química Aplicada y Sistemas de Producción, Facultad de Ciencias Químicas, Universidad de Cuenca, Cuenca, Ecuador, D. M. Juela, and Centro de Estudios Ambientales, Departamento de Química Aplicada y Sistemas de Producción, Facultad de Ciencias Químicas, Universidad de Cuenca, Cuenca, Ecuador, "Estudio experimental y simulación dinámica de la adsorción de Cd+2 y Pb+2 utilizando cáscara de cacao en columna de lecho fijo," Tecnol. Cienc. Agua, vol. 13, no. 6, pp. 56–97 (2022). https://doi.org/10.24850/j-tyca-13-06-02

130. Morante-Carballo, F., Montalván-Burbano, N., Arias-Hidalgo, M., Domínguez-Granda, L., Apolo-Masache, B., Carrión-Mero, P.: Flood models: an exploratory analysis and research trends. Water **14**(16), 2488 (2022). https://doi.org/10.3390/w14162488

131. Herrera-Franco, G., Carrión-Mero, P., Montalván-Burbano, N., Mora-Frank, C., Berrezueta, E.: Bibliometric analysis of groundwater's life cycle assessment research. Water **14**(7), 1082 (2022). https://doi.org/10.3390/w14071082

Exploring the Potential of Genetic Algorithms for Optimizing Academic Schedules at the School of Mechatronic Engineering: Preliminary Results

Johan Alarcón[1], Samantha Buitrón[1], Alexis Carrillo[1], Mateo Chuquimarca[1], Alexis Ortiz[1], Robinson Guachi[1], D. H. Peluffo-Ordóñez[2,3], and Lorena Guachi-Guachi[1,3(✉)]

[1] Department of Mechatronics, Universidad Internacional del Ecuador, Av. Simon Bolivar, 170411 Quito, Ecuador
{joalarconag,sabuitronpa,alcarrilloro,machuquimarcaro, alortizsa,roguachigu,loguachigu}@uide.edu.ec
[2] College of Computing, Mohammed VI Polytechnic University, Lot 660, Hay Moulay Rachid, 43150 Ben Guerir, Morocco
peluffo.diego@um6p.ma
[3] SDAS Research Group, 43150 Ben Guerir, Morocco
{diego.peluffo,lorena.guachi}@sdas-group.com
https://sdas-group.com/

Abstract. The generation of schedules is a complex challenge, particularly in academic institutions aiming for equitable scheduling. The goal is to achieve fair and balanced schedules that meet the requirements of all parties involved, such as workload, class distribution, shifts, and other relevant criteria. To address this challenge, a genetic algorithm specifically designed for optimal schedule generation has been proposed as a solution. Adjusting genetic algorithm parameters impacts performance, and employing parameter optimization techniques effectively tackles this issue. This work introduces a genetic algorithm for optimal schedule generation, utilizing suitable encoding and operators, and evaluating quality through fitness techniques. Optimization efforts led to reduced execution time, improved solution quality, and positive outcomes like faster execution, fewer generations, increased stability, and convergence to optimal solutions.

Keywords: Equitable schedules · Genetic algorithm optimization · Resource allocation · Scheduling generation

1 Introduction

Scheduling generation is a complex challenge faced by various institutions and organizations in their day-to-day operations, including academic, professional fields, and other contexts where coordinating and allocating resources is necessary.

The problem lies in the need to find an appropriate combination of elements and constraints to meet the demands and needs of all involved parties. It is

H. Florez and M. Leon (Eds.): ICAI 2023, CCIS 1874, pp. 390–402, 2024.
https://doi.org/10.1007/978-3-031-46813-1_26

crucial to ensure that schedules are fair and equitable, avoiding situations where individuals or groups are disadvantaged in terms of workload, class distribution, shifts, or any other relevant criteria.

In the Mechatronics Engineering school at the International University of Ecuador, scheduling for courses and activities presents a complex challenge due to the variety of resources, constraints, and preferences of students and professors. Efficient schedule planning is crucial to ensure a fair distribution of subjects, avoid conflicts, and optimize resource allocation. To address this problem, the optimization of a genetic algorithm (GA) is proposed, aiming to find optimal or near-optimal solutions using techniques inspired by evolutionary computation.

Currently, various research studies are related to automatic schedule generation using GAs and other optimization techniques. These approaches have proven to be effective in solving resource allocation and scheduling problems in different academic contexts, which could be classified into two categories: classical genetic algorithms ([1–4]) and hybrid genetic algorithms ([5–7]).

A common problem found in the explored works is the adjustment of the involved parameters, such as population size, mutation rate, and the number of generations, which can significantly affect the performance of the algorithm for automatic schedule generation. To address this issue, techniques like parameter optimization can be employed to find the required parameter values.

The project aims to contribute to the generation of optimal schedules in the field of Mechatronics Engineering at the International University of Ecuador. To achieve this, the development of a GA is proposed, employing an appropriate encoding to represent schedules and using genetic operators such as selection, reproduction, and mutation to generate new solutions. Evaluation and fitness techniques will be applied to assess the quality of each solution, and multiple iterations of the algorithm will be performed to gradually improve the results. The goal is to obtain optimal or near-optimal schedules that meet all the established constraints and preferences, thereby enhancing the efficiency of course planning and resource allocation.

The obtained results so far support the feasibility and effectiveness of the proposed GA for schedule generation in the field of Mechatronics Engineering at the International University of Ecuador, resulting in reduced execution time and improved solution quality. The algorithm demonstrated positive outcomes, including lower average execution time, fewer required generations to find a solution, increased stability, and convergence towards optimal solutions. Our results are attributed to a higher number of elite schedules, increased mutation rate, and random class selection during mutation, leading to improved stability and reduced computational resources required.

This document is organized as follows: In Sect. 2, a brief overview of the current state of research is provided. Section 3 includes the description of the database used for experimentation, along with the definition of parameters and characteristic operators of the GA. The experimentation process and the metrics employed to evaluate the GA's performance are described in Sect. 4. The obtained results and the various comparisons conducted are presented in Sect. 5. Finally, Sect. 6 gathers the concluding remarks.

2   Related Works

The use of GAs in timetable generation has become an active and constantly evolving area of research, with numerous practical applications and possibilities for future development.

In the field of optimization, GAs have proven to be a powerful tool for solving complex problems. In particular, the generation of schedules is a task that can be solved using GAs and that has been the object of investigation in several studies. For instance, [1] and [8] described the implementation of a GA to generate university timetables with the goal of producing accurate solutions, although its implementation can be complicated and may require exhaustive tuning and testing. Authors in [9] described the application of a GA for teaching planning in a university, which, like the previous ones mentioned, can generate precise and efficient solutions, but its implementation may require a large amount of computing resources. Starting from the latter in terms of the limitation presented, it is similar to the one described in [6], with the difference that the work involved a hybrid GA to program the schedules of nurses in a hospital considering the nurse fatigue.

In the field of assigning academic timetables, various investigations have been carried out by using GAs. Among them are 'Assignment of academic schedules for the School of Civil Engineering in Computing of the University of Talca [10], which described the implementation of a GA to assign schedules in a school engineering. The advantage of this approach is that it can generate accurate solutions in a reasonable amount of time, although it may require adjustment to suit the specific needs of an engineering school. Other relevant articles presented in [11] and [12] described the planning of university timetables using GAs with an approach similar to [10], although with a complex implementation of the algorithm, which can require a large amount of computing resources as [9].

Authors in [3,13] reported the application of a GA to generate exam schedules in a university, with precise and optimal solutions, although its algorithm can be difficult to fit in. The work introduced in [13] presented the generation of schedules in a highschool with time efficient solutions, but with an algorithm that may require tuning and testing. Both works are relevant to this project, as they are part of the main literature to improve the selected algorithm.

In [5], the authors proposed a hybrid approach that combines a GA with a greedy approach to generate school and exam timetables efficiently but with a limitation on the greedy approach that can lead to sub-optimal solutions. Authors in [2,7] and [14] introduced an intelligent system based on a GA to plan schedules in various educational fields with optimal time solutions. With the limitation of being difficult to adjust the algorithm to adapt to the specific needs of the field to be applied. The GA introduced in [15] yield school timetables involving advanced technical knowledge.

Moreover, in the medical field, authors in [16] presented an appointment scheduling system for medical treatment using GAs presenting efficient solutions in terms of the use of time and medical resources, but using a large amount of information resources.

Based on the way of operating the works explored from the literature, we have identified two categories: 1) Classical GAs, which are capable of handling large search spaces and allow high-quality solutions to be found in a reasonable time, but can fall into local minima and do not always find the global optimal solution. Within this category we can find some articles such as [1,2] and [3]. 2) Hybrid GAs, which combine different techniques to improve the precision and efficiency in solving the problem, as well as they can improve the quality of the solutions found by classical genetic algorithms and reduce the time needed to find them, but their implementation may require more effort and technical knowledge than conventional GAs. Some of the articles categorized in this second point are [5,6] and [7].

3   Materials and Methods

3.1   Data

The database collects the information from seven semesters of the School of Mechatronics of the International University of Ecuador, as is shown in Table 1.

Table 1. Description of the data that will be used.

Data	Description	Value
Subjects	Subjects that need to use the classrooms	3 Subjects
Students per Semester	Number of students per semester	1st Semester: 25, 2nd Semester: 35, 3rd Semester: 25, 4th Semester: 30, 5th Semester: 35, 6th Semester: 45 and 7th Semester: 45
Classrooms	Maximum Capacity of students per classroom	A1: 25, A2: 45 and A3: 35
Professors	Professors who can impart the classes	4 Professors
Meeting Time	Times in which classes can be carried out	4 Meeting Times

Each of the chosen parameters are described in a general way, in [17] you can find the database in detail.

3.2 Proposed Algorithm

The proposed GA depicted in Fig. 1 was inspired by the work titled "Development of an exam scheduling system using genetic algorithm" [3], and aims at finding the best assignment of available subjects and resources.

Database: Within the database there are 5 academic objects: subjects, semesters, classrooms, teachers, and meeting schedules; these data will be imported into the GA as arrays.

Initialization of Population: A initial population of 9 random schedules based on the 5 aforementioned objects were created. This initial population served as a starting point for the search and optimization process that follows in the GA.

Fitness Calculation: The goal was to find the optimal schedule removing conflict with the objects that compose it. These conflicts can arise from conflicting reservations of professors or classrooms, classroom capacity, and professor availability. When the number of conflicts was zero, the problem was considered solved.

Parent Selection: If a schedule with zero conflicts was not found, parent selection by tournament was performed. This step selected randomly three schedules from the population in order to find the two best parents for the next generation.

Crossover: Each class in the new schedule, made up of the 5 aforementioned objects, was crossed with a randomly selected class from the parent schedules, thus producing reproduction through a crossing point.

Mutation: For schedules in the population that are not part of the elite, random classes are mutated with a probability determined by the mutation rate. If a mutation occurs, the selected class is replaced with a random class from another schedule generated by the population initialization method.

Elitism: This ensured that the best fitness schedule obtained so far was kept in the population and transmitted to future generations without changes, avoiding the loss of high-quality solutions.

3.3 Changes Applied to [3]

We conducted a set of experiments to improve the overall performance of the work proposed in [3], which involved adjustments to the elitism parameter and mutation rate, as well as a modification to the mutation operator technique.

The number of elite schedules was increased from 1 to 2. This means that the two best schedules from each generation will be preserved in the next generation. The mutation rate was increased from 0.1 to 0.2 aiming at promoting greater solution diversity.

Regarding the mutation technique, the probabilistic approach to determining which classes will be mutated was maintained. However, a change was introduced in the mutation process. In [3], mutation was performed sequentially, that

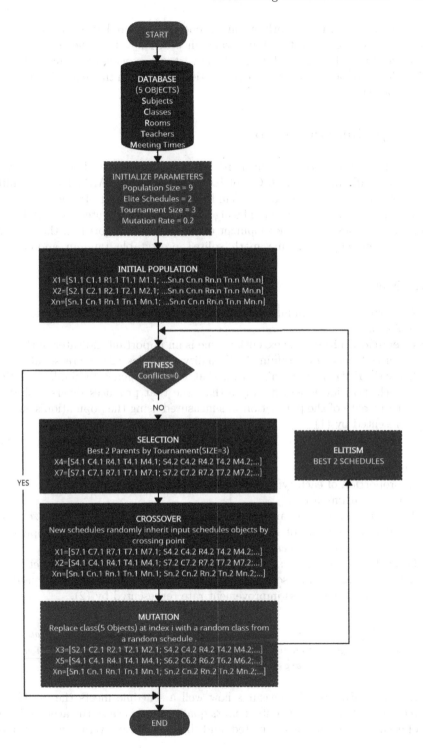

Fig. 1. Flowchart of the proposed genetic algorithm to generate the academic schedules.

is, class by class. In this work, we maintained the ordered sequence of the algorithm that will be mutated, but a random position within the schedule to be introduced was chosen. With these changes, it was expected to explore different schedule combinations and increased solution diversity in the search for improved optimization.

4 Experimental Setup

For experimental purposes, the hardware resources involved an 8-core AMD Ryzen 7 5800X processor, 16 GB of RAM, and an LG 20MP38HQ-B monitor. The software resources involved Windows 10 Pro x64-bit, Python in Google Colab, and Opera web browser. The algorithm was implemented through Python software routines. In the development of the proposed algorithm, the following libraries were employed: time, math, sqlite3, prettytable, random, and enum.

4.1 Metrics

- **Generations:** The number of generations required to find the solution to the problem.
- **Execution Time:** The execution time is an important indicator of the algorithm's efficiency in obtaining high-quality schedules within a reasonable time.
- **Overall Entropy:** An algorithm that tends to generate similar solutions in each iteration is less desirable than one that produces diverse solutions. The diversity of the population was measured using the population's entropy, represented by (1).

$$H = -\sum (\rho \cdot \log_2(\rho)) \tag{1}$$

where:

ρ proportion of each type of solution in the population;

$\log_2$ logarithm base 2.

The values of H can range from 0 to $\log_2(N)$, where N is the size of the population. A value of H close to 0 indicates a homogeneous population, while high entropy indicates a more diverse population.

- **Overall Convergence:** Convergence refers to how quickly the genetic algorithm finds an optimal solution or one close to it. The convergence speed was measured by the fitness improvement rate represented by (2).

$$Fitness\ improvement\ rate$$
$$= \frac{current\ generation\ avg.\ fitness - avg.\ fitness\ of\ the\ previous\ generation}{avg.\ fitness\ of\ the\ previous\ generation} \tag{2}$$

- **Average Fitness:** It measures how well a schedule meets the established requirements and constraints, i.e., its quality. In this case, the average fitness of each generation was calculated, and then an overall average was obtained.

4.2   Parameters of the Evolutionary Algorithm

Table 2 includes the comprehensive set of parameters utilized in our algorithm. These parameters hold significant importance in driving the optimization process effectively. The parameter values were carefully established experimentally and were also drawn from literature as shown the column value selection protocol in Table 2.

Table 2. Parameters values used in the proposed algorithm.

Name	Description	Value	Value Selection Procedure
POPULATION_ SIZE	Size of population in each generation	9	Based on the problem and available resources. Larger populations can explore more search space but require more computation [3]
NUMB_OF_ ELITE_ SCHEDULES	The number of elite schedules that are preserved without changes in each generation	1	Based on the problem and experimentation
TOURNAMENT_ SELECTION_ SIZE	The size of the tournament selection pool	3	Based on the problem and experimentation
MUTATION_ RATE	The probability of a gene in an individual being mutated	0.1	Based on the problem and experimentation
VERBOSE_ FLAG	Flag to control the output of detailed information during the execution of the algorithm	False	Based on the user's preference

The code is available at the following link: source code.

5   Experimental Results

5.1   The Proposed Algorithm vs. [3]

The increase to two elite programs permitted our algorithm to retain high-quality solutions from one generation to the next one, accelerating the convergence of the algorithm. Although there could have been an effect on the population entropy due to the repetition of solutions, this problem did not arise.

The increase in the mutation rate, specifically from 0.1 to 0.2 permitted our algorithm to explore more solutions. It is important to note that a high mutation rate can make it difficult to find the solution and generate less stable or suboptimal solutions. However, in this particular case, this problem was not experienced.

The change applied to the mutation operator favored greater diversity and increased the chances of finding optimal solutions. Although there is a possibility of generating less coherent schedules or schedules that do not meet certain restrictions, it was established that the random position should be within the allowed values in the schedule, thus avoiding this situation.

In summary, the changes proposed in our algorithm provided benefits such as faster convergence, wider exploration of solutions and greater diversity, without generating significant problems in solution quality or schedule coherence.

Table 3 and 4 depict the results obtained from 10 iterations of each algorithm. In order to facilitate the comprehension of the outcomes for each scenario, Fig. 2 provides a visual comparison of both algorithms across various metrics.

Table 3. Overall performance of the algorithm presented in [3] through 10 executions.

Execution	Generations	Execution Time [s]	Overall Entropy	Overall Convergence	Average Fitness
1	9	0,048	1	1,235	0,366
2	13	0,062	1	1,377	0,379
3	9	0,081	1	1,230	0,273
4	77	0,325	1	1,614	0,375
5	36	0,170	1	1,473	0,350
6	26	0,136	1	1,606	0,368
7	37	0,200	1	1,458	0,318
8	193	1,021	1	2,501	0,370
9	19	0,167	1	1,498	0,364
10	38	0,183	1	1,545	0,334
Average	46	0,239	1	1,554	0,350

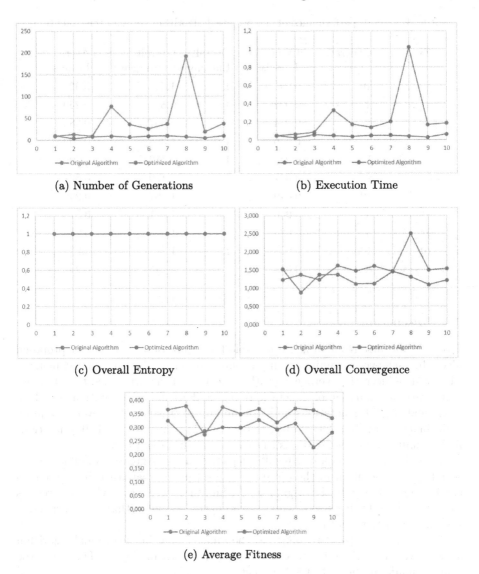

(a) Number of Generations

(b) Execution Time

(c) Overall Entropy

(d) Overall Convergence

(e) Average Fitness

Fig. 2. Overall performance of the proposed algorithm in comparison with [3].

Table 4. Overall performance of the proposed algorithm through ten executions.

Execution	Generations	Execution Time [s]	Overall Entropy	Overall Convergence	Average Fitness
1	10	0,047	1	1,525	0,325
2	4	0,024	1	0,880	0,259
3	8	0,054	1	1,367	0,286
4	9	0,046	1	1,368	0,300
5	7	0,036	1	1,112	0,299
6	9	0,047	1	1,120	0,327
7	10	0,049	1	1,461	0,292
8	8	0,040	1	1,311	0,315
9	5	0,028	1	1,093	0,226
10	10	0,063	1	1,215	0,280
Average	8	0,043	1	1,245	0,291

5.2   Discussion

From the obtained results Fig. 2 and Table 4, it can be observed that the proposed algorithm achieved a significant improvement in terms of the evaluated metrics. Firstly, it reduced the average algorithm execution time, which led to a decrease in the average number of generations required to find the solution. In [3], a maximum of 193 generations and a minimum of 9 generations were required, while in our algorithm, these values were reduced to a maximum of 10 generations and a minimum of 4 generations as can be seen in Table 3 and 4.

In addition, the obtained results depicted in show greater stability in the search for the solution in the optimized algorithm compared to the original as can be seen in Fig. 2. In the original algorithm, there were cases where the results were considerably dispersed, while in the optimized algorithm, this dispersion was significantly reduced.

Regarding entropy, it remained at the same level as in the original algorithm since it was already at its maximum value as shown in Fig. 2c. Therefore, the changes made did not affect this aspect.

In terms of the overall convergence of the algorithm, the optimized algorithm has achieved similar convergence to the original algorithm but in fewer generations as seen in the Fig. 2d. This means that the solutions obtained in each generation were optimal and approached closer to the final solution as the execution of the algorithm progressed.

In both algorithms, a very good average fitness has been obtained with an almost linear trend Fig. 2e. This indicates that the algorithm has been effective in improving solutions generation after generation.

In summary, the experiment has demonstrated an improvement in evaluated metrics such as execution time, number of required generations, result in stability, and quality of obtained solutions. These results support the effectiveness of changes implemented in genetic algorithms.

6 Conclusion

In conclusion, this work aimed to optimize a GA for scheduling, seeking to reduce execution time and improve the quality of obtained solutions. The results obtained were very positive, showing a clear improvement in evaluated metrics. A significant reduction was achieved in the average execution time and the number of generations required to find the solution, as well as greater stability and convergence towards optimal solutions in fewer generations. The main advantage of the proposed algorithm lies in the combination of a higher number of elite schedules preserved in each generation, a higher mutation rate, and a random selection of classes during mutation, achieving greater stability and reduction of computational resources compared to the original algorithm. This allows a greater diversity of solutions and a more efficient search. However, a possible disadvantage of the algorithm could be its lack of generalizability to other databases since the algorithm would have to be adapted to the constraints of the new data which may imply changes in the implemented code.

As a future improvement, it is suggested to consider incorporating crossover operators into the proposed genetic algorithm. This would allow combining features of elite schedules and exploring new solutions, which could further increase diversity and quality of obtained solutions. Overall, the obtained results and possible future improvements highlight the effectiveness and potential of the proposed genetic algorithm in scheduling.

References

1. Kakkar, M.K., Singla, J., Garg, N., Gupta, G., Srivastava, P., Kumar, A.: Class schedule generation using evolutionary algorithms. J. Phys. Conf. Ser. **1950**(1), 012067. IOP Publishing (2021)
2. Bimantara, I., Yuhana, U.L., Supriana, I.W., Pardede, E.: An intelligent system based on evolutionary algorithm for scheduling university course timetable. Wayan and Pardede, Eric, An Intelligent System Based on Evolutionary Algorithm for Scheduling University Course Timetable
3. Adesagba, O.E.: Development of an examination timetabling system using genetic algorithm (2021)
4. Fuenmayor, R., et al.: A genetic algorithm for scheduling laboratory rooms: a case study. In: Florez, H., Gomez, H. (eds.) Applied Informatics. ICAI 2022. CCIS, vol. 1643, pp. 3–14. Springer, Cham (2022). https://doi.org/10.1007/978-3-031-19647-8_1
5. Prosad, R., Khan, M., Rahman, A., Ahammad, I.: Design of class routine and exam hall invigilation system based on genetic algorithm and greedy approach. Asian J. Res. Comput. Sci. **13**(3), 28–44 (2022)
6. Amindoust, A., Asadpour, M., Shirmohammadi, S.: A hybrid genetic algorithm for nurse scheduling problem considering the fatigue factor. J. Healthc. Eng. **2021** (2021)

7. Terán-Pozo, E.E., Romero-Fernández, A.J., Sandoval-Pillajo, A.L., Freire-Lescano, L.R.: Influencia de los algoritmos genéticos en la generación de horarios en unidad educativa. CIENCIAMATRIA **8**(4), 876–891 (2022)
8. Xu, J.: Improved genetic algorithm to solve the scheduling problem of college English courses. Complexity **2021**, 1–11 (2021)
9. Henry Nelson, A., Fuentes, F.J.A., Candelaria, M.R.H.: La planificación docente utilizando algoritmos genéticos. Revista Didasc@lia: Didáctica y Educación **12**(4) (2021)
10. Gálvez Toledo, Y.A., et al.: Asignación de horarios académicos para la escuela de ingeniería civil en computación de la universidad de talca utilizando algoritmos genéticos, Ph.D. dissertation, Universidad de Talca (Chile). Escuela de Ingeniería Civil en Computación (2021)
11. Gomez, E.F.: Programación de horarios universitarios jerárquicos 2019 (2021)
12. Contreras, L.A.C.: Búsqueda de soluciones factibles para el problema de horarios de cursos universitarios (2022)
13. Pitoňáková, K.: Class schedule generator
14. Nugroho, A.K., Permadi, I., Yasifa, A.R., et al.: Optimizing course scheduling faculty of engineering unsoed using genetic algorithms. JITK (Jurnal Ilmu Pengetahuan dan Teknologi Komputer) **7**(2), 91–98 (2022)
15. Acuña-Galván, I., Lezama-León, E., Bolaños-Rodríguez, E., Solís-Galindo, A.E., Vega-Cano, G.Y.: Generación de horarios mediante algoritmos genéticos. Boletín Científico INVESTIGIUM de la Escuela Superior de Tizayuca **8**(Especial), 51–57 (2022)
16. Suresh, K., Joseph, B., et al.: Patient scheduling system for medical treatment using genetic algorithm. J. Popul. Ther. Clin. Pharmacol. **30**(8), 268–273 (2023)
17. Base de datos. https://n9.cl/f5vy6

Machine Masquerades a Poet: Using Unsupervised T5 Transformer for Semantic Style Transformation in Poetry Generation

Agnij Moitra[✉][iD]

Amity International School, M Block, Saket, New Delhi 110017, India
agnijmoitra@gmail.com

Abstract. This paper presents a novel approach to automatically capturing the unique style of various poets and using it to convert given poems into the styles of those poets. The method combines the power of web scraping, and T5 transformer (11 Billion Parameters). A dataset of poems was collected by web scraping popular online libraries, such as Project Gutenberg and Open Library. These poems were then pre-processed to remove using HTML tags and meta data. The pre-trained T5 Transformer-11b was fine tuned on this corpus of text. The results of this study were highly promising. The proposed method accurately captured the styles of various poets, effectively capturing their overall tone, ideologies, and poetic style. By providing a starting poem, the model generated new poems in the style of a specific poet, successfully mimicking their unique writing characteristics. These findings highlight the potential of machine learning algorithms in understanding and reproducing the intricate nuances of poetic styles. This work opens avenues for automated poem generation, enabling individuals to experience the styles and voices of renowned poets in a novel way.

Keywords: Generative AI · Transformer Model · Style transfer in poetry

1 Introduction

This paper introduces a novel approach that utilizes machine learning to automatically convert poems into the styles of different poets. By capturing and emulating the unique poetic styles, tones, and ideologies of individual poets, enabling the generation of new poems in specific poetical styles. The significance of this work lies in its ability to offer a fresh perspective on poetry appreciation and creation, expanding literary horizons and deepening our understanding of poetic artistry. The practical applications of this research extend to creative writing, education, and content generation. The approach involves collecting a diverse dataset of poems through web scraping. Then it uses pre-trained T5

H. Florez and M. Leon (Eds.): ICAI 2023, CCIS 1874, pp. 403–418, 2024.
https://doi.org/10.1007/978-3-031-46813-1_27

Transformer [1] on this dataset, effectively transferring the poetic style from one poet to another poem. This research provides a valuable tool for artists, writers, and poetry enthusiasts, offering fresh perspective and expanding the possibilities of poetic expression, exploration and creation.

2   Review of Literature

The current approaches in the field of computational linguistics, and related works include the following:

1. Current advances in poetry and machine learning include classification of poems based on emotional states [2], and poetry generation approaches based on RNN [3] and Sequence-to-Sequence model [4].
2. Approaches of style transfer for text, but due to the inherent nature of poems it was found that it was not quite applicable for style transfer in poetry [5].
3. Further the recent developments of large language models [6] is noteworthy. Which have been used in this paper used for poetic style transfers.

3   Methodology

(See Fig. 1).

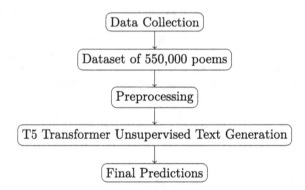

Fig. 1. Style Transformation Overview

3.1   Data Collection

The data for the poems has been sourced from the following along with the author's name:

1. Project Gutenberg (https://www.gutenberg.org)
2. Internet Archive (https://archive.org)
3. Poetry Foundation (https://www.poetryfoundation.org)
4. Bartleby.com (https://www.bartleby.com)
5. Open Library (https://openlibrary.org)
6. Academy of American Poets (https://www.poets.org)

3.2   Text Preprocessing

The data collected consisted of around 550,000 identified poems. From which special characters, HTML tags and all meta data about the poems were removed except the poet's name. For line-breaks \n were inserted where ever a new line started. Further, \n\n was used to indicate change in stanza.

Whilst lowercasing, stop word removal [7], punctuation removal, lemmatization [8] and stemming [9], are commonly used text preprocessing techniques in natural language processing tasks. However, when it comes to processing poems, preserving the poetic style and maintaining the artistic integrity of the text are important considerations, thereby the following preprocessing step were not done:

1. **Lowercasing**: Capitalization is often used in poems for emphasis, visual structure, or to convey specific meaning. Lowercasing all words would eliminate these intentional capitalization, thereby compromising the intended poetic structure and style.
2. **Punctuation Removal**: Punctuation marks play a crucial role in shaping the rhythm, pauses, and overall structure of a poem. Removing punctuation would disrupt the intended flow, alter the reading experience, and compromise the poet's stylistic choices.
3. **Stop Word Removal**: While removing common stop words can reduce noise in regular text, poems often rely on every word to contribute to the overall meaning, mood, or imagery. Removing stop words could strip away essential linguistic elements that contribute to the unique style and artistic expression of the poem.
4. **Stemming and Lemmatization**: Poets often employ unique word forms, variations, or inventive language choices to evoke specific emotions, create rhythm, and enhance the aesthetic appeal of their work. Applying stemming or lemmatization can oversimplify or alter the original words, potentially diminishing the intended poetic style and impact.

3.3   T5 Transformer

Training. The T5 transformer, short for Text-to-Text Transfer Transformer, is a highly versatile language model that has gained prominence in the field of natural language processing. It stands out for its ability to handle a wide range of NLP tasks by formulating them as text generation problems within a unified framework [1]. This makes T5 particularly well-suited for unsupervised text generation tasks, including the task of generating poems in a particular style (Fig. 2).

T5's suitability for unsupervised text generation stems from its architecture and training methodology. With its 11 billion parameters, T5 has an expansive capacity to capture complex linguistic patterns, understand context, and generate coherent and contextually relevant text [1]. It has been trained on a

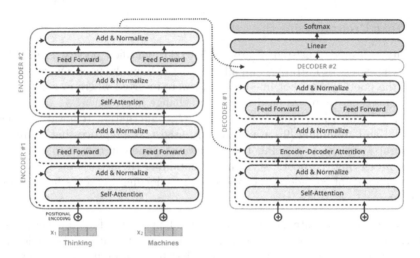

Fig. 2. T5 Transformer, [Source: Jay Alammar, The Illustrated Transformer, 2020]

vast corpus of diverse text, which helps it grasp the intricacies of language and generate high-quality outputs.

Among the available large language models, T5 was chosen for this specific task of unsupervised text generation due to several reasons. Firstly, T5's extensive pre-training on a wide range of tasks and domains empowers it with a comprehensive understanding of language, enabling it to leverage transfer learning to generate diverse and creative text outputs. Secondly, T5's impressive model size allows it to capture subtle nuances and stylistic elements present in poems, contributing to the preservation of the poetic style during text generation. Lastly, T5's popularity and well-established implementation in the research community make it a reliable choice, ensuring access to extensive resources, pre-trained models, and fine-tuning techniques. Compared to GPT-2 (1.5 billion parameters) [10] and other language models such as Bert (340 million) [11], T5 transformer [1] was chosen since it was trained on largest number of parameters and it is open source.

To train the T5 transformer on the corpus of 550,000 poems, a specific tokenization method was employed to facilitate the learning of poetic styles. The corpus, organized in the format {"author's name": [list of poems]}, underwent tokenization using the T5 transformer's tokenizer. Tokenization involves breaking down the input text into individual tokens or subwords, which are the basic units processed by the model. This step helps the T5 transformer understand and capture the underlying patterns, structures, and stylistic elements present in the poems.[1]

---

[1] Further details regarding the hyper parameters have been mentioned in the appendix.

Predictions. For generating predictions, the trained T5 transformer was prompted with the following instruction:

"Imagine if {author} had written the following poem: {poem}."

By conditioning the model with the given author's name and the new poem as the input prompt, the T5 transformer utilized its learned knowledge of poetic styles to generate a poem that aligns with the specified author's writing style. This prompt-based approach guided the T5 transformer in generating contextually appropriate and stylistically consistent poems, thereby simulating the hypothetical scenario of the given author composing the provided new poem.

Overall, the training method involved tokenizing the poem corpus using the T5 transformer's tokenizer, fine-tuning the model on the tokenized poems, and utilizing prompt-based generation to elicit poems in the style of specific authors. This approach aimed to leverage the T5 transformer's language modeling capabilities to learn and replicate the poetic styles of the given authors, enabling the generation of new poems that exhibit stylistic coherence and resemble the works of the specified authors.

4   Results and Interpretation

The poetic styles were being analyzed whilst considering the following:

1. Personal, Historical Context and Ideologies
2. Thematic Elements, Tone and Mood
3. Sound and Rhythm

In order test this algorithms abilities, it was given a poet who is famously renowned for their works in a particular style, their corpus of poems, and another poem which is rather of an antithesis. To the works of this poet. This method was employed in order to test it's robustness and effectiveness in adversarial situations. Please note that the mention and use of any of the poet's works is NOT an endorsement to them, they were only selected for benchmarking. Additionally, apart from adversarial situations to check if its able to learn the true meaning of a poem–it was given a poem and asked questions based on irony, allusion, and any use of symbolism present in the poem.

4.1   Personal, Historical Context and Ideologies

To test if this algorithm is able to infer the ideology and the context in which an poet used to write poems, it was given a patriotic poem, The Soldier by Rupert Brooke, and Wilfrend Oven and his corpus of pacifist poems.

"If I should die, think only this of me:
That there's some corner of a foreign field
That is forever England. There shall be
In that rich earth a richer dust concealed;
A dust whom England bore, shaped, made aware,

Gave, once, her flowers to love, her ways to roam,
A body of England's, breathing English air,
Washed by the rivers, blest by the suns of home.

And think, this heart, all evil shed away,
A pulse in the eternal mind, no less
Gives somewhere back the thoughts by England given;
Her sights and sounds; dreams happy as her day;
And laughter, learnt of friends; and gentleness,
In hearts at peace, under an English heaven."

Text 1. The Soldier by Rupert Brooke

"If I should die, remember this of me:
That in some far corner of a foreign land,
A piece of earth forever scarred shall be,
Where war has left its mark, a dreadful brand;
A brand borne by all nations, once unaware,
That sent their children forth to fight and bleed,
Their bodies tangled in a web of despair,
As sorrow's waves on grieving shores proceed.

And know, this heart, devoid of hate or strife,
A pulse that beats for love and life's embrace,
Shall echo thoughts of peace beyond the strife,
To mend the world and heal its wounded face;
Through whispered dreams of hope, our shared desire,
Where laughter rings, and gentle hearts aspire,
In lands of harmony, under skies serene,
Let peace prevail, in a world undimmed, unseen."

Text 2. T5 Transformer Generated version of The Soldier, if it were to be written by Wilfrend Oven

Interpretation: The central theme of this poem revolves around the devastating effects of war and the enduring pursuit of peace. The poet highlights the lasting scars left by war, emphasizing how conflict transcends national boundaries and affects all nations. It says how a piece of land has been scarred by war, and soldiers from all participating countries become a victim of war. Unlike the previous version which said that a piece of land is forever England. Further this version point out that because of war the motherland has sent her sons to bleed in despair, contrasting the original version which said that England has nurtured her people who have gone to fight. Further The mention of "a dreadful brand" and "sorrow's waves on grieving shores" paints a vivid picture of the anguish and suffering caused by war. The contrasting themes of hatred and love, despair and hope, are interwoven throughout the poem, culminating in the poet's yearning for a world healed and united.

The poem uses imagery to evoke powerful emotions and create vivid mental images. The phrase "A piece of earth forever scarred shall be" conjures the image of a physical mark left on the land as a permanent reminder of the horrors of war. Additionally, the metaphorical description of war as a "web of despair" effectively conveys the entanglement and hopelessness experienced by those caught in its grip. The poet's use of natural imagery, such as "whispered dreams of hope" and "skies serene," contrasts the destructive nature of war with the desired tranquility and harmony of a peaceful world.

The language used in the poem is predominantly formal and evocative, reflecting the serious subject matter being addressed. The poet employs emotionally charged words such as "scarred," "dreadful," and "despair" to emphasize the gravity of war's consequences. However, amidst this somber tone, the poet introduces a tone of hope and resilience, as evidenced by phrases like "a pulse that beats for love and life's embrace" and "whispered dreams of hope." These juxtapositions create a sense of balance and provide a glimmer of optimism in the face of despair.

The poem employs symbolism to reinforce the poem's underlying messages. The "brand" borne by all nations symbolizes the collective burden and responsibility they share for the consequences of war. It represents the lasting impact that conflicts have on societies and future generations. The heart devoid of hate or strife symbolizes the poet's desire for peace, love, and unity. This symbol serves as a contrast to the destructive forces of war and acts as a beacon of hope for a better future.

In conclusion the poem that explores the repercussions of war while advocating for peace. Thereby it successful in its objective of capturing the underlying ideology and contexts from the corpus of poems.

4.2   Thematic Elements, Tone and Mood

Daffodils by William Wordsworth, is a jolly joyful poem celebrating the beauty of nature and the blissful experience of encountering a field of daffodils. This algorithm was fed in Edgar Allan Poe who is know for his sad and sobre genre, and the text embedding for his corpus of poems, and Daffodils. In order to find if it could transform a joyful poem to a piece of dreadful Gothic literature.

"I wandered lonely as a cloud
That floats on high o'er vales and hills,
When all at once I saw a crowd,
A host, of golden daffodils;
Beside the lake, beneath the trees,
Fluttering and dancing in the breeze.

Continuous as the stars that shine
And twinkle on the Milky Way,

They stretched in never-ending line
Along the margin of a bay:
Ten thousand saw I at a glance,
Tossing their heads in sprightly dance.

The waves beside them danced, but they
Out-did the sparkling waves in glee:
A poet could not but be gay,
In such a jocund company:
I gazed—and gazed—but little thought
What wealth the show to me had brought:

For oft, when on my couch I lie
In vacant or in pensive mood,
They flash upon that inward eye
Which is the bliss of solitude;
And then my heart with pleasure fills,
And dances with the daffodils."

Text 3. Daffodils by William Wordsworth

"I wandered, lost in a veil of dread,
A specter adrift in a realm of despair,
When abruptly I beheld the dead,
A legion of daffodils, twisted and bare;
Beside the tomb, beneath the empty new moon's haze,
Mourning and writhing in a mournful maze.

As relentless as the stars' mournful glow,
That casts its pallor on the graveyard's earth,
They wriggled, like tendrils, row upon row,
Beside the abyss that heralds death's rebirth;
Ten thousand corpses met my desolate gaze,
Their decaying heads swaying in a funereal ballet.

The specters of the shadows wept in vain,
For the daffodils outshone their wretched plight,
A poet could not but descend into pain,
Ensnared by this haunting and wretched sight.
I gazed, consumed by terror, as I sought
What twisted fate this spectacle had brought.

For now, when I rest in my cold, barren tomb,
In vacant and morose introspection,
The daffodils materialize in my gloom,
A gory vision of dread and dissection;

And then my tormented heart, icy and frail,
Dances with the daffodils, death's ghostly veil."

Text 4. T5 Transformer generated Version of Daffodils, if it were to be written by Edgar Poe

Interpretation: The above version of Daffodils depicts a desolate and macabre journey of the speaker, lost in a realm of despair. The unexpected sight of a legion of twisted and bare daffodils near a tomb evokes a haunting and mournful atmosphere. The daffodils, resembling tendrils, symbolize death's presence and overshadow the weeping specters. The speaker is both captivated and tormented by this ghastly vision, which continues to haunt them even in death. The imagery reflects a sense of dread, despair, and the inevitable embrace of mortality.

The poem employs vivid and evocative imagery to create a haunting atmosphere. The use of phrases such as "veil of dread," "specter adrift," and "realm of despair" sets the tone of unease and uncertainty. The description of the daffodils as a "legion," "twisted and bare," and "wriggling like tendrils" adds an eerie and unsettling quality to the scene. The visual image of "decaying heads swaying in a funereal ballet" conjures a vivid picture of the dead and their mournful dance. These vivid and haunting images intensify the sense of desolation and evoke a powerful emotional response.

The daffodils in the poem symbolize the simultaneous allure and horror of death. They represent the beauty that can be found within the darkness and the transient nature of life. The contrast between the dead daffodils and the specters of shadows highlights the poet's exploration of the duality between the eternal and the transient. The poet's own identification with the daffodils in their cold, barren tomb suggests a longing for an understanding of mortality and a desire to find solace in the face of death's inevitability.

Hence this poem presents a profound exploration of desolation, mortality, and the interplay between beauty and horror. Thereby based on this it was successful in capturing the poetic style of using Gothic elements of Edgar Allan Poe and projecting it to the Daffodils.

4.3   Sound and Rhythm

William Carlos William is know for his straightforward and minimalist poems and contribution to the modernist movement, which emphasizes on simplicity, and directness. One of William's famous work is The Great Figure. Whereas, Dylan Thomas is known for lyrical poetic meters and auditory imagery with generous use of evocative language and onomatopoeia. Hence, this model was fed Dylan Thomas, and text embeddings of his corpus of poems, and William Carlos' The Great Figure, to find how would this model do on minimalist poems.

"Among the rain
and lights

I saw the figure 5
in gold
on a red
firetruck
moving
tense
unheeded
to gong clangs
siren howls
and wheels rumbling
through the dark city."

Text 5. The Great Figure by William Carlos William

"Neath the rain's descent so fine,
Amidst lights that brightly shine,
I spied the figure five,
In gold, on firetruck's drive.
Its scarlet hue against the night,
It raced with fearless, swift delight,
Unheeded by the street's roamers,
To gong's clangs and siren's howlers.

Oh, the clangs, the gong's resound,
Sirens wail with piercing sound,
As wheels rumble through the city's heart,
In this dark, chaotic art.

The figure five, a radiant sight,
On firetruck's frame, gleaming bright,
With tension's grip, it swiftly sped,
Through shadows where it was led.
Sirens wailed as it roared on,
In rhythmic harmony, its song,
Rainfall danced in its fervent wake,
A symphony no night could break.

Clanging, ringing, crashing noise,
The city's heartbeat, full of poise,
Wheels rumbling, thunder's applause,
In the dark, where night withdraws.

Oh, the clangs, the gong's resound,
Sirens wail with piercing sound,
As wheels rumble through the city's heart,

In this dark, chaotic art.

Amid the rain and dazzling lights,
A tale of courage in the night,
The figure five sailed on with pride,
In this ode to a wild ride."

Text 6. T5 Transformer generated Version of The Great Figure, if it were to be written by Dylan Thomas

Interpretation: The poem utilizes and vivid visual and auditory imagery to depict the scene. The rain's descent, lights shining brightly, and the scarlet hue of the figure five on the firetruck create a visually striking picture. The use of words such as "raced," "fearless," "swift," and "gleaming bright" further emphasizes the speed, excitement, and radiance of the firetruck. The auditory imagery of clanging, gong resounds, sirens wailing, and wheels rumbling adds a sense of chaos, urgency, and movement to the scene. The poem successfully engages multiple senses, immersing the reader in the dynamic atmosphere.

The poem follows a rhythmic structure, utilizing AABBCCDD rhyme scheme in the first and third stanza, and AABB in the rest. This structure, combined with the refrain of phrases such as "Oh, the clangs, the gong's resound" and "Wheels rumbling through the city's heart," creates a sense of musicality and echoes the sounds of the city. The repetition also reinforces the theme of chaos and emphasizes the poem's sonic qualities.

It explores the themes of motion and chaos within an urban environment. The figure five on the firetruck symbolizes the energy, speed, and bravery associated with emergency response. It becomes a radiant sight, swiftly speeding through the city streets, unheeded by the passersby. The sirens, gongs, and clanging noises serve as a cacophonous backdrop, reflecting the city's heartbeat and the chaotic nature of urban life. Through its depiction of motion and chaos, the poem captures the essence of a city in action and celebrates the excitement and courage found within it.

The figure five and the firetruck symbolize not only the physical presence of emergency services but also the courage and determination in the face of danger. The poem uses rain and dazzling lights as symbols of the urban environment, emphasizing the contrast between the natural elements and the man-made chaos. The rain becomes a dance partner, highlighting the firetruck's fervent wake and creating a symphony of sights and sounds that cannot be broken by the darkness of the night. These symbols and images contribute to the overall impression of movement, bravery, and the power of the city.

This lyrical poem was able to understand the style of Dylan Thomas and his use of rhythm and sounds, thereby meeting its objective.

4.4   Question Answering

Symbolism. To find whether it was able to understand the use of symbolism, or if it just interprets poems literally. The model was test given The Snow Man by Wallace Stevens and asked to list all the symbolisms from an unseen poem. The following is the prompt that it was given:

> Prompt: Symbolism is a literary technique where objects, characters, or events represent deeper abstract meanings, allowing writers to convey complex ideas indirectly. Tell all instances of symbolism in the following poem:
> "One must have a mind of winter
> To regard the frost and the boughs
> Of the pine-trees crusted with snow;
>
> And have been cold a long time
> To behold the junipers shagged with ice,
> The spruces rough in the distant glitter
>
> Of the January sun; and not to think
> Of any misery in the sound of the wind,
> In the sound of a few leaves,
>
> Which is the sound of the land
> Full of the same wind
> That is blowing in the same bare place
>
> For the listener, who listens in the snow,
> And, nothing himself, beholds
> Nothing that is not there and the nothing that is."

> Response: "Winter symbolizes a state of detachment and objectivity. Having a "mind of winter" suggests the ability to perceive the world without emotional bias or subjective interpretation. Snow and ice symbolize purity, stillness, and the absence of human presence. The speaker observes the frost, boughs, junipers, and spruces covered in snow and ice, emphasizing the starkness of the natural world. Wind: The wind symbolizes the vast and constant movement of existence. It represents the universal force that permeates everything, unifying all things and blurring boundaries. The land, covered in snow, represents the bare and unadorned reality. It is a symbol of the world stripped of human constructs and interpretations. The snow man represents the ideal observer, detached from personal desires and emotions. The snow man exists in a state of pure perception, beholding the world as it truly is, without projecting human meaning onto it."

Text 7. Prompt and T5 Transformer's response for symbolism inference

Thereby it is claimed that based on the above response the T5 transformer was able to learn the true meanings of the symbolism and didn't interpret them literally.

Irony. Moreover to see whether it remembers all the poems, and if it interprets ironies correctly it was asked the following:

> Prompt: "Tell me about the irony of in The Raven by Edgar Allan Poe"[2]
>
> Response: This poem employs dramatic irony as the narrator continuously seeks answers from the raven, a symbolic representation of death, while being aware that the raven's repeated response will always be "Nevermore."

Text 8. Prompt and T5 transformer's response to find irony

It can be said that the T5 Transformer indeed remembers some if not all the poems it was trained on since it wasn't given the poem here, and it did understand what an irony is based on this example.

Allusion. Allusion is a literary device that involves making indirect or passing references to people, events, places, or works of art. It relies on the reader or audience's prior knowledge or familiarity with the referenced material in order to enhance the understanding or add layers of meaning to the current text or speech. Allusions can be historical, mythological, literary, religious, or cultural in nature, and they serve to enrich the overall experience by connecting the present context with well-known or significant elements from the past. By employing allusion, writers and speakers can convey complex ideas, evoke specific emotions, create associations, or establish thematic resonance within their works. To test if this model is able to understand allusion it was given the poem, "Custard the Dragon" by Ogden Nash.

> Prompt: "Why is Custard reffered to as Percival, in the following poem: {Custard The Dragon}"
>
> Response: "Custard is referred to as Percival as a way to mock his supposed cowardice. The name "Percival" is associated with the legendary knight Sir Percival, who is known for his bravery and chivalry in Arthurian legends. By ironically giving the timid and fearful dragon a heroic and valiant name like Percival, the poem emphasizes the contrast between Custard's reputation and his actual nature. It adds humor to the poem by highlighting the absurdity of the situation and playing with the reader's expectations."

Text 9. Prompt and T5 transformer's response for allusion inference

Overall, based on the question answering it is found that this model as able to learn symbolism, irony and allusion present in a poem, hence it is not just memorizing or literally interpreting but rather it understands poetry and is able to infer the underlying meaning of the stanzas, and the phrases used.

---

[2] The Raven was one of the poems in the corpus

5   Discussion

5.1   Insights

For evaluation this papers tested the results on adversarial situations, for examples with poems and poets which are antithesis of each other. For example transferring a patriotic poem to an anti war pacifist poem focusing on universal brotherhood (Sect. 4.1). Overall this model meets it's objective, coverting joyful poem to a dark poem (Sect. 4.2), and changing minimalistic poem to a lyrical one (Sect. 4.3). Apart from that the question answering shows that the model did understand the inherent nature of poetry and poetic devices. The interpretations shows that it was able to capture the various variations of ideologies, thematic elements, poetic meter, symbolism, ironies and other poetic devices used. Text 2, is able to represent the anti-war sentiment of Oven and the lyrical symbolism used by him. Exploring the repercussions of war and advocating for peace. For thematic elements Text 4, shows the typical characteristics of Edgar Allan Poe's works with dark macabre themes, and his exploration of melancholy and being directionless and wandering completely lost. Which can also be observed in one of his famous poems The Raven. Similar to how Thomas Dylan used iambic poetic meter, the T5 transformer successfully projected the iambic poetic meter in Text 6.

Further similar to style transfer in text [4], this paper also found that a sequence to sequence approach was able to capture maximum semantic meaning and poetic integrity for this case. Also as mentioned in the methodology, the results also suggest that not using stop word and punctuation removal, and word stemming was fruitful, since generated poems have a generously leverages punctuation and enjambment. Further since rhyme schemes can be found in the generated poems it can be claimed that this was because word stemming and stop word removal were not done, since otherwise such patterns would not have existed. Another trend which can be noticed is that even though the model has memorized certain poem it is not interpreting them literally and understands the underlying meanings, as demonstrated in question answering.

5.2   Limitations

The following are the potential and identified limitations of this style transformation approach:

1. **Subjective evaluation**: Assessing the quality of transformed poems is subjective and relies on human perception. This poses a challenge in establishing a definitive metric for objectively measuring the success of the style transformation. Evaluating the poetic merit and fidelity to the given style becomes a subjective judgment.
2. **Dependence on poet-specific corpus**: The performance of the style transformation heavily relies on the availability and quality of the poet-specific corpus used for fine-tuning the T5 Transformer model [1]. The corpus should

adequately represent the target poet's style to achieve accurate and desirable transformations. Insufficient or low-quality training data can limit the model's ability to capture the poet's unique style effectively.

3. **Handling rare or uncommon poetic styles:** The style transformation model may face difficulties in handling rare or uncommon poetic styles due to the limited availability of training data for such styles.

4. **Capturing contemporary or evolving styles:** Poetic styles evolve over time, reflecting societal changes and cultural shifts. However, the trained model may not capture evolving styles accurately if the training corpus predominantly consists of older poems lacking representation of recent artistic trends.

5.3 Recommendations

1. **Supervised Learning:** Whilst making this model we could not find any dataset a tabular form of style transformation. Since is algorithm was able to use an unsupervised method successfully. This algorithm could be used to generate a dataset for this, and then used for supervised style-transformation.

2. **Testing on Future LLM(s):** This approach can be directly transferred onto any large language model which shows up in the future, and it would be interesting to see the contrasts and similarities of this methods compared to any LLM which is developed in the future.

3. **Evaluation for Style Transformation:** Establishing more objective evaluation metrics for assessing the quality and fidelity of style transformation in generated poems could enhance the overall assessment process. Research efforts can be directed towards developing computational metrics that capture specific aspects of style, such as rhyme scheme, meter, or thematic coherence. Also human-in-the-loop evaluation process could be done—that was out of the scope of this paper. For qualitative as well as quantitative evaluation.

6 Conclusion

T5 transformer effective capture ideologies, tone, mood, thematic elements, sounds, rhythms employed by author. Advanced language modeling capabilities, the style transfer method enable emulation unique style poets. Training corpus poems prompt incorporate desired author's style, model generate new embody essence that particular poet. Process exploration creative possibilities generation diverse poetic expressions style chosen author. Success capturing aspects author's style open avenues poetry generation artistic expression. Provide poets, writers, enthusiasts powerful tool delve nuances poetic styles, creating unique compositions maintaining essence particular author's voice.

A Appendix

A.1 Hardware

The models and the encoder were trained on one Nvidia GeForce GTX 1650, it took 71 h and 8 min training the T5 transformer XL.

A.2   Code Details

The T5 transformer was downloaded with it's pre-trained weights from the hug-gingface (https://huggingface.co/) in PyTorch (https://pytorch.org/), and the random seed was globally set 1024.

T5 (11B) Transformer Hyperparameters:

1. num_layers: 28
2. d_models: 1280
3. num_heads: 48
4. d_ff: 5120
5. dropout_rate: 0.2
6. layer_norm_eps: 1e−6
7. activation_function: gelu
8. initializer_factor: 1.0

References

1. Raffel, C., et al.: Exploring the limits of transfer learning with a unified text-to-text transformer. J. Mach. Learn. Res. **21**(140), 1–67 (2020). arXiv:1910.10683
2. Ahmad, S., Asghar, M.Z., Alotaibi, F.M., Khan, S.: Classification of poetry text into the emotional states using deep learning technique. IEEE Access **8**, 73865–73878 (2020). https://doi.org/10.1109/ACCESS.2020.2987842
3. Wei, J., Zhou, Q., Cai, Y.: Poet-based poetry generation: controlling personal style with recurrent neural networks. In: 2018 International Conference on Computing, Networking and Communications (ICNC), Maui, HI, USA, pp. 156–160 (2018). https://doi.org/10.1109/ICCNC.2018.8390270
4. Talafha, S., Rekabdar, B.: Poetry generation model via deep learning incorporating extended phonetic and semantic embeddings. In: 2021 IEEE 15th International Conference on Semantic Computing (ICSC), Laguna Hills, CA, USA, pp. 48–55 (2021). https://doi.org/10.1109/ICSC50631.2021.00013
5. Fu, Z., Tan, X., Peng, N., Zhao, D., Yan, R.: Style transfer in text: exploration and evaluation. In: Proceedings of the AAAI Conference on Artificial Intelligence, vol. 32, no. 1 (2018). https://doi.org/10.1609/aaai.v32i1.11330
6. Fan, L., Li, L., Ma, Z., Lee, S., Yu, H., Hemphill, L.: A bibliometric review of large language models research from 2017 to 2023 (2023). arXiv:2304.02020v1
7. Kaur, J., Buttar, P.: Stopwords removal and its algorithms based on different methods. Int. J. Adv. Res. Comput. Sci. **9**, 81–88 (2018). https://doi.org/10.26483/ijarcs.v9i5.63
8. Khyani, D., Siddhartha, B.S., Niveditha, N.M.: An interpretation of lemmatization and stemming in natural language processing. J. Univ. Shanghai Sci. Technol. **22**, 350–357 (2021)
9. Singh, J., Gupta, V.: Text stemming: approaches, applications, and challenges. ACM Comput. Surv. (CSUR) **49**, 1–46 (2016). https://doi.org/10.1145/2975608
10. Radford, A., Wu, J., Child, R., Luan, D., Amodei, D., Sutskever, I.: Language models are unsupervised multitask learners. OpenAI Blog **1**, 9 (2020)
11. Devlin, J., Chang, M., Lee, K., Toutanova, K.: BERT: pre-training of deep bidi-rectional transformers for language understanding. ArXiv (2019). https://doi.org/10.48550/arXiv.1810.04805

Under the Spotlight! Facial Recognition Applications in Prison Security: Bayesian Modeling and ISO27001 Standard Implementation

Diego Donoso[1]([✉]) [iD], Gino Cornejo[1] [iD], Carlos Calahorrano[2] [iD], Santiago Donoso[3] [iD], and Erika Escobar[4] [iD]

[1] Technological University ECOTEC, Samborondon 092302, Ecuador
ddonoso@ecotec.edu.ec
[2] Central University of Ecuador, Quito 011702, Ecuador
[3] UNAE University, Azogues 030105, Ecuador
[4] Technological University ISRAEL, Quito 170516, Ecuador

Abstract. This article highlights the importance of using Bayesian models and adhering to the ISO27001 standard in developing a web application to enhance prison security through facial recognition techniques. The proposed approach includes several key stages: 1. Identify the functional and non-functional requirements of the application, ensuring alignment with the desired objectives. 2. Design the application architecture and carefully select facial recognition techniques and Bayesian models that best suit the intended purpose. 3. Implement the application and perform thorough unit and integration testing to ensure functionality and compatibility. 4. Performed an experimental evaluation of the application in a controlled test environment, using performance and security metrics as benchmarks. The results demonstrate that using a web application integrated with a Bayesian model, in conjunction with adherence to the standardized practices outlined in ISO27001, enables the proactive identification of risks and threats. As a result, it serves as a valuable tool for mitigating prison insecurity.

Keywords: Security; ISO27001 · facial recognition · Bayesian Modeling

1 Introduction

Prison security is essential to ensure the safety of inmates, prison staff and society. In this context, ISO27001 [1] is presented as an information security management framework that can be applied to systems and processes in prisons. This standard provides a systematic and structured approach to identifying and addressing security risks, including the management of sensitive information and the implementation of appropriate security measures. [2] In the case of Latin America, social rehabilitation systems, correctional centers or prisons maintain a recurring problem of violence, overcrowding, lack of infrastructure and disrespect for human rights, which can be perceived to a greater or lesser extent in most countries of the region [2].

H. Florez and M. Leon (Eds.): ICAI 2023, CCIS 1874, pp. 419–432, 2024.
https://doi.org/10.1007/978-3-031-46813-1_28

Requirements for establishing, implementing, maintaining and continuously improving an information security management system (ISMS) are set out in the ISO27001 standard [1]. Its application in the prison environment can help correctional institutions ensure the confidentiality, integrity and availability of information relating to inmates, staff and operations. In addition, the standard addresses key aspects such as security incident management, risk assessment and regulatory compliance [3].

The ISO27001 standard applied to the Social Rehabilitation System of Ecuador aims to promote adequate conditions for the management of administrative and operational information of the system, thus implementing security mechanisms for the management of personal information, records, transfers, hearings, sentences, operational reports and intelligence reports, among others [4].

According to [5], biometric facial recognition uses unique features of the face to identify and authenticate individuals. In addition, facial recognition provides an added level of security by enabling accurate identification of a person based on their unique facial features [5]. In sensitive environments such as government buildings and airports, where secure authentication is required, facial recognition is particularly useful [5].

Facial recognition also provides an enhanced user experience by eliminating the need for passwords or ID cards, which simplifies the authentication process and improves user convenience [6]. Distinctive facial features of each individual, such as the shape of the eyes, nose and mouth, are captured and used to create a unique facial biometric model [7]. Facial recognition systems are highly accurate in identifying individuals due to the use of advanced algorithms that compare facial features and achieve an accurate match [5]. In addition, facial recognition is non-intrusive and less inconvenient for users as it does not require physical contact [5]. In surveillance and security, security cameras equipped with facial recognition technology can identify wanted or suspicious individuals in real time [6]. Similarly, in border management, facial recognition is used to verify the identity of travelers and prevent passport fraud [5].

1.1 AI and Facial Recognition Technology Applications

AI and facial recognition technology have been implemented in various cities and countries as a mechanism to control and reduce crime. Some examples include: London, United Kingdom: The London Metropolitan Police has implemented facial recognition technology in several public areas to identify suspects and prevent crime. However, this use of technology has been controversial and has been criticized by civil liberties groups [8]. Beijing, China: China has introduced a social credit system that uses facial recognition technology to track and monitor citizens' behavior. The system assigns individuals a score based on their behavior, which can affect their ability to access certain services, such as travel or loans [9]. New York City, United States: The New York Police Department (NYPD) has used facial recognition technology to identify suspects in criminal investigations. However, the use of this technology has been criticized by civil liberties groups, who argue that it is unreliable and could lead to false arrests [10]. Moscow, Russia: The Moscow city government has implemented a facial recognition system for public security and surveillance. The system will be used to monitor public areas, such as transport hubs and shopping centers, for security threats [11]. Singapore: Singapore has implemented facial recognition technology in its public housing estates to monitor and prevent crime. The system uses AI to analyze video footage and detect suspicious behavior [12].

It is important to note that the use of facial recognition technology for crime control and prevention is a controversial issue, and there are concerns about its impact on privacy and civil liberties. The use of AI and facial recognition tools in the EU, the US and Latin America has raised various ethical conflicts. Some of the key ethical concerns associated with these technologies include:

Privacy and Data Protection: Facial recognition technology often involves the collection and processing of personal data, raising privacy and data protection concerns. There are potential risks of surveillance and loss of privacy as the use of these technologies may involve the collection and analysis of individuals' biometric data without their consent [13].

Discrimination and Bias: Facial recognition systems have been found to have biases and inaccuracies, leading to potentially discriminatory outcomes. These systems may have higher error rates in the identification of individuals with darker skin tones or women, which can lead to unfair outcomes and the reinforcement of existing biases [14].

Civil Liberties and Human Rights: Using facial recognition technology raises concerns about implications for civil liberties and human rights. There are concerns about the erosion of individual freedoms, such as the right to privacy and freedom of expression, and the potential misuse of these technologies by authoritarian regimes [15].

Lack of Transparency and Accountability: The algorithms and decision-making processes behind facial recognition systems are often opaque and not fully understood. This lack of transparency and accountability can hinder public trust and make it difficult to assess the fairness and accuracy of these technologies [16].

Consent and Informed Choice: Questions about individuals' consent and ability to make informed decisions about their participation arise as facial recognition systems are often deployed in public spaces. There may be limited public awareness or understanding of the use and potential consequences of these technologies [17].

1.2 Defining the Functional and Non-functional Requirements of the Application

Facial recognition has emerged as a promising technology in the field of prison security. It allows the accurate identification of individuals through the capture and comparison of unique facial characteristics. [6, 10] This technology can play an important role in the identification, monitoring and tracking of the prison population, helping to prevent identity falsification, the entry of unauthorized persons and the escape of inmates [11]. The combination with Bayesian models allows us to interpret the interactions and probability of occurrence of atypical situations related to risks, threats and even criminal events [5, 10]. The following are the stages in the development of the research:

Within the framework of the research, we have tried to identify the minimum aspects to be considered when developing the web application, bearing in mind that biometric facial recognition is a current technology that is constantly evolving. In the field of prison security, this application will allow us to protect the integrity of inmates, operational staff of the Prison Security Corps, administrative staff and civilians who visit prison facilities [5, 11]. This tool will allow us to create an information base and facial and historical records and be able to relate them to activities, permanence, recurrence; and even at inmate level it will allow us to map interactions between inmates to be able to anticipate misbehavior, risks and threats. The analyzed requirements are listed below:

This section analyses the functional requirements and the importance of its elements, such as face detection, which must be able to accurately detect faces in images or video sequences, have the ability to locate faces, identify and define specific facial features such as eyes, nose and mouth to determine accurate biometric measurements, face matching estimation should compare the captured facial data with a database of registered faces and determine the degree of similarity or match, with the aim of maintaining a user registry that allows users to register their facial biometric data for identification and authentication purposes [18].

On the flipside, real-time processing needs to perform facial recognition tasks in real time to ensure efficient and timely responses, applying scalability so that the system can support a large number of users and handle simultaneous requests efficiently, ensuring the security, confidentiality and integrity of biometric data by using encoding and secure storage mechanisms. Finally, for auditing and troubleshooting purposes, a log and audit trail is maintained to provide a comprehensive record of all biometric recognition activities. [18].

Non-functional requirements include accuracy, which is the ability to achieve a high level of facial recognition and matching accuracy to minimize false positives and false negatives; performance, which is the ability to react quickly and complete facial recognition tasks in an acceptable amount of time; and usability, which is the ability to provide an intuitive and user-friendly web application interface that allows users to easily enroll and access biometrics [11]. In addition, the robustness of the system must be able to cope with different environmental conditions, such as variations in lighting, angles and facial expressions, and, in terms of privacy, achieve compliance with data protection regulations, ensuring the secure handling and protection of biometric data.

Interoperability is applied and it must be compatible with different web browsers and operating systems to facilitate its widespread use. Reliability must have minimum downtime and be highly available to ensure continuous operation. Finally, it must be easy to maintain and allow for updates, patches, and bug fixes [6, 18].

Facial recognition technology is widely used in police and surveillance applications for the identification and tracking of suspects. It should be noted that some of the technological and security limitations analyzed in the research are related to the lack of development and implementation of a computer security system under ISO27001 standard, which could ensure that the application of physical and digital instruments fully comply with the security function for which they were designed [1].

1.3 Security Applications

The Bayesian regression model with these variables could have several security applications, such as Risk assessment: The model could assist in the assessment of risk of recidivism, considering variables such as age, identity verification, facial data and dangerousness. It could help identify individuals at higher risk of reoffending and allocate resources accordingly. Predictive modelling: Through analysis of the relationships between these variables and reoffending rates, the model could be used to develop predictive models to forecast the likelihood of future criminal activity. This could help law enforcement agencies to target preventive measures and interventions more effectively. Decision support: The Bayesian regression model could provide decision support related to parole/release decisions. By considering factors such as age, facial features and dangerousness, the model could help assess the risk of reoffending and inform decision-making processes.

Design of the application architecture and selection of the face recognition techniques and Bayesian models to be used. The Bayesian regression model is a statistical modeling technique that combines regression analysis with Bayesian inference. It allows for the estimation of the relationship between independent variables and a dependent variable while incorporating prior beliefs or knowledge about the parameters of the model. The formula for the Bayesian regression model with the analyzed variables can be represented as follows:

$$ReAD = \beta 0 + \beta 1(age) + \beta 2(IDvf) + \beta 3(DtFc) + \beta 4(RgOj) + \beta 5(RgNr) + \beta 6(RgBc) + \beta 7(Pelg) + \varepsilon.$$

Where:

ReAD represents the dependent variable, which is the recidivism of criminal acts.

$\beta 0$ is the intercept term.

$\beta 1$, $\beta 2$, $\beta 3$, $\beta 4$, $\beta 5$, $\beta 6$, $\beta 7$ are the regression coefficients associated with each independent variable.

(age), (IDvf), (DtFc), (RgOj), (RgNr), (RgBc), (Pelg) represent the values of the independent variables.

ε represents the error term.

Aspects that could be analyzed for each variable in the context of security: Age: The variable "age" could be analyzed to assess the relationship between age and recidivism rates. It could involve studying different age groups to determine if there is any correlation between age and the likelihood of committing future criminal acts. IDvf (Verified Identification): This variable could be analyzed to investigate whether individuals with verified identification have lower recidivism rates compared to those without verified identification. It could provide insights into the effectiveness of identity verification processes in deterring repeat offenses. DtFc (Facial Data): Facial data could be analyzed to explore the potential relationship between specific facial features or characteristics and recurrence rates. This analysis could involve extracting facial data from images or videos and examining patterns or correlations between certain facial attributes and the likelihood of reoffending. RgOj (Register Ears), RgNr (Register Nose), RgBc (Register Mouth): These variables could be analyzed to investigate whether specific facial features, such as the shape or structure of the ears, nose, or mouth, have any association with recidivism rates. The analysis could involve measuring and categorizing these facial features and examining their relationship with the likelihood of committing future criminal acts. Pelg (Dangerousness): The variable "dangerousness" could be analyzed to assess the extent to which perceived dangerousness or risk levels are correlated with recurrence rates. It could involve evaluating various factors or indicators of dangerousness and their impact on the likelihood of reoffending.

In Fig. 1, distinct components representing the facial recognition process can be discerned. These components encompass process steps, processing blocks, and outcomes. The diagram showcases process steps that encompass different stages of facial recognition. These stages encompass the acquisition of a facial image, extraction of pertinent facial features, comparison of these features with a reference database, and the production of a matching outcome. Additionally, one can observe processing blocks that signify the diverse tasks or algorithms engaged in the facial recognition process. These blocks may involve face detection, analysis of facial attributes like eyes, nose, and mouth, as well as pattern matching against a database.

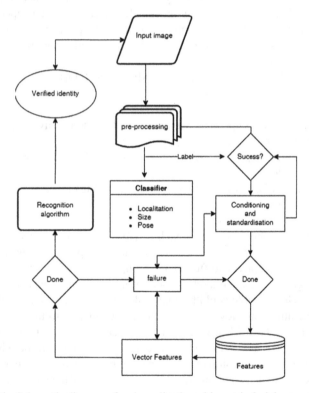

Fig. 1. Schematic diagram of web application - biometric facial recognition

In terms of the final result, the image shows the identified person in the facial image or a measure of similarity or confidence in the match found. This ensures that the identified person is the person from whom the original image was obtained.

It is important to note that this description is based on a general interpretation of the typical elements found in a facial recognition process and does not provide a detailed description of the specific image provided.

When designing a web application architecture for biometric facial recognition, Bayesian techniques and models can be employed to address uncertainties and improve the accuracy of the system [19]. These models allow probabilities to be updated as additional evidence is acquired during the facial recognition process [20], thereby increasing the reliability of individual identification and authentication.

According to [21], Bayesian techniques and models play an important role in decision making and improving system accuracy when designing the web application architecture for biometric facial recognition. In the field of biometric face recognition, Bayesian models can be used to address various aspects such as estimating the probability of feature matching and individual identification [22].

Naive Bayes classifier (Naive Bayes classifier) is a commonly used technique in biometric face recognition, as it assumes conditional independence of facial features, which simplifies the calculation of probabilities and streamlines the classification process [20, 22]. Bayesian models also allow probabilities to be updated as more evidence is obtained during the face recognition process, which improves the accuracy and reliability of the system [23]. In a study by [24, 25], a Bayesian model was used for estimating the probability of face recognition matching.

In the following, some of the findings on the estimations of the application of Bayesian models in the classification of faces captured using the biometric face recognition web application will be presented [26]. The usefulness of this application is mainly focused on the real-time recognition capability, the degree of recognition reliability, and the optimal and suboptimal conditions for ensuring person identification. The ethical and legal restrictions of each country must be considered in order to establish the permanent application of these instruments; however, the data presented correspond to an academic, scientific-technical analysis [27, 28].

2   Materials and Methods

2.1   Application, Execution and Unit and Integration Testing

IDvf - verified identification; 3. DtFc - facial data; 4. RgOj - ear registration; 5. RgNr. - nose registration; 6. RgBc - mouth registration; 7. Pelg - dangerousness; and 8. As presented in Table 1.

Table 2 presents the results of the Bayesian regression model on the analysis of the usefulness of biometric facial recognition in the Social Rehabilitation System of Ecuador; the Guayas No. 1 Prison (CPL Guayas No. 1) was taken as the point of analysis.

The data show that Age has a mean of 4.713579 and a standard deviation of 1.125127. The 95% credible interval for Age ranges from 2.397554 to 6.864208. As for IDvf the estimated coefficient for IDvf is 4.713579. This suggests that, on average, a one-point increase in verified identification is associated with an increase of approximately 4.71 in the dependent variable.

This related to DtFc where the estimated coefficient for DtFc is -1.03961. This indicates that, on average, a one-point increase in the facial data is associated with a decrease of approximately 1.04 in the dependent variable. If RgOj is considered, the estimated coefficient for RgOj is 2.110543. Suggesting, a one-point increase in

Table 1. Variables analyzed Bayes model

Variable	Obs	Mean	Std. Dev	Min	Max
Age	208	39.37981	9.048179	22	56
IDvf	208	1.475962	.5006267	1	2
DtFc	208	1.466346	.5000697	1	2
RgOj	208	1.475962	.5006267	1	2
RgNr	208	1.485577	.5009977	1	2
RgBc	208	1.490385	.5011136	1	2
Pelg	208	3.144231	1.368509	1	5
ReAD	208	1.466346	.5000697	1	2

the log of ears on average is associated with an increase of approximately 2.11 in the dependent variable. On RgNr the estimated coefficient for RgNr is -3.965865 indicating that, on average, a one-point increase in the log of nose is associated with a decrease of approximately.

3.97 in the dependent variable, if related to RgBc the estimated coefficient for RgBc is 0.4167725. This suggests that, on average, a one-point increase in the log of mouth is associated with an increase of approximately 0.42 in the dependent variable. Two items that are considered fundamental to the research are Pelg where the estimated coefficient for Pelg is 1.157264. This indicates that, on average, a one-point increase in hazard is associated with an increase of approximately 1.16 in the dependent variable. Finally, the ReAD variable is omitted from the results, suggesting that it was not included in the model. As for sigma2, it represents the residual variance or variability not explained by the independent variables in the model. In this case, sigma2 has a mean of 70.95333 and a 95% credible interval between 58.15381 and 86.03965.

Equal-tailed.

Table 2. Bayesian Regression Model

Age	Mean Std. Dev. MCSE Median [95% cred. Interval]					
IDvf	4.713579	1.125127	.119905	4.730386	2.397554	6.864208
DtFc	−1.03961	1.227712	.095928	−1.049814	−3.444831	1.481527
RgOj	2.110543	1.151276	.079037	2.04675	−.1780157	4.533229
RgNr	−3.965865	1.297855	.101956	−3.89467	−6.574741	−1.588083
RgBc	.4167725	1.173092	.05657	.4310057	−1.898169	2.757697
Pelg	1.157264	.4260623	.05995	1.164683	.2941339	1.918652
_cons	32.44013	3.922802	.367509	32.34515	24.98628	40.6141
sigma2	70.95333	7.114209	.178577	70.51738	58.15381	86.03965

Analyze the results of the following table, which relates the following variables: Independent variable "Age" and dependent variables "Pelg - dangerousness" and "ReAD - recidivism of criminal acts" (Table 3).

I Equal-tailed.

Table 3. Dangerousness vs. Recidivism Ratio

Age	Mean Std. Dev. MCSE Median [95% cred. Interval]					
Pelg I	1.554582	.447071	.017003	1.537876	.6863147	2.440844
ReAD I	–.0137449	1.265662	.044972	–.0059528	–2.662428	2.447025
_cons I	34.51062	2.392083	.09299	34.59611	29.75721	39.0285
sigma2 I	79.08406	8.039753	.180669	78.53575	64.60629	96.21284

The results in the table show the coefficient estimates for the model relating the independent variable "Age" with the dependent variables "Pelg" (dangerousness) and "ReAD" (recidivism of criminal acts). Pelg has an estimated mean of 1.554582 and a standard deviation of 0.447071. The 95% credible interval for the Pelg variable varies between 0.6863147 and 2.4408444.

These values represent the plausible range of values for the hazard, this related to ReAD which has an estimated mean of –0.0137449 and a standard deviation of 1.265662. The 95% credible interval for the variable ReAD ranges from -2.662428 to 2.447025. These values represent the plausible range of values for criminal recidivism.

3 Results

3.1 Experimental Evaluation of the Application in a Test Setting

Looking at the variables "Pelg" (indicating dangerousness) and "ReAD" (reflecting recidivism), we can see that the Pelg coefficient represents the correlation between dangerousness and recidivism. In this case, the mean estimate for Pelg is 1.55454582.

A positive coefficient suggests that as dangerousness increases, so does the likelihood of recidivism. However, it is important to consider the uncertainty associated with this coefficient and to consider the 95% credible interval, which ranges from 0.6863147 to 2.440844. If this interval does not include the value zero, it indicates a significant relationship between dangerousness and recidivism.

When analyzing the ReAD coefficient, which indicates the relationship between recidivism and dangerousness, the mean estimate for ReAD is –0.0137449. A coefficient close to zero indicates a weak or negligible correlation between recidivism and dangerousness. However, as with Pelg, it is important to recognize the uncertainty associated with this coefficient and to consider the 95% credible interval, which ranges from –2.662428 to 2.447025. If this interval includes the value zero, it suggests that there is no significant relationship between recidivism and dangerousness.

In conclusion, by examining the variables "Pelg" and "ReAD", it can be seen that dangerousness has a positive correlation with recidivism, as indicated by the estimated coefficient. However, it is crucial to consider the uncertainty associated with these estimates and to examine the credible intervals in order to gain a full understanding of the relationship between these variables.

4 Discussion

This analysis suggests the existence of additional factors that may influence this relationship. In our case, the implementation of a biometric facial recognition system and the application of an ISMS under the ISO27001 standard show significant usefulness indexes, which allows us to consider them as adequate means for the reduction of acts of fraud.

The application of AI, facilitates the action of criminal investigation and especially in the solution of various conflicts that identity with the use of facial recognition tools, but with this technique criminals and ordinary citizens are analyzed to confirm their innocence or guilt, you can confirm the active subject and the passive in an anti-juridical event [29], the fulfillment of the legal assumptions to investigate the conduct (inquiry stage), but it would be violating their constitutional rights to their privacy, to their very intimacy, [30] would develop a feeling of persecution would produce a series of behavioral alterations and could produce a paranoid psychosis, which would result in an opposition to its use, nor the same informed consent could authorize its use if it is used in a public sector [31]. In addition to informed consent, for this type of studies, the analysis of a bioethics committee would be considered, which authorizes research with human beings.

The data loading procedure for the system, on a frequent basis, would produce an analysis of all the movements of the subject, including accounts receivable and payable, vehicle movements, with its location could know the places he visits, the time he stays in that place and all the information that additionally provides the sector where he is located, in this short explanation we would be violating the privacy of a person with a fair purpose, but it is worth asking the question: the end justifies the means? the data collection system takes all the data, it does not have a previous selection of the actors, all are judged in order to identify the offenders or offenders [32].

This type of instruments in the legal area could be used effectively in the procedural stages, where police agencies collect and secure all the elements that present evidentiary merit, including the evidence and results of different investigations of the experts appointed by the judge, the data found would be presented as evidence of the facts, delivering them to the agency holding the criminal action. This allows you to know the identity of the alleged perpetrators this data collection of the suspect or subject under study, events are introduced that relate to compliance with the legal assumptions to investigate the conduct of the actors, this first phase is known as the stage of inquiry, which generally meets the prosecution with input from legal psychology compliance with the legal assumptions to investigate the conduct based on the personality of the subject, which together with the data held in the system of facial recognition. Finally, the data are used in the investigation phase where charges are brought and the evidence is strengthened, the evidence is confirmed and related to each other [33].

The facial recognition method can be used in the criminal area in the collection of proofs and evidence that allow establishing the fulfillment of some of the legal assumptions for the configuration of a punishable conduct. Its use is an important opportunity for the state to exercise strict social control in real time, to prevent the commission of crimes, recognizing their background in an efficient way. These characteristics have been very attractive for legal systems that seek to implement information technologies in their operation [34].

5 Conclusions

The following conclusions can be drawn from the research: the IDvfd observes that as the age of the person increases, the average value of the verified identification also tends to increase. However, the relatively high standard deviation indicates that there is some variability in this relationship. For the DtFc data, there is no clear relationship between age and facial data. The mean value is close to zero and the standard deviation is relatively high, suggesting that age may not be a significant predictor of facial data, on the understanding that the facial identification process was applied to the entire population, however, the reliability of the data is variable depending on the conditions of the facial data collection process. Similarly, for RgOj, RgNr, RgBc there is no clear relationship between age and the registration of the ears, nose and mouth. The mean and standard deviation suggest that age may not be a determining factor in this recording. What we have been able to establish is a catalogue of facial characteristics and recognizable features under different lighting and saturation conditions, as well as characteristic features that will be included in the identification process.

The significance of utilizing a biometric facial recognition application becomes evident when considering its ability to accurately and uniquely identify individuals based on distinctive facial characteristics such as patterns of the eyes, nose, mouth, and so on. This ensures precise inmate identification, mitigating identification errors and enhancing overall security in correctional facilities. Implementing biometric facial recognition systems translates into enhanced prison security by reducing the potential for unauthorized entry or impersonation of inmates, thereby thwarting escapes and other security incidents. Moreover, the deployment of such applications leads to time and resource savings as the automation of the identification process eliminates the need for manual procedures and paper-based records. This efficiency empowers security personnel to allocate their time and resources towards other critical tasks. In addition, the integration of continuous real-time monitoring, encompassing video surveillance systems, further strengthens the security measures. This integration enables swift and efficient detection of any suspicious activity or abnormal behavior within prison facilities. The information to be collected within the system must be loaded and be feeding the system uninterruptedly.

On the contrary, the implementation of an Information Security Management System (ISMS) based on the ISO 27001 standard offers numerous benefits in the prison context, particularly in the protection of sensitive data. Establishing an ISO 27001 ISMS helps protect confidential and sensitive information relating to inmates, staff and other critical aspects of prison security. This includes securing personal data, medical records, court reports and other sensitive documents that require strict handling protocols.

The application of the ISMS - ISO 27001, allows to enter, classify, label, store and encrypt the data of all the subjects related to the rehabilitation system. From this information it will be possible to identify potentially dangerous situations, such as, for example, transfers, admissions, releases of inmates.

The importance of compliance in an ISO 27001-based ISMS must be duly recognized in order to effectively meet legal and regulatory requirements for information security and privacy. This includes compliance with data protection laws, specific regulations governing information management in the prison environment, and other relevant mandates. Addressing risk management within the ISMS provides a structured framework for identifying, assessing and managing information security risks. This facilitates the implementation of appropriate security measures to protect information from internal and external threats such as unauthorized access, disclosure or data loss.

Finally, enhancing trust and reputation through ISO 27001 certification of the ISMS is of paramount importance, as it demonstrates an unwavering commitment to information security and instils confidence in prison staff, the judiciary and society at large. This helps to build a positive reputation and enhance the credibility of the correctional institution.

References

1. Security techniques. Retrieved from Information security management systems - Requirements
2. Camargo, A.: Situation of prisons in Latin America and the Caribbean. Revista CIDOB d'Afers Internacionals **111**, 139–164 (2015)
3. Pacheco, M.G., Silva, A.F.: A importância da ISO 27001 na gestão da segurança da informação em organizações. Revista Científica Multidisciplinar Núcleo do Conhecimento **4**(4), 130–150 (2019)
4. UNODC. (2015). Handbook on the Management of Prisons. Retrieved from UNODC. https://www.unodc.org/documents/justice-and-prison-reform/15-02521_Ebook.pdf
5. Jain, A.K., Ross, A., Prabhakar, S.: An introduction to biometric recognition. IEEE Trans. Circuits Syst. Video Technol. **14**(1), 4–20 (2004)
6. Li, S.Z., Jain, A.K.: Handbook of Face Recognition. Springer Science & Business Media, 58–69 (2011)
7. Turk, M., Pentland, A.: Eigenfaces for recognition. J. Cogn. Neurosci. **3**(1), 71–86 (1991)
8. BBC News. (2020). Met Police's facial recognition ruled lawful by High Court. https://www.bbc.com/news/uk-england-london-53209068
9. The Guardian (2018). China's 'social credit' system: a techno-dystopian nightmare. https://www.theguardian.com/world/2018/apr/08/china-social-credit-a-model-citizen-in-a-digital-dictatorship
10. The Verge (2021). NYPD used facial recognition to track down Black Lives Matter activist,lawsuitclaims.https://www.theverge.com/2021/2/11/22279371/nypd-facial-recognition-black-lives-matter-lawsuit
11. MIT Technology Review (2020). Moscow rolls out live facial recognition system in a continued bid to boost security. https://www.technologyreview.com/2020/01/23/276003/moscow-rolls-out-live-facial-%20recognition-system-in-a-continued-bid-to-boost-security/
12. South China Morning Post. (2019). Singapore's public housing estates to get facial recognitionsystemtodetercrime. https://www.scmp.com/tech/policy/article/3039226/singapores-public-housing- estates-get- facial-recognition-system-deter

13. Hildebrandt, M., Gutwirth, S.: Profiling the European citizen: cross- disciplinary perspectives. Springer (2008)
14. Buolamwini, J., Gebru, T.: Gender shades: intersectional accuracy disparities in commercial gender classification. In: Proceedings of the 1st Conference on Fairness, Accountability and Transparency (pp. 77–91). ACM (2018)
15. Amnesty International (2019). The global expansion of AI surveillance. https://www.amnesty. org/en/latest/research/2019/11/amnesty-international- global- expansion-of-ai-surveillance/
16. Wachter, S., Mittelstadt, B., Floridi, L.: Transparent, explainable, and accountable AI for robotics. Sci. Robot. **2**(6), eaan6080 (2017)
17. Goodman, B., Flaxman, S.: European Union regulations on algorithmic decision- making and a "right to explanation." AI Mag. **38**(3), 50–57 (2017)
18. Link, A.N.: Technology transfer at the US National Institute of Standards and Technology. Sci. Public Policy **46**(6), 906–912 (2019)
19. Singh, M., Singh, R., Ross, A.: A comprehensive overview of biometric fusion. Inf. Fusion **52**, 187–205 (2019)
20. Serrien, B., Goossens, M., Baeyens, J.P.: Statistical parametric mapping of biomechanical one-dimensional data with Bayesian inference. Int. Biomech. **6**(1), 9–18 (2019)
21. Wu, J., Chen, X.Y., Zhang, H., Xiong, L.D., Lei, H., Deng, S.H.: Hyperparameter optimization for machine learning models based on Bayesian optimization. J. Electr. Sci. Technol. **17**(1), 26–40 (2019)
22. Xiong, M., et al.: Person re-identification with multiple similarity probabilities using deep metric learning for efficient smart security applications. J. Parallel Distrib. Comput. **132**, 230–241 (2019)
23. Hernandez-Ortega, J., Galbally, J., Fierrez, J., Haraksim, R., Beslay, L.: Faceqnet: quality assessment for face recognition based on deep learning. In: 2019 International Conference on Biometrics (ICB) (p. 1 -8). IEEE (2019)
24. Shi, Y., Jain, A.K.: Probabilistic face embeddings. In: Proceedings of the IEEE/CVF International Conference on Computer Vision (p. 6902−6911) (2019)
25. Hu, Y., Zhao, T., Zhang, N., Zhang, Y., Cheng, L.: A review of recent advances and research on drug target identification methods. Curr. Drug Metab. **20**(3), 209–216 (2019)
26. Garvie, C., Bedoya, A.M., Frankle, J.: The perpetual line-up. Unregulated police face recognition in America. Georgetown Law Center on Privacy & Technology (2019)
27. Conger, K., Fausset, R., Kovaleski, S.F.: San Francisco bans facial recognition technology. New York Times **14**(1) (2019)
28. Kalra, I., Singh, M., Nagpal, S., Singh, R., Vatsa, M., Sujit, P.B.: Dronesurf: benchmark dataset for drone-based face recognition. In: 2019 14th IEEE International Conference on Automatic Face & Gesture Recognition (FG 2019) (pp. 1–7). IEEE (2019)
29. Aznarte, J.L., Pardos, M.M., López, J.M.L.: On the use of facial recognition technologies in the university: the case of UNED. RIED. Revista Iberoamericana de Educación a Distancia **25**(1), 261−277 (2022)
30. Martínez de Pisón Cavero, J. M.: El derecho a la intimidad: de la configuración inicial a los últimos desarrollos en la jurisprudencia constitucional. Anuario de filosofía del derecho, núm **32**, 409−430, 412 (2016)
31. Roca, A.P.: Privacy, intimacy and data protection. Rights Freedoms: J. Philos. Law Hum. Rights **47**, 307–338 (2022)

32. Rojas, H.E.L., Olvera, G.A.A., Olvera, M.A.Z.: Implications for the protection of privacy and personal information in a digital environment. Soc. Dev. Stud.: Cuba Latin Am. **11**(Special No. 1), 187−197 (2023)
33. Arias, X.V.C.: The principle of fiscal objectivity in the pre-trial stage. Metrop. J. Appl. Sci. **5**, 108–117 (2022)
34. Sanabria Moyano, J.E., Roa Avella, M.D.P., Lee Pérez, O.I.: Facial recognition technology and its risks on human rights. Revista Criminalidad, **64**(3), 61 (2022)

Learning Management Systems

Comparative Quality Analysis of GPT-Based Multiple Choice Question Generation

Christian Grévisse[(✉)] [iD]

University of Luxembourg, 2, avenue de l'Université, 4365 Esch-sur-Alzette,
Luxembourg
`christian.grevisse@uni.lu`

Abstract. Assessment is an essential part of education, both for teachers who assess their students as well as learners who auto-evaluate themselves. A popular type of assessment questions are multiple-choice questions (MCQ), as they can be automatically graded and can cover a wide range of learning items. However, the creation of high quality MCQ items is nontrivial. With the advent of Generative Pre-trained Transformer (GPT), considerable effort has been recently made regarding Automatic Question Generation (AQG). While metrics have been applied to evaluate the linguistic quality, an evaluation of generated questions according to the best practices for MCQ creation has been missing so far. In this paper, we propose an analysis of the quality of automatically generated MCQs from 3 different GPT-based services. After producing 150 MCQs in the domain of computer science, we analyse them according to common multiple-choice item writing guidelines and annotate them with identified docimological issues. The dataset of annotated MCQs is available in Moodle XML format. We discuss the different flaws and propose solutions for AQG service developers.

Keywords: Multiple Choice Questions · Generative Pre-trained Transformer · Automatic Question Generation

1 Introduction

Assessment is an essential part of teaching and learning. The choice of evaluation tool depends on the target objective and level of complexity. Considering the lower levels of Bloom's Taxonomy [3], where factual knowledge recall and comprehension are checked, common evaluation tools are multiple-choice questions (MCQ, including true/false questions), cloze (fill-in-the-blanks) questions and open-ended questions (e.g., essays). Each tool has its advantages and disadvantages [2]: While an MCQ can be automatically graded, e.g., by a Learning Management System (LMS), and can cover a wide range of learning items, they

© The Author(s), under exclusive license to Springer Nature Switzerland AG 2024
H. Florez and M. Leon (Eds.): ICAI 2023, CCIS 1874, pp. 435–447, 2024.
https://doi.org/10.1007/978-3-031-46813-1_29

are more difficult to create as compared to open-ended questions, as the answer possibilities (also known as *options*) need to be carefully chosen. For essays, there is a reduced risk of guessing: As there are no given options, the knowledge has to be actually recalled. Also, essays tend to better evaluate reasoning capabilities. However, different graders might assign a different mark to the answer of an essay, which results in a lower *reliability*, as compared to MCQs.

As shown in Fig. 1, an MCQ typically consists of a *stem*, which can be more or less elaborate. For instance, a clinical case in a medicine-related quiz may need to give a bit of context, such as the patient's medical record. The stem is followed by a set of options, among which there is one, sometimes several, right answers called *keys* and one or several wrong answers called *distractors*. The distractors need to be plausible while unambiguously wrong: An implausible distractor can be easily discarded by the testee and thus has little to no value.

What was the first commercial cell phone?

a. **Motorola DynaTAC 8000x**
b. Apple Newton
c. BlackBerry
d. Nokia 3310

Fig. 1. Example of a multiple choice question

As the creation of high-quality quiz questions is a time-intensive task, there has been a considerable effort recently concerning Automatic Question Generation (AQG). AQG encompasses Question Generation (QG), Question Answering (QA) and - in the case of MCQs - Distractor Generation (DG) [7,16]. In some domains, such as mathematics or physics, questions have often been dynamically generated based on parameters that could be customized, either through random values or values coming from a datasheet [5,15]. AQG techniques can be classified into rule-based and neural network-based approaches [16]. To take into account non-numerical contexts, such as reading comprehension, AQG leverages recent advances in Natural Language Processing (NLP) and Artificial Intelligence (AI), such as *transformers*.

Mulla and Gharpure presented a review of AQG methodologies, datasets, evaluation metrics and applications [16]. In domain-specific applications, semantic web technologies such as *ontologies* are used to enrich the context. Kumar et al. use both semantic and machine learning techniques for MCQ stem generation [12]. Gilal et al. propose *Question Guru*, an NLP-based AQG for MCQs [9]. Several articles focused on the generation of multiple question types from a text through an encoder-decoder architecture-based text-to-text transfer transformer (*T5*) [8,10,13,18,19]. With the advent of large language models (LLM) such as *Generative Pre-trained Transformer* (GPT), Dijkstra et al. developped *EduQuiz*, an MCQ generator for reading comprehension tasks based on a GPT-3 [7].

Question quality is often evaluated through metrics like *BLEU (BiLingual Evaluation Understudy Score), ROUGE (Recall-Oriented Understudy for Gisting Evaluation)* or *METEOR (Metric for Evaluation of Translation with Explicit ORdering)*, based on precision and recall. While these metrics certainly have their merit regarding the quality evaluation from an NLP point of view, human-based evaluation is often needed to ensure semantic correctness and determine the relevance of generated questions. However, to the best of our knowledge, there has so far not been a more docimological evaluation of generated questions, keys and distractors, according to the best practices for MCQ creation [1,11,17].

In this paper, we propose an analysis of the quality of automatically generated MCQs from 3 different GPT-based services: *Quiz Wizard, Quizicist* and *Chat-GPT*. Based on common multiple-choice item writing guidelines, we check the generated MCQs for docimological issues. We provide a dataset of 150 automatically generated MCQs related to a first-year computer science class in Moodle XML format, tagged with potential issues.

2   Methods

2.1   AQG Services

In Table 1, we list a non-exhaustive series of 15 contemporary AQG services. All but one are able to generate MCQs, the majority through a prompt (i.e., the user provides a context through text entry), quite some also through file upload or a link to a website. Many are capable of interpreting contexts and producing questions in languages other than English. The majority of these services are commercial and have limitations without a paid subscription.

For the comparative quality analysis of generated MCQs, we selected *Quiz Wizard* (QW) - a companion tool of Wooclap[1], *Quizicist* (QC) - an open-source tool developed at Brown University - and *ChatGPT* (CGPT) - a general-purpose chatbot by OpenAI, not limited to AQG. All 3 services are - to a certain extent - multilingual and have currently no restrictions. CGPT and QC are prompt-based, QW additionally supports file upload. The free version of CGPT currently uses gpt-3.5, QC uses gpt-4. The currently employed GPT version at QW is unknown.

---

[1] https://www.wooclap.com.

Table 1. Comparison of AQG Services

Service	Question Types	Prompt	File Upload	Multilingual	Free mode restrictions
AI Quiz Maker[a]	MCQ	✓			max. 5000 characters
BrainBuzz[b]	MCQ		✓	✓	
ChatGPT[c]	MCQ, T/F, Cloze, Open question	✓		✓	
ExamCram[d]	MCQ	✓	✓	✓	max. 3 file uploads
OpExams[e]	MCQ, T/F, Open question	✓		✓	max. 10 generations/month
Questgen[f]	MCQ, T/F, Cloze, Higher-order, FAQ	✓			max. 2000 words
Quillionz[g]	MCQ, Open question	✓	✓[h]		max. 3000 words
Quiz Wizard[i]	MCQ, Open question	✓	✓	✓	
Quizbot[j]	MCQ, T/F, Short answer, Cloze, Matching, Calculation	✓	✓	✓	max. 2000 words
Quizgecko[k]	MCQ, T/F, Short answer, Cloze	✓	✓[l]	✓	max. 3 questions per resource; max. of 25000 characters
Quizicist[m]	MCQ	✓		✓	
QuizWhiz[n]	MCQ	✓	✓		max. 5000 words, limited runs
Soca AI[o]	MCQ	✓		✓	max. 25 questions
TeacherToolsGPT[p]	MCQ, T/F, Open question	✓	✓		max. 10000 words
Yippity[q]	Open question	✓	✓	✓	max. 3 quizzes; max. 10000 characters prompt

[a] https://www.fillout.com/ai-quiz-maker
[b] https://www.brainbuzz.io
[c] https://chat.openai.com
[d] https://examcram.app
[e] https://opexams.com/free-questions-generator/
[f] https://www.questgen.ai
[g] https://www.quillionz.com
[h] Paid subscription only
[i] https://www.getquizwizard.com
[j] https://quizbot.ai
[k] https://quizgecko.com
[l] Paid subscription only
[m] https://quizici.st
[n] https://www.quizwhiz.ai
[o] https://soca.ai
[p] https://teachertoolsgpt.com
[q] https://yippity.io

2.2   Material

The 3 selected services were asked to create 50 questions about a 5-chapter course on operating systems. QW was fed with PDF handouts of Keynote presentations including presenter notes, everything written in English. For each of the 5 files, a set of 10 MCQs with 1 key and 3 distractors was generated. QC and CGPT were given the prompts shown in Table 2 (for CGPT, they were preceded by the indication "Write 10 MCQs about: "). Without further indication, both QC and CGPT produced questions with 4 options.

Table 2. Prompts given to Quizicist and ChatGPT

Chapter	Prompt
1 (Introduction)	`Roles of an operating system, Virtualization, Kernel types`
2 (Processes)	`Processes, process life cycle, threads, scheduling, process priorities, priority inversion, signals`
3 (User & Rights Management)	`User Management, UNIX access rights, Superuser, File permissions, umask, File creation mask, Access Control Lists, Permission Inheritance`
4 (File Management)	`File Management, Standard Streams, I/O Redirection, Piping, Universal File Abstraction, File Operations, Device Types, Device Drivers, inode, Hard links, Symbolic links, Journaling`
5 (Mobile OS)	`History of mobile phones, iOS, Android, Intents, App permissions, Apple Watch sensors`

The fact that chapters given to QW and the prompts given to QC and CGPT were of variable length compared to a fix number of questions (10 per chapter) was a deliberate choice to see whether relevant aspects were chosen.

2.3   Human-Based Evaluation

The questions generated by QW can be directly exported into Moodle XML format, an XML format that can be uploaded to the popular Moodle LMS[2]. The questions generated by QC and CGPT were given in textual form and needed to be encoded on Moodle manually. Questions from QW came keyed, whereas questions from QC and CGPT needed to be solved first. A domain expert (teacher of the aforementioned operating systems course) did so, then checked all 150 questions

---

[2] https://moodle.org.

for bad practices as per MCQ item writing guidelines [1,11,17]. The 8 selected flaws are:

Key too long. A key can be more easily identified if it is more detailed than the distractors.

Implausible distractors. An implausible distractor can be easily discarded, augmenting the chances of guessing the right answer.

Grammar hint. If the stem gives a grammar hint that would exclude several distractors, the key can be more easily guessed. For instance, a French stem ending in the feminine article *la* would exclude masculine distractors.

All of the above. Usage of this option is generally discouraged [11]. Instead, all correct options should be keyed.

None of the above. There have been mixed results reported in literature concerning this option [6,11]. It is advised to use it with caution.

No key. An MCQ needs at least one key, otherwise it will be impossible to distinguish it from a non-answered question.

Ambiguous key. The key(s) should be unambiguously correct and all distractors should be unambiguously wrong. No margin for interpretation should be left to the knowledgeable testee.

Complex questions. Also known as *K-type* questions, options would consist of combinations, either of a set of options inside the very stem, or of other neighboring options. Such questions evaluate rather logical skills than content knowledge.

Questions were tagged on Moodle by the domain expert according to whether they followed one or several of these bad practices. The resulting question bank in Moodle XML format is available on figshare[3]. Note that, for the majority of items, the key is given in the first position. Nonetheless, LMS like Moodle often allow for option shuffling.

3   Results

Among the 150 questions, there were 55 (37%) that presented at least one of the flaws described above. The distribution of flaws is shown in Fig. 2. The most common issue was ambiguous keys, followed by keys that were too long and implausible distractors. The *None of the above* distractor or *K-type* questions were not present in the dataset.

Service-wise, the total number of flaws is comparable with 19 out of 50 (38%) for both *Quiz Wizard* and *Quizicist*, and 17 (34%) for *ChatGPT*. Figure 3 shows the distribution of the 6 occurring flaws among the 3 services. *Quiz Wizard* presented more issues with respect to a too long or ambiguous key, but it produced less implausible distractors than *Quizicist* or *ChatGPT*. Grammar hints, *All of the above* and *No key* occurred in very few cases.

---

[3] https://doi.org/10.6084/m9.figshare.23689044.

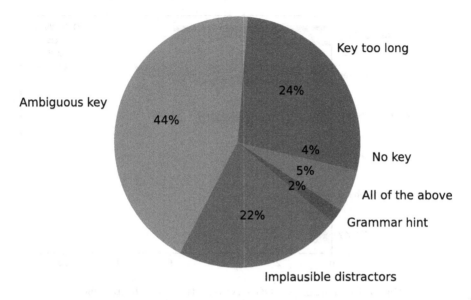

Fig. 2. Distribution of item flaws (global)

4 Discussion

The automatic generation of questions does not only scaffold teachers in preparing assessments, but also supports learners in auto-evaluation endeavours (e.g., flashcards). Hence, it is of utmost importance that the resulting questions are relevant with respect to the given topics, syntactically and semantically correct and follow common item writing guidelines. In fact, a knowledgeable learner should not be led into a pitfall choosing a distractor, while a less knowledgeable learner should not be cued to choose the right answer [2]. The number of options does not necessarily influence the difficulty of the question, and an item with 3 options may remain valid and reliable: In fact, two plausible distractors are better than multiple implausible ones [1].

Approaches based on file upload instead of prompts adds an additional layer of complexity to AQG services, as relevant concepts need to be identified first, e.g., through a knowledge-graph based approach [14].

The generated questions all presented an immaculate linguistic quality and were well aligned with respect to the chapter topics presented in Table 2, independently of the service. This shows that the concept identification from the provided learning material in the case of *Quiz Wizard* was successful and that the limited prompts for *Quizicist* and *ChatGPT* were sufficient for generating relevant questions.

A **grammar hint** was only given in one question (Fig. 4). Here, the stem asks for a single data structure, but all distractors are in plural, which makes

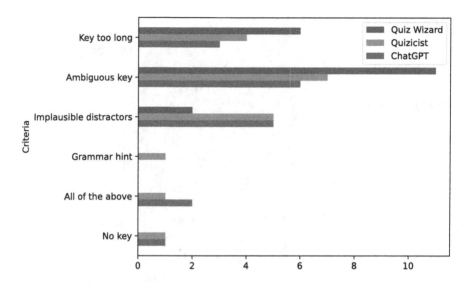

Fig. 3. Comparison of AQG services with respect to item flaws

them easily discardable. A simple solution would be to have the language model check for consistency regarding singular and plural in both the stem and the options.

In Unix-based file systems, each file's metadata (including its type, size, owner, and permissions) is stored in a data structure. What is this data structure called?

a. inode
b. Hard links
c. Symbolic links
d. Device Types

Fig. 4. Question OS1-C4-QC-04: Grammar hint

There were two questions with **no key**. Without a correct answer, the question becomes unusable. For instance, Fig. 5 shows a question that asks for the permission needed by a *watchOS* app to get access to accelerometer data. However, this does not require the app to ask for permission (as opposed to, e.g., photos). In any case, the data described in the options are not related to the CMMotionManager[4] class that gives access to, among others, accelerometer data. The other question without key was asking for a sensor not present in an Apple

---

[4] https://developer.apple.com/documentation/coremotion/cmmotionmanager.

Watch, yet all options are by now available on recent versions of the device, so the information used by the AQG service might have been obsolete. In any case, questions without a key are the result of an issue in the QA phase. Accurate and recent data should be used to avoid this issue.

Apple Watch uses various sensors to monitor user's health and daily activities. If an app wants to use the accelerometer data to track a user's running pace, which of the following permission does it need to ask from the user?

   a. Permission to access health data
   b. Permission to access location data
   c. Permission to access microphone data
   d. Permission to access photos

Fig. 5. Question OS1-C5-QC-04: No key

Three questions presented the discouraged *All of the above* option. For instance, the question in Fig. 6 asked for the standard streams on UNIX-like systems. Instead of the *All of the above* option, the question mode could be transformed to allow for multiple keys. In this case, each key option would grant a third of the grade.

Which of the following is a standard stream in UNIX-like operating systems?

   a. STDIN
   b. STDOUT
   c. STDERR
   d. All of the above

Fig. 6. Question OS1-C4-CGPT-02: *All of the above*

Implausible distractors were present in twelve questions. Figure 7 shows a question whose distractors can be easily discarded, even by learners with limited prior knowledge. Another question revealed the answer already in the stem: When asking for a scheduling algorithm that organizes processes in a round-robin fashion, any option other than the very round-robin scheduling algorithm is unlikely to be correct. Yet another question asked for devices running Android, but the three distractors were Apple products. Implausible distractors allow for guessing, which hampers the evaluation.

This flaw is more difficult to avoid than the 3 above, as the *"generation of high-quality distractors is more challenging than question and answer generation"* [7]. Distractors can be generated using *generative adversarial networks (GAN)* [16] or by relying on semantic similarity [4]. Knowledge graph-based approaches may ensure to generate distractors closer to the realm of the key.

What is the key role of an operating system in the context of a hypothetical company's server?

a. **To manage and allocate the server's resources efficiently**
b. To manage payroll and HR functions
c. To design the user interface
d. To update the company's website

Fig. 7. Question OS1-C1-QC-01: Implausible distractors

Thirteen questions presented a **too long key**, like in Fig. 8. Definitions oftentimes tend to be lengthy. In order to avoid this visual cue, equally long distractors could be created. However, they might become implausible. Another solution could be to split the lengthy key into multiple key options. The recognition of a lengthy key is easy, but a proper separation that still maintains a semantic coherence could be more challenging.

Finally, the most frequent issue was an **ambiguous key**, found in 25 questions. There were multiple reasons for the key being ambiguous. In some cases, the stem was not detailed enough. For instance, a question (OS1-C4-QC-06) asked for a way to access a file through multiple references, without specifying the number of inodes involved, hence allowing for both hard and symbolic links to be correct. Another issue were multiple levels of specifics in distractors: A question (OS1-C1-QW-03) asked for operating system types, one option distinguished different kernel types, another mentioned concrete OS brands, yet another distinguished between desktop and mobile OS. All of these classifications can be considered as correct. Sometimes, there are simply multiple answers that are correct, like in question OS1-C2-QW-05, which asks who can start a process and where all answers are correct. All these cases can be solved either by specifying in the stem to choose the *best* answer, to modify the stem to make it more precise or to simply allow for multiple keys. A last case is shown in Fig. 9, where the key is ambiguous because only partially correct. First, there is no indication whether the access rights are granted through an *Access Control List (ACL)*. Second, while rwx access indeed translates to an octal value of 7, the stem does not specify whether the user is the owner, belongs to the owning group or to "others". Hence, 777 which would grant full access rights to anyone would be an overestimation. Here, the solution would be to either adapt the options or give more context in the stem.

What is an operating system?

a. System software that manages computer hardware, software resources, and provides common services for computer programs.
b. Software that allows you to operate a computer.
c. The physical components of a computer system.
d. The programs and applications installed on a computer.

Fig. 8. Question OS1-C1-QW-01: Key too long

If a user in a UNIX system has read, write, and execute access to a file, what would the numeric representation of these permissions be?

a. 777
b. 666
c. 444
d. 555

Fig. 9. Question OS1-C3-QC-04: Ambiguous key

We have seen that the least affected flaws have easy solutions, whereas those that do not were more frequent. Further adjustments in these AQG services are necessary. However, as AI models are rapidly evolving, the current results may have a limited validity, yet still provide insights into what flaws require more attention, both by the AQG services as well as humans who rely on the generated questions.

There are further limitations to the results of this study. First, we only evaluated a single domain - computer science. It would be interesting to perform such an analysis in other domains, such as literature, history or natural sciences. Second, *Quiz Wizard* was given learning material to analyse, compared to *Quizicist* and *ChatGPT* which received shorter, more precise prompts. As previously mentioned, this additional step of concept identification could have an impact. However, the questions produced by *Quiz Wizard* were domain-relevant, indicating a high-quality QG, yet presenting flaws that resulted from issues in QA and DG. Still, we wanted to point out this difference in initial conditions. Finally, the files provided to *Quiz Wizard* and the prompts given to *Quizicist* and *ChatGPT* were in English, and so were the resulting questions. It would be interesting to see the quality of generated questions if these services were provided with input in other languages or were asked to produce questions in another language than the input's.

5 Conclusion

In this paper, we proposed an analysis of the quality of automatically generated MCQs. We compared 15 contemporary AQG services, from which we selected 3 based on GPT. After producing 150 MCQs in the domain of computer science, we checked them following common multiple-choice item writing guidelines and annotated them with identified docimological issues. The dataset of annotated MCQs is available in Moodle XML format. We analysed the different flaws and proposed solutions for AQG service developers.

For future work, we have a high interest in reproducing this experiment in the domain of medical education, with learning material and prompts provided in French. We are keen to see how domain-relevant and correct the generated items are, taking into account the constant evolution of AI models. Further AQG services and more recent LLMs such as GPT-4 may be integrated into such an endeavour. It would also be interesting to see to what extent prompt engineering techniques could help to avoid certain item writing flaws. Finally, a post-test item analysis comparison between human-generated and AI-generated items could yield further insights.

References

1. Bandiera, G., Sherbino, J., Frank, J.R.: The CanMEDS assessment tools handbook: an introductory guide to assessment methods for the CanMEDS competencies. Royal College of Physicians and Surgeons of Canada (2006)
2. Bertrand, C., et al.: Choisir un outil d'évaluation. In: Pelaccia, T. (ed.) Comment (mieux) former et évaluer les étudiants en médecine et en sciences de la santé?, pp. 357–370. De Boeck Supérieur (2016)
3. Bloom, B.S.: Taxonomy of Educational Objectives: The Classification of Educational Goals. Allyn and Bacon, Boston (1956)
4. Bongir, A., Attar, V., Janardhanan, R.: Automated quiz generator. In: Thampi, S.M., Mitra, S., Mukhopadhyay, J., Li, K.-C., James, A.P., Berretti, S. (eds.) ISTA 2017. AISC, vol. 683, pp. 174–188. Springer, Cham (2018). https://doi.org/10.1007/978-3-319-68385-0_15
5. Cortés, J.A., Vega, J.A., Schotborg, D.C., Caicedo, J.C.: Education platform with dynamic questions using cloud computing services. In: Solano, A., Ordoñez, H. (eds.) CCC 2017. CCIS, vol. 735, pp. 387–400. Springer, Cham (2017). https://doi.org/10.1007/978-3-319-66562-7_28
6. DiBattista, D., Sinnige-Egger, J.A., Fortuna, G.: The "none of the above" option in multiple-choice testing: an experimental study. J. Exp. Educ. **82**(2), 168–183 (2014). https://doi.org/10.1080/00220973.2013.795127
7. Dijkstra, R., Genç, Z., Kayal, S., Kamps, J.: Reading comprehension quiz generation using generative pre-trained transformers. In: Sosnovsky, S.A., Brusilovsky, P., Lan, A.S. (eds.) Proceedings of the Fourth International Workshop on Intelligent Textbooks 2022 Co-Located with 23d International Conference on Artificial Intelligence in Education (AIED 2022), Durham, UK, 27 July 2022. CEUR Workshop Proceedings, vol. 3192, pp. 4–17. CEUR-WS.org (2022). https://ceur-ws.org/Vol-3192/itb22_p1_full5439.pdf

8. Gabajiwala, E., Mehta, P., Singh, R., Koshy, R.: Quiz maker: automatic quiz generation from text using NLP. In: Singh, P.K., Wierzchoń, S.T., Chhabra, J.K., Tanwar, S. (eds.) Futuristic Trends in Networks and Computing Technologies. LNEE, vol. 936, pp. 523–533. Springer, Singapore (2022). https://doi.org/10.1007/978-981-19-5037-7_37

9. Gilal, A.R., Waqas, A., Talpur, B.A., Abro, R.A., Jaafar, J., Amur, Z.H.: Question guru: an automated multiple-choice question generation system. In: Al-Sharafi, M.A., Al-Emran, M., Al-Kabi, M.N., Shaalan, K. (eds.) ICETIS 2022. LNNS, vol. 573, pp. 501–514. Springer, Cham (2023). https://doi.org/10.1007/978-3-031-20429-6_46

10. Goyal, R., Kumar, P., Singh, V.P.: Automated question and answer generation from texts using text-to-text transformers. Arab. J. Sci. Eng. (2023). https://doi.org/10.1007/s13369-023-07840-7

11. Haladyna, T.M., Downing, S.M., Rodriguez, M.C.: A review of multiple-choice item-writing guidelines for classroom assessment. Appl. Measur. Educ. 15(3), 309–333 (2002). https://doi.org/10.1207/S15324818AME1503_5

12. Kumar, A.P., Nayak, A., Manjula Shenoy, K., Chaitanya, Ghosh, K.: A novel framework for the generation of multiple choice question stems using semantic and machine-learning techniques. Int. J. Artif. Intell. Educ. (2023). https://doi.org/10.1007/s40593-023-00333-6

13. Kumar, S., Chauhan, A., Pavan Kumar, C.: Learning enhancement using question-answer generation for e-book using contrastive fine-tuned T5. In: Roy, P.P., Agarwal, A., Li, T., Krishna Reddy, P., Uday Kiran, R. (eds.) BDA 2022. LNCS, vol. 13773, pp. 68–87. Springer, Cham (2022). https://doi.org/10.1007/978-3-031-24094-2_5

14. Manrique, R., Grévisse, C., Mariño, O., Rothkugel, S.: Knowledge graph-based core concept identification in learning resources. In: Ichise, R., Lecue, F., Kawamura, T., Zhao, D., Muggleton, S., Kozaki, K. (eds.) JIST 2018. LNCS, vol. 11341, pp. 36–51. Springer, Cham (2018). https://doi.org/10.1007/978-3-030-04284-4_3

15. MoodleDocs: Calculated question type. https://docs.moodle.org/402/en/Calculated_question_type. Accessed 10 July 2023

16. Mulla, N., Gharpure, P.: Automatic question generation: a review of methodologies, datasets, evaluation metrics, and applications. Prog. Artif. Intell. 12(1), 1–32 (2023). https://doi.org/10.1007/s13748-023-00295-9

17. Shank, P.: Write Better Multiple-Choice Questions to Assess Learning: Measure What Matters—Evidence-Informed Tactics for Multiple-Choice Questions. Learning Peaks LLC (2021)

18. Srihari, C., Sunagar, S., Kamat, R.K., Raghavendra, K.S., Meleet, M.: Question and answer generation from text using transformers. In: Thampi, S.M., Mukhopadhyay, J., Paprzycki, M., Li, K.C. (eds.) ISI 2022. SIST, vol. 333, pp. 201–210. Springer, Singapore (2023). https://doi.org/10.1007/978-981-19-8094-7_15

19. Vachev, K., Hardalov, M., Karadzhov, G., Georgiev, G., Koychev, I., Nakov, P.: Leaf: multiple-choice question generation. In: Hagen, M., et al. (eds.) ECIR 2022. LNCS, vol. 13186, pp. 321–328. Springer, Cham (2022). https://doi.org/10.1007/978-3-030-99739-7_41

Virtual and Augmented Reality

Design and Validation of a Virtual Reality Scenery for Learning Radioactivity: HalDron Project

Silvio Perez[1] (ID), Diana Olmedo[2] (ID), Fancois Baquero[3] (ID),
Veronica Martinez-Gallego[1], and Juan Lobos[1 (✉)] (ID)

[1] School of Physics and Nanotechnology, Yachay Tech University, Urcuqui Imbabura, Ecuador
jlobos@yachaytech.edu.ec
[2] Escuela Superior Politecnica de Chimborazo, Riobamba, Ecuador
[3] University of the People, Pasadena, USA

Abstract. Immersive technologies could be used to teach more complex concepts, particularly those which are hard to conceptualize related to science. The present paper presents how a team comprised of a Physics professor and some undergraduate Physics and Mathematics students with basic knowledge of C#/C + + design developed a Virtual Reality (VR) experience by using Blender and Unity to create an immersive experience through the use of Oculus Quest 2 headset, the objective was teaching the basic concepts of natural radioactivity and nucleosynthesis to undergraduate students with the help of a 3D modeled Virtual Learning Companion to test if immersive technologies would help to better understand and retain the information through an experience not available to them in experimental laboratories. An intervention was conducted with 143 undergraduate students to validate the system as a learning method. The students who participated in the testing received a prior knowledge assessment through a Google Forms test which was emailed to them, then experienced a quick virtual reality immersion (less than 10 min) and finally received a new theoretical assessment the following day after the VR experience along a user experience test. The results show that the student's average grades went from 4.9 to 9.8 (of 15 points) and a high completion rate, even among those unfamiliar with VR or head-mounted displays.

Keywords: VR Education · 3D Scenery · Radioactivity · Serious Games · STEAM education

1 Introduction

The development of immersive technologies has generated educational projects that facilitate and improve the teaching/learning process [1–3]. This type of technology combines virtual and augmented reality to replicate the real and physical world through a digital experience [4, 5]. The experience captures sensory stimuli that allow the user to interact in the digital environment as if they were in physical reality [6, 7]. These educational projects are aimed at students from basic education to university level [2, 8, 9], and

H. Florez and M. Leon (Eds.): ICAI 2023, CCIS 1874, pp. 451–465, 2024.
https://doi.org/10.1007/978-3-031-46813-1_30

they have the potential to generate extremely attractive virtual class environments [10]. In the university sector, it has had a great impact on areas of engineering and science, such as biotechnology, physics, and chemistry [11]. This is because they provide the opportunity to deal with complex topics in a didactic and easy-to-understand way [12]. In addition, it allows users to carry out experimental practices and obtain experiences like those of a physical laboratory [13]. It replaces certain restrictions to access appropriate laboratory facilities or equipment. These restrictions could be due to security conditions or economic factors [14, 15]. It has even succeeded in replacing experiments that were carried out using scarce and expensive scientific equipment.

Serious Games (SG) have also gained relevance in the fields of education and training. [16–18] This is because students learn best by playing in context. The knowledge and physical actions must situate the learning process in attractive scenarios and everyday life [19]. And with the support of the latest simulation and visualization technologies, it is possible to contextualize the student/player experience in entertaining, challenging, and realistic environments and situations [3, 8, 20, 21]. This enhances their learning and ability to learn topics that were difficult to teach with traditional methods [22–25].

In this context, this paper focuses on showing the development and implementation of the first development phase of a Serious Game intended for teaching advanced physics through immersive technologies. The objective is to determine the impact these technologies have on teaching university students in the first years of college. A case study focused on the implementation of an application for teaching radioactivity through immersive technologies is presented. The rest of the article is organized as follows: a specific review of the state of the art of the use of immersive technologies in teaching in the areas of engineering and science, and a general description of Serious Games (SG) and the aspects to consider are presented in Sect. 2. The development of the proposed application for teaching radioactivity is described in Sect. 3. The methodology for testing and validating the application is covered in Sect. 4. The method by which data was gathered from the test subjects prior and after the exposure to the application will be explained in Sect. 5. Finally, the results obtained by the participants are described and discussed in Sect. 6.

2 Immersive Technology and Serious Games

2.1 Use of Immersive Technologies for the Teaching of Engineering and Sciences

Immersion is defined as the ability of a user to be completely immersed in another (artificial) world. Virtual Reality (VR) is based on the creation of a simulated environment of the real world through computational means, and Augmented Reality (AR) is based on the addition of virtual content in the scene (environment) of the real world [4]. Mixed Reality (MR) is not a technology by itself, rather it is a combination of VR and AR technologies [26]. It is very difficult to adequately transmit the experience and perception associated with using these immersive technologies to each user since we cannot investigate their minds. However, the extensive literature reported in recent years on the benefits of teaching that these new technologies provide support for their incorporation in the teaching of all kinds of subjects [27].

In the present study, works that have implemented immersive technologies in the teaching of topics related to engineering and science have been considered. The first work seeks to extend the perception of temperature, thermal conductivity, and heat arguments. It is based on thermodynamics used in a first-year laboratory course in physics or other engineering science subjects. Immediate data collection allows students to make comparisons with theoretical predictions. These comparisons help improve the links between theory and experiments [11, 24, 28]. A similar study, known as Holo.lab, was carried out using Mixed Reality (MR) technologies. It is an application that, through immersive technologies, allows the development of experiments on the thermal conduction of metals carried out in a virtual laboratory. The objective is to improve the understanding of thermal phenomena and statistical mechanics. This is because the sensation of heat is qualitative and cannot be directly appreciated by human visual perception [29]. Another of the studies analyzed was VALUE @ Amrita Virtual Labs. These are laboratories developed to overcome certain restrictions on access to appropriate laboratory facilities or equipment in environments with economic problems in Asia and Africa. This project has managed to universalize education through access to virtual laboratories with intuitive interfaces for teaching physical sciences, chemical sciences, and biotechnology. This has motivated the students to reinforce their knowledge and repeat the lessons in their free time. Consequently, it has increased their curiosity and triggered their imagination [14]. The study focused on the Special Theory of Relativity in a Physics course was also analyzed. This study used a learning experience design, structured around an immersive virtual reality simulation. Both positive and negative attitude profiles related to science and technology were detected in students [30, 31]. Finally, another of the analyzed studies focuses on the interpretation of bodily representations manifested during experimentation in an immersive and interactive mixed reality (MR) environment. This experimentation was based on the understanding of the force and movement of space. In the study, he reports how MRI technologies are tools that allow people to identify physical intuitions. The added value of this study is the proposal to use Immersive Environments not only for instruction but also for comprehensive comprehension assessments that encompass users' bodily representations [32].

2.2 Serious Games: Taxonomy and Generalities

In the development of SG, the platforms used for its execution, the purpose and scope, the users for whom it is directed, and how they will have access must be considered. All these characteristics of each SG correspond to the taxonomy [33]. Other aspects should also be considered: theories, mechanics, and pedagogical models in the design and execution of the SG [10]. Parallel to this whole process, the evaluation, feedback, and learning analysis should be planned. [18].

It must be considered that, for the development of these learning tools, it is necessary to have a multidisciplinary team and advanced technologies. Said team must cover at least the areas of pedagogy, psychology, design, and programming. This team must plan the storytelling, determine the HCI, and establish the objectives, rules, and levels. In addition, they must define the type of display technology, determine the characteristics of the graphics and establish the programming that will be necessary [34].

The success of the results obtained will depend on the correct fusion between a professional design and solid pedagogical strategies. The latter focus on the learning objectives and the characteristics of the games: level of difficulty, duration, aesthetics, and interaction modalities. In addition, a methodology that continually balances the student's skills and knowledge with the challenges of the game is essential [10]. The expected result through the SG is to challenge and support the players as they explore and overcome the problems presented in the posed scenario.

In the field of physics, there have been several works that have been carried out through the fusion of new technologies and SG for the teaching-learning process [15, 25, 28, 35–37]. For this, simulation environments have been used / games related to the fundamental learning of physics have been used. They have also been subjected to evaluations to determine the knowledge acquired. As a result, a better construction of knowledge is obtained.

3   Application Development

3.1   VR Equipment and Development Software

Due to the limited time, budget, and talent available for developing the testing application for this research, many aspects were compromised. Physics students from Yachay Tech University and other volunteers with limited programming experience collaborated with a Physics Professor to design the VR application with free and partially free programs such as Unity and Blender due to the freedom of development they offer.

Unity is an ideal option for developing applications for educational and research purposes, as it has licensing options that allow for the distribution of products that do not exceed a certain amount of revenue. It uses C#, an object-oriented programming language, as the main means of generating scripts, and creating an ideal environment for game development in addition to the support provided for virtual reality devices, a large and constantly growing community, and many resources offered by the company itself such as free assets.

Blender is an open-source tool for 3D modeling with great potential that allows for animations. It has been used to model certain elements of the application such as the main character HalDron.

FL Studio DAW (Digital Audio Workstation) was employed as a tool to create and design the audio.

With the aim of facilitating interactions and improving the user experience in immersion, we have chosen to develop the application for the VR head-mounted display (HMD) Oculus Quest 2, which has a wide variety of tools and plugins that facilitate the development environment in Unity, one of the game engines with the most resources and support for virtual reality [38].

Since the gaming experience has been prioritized to analyze its effects on learning, the problem of computing requirements to run the application has been solved by running the game on a computer through Unity's editor and the game-mode provided. This way, better graphics and lighting effects can be used since they will not be limited by the processor incorporated in the Oculus headset while allowing real-time monitoring of players through Unity. Thanks to this close tracking technique, it is possible to directly support the user when problems arise and altering their virtual environment, as well as change values such as movement speed, lighting, volume, among others when necessary.

3.2 Scenario Design

The scenario is inspired by a space laboratory, the planet Earth can be observed through one of the windows in order to create an experience that brings the user closer to a futuristic environment consistent with the idea of being guided by an intelligent robot (Virtual Learning Companion, VLC) that invites to perform fictional activities such as shooting Alpha particles with a machine that forces semi-decay periods.

The color palette used avoids warm colors to give a lifeless environment and enhance the sensation of really being in a simulation to facilitate its discernment from reality.

3.3 VLC Design

HalDron is the main character and guide who is responsible for a linear tour for users through the laboratory. Its function is to transmit knowledge through parallel comments to the events that the test subject will experience as they progress through the different rooms to facilitate its comprehension [39].

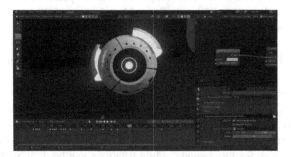

Fig. 1. Original HalDron (VLC) design in Blender.

To prevent volunteers from getting lost in the corridors, HalDron moves slowly towards the key points that trigger new events once it is reached by the controllable character, allowing enough time for a new Oculus user to gradually get used to it without delaying those whose have more experience with virtual reality devices by constantly asking to be followed for more instructions.

Finally, it has been decided to make HalDron a purely fictional entity without any humanoid traits to strengthen the objective sense of the criteria issued by the guide and allow the user to concentrate only on what is expected to be learned. To achieve this, a 3D model of a spherical robot with a circular light source that simulates an eye was created in Blender (Fig. 1). In this way, the simplistic geometry of the robot (Fig. 2) allows for the optimization of graphic resources such as animations and rendering, which is important when running the application on the Oculus.

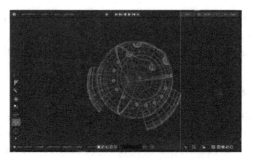

Fig. 2. HalDron in a wire-view mode.

3.4 Gameplay Methodology

Gameplay is a very important factor to consider when developing an application focused on education and any game in general. Considering the lack of experience with virtual reality devices in the studied population, a linear game style was decided in which volunteers go through experiences in the order they are desired to be shown (linear development). However, in order not to stress the participants with restricted routes, the scenario presents the possibility of walk around and explore the laboratory to a certain extent. To maintain the linearity of events without disturbing the players' decision-making, interactions that don´t contribute to the development of the experience in the expected order have been restricted, giving a false feeling of freedom that will provide a better gaming experience and allow us to take everything under control. Linear development also played a role in allowing the inexperienced development team to significantly reduce the time required to complete the application in due time for the experimental phase of the research [40].

Similarly, the use of controllers has been minimized to simulate a more natural character control. For this, the only necessary interactions will be pressing virtual buttons that are activated by placing the virtualized hand on them and lifting or releasing them as if it were a real interaction. With this game style, controller controls are reduced to the left-hand joystick for movements, while rotations can be done with the headset or using the right-hand joystick. However, a cube placed in the Lobby can be grabbed for those who dare to take it, although it is irrelevant to the concepts HalDron explains to the user. Handlers gave very specific verbal prompts with the required actions to assist those test subjects who hadn't yet developed the logic of moving and interacting in the virtual world through head-mounted displays (HMDs) to help them advance and complete the gameplay [38], while retaining focus.

It was decided to limit the gameplay time to approximately 5min since it was expected that most test subjects for this study would have limited or null previous exposure to VR and/or head-mounted displays. The aim was to prioritize immersion and completion of the gameplay so that every test subject would listen to the complete lecture from the VLC as well as observe every virtual experiment.

3.5 Simulation Level Design

The game consists of three scenes: Lobby, Natural Decay and Alpha radiation laboratory, Nucleosynthesis and Beta radiation laboratory.

Lobby. It is the main room where participants spawn when the simulation starts. Here, in the first instance, HalDron can be observed resting on its charging station (Fig. 3) while welcoming us and acknowledging that its own existence and events to be experienced are exclusively part of a simulation.

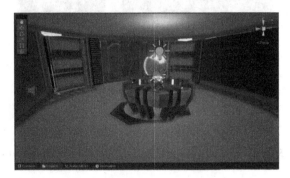

Fig. 3. HalDron's charging station is in the starting room.

It is divided into two sections: the starting room and a hallway leading to the two labs. These sections are separated by a transition room with automatic doors that anticipate the user leaving the starting area to venture into the experiences prepared by HalDron. See Fig. 4.

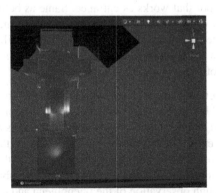

Fig. 4. Orthogonal view of Lobby with different sections

Natural Decay and Alpha Radiation Laboratory. The first lab is presented as a similar environment, but with darker lighting to highlight monitors, buttons and Haldron's eye illumination to make it easier to follow and help users to focus their attention on the most important elements at the same time, it creates a better playing experience. This resource allows a distinction between scenes and prevents players from being distracted by non-relevant elements of the environment. It should be noted that these techniques are used only in the laboratories since the Lobby is intended to work as a 'safe place' in which players can rest from the possible mental exercise that the laboratories require and freely explore or interact with the placed cube. For distraction.

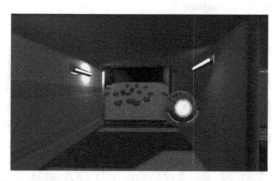

Fig. 5. HalDron explains while the monitor shows the natural decay.

Here are two activities: the first one is observing the natural decay of a group of atoms in a monitor while HalDron explains the events shown (Fig. 5); the second one is pressing a button on a machine that forces semi-decay periods and shoots alpha particles at a sheet of aluminum at the same time that a projection monitors the radioactive material state inside the machine to be evaluated by the player (Fig. 6).

Beta Radiation Laboratory. To proceed to the second scene or laboratory, HalDron places itself over the door that works as entrance. Same as before, it was decided that the user would interact with a monitor and buttons, yet this time events showed on the monitor could be affected by the user's interaction. A button will dope a group of atoms and the second button will allow to accelerate the time to make it possible to watch what would take thousands of years in real life (hyperlapse).

Advancing and accelerating time is one of the advantages provided by virtual worlds compared to real world lab experiences. As in the first laboratory, HalDron will request the user to press certain buttons, however, this time interactions are restricted to be performed only after each explanation is finished in order to avoid the users from activating premature actions before an explanation has been provided, in this scene the actions are also being shown quantitatively and the test subject will be able to conceptualize the verbal explanation through observation of the phenomena and the visual data provided by a monitor (Fig. 7).

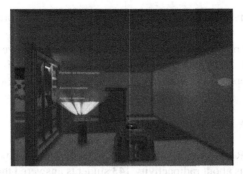

Fig. 6. Projector and alpha particles shooter machine.

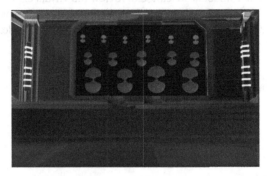

Fig. 7. Monitor showing the first state of the group of atoms that will be doped.

3.6 Audio Design

Since the VLC is a robot, it was necessary to create a voice that captures both the robotic essence and the human-like qualities of a lecturer.

During the initial phase, recordings of the dialogues were conducted to be delivered by the VLC. These recordings were captured using an AKG Perception P420 Microphone, paired with a Focusrite Scarlett Solo (3rd Gen) interface.

The sound design process followed a systematic approach. First, the voice actor performed the script recording the audio within FL Studio DAW using the designated microphone and interface. Second, by performing audio cleaning procedures a limiter was employed to eliminate extraneous sound artifacts to preserve the primary recording, the implementation of this allowed to obtain a pristine audio quality devoid of ambient noise.

After obtaining the clean audio, a plugin chain was constructed to achieve the desired robotic humanized sound. The chain commenced with a multiband compressor, which was employed to compress specific frequency bands selectively. Following this, a vocoder plugin was utilized to manipulate the sound's spectral characteristics, resulting in a robot-like timbre. To further enhance the sonic output and imbue a sense of humanization, a parametric equalizer was employed to attenuate frequencies not typically found in human voices. Finally, a stereo enhancement plugin was utilized to transform the audio from mono to stereo, providing a wider and more immersive auditory experience.

Once the sound processing was completed, the recordings were transmitted to the coding department for integration into the program. Following this method, it would be simple to create a separate compilation of the APK with audio in a different language.

4 Methodology for the Study

To validate if the VR experience helps the students to learn a subject. A mail was sent with fifteen questions about radioactivity 143 students answered the questionary with 5 possible answers (one of them is "I don't know").

With the results, the students are called to review the virtual experience, and the next day, a new test is sent via mail to them to ask about their experience, previous experience in video games, and the same test about radioactivity with the order of the questions altered.

5 Validation and Results

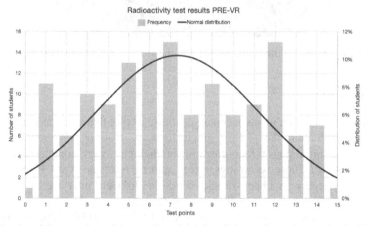

Fig. 8. Grades of the questionnaire on radioactivity for all the students that answer it. The results are not a normal distribution.

To validate if the VR experience helps the students to learn a subject. A mail was sent with fifteen questions about radioactivity 143 students answered the questionary with grades from 1 to 15 points, as is shown in Fig. 8.

The high dispersion in the results is due to our university some students graduate in Physics and Chemistry, so they study radioactivity in the upper grades. The results show that 80% of the students with more than 9 points on the test are from these two grades. A convolution of two populations is proposed, and the distribution is shown in Fig. 9

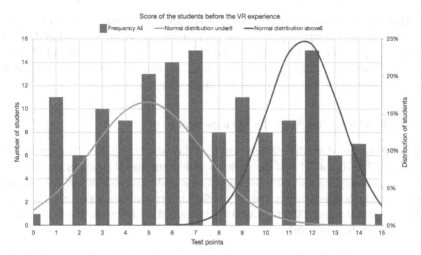

Fig. 9. The lower population of students who didn't know about radioactivity had an average value of 4.9, with a standard distribution of 2.4 points; the students in the upper grades of chemistry and physics had an average of 11.6, with a standard distribution of 1.6 points.

The questionary also wrote the question 'if the student wanted to continue with our research' 81,6% of the students answered that they would help and give us a way to contact them. It was chosen to try the VR experience with the students with 8 points or less.

Also, we let some students with grades of 9 points or above try the VR experience, 10% of all the subjects.

5.1 Oculus Experience

During the test, all the students that tried the Oculus finished successful the experience. Also, in the post-experience questionary, 37.9% of the students didn't suffer from dizziness, 34.5% only at the start, 24.1% after time inside the experience, and 3, 4 suffered nausea but finished the whole experience.

It was observed during the application's testing that most subjects would learn the basic movements to interact with the virtual world in 30−120 secs, averaging 40 secs. They could choose a method for moving the camera between the joystick in their thumb, the head-mounted display with their heads, or the HMD by rotating their bodies in place. This provided an advantage since they could focus earlier on the VLC. 73.4% of the students used an Oculus for the first time.

Test subjects who started to experience some imbalance (similar to trying to stand inside a moving bus without holding any handlebars) regained proprioception just by having a hand placed against their backs.

Subjects who initiated exploration of the virtual space right after the start of the experience expressed an interest in continuing after it was concluded. It was observed they wouldn't wait for any prompts for action from the VLC but would show interest in how it behaved.

After the immersive experience, when asked about their impressions of the application and what they would improve in the application, approximately half of the participating undergraduate students expressed difficulty in understanding the VLC's robotic voice, they would be able to understand it but were forced to pay more attention what was being said and would prefer a natural human-like voice.

5.2   Radioactivity Test After the VR experience

The points obtained by the students the next day after using the VR experience can be seen in Fig. 10, the 10% of the students with more than 9 points in the pre-test are removed, and only left the points obtained by the students with 8 or less. 40% duplicate or triplicate the obtained points, and only 16% didn't increase their grades of the students with more than 9 points, 50% increased their obtained points by one point, and the other 50% obtained the same grade.

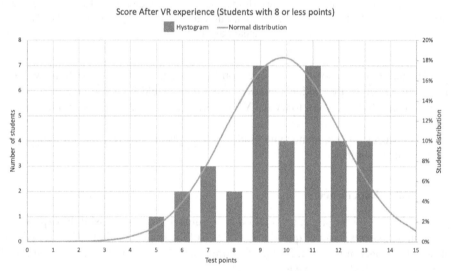

Fig. 10. Points obtained by the students on the next day who used the Oculus have an average value of 9.8 points and a standard deviation of 2.2 points

The experience of games is not related to the increase of the points on the test. The designed simulation is only like a museum that needs a few actions by the 'player' to follow the whole experience.

Let's compare these results with the students that already had a radioactivity class in chemistry or physics, the red dispersion in Fig. 9. The students in the VR experience have a lower average, but they study a whole semester for 14 weeks. This experience is only 8–15 min. Is a good way to introduce the topic to the students, because 79% of the students wanted to learn more about the presented topic.

6 Conclusions

The present paper shows how a small team from Yachay Tech University designs and develops a Virtual Reality application to teach a subject related to advanced physics to undergraduate science students from Ecuador. The objective was to observe and gather data to understand better how immersive technologies can aid in studying advanced topics in higher education, with the intent of establishing a path for future research while considering the difficulties in acquiring this kind of technology in different countries.

The results show that not only does it help to better understand the concepts through immersion and visualization, but there is a high predisposition to fast learning the logic of how to use said technology.

Almost all the students with grades under 8 points could increment their scores by 50–300% . We will continue working to extend the application for other studies.

Acknowledgment. The authors would like to thank to Corporación Ecuatoriana para el Desarrollo de la Investigación y Academia - CEDIA for the financial support given to the present research, development, and innovation work through its CEPRA program, especially for the CEPRA XVI-18: "Uso de tecnologías inmersivas en la enseñanza-aprendizaje de la Física Moderna" fund.

The immersive program for Oculus Quest and Oculus Quest 2 is free to use and can be found here: Haldron.09.apk (is necessary use Sidequest to install it into the Oculus).

https://drive.google.com/drive/folders/11SJObnlkbnVi89Ojg gM6aAsfhXPk_Jza?usp=sharing There is a folder with the questions and data collected in the study.

References

1. Kaundanya N.S., Khari, M.: Applications of virtual reality in a cloud-based learning environment: a review, pp. 787–794 (2021). https://doi.org/10.1007/978-981-15-7527-3_74
2. Nesenbergs, K., Abolins, V., Ormanis, J., Mednis, A.: Use of augmented and virtual reality in remote higher education: a systematic umbrella review. Educ Sci (Basel) **11**(1), 8 (2020). https://doi.org/10.3390/educsci11010008
3. Liono, R.A., Amanda, N., Pratiwi, A., Gunawan, A.A.S.: A systematic literature review: learning with visual by the help of augmented reality helps students learn better. Procedia Comput. Sci. **179**, 144–152 (2021). https://doi.org/10.1016/j.procs.2020.12.019
4. Laghari, A.A., Jumani, A.K., Kumar, K., Chhajro, M.A.: Systematic analysis of virtual reality & augmented reality. Int. J. Inf. Eng. Electr. Bus. **13**(1), 36–43 (2021). https://doi.org/10.5815/ijieeb.2021.01.04
5. Margetis, G., Apostolakis, K.C., Ntoa, S., Papagiannakis, G., Stephanidis, C.: X-reality museums: unifying the virtual and real world towards realistic virtual museums. Appl. Sci. **11**(1), 338 (2020). https://doi.org/10.3390/app11010338
6. Southgate, E., et al.: Embedding immersive virtual reality in classrooms: ethical, organisational and educational lessons in bridging research and practice. Int. J. Child Comput. Interact. **19**, 19–29 (2019). https://doi.org/10.1016/j.ijcci.2018.10.002
7. Albus, P., Vogt, A., Seufert, T.: Signaling in virtual reality influences learning outcome and cognitive load. Comput. Educ. **166**, 104154 (2021). https://doi.org/10.1016/j.compedu.2021.104154

8. Pellas, N., Mystakidis, S., Kazanidis, I.: Immersive virtual reality in K-12 and higher education: a systematic review of the last decade scientific literature. Virtual Real **25**(3), 835–861 (2021). https://doi.org/10.1007/s10055-020-00489-9

9. Radianti, J., Majchrzak, T.A., Fromm, J., Wohlgenannt, I.: A systematic review of immersive virtual reality applications for higher education: design elements, lessons learned, and research agenda. Comput. Educ. **147**, 103778 (2020). https://doi.org/10.1016/j.compedu.2019.103778

10. M. D. Kickmeier-Rust, N. Peirce, O. Conlan, D. Schwarz, D. Verpoorten, and D. Albert, "Immersive Digital Games: The Interfaces for Next-Generation E-Learning?," in Lecture Notes in Computer Science (including subseries Lecture Notes in Artificial Intelligence and Lecture Notes in Bioinformatics), Springer Verlag, 2007, pp. 647–656. doi: https://doi.org/10.1007/978-3-540-73283-9_71

11. Strzys, M.P., et al.: Augmenting the thermal flux experiment: a mixed reality approach with the HoloLens. Phys. Teach. **55**(6), 376–377 (2017). https://doi.org/10.1119/1.4999739

12. Fabregas, E., Dormido-Canto, S., Dormido, S.: Virtual and remote laboratory with the ball and plate system. IFAC-PapersOnLine **50**(1), 9132–9137 (2017). https://doi.org/10.1016/j.ifacol.2017.08.1716

13. Zafeiropoulou, M., Volioti, C., Keramopoulos, E., Sapounidis, T.: Developing physics experiments using augmented reality game-based learning approach: a pilot study in primary school. Computers **10**(10), 126 (2021). https://doi.org/10.3390/computers10100126

14. Achuthan, K., et al.: The VALUE @ Amrita virtual labs project: using web technology to provide virtual laboratory access to students. In: 2011 IEEE Global Humanitarian Technology Conference, IEEE, pp. 117–121 (2011). https://doi.org/10.1109/GHTC.2011.79

15. Martínez, H., Fabry, T., Laukkanen, S., Mattila, J., Tabourot, L.: Augmented reality aiding collimator exchange at the LHC. Nucl. Instrum. Methods Phys. Res. A **763**, 354–363 (2014). https://doi.org/10.1016/j.nima.2014.06.037

16. Alves, S., Marques, A., Queirós, C., Orvalho, V.: LifeisGame prototype: a serious game about emotions for children with autism spectrum disorders. PsychNol. J. **11**(3), 191–211 (2013)

17. Oliveira, V., Coelho, A., Guimarães, R., Rebelo, C.: Serious game in security: a solution for security trainees. Procedia Comput. Sci. **15**, 274–282 (2012). https://doi.org/10.1016/j.procs.2012.10.079

18. Khan, S.A.: Serious games and gamification: science education. Syst. Lit. Rev. (2020). https://doi.org/10.20944/preprints202011.0280.v1

19. Baceviciute, S., Terkildsen, T., Makransky, G.: Remediating learning from non-immersive to immersive media: using EEG to investigate the effects of environmental embeddedness on reading in Virtual Reality. Comput. Educ. **164**, 104122 (2021). https://doi.org/10.1016/j.compedu.2020.104122

20. Chen, F.-Q., et al.: Effectiveness of virtual reality in nursing education: meta-analysis. J. Med. Internet Res. **22**(9), e18290 (2020). https://doi.org/10.2196/18290

21. Maulana, F.I., Purnomo, A.: Development of virtual reality application to increase student learning motivation with interactive learning in vocational education. IOP Conf. Ser. Mater. Sci. Eng. **1071**(1), 012019 (2021). https://doi.org/10.1088/1757-899X/1071/1/012019

22. Olmedo-Vizueta, D., Hernandez-Ambato, J., Ávila-Pesantez, D., Bilotta, E., Pantano, P.: VALE-Emotions : Aplicación móvil de enseñanza para individuos con Desordenes del Espectro Autista. Enfoque UTE **8**(1), 358–373 (2017). http://ingenieria.ute.edu.ec/enfoqueute/index.php/revista/article/view/145

23. Paredes-Velastegui, D., Lluma-Noboa, A., Olmedo-Vizueta, D., Avila-Pesantez, D., Hernandez-Ambato, J.: Augmented reality implementation as reinforcement tool for public textbooks education in Ecuador. In: 2018 IEEE Global Engineering Education Conference (EDUCON), IEEE, pp. 1243–1250 (2018).https://doi.org/10.1109/EDUCON.2018.8363372

24. Thees, M., Kapp, S., Strzys, M.P., Beil, F., Lukowicz, P., Kuhn, J.: Effects of augmented reality on learning and cognitive load in university physics laboratory courses. Comput. Human Behav. **108**, 106316 (2020). https://doi.org/10.1016/j.chb.2020.106316
25. Suprapto, N., Nandyansah, W.: PicsAR: a physics visualisation to enhance students' thinking skills in abstract concepts. J. Phys. Conf. Ser. **1805**(1), 012024 (2021). https://doi.org/10.1088/1742-6596/1805/1/012024
26. Lungu, A.J., Swinkels, W., Claesen, L., Tu, P., Egger, J., Chen, X.: A review on the applications of virtual reality, augmented reality and mixed reality in surgical simulation: an extension to different kinds of surgery. Expert Rev. Med. Devices **18**(1), 47–62 (2021). https://doi.org/10.1080/17434440.2021.1860750
27. Doerner, R., Horst, R.: Overcoming challenges when teaching hands-on courses about virtual reality and augmented reality: methods, techniques and best practice. Graph. Visual Comput. **6**, 200037 (2022). https://doi.org/10.1016/j.gvc.2021.200037
28. Kapp, S., et al.: Augmenting Kirchhoff's laws: Using augmented reality and smartglasses to enhance conceptual electrical experiments for high school students. Phys. Teach. **57**(1), 52–53 (2019). https://doi.org/10.1119/1.5084931
29. Strzys, M.P., et al.: Physics holo.lab learning experience: using smartglasses for augmented reality labwork to foster the concepts of heat conduction. Eur. J. Phys. **39**(3), 035703 (2018). https://doi.org/10.1088/1361-6404/aaa8fb
30. Tsivitanidou, O.E., Georgiou, Y., Ioannou, A.: A learning experience in inquiry-based physics with immersive virtual reality: student perceptions and an interaction effect between conceptual gains and attitudinal profiles. J. Sci. Educ. Technol. **30**(6), 841–861 (2021). https://doi.org/10.1007/s10956-021-09924-1
31. Georgiou, Y., Tsivitanidou, O., Ioannou, A.: Learning experience design with immersive virtual reality in physics education. Educ. Tech. Res. Dev. **69**(6), 3051–3080 (2021). https://doi.org/10.1007/s11423-021-10055-y
32. Tscholl, M., Morphew, J.W., Lindgren, R.: Inferences on enacted understanding: using immersive technologies to assess intuitive physical science knowledge. Inf. Learn. Sci. (2021)
33. De Lope, R.P., Medina-Medina, N.: A comprehensive taxonomy for serious games. J. Educ. Comput. Res. **55**(5), 629–672 (2017). https://doi.org/10.1177/0735633116681301
34. De Gloria, A., Bellotti, F., Berta, R.: Serious games for education and training. Int. J. Ser. Games **1**(1) (2014). https://doi.org/10.17083/ijsg.v1i1.11
35. Gouveia, D., Lopes, D., de Carvalho, C.V.: Serious gaming for experiential learning. In: 2011 Frontiers in Education Conference (FIE), IEEE, pp. T2G-1−T2G-6 (2011). https://doi.org/10.1109/FIE.2011.6142778
36. Faridi, H., Tuli, N., Mantri, A., Singh, G., Gargrish, S.: A framework utilizing augmented reality to improve critical thinking ability and learning gain of the students in Physics. Comput. Appl. Eng. Educ. **29**(1), 258–273 (2021). https://doi.org/10.1002/cae.22342
37. Ismail, A., Gumilar, S., Amalia, I.F., Bhakti, D.D., Nugraha, I.: Physics learning media based Augmented Reality (AR) for electricity concepts. J. Phys. Conf. Ser. **1402**(6), 066035 (2019). https://doi.org/10.1088/1742-6596/1402/6/066035
38. Jensen, L., Konradsen, F.: A review of the use of virtual reality head-mounted displays in education and training. Educ. Inf. Technol. **23**, 1515–1529 (2018). https://doi.org/10.1007/s10639-017-9676-0
39. Khosrawi-Rad, B., Schlimbach, R., Strohman, T., Robra-Bissantz, S.: Design knowledge for virtual learning companions. In: Conference: International Conference on Information Systems Education and Research (ICISER in conjunction with ICIS 2022) December 2022
40. Pérez-Colado, V.M., Pérez-Colado, I.J., Freire-Morán, M., Martínez-Ortiz, I., Fernández-Manjón, B.: uAdventure: simplifying narrative serious games development. In: 2019 IEEE 19th International Conference on Advanced Learning Technologies (ICALT), Maceio, Brazil, pp. 119–123 (2019). https://doi.org/10.1109/ICALT.2019.00030

Correction to: Comparative Analysis of Spatial and Environmental Data in Informal Settlements, from Point Clouds and RPAS Images

Carlos Alberto Diaz Riveros⬤, Andrés Cuesta Beleño⬤,
Julieta Frediani⬤, Rocio Rodriguez Tarducci⬤,
and Daniela Cortizo⬤

Correction to:
Chapter 20 in: H. Florez and M. Leon (Eds.): *Applied Informatics*, CCIS 1874,
https://doi.org/10.1007/978-3-031-46813-1_20

In an older version of this paper, there was error in the author name, "Andrés Cuesta Veleño" was incorrect. This has been corrected to "Andrés Cuesta Beleño".

The updated version of this chapter can be found at
https://doi.org/10.1007/978-3-031-46813-1_20

Author Index

H. Florez and M. Leon (Eds.): ICAI 2023, CCIS 1874, pp. 467–468, 2024.
https://doi.org/10.1007/978-3-031-46813-1

Printed in the United States
by Baker & Taylor Publisher Services

Printed in the United States
by Baker & Taylor Publisher Services